Foundations of Business

4e

William M. Pride
Texas A&M University

Robert J. Hughes
Dallas County Community Colleges

Jack R. Kapoor
College of DuPage

CENGAGE
Learning®

Australia • Brazil • Mexico • Singapore • United Kingdom • United States

Foundations of Business, Fourth edition
William M. Pride, Robert J. Hughes,
Jack R. Kapoor

Senior Vice President, Global Product Manager,
Higher Education: Jack W. Calhoun

Vice President, General Manager, Social Science
& Qualitative Business: Erin Joyner

Product Director: Mike Schenk

Product Manager: Jason Fremder

Sr. Content Developer: Joanne Dauksewicz

Product Assistant: Megan Fischer

Marketing Manager: Robin LeFevre

Content Project Manager: Darrell E. Frye

Media Developer: Kristin Meere

Manufacturing Planner: Ron Montgomery

Marketing Coordinator: Christopher Walz

Production Service: PreMediaGlobal

Sr. Art Director: Stacy Jenkins Shirley

Internal Designer: Joe Devine, Red Hangar
Design

Cover Designer: Kathy Heming

Cover Image: ©J. Bieking/Shutterstock

Rights Acquisitions Specialist: John Hill

For product information and technology assistance, contact us at
Cengage Learning Customer & Sales Support, 1-800-354-9706

For permission to use material from this text or product,
submit all requests online at **www.cengage.com/permissions**
Further permissions questions can be emailed to
permissionrequest@cengage.com

Library of Congress Control Number: 2013951070

ISBN-978-1-285-19394-6

ISBN-10: 1-285-19394-6

Cengage Learning
200 First Stamford Place, 4th Floor
Stamford, CT 06902
USA

Cengage Learning is a leading provider of customized learning solutions with office locations around the globe, including Singapore, the United Kingdom, Australia, Mexico, Brazil, and Japan. Locate your local office at:
www.cengage.com/global

Cengage Learning products are represented in Canada by Nelson Education, Ltd.

To learn more about Cengage Learning Solutions, visit **www.cengage.com**

Purchase any of our products at your local college store or at our preferred online store **www.cengagebrain.com**

Printed in the United States of America
1 2 3 4 5 6 7 17 16 15 14 13

To Nancy, Allen, Michael, Ashley, Charlie, and James Robinson Pride

To my wife Peggy and to my mother Barbara Hughes

To my wife Theresa; my children Karen, Kathryn, and Dave; and in memory of my parents Ram and Sheela Kapoor

Brief Contents

Contents

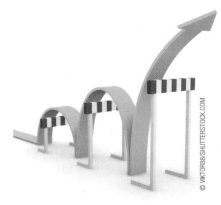

PART 1   The Environment of Business   1

Chapter 3: Exploring Global Business 65

PART 2 Business Ownership and Entrepreneurship 100

© ANDY DEAN PHOTOGRAPHY/SHUTTERSTOCK.COM

Chapter 4: Choosing a Form of Business Ownership 100

© ANDY DEAN PHOTOGRAPHY/SHUTTERSTOCK.COM

PART 3 Management and Organization 159

Chapter 8: **Producing Quality Goods and Services 206**

© ANDY DEAN PHOTOGRAPHY/SHUTTERSTOCK.COM

PART 4 Human Resources 238

Chapter 9: **Attracting and Retaining the Best Employees 238**

PART 5 Marketing 297

© ANDY DEAN PHOTOGRAPHY/SHUTTERSTOCK.COM

PART 6 Information, Accounting, and Finance 394

About the Authors

William M. Pride Texas A&M University

William M. Pride is professor of marketing, Mays Business School at Texas A&M University. He received his PhD from Louisiana State University. He is the author of Cengage Learning's *Marketing*, 15th edition, and a market leader. Dr. Pride's research interests are in advertising, promotion, and distribution channels. His research articles have appeared in major journals in the fields of advertising and marketing, such as *Journal of Marketing, Journal of Marketing Research, Journal of the Academy of Marketing Science*, and the *Journal of Advertising*. Dr. Pride is a member of the American Marketing Association, Academy of Marketing Science, Association of Collegiate Marketing Educators, Society for Marketing Advances, and the Marketing Management Association. He has taught principles of marketing and other marketing courses for more than 30 years at both the undergraduate and graduate levels.

Robert J. Hughes Richland College, Dallas County Community Colleges

Robert J. Hughes (PhD, University of North Texas) specializes in business administration and college instruction. He has taught Introduction to Business for more than 35 years both on campus and online for Richland College—one of the seven campuses that are part of the Dallas County Community College District. In addition to *Business* and *Foundations of Business*, published by Cengage Learning, he has authored college textbooks in personal finance and business mathematics; served as a content consultant for two popular national television series, *It's Strictly Business* and *Dollars & Sense: Personal Finance for the 21st Century*; and is the lead author for a business math project utilizing computer-assisted instruction funded by the ALEKS Corporation. He is also active in many academic and professional organizations and has served as a consultant and investment advisor to individuals, businesses, and charitable organizations. Dr. Hughes is the recipient of three different Teaching in Excellence Awards at Richland College. According to Dr. Hughes, after 35 years of teaching Introduction to Business, the course is still exciting: "There's nothing quite like the thrill of seeing students succeed, especially in a course like Introduction to Business, which provides the foundation for not only academic courses, but also life in the real world."

Jack R. Kapoor College of DuPage

Jack R. Kapoor (EdD, Northern Illinois University) is professor of business and economics in the Business and Technology Division at the College of DuPage, where he has taught Introduction to Business, Marketing, Management, Economics, and Personal Finance since 1969. He previously taught at Illinois Institute of Technology's Stuart School of Management, San Francisco State University's School of World Business, and other colleges. Professor Kapoor was awarded the Business and Services Division's Outstanding Professor Award for 1999–2000. He served as an Assistant National Bank Examiner for the U.S. Treasury Department and as an international trade consultant to Bolting Manufacturing Co., Ltd., Mumbai, India.

He is known internationally as a coauthor of several textbooks, including *Foundations of Business*, 3rd edition (Cengage Learning), has served as a content consultant for the popular national television series *The Business File: An Introduction to Business*, and developed two full-length audio courses in business and personal finance. He has been quoted in many national newspapers and magazines, including *USA Today, U.S. News & World Report*, the *Chicago Sun-Times, Crain's Small Business*, the *Chicago Tribune*, and other publications.

Dr. Kapoor has traveled around the world and has studied business practices in capitalist, socialist, and communist countries.

Acknowledgments

The quality of this book and its supplements program has been helped immensely by the insightful and rich comments of a special set of instructors. Their thoughtful and helpful comments had real impact in shaping the final product. In particular, we wish to thank:

John Adams,
San Diego Mesa College

Ken Anglin,
Minnesota State University, Mankato

Ellen A. Benowitz,
Mercer County Community College

Michael Bento,
Owens Community College

Patricia Bernson,
County College of Morris

Laura Bulas,
Central Community College, NE

Brennan Carr,
Long Beach City College

Paul Coakley,
The Community College of Baltimore County

Jean Condon,
Mid-Plains Community College

Mary Cooke,
Surry Community College

Dean Danielson,
San Joaquin Delta College

John Donnellan,
Holyoke Community College

Gary Donnelly,
Casper College

Karen Edwards,
Chemeketa Community College

Donna K. Fisher,
Georgia Southern University

Charles R. Foley,
Columbus State Community College

Mark Fox,
Indiana University South Bend

Connie Golden,
Lakeland Community College

Karen Gore,
Ivy Tech Community College—Evansville

Carol Gottuso,
Metropolitan Community College

John Guess,
Delgado Community College

Frank Harber,
Indian River State College

Linda Hefferin,
Elgin Community College

Tom Hendricks,
Oakland Community College

Chip Izard,
Richland College

Eileen Kearney,
Montgomery Community College

Anita Kelley,
Harold Washington College

Mary Beth Klinger,
College of Southern Maryland

Natasha Lindsey,
University of North Alabama

Robert Lupton,
Central Washington University

John Mago,
Anoka Ramsey Community College

Rebecca J. Mahr,
Western Illinois University

Pamela G. McElligott,
St. Louis Community College Meramec

Myke McMullen,
Long Beach City College

Carol Miller,
Community College of Denver

Jadeip Motwani,
Grand Valley State

Mark Nagel,
Normandale Community College

Dyan Pease,
Sacramento City College

Jeffrey D. Penley,
Catawba Valley Community College

Angela J. Rabatin,
Prince George's Community College

Anthony Racka,
Oakland Community College—Auburn Hills Campus

Dwight Riley,
Richland College

Kim Rocha,
Barton College

Carol Rowey,
Community College of Rhode Island

Christy Shell,
Houston Community College

Cindy Simerly,
Lakeland Community College

Yolanda I. Smith,
Northern Virginia Community College

Gail South,
Montgomery College

Rieann Spence-Gale,
Northern Virginia Comm. College—Alexandria Campus

Kurt Stanberry,
University of Houston, Downtown

John Striebich,
Monroe Community College

Keith Taylor,
Lansing Community College

Tricia Troyer,
Waubonsee Community College

Leo Trudel,
University of Maine—Fort Kent

Randy Waterman,
Richland College

Leslie Wiletzky,
Pierce College—Ft. Steilacoom

Anne Williams,
Gateway Community College

We also wish to acknowledge Colette Wolfson and Linda Hoffman of Ivy Tech Community College for their contributions to the *Instructor's Resource Manual*, as well as Julie Boyles of Portland State University for her help in developing the Test Bank. We thank Instructional Designer, Tiana Tagami, and ANSR Source for their excellent work on the PowerPoint program. For our CengageNOW and CourseMate content, we would again like to thank Julie Boyles as well as LuAnn Bean of the Florida Institute of Technology, Amit Shah of Frostburg State University, and ANSR Source. We thank the Dallas Center for Distance Learning Solutions for their Telecourse partnership and for providing the related student and instructor materials. Finally, we thank the following people for their professional and technical assistance: Stacy Landreth Grau, Marian Wood, Amy Ray, Elisa Adams, Jennifer Jackson, Jamie Jahns, Eva Tweety, Carolyn Phillips, Laurie Marshall, Clarissa Means, Theresa Kapoor, David Pierce, Kathryn Thumme, Margaret Hill, Nathan Heller, Karen Tucker, and Dave Kapoor.

Many talented professionals at Cengage Learning have contributed to the development of *Foundations of Business*, *4e*. We are especially grateful to Erin Joyner, Mike Schenk, Jason Fremder, Kristen Hurd, Joanne Dauksewicz, Darrell Frye, Stacy Shirley, Kristen Meere, and Megan Fischer. Their inspiration, patience, support, and friendship are invaluable.

W. M. P.

R. J. H

J. R. K

Advisory Board
Pride/Hughes/Kapoor, FOUNDATIONS OF BUSINESS, 3e
(Conducted in-depth reviews, attended focus groups, responded to quick mini-surveys)

Michael Bento
Owens Community College
Patricia Bernson
County College of Morris
Brennan Carr
Long Beach City College
Paul Coakley
The Community College of Baltimore County
Donna K. Fisher
Georgia Southern University
Charles R. Foley
Columbus State Community College
Connie Golden
Lakeland Community College
John Guess
Delgado Community College
Frank Harber
Indian River State College

Anita Kelley
Harold Washington College
Mary Beth Klinger
College of Southern Maryland
Pamela G. McElligott
St Louis Community College Meramec
Mark Nagel
Normandale Community College
Angela J. Rabatin
Prince George's Community College
Anthony Racka
Oakland Community College— Auburn Hills Campus
Carol Rowey
Community College of Rhode Island
Christy Shell
Houston Community College

Cindy Simerly
Lakeland Community College
Yolanda I. Smith
Northern Virginia Community College
Gail South
Montgomery College
Rieann Spence-Gale
Northern Virginia Community College—Alexandria Campus
Kurt Stanberry
University of Houston, Downtown
John Striebich
Monroe Community College
Keith Taylor
Lansing Community College
Tricia Troyer
Waubonsee Community College

© EDHAR/SHUTTERSTOCK.COM

Exploring the World of Business and Economics

Learning Objectives

What you will be able to do once you complete this chapter:

1 Discuss what you must do to be successful in the world of business.

2 Define *business* and identify potential risks and rewards.

3 Define *economics* and describe the two types of economic systems: capitalism and command economy.

4 Identify the ways to measure economic performance.

5 Examine the different phases in the typical business cycle.

6 Outline the four types of competition.

7 Summarize the factors that affect the business environment and the challenges that American businesses will encounter in the future.

Why Should You Care?

Studying business will help you to choose a career, become a successful employee or manager, start your own business, and become a more informed consumer and better investor.

How Starbucks Brews Up Global Profits

Starbucks was a small, decade-old business in 1981 when Howard Schultz happened to be in its store in Seattle's Pike Place Market and sipped the founder's freshly brewed coffee. Intrigued by the product and the possibilities, he soon joined the firm. Then he traveled to Italy and got a first hand taste of the robust espressos and the welcoming ambiance in local coffeehouses. Back home, Schultz decided to start his own company, opening European-style cafés serving premium coffees brewed to order. A few years later, he and a group of investors bought Starbucks and began opening cafés all across America. To raise millions of dollars for funding new cafés and creating new products, Starbucks sold stock and became a publicly traded corporation in 1992.

Now, after 25 years of aggressive growth, Starbucks has spread its unique brand of coffee culture around the country and around the world. The company's familiar green-and-white mermaid logo appears on its nearly 18,000 cafés in 60 countries, with future openings planned throughout Asia, Northern Europe, and beyond. The ever-expanding menu includes hot and iced coffees and teas, fruit juices and chilled drinks, and an assortment of pastries, wraps, and yogurts. Thanks to acquisitions and partnerships, the Starbucks empire also includes packaged coffee beans, coffee ice cream, coffee drinks, and fruit juices sold in supermarkets, as well as high-tech coffeemakers for home and office.

Starbucks is a company with a conscience. It provides health-care coverage to both full-time and part-time employees, a benefit that many companies offer to full-timers only. It also emphasizes environment-friendly practices such as composting coffee grounds, conserving water, and recycling paper, glass, and plastic. In addition, Starbucks is piloting the development of smaller, certified energy-efficient stores constructed from locally available materials. Looking ahead, how will Starbucks handle such critical challenges as intense competition and economic uncertainty?[1]

Did You Know?

Starbucks rings up more than $13 billion in annual revenue through nearly 18,000 cafés in 60 nations.

Wow! What a challenging world we live in. Just for a moment, think about how you would answer the question below.

In the future, which of the following is the most serious problem facing Americans?

a. The national debt.
b. The high unemployment rate.
c. A volatile stock market.
d. Consumer pessimism.
e. An unstable economy and business environment.

Unfortunately there is no one best answer because all of the above options are serious problems facing you, American businesses, and the nation. Ask almost anyone, and they will tell you that they are worried about at least one or more of the above problems. At the time of the publication of your text, there are signs of economic improvement when compared to the last five years, but people still worry about their future and the future of the nation. Still, it is important to remember the old adage, "History is a great teacher." Both the nation and individuals should take a look at what went wrong to avoid making the same mistakes in the future.

In addition, it helps to keep one factor in mind: Our economy continues to adapt and change to meet the challenges of an ever-changing world and to provide opportunities for those who want to achieve success. Our economic system provides an amazing amount of freedom that allows businesses like Starbucks—the company profiled in the Inside Business opening case for this chapter—to adapt to changing business environments. Despite troubling economic times and a weak economy, Starbucks—and its employees—is a success because it was able to introduce new products, open new stores, meet the needs of its customers, earn a profit, and sell stock to the general public.

Within certain limits, imposed mainly to ensure public safety, the owners of a business can produce any legal good or service they choose and attempt to sell it at the price they set. This system of business, in which individuals decide what to produce, how to produce it, and at what price to sell it, is called **free enterprise.** Our free-enterprise system ensures, for example, that Amazon.com can sell everything from televisions, toys, and tools to computers, cameras, and clothing. Our system gives Amazon's owners and stockholders the right to make a profit from the company's success. It gives Amazon's management the right to compete with bookstore rival Barnes & Noble and electronics giant Sony. It also gives you—the consumer—the right to choose.

In this chapter, we look briefly at what business is and how it became that way. First, we discuss what you must do to be successful in the world of business and explore some important reasons for studying business. Then we define *business*, noting how business organizations satisfy their customers' needs and earn profits. Next, we examine how capitalism and command economies answer four basic economic questions. Then our focus shifts to how the nations of the world measure economic performance, the phases in a typical business cycle, and the four types of competitive situations. Next, we look at the events that helped shape today's business system, the current business environment, and the challenges that businesses face.

free enterprise the system of business in which individuals are free to decide what to produce, how to produce it, and at what price to sell it

YOUR FUTURE IN THE CHANGING WORLD OF BUSINESS

Learning Objective

1 Discuss what you must do to be successful in the world of business.

The key word in this heading is *changing*. When faced with both economic problems and increasing competition not only from firms in the United States but also from international firms located in other parts of the world, employees and managers began to ask the question: What do we do now? Although this is a fair question, it is difficult to answer. Certainly, for a college student taking business courses or an employee just starting a career, the question is even more difficult to answer. Yet there are still opportunities out there for people who are willing to work hard, continue to learn, and possess the ability to adapt to change. Let's begin our discussion in this section with three basic concepts.

- What do you want?
- Why do you want it?
- Write it down!

During a segment on a national television talk show, Joe Dudley, one of the world's most respected black business owners, gave the preceding advice to anyone who wanted to succeed in business. His advice can help you achieve success. What is so amazing about Dudley's success is that he started a manufacturing business in his own kitchen, with his wife and children serving as the new firm's only employees. He went on to develop his own line of hair-care and cosmetic products sold directly to cosmetologists, barbers, beauty schools, and consumers in the United States and 18 foreign countries. Today, Mr. Dudley has a multimillion-dollar empire—one of the most successful minority-owned companies in the nation. He is not only a successful business owner but also a winner of the Horatio Alger Award—an award given to outstanding individuals who have succeeded in the face of adversity.[2]

Although many people would say that Joe Dudley was just lucky or happened to be in the right place at the right time, the truth is that he became a success because he had a dream and worked hard to turn his dream into a reality. He would be the first to tell you that you have the same opportunities that he had. According to Mr. Dudley, "Success is a journey, not just a destination."[3]

Whether you want to obtain part-time employment to pay college and living expenses, begin your career as a full-time employee, or start a business, you must *bring* something to the table that makes you different from the next person. Employers and

Improve Your Productivity!

No matter what career you choose, you'll be much more effective on the job if you use these five keys to higher productivity.

1. *Focus on one task at a time.* If you divide your attention, you can't apply as much mental muscle to complex projects or difficult challenges.

2. *Make your workload more manageable.* Divide large tasks into small steps so you won't feel as intimidated by all you have to accomplish. Just as important, you can determine which steps should be completed now and which can wait for another day.

3. *Organize your work space and your work day.* It's easier to focus and put your hands on the materials you need when you're not surrounded by clutter. Keep yourself on track by making notes (electronically or on paper) about what you plan to do and when. If you don't complete your daily or weekly "to do" list, check again to see what should take priority and what you can cut out or postpone.

4. *Structure your time.* Plan to avoid distractions and interruptions during some parts of every work day. Turn off your e-mail, close the web browser, and settle down to concentrate for a set period.

5. *Give your brain a break.* Treat yourself to a brief break every few hours. Stand up, stretch, walk around if you can, and think about something else for a couple of minutes. When you return to the task at hand, you'll feel more refreshed—and you may even have some fresh ideas.

Sources: Based on information in Daniel Bortz, "10 Ways to Be More Productive at Work," *U.S. News & World Report*, May 4, 2012, http://money.usnews.com; Sabah Karimi, "7 Ways to Jump-Start Your Productivity at Work," *U.S. News & World Report*, February 27, 2012, http://money.usnews.com; Eilene Zimmerman, "Distracted? It's Time to Hit the Reset Button," *New York Times*, November 19, 2011, www.nytimes.com; Daniel McGinn, "Being More Productive," *Harvard Business Review*, May 2011, http://hbr.org.

our economic system are more demanding than ever before. Ask yourself: What can I do that will make employers want to pay me a salary? What skills do I have that employers need? With these two questions in mind, we begin the next section with another basic question: Why study business?

Why Study Business?

The potential benefits of higher education are enormous. To begin with, there are economic benefits. Over their lifetimes, college graduates on average earn much more than high school graduates. Although lifetime earnings are substantially higher for college graduates, so are annual income amounts (see Figure 1-1). In addition to higher income, you will find at least five compelling reasons for studying business.

FOR HELP IN CHOOSING A CAREER What do you want to do with the rest of your life? Like many people, you may find it a difficult question to answer. This business course will introduce you to a wide array of employment opportunities. In private enterprise, these range from small, local businesses owned by one individual to large companies such as American Express and Marriott International that are owned by thousands of stockholders. There are also employment opportunities with federal, state, county, and local governments and with charitable organizations such as the Red Cross and Save the Children. For help in deciding which career might be right for you, read Appendix B: Careers in Business, which appears on the text website. To view this information:

1. Go to www.cengagebrain.com.
2. At the CengageBrain.com home page, search for the ISBN for your book (located on the back cover of your book) using the search box at the top of the page. This will take you to the product page where companion resources can be found.

FIGURE 1-1 Who Makes the Most Money?

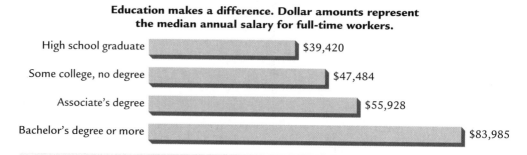

Education makes a difference. Dollar amounts represent the median annual salary for full-time workers.

High school graduate	$39,420
Some college, no degree	$47,484
Associate's degree	$55,928
Bachelor's degree or more	$83,985

Source: "Educational Attainment of Householder—Households with Householder 25 Years Old and Over by Median and Mean Income," The U.S. Census Bureau at www.census.gov (accessed January 2, 2013).

In addition to career information in Appendix B, a number of additional websites provide information about career development. For more information, visit the following sites:

- Career Builder at www.careerbuilder.com
- Career One Stop at www.careeronestop.org
- Monster at www.monster.com

To click your career into high gear, you can also use online networking to advance your career. Websites like Facebook, Twitter, LinkedIn, and other social media sites can help you locate job openings, help prospective employers to find you, and make a good impression on current and future employers. To make the most of online networking, begin by identifying and joining sites where you can connect with potential employers, former classmates, and others who may have or may hear of job openings. Next, be sure your online profiles, photographs, and posts communicate your abilities and interests. Finally, be ready to respond quickly when you spot a job opening.

One thing to remember as you think about what your ideal career might be is that a person's choice of a career ultimately is just a reflection of what he or she values and holds most important. What will give one individual personal satisfaction may not satisfy another. For example, one person may dream of a career as a corporate executive and becoming a millionaire before the age of 30. Another may choose a career that has more modest monetary rewards but that provides the opportunity to help others. What you choose to do with your life will be based on what you feel is most important. And *you* are a very important part of that decision.

TO BE A SUCCESSFUL EMPLOYEE Deciding on the type of career you want is only the first step. To get a job in your chosen field and to be successful at it, you will have to develop a plan, or a road map, that ensures that you have the skills and knowledge the job requires. You will also be expected to have the ability to work well with many types of people in a culturally diverse workforce. **Cultural (or workplace) diversity** refers to the differences among people in a workforce owing to race, ethnicity, and gender. These skills and an appreciation for a culturally diverse workplace, can give you an inside edge when you are interviewing with a prospective employer.

This course, your instructor, and all of the resources available at your college or university can help you to acquire the skills and knowledge you will need for a successful career. But do not underestimate your part in making your dream a reality. In addition to the job-related skills and knowledge you'll need to be successful in a specific job, employers will also look for the following characteristics when hiring a new employee or promoting an existing employee:

- Honesty and integrity
- Willingness to work hard
- Dependability
- Time management skills
- Self-confidence
- Motivation
- Willingness to learn
- Communication skills
- Professionalism

Employers will also be interested in any work experience you may have had in cooperative work/school programs, during summer vacations, or in part-time jobs during the school year. These things can make a difference when it is time to apply for the job you really want.

Personal Apps

Sometimes you have to reach for success!

There's an old saying that if you choose a career you like, you never have to work a day in your life. For most people, the first decision is choosing a career. Then the material in the sections "To Be a Successful Employee" and "To Improve Your Management Skills" can help you achieve success.

© SPECTRAL-DESIGN/SHUTTERSTOCK.COM

cultural (or workplace) diversity differences among people in a workforce owing to race, ethnicity, and gender

© ALMAGAMI/SHUTTERSTOCK.COM

A life changing decision! Often the most important factor to consider when choosing a career is what you think is important. For some people, more responsibility, promotions, and money may be important. For others, more free time and the opportunity to help others may be more important. Ultimately, it's your choice—an important choice that can affect the rest of your life.

TO IMPROVE YOUR MANAGEMENT SKILLS Many employees want to become managers because managers often receive higher salaries and can earn promotions within an organization. Although management obviously can be a rewarding career, what is not so obvious is the amount of time and hard work needed to achieve the higher salaries and promotions. For starters, employers expect more from managers and supervisors than ever before. Typically, the heavy workload requires that managers work long hours, and most do not get paid overtime. They also face increased problems created by an unstable economy, increased competition, employee downsizing, the quest for improved quality, and the need for efficient use of the firm's resources.

To be an effective manager, managers must be able to perform four basic management functions: planning, organizing, leading and motivating, and controlling. All four topics are discussed in Chapter 6, Understanding the Management Process. To successfully perform these management functions, managers must possess four very important skills.

- *Interpersonal skills*—The ability to deal effectively with individual employees, other managers within the firm, and people outside the firm.
- *Analytic skills*—The ability to identify problems correctly, generate reasonable alternatives, and select the "best" alternatives to solve problems.
- *Technical skills*—The skill required to accomplish a specific kind of work being done in an organization. Although managers may not actually perform the technical tasks, they should be able to train employees and answer technical questions.
- *Conceptual skills*—The ability to think in abstract terms in order to see the "big picture." Conceptual skills help managers understand how the various parts of an organization or idea can fit together.

In addition to the four skills just described, a successful manager will need many of the same characteristics that an employee needs to be successful.

TO START YOUR OWN BUSINESS Some people prefer to work for themselves, and they open their own businesses. To be successful, business owners must possess many of the same characteristics that successful employees have, and they must be willing to work hard and put in long hours.

It also helps if your small business can provide a product or service that customers want. For example, Steve Demeter, the CEO and founder of the software development firm Demiforce, began his career by creating the *Trism* application for the Apple iPhone. *Trism* was an immediate sensation and sold 50,000 copies at $4.99 in its first two months on Apple's App Store. Now Demeter and the employees at Demiforce are working with a number of promising ideas in the works all with one goal in mind: to provide games and applications that people want.[4]

Unfortunately, many small-business firms fail: Approximately 70 percent of them fail within the first ten years. Typical reasons for business failures include undercapitalization (not enough money), poor business location, poor customer service, unqualified or untrained employees, fraud, lack of a proper business plan, and failure to seek outside professional help. The material in Chapter 5, Small Business, Entrepreneurship, and Franchises, and selected topics and examples throughout this text will help you to decide whether you want to open your own business. This material will also help you to overcome many of these problems.

TO BECOME A BETTER INFORMED CONSUMER AND INVESTOR The world of business surrounds us. You cannot buy a home, a new Ford Fusion Hybrid from the local Ford dealer, a pair of jeans at Gap Inc., or a hot dog from a street vendor without entering into a business transaction. Because you no doubt will engage in business transactions almost every day of your life, one very good reason for studying business is to become a more fully informed consumer.

Many people also rely on a basic understanding of business to help them to invest for the future. According to Julie Stav, Hispanic stockbroker-turned-author/radio personality, "Take $25, add to it drive plus determination and then watch it multiply into

Concept Check

✓ What reasons would you give if you were advising someone to study business?

✓ What factors affect a person's choice of careers?

✓ Once you have a job, what steps can you take to be successful?

an empire."[5] The author of *Get Your Share* believes that it is important to learn the basics about the economy and business, stocks, mutual funds, and other alternatives before investing your money. She also believes that it is never too early to start investing. Although this is an obvious conclusion, just dreaming of being rich does not make it happen. In fact, like many facets of life, it takes planning and determination to establish the type of investment program that will help you to accomplish your financial goals.

Special Note to Business Students

It is important to begin reading this text with one thing in mind: *This business course does not have to be difficult.* We have done everything possible to eliminate the problems that you encounter in a typical class. All of the features in each chapter have been evaluated and recommended by instructors with years of teaching experience. In addition, business students were asked to critique each chapter component. Based on this feedback, the text includes the following features:

- *Learning objectives* appear at the beginning of each chapter.
- *Inside Business* is a chapter-opening case that highlights how successful companies do business on a day-to-day basis.
- *Margin notes* are used throughout the text to reinforce both learning objectives and key terms.
- *Boxed features* in each chapter highlight how both employees and entrepreneurs can be ethical and successful.
- *Two Personal Apps* in each chapter provide special student-centered examples and explanations that help you immediately grasp and retain the material.
- *Sustaining the Planet* features provide information about companies working to protect the environment.
- *Social Media* features provide examples of how businesses and individuals are using social networking and social media sites.
- *Concept Checks* at the end of each major section within a chapter help you test your understanding of the major issues just discussed.
- *End-of-chapter materials* provide a chapter summary, a list of key terms, discussion questions, a Test Yourself Quiz, and a video case about a successful, real-world company.
- The last section of every chapter is entitled *Building Skills for Career Success* and includes exercises devoted to enhancing your social media skills, building team skills, and researching different careers.
- *End-of-part materials* provide a continuing video case about Graeter's Ice Cream, a company that operates a chain of retail outlets in the Cincinnati, Ohio, area and sells to Kroger Stores and other retailers throughout the country. Also, at the end of each major part is an exercise designed to help you to develop the components that are included in a typical business plan.

In addition to the text, a number of student supplements will help you to explore the world of business. We are especially proud of the website that accompanies this edition. There, you will find online study aids, such as interactive quizzes, key terms and definitions, student PowerPoint slides, crossword puzzles, and links to the videos for each chapter. If you want to take a look at the Internet support materials available for this edition of *Business*,

1. Go to www.cengagebrain.com.
2. At the CengageBrain.com home page, search for the ISBN for your book (located on the back cover of your book) using the search box at the top of the page. This will take you to the textbook website where companion resources can be found.

As authors, we want you to be successful. We know that your time is valuable and that your schedule is crowded with many different activities. We also appreciate the fact that textbooks are expensive. Therefore, we want you to use this text and get the most out of your investment. To help you get off to a good start, a number of suggestions for developing effective study skills and using this text are provided in Table 1-1.

TABLE 1-1 Seven Ways to Use This Text and Its Resources

1. Prepare before you go to class.	Early preparation is the key to success in many of life's activities. Certainly, early preparation for this course can help you to participate in class, ask questions, and improve your performance on examinations.
2. Read the chapter.	Although it may seem like an obvious suggestion, many students never take the time to really read the material. Find a quiet space where there are no distractions, and invest enough time to become a "content expert."
3. Underline or highlight important concepts.	Make this text yours. Do not be afraid to write on the pages of your text or highlight important material. It is much easier to review material if you have identified important concepts.
4. Take notes.	While reading, take the time to jot down important points and summarize concepts in your own words. Also, take notes in class.
5. Apply the concepts.	Learning is always easier if you can apply the content to your real-life situation. Think about how you could use the material either now or in the future.
6. Practice critical thinking.	Test the material in the text. Do the concepts make sense? To build critical-thinking skills, answer the discussion questions and the questions that accompany the cases at the end of each chapter. Also, many of the exercises in the Building Skills for Career Success require critical thinking.
7. Prepare for the examinations.	Allow enough time to review the material before the examinations. Check out the concept check questions at the end of each major section in the chapter and the summary at the end of the chapter. Then use the resources on the text website.

© CENGAGE LEARNING 2015

Because a text should always be evaluated by the students and instructors who use it, we would welcome and sincerely appreciate your comments and suggestions. Please feel free to contact us by using one of the following e-mail addresses:

Bill Pride: w-pride@tamu.edu

Bob Hughes: bhughes@dcccd.edu

Jack Kapoor: kapoorj@cod.edu

Learning Objective

2 Define *business* and identify potential risks and rewards.

business the organized effort of individuals to produce and sell, for a profit, the goods and services that satisfy society's needs

BUSINESS: A DEFINITION

Business is the organized effort of individuals to produce and sell, for a profit, the goods and services that satisfy society's needs. The general term *business* refers to all such efforts within a society (as in "American business"). However, *a business* is a particular organization, such as Kraft Foods, Inc., or Cracker Barrel Old Country Stores. To be successful, a business must perform three activities. It must be organized, it must satisfy needs, and it must earn a profit.

The Organized Effort of Individuals

For a business to be organized, it must combine four kinds of resources: material, human, financial, and informational. *Material* resources include the raw materials used in manufacturing processes as well as buildings and machinery. For example, Mrs. Fields Cookies needs flour, sugar, butter, eggs, and other raw materials to produce the food products it sells worldwide. In addition, this Colorado-based company needs human, financial, and informational resources. *Human* resources are the people who furnish their labor to the business in return for wages. The *financial* resource is the money required to pay employees, purchase materials, and generally keep the business operating. *Information* is the resource that tells the managers of the business how effectively the other three resources are being combined and used (see Figure 1-2).

Today, businesses are usually organized as one of three specific types. *Service businesses* produce services, such as haircuts, legal advice, or tax preparation. H&R Block provides tax preparation, retail banking, and software and digital products to both businesses and consumers in the United States, Canada, and Australia.

FIGURE 1-2 Combining Resources

A business must combine all four resources effectively to be successful.

© CENGAGE LEARNING 2015

Manufacturing businesses process various materials into tangible goods, such as delivery trucks, towels, or computers. Intel, for example, produces computer chips that, in turn, are sold to companies that manufacture computers. Finally, some firms called *marketing intermediaries* buy products from manufacturers and then resell them. Sony Corporation is a manufacturer that produces stereo equipment, televisions, and other electronic products. These products may be sold to a marketing intermediary such as Best Buy or Walmart, which then resells the manufactured goods to consumers in their retail stores.

Satisfying Needs

The ultimate objective of every firm must be to satisfy the needs of its customers. People generally do not buy goods and services simply to own them; they buy goods and services to satisfy particular needs. Some of us may feel that the need for transportation is best satisfied by an air-conditioned BMW with navigation system, stereo system, heated and cooled seats, automatic transmission, power windows, and remote-control side mirrors. Others may believe that a Chevrolet Sonic with a stick shift will do just fine. Both products are available to those who want them, along with a wide variety of other products that satisfy the need for transportation.

When firms lose sight of their customers' needs, they are likely to find the going rough. However, when businesses understand their customers' needs and work to satisfy those needs, they are usually successful. Back in 1962, Sam Walton opened his first discount store in Rogers, Arkansas. Although the original store was quite different from the Walmart Superstores you see today, the basic ideas of providing customer service and offering goods that satisfied needs at low prices are part of the reason why this firm has grown to become the largest retailer in the world.

BLOOMBERG/GETTY IMAGES

Do you recognize these two entrepreneurs?
Although you may not recognize the two people in this photo, there's a good chance that you will recognize the businesses that they started. On the left is Jack Dorsey—one of the co-founders of Twitter and Square, Inc. On the right is Howard Schultz—the founder and CEO of Starbucks. Both are known for the ideas that helped make their companies a success.

Business Profit

A business receives money (sales revenue) from its customers in exchange for goods or services. It must also pay out money to cover the expenses involved in doing business. If the firm's sales revenues are greater than its expenses, it has earned a profit. More specifically, as shown in Figure 1-3, **profit** is what remains after all business expenses have been deducted from sales revenue.

A negative profit, which results when a firm's expenses are greater than its sales revenue, is called a *loss*. A business cannot continue to operate at a loss for an indefinite period of time. Management and employees must find some way to increase sales revenues and reduce expenses to return to profitability. If some specific actions are not taken to eliminate losses, a firm may be forced to close

profit what remains after all business expenses have been deducted from sales revenue

FIGURE 1-3 The Relationship Between Sales Revenue and Profit

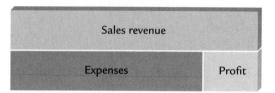

Profit is what remains after all business expenses have been deducted from sales revenue.

© CENGAGE LEARNING 2015

its doors or file for bankruptcy protection. Although many people—especially stockholders and business owners—believe that profit is literally the bottom line or most important goal for a business, many stakeholders may be just as concerned about a firm's social responsibility record. The term **stakeholders** is used to describe all the different people or groups of people who are affected by an organization's policies, decisions, and activities. Many corporations, for example, are careful to point out their efforts to sustain the planet, participate in the green ecological movement, and help people to live better lives in an annual social responsibility report. In its latest social responsibility report, General Mills describes how it contributes $2 million each week to a wide variety of causes, including support for programs that feed the hungry and non profit organizations in the United States and around the globe.[6] Although stockholders and business owners sometimes argue that the money that a business contributes to charitable causes could have been used to pay larger dividends to stockholders or increase the return on the owners' investment, the fact is that most socially responsible business firms feel social responsibility is the right thing to do and is good for business.

The profit earned by a business becomes the property of its owners. Thus, in one sense, profit is the reward business owners receive for producing goods and services that customers want. Profit is also the payment that business owners receive for assuming the considerable risks of business ownership. One of these is the risk of not being paid. Everyone else—employees, suppliers, and lenders—must be paid before the owners.

A second risk that owners undertake is the risk of losing whatever they have invested into the business. A business that cannot earn a profit is very likely to fail, in which case the owners lose whatever money, effort, and time they have invested.

To satisfy society's needs and make a profit, a business must operate within the parameters of a nation's economic system. In the next section, we define economics and describe two different types of economic systems.

stakeholders all the different people or groups of people who are affected by an organization's policies, decisions, and activities

Concept Check

✓ Describe the four resources that must be combined to organize and operate a business.

✓ What is the difference between a manufacturing business, a service business, and a marketing intermediary?

✓ Explain the relationship among profit, business risk, and the satisfaction of customers' needs.

Learning Objective

3 Define *economics* and describe the two types of economic systems: capitalism and command economy.

economics the study of how wealth is created and distributed

TYPES OF ECONOMIC SYSTEMS

Economics is the study of how wealth is created and distributed. By *wealth*, we mean "anything of value," including the goods and services produced and sold by business. *How wealth is distributed* simply means "who gets what." Experts often use economics to explain the choices we make and how these choices change as we cope with the demands of everyday life. In simple terms, individuals, businesses, governments, and society must make decisions that reflect what is important to each group at a particular time. For example, suppose you want to take a weekend trip to some exotic vacation spot, and you also want to begin an investment program. Because of your financial resources, though, you cannot do both, so you must decide what is most important. Business firms, governments, and to some extent society face the same types of decisions. Each group must deal with scarcity when making important decisions. In this case, *scarcity* means "lack of resources"—money, time, natural resources, and so on—that are needed to satisfy a want or need.

Today, experts often study economic problems from two different perspectives: microeconomics and macroeconomics. **Microeconomics** is the study of the decisions made by individuals and businesses. Microeconomics, for example, examines how the prices of homes affect the number of homes individuals will buy. On the other hand, **macroeconomics** is the study of the national economy and the global economy. Macroeconomics examines the economic effect of national income, unemployment, inflation, taxes, government spending, interest rates, and similar factors on a nation and society.

The decisions that individuals, business firms, government, and society make, and the way in which people deal with the creation and distribution of wealth determine the kind of economic system, or **economy**, that a nation has.

Over the years, the economic systems of the world have differed in essentially two ways: (1) the ownership of the factors of production and (2) how they answer four basic economic questions that direct a nation's economic activity.

Factors of production are the resources used to produce goods and services. There are four such factors:

- *Land and natural resources*—elements that can be used in the production process to make appliances, automobiles, and other products. Typical examples include crude oil, forests, minerals, land, water, and even air.
- *Labor*—the time and effort that we use to produce goods and services. It includes human resources such as managers and employees.
- *Capital*—the money, facilities, equipment, and machines used in the operation of organizations. Although most people think of capital as just money, it can also be the manufacturing equipment in a Pepperidge Farm production facility or a computer used in the corporate offices of McDonald's.
- *Entrepreneurship*—the activity that organizes land and natural resources, labor, and capital. It is the willingness to take risks and the knowledge and ability to use the other factors of production efficiently. An **entrepreneur** is a person who risks his or her time, effort, and money to start and operate a business.

A nation's economic system significantly affects all the economic activities of its citizens and organizations. This far-reaching impact becomes more apparent when we consider that a country's economic system determines how the factors of production are used to meet the needs of society. Today, two different economic systems exist: capitalism and command economies. The way each system answers the four basic economic questions listed here determines a nation's economy.

1. *What* goods and services—and how much of each—will be produced?
2. *How* will these goods and services be produced?
3. *For whom* will these goods and services be produced?
4. *Who* owns and who controls the major factors of production?

© MIKER/SHUTTERSTOCK.COM

Saving natural resources one bus at a time. While "green" used to refer to a color in a box of crayons, now it has taken on a whole new meaning. For consumers, the government, *and* businesses, green means a new way to save natural resources, to protect the environment, and often to reduce our dependence on oil from foreign countries.

microeconomics the study of the decisions made by individuals and businesses

macroeconomics the study of the national economy and the global economy

economy the way in which people deal with the creation and distribution of wealth

factors of production resources used to produce goods and services

entrepreneur a person who risks time, effort, and money to start and operate a business

Entrepreneurial Success

Building a Million-Dollar App Business

Nick D'Aloisio, who lives in the south of London, England, created his first iPhone app when he was 12. Two apps later, teen entrepreneur D'Aloisio hit upon a new app idea that has brought him into the major leagues of the app business world.

D'Aloisio was searching the Internet for information for a term paper when he realized how much time it takes to determine the content of each web page. To speed things up, he developed an algorithm that summarizes the key points in a few words. He named this app Trimit, priced it at 99 cents per download, released it on Apple's App Store, and earned $1,600 within the first three days.

To accelerate Trimit's momentum, D'Aloisio decided to give it away free instead of charging for it. The app's download numbers skyrocketed, bringing it to the attention of Horizon Ventures, a firm that invests in businesses when they're in the early stages of growth. Horizon invested $250,000 to commercialize the app, which was renamed Summly and relaunched a few months later. As Summly, the app was downloaded 30,000 times in the first week alone, putting D'Aloisio squarely on the path toward his goal of building a $1 million app business.

Sources: Based on information in the Summly website at www.summly.com (accessed January 7, 2013), Jane Wakefield, "British Teenage Designer of Summly App Hits Jackpot," *BBC News*, December 28, 2011, www.bbc.co.uk; Parmy Olson, "Teen Programmer Hopes to Make a Million from A.I. App," *Forbes*, September 1, 2011, www.forbes.com; Kit Eaton, "The 15-year-old Creator of the Trimit App Makes Regular Old Entrepreneurs Seem Like Slackers," *Fast Company*, August 11, 2011, www.fastcompany.com.

capitalism an economic system in which individuals own and operate the majority of businesses that provide goods and services

invisible hand a term created by Adam Smith to describe how an individual's personal gain benefits others and a nation's economy

Capitalism

Capitalism is an economic system in which individuals own and operate the majority of businesses that provide goods and services. Capitalism stems from the theories of the 18th-century Scottish economist Adam Smith. In his book *Wealth of Nations*, published in 1776, Smith argued that a society's interests are best served when the individuals within that society are allowed to pursue their own self-interest. According to Smith, when individuals act to improve their own fortunes, they indirectly promote the good of their community and the people in that community. Smith went on to call this concept the "invisible hand." The **invisible hand** is a term created by Adam Smith to describe how an individual's own personal gain benefits others and a nation's economy. For example, the only way a small-business owner who produces shoes can increase personal wealth is to sell shoes to customers. To become even more prosperous, the small-business owner must hire workers to produce even more shoes. According to the invisible hand, people in the small-business owner's community not only would have shoes but also would have jobs working for the shoemaker. Thus, the success of people in the community and, to some extent, the nation's economy are tied indirectly to the success of the small-business owner.

Adam Smith's capitalism is based on the following fundamental issues—also see Figure 1-4.

1. The creation of wealth is properly the concern of private individuals, not the government.
2. Private individuals must own private property and the resources used to create wealth.
3. Economic freedom ensures the existence of competitive markets that allow both sellers and buyers to enter and exit the market as they choose.
4. The role of government should be limited to providing defense against foreign enemies, ensuring internal order, and furnishing public works and education.

One factor that Smith felt was extremely important was the role of government. He believed that government should act only as rule maker and umpire. The French term *laissez-faire* describes Smith's capitalistic system and implies that there should

FIGURE 1-4 Basic Assumptions of Adam Smith's Laissez-Faire Capitalism

Laissez-Faire capitalism

Right to create wealth

Right to own private property and resources

Right to economic freedom and freedom to compete

Right to limited government intervention

© CENGAGE LEARNING 2015

be no government interference in the economy. Loosely translated, this term means "let them do" (as they see fit).

Adam Smith's laissez-faire capitalism is also based on the concept of a market economy. A **market economy** (sometimes referred to as a *free-market economy*) is an economic system in which businesses and individuals decide what to produce and buy, and the market determines prices and quantities sold. The owners of resources should be free to determine how these resources are used and also to enjoy the income, profits, and other benefits derived from ownership of these resources.

market economy an economic system in which businesses and individuals decide what to produce and buy, and the market determines quantities sold and prices

Capitalism in the United States

Our economic system is rooted in the laissez-faire capitalism of Adam Smith. However, our real-world economy is not as laissez-faire as Smith would have liked because government participates as more than umpire and rule maker. Our economy is, in fact, a **mixed economy**, one that exhibits elements of both capitalism and socialism.

In a mixed economy, the four basic economic questions discussed at the beginning of this section (*what, how, for whom,* and *who*) are answered through the interaction of households, businesses, and governments. The interactions among these three groups are shown in Figure 1-5.

mixed economy an economy that exhibits elements of both capitalism and socialism

HOUSEHOLDS Households, made up of individuals, are the consumers of goods and services as well as owners of some of the factors of production. As *resource owners*, the members of households provide businesses with labor, capital, and other resources. In return, businesses pay wages, rent, and dividends and interest, which households receive as income.

FIGURE 1-5 The Circular Flow in Our Mixed Economy

Our economic system is guided by the interaction of buyers and sellers, with the role of government being taken into account.

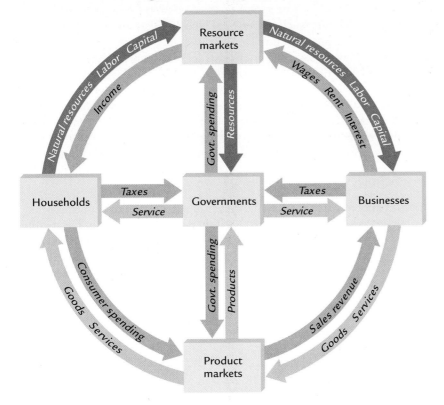

© CENGAGE LEARNING 2015

Why is Apple successful? The answer: The company has a history of introducing state-of-the-art consumer products like the iPhone and iPad. In fact, consumers often line up and wait for hours to get Apple's latest products.

consumer products goods and services purchased by individuals for personal consumption

As *consumers*, household members use their income to purchase the goods and services produced by business. Today, approximately 70 percent of our nation's total production consists of **consumer products**—goods and services purchased by individuals for personal consumption.[7] This means that consumers, as a group, are the biggest customers of American business.

BUSINESSES Like households, businesses are engaged in two different exchanges. They exchange money for natural resources, labor, and capital and use these resources to produce goods and services. Then they exchange their goods and services for sales revenue. This sales revenue, in turn, is exchanged for additional resources, which are used to produce and sell more goods and services.

Along the way, of course, business owners would like to remove something from the circular flow in the form of profits. When business profits are distributed to business owners, these profits become household income. (Business owners are, after all, members of households.) Households try to retain some income as savings. But are profits and savings really removed from the flow? Usually not! When the economy is running smoothly, households are willing to invest their savings in businesses. They can do so directly by buying stocks issued by businesses, by purchasing shares in mutual funds that purchase stocks in businesses, or by lending money to businesses. They can also invest indirectly by placing their savings in bank accounts. Banks and other financial institutions then invest these savings as part of their normal business operations. Thus, business profits, too, are retained in the business system, and the circular flow in Figure 1-5 is complete. How, then, does government fit in?

GOVERNMENTS The numerous government services are important but they (1) would either not be produced by private business firms or (2) would be produced only for those who could afford them. Typical services include national defense, police, fire protection, education, and construction of roads and highways. To pay for all these services, governments collect a variety of taxes from households (such as personal income taxes and sales taxes) and from businesses (corporate income taxes).

Figure 1-5 shows this exchange of taxes for government services. It also shows government spending of tax dollars for resources and products required to provide these services.

Actually, with government included, our circular flow looks more like a combination of several flows. In reality, it is. The important point is that together the various flows make up a single unit—a complete economic system that effectively provides answers to the basic economic questions. Simply put, the system works.

Command Economies

command economy an economic system in which the government decides what goods and services will be produced, how they will be produced, for whom available goods and services will be produced, and who owns and controls the major factors of production

A **command economy** is an economic system in which the government decides *what* goods and services will be produced, *how* they will be produced, *for whom* available goods and services will be produced, and *who* owns and controls the major factors of production. The answers to all four basic economic questions are determined, at least to some degree, through centralized government planning. Today, two types of economic systems—*socialism* and *communism*—serve as examples of command economies.

SOCIALISM In a socialist economy, the key industries are owned and controlled by the government. Such industries usually include transportation, utilities, communications, banking, and industries producing important materials such as steel. Land, buildings, and raw materials may also be the property of the state in a socialist economy. Depending on the country, private ownership of smaller businesses is permitted to varying degrees. Usually, people may choose their own occupations, although many work in state-owned industries.

What to produce and how to produce it are determined in accordance with national goals, which are based on projected needs and the availability of resources. The distribution of goods and services—who gets what—is also controlled by the state to the extent that it controls taxes, rents, and wages. Among the professed aims of socialist countries are the equitable distribution of income, the elimination of poverty, and the distribution of social services (such as medical care) to all who need them. The disadvantages of socialism include increased taxation and loss of incentive and motivation for both individuals and business owners.

Today, many of the nations that have been labeled as socialist nations traditionally, including France, Sweden, and India, are transitioning to a free-market economy. Currently, many countries that were once thought of as communist countries are now often referred to as socialist countries. Examples of former communist countries often referred to as socialists (or even capitalists) include most of the nations that were formerly part of the Union of Soviet Socialist Republics, China, and Vietnam.

COMMUNISM If Adam Smith was the father of capitalism, Karl Marx was the father of communism. In his writings during the mid-19th century, Marx advocated a classless society whose citizens together owned all economic resources. All workers would then contribute to this *communist* society according to their ability and would receive benefits according to their need.

Since the breakup of the Soviet Union and economic reforms in China and most of the Eastern European countries, the best remaining examples of communism are North Korea and Cuba. Today these so-called communist economies seem to practice a strictly controlled kind of socialism. The basic four economic questions are answered through centralized government plans. Emphasis is placed on the production of goods the government needs rather than on the products that consumers might want, so there are frequent shortages of consumer goods.

MEASURING ECONOMIC PERFORMANCE

Consider for just a moment the following questions:

- Is the gross domestic product for the United States increasing or decreasing?
- Why is the unemployment rate important?
- Are U.S. workers as productive as workers in other countries?

The information needed to answer these questions is easily obtainable from many sources. More important, the answers to these and other questions can be used to gauge the economic health of the nation. For individuals, the health of the nation's economy can affect:

- the financing you need to continue your education;
- your ability to get a job; and
- the amount of interest you pay for credit card purchases, automobiles, homes, and other credit transactions.

The Importance of Productivity in the Global Marketplace

One way to measure a nation's economic performance is to assess its productivity. While there are other definitions of productivity, for our purposes, **productivity** is the average level of output per worker per hour.

Concept Check

✓ What are the four basic economic questions? How are they answered in a capitalist economy?

✓ Describe the four basic assumptions required for a laissez-faire capitalist economy.

✓ Why is the American economy called a mixed economy?

✓ How does capitalism differ from socialism and communism?

Learning Objective

4 Identify the ways to measure economic performance.

productivity the average level of output per worker per hour

One way to reduce costs is to manufacture products in a foreign country. In this photo, a Chinese worker assembles an electronic keyboard. To compete with foreign competition, manufacturers in the United States use sophisticated equipment and the latest technology to reduce costs, increase profits, *and* improve productivity.

An increase in productivity results in economic growth because a larger number of goods and services are produced by a given labor force. To see how productivity affects you and the economy, consider the following three questions:

Question: *How does productivity growth affect the economy?*

Answer: Because of increased productivity, it now takes fewer workers to produce more goods and services. As a result, employers have reduced costs, earned more profits, and sold their products for less. Finally, productivity growth helps American business to compete more effectively with other nations in a competitive world.

Question: *How does a nation improve productivity?*

Answer: Reducing costs and enabling employees to work more efficiently are at the core of all attempts to improve productivity. Methods that can be used to increase productivity are discussed in detail in Chapter 8, Producing Quality Goods and Services.

Question: *Is productivity growth always good?*

Answer: Fewer workers producing more goods and services can lead to higher unemployment rates. In this case, increased productivity is good for employers but not good for unemployed workers seeking jobs in a very competitive work environment.

The Nation's Gross Domestic Product

In addition to productivity, a measure called *gross domestic product* can be used to measure the economic well-being of a nation. **Gross domestic product (GDP)** is the total dollar value of all goods and services produced by all people within the boundaries of a country during a one-year period. For example, the values of automobiles produced by employees in an American-owned General Motors plant and a Japanese-owned Toyota plant in the United States are both included in the GDP for the United States. The U.S. GDP was $15.7 trillion in 2012.[8] (*Note:* At the time of publication, 2012 was the last year for which complete statistics were available.)

The GDP figure facilitates comparisons between the United States and other countries because it is the standard used in international guidelines for economic accounting. It is also possible to compare the GDP for one nation over several different time periods. This comparison allows observers to determine the extent to which a nation is experiencing economic growth. For example, government experts project that GDP will grow to $23.7 trillion by the year 2020.[9]

To make accurate comparisons of the GDP for different years, we must adjust the dollar amounts for inflation. **Inflation** is a general rise in the level of prices. (The opposite of inflation is deflation.) **Deflation** is a general decrease in the level of prices. By using inflation-adjusted figures, we are able to measure the *real* GDP for a nation. In effect, it is now possible to compare the products and services produced by a nation in constant dollars—dollars that will purchase the same amount of goods and services. Figure 1-6 depicts the GDP of the United States in current dollars and the real GDP in inflation-adjusted dollars. Note that between 1990 and 2012, America's real GDP grew from $8 trillion to $13.6 trillion.[10]

Important Economic Indicators That Measure a Nation's Economy

In addition to productivity, GDP, and real GDP, other economic measures exist that can be used to evaluate a nation's economy. Because of the recent economic crisis, one very important statistic is the unemployment rate. The **unemployment rate** is the percentage of a nation's labor force unemployed at any time. Although the unemployment rate for the United States is typically about 4 to 6 percent, it peaked during the recent economic crisis. Despite both federal and state programs to reduce the unemployment rate for the United States, it is still hovering between 7 and 8 percent

---

gross domestic product (GDP) the total dollar value of all goods and services produced by all people within the boundaries of a country during a one-year period

inflation a general rise in the level of prices

deflation a general decrease in the level of prices

unemployment rate the percentage of a nation's labor force unemployed at any time

---

Concept Check

✓ How does an increase in productivity affect business?

✓ Define gross domestic product. Why is this economic measure significant?

✓ How does inflation affect the prices you pay for goods and services?

✓ How is the producer price index related to the consumer price index?

FIGURE 1-6 GDP in Current Dollars and in Inflation-Adjusted Dollars

The change in GDP and real GDP for the United States from one year to another year can be used to measure economic growth.

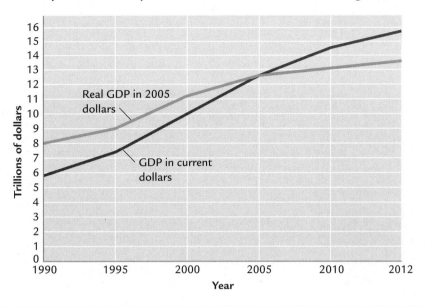

Source: U.S. Bureau of Economic Analysis website at www.bea.gov (accessed January 30, 2013).

at the time of publication. This is an especially important statistic—especially if you are unemployed.

The **consumer price index (CPI)** is a monthly index that measures the changes in prices of a fixed basket of goods purchased by a typical consumer in an urban area. Goods listed in the CPI include food and beverages, transportation, housing, clothing, medical care, recreation, education, communication, and other goods and services. Economists often use the CPI to determine the effect of inflation on not only the nation's economy but also individual consumers. Another monthly index is the producer price index. The **producer price index (PPI)** measures prices that producers receive for their finished goods. Because changes in the PPI reflect price increases or decreases at the wholesale level, the PPI is an accurate predictor of both changes in the CPI and prices that consumers will pay for many everyday necessities.

Some additional economic measures are described in Table 1-2. Like the measures for GDP, real GDP, unemployment rate, and price indexes, these measures can be used to compare one economic statistic over different periods of time.

THE BUSINESS CYCLE

All industrialized nations of the world seek economic growth, full employment, and price stability. However, a nation's economy fluctuates rather than grows at a steady pace every year. In fact, if you were to graph the economic growth rate for a country like the United States, it would resemble a roller-coaster ride with peaks (high points) and troughs (low points). These fluctuations are generally referred to as the **business cycle**, that is, the recurrence of periods of growth and recession in a nation's economic activity.

At the time of publication, many experts believed that the U.S. economy was showing signs of improvement. However, the nation's unemployment rate is still high and people are reluctant to spend money on many consumer goods. Although the federal government has enacted a number of stimulus plans to help unemployed

consumer price index (CPI) a monthly index that measures the changes in prices of a fixed basket of goods purchased by a typical consumer in an urban area

producer price index (PPI) an index that measures prices that producers receive for their finished goods

Learning Objective

5 Examine the different phases in the typical business cycle.

business cycle the recurrence of periods of growth and recession in a nation's economic activity

TABLE 1-2 Common Measures Used to Evaluate a Nation's Economic Health

Economic Measure	Description
1. Balance of trade	The total value of a nation's exports minus the total value of its imports over a specific period of time.
2. Consumer confidence index	A measure of how optimistic or pessimistic consumers are about the nation's economy. This measure is usually reported on a monthly basis.
3. Corporate profits	The total amount of profits made by corporations over selected time periods.
4. Inflation rate	An economic statistic that tracks the increase in prices of goods and services over a period of time. This measure is usually calculated on a monthly or an annual basis.
5. National income	The total income earned by various segments of the population, including employees, self-employed individuals, corporations, and other types of income.
6. New housing starts	The total number of new homes started during a specific time period.
7. Prime interest rate	The lowest interest rate that banks charge their most credit-worthy customers.

© CENGAGE LEARNING 2015

recession two or more consecutive three-month periods of decline in a country's GDP

© IQONCEPT/SHUTTERSTOCK.COM

Just push the red button.
Unfortunately, it's not that easy to stop a recession and restore a nation's economy. A recession—two or more consecutive three-month period of decline in a country's gross domestic products—can impact both what consumers buy and what businesses produce.

depression a severe recession that lasts longer than a typical recession and has a larger decline in business activity when compared to a recession

monetary policies Federal Reserve's decisions that determine the size of the supply of money in the nation and the level of interest rates

fiscal policy government influence on the amount of savings and expenditures; accomplished by altering the tax structure and by changing the levels of government spending

workers, to shore up the nation's financial system, and to reduce the number of home foreclosures, many experts still believe that we have serious financial problems. For one, the size of the national debt—a topic described later in this section—is a concern. To make matters worse, the recent economic crisis did not affect just the U.S. economy but also the economies of countries around the world.

The changes that result from either economic growth or economic downturn affect the amount of products and services that consumers are willing to purchase and, as a result, the amount of products and services produced by business firms. Generally, the business cycle consists of four phases: the peak (sometimes called prosperity), recession, the trough, and recovery (sometimes called expansion).

During the *peak period* (prosperity), the economy is at its highest point and unemployment is low. Total income is relatively high. As long as the economic outlook remains prosperous, consumers are willing to buy products and services. In fact, businesses often expand and offer new products and services during the peak period to take advantage of consumers' increased buying power.

Generally, economists define a **recession** as two or more consecutive three-month periods of decline in a country's GDP. Because unemployment rises during a recession, total buying power declines. The pessimism that accompanies a recession often stifles both consumer and business spending. As buying power decreases, consumers tend to become more value conscious and reluctant to purchase frivolous or nonessential items. And companies and government at all levels often postpone or go slow on major projects during a recession. In response to a recession, many businesses focus on producing the products and services that provide the most value to their customers.

Economists define a **depression** as a severe recession that lasts longer than a typical recession and has a larger decline in business activity when compared to a recession. A depression is characterized by extremely high unemployment rates, low wages, reduced purchasing power, lack of confidence in the economy, lower stock values, and a general decrease in business activity.

The third phase of the business cycle is the *trough*. The trough of a recession or depression is the turning point when a nation's production and employment bottom out and reach their lowest levels. To offset the effects of recession and depression, the federal government uses both monetary and fiscal policies. **Monetary policies** are the Federal Reserve's decisions that determine the size of the supply of money in the nation and the level of interest rates. Through **fiscal policy**, the government can influence the amount of savings and expenditures by altering the tax structure and changing the levels of government spending.

Although the federal government collects over $2 trillion in annual revenues, the government usually spends more than it receives, resulting in a **federal deficit**. For example, the government had a federal deficit for each year between 2002 and 2012. The total of all federal deficits is called the **national debt**. Today, the U.S. national debt is $16.4 trillion or approximately $52,000 for every man, woman, and child in the United States.[11]

Since World War II, business cycles have lasted from three to five years from one peak period to the next peak period. During the same time period, the average length of recessions has been 11 months.[12] Some experts believe that effective use of monetary and fiscal policies can speed up recovery and reduce the amount of time the economy is in recession. *Recovery* (or *expansion*) is the movement of the economy from recession or depression to prosperity. High unemployment rates decline, income increases, and both the ability and the willingness to buy rise.

At the time of publication, many business leaders, politicians, and consumers are still worried about the health and stability of the U.S. economy. Unfortunately, many of the problems that caused the recent economic crisis are still there, and they will take years to correct and resolve.

federal deficit a shortfall created when the federal government spends more in a fiscal year than it receives

national debt the total of all federal deficits

Concept Check

✓ What are the four phases in the typical business cycle?

✓ At the time you are studying the material in this chapter, which phase of the business cycle do you think the U.S. economy is in? Justify your answer.

✓ How can the government use monetary policy and fiscal policy to reduce the effects of an economic crisis?

TYPES OF COMPETITION

Our capitalist system ensures that individuals and businesses make the decisions about what to produce, how to produce it, and what price to charge for the product. Mattel, Inc., for example, can introduce new versions of its famous Barbie doll, license the Barbie name, change the doll's price and method of distribution, and attempt to produce and market Barbie in other countries or over the Internet at www.mattel.com. Our system also allows customers the right to choose between Mattel's products and those produced by competitors.

As a consumer, you get to choose which products or services you want to buy. Competition like that between Mattel and other toy manufacturers is a necessary and extremely important by-product of capitalism. Business **competition** is essentially a rivalry among businesses for sales to potential customers. In a capitalistic economy, competition also ensures that a firm will survive only if it serves its customers well by providing products and services that meet needs. Economists recognize four different degrees of competition ranging from ideal, complete competition to no competition at all. These are perfect competition, monopolistic competition, oligopoly, and monopoly. For a quick overview of the different types of competition, including numbers of firms and examples for each type, look at Table 1-3.

Learning Objective

6 Outline the four types of competition.

competition rivalry among businesses for sales to potential customers

perfect (or pure) competition the market situation in which there are many buyers and sellers of a product, and no single buyer or seller is powerful enough to affect the price of that product

Perfect Competition

Perfect (or pure) competition is the market situation in which there are many buyers and sellers of a product, and no single buyer or seller is powerful enough to affect the price of that product. For perfect competition to exist, there are five very important concepts.

- We are discussing the market for a single product, such as bushels of wheat.
- There are no restrictions on firms entering the industry.
- All sellers offer essentially the same product for sale.

Competition often gives consumers a choice. Often wonder why there are so many soap products? It's called competition. Different manufacturers use product differentiation to develop and promote the differences between their products and all similar products. Not only does product differentiation help their products stand out from the competition, it gives you—the consumer—a choice.

TABLE 1-3 Four Different Types of Competition

The number of firms determines the degree of competition within an industry.

Type of Competition	Number of Business Firms or Suppliers	Real-World Examples
1. Perfect	Many	Corn, wheat, peanuts
2. Monopolistic	Many	Clothing, shoes
3. Oligopoly	Few	Automobiles, cereals
4. Monopoly	One	Software protected by copyright, many local public utilities

© CENGAGE LEARNING 2015

- All buyers and sellers know everything there is to know about the market (including, in our example, the prices that all sellers are asking for their wheat).
- The overall market is not affected by the actions of any one buyer or seller.

When perfect competition exists, every seller should ask the same price that every other seller is asking. Why? Because if one seller wanted 50 cents more for his products than all the others, that seller would not be able to sell a single product. Buyers could—and would—do better by purchasing the same products from the competition. On the other hand, a firm willing to sell below the going price would sell all its products quickly. However, that seller would lose sales revenue (and profit) because buyers are actually willing to pay more.

In perfect competition, then, sellers—and buyers as well—must accept the going price. The price of each product is determined by the actions of all buyers and all sellers together through the forces of supply and demand.

supply the quantity of a product that producers are willing to sell at each of various prices

THE BASICS OF SUPPLY AND DEMAND The **supply** of a particular product is the quantity of the product that producers are willing to sell at each of various prices. Producers are rational people, so we would expect them to offer more of a product for sale at higher prices and to offer less of the product at lower prices, as illustrated by the supply curve in Figure 1-7.

FIGURE 1-7 Supply Curve and Demand Curve

The intersection of a supply curve and a demand curve is called the *equilibrium*, or *market price*. This intersection indicates a single price and quantity at which suppliers will sell products and buyers will purchase them.

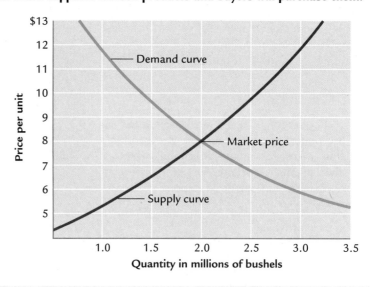

© CENGAGE LEARNING 2015

The **demand** for a particular product is the quantity that buyers are willing to purchase at each of various prices. Buyers, too, are usually rational, so we would expect them—as a group—to buy more of a product when its price is low and to buy less of the product when its price is high, as depicted by the demand curve in Figure 1-7.

THE EQUILIBRIUM, OR MARKET, PRICE There is always one certain price at which the demand for a product is exactly equal to the quantity of that product produced. Suppose that producers are willing to *supply* two million bushels of wheat at a price of $8 per bushel and that buyers are willing to *purchase* two million bushels at a price of $8 per bushel. In other words, supply and demand are in balance, or in equilibrium, at the price of $8. Economists call this price the *market price*. The **market price** of any product is the price at which the quantity demanded is exactly equal to the quantity supplied.

In theory and in the real world, market prices are affected by anything that affects supply and demand. The *demand* for wheat, for example, might change if researchers suddenly discovered that it offered a previously unknown health benefit. Then buyers would demand more wheat at every price. Or the *supply* of wheat might change if new technology permitted the production of greater quantities of wheat from the same amount of acreage. Other changes that can affect competitive prices are shifts in buyer tastes, the development of new products, fluctuations in income owing to inflation or recession, or even changes in the weather that affect the production of wheat.

Perfect competition is quite rare in today's world. Many real markets, however, are examples of monopolistic competition.

GERARD FRITZ/PHOTOGRAPHER'S CHOICE/GETTY IMAGES

Monopolistic Competition

Monopolistic competition is a market situation in which there are many buyers along with a relatively large number of sellers. The various products available in a monopolistically competitive market are very similar in nature, and they are all intended to satisfy the same need. However, each seller attempts to make its product different from the others by providing unique product features, an attention-getting brand name, unique packaging, or services such as free delivery or a lifetime warranty.

Product differentiation is the process of developing and promoting differences between one's products and all competitive products. It is a fact of life for the producers of many consumer goods, from soaps to clothing to furniture to shoes. A furniture manufacturer such as Thomasville sees what looks like a mob of competitors, all trying to chip away at its share of the market. By differentiating each of its products from all similar products produced by competitors, Thomasville obtains some limited control over the market price of its product.

Oligopoly

An **oligopoly** is a market (or industry) situation in which there are few sellers. Generally, these sellers are quite large, and sizable investments are required to enter into their market. Examples of oligopolies are the automobile, airline, car rental, cereal, and farm implement industries.

Because there are few sellers in an oligopoly, the market actions of each seller can have a strong effect on competitors' sales and prices. If General Motors, for example, reduces its automobile prices, Ford, Honda, Toyota, and Nissan usually do the same to retain their market shares. In the absence of much price competition, product differentiation becomes the major competitive weapon; this is very evident in the advertising of the major automobile manufacturers. For instance, when Ford and General Motors began offering cash incentives to encourage consumers to

demand the quantity of a product that buyers are willing to purchase at each of various prices

market price the price at which the quantity demanded is exactly equal to the quantity supplied

monopolistic competition a market situation in which there are many buyers along with a relatively large number of sellers who differentiate their products from the products of competitors

product differentiation the process of developing and promoting differences between one's products and all competitive products

oligopoly a market (or industry) in which there are few sellers

purchase a new automobile at the end of 2012, Chrysler, Honda, Nissan, and Toyota began offering similar incentives and for the same reason—to attract new-car buyers.

Monopoly

A **monopoly** is a market (or industry) with only one seller, and there are barriers to keep other firms from entering the industry. In a monopoly, there is no close substitute for the product or service. Because only one firm is the supplier of a product, it would seem that it has complete control over price. However, no firm can set its price at some astronomical figure just because there is no competition; the firm would soon find that it has no customers or sales revenue either. Instead, the firm in a monopoly position must consider the demand for its product and set the price at the most profitable level.

Classic examples of monopolies in the United States are public utilities, including companies that provide local gas, water, or electricity. Each utility firm operates in a *natural monopoly*, an industry that requires a huge investment in capital and within which any duplication of facilities would be wasteful. Natural monopolies are permitted to exist because the public interest is best served by their existence, but they operate under the scrutiny and control of various state and federal agencies. Although many public utilities are still classified as natural monopolies, there is increased competition in many areas of the country. For example, there have been increased demands for consumer choice when selecting a company that provides electrical service to both homes and businesses.

A legal monopoly—sometimes referred to as a *limited monopoly*—is created when a government entity issues a franchise, license, copyright, patent, or trademark. For example, a copyright exists for a specific period of time and can be used to protect the owners of written materials from unauthorized use by competitors that have not shared in the time, effort, and expense required for their development. Because Microsoft owns the copyright on its popular Windows software, it enjoys a legal-monopoly position. Except for natural monopolies and legal monopolies, federal antitrust laws prohibit both monopolies and attempts to form monopolies.

Concept Check

✓ Is competition good for business? Is it good for consumers?

✓ Compare the four forms of competition.

✓ What is the relationship between supply and demand?

✓ Explain how the equilibrium, or market, price of a product is determined.

AMERICAN BUSINESS TODAY

Although our economic system is far from perfect, it provides Americans with a high standard of living compared with people in other countries throughout the world. **Standard of living** is a loose, subjective measure of how well off an individual or a society is, mainly in terms of want satisfaction through goods and services. Also, our economic system offers solutions to many of the problems that plague society and provides opportunities for people who are willing to work and to continue learning.

To understand the current business environment and the challenges ahead, it helps to understand how business developed.

Early Business Development

Our American business system has its roots in the knowledge, skills, and values that the earliest settlers brought to this country. The first settlers in the United States were concerned mainly with providing themselves with basic necessities—food, clothing, and shelter. Almost all families lived on farms, and the entire family worked at the business of surviving. They used their surplus for trading, mainly by barter, among themselves and with the English trading ships that called at the colonies. **Barter** is a system of exchange in which goods or services are traded directly for other goods or services without using money. As this trade increased, small businesses began to appear. Some settlers were able to use their skills and their excess time to work under the domestic system of production. The **domestic system** was a method of manufacturing in which an entrepreneur distributed raw materials to various homes, where families would process them into finished goods. The entrepreneur then offered the goods for sale.

Then, in 1793, a young English apprentice mechanic named Samuel Slater set up a textile factory in Pawtucket, Rhode Island, to spin raw cotton into thread. Slater's ingenuity resulted in America's first use of the **factory system** of manufacturing, in which all the materials, machinery, and workers required to manufacture a product are assembled in one place. The Industrial Revolution in America was born. A manufacturing technique called *specialization* was used to improve productivity. **Specialization** is the separation of a manufacturing process into distinct tasks and the assignment of the different tasks to different individuals.

The years from 1820 to 1900 were the golden age of invention and innovation in machinery. At the same time, new means of transportation greatly expanded the domestic markets for American products. Certainly, many basic characteristics of our modern business system took form during this time period.

Business Development in the 1900s

Industrial growth and prosperity continued well into the 20th century. Henry Ford's moving automotive assembly line, which brought the work to the worker, refined the concept of specialization and helped spur on the mass production of consumer goods. Fundamental changes occurred in business ownership and management as well. No longer were the largest businesses owned by one individual; instead, ownership was in the hands of thousands of corporate shareholders who were willing to invest in—but not to operate—a business.

The Roaring Twenties ended with the sudden crash of the stock market in 1929 and the near collapse of the economy. The Great Depression that followed in the 1930s was a time of misery and human suffering. People lost their faith in business and its ability to satisfy the needs of society without government involvement. After Franklin D. Roosevelt became president in 1933, the federal government devised a number of programs to get the economy moving again. In implementing these programs, the government got deeply involved in business for the first time.

To understand the major events that shaped the United States during the remainder of the 20th century, it helps to remember that the economy was compared to a roller-coaster ride earlier in this chapter—periods of economic growth followed by periods of economic slowdown. The following are major events that shaped the nation's economy during the period from 1940 to 2000:

- World War II, the Korean War, and the Vietnam War
- Rapid economic growth and higher standard of living during the 1950s and 1960s
- The social responsibility movement during the 1960s
- A shortage of crude oil and higher prices for most goods in the mid-1970s
- High inflation, high interest rates, and reduced business profits during the early 1980s
- Sustained economic growth in the 1990s

During the last part of the 20th century, the Internet became a major force in the economy. e-Business—a topic we will continue to explore throughout this text—became an accepted method of conducting business.

Unfortunately, by the last part of the 20th century, a larger number of business failures and declining stock values were initial signs that larger economic problems were on the way.

EVERETT COLLECTION/SUPERSTOCK

Gas shortages—could it happen again? For an industrialized economy like the United States, crude oil is an essential natural resource. When the nation experienced a shortage of crude oil during the mid-1970s, it was common to see signs like the one in this photo. Even now, both the supply and price for a gallon of gasoline are still concerns as the nation begins to rebound from the recent economic crisis.

factory system a system of manufacturing in which all the materials, machinery, and workers required to manufacture a product are assembled in one place

specialization the separation of a manufacturing process into distinct tasks and the assignment of the different tasks to different individuals

A New Century: 2000 and Beyond

According to many economic experts, the first part of the 21st century might be characterized as the best of times and the worst of times rolled into one package. On the plus side, technology became available at an affordable price. Both individuals and businesses could now access information with the click of a button. They also could buy and sell merchandise online.

In addition to information technology, the growth of service businesses also changed the way American firms do business in the 21st century. Because service businesses employ approximately 85 percent of the nation's workforce, we now have a service economy.[13] A **service economy** is an economy in which more effort is devoted to the production of services than to the production of goods. Typical service businesses include restaurants, laundries and dry cleaners, real estate, movie theaters, repair companies, and other services that we often take for granted. More information about how service businesses affect the economy is provided in Chapter 8, Producing Quality Goods and Services.

On the negative side, it is hard to watch television, surf the Web, listen to the radio, or read the newspaper without hearing some news about the economy. Because many of the economic indicators described in Table 1-2 on page 18 indicate troubling economic problems, there is still a certain amount of pessimism surrounding the economy.

service economy an economy in which more effort is devoted to the production of services than to the production of goods

The Current Business Environment

Before reading on, answer the following question:

In today's competitive business world, which of the following environments affects business?

a. The competitive environment
b. The global environment
c. The technological environment
d. The economic environment
e. All of the above

Correct Answer: e. All the environments listed in the above question affect business today.

THE COMPETITIVE ENVIRONMENT As noted earlier in this chapter, competition is a basic component of capitalism. Every day, business owners must figure out what makes their businesses successful and how the goods and services they provide are different from the competition. Often, the answer is contained in the basic definition of business provided on page 8. Just for a moment, review the definition:

Business is the organized effort of individuals to produce and sell, for a profit, the goods and services that satisfy society's needs.

In the definition of business, note the phrase *satisfy society's needs*. These three words say a lot about how well a successful firm competes with competitors. If you meet customer needs, then you have a better chance at success.

THE GLOBAL ENVIRONMENT Related to the competitive environment is the global environment. Not only do American businesses have to compete with other American businesses, but they also must compete with businesses from all over the globe. According to global experts, China is one of the fastest-growing economies in the world. And China is not alone. Other countries around the world also compete with U.S. firms. There was once a time when the label

"Made in the United States" gave U.S. businesses an inside edge both at home and in the global marketplace. Today, because business firms in other countries manufacture and sell goods, the global marketplace has never been more competitive.

While many foreign firms are attempting to sell goods and services to U.S. customers, U.S. firms are also increasing both sales and profits by selling goods and services to customers in other countries. In fact there are many "potential" customers in developing nations that will buy goods and services manufactured by U.S. firms. For example, Procter & Gamble sells laundry detergent, soap, and diapers in Nigeria and has plans to do business in more than 50 African countries.[14] And Procter & Gamble is not alone. Unilever, DuPont, Johnson & Johnson, General Motors, and many more U.S. companies are also selling goods and services to customers in countries all over the globe.

THE TECHNOLOGY ENVIRONMENT Although increased global competition and technological innovation has changed the way we do business, the technology environment for U.S. businesses has never been more challenging. Changes in manufacturing equipment, distribution of products, and communication with customers are all examples of how technology has changed everyday business practices. For example, many businesses are now using social media to provide customers with information about products and services. If you ask different people, you will often find different definitions for social media, but for our purposes **social media** is defined as online interaction that allows people and businesses to communicate and share ideas, personal information, and information about products or services. To illustrate how popular social media is, consider that Facebook with over one billion active users was launched in 2004 and Twitter with approximately 200 million active users was launched in 2006. Because of rapid developments in social media and the increased importance of technology and information, businesses will need to spend additional money to keep abreast of an ever-changing technology environment and even more money to train employees to use the new technology.

social media the online interaction that allows people and businesses to communicate and share ideas, personal information, and information about products or services

THE ECONOMIC ENVIRONMENT The economic environment must always be considered when making business decisions. This fact is especially important when the nation's economy takes a nosedive or an individual firm's sales revenue and profits are declining. For example, both small and large business firms reduced both spending and hiring new employees over the last five years because of the nation's unstable economy.

In addition to economic pressures, today's socially responsible managers and business owners must be concerned about the concept of sustainability. According to the U.S. Environmental Protection Agency, **sustainability** means creating and maintaining the conditions under which humans and nature can exist in productive harmony while fulfilling the social, economic, and other requirements of present and future generations.[15] Although the word *green* used to mean a color in a box of crayons, today green means a new way of doing business. As a result, a combination of forces, including economic factors, growth in population, increased energy use, and concerns for the environment, is changing the way individuals live and businesses operate.

sustainability creating and maintaining the conditions under which humans and nature can exist in productive harmony while fulfilling the social, economic, and other requirements of present and future generations

When you look back at the original question we asked at the beginning of this section, clearly, each different type of environment—competitive, global, technological, and economic—affects the way a business does *business*. As a result, there are always opportunities for improvement and challenges that must be considered.

The Challenges Ahead

There it is—the American business system in brief.

When it works well, it provides jobs for those who are willing to work, a standard of living that few countries can match, and many opportunities for personal advancement for those willing to work hard and continue to learn. However, like every other system devised by humans, it is not perfect. Our business system may give us prosperity, but it also gave us the Great Depression of the 1930s, the economic problems of the 1970s and the early 1980s, and the recent economic crisis.

Obviously, the system can be improved. Certainly, there are plenty of people who are willing to tell us exactly what they think the American economy needs. However, these people often provide us only with conflicting opinions. Who is right and who is wrong? Even the experts cannot agree.

The experts do agree, however, that several key issues will challenge our economic system (and our nation) over the next decade. Some of the questions to be resolved include:

- How can we create a more stable economy and create new jobs for the unemployed?
- How do we reduce the national debt and still stimulate business growth?
- How do we restore investor confidence in the financial system?
- How can we use technology to make American workers more productive and American firms more competitive in the global marketplace?
- How can we preserve the benefits of competition and small business in our American economic system?
- How can we conserve natural resources and sustain our environment?
- How can we meet the needs of two-income families, single parents, older Americans, and the less fortunate who need health care and social programs to exist?
- How can we defeat terrorism and resolve conflict with Iran, North Korea, and other countries throughout the world?

The answers to these questions are anything but simple. In the past, Americans have always been able to solve their economic problems through ingenuity and creativity. Now, as we continue the journey through the 21st century, we need that same ingenuity and creativity not only to solve our current problems but also to compete in the global marketplace and build a nation and economy for future generations.

The American business system is not perfect by any means, but it does work reasonably well. We discuss some of its problems in Chapter 2 as we examine the topics of social responsibility and business ethics.

Concept Check

✓ How does your standard of living affect the products or services you buy?

✓ What is the difference between the domestic system and the factory system?

✓ Choose one of the environments that affect business and explain how it affects a small electronics manufacturer located in Portland, Oregon.

✓ What do you consider the most important challenge that will face people in the United States in the years ahead?

Looking for Success? *Get Flashcards, Quizzes, Games, Crosswords, and more @ www.cengagebrain.com.*

Summary

1 Discuss what you must do to be successful in the world of business.

For many years, people in business—both employees and managers—assumed that prosperity would continue. When faced with both economic problems and increased competition, a large number of these people began to ask the question: What do we do now? Although this is a fair question, it is difficult to answer. Certainly, for a college student taking business courses or an employee just starting a career, the question is even more difficult to answer. And yet there are still opportunities out there for people who are willing to work hard, continue to learn, and possess the ability to adapt to change. The kind of career you choose ultimately will depend on your own values and what you feel is most important in life. By studying business, you can become a better employee or manager or you may decide to start your own business. You can also become a better consumer and investor.

2 Define *business* and identify potential risks and rewards.

Business is the organized effort of individuals to produce and sell, for a profit, the goods and services that satisfy society's needs. Four kinds of resources—material, human, financial, and informational—must be combined to start and operate a business. The three general types of businesses are service businesses, manufacturers, and marketing intermediaries. Profit is what remains after all business expenses are deducted from sales revenue. It is the payment that owners receive for assuming the risks of business—primarily the risks of not receiving payment and of losing whatever has been invested in the firm. Although many people believe that profit is literally the bottom line or most important goal for a business, the ultimate objective of a successful business is to satisfy the needs of its customers. In addition to profit, many corporations are careful to point out their efforts to sustain the planet, participate in the green ecological movement, and help people to live better lives.

3. Define *economics* and describe the two types of economic systems: capitalism and command economy.

Economics is the study of how wealth is created and distributed. An economic system must answer four questions: *What* goods and services will be produced? *How* will they be produced? *For whom* will they be produced? *Who* owns and who controls the major factors of production? The factors of production are land and natural resources, labor, capital, and entrepreneurship. Capitalism (on which our economic system is based) is an economic system in which individuals own and operate the majority of businesses that provide goods and services. Capitalism stems from the theories of Adam Smith. Smith's pure laissez-faire capitalism is an economic system in which the factors of production are owned by private entities and all individuals are free to use their resources as they see fit; prices are determined by the workings of supply and demand in competitive markets; and the economic role of government is limited to rule maker and umpire.

Our economic system today is a mixed economy and exhibits elements of both capitalism and socialism. In the circular flow that characterizes our business system (see Figure 1-5), households and businesses exchange resources for goods and services, using money as the medium of exchange. In a similar manner, the government collects taxes from businesses and households and purchases products and resources with which to provide services.

In a command economy, government, rather than individuals, owns many of the factors of production and provides the answers to the three other economic questions. Socialist and communist economies are—at least in theory—command economies.

4. Identify the ways to measure economic performance.

One way to evaluate the performance of an economic system is to assess changes in productivity, which is the average level of output per worker per hour. Gross domestic product (GDP) can also be used to measure a nation's economic well-being and is the total dollar value of all goods and services produced by all people within the boundaries of a country during a one-year period. It is also possible to adjust GDP for inflation and thus to measure real GDP. In addition to GDP, other economic indicators include a nation's balance of trade, consumer confidence index, consumer price index (CPI), corporate profits, inflation rate, national income, new housing starts, prime interest rate, producer price index (PPI), and unemployment rate.

5. Examine the different phases in the typical business cycle.

A nation's economy fluctuates rather than grows at a steady pace every year. These fluctuations are generally referred to as the business cycle. Generally, the business cycle consists of four states: the peak (sometimes called prosperity), recession, the trough, and recovery (sometimes called expansion). Some experts believe that effective use of monetary policy (the Federal Reserve's decisions that determine the size of the supply of money and the level of interest rates) and fiscal policy (the government's influence on the amount of savings and expenditures) can speed up recovery.

A federal deficit occurs when the government spends more than it receives in taxes and other revenues. At the time of publication, the national debt is over $16.4 trillion or approximately $52,000 for every man, woman, and child in the United States.

6. Outline the four types of competition.

Competition is essentially a rivalry among businesses for sales to potential customers. In a capitalist economy, competition works to ensure the efficient and effective operation of business. Competition also ensures that a firm will survive only if it serves its customers well by providing products and services that meet their needs. Economists recognize four degrees of competition. Ranging from most to least competitive, the four degrees are perfect competition, monopolistic competition, oligopoly, and monopoly. The factors of supply and demand generally influence the price that customers pay producers for goods and services.

7. Summarize the factors that affect the business environment and the challenges that American businesses will encounter in the future.

From the beginning of the Industrial Revolution to the phenomenal expansion of American industry in the 19th and early 20th centuries, our government maintained an essentially laissez-faire attitude toward business. However, during the Great Depression of the 1930s, the federal government began to provide a number of social services to its citizens.

To understand the major events that shaped the United States during the remainder of the 20th and 21st century, it helps to remember that the economy was compared to a roller-coaster ride earlier in this chapter—periods of economic growth followed by periods of economic slowdown. Events and a changing business environment including wars, rapid economic growth, the social responsibility movement, a shortage of crude oil, high inflation, high interest rates, reduced business profits, increased use of technology, e-business, and social media all have shaped business and the economy.

Now more than ever before, the way a business operates is affected by the competitive environment, global environment, technological environment, and economic environment. As a result, business has a number of opportunities for improvement and challenges for the future.

Key Terms

You should now be able to define and give an example relevant to each of the following terms:

free enterprise (3)
cultural (or workplace) diversity (5)
business (8)
profit (9)
stakeholders (10)
economics (10)
microeconomics (11)
macroeconomics (11)
economy (11)
factors of production (11)
entrepreneur (11)
capitalism (12)

invisible hand (12)
market economy (13)
mixed economy (13)
consumer products (14)
command economy (14)
productivity (15)
gross domestic product (GDP) (16)
inflation (16)
deflation (16)
unemployment rate (16)
consumer price index (CPI) (17)

producer price index (PPI) (17)
business cycle (17)
recession (18)
depression (18)
monetary policies (18)
fiscal policy (18)
federal deficit (19)
national debt (19)
competition (19)
perfect (or pure) competition (19)
supply (20)
demand (21)

market price (21)
monopolistic competition (21)
product differentiation (21)
oligopoly (21)
monopoly (22)
standard of living (22)
barter (22)
domestic system (22)
factory system (23)
specialization (23)
service economy (24)
social media (25)
sustainability (25)

Discussion Questions

1. In what ways have the problems caused by the recent economic crisis affected business firms? In what ways have these problems affected employees and individuals?
2. What factors caused American business to develop into a mixed economic system rather than some other type of economic system?
3. Does an individual consumer really have a voice in answering the basic four economic questions?
4. Is gross domestic product a reliable indicator of a nation's economic health? What might be a better indicator?
5. Discuss this statement: "Business competition encourages improved product quality and increased customer satisfaction."
6. Is government participation in our business system good or bad? What factors can be used to explain your position.
7. Choose one of the challenges listed on page 26 and describe possible ways in which business and society could help to solve or eliminate the problem in the future.

Test Yourself

Matching Questions

1. _____ Materials, machinery, and workers are assembled in one place.
2. _____ The government spends more than it receives.
3. _____ System of exchange.
4. _____ The process of distinguishing Colgate from Crest toothpaste.
5. _____ The average level of output per worker per hour.
6. _____ A study of how wealth is created and distributed.
7. _____ An organized effort to produce and sell goods and services for a profit.
8. _____ A system where individuals own and operate the majority of businesses.
9. _____ A person who takes the risk and invests in a business.
10. _____ Value of all goods and services produced within a country during a one-year period.

a. capitalism
b. economics
c. federal deficit
d. productivity
e. product differentiation
f. business
g. factory system
h. entrepreneur
i. gross domestic product
j. barter

True False Questions

11. **T F** The majority of small business firms are successful at the end of ten years.

12. **T F** For a business to be organized, it must combine four types of resources: workers, natural resources, capital, and ownership.

13. **T F** The equilibrium price means that the supply and demand for a product are in balance.

14. **T F** Under communism, individual consumers determine what will be produced.

15. **T F** Hewlett-Packard Corporation and Dell Computer use product differentiation in the marketplace.

16. **T F** If a firm's sales revenues exceed its expenses, the firm has earned a profit.

17. **T F** Fiscal policy determines the level of interest rates.

18. **T F** The ultimate objective of business firms should be to satisfy the needs of their customers.

19. **T F** Adam Smith is the father of communism and advocated a classless society.

20. **T F** A business cycle consists of four states: peak, recession, trough, and recovery.

Multiple-Choice Questions

21. _____ Demand is a
   a. relationship between prices and the quantities purchased by buyers.
   b. relationship between prices and the quantities offered by producers.
   c. quantity of goods available for purchase.
   d. is measured by comparing the gross domestic product with supply.
   e. by-product of communism.

22. _____ The process of separating work into distinct tasks is called
   a. bartering.
   b. networking.
   c. specialization.
   d. a factory system.
   e. a domestic system.

23. _____ What term implies that there shall be no government interference in the economy?
   a. market economy
   b. free-market economy
   c. command economy
   d. laissez-faire
   e. socialism

24. _____ When the level of prices in an economy rise, it's called
   a. prosperity.
   b. recession.
   c. depression.
   d. recovery.
   e. inflation.

25. _____ The total of all federal deficits is called
   a. depression.
   b. fiscal policy.
   c. gross domestic product.
   d. national debt.
   e. business cycle.

26. _____ The ability to work well with many types of people in the workplace is referred to as
   a. workplace differentiation.
   b. cultural diversity.
   c. economic stability.
   d. career unity.
   e. employee magnification.

27. _____ Best Buy and Walmart are both examples of
   a. production intermediaries.
   b. manufacturing businesses.
   c. service businesses.
   d. marketing intermediaries.
   e. small businesses.

28. _____ The study of the national economy and the global economy is referred to as
   a. factors of the economy.
   b. microeconomics.
   c. macroeconomics.
   d. laissez-faire capitalism.
   e. a command economy.

29. _____ How well off an individual or a society is, mainly in terms of want satisfaction through goods and services is referred to as
   a. microeconomics.
   b. national satisfaction index.
   c. economic standard.
   d. standard of living.
   e. global comparison measure.

30. _____ A monthly index that measures changes in prices that consumers pay for goods is referred to as the
   a. prosperity index.
   b. producer's price index.
   c. prosperity price predictor.
   d. inflation rate index.
   e. consumer price index.

Answers to the Test Yourself questions appear at the end of the book on page TY-1.

Video Case

KlipTech Turns Recycled Paper into Products and Profits

Joel Klippert became an entrepreneur at the urging of his wife, LeeAnn Klippert, who believed in his unusual idea of turning recycled paper into a superstrong surface for skateboard ramps. For months he had tried, without success, to find a manufacturer willing to work with him in developing a durable composite ramp surface made from recycled and eco-friendly materials. Even his closest friends were skeptical. However, because Klippert and his wife were convinced that there was a viable market for this kind of sustainable product, they moved ahead to form KlipTech (http://kliptech.com) in 2000.

For the next two years, Klippert wrote and fine-tuned a business plan as he had manufacturing experts test various materials and production processes for transforming his invention from an idea to a reality. Despite unenthusiastic responses from most of the bankers he approached for possible financing, Klippert introduced his new skateboard ramp surface product in 2002. Later that same year, he pioneered yet another green product by introducing kitchen countertops made from a composite of recycled materials.

Despite ever-higher sales of these products, Klippert still faced the challenge of enhancing the aesthetic appearance of his paper-based composite countertops for home use. At the time, such composites were produced only in dark colors because of the resins used in the manufacturing process. Klippert recognized that a broader range of colors would make the countertops more appealing to more consumers. Working with a new supplier, he created an innovative countertop composite made with both recycled paper and bamboo and capable of being dyed in either light or dark colors. This new type of countertop attracted the attention of mainstream buyers, not just green-minded buyers, and gave KlipTech the edge it needed to compete more effectively with some of the biggest names in the industry.

KlipTech continues to build revenues and profits by introducing new products made from recycled paper. Most recently, it launched EcoClad, a line of composites used for exterior siding on commercial buildings and residences. Not only is EcoClad attractive and durable, it also helps buildings qualify as green under the U.S. Green Building Council's standards, confirming its environmentally-sound qualities.

Today, KlipTech is a profitable small business with multiple product lines, a global customer base, and a reputation for dedication to sustainability. What lessons has Joel Klippert learned in the years since becoming a successful entrepreneur? First, he found out first hand that an entrepreneur must have the confidence, patience, and perseverance to take the practical steps necessary to turn a good idea into an actual product that can meet customers' needs. It took many months of experimentation to perfect the skateboard ramp surface that gave KlipTech its start in the business world, but Klippert never gave up.

Second, the product must be unique so the company can, in effect, make its own market rather than go head-to-head with major competitors in an established market. When Klippert introduced his first skateboard ramp surface, no one else was making such products from recycled paper. The same was true for KlipTech's first kitchen counter surface, as well as its later products. KlipTech's innovations resulted in unique products that really fit the needs of its customers.

Third, Klippert learned that a nimble startup has an important advantage over large competitors. "The great part about being a small business is you're like a speed boat on the water," he explains. This means KlipTech can respond very quickly, "on the fly," to emerging trends in the business environment. In contrast, big rivals need more time to make and implement decisions about adapting to the same changes in the business environment.

Klippert also advises entrepreneurs to do their homework early on legal issues and financing possibilities, so they have experts and resources in place before problems arise. From experience, he knows that small business owners must understand finance and plan to pay vendors and employees before paying themselves. He's always thinking about how to improve one of his products or listening to customers talk about a new product they'd like to see. Succeeding in the global economy is far from easy, but Klippert remains enthusiastic about the opportunities he faces every day as the co-founder and co-owner of a successful small business.[16]

Questions

1. Joel Klippert says he pays himself last, after he pays his vendors and employees. Explain this decision in terms of the principle of business profit. Do you agree with his payment priorities?

2. When compared to larger manufacturing firms in the building products industry, what advantages have helped KlipTech become successful?

3. How have the competitive, global, technological, and economic environments helped KlipTech to become a successful small business? Which of the above environments might pose the most challenges in the next few years, and why?

Building Skills for Career Success

1. Social Media Exercise

Today, many companies have a social media presence on Facebook, Twitter, Flickr, and other sites beyond their corporate website. Think of three of your favorite car companies and conduct a quick search using a search engine like Google or Yahoo! Then answer the following:

1. Name the social networks for each company.
2. Compare each of their Facebook pages. How many "likes" does each company have? Are there multiple pages for the company? How much interaction (or engagement) is on each Facebook page?
3. What business goals do you think each company is trying to reach through their Facebook presence?

2. Building Team Skills

Over the past few years, employees have been expected to function as productive team members instead of working alone. People often believe that they can work effectively in teams, but many people find working with a group of people to be a challenge.

College classes that function as teams are more interesting and more fun to attend, and students generally learn more about the topics in the course. One way to begin creating a team is to learn something about each student in the class. This helps team members to feel comfortable with each other and fosters a sense of trust.

Assignment

1. Find a partner, preferably someone you do not know.
2. Each partner has two to three minutes to answer the following questions:
   a. What is your name, and where do you work?
   b. What interesting or unusual thing have you done in your life? (Do not talk about work or college; rather, focus on such things as hobbies, travel, family, and sports.)
   c. Why are you taking this course, and what do you expect to learn? (Satisfying a degree requirement is not an acceptable answer.)
3. Introduce your partner to the class. Use one to two minutes, depending on the size of the class.

3. Researching Different Careers

In this chapter, *entrepreneurship* is defined as the willingness to take risks and the knowledge and ability to use the other factors of production efficiently. An *entrepreneur* is a person who risks time, effort, and money to start and operate a business. Often, people believe that these terms apply only to small business. However, employees with entrepreneurial attitudes have recently advanced more rapidly in large companies as well.

Assignment

1. Go to the local library or use the Internet to research how large firms, especially corporations, are rewarding employees who have entrepreneurial skills.
2. Find answers to the following questions:
   a. Why is an entrepreneurial attitude important in large corporations today?
   b. What makes an entrepreneurial employee different from other employees?
   c. How are these employees being rewarded, and are the rewards worth the effort?
3. Write a two-page report that summarizes your findings.

Endnotes

1. Based on information in Lauren Torrisi, "Starbucks Unveils New Menu Items in Calif. Stores," *ABC News*, October 8, 2012, http://abcnews .go.com; "An Experimental New Starbucks Store," *Fast Company Design*, October 1, 2012, www.fastcodesign.com; James Callan, "Starbucks Adds Stores in Scandinavia to Spur European Sales," *Bloomberg*, September 26, 2012, www.bloomberg.com; "Starbucks: #73 *Fortune* 100 Best Companies to Work For," *Fortune*, February 6, 2012, http://money.cnn.com; Leslie Patton, "Starbucks Falls After Cutting Forecast Below Estimate," *Bloomberg*, August 14, 2012, www.bloomberg.com; www.starbucks.com.
2. The Horatio Alger website at www.horatioalger.org (accessed April 23, 2011).
3. Ibid.
4. The 66Apps website at www.66apps.com (accessed January 11, 2012).
5. Idy Fernandez, "Julie Stav," *Hispanic*, June–July 2005, 204.
6. The General Mills website at www.generalmills.com (accessed January 3, 2013).
7. The Bureau of Economic Analysis website at www.bea.gov (accessed January 3, 2013).
8. The Bureau of Economic Analysis website at www.bea.gov (accessed January 3, 2013).
9. The Bureau of Labor Statistics website at www.bls.gov (accessed January 7, 2013).
10. The Bureau of Economic Analysis website at www.bea.gov (accessed January 30, 2013).
11. The Treasury Direct website at www.treasurydirect.gov (accessed January 9, 2012) and the U.S. Census Bureau website at www.census .gov (accessed January 7, 2013).
12. The Investopedia website at www.investopedia.com (accessed January 3, 2013).
13. The Bureau of Labor Statistics website at www.bls.gov (accessed January 3, 2013).
14. Les Dlabay, "The Future of Global Business at 'Base of the Pyramid,'" *The Daily Herald Business Ledger*, November 29, 2011, p. 22.
15. The Environmental Protection Agency website at www.epa.gov (accessed January 3, 2013).
16. Sources: Based on information in "Editor's Choice: The Hot 50 Products 2012," *Green Builder*, February 2012, www.greenbuildermag .com/hot502012; Wanda Lau, "KlipTech EcoClad XP," *Architect*, January 2012, www.architectmagazine.com; Kevin O'Donnell, "Stories of Sustainability: KlipTech," *Current TV*, January 19, 2010, http://current.com; and the Cengage video, "The Entrepreneurial Life: KlipTech."

Being Ethical and Socially Responsible

Why Should You Care?

Business ethics and social responsibility issues have become extremely relevant in today's business world. Business schools teach business ethics to prepare managers to be more responsible. Corporations are developing ethics and social responsibility programs to help meet these needs in the work place.

Learning Objectives

Once you complete this chapter, you will be able to:

1 Understand what is meant by *business ethics.*

2 Identify the types of ethical concerns that arise in the business world.

3 Discuss the factors that affect the level of ethical behavior in organizations.

4 Explain how ethical decision making can be encouraged.

5 Describe how our current views on the social responsibility of business have evolved.

6 Explain the two views on the social responsibility of business and understand the arguments for and against increased social responsibility.

7 Discuss the factors that led to the consumer movement and list some of its results.

8 Analyze how present employment practices are being used to counteract past abuses.

9 Describe the major types of pollution, their causes, and their cures.

10 Identify the steps a business must take to implement a program of social responsibility.

Get Flashcards, Quizzes, Games, Crosswords, and more @ www.cengagebrain.com.

Chipotle Mexican Grill's "Food with Integrity"

When Steve Ells founded Chipotle Mexican Grill (www.chipotle.com) in 1993, most fast-food restaurants were competing on the basis of trendy new menu items and glitzy advertising. Ells, a trained chef, saw an opportunity for an entrepreneurial company to take fast food upscale. He developed recipes for boldly flavored burritos, tacos, and toppings, all made fresh from quality ingredients, and named his Denver restaurant after a smoked chili pepper. Customers crowded in, attracted by the authentic tastes and popular prices, and soon Ells was opening a couple of new Chipotle restaurants every year, with barely any menu changes and almost no advertising. By the end of 2006, Chipotle was a very successful publicly traded corporation, opening more than 100 new restaurants a year.

As the company grew and needed to buy larger quantities of fresh meats, vegetables, and beans, Ells took a closer look at where these ingredients come from. He became convinced that foods produced in a sustainable, humane way would be better for the planet and would taste better. Starting in 1999, Chipotle began buying naturally raised beef, later adding naturally raised pork and chicken as well as dairy products from pasture-raised cows. It's also become a big buyer of organic produce, preferring to work with local suppliers and family farms in particular.

Chipotle is so dedicated to the concept of "food with integrity" that it's trademarked the phrase, making ethical sourcing and sustainability the cornerstone of all customer communications. Not long ago, the company commissioned a two-minute animated video titled "Back to the Start," about a farmer who goes from family farming to large-scale industrial farming and finally chooses back-to-the-earth sustainable farming. The video was first released online, then aired as a commercial during the Grammy Awards. It reached tens of millions of viewers and made a big social media splash by putting the spotlight squarely on Chipotle's long-term commitment to ethics and social responsibility.[1]

Did You Know?

Serving "food with integrity," Chipotle has expanded beyond 1,300 restaurants worldwide and increased annual sales above $2 billion.

Obviously, organizations like Chipotle want to be recognized as responsible corporate citizens. Such companies recognize the need to harmonize their operations with environmental demands and other vital social concerns. Not all firms, however, have taken steps to encourage a consideration of social responsibility and ethics in their decisions and day-to-day activities. Some managers still regard such business practices as a poor investment, in which the cost is not worth the return. Other managers—indeed, most managers—view the cost of these practices as a necessary business expense, similar to wages or rent.

Most managers today, like those at Chipotle, are finding ways to balance a growing agenda of socially responsible activities with the drive to generate profits. This also happens to be a good way for a company to demonstrate its values and to attract like-minded employees, customers, and stockholders. In a highly competitive business environment, an increasing number of companies are, like Chipotle, seeking to set themselves apart by developing a reputation for ethical and socially responsible behavior.

We begin this chapter by defining *business ethics* and examining ethical issues. Next, we look at the standards of behavior in organizations and how ethical behavior can be encouraged. We then turn to the topic of social responsibility. We compare and contrast two present-day models of social responsibility and present arguments for and against increasing the social responsibility of business. We then examine the major elements of the consumer movement. We discuss how social responsibility in business has affected employment practices and environmental concerns. Finally, we consider the commitment, planning, and funding that go into a firm's program of social responsibility.

Learning Objective

1 **Understand what is meant by** *business ethics.*

ethics the study of right and wrong and of the morality of the choices individuals make

business ethics the application of moral standards to business situations

BUSINESS ETHICS DEFINED

Ethics is the study of right and wrong and of the morality of the choices individuals make. An ethical decision or action is one that is "right" according to some standard of behavior. **Business ethics** is the application of moral standards to business situations. Recent court cases involving unethical behavior have helped to make business ethics a matter of public concern. In one such case, Copley Pharmaceutical, Inc., pled guilty to federal criminal charges (and paid a $10.65 million fine) for falsifying drug manufacturers' reports to the Food and Drug Administration. In another much-publicized case, lawsuits against tobacco companies have led to $246 billion in settlements, although there has been only one class-action lawsuit filed on behalf of all smokers. The case, *Engle v. R. J. Reynolds,* could cost tobacco companies an estimated $500 billion. In yet another case, Adelphia Communications Corp., the nation's fifth-largest cable television company, agreed to pay $715 million to settle federal investigations stemming from rampant earnings manipulation by its founder John J. Rigas, and his son, Timothy J. Rigas. Prosecutors and government regulators charged that both father and son had misappropriated $2.3 billion of Adelphia funds for their own use and had failed to pay the corporation for securities they controlled. Consequently, investors lost more than $60 billion when Adelphia declared bankruptcy. The tax evasion charge against the Rigases was dismissed in early 2012. John Rigas and Timothy Rigas are serving 12 years and 17 years in prison, respectively. John Rigas applied for a presidential pardon in January 2009, but George W. Bush left office without making a decision on Rigas's request. Mr. Rigas is scheduled to be released from federal prison in 2018. The Rigases have appealed their convictions to the Second Court of Appeals and they are awaiting a date from the court for oral arguments.[2]

Learning Objective

2 **Identify the types of ethical concerns that arise in the business world.**

ETHICAL ISSUES

Ethical issues often arise out of a business's relationship with investors, customers, employees, creditors, or competitors. Each of these groups has specific concerns and usually exerts pressure on the organization's managers. For example, investors want management to make sensible financial decisions that will boost sales, profits, and returns on their investments. Customers expect a firm's products to be safe, reliable, and reasonably priced. Employees demand to be treated fairly in hiring, promotion, and compensation decisions. Creditors require accounts to be paid on time and the accounting information furnished by the firm to be accurate. Competitors expect the firm's competitive practices to be fair and honest. Consider TAP Pharmaceutical Products, Inc., whose sales representatives offered every urologist in the United States a big-screen TV, computers, fax machines, and golf vacations if the doctors prescribed TAP's new prostate cancer drug Lupron. Moreover, the sales representatives sold Lupron at cut-rate prices or gratis while defrauding Medicare. Recently, the federal government won an $875 million judgment against TAP when a former TAP vice president of sales, Douglas Durand, and Dr. Joseph Gerstein blew the whistle.[3]

In late 2006, Hewlett-Packard Co.'s chairman, Patricia Dunn, and general counsel, Ann Baskins, resigned amid allegations that the company used intrusive tactics in observing the personal lives of journalists and the company's directors, thus tarnishing Hewlett-Packard's reputation for integrity. According to Congressman John Dingell of Michigan, "We have before us witnesses from Hewlett-Packard to discuss a plunderers' operation that would make (former president) Richard Nixon blush were he still alive." Alternatively, consider Bernard Madoff, former stockbroker, financial advisor, and chairman of the NASDAQ stock exchange. In 2009, he was convicted of securities and other frauds, including a Ponzi scheme that defrauded clients of $65 billion. Madoff was sentenced to 150 years in prison.

Businesspeople face ethical issues every day, and some of these issues can be difficult to assess. Although some types of issues arise infrequently, others occur regularly. Let's take a closer look at several ethical issues.

Fairness and Honesty

Fairness and honesty in business are two important ethical concerns. Besides obeying all laws and regulations, businesspeople are expected to refrain from knowingly deceiving, misrepresenting, or intimidating others. The consequences of failing to do so can be expensive. Recently, for example, Keith E. Anderson and Wayne Anderson, the leaders of an international tax shelter scheme known as Anderson's Ark and Associates, were sentenced to as many as 20 years in prison. The Andersons; Richard Marks, their chief accounting officer; and Karolyn Grosnickle, the chief administrative officer, were ordered to pay more than $200 million in fines and restitution.[4] More than 1,500 clients of Anderson's Ark and Associates lost about $31 million. In yet another case, the accounting firm PricewaterhouseCoopers LLP agreed to pay the U.S. government $42 million to resolve allegations that it made false claims in connection with travel reimbursements it collected for several federal agencies.[5]

Deere & Company requires each employee to deal fairly with its customers, suppliers, competitors, and employees. "No employee should take unfair advantage of anyone through manipulation, concealment, abuse of privileged information, misrepresentation of material facts or any other unfair dealing practice." Employees are encouraged to report possible violations of company ethics policies using a 24-hour hotline or anonymous e-mails. Reporting is not only encouraged; it is an accepted and protected behavior.[6]

Personal data security breaches have become a major threat to personal privacy in the new millennium. Can businesses keep your personal data secure?

Organizational Relationships

A businessperson may be tempted to place his or her personal welfare above the welfare of others or the welfare of the organization. For example, in late 2002, former CEO of Tyco International, Ltd, Leo Dennis Kozlowski, was indicted for misappropriating $43 million in corporate funds to make philanthropic contributions in his own name, including $5 million to Seton Hall University, which named its new business-school building Kozlowski Hall. Furthermore, according to Tyco, the former CEO took $61.7 million in interest-free relocation loans without the board's permission. He allegedly used the money to finance many personal luxuries, including a $15 million yacht and a $3.9 million Renoir painting, and to throw a $2 million party for his wife's birthday. Mr. Kozlowski, currently serving up to 25 years in prison, paid $134 million in restitution to Tyco and criminal fines of $70 million. In 2009, the U.S. Supreme Court denied his petition for a judicial review.[7]

Relationships with customers and co-workers often create ethical problems. Unethical behavior in these areas includes taking credit for others' ideas or work, not meeting one's commitments in a mutual agreement, and pressuring others to behave unethically.

RJ CAPAK/WIREIMAGE/GETTY IMAGES

Conflict of Interest

Conflict of interest results when a businessperson takes advantage of a situation for his or her own personal interest rather than for the employer's interest. Such conflict may occur when payments and gifts make their way into business deals. A wise rule to remember is that anything given to a person that might unfairly influence that person's business decision is a bribe, and all bribes are unethical.

For example, at Procter & Gamble Company (P&G), all employees are obligated to act at all times solely in the best interests of the company. A conflict of interest arises when an employee has a personal relationship or financial or other interest that could interfere with this obligation, or when an employee uses his or her position with the company for personal gain. P&G requires employees to disclose all potential conflicts of interest and to take prompt actions to eliminate a conflict when the company asks them to do so. Generally, it is not acceptable to receive gifts, entertainment, or other gratuities from people with whom P&G does business because doing so could imply an obligation on the part of the company and potentially pose a conflict of interest.

Communications

Business communications, especially advertising, can present ethical questions. False and misleading advertising is illegal and unethical, and it can infuriate customers. Sponsors of advertisements aimed at children must be especially careful to avoid misleading messages. Advertisers of health-related products also must take precautions to guard against deception when using such descriptive terms as *low fat*, *fat free*, and *light*. In fact, the Federal Trade Commission has issued guidelines on the use of these labels.

Concept Check

✓ What is meant by business ethics?

✓ What are the different types of ethical concerns that may arise in the business world?

✓ Explain and give an example of how advertising can present ethical questions.

Learning Objective

3 Discuss the factors that affect the level of ethical behavior in organizations.

FACTORS AFFECTING ETHICAL BEHAVIOR

Is it possible for an individual with strong moral values to make ethically questionable decisions in a business setting? What factors affect a person's inclination to make either ethical or unethical decisions in a business organization? Although the answers to these questions are not entirely clear, three general sets of factors do appear to influence the standards of behavior in an organization. As shown in Figure 2-1, the sets consist of individual factors, social factors, and opportunities.

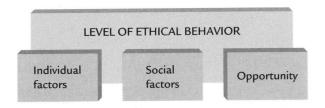

LEVEL OF ETHICAL BEHAVIOR

Individual factors	Social factors	Opportunity

Source: Based on O. C. Ferrell and Larry Gresham, "A Contingency Framework for Understanding Ethical Decision Making in Marketing," *Journal of Marketing* (Summer 1985), 89.

Individual Factors Affecting Ethics

Several individual factors influence the level of ethical behavior in an organization.

- *Individual knowledge of an issue.* How much an individual knows about an issue is one factor. A decision maker with a greater amount of knowledge regarding a situation may take steps to avoid ethical problems, whereas a less-informed person may take action unknowingly that leads to an ethical quagmire.
- *Personal values.* An individual's moral values and central, value-related attitudes also clearly influence his or her business behavior. Most people join organizations to accomplish personal goals.
- *Personal goals.* The types of personal goals an individual aspires to and the manner in which these goals are pursued have a significant impact on that individual's behavior in an organization. The actions of specific individuals in scandal-plagued companies, such as Adelphia, Arthur Anderson, Enron, Halliburton, Qwest, and WorldCom, often raise questions about individuals' personal character and integrity.

Social Factors Affecting Ethics

Many social factors can affect ethical behavior within a firm, including cultural norms, actions and decisions of co-workers, values and attitudes of "significant others," and the use of the Internet.

- *Cultural norms.* A person's behavior in the workplace, to some degree, is determined by cultural norms, and these social factors vary from one culture to another. For example, in some countries it is acceptable and ethical for customs agents to receive gratuities for performing ordinary, legal tasks that are a part of their jobs, whereas in other countries these practices would be viewed as unethical and perhaps illegal.
- *Co-workers.* The actions and decisions of co-workers constitute another social factor believed to shape a person's sense of business ethics. For example, if your co-workers make long-distance telephone calls on company time and at company expense, you might view that behavior as acceptable and ethical because everyone does it.
- *Significant others.* The moral values and attitudes of "significant others"—spouses, friends, and relatives, for instance—also can affect an employee's perception of what is ethical and unethical behavior in the workplace.

- *Use of the Internet.* Even the Internet presents new challenges for firms whose employees enjoy easy access to sites through convenient high-speed connections at work. An employee's behavior online can be viewed as offensive to co-workers and possibly lead to lawsuits against the firm if employees engage in unethical behavior on controversial websites not related to their job. Interestingly, one recent survey of employees found that most workers assume that their use of technology at work will be monitored. A large majority of employees approved of most monitoring methods such as monitoring faxes and e-mail, tracking Web use, and even recording telephone calls.

"Opportunity" as a Factor Affecting Ethics

Several "opportunity" factors affect ethics in an organization.

- *Presence of opportunity. Opportunity* refers to the amount of freedom an organization gives an employee to behave unethically if he or she makes that choice. In some organizations, certain company policies and procedures reduce the opportunity to be unethical. For example, at some fast-food restaurants, one employee takes your order and receives your payment, and another fills the order. This procedure reduces the opportunity to be unethical because the person handling the money is not dispensing the product, and the person giving out the product is not handling the money.
- *Ethical codes.* The existence of an ethical code and the importance management places on this code are other determinants of opportunity (codes of ethics are discussed in more detail in the next section).
- *Enforcement.* The degree of enforcement of company policies, procedures, and ethical codes is a major force affecting opportunity. When violations are dealt with consistently and firmly, the opportunity to be unethical is reduced.

Do you make personal telephone calls on company time? Many individuals do. Although most employees limit personal calls to a few minutes, some make personal calls in excess of 30 minutes. Whether you use company time and equipment to make personal calls is an example of a personal ethical decision.

Now that we have considered some of the factors believed to influence the level of ethical behavior in the workplace, let us explore what can be done to encourage ethical behavior and to discourage unethical behavior.

ENCOURAGING ETHICAL BEHAVIOR

Most authorities agree that there is room for improvement in business ethics. A more problematic question is: Can business be made more ethical in the real world? The majority opinion on this issue suggests that government, trade associations, and individual firms indeed can establish acceptable levels of ethical behavior.

Government's Role in Encouraging Ethics

The government can encourage ethical behavior by legislating more stringent regulations. For example, the landmark **Sarbanes–Oxley Act of 2002** provides sweeping new legal protection for those who report corporate misconduct. At the signing ceremony, President George W. Bush stated, "The act adopts tough new provisions to deter and punish corporate and accounting fraud and corruption, ensure justice for wrongdoers, and protect the interests of workers and shareholders." Among other things, the law deals with corporate responsibility, conflicts of interest, and corporate accountability. However, rules require enforcement, and the unethical businessperson frequently seems to "slip something by" without getting caught. Increased regulation may help, but it surely cannot solve the entire ethics problem.

Concept Check

✓ Describe several individual factors that influence the level of ethical behavior in an organization.

✓ Explain several social factors that affect ethics in an organization.

✓ How does "opportunity" influence the level of ethical behavior in the workplace?

Learning Objective

4 **Explain how ethical decision making can be encouraged.**

Sarbanes–Oxley Act of 2002 provides sweeping new legal protection for employees who report corporate misconduct

Trade Associations' Role in Encouraging Ethics

Trade associations can and often do provide ethical guidelines for their members. These organizations, which operate within particular industries, are in an excellent position to exert pressure on members who stoop to questionable business practices. For example, recently, a pharmaceutical trade group adopted a new set of guidelines to halt the extravagant dinners and other gifts sales representatives often give to physicians. However, enforcement and authority vary from association to association. Because trade associations exist for the benefit of their members, harsh measures may be self-defeating.

Individual Companies' Role in Encouraging Ethics

Codes of ethics that companies provide to their employees are perhaps the most effective way to encourage ethical behavior. A **code of ethics** is a written guide to acceptable and ethical behavior as defined by an organization; it outlines uniform policies, standards, and punishments for violations. Because employees know what is expected of them and what will happen if they violate the rules, a code of ethics goes a long way toward encouraging ethical behavior. However, codes cannot possibly cover every situation. Companies also must create an environment in which employees recognize the importance of complying with the written code. Managers must provide direction by fostering communication, actively modeling and encouraging ethical decision making, and training employees to make ethical decisions.

During the 1980s, an increasing number of organizations created and implemented ethics codes. In a recent survey of *Fortune* 1000 firms, 93 percent of the companies that responded reported having a formal code of ethics. Some companies are now even taking steps to strengthen their codes. For example, to strengthen its accountability, the Healthcare Financial Management Association recently revised its code to designate contact persons who handle reports of ethics violations, to clarify how its board of directors should deal with violations of business ethics, and to guarantee a fair hearing process. S. C. Johnson & Son, makers of Pledge®,

code of ethics a guide to acceptable and ethical behavior as defined by the organization

Meet Senators Sarbanes and Oxley. The Sarbanes-Oxley Act of 2002 adopted tough new provisions to deter and punish corporate and accounting fraud and corruption. The legislation passed with near unanimous support.

SCOTT J. FERRELL/CONGRESSIONAL QUARTERLY/GETTY IMAGES

Drano®, Windex®, and many other household products, is another firm that recognizes that it must behave in ways the public perceives as ethical; its code includes expectations for employees and its commitment to consumers, the community, and society in general. As shown in Figure 2-2, the ethics code of electronics giant Texas

FIGURE 2-2 Defining Acceptable Behavior: Texas Instruments' Code of Ethics

Texas Instruments encourages ethical behavior through an extensive training program and a written code of ethics and shared values.

TEXAS INSTRUMENTS CODE OF ETHICS

"Integrity is the foundation on which TI is built. There is no other characteristic more essential to a TIer's makeup. It has to be present at all levels. Integrity is expected of managers and individuals when they make commitments. They are expected to stand by their commitments to the best of their ability.

One of TI's greatest strengths is its values and ethics. We had some early leaders who set those values as the standard for how they lived their lives. And it is important that TI grew that way. It's something that we don't want to lose. At the same time, we must move more rapidly. But we don't want to confuse that with the fact that we're ethical and we're moral. We're very responsible, and we live up to what we say."

Tom Engibous, President and CEO
Texas Instruments, 1997

We Respect and Value People By:

Treating others as we want to be treated.

- Exercising the basic virtues of respect, dignity, kindness, courtesy and manners in all work relationships.
- Recognizing and avoiding behaviors that others may find offensive, including the manner in which we speak and relate to one another and the materials we bring into the workplace, both printed and electronically.
- Respecting the right and obligation of every TIer to resolve concerns relating to ethics questions in the course of our duties without retribution and retaliation.
- Giving all TIers the same opportunity to have their questions, issues and situations fairly considered while understanding that being treated fairly does not always mean that we will all be treated the same.
- Trusting one another to use sound judgment in our use of TI business and information systems.
- Understanding that even though TI has the obligation to monitor its business information systems activity, we will respect privacy by prohibiting random searches of individual TIers' communications.
- Recognizing that conduct socially and professionally acceptable in one culture and country may be viewed differently in another.

We Are Honest By:

Representing ourselves and our intentions truthfully.

- Offering full disclosure and withdrawing ourselves from discussions and decisions when our business judgment appears to be in conflict with a personal interest.
- Respecting the rights and property of others, including their intellectual property. Accepting confidential or trade secret information only after we clearly understand our obligations as defined in a nondisclosure agreement.
- Competing fairly without collusion or collaboration with competitors to divide markets, set prices, restrict production, allocate customers or otherwise restrain competition.
- Assuring that no payments or favors are offered to influence others to do something wrong.
- Keeping records that are accurate and include all payments and receipts.
- Exercising good judgment in the exchange of business courtesies, meals and entertainment by avoiding activities that could create even the appearance that our decisions could be compromised.
- Refusing to speculate in TI stock through frequent buying and selling or through other forms of speculative trading.

Source: Courtesy of Texas Instruments, http://www.ti.com/corp/docs/csr/corpgov/ethics (accessed February 3, 2013).

Instruments (TI) includes issues relating to policies and procedures; laws and regulations; relationships with customers, suppliers, and competitors; conflicts of interest; handling of proprietary information; and code enforcement.

Assigning an ethics officer who coordinates ethical conduct gives employees someone to consult if they are not sure of the right thing to do. An ethics officer meets with employees and top management to provide ethical advice, establishes and maintains an anonymous confidential service to answer questions about ethical issues, and takes action on ethics code violations.

Sometimes even employees who want to act ethically may find it difficult to do so. Unethical practices can become ingrained in an organization. Employees with high personal ethics may then take a controversial step called *whistle-blowing*. **Whistle-blowing** is informing the press or government officials about unethical practices within one's organization.

Whistle-blowing could have averted disaster and prevented needless deaths in the *Challenger* space shuttle disaster, for example. How could employees have known about life-threatening problems and let them pass? Whistle-blowing, however, can have serious repercussions for employees: Those who "blow whistles" sometimes lose their jobs. However, the Sarbanes–Oxley Act of 2002 protects whistle-blowers who report corporate misconduct. Any executive who retaliates against a whistle-blower can be held criminally liable and imprisoned for up to ten years.

The Whistleblower Protection Act of 1989 protects federal employees who report an agency's misconduct. The Obama administration is attempting to pass a law that would further protect the government whistle-blowers.[8]

When firms set up anonymous hotlines to handle ethically questionable situations, employees actually may be more likely to engage in whistle-blowing. When firms instead create an environment that educates employees and nurtures ethical behavior, fewer ethical problems arise. Ultimately, the need for whistle-blowing is greatly reduced.

It is difficult for an organization to develop ethics codes, policies, and procedures to deal with all relationships and every situation. When no company policies or procedures exist or apply, a quick test to determine if a behavior is ethical is to see if others—co-workers, customers, and suppliers—approve of it. Ethical decisions will always withstand scrutiny. Openness and communication about choices will often build trust and strengthen business relationships. Table 2-1 provides some general guidelines for making ethical decisions.

whistle-blowing informing the press or government officials about unethical practices within one's organization

TABLE 2-1 Guidelines for Making Ethical Decisions

1. Listen and learn.	Recognize the problem or decision-making opportunity that confronts your company, team, or unit. Don't argue, criticize, or defend yourself—keep listening and reviewing until you are sure that you understand others.
2. Identify the ethical issues.	Examine how co-workers and consumers are affected by the situation or decision at hand. Examine how you feel about the situation, and attempt to understand the viewpoint of those involved in the decision or in the consequences of the decision.
3. Create and analyze options.	Try to put aside strong feelings such as anger or a desire for power and prestige and come up with as many alternatives as possible before developing an analysis. Ask everyone involved for ideas about which options offer the best long-term results for you and the company. Then decide which option will increase your self-respect even if, in the long run, things don't work out the way you hope they will.
4. Identify the best option from your point of view.	Consider it and test it against some established criteria, such as respect, understanding, caring, fairness, honesty, and openness.
5. Explain your decision and resolve any differences that arise.	This may require neutral arbitration from a trusted manager or taking "time out" to reconsider, consult, or exchange written proposals before a decision is reached.

Source: Based on information in Tom Rusk with D. Patrick Miller, "Doing the Right Thing," *Sky* (Delta Airlines), August 1993, 18–22.

SOCIAL RESPONSIBILITY

Social responsibility is the recognition that business activities have an impact on society and the consideration of that impact in business decision making. In the first few days after Hurricane Sandy hit the East Coast, Walmart pledged $1.5 million to help with the relief efforts in the hardest hit areas. In addition to providing food and personal care products, the company delivered about one million bottles of water in New York City and to the state of New Jersey. Obviously, social responsibility costs money. It is perhaps not so obvious—except in isolated cases—that social responsibility is also good business. Customers eventually find out which firms act responsibly and which do not. Just as easily as they can purchase a product made by a company that is socially responsible, they can choose against buying from the firm that is not.

Consider the following examples of organizations that are attempting to be socially responsible:

- Social responsibility can take many forms—including flying lessons. Through Young Eagles, underwritten by S. C. Johnson, Phillips Petroleum, Lockheed Martin, Jaguar, and other corporations, 22,000 volunteer pilots have taken a half million youngsters on free flights designed to teach flying basics and inspire excitement about flying careers. Young Eagles is just one of the growing number of education projects undertaken by businesses building solid records as good corporate citizens.

- The General Mills Foundation, created in 1954, is one of the nation's largest company-sponsored foundations. Since the General Mills Foundation was created, it has awarded more than $1 billion to its communities.

  Since its inception in the mid-1990s, General Mills Box Tops for Education has raised more than $400 million to provide schools with funding for whatever students need, everything from playground equipment to paint, computers to clarinets.[9]

- As part of Dell's commitment to the community, the Dell Foundation contributes significantly to the quality of life in communities where Dell employees live and work. The Dell Foundation supports innovative and effective programs that provide fundamental prerequisites to equip youth to learn and excel in a world driven by the digital economy. The Dell Foundation supports a wide range of programs that benefit children from newborn to 17 years of age in Dell's principal U.S. locations and welcomes proposals from nonprofit organizations that address health and human services, education, and technology access for youth. In partnership with the University of Texas, Dell invites college students from around the world to join its strong community of support and to present their innovative ideas for solving social problems into the Dell Social Innovation Challenge.

  Globally, the Michael and Susan Dell Foundation has contributed more than $850 million to improve student performance and increase access to education so that all children have the opportunity to achieve their dreams.[10]

- Improving public schools around the world continues to be IBM's top social priority. Its efforts are focused on preparing the next generation of leaders and workers. Through Reinventing Education and other strategic efforts, IBM is solving education's toughest problems with solutions that draw on advanced information technologies and the best minds IBM can apply. Its programs are paving the way for reforms in school systems around the world.

  IBM launched the World Community Grid in November 2004. It combines excess processing power from thousands of computers into a virtual supercomputer. This grid enables researchers to gather and analyze unprecedented quantities of data aimed at advancing research on genomics, diseases, and natural disasters. The first project, the Human Proteome Folding Project, assists in identifying cures for diseases such as malaria and tuberculosis and has registered more than 150,000 devices around the world to date.[11]

Social responsibility is good business. When Hurricane Sandy hit the East Coast, Walmart provided food, personal care products, and delivered about one million bottles of water in New York City and to the state of New Jersey.

- General Electric Company (GE) has a long history of supporting the communities where its employees work and live through GE's unique combination of resources, equipment, and employees' and retirees' hearts and souls. Today GE's responsibility extends to communities around the world.

  For example, the GE Foundation matches GE employee and retiree gifts to disaster relief organizations such as the International Red Cross, UNICEF, AmeriCares, and Save the Children. Recently, the GE employees and retirees around the world contributed 1.3 million hours through company-sponsored programs. GE's network of more than 220 Volunteer Councils in 51 countries completed 6,200 projects of support and tutoring, cleanups, and paint-and-fix.[12]

- With the help of dedicated Schwab volunteers, the Charles Schwab Foundation provides programs and funding to help individuals fill the information gap. For example, Schwab MoneyWise helps adults teach—and children learn—the basics of financial literacy. Interactive tools are available at http://schwabmoneywise .com, and local workshops cover topics such as getting kids started on a budget. In addition to these efforts, widely distributed publications and news columns by foundation President Carrie Schwab Pomerantz promote financial literacy on a wide range of topics—from saving for a child's education to bridging the health insurance gap for retirees. Since its founding in 1993, Charles Schwab Foundation has made contributions averaging $4 million a year to more than 2,300 nonprofit organizations.[13]

- ExxonMobil's commitment to education spans all levels of achievement. One of its corporate primary goals is to support basic education and literacy programs in the developing world. In areas of the world where basic education levels have been met, ExxonMobil supports education programs in science, technology, engineering, and mathematics.

  In recognition of 2011 International Women's Day, ExxonMobil granted $6 million to support economic opportunities for women around the world. In announcing the grant, Suzanne McCarron, president of ExxonMobil Foundation said, "Research tells us that the success of women entrepreneurs is key to building communities. When women thrive economically, entire societies are transformed by becoming healthier, more stable and more prosperous." Recently, ExxonMobil Corporation, its employees, retirees, and the ExxonMobil Foundation provided $278.4 million in cash, goods, and services around the world.[14]

- AT&T has built a tradition of supporting education, health and human services, the environment, public policy, and the arts in the communities it serves since Alexander Graham Bell founded the company over a century ago. Since 1984, AT&T has invested more than $900 million in support of education. Currently, more than half the company's contribution dollars, employee volunteer time, and community-service activities are directed toward education. Since 1911, AT&T has been a sponsor to the Telephone Pioneers of America, the world's largest industry-based volunteer organization consisting of nearly 620,000 employees and retirees from the telecommunications industry. Each year, the Pioneers volunteer millions of hours and raise millions of dollars for health and human services and the environment. In schools and neighborhoods, the Pioneers strengthen connections and build communities.

  In 2012, AT&T developed the "Texting and Driving: 'It Can Wait'" Simulator to show the dangers of texting behind the wheel. AT&T and its 240,000 employees urge all drivers to go to www.itcanwait.com to take the no-texting-and-driving pledge and then share their promise with others via Twitter (# itcanwait) and Facebook. According to AT&T Chairman and CEO, Randall Stephenson, "More than 100,000 times each year an automobile crashes and people are injured or die while a driver was texting and driving. Our goal is to save lives." In 2013, AT&T was developing preload no-texting-while-driving technology for all AT&T smartphones. Many manufacturers, including Samsung and HTC, have plans to preload DriveMode onto future smartphones in 2013.[15]

- At Merck & Co., Inc., the Patient Assistance Program makes the company's medicines available to low-income Americans and their families at no cost. When patients do not have health insurance or a prescription drug plan and are unable to afford the Merck medicines their doctors prescribe, they can work with their physicians to contact the Merck Patient Assistance Program. For more than 50 years, Merck has provided its medicines completely free of charge to people in need through this program. Patients can get information through www.merck.com; by calling a toll-free number, 1-800-727-5400; or from their physician's office. For eligible patients, the medicines are shipped directly to their home or the prescribing physician's office. Each applicant may receive up to one year of medicines, and patients may reapply to the program if their need continues. In its annual survey of philanthropic giving by U.S. corporations, *The Chronicle of Philanthropy* ranked Merck third in corporate donations of cash and products among some of the country's largest corporations.

  Education programs often link social responsibility with corporate self-interest. For example, Bayer and Merck, two major pharmaceuticals firms, promote science education as a way to enlarge the pool of future employees. Students who visit the Bayer Science Forum in Elkhart, Indiana, work alongside scientists conducting a variety of experiments. Workshops created by the Merck Institute for Science Education show teachers how to put scientific principles into action through hands-on experiments.

These are just a few illustrations from the long list of companies, big and small, that attempt to behave in socially responsible ways. In general, people are more likely to want to work for and buy from such organizations.

Concept Check

✓ How can the government encourage the ethical behavior of organizations?

✓ What is trade associations' role in encouraging ethics?

✓ What is whistle-blowing? Who protects the whistle-blowers?

✓ What is social responsibility? How can business be socially responsible?

Learning Objective

5 **Describe how our current views on the social responsibility of business have evolved.**

THE EVOLUTION OF SOCIAL RESPONSIBILITY IN BUSINESS

Business is far from perfect in many respects, but its record of social responsibility today is much better than that in past decades. In fact, present demands for social responsibility have their roots in outraged reactions to the abusive business practices of the early 1900s.

Historical Evolution of Business Social Responsibility

During the first quarter of the 20th century, businesses were free to operate pretty much as they chose. Government protection of workers and consumers was minimal. As a result, people either accepted what business had to offer or they did without. Working conditions often were deplorable by today's standards. The average workweek in most industries exceeded 60 hours, no minimum-wage law existed, and employee benefits were almost nonexistent. Work areas were crowded and unsafe, and industrial accidents were the rule rather than the exception. To improve working conditions, employees organized and joined labor unions. During the early 1900s, however, businesses—with the help of government—were able to use court orders, brute force, and even the few existing antitrust laws to defeat union attempts to improve working conditions.

During this period, consumers generally were subject to the doctrine of **caveat emptor**, a Latin phrase meaning "let the buyer beware." In other words, "what you see is what you get," and if it is not what you expected, too bad. Although victims of unscrupulous business practices could take legal action, going to court was very expensive, and consumers rarely won their cases. Moreover, no consumer groups or government agencies existed to publicize their consumers' grievances or to hold sellers accountable for their actions.

caveat emptor a Latin phrase meaning "let the buyer beware"

Before the 1930s, most people believed that competition and the action of the marketplace would, in time, correct abuses. Government, therefore, became involved in day-to-day business activities only in cases of obvious abuse of the free-market system. Six of the most important business-related federal laws passed between 1887 and 1914 are described in Table 2-2. As you can see, these laws were aimed more at encouraging competition than at correcting abuses, although two of them did deal with the purity of food and drug products.

The collapse of the stock market on October 29, 1929, triggered the Great Depression and years of dire economic problems for the United States. Factory production fell by almost half, and up to 25 percent of the nation's workforce was unemployed. Before long, public pressure mounted for the government to "do something" about the economy and about worsening social conditions.

Soon after Franklin D. Roosevelt became president in 1933, he instituted programs to restore the economy and improve social conditions. The government passed laws to correct what many viewed as the monopolistic abuses of big business, and

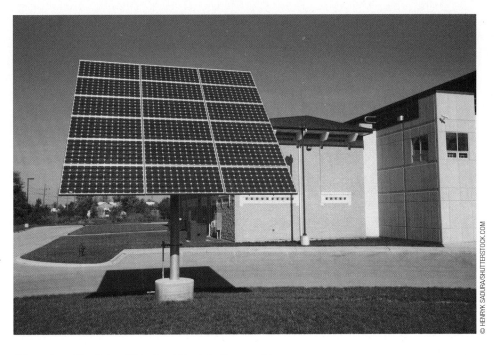

Breaking away from fossil fuels. Today's businesses (and consumers) are more open to alternative sources of energy, such as the solar energy, because they are concerned about the negative impact of conventional energy sources.

TABLE 2-2 Early Government Regulations That Affected American Business

Government Regulation	Major Provisions
Interstate Commerce Act (1887)	First federal act to regulate business practices; provided regulation of railroads and shipping rates
Sherman Antitrust Act (1890)	Prevented monopolies or mergers where competition was endangered
Pure Food and Drug Act (1906)	Established limited supervision of interstate sales of food and drugs
Meat Inspection Act (1906)	Provided for limited supervision of interstate sales of meat and meat products
Federal Trade Commission Act (1914)	Created the Federal Trade Commission to investigate illegal trade practices
Clayton Antitrust Act (1914)	Eliminated many forms of price discrimination that gave large businesses a competitive advantage over smaller firms

© CENGAGE LEARNING 2015

provided various social services for individuals. These massive federal programs became the foundation for increased government involvement in the dealings between business and society.

As government involvement has increased, so has everyone's awareness of the social responsibility of business. Today's business owners are concerned about the return on their investment, but at the same time most of them demand ethical behavior from employees. In addition, employees demand better working conditions, and consumers want safe, reliable products. Various advocacy groups echo these concerns and also call for careful consideration of Earth's delicate ecological balance. Therefore, managers must operate in a complex business environment— one in which they are just as responsible for their managerial actions as for their actions as individual citizens. Interestingly, today's high-tech and Internet-based firms fare relatively well when it comes to environmental issues, worker conditions, the representation of minorities and women in upper management, animal testing, and charitable donations.

Concept Check

✓ Outline the historical evolution of business social responsibility.

✓ What is the doctrine of caveat emptor?

✓ What are the six important business-related federal laws passed between 1887 and 1914?

Learning Objective

6 **Explain the two views on the social responsibility of business and understand the arguments for and against increased social responsibility.**

TWO VIEWS OF SOCIAL RESPONSIBILITY

Government regulation and public awareness are *external* forces that have increased the social responsibility of business. However, business decisions are made within the firm—there, social responsibility begins with the attitude of management. Two contrasting philosophies, or models, define the range of management attitudes toward social responsibility.

The Economic Model

According to the traditional concept of business, a firm exists to produce quality goods and services, earn a reasonable profit, and provide jobs. In line with this concept, the **economic model of social responsibility** holds that society will benefit most when business is left alone to produce and market profitable products that society needs. The economic model has its origins in the 18th century, when businesses were owned primarily by entrepreneurs or owner-managers. Competition was vigorous among small firms, and short-run profits and survival were the primary concerns.

To the manager who adopts this traditional attitude, social responsibility is someone else's job. After all, stockholders invest in a corporation to earn a return

economic model of social responsibility the view that society will benefit most when business is left alone to produce and market profitable products that society needs

on their investment, not because the firm is socially responsible, and the firm is legally obligated to act in the economic interest of its stockholders. Moreover, profitable firms pay federal, state, and local taxes that are used to meet the needs of society. Thus, managers who concentrate on profit believe that they fulfill their social responsibility indirectly through the taxes paid by their firms. As a result, social responsibility becomes the problem of the government, various environmental groups, charitable foundations, and similar organizations.

The Socioeconomic Model

In contrast, some managers believe that they have a responsibility not only to stockholders but also to customers, employees, suppliers, and the general public. This broader view is referred to as the **socioeconomic model of social responsibility**, which places emphasis not only on profits but also on the impact of business decisions on society.

socioeconomic model of social responsibility the concept that business should emphasize not only profits but also the impact of its decisions on society

Recently, increasing numbers of managers and firms have adopted the socioeconomic model, and they have done so for at least three reasons. First, business is dominated by the corporate form of ownership, and the corporation is a creation of society. If a corporation does not perform as a good citizen, society can and will demand changes. Second, many firms have begun to take pride in their social responsibility records, among them Starbucks Coffee, Hewlett-Packard, Colgate-Palmolive, and Coca-Cola. Each of these companies is a winner of a Corporate Conscience Award in the areas of environmental concern, responsiveness to employees, equal opportunity, and community involvement. Of course, many other corporations are much more socially responsible today than they were ten years ago. Third, many businesspeople believe that it is in their best interest to take the initiative in this area. The alternative may be legal action brought against the firm by some special-interest group; in such a situation, the firm may lose control of its activities.

The Pros and Cons of Social Responsibility

Business owners, managers, customers, and government officials have debated the pros and cons of the economic and socioeconomic models for years. Each side seems to have four major arguments to reinforce its viewpoint.

ARGUMENTS FOR INCREASED SOCIAL RESPONSIBILITY Proponents of the socioeconomic model maintain that a business must do more than simply seek profits. To support their position, they offer the following arguments:

1. Because business is a part of our society, it cannot ignore social issues.
2. Business has the technical, financial, and managerial resources needed to tackle today's complex social issues.
3. By helping resolve social issues, business can create a more stable environment for long-term profitability.
4. Socially responsible decision making by firms can prevent increased government intervention, which would force businesses to do what they fail to do voluntarily.

These arguments are based on the assumption that a business has a responsibility not only to its stockholders but also to its customers, employees, suppliers, and the general public.

ARGUMENTS AGAINST INCREASED SOCIAL RESPONSIBILITY Opponents of the socioeconomic model argue that business should do what it does best: earn a profit by manufacturing and marketing products that people want. Those who support this position argue as follows:

1. Business managers are responsible primarily to stockholders, so management must be concerned with providing a return on owners' investments.
2. Corporate time, money, and talent should be used to maximize profits, not to solve society's problems.

TABLE 2-3 A Comparison of the Economic and Socioeconomic Models of Social Responsibility as Implemented in Business

Economic Model Primary Emphasis		Socioeconomic Model Primary Emphasis
1. Production		1. Quality of life
2. Exploitation of natural resources		2. Conservation of natural resources
3. Internal, market-based decisions	Middle ground	3. Market-based decisions, with some community controls
4. Economic return (profit)		4. Balance of economic return and social return
5. Firm's or manager's interest		5. Firm's and community's interests
6. Minor role for government		6. Active government

Source: Adapted from Keith Davis, William C. Frederick, and Robert L. Blomstron, *Business and Society: Concepts and Policy Issues* (New York: Mcgraw-Hill, 1980), 9. Used by permission of Mcgraw-Hill Book Company.

3. Social problems affect society in general, so individual businesses should not be expected to solve these problems.
4. Social issues are the responsibility of government officials who are elected for that purpose and who are accountable to the voters for their decisions.

These arguments obviously are based on the assumption that the primary objective of business is to earn profits and that government and social institutions should deal with social problems.

Table 2-3 compares the economic and socioeconomic viewpoints in terms of business emphasis. Today, few firms are either purely economic or purely socioeconomic in outlook; most have chosen some middle ground between the two extremes. However, our society generally seems to want—and even to expect—some degree of social responsibility from business. Thus, within this middle ground, businesses are leaning toward the socioeconomic view. In the next several sections, we look at some results of this movement in four specific areas: consumerism, employment practices, concern for the environment, and implementation of social responsibility programs.

Concept Check

✓ Explain the two views on the social responsibility of business.

✓ What are the arguments for increased social responsibility?

✓ What are the arguments against increased social responsibility?

Learning Objective

7 Discuss the factors that led to the consumer movement and list some of its results.

consumerism all activities undertaken to protect the rights of consumers

CONSUMERISM

Consumerism consists of all activities undertaken to protect the rights of consumers. The fundamental issues pursued by the consumer movement fall into three categories: environmental protection, product performance and safety, and information disclosure. Although consumerism has been with us to some extent since the early 19th century, the consumer movement became stronger in the 1960s. It was then that President John F. Kennedy declared that the consumer was entitled to a new "Bill of Rights."

The Six Basic Rights of Consumers

President Kennedy's Consumer Bill of Rights asserted that consumers have a right to safety, to be informed, to choose, and to be heard. Two additional rights added since 1975 are the right to consumer education and the right to courteous service. These six rights are the basis of much of the consumer-oriented legislation passed during the last 45 years. These rights also provide an effective outline of the objectives and accomplishments of the consumer movement.

THE RIGHT TO SAFETY The consumers' right to safety means that the products they purchase must be safe for their intended use, must include thorough and explicit directions for proper use, and must be tested by the manufacturer to ensure product quality and reliability. There are several reasons why American business firms must be concerned about product safety.

Corrective Actions Can Be Expensive. Federal agencies, such as the Food and Drug Administration and the Consumer Product Safety Commission, have the power to force businesses that make or sell defective products to take corrective actions. Such actions include offering refunds, recalling defective products, issuing public warnings, and reimbursing consumers—all of which can be expensive.

Increasing Number of Lawsuits. Business firms also should be aware that consumers and the government have been winning an increasing number of product-liability lawsuits against sellers of defective products. Moreover, the amount of the awards in these suits has been increasing steadily. Fearing the outcome of numerous lawsuits filed around the nation, tobacco giants Philip Morris and R. J. Reynolds, which for decades had denied that cigarettes cause illness, began negotiating in 1997 with state attorneys general, plaintiffs' lawyers, and antismoking activists. The tobacco giants proposed sweeping curbs on their sales and advertising practices and the payment of hundreds of billions of dollars in compensation.

Consumer Demand. Yet another major reason for improving product safety is consumers' demand for safe products. People simply will stop buying a product they believe is unsafe or unreliable.

THE RIGHT TO BE INFORMED The right to be informed means that consumers must have access to complete information about a product before they buy it. Detailed information about ingredients and nutrition must be provided on food containers, information about fabrics and laundering methods must be attached to clothing, and lenders must disclose the true cost of borrowing the money they make available to customers who purchase merchandise on credit.

In addition, manufacturers must inform consumers about the potential dangers of using their products. Manufacturers that fail to provide such information can be held responsible for personal injuries suffered because of their products. For example, Maytag provides customers with a lengthy booklet that describes how they should use an automatic clothes washer. Sometimes such warnings seem excessive, but they are necessary if user injuries (and resulting lawsuits) are to be avoided.

THE RIGHT TO CHOOSE The right to choose means that consumers must have a choice of products, offered by different manufacturers and sellers, to satisfy a particular need. The government has done its part by encouraging competition through antitrust legislation. The greater the competition, the greater is the choice available to consumers.

Competition and the resulting freedom of choice provide additional benefits for customers by reducing prices. For example, when personal computers were introduced, they cost more than $5,000. Thanks to intense competition and technological advancements, personal computers today can be purchased for less than $500.

THE RIGHT TO BE HEARD This fourth right means that someone will listen and take appropriate action when customers complain. Actually, management began to listen to consumers after World War II, when competition between businesses that manufactured and sold consumer goods increased. One way that firms got a competitive edge was to listen to consumers and provide the products they said they wanted and needed. Today, businesses are listening even more attentively, and many larger firms have consumer relations departments that can be contacted easily via toll-free telephone numbers.

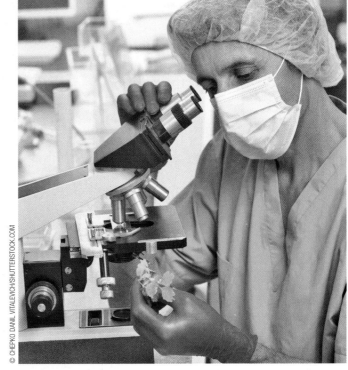

© CHEPKO DANIL VITALEVICH/SHUTTERSTOCK.COM

The right to safety. The Consumer Bill of Rights asserts consumers' basic rights. The right to safety means that products must be safe for their intended use and must be tested by the processor to ensure product quality and safety.

Do you always know what you're buying?

© ANDRESR/SHUTTERSTOCK.COM

Keep these consumer rights in mind when you shop around for goods or services, buy something, or have a problem with a purchase. You're entitled to be informed, to have choices, to be heard, to buy safe products, to have responsive service, and to know your rights.

Concept Check

✓ Describe the six basic rights of consumers.

✓ What are the major forces in consumerism today?

✓ What are some of the federal laws enacted in the last 50 years to protect your rights as a consumer?

Learning Objective

⑧ **Analyze how present employment practices are being used to counteract past abuses.**

Other groups listen, too. Most large cities and some states have consumer affairs offices to act on citizens' complaints.

ADDITIONAL CONSUMER RIGHTS In 1975, President Gerald Ford added to the Consumer Bill of Rights the right to consumer education, which entitles people to be fully informed about their rights as consumers. In 1994, President Bill Clinton added a sixth right, the right to service, which entitles consumers to convenience, courtesy, and responsiveness from manufacturers and sellers of consumer products.

Major Consumerism Forces

The major forces in consumerism are individual consumer advocates and organizations, consumer education programs, and consumer laws. Consumer advocates, such as Ralph Nader, take it on themselves to protect the rights of consumers. They band together into consumer organizations, either independently or under government sponsorship. Some organizations, such as the National Consumers' League and the Consumer Federation of America, operate nationally, whereas others are active at state and local levels. They inform and organize other consumers, raise issues, help businesses to develop consumer-oriented programs, and pressure lawmakers to enact consumer protection laws. Some consumer advocates and organizations encourage consumers to boycott products and businesses to which they have objections. Today, the consumer movement has adopted corporate-style marketing and addresses a broad range of issues. Current campaigns include efforts (1) to curtail the use of animals for testing purposes, (2) to reduce liquor and cigarette billboard advertising in low-income, inner-city neighborhoods, and (3) to encourage recycling.

Educating consumers to make wiser purchasing decisions is perhaps one of the most far-reaching aspects of consumerism. Increasingly, consumer education is becoming a part of high school and college curricula and adult-education programs. These programs cover many topics—for instance, what major factors should be considered when buying specific products, such as insurance, real estate, automobiles, appliances and furniture, clothes, and food; the provisions of certain consumer-protection laws; and the sources of information that can help individuals become knowledgeable consumers.

Major advances in consumerism have come through federal legislation. Some laws enacted in the last 50 years to protect your rights as a consumer are listed and described in Table 2-4.

Most businesspeople now realize that they ignore consumer issues only at their own peril. Managers know that improper handling of consumer complaints can result in lost sales, bad publicity, and lawsuits.

EMPLOYMENT PRACTICES

Managers who subscribe to the socioeconomic view of a business's social responsibility, together with significant government legislation enacted to protect the buying public, have broadened the rights of consumers. The last five decades have seen similar progress in affirming the rights of employees to equal treatment in the workplace.

Everyone should have the opportunity to land a job for which he or she is qualified and to be rewarded on the basis of ability and performance. This is an important issue for society, and it also makes good business sense. Yet, over the years, this opportunity

TABLE 2-4 Major Federal Legislation Protecting Consumers Since 1960

Legislation	Major Provisions
Federal Hazardous Substances Labeling Act (1960)	Required warning labels on household chemicals if they were highly toxic
Kefauver–Harris Drug Amendments (1962)	Established testing practices for drugs and required manufacturers to label drugs with generic names in addition to trade names
Cigarette Labeling Act (1965)	Required manufacturers to place standard warning labels on all cigarette packages and advertising
Fair Packaging and Labeling Act (1966)	Called for all products sold across state lines to be labeled with net weight, ingredients, and manufacturer's name and address
Motor Vehicle Safety Act (1966)	Established standards for safer cars
Truth in Lending Act (1968)	Required lenders and credit merchants to disclose the full cost of finance charges in both dollars and annual percentage rates
Credit Card Liability Act (1970)	Limited credit-card holder's liability to $50 per card and stopped credit-card companies from issuing unsolicited cards
Fair Credit Reporting Act (1971)	Required credit bureaus to provide credit reports to consumers regarding their own credit files; also provided for correction of incorrect information
Consumer Product Safety Commission Act (1972)	Established an abbreviated procedure for registering certain generic drugs
Fair Credit Billing Act (1974)	Amended the Truth in Lending Act to enable consumers to challenge billing errors
Equal Credit Opportunity Act (1974)	Provided equal credit opportunities for males and females and for married and single individuals
Magnuson–Moss Warranty–Federal Trade Commission Act (1975)	Provided for minimum disclosure standards for written consumer-product warranties for products that cost more than $15
Amendments to the Equal Credit Opportunity Act (1976, 1994)	Prevented discrimination based on race, creed, color, religion, age, and income when granting credit
Fair Debt Collection Practices Act (1977)	Outlawed abusive collection practices by third parties
Nutrition Labeling and Education Act (1990)	Required the Food and Drug Administration to review current food labeling and packaging focusing on nutrition label content, label format, ingredient labeling, food descriptors and standards, and health messages
Telephone Consumer Protection Act (1991)	Prohibited the use of automated dialing and prerecorded-voice calling equipment to make calls or deliver messages
Consumer Credit Reporting Reform Act (1997)	Placed more responsibility for accurate credit data on credit issuers; required creditors to verify that disputed data are accurate and to notify a consumer before reinstating the data
Children's Online Privacy Protection Act (2000)	Placed parents in control over what information is collected online from their children younger than 13 years; required commercial website operators to maintain the confidentiality, security, and integrity of personal information collected from children
Do Not Call Implementation Act (2003)	Directed the FCC and the FTC to coordinate so that their rules are consistent regarding telemarketing call practices including the Do Not Call Registry and other lists, as well as call abandonment
Credit Card Accountability, Responsibility, and Disclosure Act (2009)	Provided the most sweeping changes in credit card protections since the Truth in Lending Act of 1968
Dodd–Frank Wall Street Reform and Consumer Protection Act of 2010	Promoted the financial stability of the United States by improving accountability and responsibility in the financial system; established a new Consumer Financial Protection Agency to regulate home mortgages, car loans, and credit cards; became Public Law on July 21, 2010

minority a racial, religious, political, national, or other group regarded as different from the larger group of which it is a part and that is often singled out for unfavorable treatment

has been denied to members of various minority groups. A **minority** is a racial, religious, political, national, or other group regarded as different from the larger group of which it is a part and that is often singled out for unfavorable treatment.

The federal government responded to the outcry of minority groups during the 1960s and 1970s by passing a number of laws forbidding discrimination in the workplace. (These laws are discussed in Chapter 9 in the context of human resources management.) Now, almost 50 years after passage of the first of these (the Civil Rights Act of 1964), abuses still exist. An example is the disparity in income levels for whites, blacks, Hispanics, and Asians, as illustrated in Figure 2-3. Lower incomes and higher unemployment rates also characterize Native Americans, handicapped persons, and women. Responsible managers have instituted a number of programs to counteract the results of discrimination.

Affirmative Action Programs

affirmative action program a plan designed to increase the number of minority employees at all levels within an organization

An **affirmative action program** is a plan designed to increase the number of minority employees at all levels within an organization. Employers with federal contracts of more than $50,000 per year must have written affirmative action plans. The objective of such programs is to ensure that minorities are represented within the organization in approximately the same proportion as in the surrounding community. If 25 percent of the electricians in a geographic area in which a company is located are African Americans, then approximately 25 percent of the electricians it employs also should be African Americans. Affirmative action plans encompass all areas of human resources management: recruiting, hiring, training, promotion, and pay.

Unfortunately, affirmative action programs have been plagued by two problems. The first involves quotas. In the beginning, many firms pledged to recruit and hire a certain number of minority members by a specific date. To achieve this goal, they were forced to consider only minority applicants for job openings; if they

FIGURE 2-3 Comparative Income Levels

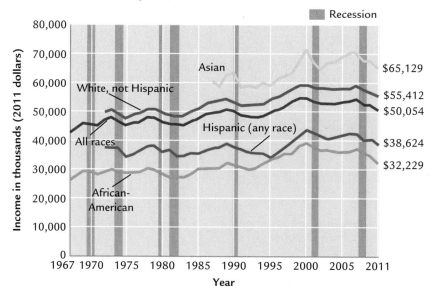

This chart shows the median household incomes of Asian, white, Hispanic, and African-American workers in 2011.

Source: U.S. Census Bureau, Current Population Report, 1968 to 2012 Annual Social and Economic Supplements, *Income, Poverty, and Health Insurance Coverage in the United States: 2012*, issued September 2012, U.S. Census Bureau, U.S. Department of Commerce, 5, http://www.census.gov/prod/2012pubs/p60-243pdf (accessed February 4, 2013).

hired nonminority workers, they would be defeating their own purpose. However, the courts have ruled that such quotas are unconstitutional even though their purpose is commendable. They are, in fact, a form of discrimination called *reverse discrimination.*

The second problem is that although most such programs have been reasonably successful, not all businesspeople are in favor of affirmative action programs. Managers not committed to these programs can "play the game" and still discriminate against workers. To help solve this problem, Congress created (and later strengthened) the **Equal Employment Opportunity Commission (EEOC)**, a government agency with the power to investigate complaints of employment discrimination and sue firms that practice it.

The threat of legal action has persuaded some corporations to amend their hiring and promotional policies, but the discrepancy between men's and women's salaries still exists, as illustrated in Figure 2-4. For more than 50 years, women have consistently earned only about 77 cents for each dollar earned by men.

Training Programs for the Hard-Core Unemployed

For some firms, social responsibility extends far beyond placing a help-wanted advertisement in the local newspaper. These firms have assumed the task of helping the **hard-core unemployed,** workers with little education or vocational training and a long history of unemployment. For example, a few years ago, General Mills helped establish Siyeza, a frozen soul-food processing plant in North Minneapolis. Through the years, Siyeza has provided stable, high-quality full-time jobs for a permanent core of 80 unemployed or underemployed minority inner-city residents. In addition, groups of up to 100 temporary employees are called in when needed. In the past, such workers often were turned down routinely by personnel managers, even for the most menial jobs.

Meet Sam's Club president and CEO.
In early 2012, Rosalind Brewer became the first African-American woman to hold a CEO position at one of the company's business units.

Equal Employment Opportunity Commission (EEOC) a government agency with the power to investigate complaints of employment discrimination and the power to sue firms that practice it

hard-core unemployed workers with little education or vocational training and a long history of unemployment

FIGURE 2-4 Relative Earnings of Male and Female Workers

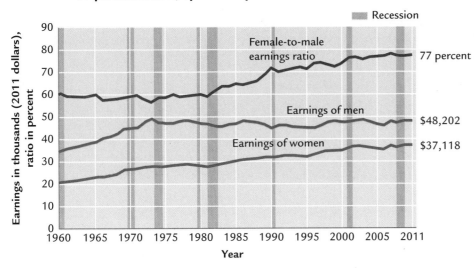

The ratio of women's to men's annual full-time earnings was 77 percent in 2011, up from 74 percent first reached in 1996.

Earnings in thousands (2011 dollars), ratio in percent

- Female-to-male earnings ratio — 77 percent
- Earnings of men — $48,202
- Earnings of women — $37,118

Year (1960–2011)

Concept Check

✓ What is an affirmative action program? What is its purpose?

✓ Why did Congress create (and later strengthen) the Equal Employment Opportunity Commission?

Source: U.S. Census Bureau, Current Population Survey, 1960 to 2011 Annual Social and Economic Supplements, *Income, Poverty, and Health Insurance Coverage in the United States: 2011*, issued September 2012, U.S. Census Bureau, U.S. Department of Commerce, 9, http://www.census.gov/prod/2012pubs/p60-243.pdf (accessed February 4, 2013).

pollution the contamination of water, air, or land through the actions of people in an industrialized society

CONCERN FOR THE ENVIRONMENT

The social consciousness of responsible business managers, the encouragement of a concerned government, and an increasing concern on the part of the public have led to a major effort to reduce environmental pollution, conserve natural resources, and reverse some of the worst effects of past negligence in this area. **Pollution** is the contamination of water, air, or land through the actions of people in an industrialized society. For several decades, environmentalists have been warning us about the dangers of industrial pollution. Unfortunately, business and government leaders either ignored the problem or were not concerned about it until pollution became a threat to life and health in America. Today, Americans expect business and government leaders to take swift action to clean up our environment—and to keep it clean.

Effects of Environmental Legislation

As in other areas of concern to our society, legislation and regulations play a crucial role in pollution control. The laws outlined in Table 2-5 reflect the scope of current environmental legislation: laws to promote clean air, clean water, and even quiet work and living environments. Of major importance was the creation of the Environmental Protection Agency (EPA), the federal agency charged with enforcing laws designed to protect the environment.

TABLE 2-5 Summary of Major Environmental Laws

Legislation	Major Provisions
National Environmental Policy Act (1970)	Established the Environmental Protection Agency (EPA) to enforce federal laws that involve the environment
Clean Air Amendment (1970)	Provided stringent automotive, aircraft, and factory emission standards
Water Quality Improvement Act (1970)	Strengthened existing water pollution regulations and provided for large monetary fines against violators
Resource Recovery Act (1970)	Enlarged the solid-waste disposal program and provided for enforcement by the EPA
Water Pollution Control Act Amendment (1972)	Established standards for cleaning navigable streams and lakes and eliminating all harmful waste disposal by 1985
Noise Control Act (1972)	Established standards for major sources of noise and required the EPA to advise the Federal Aviation Administration on standards for airplanes
Clean Air Act Amendment (1977)	Established new deadlines for cleaning up polluted areas; also required review of existing air-quality standards
Resource Conservation and Recovery Act (1984)	Amended the original 1976 act and required federal regulation of potentially dangerous solid-waste disposal
Clean Air Act Amendment (1987)	Established a national air-quality standard for ozone
Oil Pollution Act (1990)	Expanded the nation's oil-spill prevention and response activities; also established the Oil Spill Liability Trust Fund
Clean Air Act Amendments (1990)	Required that motor vehicles be equipped with onboard systems to control about 90 percent of refueling vapors
Food Quality Protection Act (1996)	Amended the Federal Insecticide, Fungicide and Rodenticide Act and the Federal Food Drug and Cosmetic Act; the requirements included a new safety standard—reasonable certainty of no harm—that must be applied to all pesticides used on foods
American Recovery and Reinvestment Act (2009)	Provided $7.22 billion to the EPA to protect and promote "green" jobs and a healthier environment

© CENGAGE LEARNING 2015

When they are aware of a pollution problem, many firms respond to it rather than wait to be cited by the EPA. Other owners and managers, however, take the position that environmental standards are too strict. (Loosely translated, this means that compliance with present standards is too expensive.) Consequently, it often has been necessary for the EPA to take legal action to force firms to install antipollution equipment and to clean up waste storage areas.

Experience has shown that the combination of environmental legislation, voluntary compliance, and EPA action can succeed in cleaning up the environment and keeping it clean. However, much still remains to be done.

WATER POLLUTION The Clean Water Act has been credited with greatly improving the condition of the waters in the United States. This success comes largely from the control of pollutant discharges from industrial and wastewater treatment plants. Although the quality of our nation's rivers, lakes, and streams has improved significantly in recent years, many of these surface waters remain severely polluted. Currently, one of the most serious water-quality problems results from the high level of toxic pollutants found in these waters.

Among the serious threats to people posed by water pollutants are respiratory irritation, cancer, kidney and liver damage, anemia, and heart failure. Toxic pollutants also damage fish and other forms of wildlife. In fish, they cause tumors or reproductive problems; shellfish and wildlife living in or drinking from toxin-laden waters also have suffered genetic defects. Recently, the Pollution Control Board of Kerala in India ordered Coca-Cola to close its major bottling plant. For years, villagers in the nearby areas had accused Coke of depleting local groundwater and producing other local pollution. The village council president said, "We are happy that the government is finally giving justice to the people who are affected by the plant."

The task of water cleanup has proved to be extremely complicated and costly because of pollution runoff and toxic contamination. Yet, improved water quality is not only necessary, it is also achievable. Consider Cleveland's Cuyahoga River. A few years ago, the river was so contaminated by industrial wastes that it burst into flames one hot summer day! Now, after a sustained community cleanup effort, the river is pure enough for fish to thrive in.

Another serious issue is acid rain, which is contributing significantly to the deterioration of coastal waters, lakes, and marine life in the eastern United States. Acid rain forms when sulfur emitted by smokestacks in industrialized areas combines with moisture in the atmosphere to form acids that are spread by winds. The acids eventually fall to Earth in rain, which finds its way into streams, rivers, and lakes. The acid-rain problem has spread rapidly in recent years, and experts fear that the situation will worsen if the nation begins to burn more coal to generate electricity. To solve the problem, investigators first must determine where the sulfur is being emitted. The costs of this vital investigation and cleanup are going to be high. The human costs of having ignored the problem so long may be higher still.

AIR POLLUTION Aviation emissions are a potentially significant and growing percentage of greenhouse gases that contribute to global warming. Aircraft emissions are significant for several reasons. First, jet aircraft are the main source of human emissions deposited directly into the upper atmosphere, where they may have a greater warming

Sustain the Planet

Social Responsibility at Xerox

Over the past 40 years, Xerox has demonstrated leadership in sustainability and corporate citizenship by designing waste-free products built in waste-free plants, investing in innovations that benefit the environment, supporting community projects, and many other initiatives. Take a look at its 2012 Report on Global Citizenship, which details its environmental sustainability initiatives, corporate donations, volunteerism, and more.

http://www.xerox.com/about-xerox/citizenship/enus.html

COURTESY OF XEROX CORPORATION

© IGOR JANDRIC/SHUTTERSTOCK.COM

Worsening water and land pollution problem. Land pollution is still a serious problem in many parts of the country. It is not just the manufacturers and service businesses that produce millions of tons of waste! We, the individuals in the United States, contribute to the waste-disposal problem, too.

effect than if they were released at Earth's surface. Second, carbon dioxide—the primary aircraft emission—is the main focus of international concern. For example, it survives in the atmosphere for nearly 100 years and contributes to global warming, according to the Intergovernmental Panel on Climate Change. The carbon dioxide emissions from worldwide aviation roughly equal those of some industrialized countries. Third, carbon dioxide emissions combined with other gases and particles emitted by jet aircraft could have two to four times as great an effect on the atmosphere as carbon dioxide alone. Fourth, the Intergovernmental Panel recently concluded that the rise in aviation emissions owing to the growing demand for air travel would not be fully offset by reductions in emissions achieved solely through technological improvements.

How effective is air pollution control? The EPA estimates that the Clean Air Act and its amendments will eventually result in the removal of 56 billion of pollution from the air each year, thus measurably reducing lung disease, cancer, and other serious health problems caused by air pollution. Other authorities note that we have already seen improvement in air quality. A number of cities have cleaner air today than they did 30 years ago. Even in southern California, bad air-quality days have dropped to less than 40 days a year, about 60 percent lower than that observed just a decade ago. Numerous chemical companies have recognized that they must take responsibility for operating their plants in an environmentally safe manner; some now devote considerable capital to purchasing antipollution devices. For example, 3M's pioneering Pollution Prevention Pays (3P) program, designed to find ways to avoid the generation of pollutants, marked its 30th anniversary in 2005. Since 1975, more than 5,600 employee-driven 3P projects have prevented the generation of more than 2.2 billion pounds of pollutants and produced first-year savings of nearly $1 billion.

LAND POLLUTION Air and water quality may be improving, but land pollution is still a serious problem in many areas. The fundamental issues are (1) how to restore damaged or contaminated land at a reasonable cost and (2) how to protect unpolluted land from future damage.

The land pollution problem has been worsening over the past few years because modern technology has continued to produce increasing amounts of chemical and radioactive waste. U.S. manufacturers produce an estimated 40 to 60 million tons of contaminated oil, solvents, acids, and sludge each year. Service businesses, utility companies, hospitals, and other industries also dump vast amounts of wastes into the environment.

Individuals in the United States contribute to the waste-disposal problem, too. A shortage of landfills, owing to stricter regulations, makes garbage disposal a serious problem in some areas. Incinerators help to solve the landfill-shortage problem, but they bring with them their own problems. They reduce the amount of garbage but also leave tons of ash to be buried—ash that often has a higher concentration of toxicity than the original garbage. Other causes of land pollution include strip mining of coal, nonselective cutting of forests, and development of agricultural land for housing and industry.

To help pay the enormous costs of cleaning up land polluted with chemicals and toxic wastes, Congress created a $1.6 billion Superfund in 1980. Originally, money was to flow into the Superfund from a tax paid by 800 oil and chemical companies that produce toxic waste. The EPA was to use the money in the Superfund to finance the cleanup of hazardous waste sites across the nation. To replenish the Superfund, the EPA had two options: It could sue companies guilty of dumping chemicals at specific waste sites, or it could negotiate with guilty companies and thus completely avoid the legal system. During the 1980s, officials at the EPA came under fire because they preferred negotiated settlements. Critics referred to these settlements as "sweetheart deals" with industry. They felt that the EPA should be much more aggressive in reducing land pollution. Of course, most corporate executives believe that cleanup efficiency and quality might be improved if companies were more involved in the process.

NOISE POLLUTION Excessive noise caused by traffic, aircraft, and machinery can do physical harm to human beings. Research has shown that people who are exposed to loud noises for long periods of time can suffer permanent hearing loss. The Noise Control Act of 1972 established noise emission standards for aircraft and airports, railroads, and interstate motor carriers. The act also provided funding for noise research at state and local levels.

Noise levels can be reduced by two methods. The source of noise pollution can be isolated as much as possible. (Thus, many metropolitan airports are located outside the cities.) Engineers can also modify machinery and equipment to reduce noise levels. If it is impossible to reduce industrial noise to acceptable levels, workers should be required to wear earplugs to guard them against permanent hearing damage.

Entrepreneurial Success

Social Entrepreneurs of Tomorrow

A growing number of young entrepreneurs are starting businesses with the goal of using their skills for a socially responsible purpose: to improve the quality of life for people all over the world. Many of these social entrepreneurs are focusing on different ways to bring reliable, inexpensive sources of electricity to poverty-stricken areas.

For example, Alan Hurt, John Harkness, Jason Schwebke, and Mike Sutarik are members of Team Light Up Africa, which won $10,000 in the first Northern Illinois University Social Venture Business Plan Competition. Their Zoom Box, currently in development, is a low-cost, lightweight generator suitable for powering electric lights and charging cell phones in Africa. "We're more than a company and more than a passing idea," says Hurt. "We're a movement."

Teenage inventor Eden Full created a rotating solar panel, the SunSaluter, that turns to follow the sun throughout the day. The improved efficiency increases the amount of solar power that can be generated in an earth-friendly manner. Her SunSaluter panels are already lighting up two villages in Kenya, with more installations on the way. Full's ingenuity has won her social enterprise additional funding to refine and manufacture the product on a larger scale.

Sources: Based on information in Jack McCarthy, "NIU Students Generate Winning Idea," *Chicago Tribune*, December 11, 2011, www.chicagotribune.com; Zachary Sniderman, "4 Young Social Good Entrepreneurs to Watch," *Mashable*, December 6, 2011, http://mashable.com; "Class Launches Social Entrepreneurs," *NIU Today (Northern Illinois University)*, December 20, 2011, www.niutoday.info; Anya Kamenetz, "Peter Thiel Gives Whiz Kids $100K to Quit College, Start Businesses," *Fast Company*, May 25, 2011, www.fastcompany.com.

Who Should Pay for a Clean Environment?

Governments and businesses are spending billions of dollars annually to reduce pollution—more than $45 billion to control air pollution, $33 billion to control water pollution, and $12 billion to treat hazardous wastes. To make matters worse, much of the money required to purify the environment is supposed to come from already depressed industries, such as the chemical industry. A few firms have discovered that it is cheaper to pay a fine than to install expensive equipment for pollution control.

Who, then, will pay for the environmental cleanup? Many business leaders offer one answer—tax money should be used to clean up the environment and to keep it clean. They reason that business is not the only source of pollution, so business should not be forced to absorb the entire cost of the cleanup. Environmentalists disagree. They believe that the cost of proper treatment and disposal of industrial wastes is an expense of doing business. In either case, consumers probably will pay a large part of the cost—either as taxes or in the form of higher prices for goods and services.

Concept Check

✓ Describe the major types of pollution? What are their causes and their cures?

✓ Summarize major provisions of federal environmental laws enacted since 1970?

✓ Who should pay for a clean environment?

Learning Objective

10 Identify the steps a business must take to implement a program of social responsibility.

IMPLEMENTING A PROGRAM OF SOCIAL RESPONSIBILITY

A firm's decision to be socially responsible is a step in the right direction—but only the first step. The firm then must develop and implement a program to reach this goal. The program will be affected by the firm's size, financial resources, past record in the area of social responsibility, and competition. Above all, however, the program must have the firm's total commitment or it will fail.

Developing a Program of Social Responsibility

An effective program for social responsibility takes time, money, and organization. In most cases, developing and implementing such a program will require four steps: securing the commitment of top executives, planning, appointing a director, and preparing a social audit.

COMMITMENT OF TOP EXECUTIVES Without the support of top executives, any program will soon falter and become ineffective. For example, the Boeing Company's Ethics and Business Conduct Committee is responsible for the ethics program. The committee is appointed by the Boeing board of directors, and its members include the company chairman and CEO, the president and chief operating officer, the presidents of the operating groups, and senior vice presidents. As evidence of their commitment to social responsibility, top managers should develop a policy statement that outlines key areas of concern. This statement sets a tone of positive support and later will serve as a guide for other employees as they become involved in the program.

PLANNING Next, a committee of managers should be appointed to plan the program. Whatever form their plan takes, it should deal with each of the issues described in the top managers' policy statement. If necessary, outside consultants can be hired to help develop the plan.

APPOINTMENT OF A DIRECTOR After the social responsibility plan is established, a top-level executive should be appointed to implement the organization's plan. This individual should be charged with recommending specific policies and helping individual departments to understand and live up to the social responsibilities the firm has assumed. Depending on the size of the firm, the director may require a staff to handle the program on a day-to-day basis. For example, at the Boeing Company, the director of ethics and business conduct administers the ethics and business conduct program.

THE SOCIAL AUDIT At specified intervals, the program director should prepare a social audit for the firm. A **social audit** is a comprehensive report of what an organization has done and is doing with regard to social issues that affect it. This document provides the information the firm needs to evaluate and revise its social responsibility program. Typical subject areas include human resources, community involvement, the quality and safety of products, business practices, and efforts to reduce pollution and improve the environment. The information included in a social audit should be as accurate and as quantitative as possible, and the audit should reveal both positive and negative aspects of the program.

Today, many companies listen to concerned individuals within and outside the company. For example, the Boeing Ethics Line listens to and acts on concerns expressed by employees and others about possible violations of company policies, laws, or regulations, such as improper or unethical business practices, as well as health, safety, and environmental issues. Employees are encouraged to communicate their concerns, as well as ask questions about ethical issues. The Ethics Line is available to all Boeing employees, including Boeing subsidiaries. It is also available to concerned individuals outside the company.

social audit a comprehensive report of what an organization has done and is doing with regard to social issues that affect it

Funding the Program

We have noted that social responsibility costs money. Thus, just like any other corporate undertaking, a program to improve social responsibility must be funded. Funding can come from three sources:

1. Management can pass the cost on to consumers in the form of higher prices.
2. The corporation may be forced to absorb the cost of the program if, for example, the competitive situation does not permit a price increase. In this case, the cost is treated as a business expense, and profit is reduced.
3. The federal government may pay for all or part of the cost through tax reductions or other incentives.

Concept Check

✓ What steps must a business take to implement a program of social responsibility?

✓ What is the social audit? Who should prepare a social audit for the firm?

✓ What are the three sources of funding for a social responsibility program?

Looking for Success? *Get Flashcards, Quizzes, Games, Crosswords, and more @ www.cengagebrain.com.*

Summary

1 Understand what is meant by business ethics.

Ethics is the study of right and wrong and of the morality of choices. Business ethics is the application of moral standards to business situations.

2 Identify the types of ethical concerns that arise in the business world.

Ethical issues arise often in business situations out of relationships with investors, customers, employees, creditors, or competitors. Businesspeople should make every effort to be fair, to consider the welfare of customers and others within the firm, to avoid conflicts of interest, and to communicate honestly.

3 Discuss the factors that affect the level of ethical behavior in organizations.

Individual, social, and opportunity factors all affect the level of ethical behavior in an organization. Individual factors include knowledge level, moral values and attitudes, and personal goals. Social factors include cultural norms and the actions and values of co-workers and significant others. Opportunity factors refer to the amount of leeway that exists in an organization for employees to behave unethically if they choose to do so.

4 Explain how ethical decision making can be encouraged.

Governments, trade associations, and individual firms can establish guidelines for defining ethical behavior. Governments can pass stricter regulations. Trade associations provide ethical guidelines for their members.

Companies provide codes of ethics—written guides to acceptable and ethical behavior as defined by an organization—and create an atmosphere in which ethical behavior is encouraged. An ethical employee working in an unethical environment may resort to whistle-blowing to bring a questionable practice to light.

5 Describe how our current views on the social responsibility of business have evolved.

In a socially responsible business, management realizes that its activities have an impact on society and considers that impact in the decision-making process. Before the 1930s, workers, consumers, and government had very little influence on business activities; as a result, business leaders gave little thought to social responsibility. All this changed with the Great Depression. Government regulations, employee demands, and consumer awareness combined to create a demand that businesses act in socially responsible ways.

6 Explain the two views on the social responsibility of business and understand the arguments for and against increased social responsibility.

The basic premise of the economic model of social responsibility is that society benefits most when business is left alone to produce profitable goods and services. According to the socioeconomic model, business has as much responsibility to society as it has to its owners. Most managers adopt a viewpoint somewhere between these two extremes.

7 **Discuss the factors that led to the consumer movement and list some of its results.**

Consumerism consists of all activities undertaken to protect the rights of consumers. The consumer movement generally has demanded—and received—attention from business in the areas of product safety, product information, product choices through competition, and the resolution of complaints about products and business practices. Although concerns over consumer rights have been around to some extent since the early 19th century, the movement became more powerful in the 1960s when President John F. Kennedy initiated the Consumer Bill of Rights. The six basic rights of consumers include the right to safety, the right to be informed, the right to choose, the right to be heard, and the rights to consumer education and courteous service.

8 **Analyze how present employment practices are being used to counteract past abuses.**

Legislation and public demand have prompted some businesses to correct past abuses in employment practices—mainly with regard to minority groups. Affirmative action and training of the hard-core unemployed are two types of programs that have been used successfully.

9 **Describe the major types of pollution, their causes, and their cures.**

Industry has contributed to noise pollution and pollution of our land and water through the dumping of wastes, and to air pollution through vehicle and smokestack emissions. This contamination can be cleaned up and controlled, but the big question is: Who will pay? Present cleanup efforts are funded partly by government tax revenues, partly by business, and in the long run by consumers.

10 **Identify the steps a business must take to implement a program of social responsibility.**

A program to implement social responsibility in a business begins with total commitment by top management. The program should be planned carefully, and a capable director should be appointed to implement it. Social audits should be prepared periodically as a means of evaluating and revising the program. Programs may be funded through price increases, reduction of profit, or federal incentives.

Key Terms

You should now be able to define and give an example relevant to each of the following terms:

ethics (34)
business ethics (34)
Sarbanes–Oxley Act of 2002 (38)
code of ethics (39)
whistle-blowing (41)

social responsibility (42)
caveat emptor (45)
economic model of social responsibility (46)
socioeconomic model of social responsibility (47)

consumerism (48)
minority (52)
affirmative action program (52)
Equal Employment Opportunity Commission (EEOC) (53)

hard-core unemployed (53)
pollution (54)
social audit (58)

Discussion Questions

1. When a company acts in an ethically questionable manner, what types of problems are caused for the organization and its customers?
2. How can an employee take an ethical stand regarding a business decision when his or her superior already has taken a different position?
3. Overall, would it be more profitable for a business to follow the economic model or the socioeconomic model of social responsibility?
4. Why should business take on the task of training the hard-core unemployed?
5. To what extent should the blame for vehicular air pollution be shared by manufacturers, consumers, and government?
6. Why is there so much government regulation involving social responsibility issues? Should there be less?

Test Yourself

Matching Questions

1. _____ An application of moral standards to business situations.

2. _____ Provides legal protection for employees who report corporate misconduct.

3. _____ A guide to acceptable and ethical behavior as defined by the organization.

4. _____ All activities undertaken to protect the rights of consumers.

5. _____ Informing the press or government officials about unethical practices within one's organization.

6. _____ A Latin phrase meaning "let the buyer beware."

7. _____ A racial, religious, political, national, or other group regarded as different from the larger group of which it is a part.

8. _____ A plan designed to increase the number of minority employees at all levels within an organization.

9. _____ Workers with little education or vocational training and a long history of unemployment.

10. _____ The contamination of water, air, or land.

    a. whistle-blowing
    b. pollution
    c. social audit
    d. minority
    e. code of ethics
    f. hard-core unemployed
    g. Sarbanes–Oxley Act of 2002
    h. economic model of social responsibility
    i. affirmative action program
    j. business ethics
    k. consumerism
    l. caveat emptor

True False Questions

11. **T F** The field of business ethics applies moral standards to business situations.

12. **T F** Business ethics rarely involves the application of moral standards to the business activity of a normal company.

13. **T F** The economic model of social responsibility emphasizes the effect of business decisions on society.

14. **T F** Consumerism consists of all activities undertaken to protect the rights of consumers.

15. **T F** Manufacturers are not required by law to inform consumers about the potential dangers of using their products.

16. **T F** Affirmative-action plans encompass all areas of human resources management, including recruiting, hiring, training, promotion, and pay.

17. **T F** Hard-core unemployed workers are those with little education or vocational training.

18. **T F** The EPA was created by the government to develop new improved ways to clean and improve the environment.

19. **T F** Consumers will probably pay in large part for cleaning up our environment through increased taxes or increased product cost.

20. **T F** A key step in developing and implementing a social responsibility program is the environmental audit.

Multiple-Choice Questions

21. _____ Business ethics
    a. is laws and regulations that govern business.
    b. is the application of moral standards to business situations.
    c. do not vary from one person to another.
    d. is most important for advertising agencies.
    e. is well-defined rules for appropriate business behavior.

22. _____ Customers expect a firm's products to
    a. boost sales.
    b. be profitable.
    c. earn a reasonable return on investment.
    d. be available everywhere.
    e. be safe, reliable, and reasonably priced.

23. _____ Some AIG executives were aware of the financial problems the company was facing and yet failed to reveal this information to the public.

    These actions taken by AIG executives were
    a. moral.
    b. normal.
    c. in the best interests of shareholders.
    d. unethical.
    e. in the best interests of the employees.

24. _____ Bribes are
    a. unethical.
    b. ethical only under certain circumstances.
    c. uncommon in many foreign countries.
    d. economic returns.
    e. ethical.

25. _____ What are three sets of factors that influence the standards of behavior in an organization?
   a. Organizational norms, circumstances, morals
   b. Peer pressure, attitudes, social factors
   c. Historical factors, management attitudes, opportunity
   d. Opportunity, individual factors, social factors
   e. Financial factors, opportunity, morals

26. _____ Informing the press or government officials about unethical practices within one's organization is called
   a. unethical behavior.
   b. whistling.
   c. whistle-blowing.
   d. trumpeting.
   e. a company violation.

27. _____ Social responsibility
   a. has little or no associated costs.
   b. can be extremely expensive and provides very little benefit to a company.
   c. has become less important as businesses become more competitive.
   d. is generally a crafty scheme to put competitors out of business.
   e. is costly but provides tremendous benefits to society and the business.

28. _____ *Caveat emptor*
   a. is a French term that implies laissez-faire.
   b. implies disagreements over peer evaluations.
   c. is a Latin phrase meaning "let the buyer beware."
   d. is a Latin phrase meaning "let the seller beware."
   e. is a Latin phrase meaning "the cave is empty."

29. _____ Where does social responsibility of business have to begin?
   a. Government
   b. Management
   c. Consumers
   d. Consumer protection groups
   e. Society

30. _____ Primary emphasis in the economic model of social responsibility is on
   a. quality of life.
   b. conservation of resources.
   c. market-based decisions.
   d. production.
   e. firm's and community's interests.

Answers to the Test Yourself questions appear at the end of the book on page TY-1.

Video Case

PortionPac Chemical Is People-Friendly, Planet-Friendly

When Marvin Klein and Syd Weisberg founded PortionPac Chemical Corporation (www.portionpaccorp.com) in 1964, they were thinking "green" long before the word came to describe an international environmental movement. The partners shared the belief that cleaning solutions didn't have to be toxic or caustic to be effective. They also realized that both water and packaging went to waste when manufacturers poured premixed cleaning liquids into spray bottles that customers would throw away when empty. One more thing the cofounders agreed on: They wanted to do business with integrity, dealing with employees, suppliers, and customers in an ethical way.

With commercial customers in mind, Weisberg tested and developed concentrated cleaning formulas that did away with grease and dirt in offices, kitchens, and bathrooms without endangering people or the planet. He and Klein prepared small packages of concentrate to be mixed with water for full-strength cleaning in elementary schools, companies, factories, and correctional facilities. To be sure the cleaning solution wasn't too strong or too weak, the entrepreneurs gave custodians, janitors, and other cleaning staff careful instructions about exactly how to dilute the concentrate. And to avoid mountains of empty bottles piling up in local landfills, they had customers use refillable spray bottles.

Chicago-based PortionPac's core principles of safety and sustainability were way ahead of their time. Now that environmental issues are in the public eye, the company is thriving, with $20 million in annual sales, 84 employees, and an ever-expanding customer base. Unlike most businesses, however, PortionPac rewards its salespeople for selling only the amount of cleaning products that customers need. This policy reflects its respect for the environment as well as its emphasis on ethical business practices. If customers buy too much, they may use too much and put their staff or the environment at risk, not to mention spending more than they should. PortionPac also provides customers with on-site and online training about the proper use of cleaning products and timesaving ways to get the job done. No wonder so many of PortionPac's customers remain loyal buyers year after year.

PortionPac pays just as much attention to the needs of its employees as it does to the needs of its customers and the planet. Machines in the company's Chicago factory have been designed to operate with minimal noise, so that employees can talk or listen to music as they work. Sunshine streams through large skylights, potted plants brighten the factory floor, and thoughtful sculptures follow the themes of plumbing and cleaning. Rather than operate three shifts around the clock, PortionPac arranges family-friendly work schedules that allow managers and employees to balance their personal and professional obligations.

Once every year, on Front to Back Day, top executives and all non production managers and employees go into the factory to work side by side with frontline employees. This experience gives them a better understanding of everyday challenges and conditions on the factory floor, which, in turn, helps senior managers make more informed decisions about production. At the end of the day, the entire workforce joins in a barbecue that reinforces the company's close-knit family feeling. It's not surprising that turnover is exceptionally low. More than half the workforce has been with PortionPac for more than a decade. On the few occasions when positions do open up, employees encourage their brothers, sisters, or adult children to apply. Recognizing the company's commitment to its employees, *Inc.* magazine has named PortionPac to its list of Winning Workplaces.

Marvin Klein, who now serves as chairman, stresses that PortionPac's dedication to business ethics and integrity is actually a matter of common sense. It's also a two-way street: He wants to do business with suppliers and customers that do the right thing. As PortionPac celebrates its 50th anniversary, Klein and the entire management team are planning for a people-friendly, planet-friendly future.[16]

Questions

1. PortionPac is family-owned. How does this private ownership affect the company's ability to follow the socioeconomic model of social responsibility?
2. If you were appointed to conduct a social audit of PortionPac, what type of information would you collect? What questions would you ask? Explain your answer.
3. Do you agree with Marvin Klein's assessment of business ethics as a matter of common sense? Why or why not?

Building Skills for Career Success

1. Social Media Exercise

In 2010, Pepsi decided to develop a new social media–based project, called Pepsi Refresh Project, aimed at Millennials and allowing consumers to post ideas for improving their communities. This replaced the $20 million they spent on Superbowl advertising. The project received more than 57 million votes. Visit the website at http://www.refresheverything.com/.

1. Do you think this was an effective strategy for Pepsi? Do you think this resonated with the Millennial generation?
2. Do you think this is a good example of corporate social responsibility (CSR)? Why or why not?
3. How does this CSR example for Pepsi compare with that of its main rival Coca-Cola (see http://www.thecoca-colacompany.com/citizenship/index.html)?

2. Building Team Skills

A firm's code of ethics outlines the kinds of behaviors expected within the organization and serves as a guideline for encouraging ethical behavior in the workplace. It reflects the rights of the firm's workers, shareholders, and consumers.

Assignment

1. Working in a team of four, find a code of ethics for a business firm. Start the search by asking firms in your community for a copy of their codes, by visiting the library, or by searching and downloading information from the Internet.

2. Analyze the code of ethics you have chosen, and answer the following questions:
   a. What does the company's code of ethics say about the rights of its workers, shareholders, consumers, and suppliers? How does the code reflect the company's attitude toward competitors?
   b. How does this code of ethics resemble the information discussed in this chapter? How does it differ?
   c. As an employee of this company, how would you personally interpret the code of ethics? How might the code influence your behavior within the workplace? Give several examples.

3. Researching Different Careers

Business ethics has been at the heart of many discussions over the years and continues to trouble employees and shareholders. Stories about dishonesty and wrongful behavior in the workplace appear on a regular basis in newspapers and on the national news.

Assignment

Prepare a written report on the following:

1. Why can it be so difficult for people to do what is right?
2. What is your personal code of ethics? Prepare a code outlining what you believe is morally right. The document should include guidelines for your personal behavior.
3. How will your code of ethics affect your decisions about:
   a. The types of questions you should ask in a job interview?
   b. Selecting a company in which to work?

Endnotes

1. Based on information in Hosea Sanders, "Less Is More for Green Business," *ABC WLS-TV*, January 21, 2011, http://abclocal.go.com; Leigh Buchanan, "A Look Inside the Un-Factory," *Inc.*, June 8, 2010, www.inc.com; "Top Workplaces: PortionPac Chemical," *Inc.*, June 1, 2010, www.inc.com; Nicole J. Bowman, "PortionPac Chemical Corp.," *ISSA*, March 23, 2010, http://current.issa.com; www.portionpaccorp.com.

2. Official John Rigas website, http://johnrigas.com/AdelphiaLitigation.html (accessed February 2, 2013), http://www.time.com/time/specials/packages/articles/0,288 (accessed April 24, 2012), and the U.S. Department of Justice website at http://www.justice.gov/usao/pam/news/2012/Rigas_01_25 (accessed February 2, 2013).

3. The U.S. Department of Justice website at http://www.justice.gov/opa/pr/2001/October/513civ.htm, and http://www.justice.gov/opa/pr/2003/June/03_civ_371.htm (accessed February 2, 2013).

4. The U.S. Department of Justice website at http://www.justice.gov/tax/txdv05268.htm, and http://www.justice.gov/tax/usaopress/2007/txdv072007-122 (Creasia).pdf (accessed February 3, 2013).

5. *Frontlines* (Washington, DC: U.S. Agency for International Development, September 2005), 16.

6. Deere & Company website at http://search.deere.com/wps/dcom/en_US/corporate/our_company/investor accessed February 3, 2013).

7. U.S. Securities and Exchange Commission website at http://www.sec.gov/litigation/litre-leases/2009/lr21129.htm and http://http://www.sec.gov/litigation/complaints/complr17722.htm (accessed February 2, 2013).

8. U.S. Department of Labor website at http://www.dol.gov/compliance/laws/comp-whistleblower.htm and http://www.sec.gov/news/press/2011/2011-116.htm (accessed February 5, 2013).

9. The General Mills website at http://www.generalmills.com//media/Files/CSR/global_resp_summary_2012 (accessed February 5, 2013).

10. The Michael and Susan Dell Foundation website at http://www.msdf.org/about/ and The Dell Corporate Responsibility Report at http://www.dell.com (accessed February 2, 2013).

11. The IBM website at http://www.ibm.com/ibm/g10/us/en/world.wcgrid.html (accessed February 3, 2013).

12. The GE website at http://www.gecitizenship.com/community-engagement/volunteering/ (accessed February 5, 2013).

13. The Charles Schwab Foundation website at http://www.aboutschwab.com/about/overview/charles_schwab/foundation (accessed February 2, 2013).

14. The ExxonMobil website at http://www.exxonmobil.com/corporate/community_wwgiving.aspx (accessed February 1, 2013).

15. The AT&T website at http://www.att.com/gen/press-room?pid=2964 (accessed February 4, 2013).

16. Based on information in "NIST Visit to Chicago Spotlights Manufacturing Success," *Department of Commerce*, July 20, 2012, http://www.commerce.gov Hosea; Sanders, "Less Is More for Green Business," *ABC WLS-TV*, January 21, 2011, http://abclocal.go.com; Leigh Buchanan, "A Look Inside the Un-Factory," *Inc.*, June 8, 2010, http://www.inc.com; "Top Workplaces: PortionPac Chemical," *Inc.*, June 1, 2010, http://www.inc.com; Nicole J. Bowman, "PortionPac Chemical Corp.," *ISSA*, March 23, 2010, http://current.issa.com; http://www.portionpaccorp.com.

Exploring Global Business

Learning Objectives

Once you complete this chapter, you will be able to:

1 Explain the economic basis for international business.

2 Discuss the restrictions nations place on international trade, the objectives of these restrictions, and their results.

3 Outline the extent of international business and the world economic outlook for trade.

4 Discuss international trade agreements and international economic organizations working to foster trade.

5 Define the methods by which a firm can organize for and enter into international markets.

6 Describe the various sources of export assistance.

7 Identify the institutions that help firms and nations finance international business.

Why Should You Care?

Free trade—are you for or against it? Most economists support free-trade policies, but public support can be lukewarm, and certain groups are adamantly opposed, alleging that "trade harms large segments of U.S. workers," "degrades the environment," and "exploits the poor."

Coca-Cola

The Coca-Cola Company has been an international success story in soft drinks for more than 100 years. With $46.5 billion in annual revenues and 146,000 employees worldwide, the company sells beverages under well-known brands such as Coca-Cola, Diet Coke, Minute Maid, Sprite, and Dasani. In fact, 15 of Coca-Cola's global brands ring up $1 billion or more in annual sales.

Founded in Atlanta in 1886, Coca-Cola first expanded across the country and then looked beyond our borders for more profit opportunity. By 1912, the company's familiar hourglass bottles were on store shelves in Canada, the Caribbean, Central America, and the Philippines. Today, more than half of Coca-Cola's sales are made outside the United States. It operates in more than 200 nations and is investing $30 billion to open new bottling plants and other facilities in Africa, South America, Russia, Asia, and the Middle East.

Doing business around the world presents Coca-Cola with both opportunities and challenges. For example, aiming for higher market share in China, where soft-drink consumption is on the rise, the company created the Minute Maid Pulpy fruit drink to suit local taste preferences. The product became so popular that Coca-Cola quickly introduced it in 18 countries. On the other hand, because a high percentage of company sales come from non-U.S. markets, changes in the value of world currencies can significantly affect both revenues and profits. Moreover, Coca-Cola has to be creative in dealing with frequent power outages or unpaved roads in some developing nations.

To more effectively manage its activities, Coca-Cola has established three distinct divisions responsible for specific parts of the business: Coca-Cola Americas (covering North and South America), Coca-Cola International (covering Africa, Europe, Eurasia, and the Pacific), and the Bottling Investments Group (covering bottling units outside of North America). Looking ahead, Coca-Cola aims to build on its global success by doubling worldwide revenues by 2020.[1]

Did You Know?

Coca-Cola rings up $46.5 billion in annual revenue around the world.

Coca-Cola is just one of a growing number of companies, large and small, that are doing business with firms in other countries. Some companies, such as General Electric, sell to firms in other countries; others, such as Pier 1 Imports, buy goods around the world to import into the United States. Whether they buy or sell products across national borders, these companies are all contributing to the volume of international trade that is fueling the global economy.

Theoretically, international trade is every bit as logical and worthwhile as interstate trade between, say, California and Washington. Yet, nations tend to restrict the import of certain goods for a variety of reasons. For example, in the early 2000s, the United States restricted the import of Mexican fresh tomatoes because they were undercutting price levels of domestic fresh tomatoes.

Despite such restrictions, international trade has increased almost steadily since World War II. Many of the industrialized nations have signed trade agreements intended to eliminate problems in international business and to help less-developed nations participate in world trade. Individual firms around the world have seized the opportunity to compete in foreign markets by exporting products and increasing foreign production, as well as by other means.

Signing the Trade Act of 2002, President George W. Bush remarked, "Trade is an important source of good jobs for our workers and a source of higher growth for our economy. Free trade is also a proven strategy for building global prosperity and adding to the momentum of political freedom. Trade is an engine of economic growth. In our lifetime, trade has helped lift millions of people and whole nations out of poverty and put them on the path of prosperity."[2] In his national best seller, *The World Is Flat*, Thomas L. Friedman states, "The flattening of the world has presented us with new opportunities, new challenges, new partners but, also, alas new dangers, particularly as Americans it is imperative that we be the best global citizens that we can be—because in a flat world, if you don't visit a bad neighborhood, it might visit you."

We describe international trade in this chapter in terms of modern specialization, whereby each country trades the surplus goods and services it produces most efficiently for products in short supply. We also explain the restrictions nations place on products and services from other countries and present some of the possible advantages and disadvantages of these restrictions. We then describe the extent of international trade and identify the organizations working to foster it. We describe several methods of entering international markets and the various sources of export assistance available from the federal government. Finally, we identify some of the institutions that provide the complex financing necessary for modern international trade.

THE BASIS FOR INTERNATIONAL BUSINESS

Learning Objective

1 Explain the economic basis for international business.

International business encompasses all business activities that involve exchanges across national boundaries. Thus, a firm is engaged in international business when it buys some portion of its input from, or sells some portion of its output to, an organization located in a foreign country. (A small retail store may sell goods produced in some other country. However, because it purchases these goods from American distributors, it is not engaged in international trade.)

International business all business activities that involve exchanges across national boundaries

Absolute and Comparative Advantage

Some countries are better equipped than others to produce particular goods or services. The reason may be a country's natural resources, its labor supply, or even customs or a historical accident. Such a country would be best off if it could specialize in the production of such products so that it can produce them most efficiently. The country could use what it needed of these products and then trade the surplus for products it could not produce efficiently on its own.

Saudi Arabia thus has specialized in the production of crude oil and petroleum products; South Africa, in diamonds; and Australia, in wool. Each of these countries is said to have an absolute advantage with regard to a particular product. An **absolute advantage** is the ability to produce a specific product more efficiently than any other nation.

One country may have an absolute advantage with regard to several products, whereas another country may have no absolute advantage at all. Yet it is still worthwhile for these two countries to specialize and trade with each other. To see why this is so, imagine that you are the president of a successful manufacturing firm and that you can accurately type 90 words per minute. Your assistant can type 80 words per minute but would run the business poorly. Thus, you have an absolute advantage over your assistant in both typing and managing. However, you cannot afford to type your own letters because your time is better spent in managing the business. That is, you have a **comparative advantage** in managing. A comparative advantage is the ability to produce a specific product more efficiently than any other product.

Your assistant, on the other hand, has a comparative advantage in typing because he or she can do that better than managing the business. Thus, you spend your time managing, and you leave the typing to your assistant. Overall, the business is run as efficiently as possible because you are each working in accordance with your own comparative advantage.

absolute advantage the ability to produce a specific product more efficiently than any other nation

comparative advantage the ability to produce a specific product more efficiently than any other product

Exploiting an American advantage. The United States has long specialized in the production of wheat. Because of its natural resource, the United States and some other countries enjoy an absolute advantage—their ability to produce wheat more efficiently than countries in other parts of the world.

The same is true for nations. Goods and services are produced more efficiently when each country specializes in the products for which it has a comparative advantage. Moreover, by definition, every country has a comparative advantage in some product. The United States has many comparative advantages—in research and development, high-technology industries, and identifying new markets, for instance.

Exporting and Importing

Suppose that the United States specializes in producing corn. It then will produce a surplus of corn, but perhaps it will have a shortage of wine. France, on the other hand, specializes in producing wine but experiences a shortage of corn. To satisfy both needs—for corn and for wine—the two countries should trade with each other. The United States should export corn and import wine. France should export wine and import corn.

Exporting is selling and shipping raw materials or products to other nations. The Boeing Company, for example, exports its airplanes to a number of countries for use by their airlines. Figure 3-1 shows the top ten merchandise-exporting states in the United States.

Importing is purchasing raw materials or products in other nations and bringing them into one's own country. Thus, buyers for Macy's department stores may purchase rugs in India or raincoats in England and have them shipped back to the United States for resale.

Importing and exporting are the principal activities in international trade. They give rise to an important concept called the *balance of trade*. A nation's **balance of trade** is the total value of its exports minus the total value of its imports over some period of time. If a country imports more than it exports, its balance of trade is negative and is said to be *unfavorable*. (A negative balance of trade is unfavorable because the country must export money to pay for its excess imports.)

In 2012, the United States imported $2,736 billion worth of goods and services and exported $2,196 billion worth. It thus had a trade deficit of $540 billion. A **trade deficit** is a negative balance of trade (see Figure 3.2). However, the United States has

exporting selling and shipping raw materials or products to other nations

importing purchasing raw materials or products in other nations and bringing them into one's own country

balance of trade the total value of a nation's exports minus the total value of its imports over some period of time

trade deficit a negative balance of trade

FIGURE 3-1 The Top Ten Merchandise-Exporting States

Texas and California accounted for over one-fourth of all 2012 U.S. merchandise exports.

Billions of dollars, 2012 merchandise exports (as of November 2012).

State	Exports
Texas	$192.5
California	$164.4
New York	$77.5
Illinois	$75.6
Michigan	$70.0
Florida	$63.1
Washington	$58.0
Ohio	$47.2
New Jersey	$43.5
Pennsylvania	$42.5

Total 2012 U.S. exports: $1,416 billion (as of November 2012)

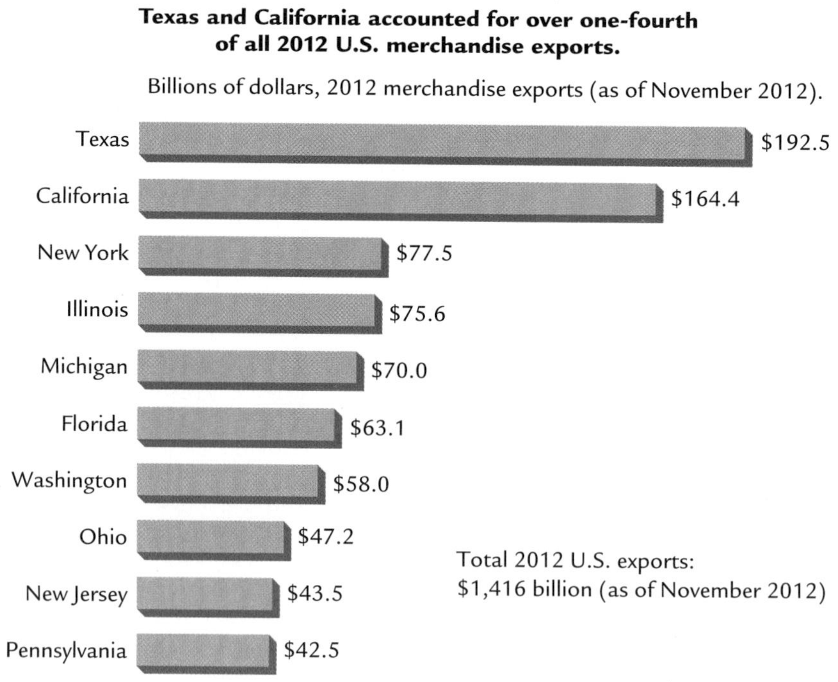

Source: www.census.gov/foreign-trade/statistics/state/zip/2012/11/zipstate.pdf (accessed February 6, 2013).

FIGURE 3-2 U.S. International Trade in Goods and Services

If a country imports more goods than it exports, the balance of trade is negative, as it was in the United States from 1987 to 2012.

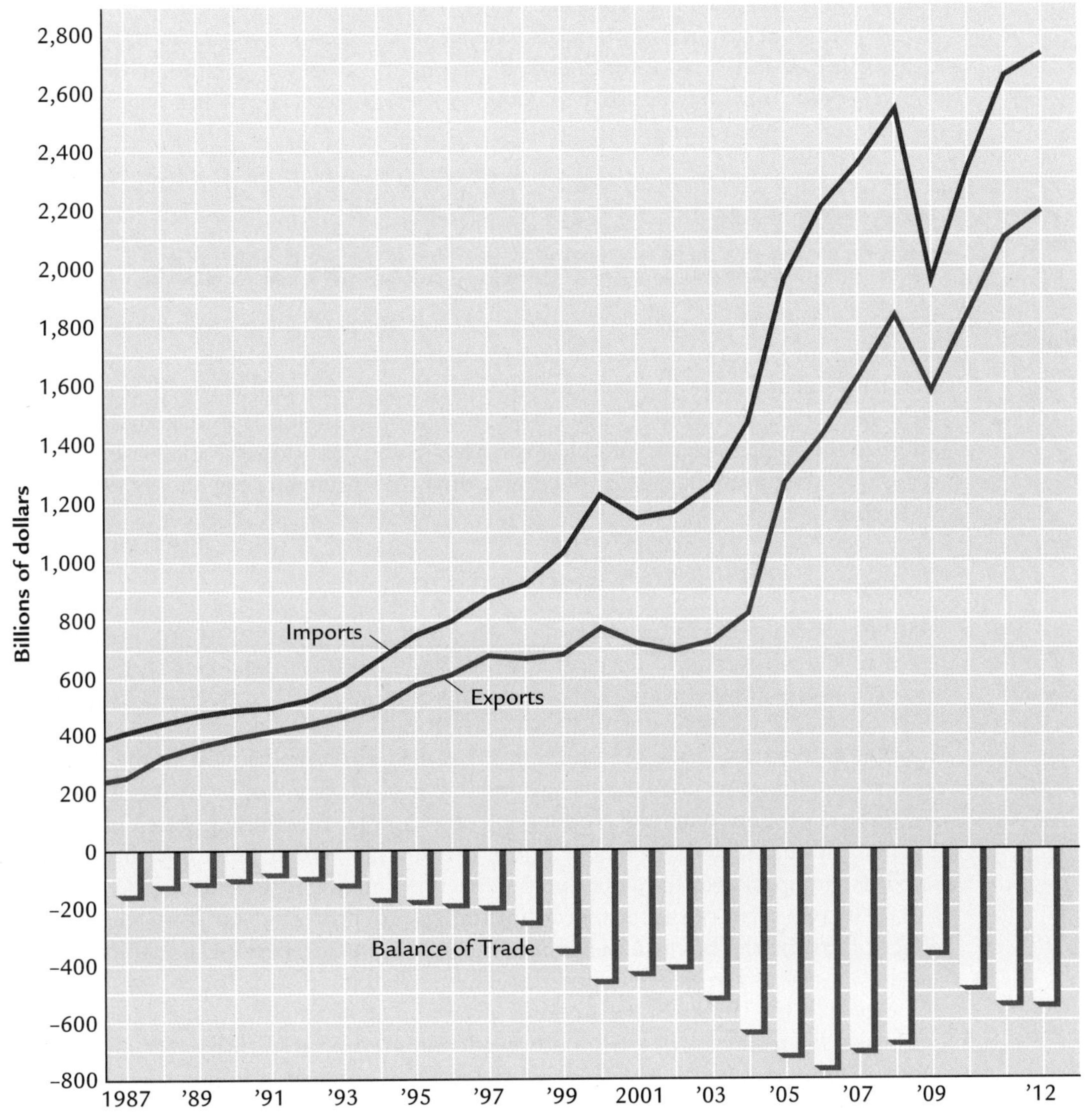

Source: U.S. Department of Commerce, International Trade Administration, U.S. Bureau of Economic Analysis, www.trade.gov/press/press-releases/2013/export-factsheet-february2013-020813.pdf (accessed August 26, 2013).

consistently enjoyed a large and rapidly growing surplus in services. For example, in 2012, the United States imported $437 billion worth of services and exported $632 billion worth, thus creating a favorable balance of $195 billion.[3]

Question: *Are trade deficits bad?*

Answer: In testimony before the Senate Finance Committee, Daniel T. Griswold, associate director of the Center for Trade Policy at the Cato Institute, remarked, "The trade deficit is not a sign of economic distress, but of rising domestic demand and investment. Imposing new trade barriers will only make Americans worse off while leaving the trade deficit virtually unchanged."

On the other hand, when a country exports more than it imports, it is said to have a favorable balance of trade. This has consistently been the case for Japan over the last two decades or so.

Concept Check

✓ Why do firms engage in international trade?

✓ What is the difference between an absolute advantage and a comparative advantage?

✓ What is the difference between balance of trade and balance of payments?

balance of payments the total flow of money into a country minus the total flow of money out of that country over some period of time

A nation's **balance of payments** is the total flow of money into a country minus the total flow of money out of that country over some period of time. Balance of payments, therefore, is a much broader concept than balance of trade. It includes imports and exports, of course. However, it also includes investments, money spent by foreign tourists, payments by foreign governments, aid to foreign governments, and all other receipts and payments.

A continual deficit in a nation's balance of payments (a negative balance) can cause other nations to lose confidence in that nation's economy. Alternatively, a continual surplus may indicate that the country encourages exports but limits imports by imposing trade restrictions.

Learning Objective

2 Discuss the restrictions nations place on international trade, the objectives of these restrictions, and their results.

RESTRICTIONS TO INTERNATIONAL BUSINESS

Specialization and international trade can result in the efficient production of want-satisfying goods and services on a worldwide basis. As we have noted, international business generally is increasing. Yet the nations of the world continue to erect barriers to free trade. They do so for reasons ranging from internal political and economic pressures to simple mistrust of other nations. We examine first the types of restrictions that are applied and then the arguments for and against trade restrictions.

Types of Trade Restrictions

Nations generally are eager to export their products. They want to provide markets for their industries and to develop a favorable balance of trade. Hence, most trade restrictions are applied to imports from other nations.

TARIFFS Perhaps the most commonly applied trade restriction is the customs (or import) duty. An **import duty** (also called a **tariff**) is a tax levied on a particular foreign product entering a country. For example, the United States imposes a 2.2 percent import duty on fresh Chilean tomatoes, an 8.7 percent duty if tomatoes are dried and packaged, and nearly 12 percent if tomatoes are made into ketchup or salsa. The two types of tariffs are revenue tariffs and protective tariffs; both have the effect of raising the price of the product in the importing nations, but for different reasons. *Revenue tariffs* are imposed solely to generate income for the government. For example, the United States imposes a duty on Scotch whiskey solely for revenue purposes. *Protective tariffs*, on the other hand, are imposed to protect a domestic industry from competition by keeping the price of competing imports level with or higher than the price of similar domestic products. Because fewer units of the product will be sold at the increased price, fewer units will be imported. The French and Japanese agricultural sectors would both shrink drastically if their nations abolished the protective tariffs that keep the price of imported farm products high. Today, U.S. tariffs are the lowest in history, with average tariff rates on all imports under 3 percent.

Some countries rationalize their protectionist policies as a way of offsetting an international trade practice called *dumping*. **Dumping** is the exportation of large quantities of a product at a price lower than that of the same product in the home market.

Thus, dumping drives down the price of the domestic item. Recently, for example, the Pencil Makers Association, which represents eight U.S. pencil manufacturers, charged that low-priced pencils from Thailand and the People's Republic of China were being sold in the United States at less than fair value prices. Unable to compete with these inexpensive imports, several domestic manufacturers had to shut down. To protect themselves, domestic manufacturers can obtain an anti-dumping duty through the government to offset the advantage of the foreign

import duty (tariff) a tax levied on a particular foreign product entering a country

dumping exportation of large quantities of a product at a price lower than that of the same product in the home market

product. Recently, for example, the U.S. Department of Commerce imposed antidumping duties of up to 99 percent on a variety of steel products imported from China, following allegations by U.S. Steel Corp. and other producers that the products were being dumped at unfair prices.

NONTARIFF BARRIERS A **nontariff barrier** is a nontax measure imposed by a government to favor domestic over foreign suppliers. Nontariff barriers create obstacles to the marketing of foreign goods in a country and increase costs for exporters. The following are a few examples of government-imposed nontariff barriers:

Restricting the trade: The Russian style. In early 2012, Russian foreign minister Sergey Lavrov speaks at a news conference in Moscow, Russia. Mr. Lavrov threatens that Moscow will not abide by its World Trade Organization's commitments in trade with the United States unless it scraps a Cold War trade law.

- An **import quota** is a limit on the amount of a particular good that may be imported into a country during a given period of time. The limit may be set in terms of either quantity (so many pounds of beef) or value (so many dollars' worth of shoes). Quotas also may be set on individual products imported from specific countries. Once an import quota has been reached, imports are halted until the specified time has elapsed.

- An **embargo** is a complete halt to trading with a particular nation or of a particular product. The embargo is used most often as a political weapon. At present, the United States has import embargoes against Iran and North Korea—both as a result of extremely poor political relations.

- A **foreign-exchange control** is a restriction on the amount of a particular foreign currency that can be purchased or sold. By limiting the amount of foreign currency importers can obtain, a government limits the amount of goods importers can purchase with that currency. This has the effect of limiting imports from the country whose foreign exchange is being controlled.

- A nation can increase or decrease the value of its money relative to the currency of other nations. **Currency devaluation** is the reduction of the value of a nation's currency relative to the currencies of other countries.

Devaluation increases the cost of foreign goods, whereas it decreases the cost of domestic goods to foreign firms. For example, suppose that the British pound is worth $2. In this case, an American-made $2,000 computer can be purchased for £1,000. However, if the United Kingdom devalues the pound so that it is worth only $1, that same computer will cost £2,000. The increased cost, in pounds, will reduce the import of American computers—and all foreign goods—into England.

On the other hand, before devaluation, a £500 set of English bone china will cost an American $1,000. After the devaluation, the set of china will cost only $500. The decreased cost will make the china—and all English goods—much more attractive to U.S. purchasers. Bureaucratic red tape is more subtle than the other forms of nontariff barriers. Yet it can be the most frustrating trade barrier of all. A few examples are the unnecessarily restrictive application of standards and complex requirements related to product testing, labeling, and certification.

CULTURAL BARRIERS Another type of nontariff barrier is related to cultural attitudes. Cultural barriers can impede acceptance of products in foreign countries. For example, illustrations of feet are regarded as despicable in Thailand. Even so simple a thing as the color of a product or its package can present a problem. In Japan, black and white are the colors of mourning, so they should not be used in packaging. In Brazil, purple is the color of death. And in Egypt, green is never used on a package because it is the national color. When customers are unfamiliar

nontariff barrier a nontax measure imposed by a government to favor domestic over foreign suppliers

import quota a limit on the amount of a particular good that may be imported into a country during a given period of time

embargo a complete halt to trading with a particular nation or in a particular product

foreign-exchange control a restriction on the amount of a particular foreign currency that can be purchased or sold

currency devaluation the reduction of the value of a nation's currency relative to the currencies of other countries

with particular products from another country, their general perceptions of the country itself affect their attitude toward the product and help to determine whether they will buy it. Because Mexican cars have not been viewed by the world as being quality products, Volkswagen, for example, may not want to advertise that some of its models sold in the United States are made in Mexico. Many retailers on the Internet have yet to come to grips with the task of designing an online shopping site that is attractive and functional for all global customers.

Gifts to authorities—sometimes quite large ones—may be standard business procedure in some countries. In others, including the United States, they are called bribes or payoffs and are strictly illegal.

Reasons for Trade Restrictions

Various reasons are given for trade restrictions either on the import of specific products or on trade with particular countries. We have noted that political considerations usually are involved in trade embargoes. Other frequently cited reasons for restricting trade include the following:

- *To equalize a nation's balance of payments.* This may be considered necessary to restore confidence in the country's monetary system and in its ability to repay its debts.
- *To protect new or weak industries.* A new, or infant, industry may not be strong enough to withstand foreign competition. Temporary trade restrictions may be used to give it a chance to grow and become self-sufficient. The problem is that once an industry is protected from foreign competition, it may refuse to grow, and "temporary" trade restrictions will become permanent. For example, a recent report by the Government Accountability Office (GAO), the congressional investigative agency, has accused the federal government of routinely imposing quotas on foreign textiles without "demonstrating the threat of serious damage" to U.S. industry. The GAO said that the Committee for the Implementation of Textile Agreements sometimes applies quotas even though it cannot prove the textile industry's claims that American companies have been hurt or jobs have been eliminated.
- *To protect national security.* Restrictions in this category generally apply to technological products that must be kept out of the hands of potential enemies. For example, strategic and defense-related goods cannot be exported to unfriendly nations.
- *To protect the health of citizens.* Products may be embargoed because they are dangerous or unhealthy (e.g., farm products contaminated with insecticides).
- *To retaliate for another nation's trade restrictions.* A country whose exports are taxed by another country may respond by imposing tariffs on imports from that country.
- *To protect domestic jobs.* By restricting imports, a nation can protect jobs in domestic industries. However, protecting these jobs can be expensive. For example, protecting 9,000 jobs in the U.S. carbon-steel industry costs $6.8 billion, or $750,000 per job. In addition, Gary Hufbauer and Ben Goodrich, economists at the Institute for International Economics, estimate that the tariffs could temporarily save 3,500 jobs in the steel industry, but at an annual cost to steel users of $2 billion, or $584,000 per job saved. Yet recently the United States imposed tariffs of up to 616 percent on steel pipes imported from China, South

Concept Check

✓ List and briefly describe the principal restrictions that may be applied to a nation's imports.

✓ What reasons are generally given for imposing trade restrictions?

✓ What are the general effects of import restrictions on trade?

Korea, and Mexico. Similarly, it is estimated that we spent more than $100,000 for every job saved in the apparel manufacturing industry—jobs that seldom paid more than $35,000 a year.

Reasons Against Trade Restrictions

Trade restrictions have immediate and long-term economic consequences—both within the restricting nation and in world trade patterns. These include the following:

- *Higher prices for consumers.* Higher prices may result from the imposition of tariffs or the elimination of foreign competition, as described earlier. For example, imposing quota restrictions and import protections adds $25 billion annually to U.S. consumers' apparel costs by directly increasing costs for imported apparel.
- *Restriction of consumers' choices.* Again, this is a direct result of the elimination of some foreign products from the marketplace and of the artificially high prices that importers must charge for products that are still imported.
- *Misallocation of international resources.* The protection of weak industries results in the inefficient use of limited resources. The economies of both the restricting nation and other nations eventually suffer because of this waste.
- *Loss of jobs.* The restriction of imports by one nation must lead to cutbacks—and the loss of jobs—in the export-oriented industries of other nations. Furthermore, trade protection has a significant effect on the composition of employment. U.S. trade restrictions—whether on textiles, apparel, steel, or automobiles—benefit only a few industries while harming many others. The gains in employment accrue to the protected industries and their primary suppliers, and the losses are spread across all other industries. A few states gain employment, but many other states lose employment.

THE EXTENT OF INTERNATIONAL BUSINESS

Learning Objective

3 Outline the extent of international business and the world economic outlook for trade.

Restrictions or not, international business is growing. Although the worldwide recessions of 1991 and 2001–2002 slowed the rate of growth, and the 2008–2009 global economic crisis caused the sharpest decline in more than 75 years, globalization is a reality of our time. In the United States, international trade now accounts for over one-fourth of Gross Domestic Product (GDP). As trade barriers decrease, new competitors enter the global marketplace, creating more choices for consumers and new opportunities for job seekers. International business will grow along with the expansion of commercial use of the Internet.

The World Economic Outlook for Trade

Although the global economy continued to grow robustly until 2007, economic performance was not equal: growth in the advanced economies slowed and then stopped in 2009, whereas emerging and developing economies continued to grow. Looking ahead, the International Monetary Fund (IMF), an international bank with 188 member nations, expected a gradual global growth to continue in 2013 and 2014 in both advanced and emerging developing economies.[4]

CANADA AND WESTERN EUROPE Our leading export partner, Canada, is projected to show a growth rate of 1.8 percent in 2013 and 2.3 percent in 2014. The euro area, which was projected to decline by 0.2 percent in 2013 is expected to grow 1.0 percent in 2014. The United Kingdom is expected to grow 1.0 percent and 1.9 percent in 2013 and 2014, respectively.

MEXICO AND LATIN AMERICA Our second-largest export customer, Mexico, suffered its sharpest recession ever in 1995, and experienced another major setback in 2009. However, its growth rate in 2013 and 2014 is expected to be 3.5 percent. Growth of about 3.5 percent and 4 percent is expected in 2013 and 2014, respectively. In general, the Latin American and the Caribbean economies are recovering at a robust pace.

JAPAN Japan's economy is regaining some momentum after suffering from an earthquake, tsunami, and nuclear plant disaster in 2011. Stronger consumer demand and business investment make Japan less reliant on exports for growth. The IMF estimates the growth for Japan at 1.2 percent in 2013 and 0.7 percent in 2014.

OTHER ASIAN COUNTRIES The economic growth in Asia remained strong in 2011 and 2012 despite the global recession. Growth was led by China, where its economy expanded by 7.8 percent in 2012, and is expected to grow at 8.2 percent and 8.5 percent in 2013 and 2014, respectively. Growth in India was 4.5 percent in 2012, and is predicted to grow at 5.9 percent and 6.4 percent in 2013 and 2014, respectively. Growth in ASEAN-5 countries—Indonesia, Malaysia, the Philippines, Thailand, and Vietnam—is expected at 5.5 percent and 5.7 percent in 2013 and 2014, respectively. In short, the key emerging economies in Asia are leading the global recovery.

China's emergence as a global economic power has been among the most dramatic economic developments of recent decades. From 1980 to 2004, China's economy averaged a real GDP growth rate of 9.5 percent and became the world's sixth-largest economy. By 2004, China had become the third-largest trading nation in dollar terms, behind the United States and Germany and just ahead of Japan. Today, China, the world's second-largest economy, generates 10 to 15 percent of world GDP, and in 2011, accounted for about 25 percent of world GDP growth. The United States now imports more goods from China than any other nation in the world. In fact, China, with almost $1.9 trillion in exports, is the world's number-one exporter.

Caterpillar in South Africa. Restrictions or not, international business is booming. Globalization is the reality of our time. As trade barriers decrease, ever increasing number of U.S. companies, such as Caterpillar, are selling in the global marketplace.

IMAGEBROKER/ALAMY

© ROBYNELAINE/SHUTTERSTOCK.COM

In 2012, China took steps to promote the international use of its currency, the renminbi.[5]

COMMONWEALTH OF INDEPENDENT STATES The growth in this region is expected to be 3.8 percent in 2013 and 4.1 percent in 2014. Strong growth is expected to continue in Azerbaijan and Armenia, whereas growth is projected to remain stable in Moldova, Tajikistan, and Uzbekistan. Table 3-1 shows the growth rate from 2011 to 2014 for most regions of the world.

EXPORTS AND THE U.S. ECONOMY In 2008, U.S. exports supported more than 10.3 million full- and part-time jobs during a historic time, when exports as a percentage of GDP reached the highest levels since 1916. The new record, 13.8 percent of GDP in 2011, shows that U.S. businesses have great opportunities in the global marketplace. Even though the global economic crisis caused the number of jobs supported by exports to decline sharply to 8.5 million in 2009, globalization represents a huge opportunity for all countries—rich or poor. Indeed, in 2011, for the first time, the U.S. exports exceeded $2.15 trillion and supported 9.7 million jobs, an increase of 1.2 million jobs since 2009.[6] The 15-fold increase in trade volume over the past 65 years has been one of the most important factors in the rise of living standards around the world. During this time, exports have become increasingly important to the U.S. economy. Exports as a percentage of U.S. GDP have increased steadily since 1985, except in the 2001 and 2008 recessions. Our exports to developing

TABLE 3-1 Global Growth Is Picking Up Gradually

Growth has been led by developing countries and emerging markets.

	Annual Percent Change			
	2011	**2012**	**Projected 2013**	**Projected 2014**
World	3.9	3.2	3.5	4.1
United States	1.8	2.3	2.0	3.0
Euro area	1.4	−0.4	−0.2	1.0
United Kingdom	0.9	−0.2	1.0	1.9
Japan	−0.6	2.0	1.2	0.7
Canada	2.6	2.0	1.8	2.3
Other advanced economies	3.3	1.9	2.7	3.3
Newly industrialized Asian economies	4.0	1.8	3.2	3.9
Emerging markets and developing countries	6.3	5.1	5.5	5.9
Developing Asia	8.0	6.6	7.1	7.5
Commonwealth of Independent States	4.9	3.6	3.8	4.1
Middle East and North Africa	3.5	5.2	3.4	3.8
Latin America and the Caribbean	4.5	3.0	3.6	3.9

Source: *International Monetary Fund: World Economic Outlook* by International Monetary Fund. Copyright 2013 by International Monetary Fund. Reproduced with permission of International Monetary Fund via Copyright Clearance Center. www.imf.org/external/pubs/ft/weo/2013/update/01/index.htm (accessed August 26, 2013).

TABLE 3-2 Value of U.S. Merchandise Exports and Imports, 2012 (as of November 2012)

Rank/Trading Partner	Exports ($ billions)	Rank/Trading Partner	Imports ($ billions)
1) Canada	270.1	1) China	390.8
2) Mexico	199.9	2) Canada	298.4
3) China	100.2	3) Mexico	257.3
4) Japan	64.0	4) Japan	134.6
5) United Kingdom	50.8	5) Germany	99.3
6) Germany	45.0	6) South Korea	54.3
7) Brazil	40.2	7) Saudi Arabia	52.0
8) South Korea	38.9	8) United Kingdom	50.6
9) Netherlands	36.8	9) France	38.3
10) France	28.4	10) India	37.7

Source: U.S. Census Bureau website, http://www.census.gov/foreign-trade/statistics/highlights/toppartners.html (accessed February 5, 2013).

Concept Check

✓ According to the IMF, what are the world economic growth projections for 2013 and 2014?

✓ What is the importance of exports to the U.S. economy?

✓ Which nations are the principal trading partners of the United States? What are the major U.S. imports and exports?

and newly industrialized countries are on the rise. Table 3-2 shows the value of U.S. merchandise exports to, and imports from, each of the nation's ten major trading partners. Note that Canada and Mexico are our best partners for our exports; China and Canada, for imports.

Figure 3-3 shows the U.S. goods export and import shares in 2012. Major U.S. exports and imports are manufactured goods, agricultural products, and mineral fuels.

FIGURE 3-3 U.S. Goods Export and Import Shares in 2012

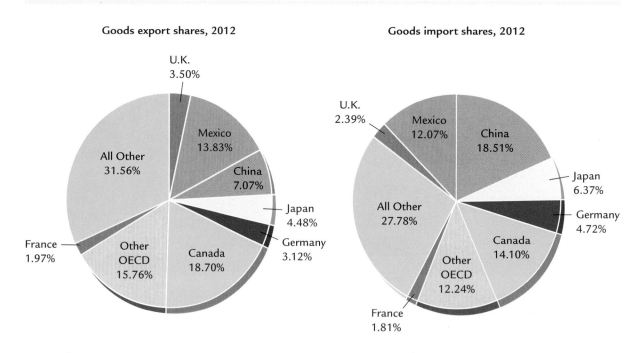

Source: Federal Reserve Bank of St. Louis, *National Economic Trends*, May 2013, p.18.

INTERNATIONAL TRADE AGREEMENTS

The General Agreement on Tariffs and Trade and the World Trade Organization

Learning Objective

4 Discuss international trade agreements and international economic organizations working to foster trade.

At the end of World War II, the United States and 22 other nations organized the body that came to be known as GATT. The **General Agreement on Tariffs and Trade (GATT)** is an international organization of 159 nations dedicated to reducing or eliminating tariffs and other barriers to world trade. These 159 nations accounted for more than 97 percent of the world's merchandise trade (see Figure 3-4). GATT, headquartered in Geneva, Switzerland, provided a forum for tariff negotiations and a means for settling international trade disputes and problems. Most-favored-nation status (MFN) was the famous principle of GATT. It meant that each GATT member nation was to be treated equally by all contracting nations. Therefore, MFN ensured that any tariff reductions or other trade concessions were extended automatically to all GATT members. From 1947 to 1994, the body sponsored eight rounds of negotiations to reduce trade restrictions. Three of the most fruitful were the Kennedy Round, the Tokyo Round, and the Uruguay Round.

THE KENNEDY ROUND (1964–1967) In 1962, the United States Congress passed the Trade Expansion Act. This law gave President John F. Kennedy the authority to negotiate reciprocal trade agreements that could reduce U.S. tariffs by as much as 50 percent. Armed with this authority, which was granted for a period of five years, President Kennedy called for a round of negotiations through GATT.

These negotiations, which began in 1964, have since become known as the Kennedy Round. They were aimed at reducing tariffs and other barriers to trade in

General Agreement on Tariffs and Trade (GATT) an international organization of 159 nations dedicated to reducing or eliminating tariffs and other barriers to world trade

FIGURE 3-4 WTO Members Share in World Merchandise Trade, 2011

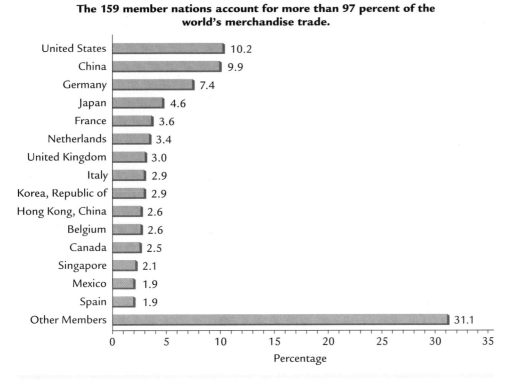

The 159 member nations account for more than 97 percent of the world's merchandise trade.

Country	Percentage
United States	10.2
China	9.9
Germany	7.4
Japan	4.6
France	3.6
Netherlands	3.4
United Kingdom	3.0
Italy	2.9
Korea, Republic of	2.9
Hong Kong, China	2.6
Belgium	2.6
Canada	2.5
Singapore	2.1
Mexico	1.9
Spain	1.9
Other Members	31.1

Source: www.wto.org/english/res_e/Statis_e/its2012_e/its12_charts_e.htm (accessed February 7, 2013).

both industrial and agricultural products. The participants succeeded in reducing tariffs on these products by an average of more than 35 percent. However, they were less successful in removing other types of trade barriers.

THE TOKYO ROUND (1973–1979) In 1973, representatives of approximately 100 nations gathered in Tokyo for another round of GATT negotiations. The *Tokyo Round* was completed in 1979. The participants negotiated tariff cuts of 30 to 35 percent, which were to be implemented over an eight-year period. In addition, they were able to remove or ease such nontariff barriers as import quotas, unrealistic quality standards for imports, and unnecessary red tape in customs procedures.

THE URUGUAY ROUND (1986–1993) In 1986, the *Uruguay Round* was launched to extend trade liberalization and widen the GATT treaty to include textiles, agricultural products, business services, and intellectual-property rights. This most ambitious and comprehensive global commercial agreement in history concluded overall negotiations on December 15, 1993, with delegations on hand from 109 nations. The agreement included provisions to lower tariffs by greater than one-third, to reform trade in agricultural goods, to write new rules of trade for intellectual property and services, and to strengthen the dispute-settlement process. These reforms were expected to expand the world economy by an estimated $200 billion annually.

World Trade Organization (WTO) powerful successor to GATT that incorporates trade in goods, services, and ideas

The Uruguay Round also created the **World Trade Organization (WTO)** on January 1, 1995. The WTO was established by GATT to oversee the provisions of the Uruguay Round and resolve any resulting trade disputes. Membership in the WTO obliges 159 member nations to observe GATT rules. The WTO has judicial powers to mediate among members disputing the new rules. It incorporates trade in goods, services, and ideas and exerts more binding authority than GATT. Its main function is to ensure that trade flows as smoothly, predictably, and freely as possible.

THE DOHA ROUND (2001) On November 14, 2001, in Doha, Qatar, the WTO members agreed to further reduce trade barriers through multilateral trade negotiations over the next three years. This new round of negotiations focuses on industrial tariffs and nontariff barriers, agriculture, services, and easing trade rules. The Doha Round has set the stage for WTO members to take an important step toward significant new multilateral trade liberalization. It is a difficult task, but the rewards—lower tariffs, more choices for consumers, and further integration of developing countries into the world trading system—are sure to be worth the effort. Some experts suggest that U.S. exporters of industrial and agricultural goods and services should have improved access to overseas markets, whereas others disagree. Negotiations between the developed and developing countries continued in 2013.

World Trade and the Global Economic Crisis

After the sharpest decline in more than 72 years, world trade was set to rebound in 2010 by growing at 9.5 percent, according to the WTO economists. In a 2012 speech, WTO Director-General Pascal Lamy stated, "The multilateral trading system has been instrumental in maintaining trade openness during the crisis, thereby avoiding even worse outcomes. Members must remain vigilant. This is not the time for go-it-alone measures. This is the time to strengthen and preserve the global trading system so that it keeps performing this vital function in the future."[7]

International Economic Organizations Working to Foster Trade

economic community an organization of nations formed to promote the free movement of resources and products among its members and to create common economic policies

The primary objective of the WTO is to remove barriers to trade on a worldwide basis. On a smaller scale, an **economic community** is an organization of nations formed to promote the free movement of resources and products among its members and to create common economic policies. A number of economic communities now exist.

THE EUROPEAN UNION The European Union (EU), also known as the European Economic Community and the Common Market, was formed in 1957 by six countries—France, the Federal Republic of Germany, Italy, Belgium, the Netherlands, and Luxembourg. Its objective was freely conducted commerce among these nations and others that might later join. As shown in Figure 3-5, many more nations have joined the EU since then.

On January 1, 2007, the 25 nations of the EU became the EU27 as Bulgaria and Romania became new members. The EU, with a population of nearly 504 million, is now an economic force with a collective economy larger than much of the United States or Japan.

In celebrating the EU's 50th anniversary in 2007, the president of the European Commission, José Manuel Durão Barroso, declared, "Let us first recognize 50 years of achievement. Peace, liberty, and prosperity, beyond the dreams of even the most optimistic founding fathers of Europe. In 1957, 15 of our 27 members were either under dictatorship or were not allowed to exist as independent countries. Now we are all prospering democracies. The EU of today is around 50 times more prosperous and with three times the population of the EU of 1957."

Since January 2002, 17 member nations of the EU have been participating in the new common currency, the euro. The euro is the single currency of the European Monetary Union nations. However, three EU members, Denmark, the United Kingdom, and Sweden, still maintain their own currencies.

THE NORTH AMERICAN FREE TRADE AGREEMENT The North American Free Trade Agreement (NAFTA) joined the United States with its first- and second-largest export trading partners, Canada and Mexico. Implementation of

FIGURE 3-5 The Evolving European Union

The evolving European Union: The European Union is now an economic force, with a collective economy larger than that of the United States or Japan.

Source: http://europa.eu/abc/european_countries/index_en.htm (accessed February 4, 2013).

NAFTA on January 1, 1994, created a market of more than 469 million people. This market consists of Canada (population 35 million), the United States (317 million), and Mexico (117 million). According to the Office of the U.S. Trade Representative, after 19 years, NAFTA has achieved its core goals of expanding trade and investment between the United States, Canada, and Mexico. For example, from 1993 to 2011, trade among the NAFTA nations more than tripled, from $297 billion to $1,058 billion.

NAFTA is built on the Canadian Free Trade Agreement, signed by the United States and Canada in 1989, and on the substantial trade and investment reforms undertaken by Mexico since the mid-1980s. Initiated by the Mexican government, formal negotiations on NAFTA began in June 1991 among the three governments. The support of NAFTA by President Bill Clinton, former Presidents Ronald Reagan and Jimmy Carter, and Nobel Prize–winning economists provided the impetus for U.S. congressional ratification of NAFTA in November 1993. By 2008, NAFTA had gradually eliminated all tariffs and quotas on goods produced and traded among Canada, Mexico, and the United States to provide for a totally free-trade area. Chile is expected to become the fourth member of NAFTA, but political forces may delay its entry into the agreement for several years.

However, NAFTA is not without its critics. Critics maintain that NAFTA

- has not achieved its goals
- has resulted in job losses
- hurts workers by eroding labor standards and lowering wages
- undermines national sovereignty and independence
- does nothing to help the environment, and
- hurts the agricultural sector

The proponents of NAFTA call the agreement a remarkable economic success story for all three partners. They maintain that NAFTA

- has contributed to significant increases in trade and investment
- has benefited companies in all three countries
- has resulted in increased sales, new partnerships, and new opportunities
- has created high-paying export-related jobs, and
- better prices and selection in consumer goods

THE CENTRAL AMERICAN FREE TRADE AGREEMENT The Central American Free Trade Agreement (CAFTA) was created in 2003 by the United States and four Central American countries—El Salvador, Guatemala, Honduras, and Nicaragua. The CAFTA became CAFTA-DR when the Dominican Republic joined the group in 2007. On January 1, 2009, Costa Rica joined CAFTA-DR as the sixth member. CAFTA-DR creates the third-largest U.S. export market in Latin America, behind only Mexico and Brazil.

THE ASSOCIATION OF SOUTHEAST ASIAN NATIONS The Association of Southeast Asian Nations, with headquarters in Jakarta, Indonesia, was established in 1967 to promote political, economic, and social cooperation among its seven member countries: Indonesia, Malaysia, the Philippines, Singapore, Thailand, Brunei, and Vietnam. With the three new members, Cambodia, Laos, and Myanmar, this region of more than 600 million people is already our fifth-largest trading partner.

THE COMMONWEALTH OF INDEPENDENT STATES The Commonwealth of Independent States was established in December 1991 by the newly independent states as an association of 11 republics of the former Soviet Union.

TRANS-PACIFIC PARTNERSHIP (TPP) On November 12, 2011, the leaders of the nine countries—Australia, Brunei Darussalam, Chile, Malaysia, New Zealand, Peru, Singapore, Vietnam, and the United States—formed the Trans-Pacific Partnership. This partnership will boost economies of the member countries, lower barriers to trade and investment, increase exports, and create more jobs. Together, these eight economies would be America's fifth-largest trading partner. According to President Obama, "We already do more than $200 billion in trade with them every year, and with nearly 500 million consumers between us, there's so much more that we can do together." The Asia-Pacific region is one of the fastest growing areas in the world and TPP will open more markets to American businesses and exports.[8]

THE COMMON MARKET OF THE SOUTHERN CONE (MERCOSUR) Headquartered in Montevideo, Uruguay, the Common Market of the Southern Cone (MERCOSUR) was established in 1991 under the Treaty of Asuncion to unite Argentina, Brazil, Paraguay, and Uruguay as a free-trade alliance; Colombia, Ecuador, Peru, Bolivia, and Chile joined later as associates. In 2012, Venezuela, an associate member since 2004, became a full member of MERCOSUR. The alliance represents more than 267 million consumers—67 percent of South America's population, making it the third-largest trading block behind NAFTA and the EU. Like NAFTA, MERCOSUR promotes "the free circulation of goods, services, and production factors among the countries" and established a common external tariff and commercial policy.

THE ORGANIZATION OF PETROLEUM EXPORTING COUNTRIES The Organization of Petroleum Exporting Countries was founded in 1960 in response to reductions in the prices that oil companies were willing to pay for crude oil. The organization was conceived as a collective bargaining unit to provide oil-producing nations with some control over oil prices.

Concept Check

✔ Define and describe the major objectives of the World Trade Organization (WTO) and the international economic communities.

✔ What is the North American Free Trade Agreement (NAFTA)? What is its importance for the United States, Canada, and Mexico?

METHODS OF ENTERING INTERNATIONAL BUSINESS

A firm that has decided to enter international markets can do so in several ways. We will discuss several different methods. These different approaches require varying degrees of involvement in international business. Typically, a firm begins its international operations at the simplest level. Then, depending on its goals, it may progress to higher levels of involvement.

Learning Objective

5 Define the methods by which a firm can organize for and enter into international markets.

licensing a contractual agreement in which one firm permits another to produce and market its product and use its brand name in return for a royalty or other compensation

Licensing

Licensing is a contractual agreement in which one firm permits another to produce and market its product and use its brand name in return for a royalty or other compensation. For example, Yoplait yogurt is a French yogurt licensed for production in the United States. The Yoplait brand maintains an appealing French image, and in return, the U.S. producer pays the French firm a percentage of its income from sales of the product.

Licensing is especially advantageous for small manufacturers wanting to launch a well-known domestic brand internationally. For example, all Spalding sporting products are licensed worldwide. The licensor, the Questor Corporation, owns the Spalding name but produces no goods itself. Licensing thus provides a simple method for expanding into a foreign market with virtually no investment. On the other hand, if the licensee does not maintain the licensor's product standards, the product's image may be damaged. Another possible disadvantage is that a licensing arrangement may not provide the original producer with any foreign marketing experience.

© STUART MILES/SHUTTERSTOCK.COM

Exporting

A firm also may manufacture its products in its home country and export them for sale in foreign markets. As with licensing, exporting can be a relatively low-risk method of entering foreign markets. Unlike licensing, however, it is not a simple method; it opens up several levels of involvement to the exporting firm.

At the most basic level, the exporting firm may sell its products outright to an *export–import merchant*, which is essentially a merchant wholesaler. The merchant assumes all the risks of product ownership, distribution, and sale. It may even purchase the goods in the producer's home country and assume responsibility for exporting the goods. An important and practical issue for domestic firms dealing with foreign customers is securing payment. This is a two-sided issue that reflects the mutual concern rightly felt by both parties to the trade deal: The exporter would like to be paid before shipping the merchandise, whereas the importer obviously would prefer to know that it has received the shipment before releasing any funds. Neither side wants to take the risk of fulfilling its part of the deal only to discover later that the other side has not. The result would lead to legal costs and complex, lengthy dealings that would waste everyone's resources. This mutual level of mistrust, in fact, makes good business sense and has been around since the beginning of trade centuries ago. The solution then was the same as it still is today—for both parties to use a mutually trusted go-between who can ensure that the payment is held until the merchandise is in fact delivered according to the terms of the trade contract. The go-between representatives employed by the importer and exporter are still, as they were in the past, the local domestic banks involved in international business.

EXPORTING TO INTERNATIONAL MARKETS American companies may manufacture their products in the United States and export them for sale in foreign markets. Exporting can be a relatively low-risk method of entering foreign markets.

Here is a simplified version of how it works. After signing contracts detailing the merchandise sold and terms for its delivery, an importer will ask its local bank to issue a **letter of credit** for the amount of money needed to pay for the merchandise. The letter of credit is issued "in favor of the exporter," meaning that the funds are tied specifically to the trade contract involved. The importer's bank forwards the letter of credit to the exporter's bank, which also normally deals in international transactions. The exporter's bank then notifies the exporter that a letter of credit has been received in its name, and the exporter can go ahead with the shipment. The carrier transporting the merchandise provides the exporter with evidence of the shipment in a document called a **bill of lading**. The exporter signs over title to the merchandise (now in transit) to its bank by delivering signed copies of the bill of lading and the letter of credit.

In exchange, the exporter issues a **draft** from the bank, which orders the importer's bank to pay for the merchandise. The draft, bill of lading, and letter of credit are sent from the exporter's bank to the importer's bank. Acceptance by the importer's bank leads to return of the draft and its sale by the exporter to its bank, meaning that the exporter receives cash and the bank assumes the risk of collecting the funds from the foreign bank. The importer is obliged to pay its bank on delivery of the merchandise, and the deal is complete.

In most cases, the letter of credit is part of a lending arrangement between the importer and its bank. Of course, both banks earn fees for issuing letters of credit and drafts and for handling the import–export services for their clients. Furthermore, the process incorporates the fact that both importer and exporter will have different local currencies and might even negotiate their trade in a third currency. The banks look after all the necessary exchanges. For example, the vast majority of international business is negotiated in U.S. dollars, even though the trade may be between countries other than the United States. Thus, although the importer may end up paying for the merchandise in its local currency and the exporter may receive payment

letter of credit issued by a bank on request of an importer stating that the bank will pay an amount of money to a stated beneficiary

bill of lading document issued by a transport carrier to an exporter to prove that merchandise has been shipped

draft issued by the exporter's bank, ordering the importer's bank to pay for the merchandise, thus guaranteeing payment once accepted by the importer's bank

in another local currency, the banks involved will exchange all necessary foreign funds in order to allow the deal to take place.

Alternatively, the exporting firm may ship its products to an *export–import agent*, which arranges the sale of the products to foreign intermediaries for a commission or fee. The agent is an independent firm—like other agents—that sells and may perform other marketing functions for the exporter. The exporter, however, retains title to the products during shipment and until they are sold.

An exporting firm also may establish its own *sales offices*, or *branches*, in foreign countries. These installations are international extensions of the firm's distribution system. They represent a deeper involvement in international business than the other exporting techniques we have discussed—and thus they carry a greater risk. The exporting firm maintains control over sales, and it gains both experience in and knowledge of foreign markets. Eventually, the firm also may develop its own sales force to operate in conjunction with foreign sales offices.

Exporting to international markets. American companies may manufacture their products in the United States and export them for sale in foreign markets. Exporting can be a relatively risk-free method of entering foreign markets.

Joint Ventures

A *joint venture* is a partnership formed to achieve a specific goal or to operate for a specific period of time. A joint venture with an established firm in a foreign country provides immediate market knowledge and access, reduced risk, and control over product attributes. However, joint-venture agreements established across national borders can become extremely complex. As a result, joint-venture agreements generally require a very high level of commitment from all the parties involved.

A joint venture may be used to produce and market an existing product in a foreign nation or to develop an entirely new product. Recently, for example, Archer Daniels Midland Company (ADM), one of the world's leading food processors, entered into a joint venture with Gruma SA, Mexico's largest corn flour and tortilla company. Besides a 22 percent stake in Gruma, ADM also received stakes in other joint ventures operated by Gruma. One of them will combine both companies' U.S. corn flour operations, which account for about 25 percent of the U.S. market. ADM also has a 40 percent stake in a Mexican wheat flour mill. ADM's joint venture increased its participation in the growing Mexican economy, where ADM already produces corn syrup, fructose, starch, and wheat flour.

Totally Owned Facilities

At a still deeper level of involvement in international business, a firm may develop *totally owned facilities*, that is, its own production and marketing facilities in one or more foreign nations. This *direct investment* provides complete control over operations, but it carries a greater risk than the joint venture. The firm is really establishing a subsidiary in a foreign country. Most firms do so only after they have acquired some knowledge of the host country's markets.

Direct investment may take either of two forms. In the first, the firm builds or purchases manufacturing and other facilities in the foreign country. It uses these facilities to produce its own established products and to market them in that country and perhaps in neighboring countries. Firms such as General Motors, Union Carbide, and Colgate-Palmolive are multinational companies with worldwide manufacturing facilities. Colgate-Palmolive factories are becoming *Eurofactories*, supplying neighboring countries as well as their own local markets.

A second form of direct investment in international business is the purchase of an existing firm in a foreign country under an arrangement that allows it to operate

Striving for Success

Services Team Up to Enter India

A growing number of U.S.-based service firms are expanding into India by forming joint ventures with local firms. Both partners bring specific strengths to the joint venture, not just their brands but also the Indian firm's in-depth knowledge of customers and the U.S. firm's service concepts.

For example, Cigna, which markets health insurance, has teamed up with TTK Group to sell insurance policies in India. TTK Group operates 1,500 retail stores and sells a variety of goods and services, including insurance. The joint venture will enable Cigna to reach consumers without creating a separate network of insurance agents—and TTK Group gains another product line to diversify its offerings.

CBS and its partner in India, Reliance Broadcast Networks, recently launched English-language channels to tap into the country's burgeoning market for television entertainment. CBS provides the content (including hit programs such as CSI) and Reliance provides its expertise in distribution and advertising sales for this joint venture, known as Big CBS.

Dunkin' Donuts has a joint venture with Jubilant Foodworks to open shops featuring an all-day menu of coffee, donuts, and other foods adapted to Indian tastes. In this partnership, "Dunkin' provides flexibility in localizing recipes, and we have strengths in food and culinary which we intend to leverage," explains Jubilant's chairman.

Sources: Based on information in Vikas Bajaj, "Cigna in Deal to Sell Health Insurance in India," *New York Times*, November 21, 2011, www.nytimes.com; Sanjeev Choudhary, "Dunkin' Donuts to Enter India with Jubilant Foodworks," *Reuters*, February 25, 2011, www.reuters.com; Nyay Bhushan, "Reliance, RTL Group Plan Joint Venture for English, Local-Language Channels," *Hollywood Reporter*, March 11, 2011, www.hollywoodreporter.com.

independently of the parent company. When Sony Corporation (a Japanese firm) decided to enter the motion picture business in the United States, it chose to purchase Columbia Pictures Entertainment, Inc., rather than start a new motion picture studio from scratch.

Strategic Alliances

strategic alliance a partnership formed to create competitive advantage on a worldwide basis

A **strategic alliance,** the newest form of international business structure, is a partnership formed to create competitive advantage on a worldwide basis. Strategic alliances are very similar to joint ventures. The number of strategic alliances is growing at an estimated rate of about 20 percent per year. In fact, in the automobile and computer industries, strategic alliances are becoming the predominant means of competing. International competition is so fierce and the costs of competing on a global basis are so high that few firms have all the resources needed to do it alone. Thus, individual firms that lack the internal resources essential for international success may seek to collaborate with other companies.

An example of such an alliance is the New United Motor Manufacturing, Inc. (NUMMI), formed by Toyota and General Motors to make automobiles of both firms. This enterprise united the quality engineering of Japanese cars with the marketing expertise and market access of General Motors.

Trading Companies

trading company provides a link between buyers and sellers in different countries

A **trading company** provides a link between buyers and sellers in different countries. A trading company, as its name implies, is not involved in manufacturing or owning assets related to manufacturing. It buys products in one country at the lowest price consistent with quality and sells to buyers in another country. An important function of trading companies is taking title to products and performing all the activities necessary to move the products from the domestic country to a foreign country. For example, large grain-trading companies operating out of home offices both in the United States and overseas control a major portion of the world's trade in basic food commodities. These trading companies sell homogeneous agricultural commodities that can be stored and moved rapidly in response to market conditions.

Countertrade

In the early 1990s, many developing nations had major restrictions on converting domestic currency into foreign currency. Therefore, exporters had to resort to barter agreements with importers. **Countertrade** is essentially an international barter transaction in which goods and services are exchanged for different goods and services. Examples include Saudi Arabia's purchase of ten 747 jets from Boeing with payment in crude oil and Philip Morris's sale of cigarettes to Russia in return for chemicals used to make fertilizers.

countertrade an international barter transaction

multinational enterprise a firm that operates on a worldwide scale without ties to any specific nation or region

Multinational Firms

A **multinational enterprise** is a firm that operates on a worldwide scale without ties to any specific nation or region. The multinational firm represents the highest level of involvement in international business. It is equally "at home" in most countries of the world. In fact, as far as the operations of the multinational enterprise are concerned, national boundaries exist only on maps. It is, however, organized under the laws of its home country.

Table 3-3 shows the ten largest foreign and U.S. public multinational companies; the ranking is based on a composite score reflecting each company's best three out of four rankings for sales, profits, assets, and market value. Table 3-4 describes steps in entering international markets.

According to the chairman of the board of Dow Chemical Company, a multinational firm of U.S. origin, "The emergence of a world economy and of the multinational corporation has been accomplished hand in hand." He sees multinational enterprises moving toward what he calls the "anational company," a firm that has no nationality but belongs to all countries. In recognition of this movement, there already have been international conferences devoted to the question of how such enterprises would be controlled.

Concept Check

✓ Two methods of engaging in international business may be categorized as either direct or indirect. How would you classify each of the methods described in this chapter? Why?

✓ What is a letter of credit? A bill of lading? A draft?

✓ In what ways is a multinational enterprise different from a large corporation that does business in several countries?

✓ What are the steps in entering international markets?

TABLE 3-3 The Ten Largest Foreign and U.S. Multinational Corporations

2012 Rank	Company	Business	Country	Revenue ($ millions)
1	Royal Dutch/Shell Group	Energy	Netherlands	484,489
2	ExxonMobil	Energy	United States	452,926
3	Walmart Stores	General merchandiser	United States	446,950
4	BP	Energy	United Kingdom	386,463
5	Sinopec Group	Energy	China	375,214
6	China Natural Petroleum	Energy	China	352,338
7	State Grid	Power grids	China	259,142
8	Chevron	Energy	United States	245,621
9	Conoco Phillips	Energy	United States	237,272
10	Toyota Motor	Automobiles	Japan	235,364

Source: http://money.cnn.com/magazine/fortune/global500/2012/snapshots/6388.html (accessed February 6, 2013).

TABLE 3-4 Steps in Entering International Markets

Step	Activity	Marketing Tasks
1	Identify exportable products.	Identify key selling features. Identify needs that they satisfy. Identify the selling constraints that are imposed.
2	Identify key foreign markets for the products.	Determine who the customers are. Pinpoint what and when they will buy. Do market research. Establish priority, or "target," countries.
3	Analyze how to sell in each priority market (methods will be affected by product characteristics and unique features of country/market).	Locate available government and private-sector resources. Determine service and backup sales requirements.
4	Set export prices and payment terms, methods, and techniques.	Establish methods of export pricing. Establish sales terms, quotations, invoices, and conditions of sale. Determine methods of international payments, secured and unsecured.
5	Estimate resource requirements and returns.	Estimate financial requirements. Estimate human resources requirements (full- or part-time export department or operation). Estimate plant production capacity. Determine necessary product adaptations.
6	Establish overseas distribution network.	Determine distribution agreement and other key marketing decisions (price, repair policies, returns, territory, performance, and termination). Know your customer (use U.S. Department of Commerce international marketing services).
7	Determine shipping, traffic, and documentation procedures and requirements.	Determine methods of shipment (air or ocean freight, truck, rail). Finalize containerization. Obtain validated export license. Follow export-administration documentation procedures.
8	Promote, sell, and be paid.	Use international media, communications, advertising, trade shows, and exhibitions. Determine the need for overseas travel (when, where, and how often?). Initiate customer follow-up procedures.
9	Continuously analyze current marketing, economic, and political situations.	Recognize changing factors influencing marketing strategies. Constantly re-evaluate.

Source: U.S. Department of Commerce, International Trade Administration, Washington, DC.

Learning Objective

6 Describe the various sources of export assistance.

SOURCES OF EXPORT ASSISTANCE

Concept Check

✓ List some key sources of export assistance. How can these sources be useful to small business firms?

In August 2010, President Obama announced the *National Export Initiative* (NEI) to revitalize U.S. exports. Under the NEI, many federal agencies assist U.S. firms in developing export-promotion programs. The export services and programs of these agencies can help American firms to compete in foreign markets and create new jobs in the United States. For example, recently the International Trade Administration coordinated 77 trade missions to 38 countries. More than 1,120 companies secured over $1.25 billion in export sales during these missions. Table 3-5 provides an overview of selected export assistance programs.

These and other sources of export information enhance the business opportunities of U.S. firms seeking to enter expanding foreign markets. Another vital energy factor is financing.

TABLE 3-5 U.S. Government Export Assistance Programs

1	U.S. Export Assistance Centers, www.sba.gov/oit/export/useac.html	Provides assistance in export marketing and trade finance
2	International Trade Administration, www.ita.doc.gov/	Offers assistance and information to exporters through its domestic and overseas commercial officers
3	U.S. and Foreign Commercial Services, www.export.gov/	Helps U.S. firms compete more effectively in the global marketplace and provides information on foreign markets
4	Advocacy Center, www.ita.doc.gov/advocacy	Facilitates advocacy to assist U.S. firms competing for major projects and procurements worldwide
5	Trade Information Center, www.ita.doc.gov/td/tic/	Provides U.S. companies information on federal programs and activities that support U.S. exports
6	STAT-USA/Internet, www.stat-usa.gov/	Offers a comprehensive collection of business, economic, and trade information on the Web
7	Small Business Administration, www.sba.gov/oit/	Publishes many helpful guides to assist small- and medium-sized companies
8	National Trade Data Bank, www.stat-usa.gov/tradtest.nsf	Provides international economic and export-promotion information supplied by more than 20 U.S. agencies

© CENGAGE LEARNING 2015

FINANCING INTERNATIONAL BUSINESS

Learning Objective

7 **Identify the institutions that help firms and nations finance international business.**

International trade compounds the concerns of financial managers. Currency exchange rates, tariffs and foreign exchange controls, and the tax structures of host nations all affect international operations and the flow of cash. In addition, financial managers must be concerned both with the financing of their international operations and with the means available to their customers to finance purchases.

Fortunately, along with business in general, a number of large banks have become international in scope. Many have established branches in major cities around the world. Thus, like firms in other industries, they are able to provide their services where and when they are needed. In addition, financial assistance is available from U.S. government and international sources.

Several of today's international financial organizations were founded many years ago to facilitate free trade and the exchange of currencies among nations. Some, such as the Inter-American Development Bank, are supported internationally and focus on developing countries. Others, such as the Export-Import Bank, are operated by one country but provide international financing.

The Export-Import Bank of the United States

The **Export-Import Bank of the United States**, created in 1934, is an independent agency of the U.S. government whose function is to assist in financing the exports of American firms. *Ex-Im Bank*, as it is commonly called, extends and guarantees credit to overseas buyers of American goods and services and guarantees short-term financing for exports. It also cooperates with commercial banks in helping American exporters to offer credit to their overseas customers. For example, in early 2013, the Ex-Im Bank guaranteed a $500 million loan to finance export of Boeing 777 jets to Aeroflot Russian Airlines. This loan created approximately 3,200 U.S. jobs.

According to Fred P. Hochberg, chairman and president of Ex-Im Bank, "Working with private lenders we are helping U.S. exporters put Americans to work producing the high quality goods and services that foreign buyers prefer. As part of President Obama's National Export Initiative, Ex-Im Bank's export financing is contributing to the goal of doubling of U.S. exports within the next five years."

Export-Import Bank of the United States an independent agency of the U.S. government whose function is to assist in financing the exports of American firms

© MILAN LJUBISAVLJEVIC/SHUTTERSTOCK.COM

Multilateral Development Banks

A **multilateral development bank (MDB)** is an internationally supported bank that provides loans to developing countries to help them grow. The most familiar is the World Bank, a cooperative of 188 member countries, which operates worldwide. Established in 1944 and headquartered in Washington, DC, the bank provides low-interest loans, interest-free credits, and grants to developing countries. The loans and grants help these countries to:

- supply safe drinking water
- build schools and train teachers
- increase agricultural productivity
- expand citizens' access to markets, jobs, and housing
- improve health care and access to water and sanitation
- manage forests and other natural resources
- build and maintain roads, railways, and ports, and
- reduce air pollution and protect the environment.[9]

Four other MDBs operate primarily in Central and South America, Asia, Africa, and Eastern and Central Europe. All five are supported by the industrialized nations, including the United States.

THE INTER-AMERICAN DEVELOPMENT BANK The Inter-American Development Bank (IDB), the oldest and largest regional bank, was created in 1959 by 19 Latin American countries and the United States. The bank, which is headquartered in Washington, DC, makes loans and provides technical advice and assistance to countries. Today, the IDB is owned by 48 member states.

THE ASIAN DEVELOPMENT BANK With 67 member nations, the Asian Development Bank (ADB), created in 1966 and headquartered in the Philippines, promotes economic and social progress in Asian and Pacific regions. The U.S. government is the second-largest contributor to the ADB's capital, after Japan.

multilateral development bank (MDB) an internationally supported bank that provides loans to developing countries to help them grow

THE AFRICAN DEVELOPMENT BANK The African Development Bank (AFDB), also known as *Banque Africaines de Development*, was established in 1964 with headquarters in Abidjan, Ivory Coast. Its members include 53 African and 24 non-African countries from the Americas, Europe, and Asia. The AFDB's goal is to foster the economic and social development of its African members. The bank pursues this goal through loans, research, technical assistance, and the development of trade programs.

EUROPEAN BANK FOR RECONSTRUCTION AND DEVELOPMENT Established in 1991 to encourage reconstruction and development in the Eastern and Central European countries, the London-based *European Bank for Reconstruction and Development* is owned by 64 countries and 2 intergovernmental institutions. Its loans are geared toward developing market-oriented economies and promoting private enterprise.

The International Monetary Fund

International Monetary Fund (IMF) an international bank with 188 member nations that makes short-term loans to developing countries experiencing balance-of-payment deficits

The **International Monetary Fund (IMF)** is an international bank with 188 member nations that makes short-term loans to developing countries experiencing balance-of-payment deficits. This financing is contributed by member nations, and it must be repaid with interest. Loans are provided primarily to fund international trade. Created in 1945 and headquartered in Washington, DC, the bank's main goals are to:

- promote international monetary cooperation
- facilitate the expansion and balanced growth of international trade

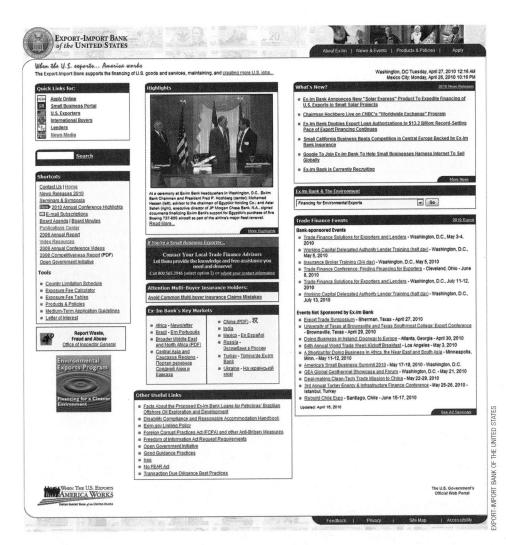

Mission possible. The Export-Import Bank of the United States (Ex-Im Bank) is the official export credit agency of the United States. Ex-Im Bank's mission is to assist in financing U.S. goods and services to international markets. With more than 78 years of experience, Ex-Im Bank has supported more than $400 billion of U.S. exports, primarily to developing markets worldwide.

- promote exchange rate stability
- assist in establishing a multilateral system of payments, and
- make resources available to members experiencing balance-of-payment difficulties.

The Challenges Ahead

In a 2012 speech at Oxford University, Pascal Lamy, Director-General of the World Trade Organization stated, "We live in a world of ever-growing independence and interconnectedness. Our interdependence has grown beyond anyone's imagination. The world of today is virtually unrecognizable from the world in which we lived one generation ago." The most striking example of globalization is Apple. Apple's iPod is designed in the United States, manufactured with components from Japan, Korea, and several other Asian countries, and assembled in China by a company from Chinese Taipei. Nowadays, most products are not "Made in the UK" or "Made in France"; they are in fact "Made in the World."[10]

In 2013, the global economic recovery remained sluggish. Financial challenges in some euro-area economies slowed the economic growth. However, WTO rules and principles have assisted governments in keeping markets open and they now provide a platform for which the trade can grow as the global economy improves. According to Mr. Lamy, "We see the light at the end of the tunnel and trade promises to be an important part of the recovery. But we must avoid derailing any economic revival through protectionism."

Concept Check

✓ What is the Export-Import Bank of the United States? How does it assist U.S. exporters?

✓ What is a multilateral development bank (MDB)? Who supports these banks?

✓ What is the International Monetary Fund? What types of loans does the IMF provide?

Summary

1 Explain the economic basis for international business.

International business encompasses all business activities that involve exchanges across national boundaries. International trade is based on specialization, whereby each country produces the goods and services that it can produce more efficiently than any other goods and services. A nation is said to have a comparative advantage relative to these goods. International trade develops when each nation trades its surplus products for those in short supply.

A nation's balance of trade is the difference between the value of its exports and the value of its imports. Its balance of payments is the difference between the flow of money into and out of the nation. Generally, a negative balance of trade is considered unfavorable.

2 Discuss the restrictions nations place on international trade, the objectives of these restrictions, and their results.

Despite the benefits of world trade, nations tend to use tariffs and nontariff barriers (import quotas, embargoes, and other restrictions) to limit trade. These restrictions typically are justified as being needed to protect a nation's economy, industries, citizens, or security. They can result in the loss of jobs, higher prices, fewer choices in the marketplace, and the misallocation of resources.

3 Outline the extent of international business and the world economic outlook for trade.

World trade is generally increasing. Trade between the United States and other nations is increasing in dollar value but decreasing in terms of our share of the world market. Exports as a percentage of U.S. GDP have increased steadily since 1985, except in the 2001 and 2008 recessions.

4 Discuss international trade agreements and international economic organizations working to foster trade.

The General Agreement on Tariffs and Trade (GATT) was formed to dismantle trade barriers and provide an environment in which international business can grow. Today, the World Trade Organization (WTO)

and various economic communities carry on this mission. These world economic communities include the European Union, the NAFTA, the CAFTA, the Association of Southeast Asian Nations, the Pacific Rim, the Commonwealth of Independent States, the Caribbean Basin Initiative, the Common Market of the Southern Cone, the Organization of Petroleum Exporting Countries, and the Organization for Economic Cooperation and Development.

5 Define the methods by which a firm can organize for and enter into international markets.

A firm can enter international markets in several ways. It may license a foreign firm to produce and market its products. It may export its products and sell them through foreign intermediaries or its own sales organization abroad, or it may sell its exports outright to an export–import merchant. It may enter into a joint venture with a foreign firm. It may establish its own foreign subsidiaries, or it may develop into a multinational enterprise.

Generally, each of these methods represents an increasingly deeper level of involvement in international business, with licensing being the simplest and the development of a multinational corporation the most involved.

6 Describe the various sources of export assistance.

Many government and international agencies provide export assistance to U.S. and foreign firms. Sources of export assistance include U.S. Export Assistance Centers, the International Trade Administration, U.S. and Foreign Commercial Services, Export Legal Assistance Network, Advocacy Center, National Trade Data Bank, and other government and international agencies.

7 Identify the institutions that help firms and nations finance international business.

The financing of international trade is more complex than that of domestic trade. Institutions such as the Ex-Im Bank and the International Monetary Fund have been established to provide financing and ultimately to increase world trade for American and international firms.

Key Terms

You should now be able to define and give an example relevant to each of the following terms:

international business (67)
absolute advantage (67)
comparative advantage (67)
exporting (68)
importing (68)
balance of trade (68)
trade deficit (68)
balance of payments (70)
import duty (tariff) (70)

dumping (70)
nontariff barrier (71)
import quota (71)
embargo (71)
foreign-exchange control (71)
currency devaluation (71)
General Agreement on
    Tariffs and Trade
    (GATT) (77)

World Trade Organization
    (WTO) (78)
economic community (78)
licensing (81)
letter of credit (82)
bill of lading (82)
draft (82)
strategic alliance (84)
trading company (84)

countertrade (85)
multinational enterprise (85)
Export-Import Bank of the
    United States (87)
multilateral development
    bank (MDB) (88)
International Monetary
    Fund (IMF) (88)

Discussion Questions

1. The United States restricts imports but, at the same time, supports the WTO and international banks whose objective is to enhance world trade. As a member of Congress, how would you justify this contradiction to your constituents?

2. What effects might the devaluation of a nation's currency have on its business firms, its consumers, and the debts it owes to other nations?

3. Should imports to the United States be curtailed by, say, 20 percent to eliminate our trade deficit? What might happen if this were done?

4. When should a firm consider expanding from strictly domestic trade to international trade? When should it consider becoming further involved in international trade? What factors might affect the firm's decisions in each case?

5. How can a firm obtain the expertise needed to produce and market its products in, for example, the EU?

Test Yourself

Matching Questions

1. _____ The total value of a nation's exports minus the total value of its imports over some period of time.

2. _____ The ability to produce a specific product more efficiently than any other nation.

3. _____ Selling and shipping raw materials or products to other nations.

4. _____ The ability to produce a specific product more efficiently than any other product.

5. _____ All business activities that involve exchanges across national boundaries.

6. _____ The total flow of money into a country minus the total flow of money out of that country over the same period of time.

7. _____ A tax levied on a particular foreign product entering a country.

8. _____ A complete halt to trading with a particular nation or in a particular product.

9. _____ An international barter transaction.

10. _____ An internationally supported bank that provides loans to developing countries to help them grow.

a. countertrade
b. foreign exchange control
c. multilateral development bank (MDB)
d. absolute advantage
e. import duty
f. embargo
g. exporting
h. international business
i. balance of trade
j. comparative advantage
k. Export-Import
l. balance of payments

True False Questions

11. **T** **F** The United States has enjoyed a trade surplus during the last two decades.

12. **T** **F** Tariff is a tax levied on a particular foreign product entering a country.

13. **T** **F** Quotas may be set on worldwide imports or on imports from a specific country.

14. **T** **F** The participants in the Kennedy Round have succeeded in reducing tariffs by less than 20 percent.

15. **T** **F** Licensing and exporting can be considered relatively low-risk methods of entering foreign markets.

16. **T** **F** A letter of credit is issued in favor of the importer.

17. **T** **F** A letter of credit is issued by the transport carrier to the exporter to prove that merchandise has been shipped.

18. **T** **F** Strategic alliances are partnerships formed to create competitive advantage on a worldwide basis.

19. **T** **F** A firm that has no ties to a specific nation or region and operates on a worldwide scale is called a national enterprise.

20. **T** **F** The International Monetary Fund (IMF) makes short-term loans to developing countries experiencing balance-of-payment deficits.

Multiple-Choice Questions

21. _____ By definition, every country has a(n) advantage in some product.
   a. relative
   b. absolute
   c. comparative
   d. superior
   e. inferior

22. _____ Purchasing products or materials in other nations and bringing them into one's own country is
   a. trading.
   b. balancing.
   c. exporting.
   d. importing.
   e. dumping.

23. _____ General Motors and Ford products produced in the United States are found around the world. The United States is these automobiles.
   a. tariffing
   b. importing
   c. exporting
   d. releasing
   e. dumping

24. _____ is the exportation of large quantities of a product at a price lower than that of the same product in the home market.
   a. Embargo
   b. Duty
   c. Dumping
   d. Export quota
   e. Dropping

25. _____ A complete halt to trading with a particular nation or in a particular product is called a(n)
   a. embargo.
   b. stoppage.
   c. stay.
   d. closure.
   e. barricade.

26. _____ Because it has not been around long enough to establish itself, the Russian automobile industry could be classified as a(n)
   a. hopeless industry.
   b. soft industry.
   c. infant industry.
   d. protected industry.
   e. toddler industry.

27. _____ The World Trade Organization was created by the
   a. Kennedy Round.
   b. United Nations.
   c. League of Nations.
   d. Tokyo Round.
   e. Uruguay Round.

28. _____ CAFTA, NAFTA, OECD, and OPEC are all examples of
   a. political organizations.
   b. peace treaties.
   c. international economic communities.
   d. World Trade Organization members.
   e. democratic organizations.

29. _____ Foreign licensing is similar to
   a. starting from scratch.
   b. franchising.
   c. wholesaling.
   d. establishing a subsidiary in another country.
   e. establishing a sales office in a foreign country.

30. _____ Established in 1944 and headquartered in Washington, D.C., the World Bank is an example of
   a. Eximbank
   b. IMF
   c. MDB
   d. EFTA
   e. LAFTA

Answers to the Test Yourself questions appear at the end of the book on page TY-1.

Video Case
Keeping Brazil's Economy Hot

It's been hot in Brazil. No, we're not talking about the country's temperature: We're talking about its economy, which has been growing at a heated pace. In 2010, the country's GDP grew by 7.5 percent. That's a growth rate developed countries such as the United States haven't experienced for years, if not decades. Although Brazil's growth rate slowed considerably in 2011 and 2012 due to the global economic crisis, it has fared better than many other nations. Recently it surpassed the United Kingdom as the sixth-largest economy in the world.

Why has Brazil done so well economically? Increased world trade is one reason why. The country has an abundant amount of natural resources firms in other countries around the world are eager to buy—especially companies in the fast-growing nation of China. Greater exports have also helped 40 million Brazilians rise up out of poverty and into the middle class. Their massive spending power is creating new markets for multinational companies ranging from McDonald's and Whirlpool to Nestlé, Avon, and Volkswagen. Brazil has become Avon's largest market. Volkswagen now sells more cars in Brazil than it does Germany, where the company is headquartered. "China may have over a billion inhabitants, but Brazil has 200,000 consumers," explains Ivan Zurita, the president of Nestle's Brazil division.

Clouds on the horizon threaten to cool off Brazil's growth, however. To begin with, the country is concerned that its trade with China is out of balance. Although China purchases more natural resources from Brazil than any other nation, it doesn't purchase near as many manufactured goods from Brazil as it exports to it.

A bigger issue is the appreciation of Brazil's currency, the real. Massive amounts of money have been flowing into Brazil to take advantage of the nation's high interest rates and growth opportunities. This has increased the demand for the real, causing its value to rise by nearly 50 percent relative to other currencies. The good news is that the stronger real has made imported products cheaper for Brazilians to buy. The bad news is that products made in Brazil have become more expensive for the rest of the world to purchase, slowing the country's exports and growth.

Businesses in Brazil have lobbied the government to weaken the real so their products are better able to compete against imports. Their efforts appear to have paid off. Recently, Guido Mantega, Brazil's minister of finance, said the country will take steps "as needed" to weaken the real. The government has also imposed tariffs on a number of imported products, including cars, shoes, chemicals, and textiles, and signed a trade deal with Mexico that put a quota on the number of automobiles imported from that country.

Imports and the value of the real are not the only clouds threatening Brazil, though. Businesses in the country face a great deal of bureaucratic red tape, heavy regulations, and tax rates that are some of the highest in the world. To deal with these problems, Brazilian President Dilma Rousseff has announced that her administration will eliminate payroll taxes for employers in industries hardest hit by imports. To further ease the nation's growing pains, Brazil's development bank, BDM, will subsidize business loans to boost the production of many products, including tablets and off-shore oil rigs. The goal is to stimulate technological innovations that will enable manufacturers to produce higher-value products so Brazil doesn't have to rely on natural resources to fuel its growth. "Look, a government isn't made on the second or third day," Rousseff has said about her administration's incremental efforts to keep Brazil's emerging economy moving forward. "It's made over time. Things mature."[11]

Questions

1. Do you think the efforts of Brazil's government to keep the economy growing will be successful? Why or why not?
2. What downsides might Brazil experience by implementing quotas, tariffs, and measures to devalue its currency?

Building Skills for Career Success

1. Social Media Exercise

Although Nike was founded in the Pacific Northwest and still has its corporate headquarters near Beaverton, Oregon, the company has become a multinational enterprise. The firm employs more than 35,000 people across six continents and is now a global marketer of footwear, apparel, and athletic equipment.

Because it operates in 160 countries around the globe and manufactures products in over 900 factories in 47 different countries, sustainability is a big initiative for Nike. Today, Nike uses the YouTube social media site to share its sustainability message with consumers, employees, investors, politicians, and other interested stakeholders. To learn about the company's efforts to sustain the planet, follow these steps:

- Make an Internet connection and go to the YouTube website (www.youtube.com).
- Enter the words "Nike" and "Sustainability" in the search window and click the search button.

1. View at least three different YouTube videos about Nike's sustainability efforts.
2. Based on the information in the videos you watched, do you believe that Nike is a good corporate citizen because of its efforts to sustain the planet? Why or why not?
3. Prepare a one to two page report that describes how Nike is taking steps to reduce waste, improve the environment, and reduce its carbon footprint while manufacturing products around the globe.

2. Building Team Skills

The North American Free Trade Agreement among the United States, Mexico, and Canada went into effect on January 1, 1994. It has made a difference in trade among the countries and has affected the lives of many people.

Assignment

1. Working in teams and using the resources of your library, investigate NAFTA. Answer the following questions:
   a. What are NAFTA's objectives?
   b. What are its benefits?
   c. What impact has NAFTA had on trade, jobs, and travel?
   d. Some Americans were opposed to the implementation of NAFTA. What were their objections? Have any of these objections been justified?
   e. Has NAFTA influenced your life? How?
2. Summarize your answers in a written report. Your team also should be prepared to give a class presentation.

3. Researching Different Careers

Today, firms around the world need employees with special skills. In some countries, such employees are not always available, and firms then must search abroad for qualified applicants. One way they can do this is through global work-force databases. As business and trade operations continue to grow globally, you may one day find yourself working in a foreign country, perhaps for an American company doing business there or for a foreign company. In what foreign country would you like to work? What problems might you face?

Assignment

1. Choose a country in which you might like to work.
2. Research the country. The National Trade Data Bank is a good place to start. Find answers to the following questions:
   a. What language is spoken in this country? Are you proficient in it? What would you need to do if you are not proficient?
   b. What are the economic, social, and legal systems like in this nation?
   c. What is its history?
   d. What are its culture and social traditions like? How might they affect your work or your living arrangements?
3. Describe what you have found out about this country in a written report. Include an assessment of whether you would want to work there and the problems you might face if you did.

Running a Business
Part 1

Let's Go Get a Graeter's!

Only a tiny fraction of family-owned businesses are still growing four generations after their founding, but happily for lovers of premium-quality ice cream, Graeter's is one of them.

Now a $30 million firm with national distribution, Graeter's was founded in Cincinnati in 1870 by Louis Charles Graeter and his wife, Regina Graeter. The young couple made ice cream and chocolate candies in the back room of their shop, sold them in the front room, and lived upstairs. Ice cream was a special treat in this era before refrigeration, and the Graeters started from scratch every day to make theirs from the freshest, finest ingredients. Even after freezers were invented, the Graeters continued to make ice cream in small batches to preserve the quality, texture, and rich flavor.

After her husband's death, Regina's entrepreneurial leadership became the driving force behind Graeter's expansion from 1920 until well into the 1950s. At a time when few women owned or operated a business, Regina opened 20 new Graeter's stores in the Cincinnati area and added manufacturing capacity to support this ambitious—and successful—growth strategy. Her sons and grandchildren followed her into the business and continued to open ice-cream shops all around Ohio and beyond. Today, three of Regina's great-grandsons run Graeter's with the same attention to quality that made the firm famous. In her honor, the street in front of the company's ultramodern Cincinnati factory is named Regina Graeter Way.

The Scoop on Graeter's Success

Graeter's fourth-generation owners are Richard Graeter II (CEO), Robert (Bob) Graeter (vice president of operations), and Chip Graeter (vice president of retail operations). They grew up in the business, learning through hands-on experience how to do everything from packing a pint of ice cream to locking up the store at night. They also absorbed the family's dedication to product quality, a key reason for the company's enduring success. "Our family has always been contented to make a little less profit in order to ensure our long-term survival," explains the CEO.

Throughout its history, Graeter's has used a unique, time-consuming manufacturing process to produce its signature ice creams in small batches. "Our competition is making thousands and thousands of gallons a day," says Chip

Graeter. "We are making hundreds of gallons a day at the most. All of our ice cream is packed by hand, so it's a very laborious process." Graeter's "French pot" manufacturing method ensures that very little air gets into the product. As a result, the company's ice cream is dense and creamy, not light and fluffy—so dense, in fact, that each pint weighs nearly a pound.

Another success factor is the use of simple, fresh ingredients like high-grade chocolate, choice seasonal fruits, and farm-fresh cream. Graeter's imports some ingredients, such as vanilla from Madagascar, and buys other ingredients from U.S. producers known for their quality. "We use a really great grade of chocolate," says Bob Graeter. "We don't cut corners on that … Specially selected great black raspberries, strawberries, blueberries, and cherries go into our ice cream because we feel that we want to provide flavor not from artificial or unnatural ingredients but from really quality, ripe, rich fruits." Instead of tiny chocolate chips, Graeter's products contain giant chunks formed when liquid chocolate is poured into the ice-cream base just before the mixture is frozen and packed into pints.

Maintaining the Core of Success

Graeter's "fanatical devotion to product quality" and its time-tested recipes have not changed over the years. The current generation of owners is maintaining this core of the company's success while mixing in a generous dash of innovation. "If you just preserve the core," Bob Graeter says, "ultimately you stagnate. And if you are constantly stimulating progress and looking for new ideas, well, then you risk losing what was important. . . . Part of your secret to long-term success is knowing what your core is and holding to that. Once you know what you're really all about and what is most important to you, you can change everything else."

One of those "important" things is giving back to the community and its families via local charities and other initiatives. "Community involvement is just part of being a good corporate citizen," observes Richard Graeter. When Graeter's celebrated a recent new store opening, for example, it made a cash donation to the neighborhood public library. It is also a major sponsor of The Cure Starts Now Foundation, a research foundation seeking a cure for pediatric brain cancer. In line with its focus on natural goodness, Graeter's has been doing its part to preserve the environment by recycling and by boosting production efficiency to conserve water, energy, and other resources.

Graeter's Looks to the Future

Even though Graeter's recipes reflect its 19th-century heritage, the company is clearly a 21st-century operation. It has 150,000 Facebook "likes," connects with brand fans on Twitter, and invites customers to subscribe to its e-mail newsletter. The company sells its products online and ships orders via United Parcel Service to ice-cream lovers across the continental United States. Its newly-opened production facility uses state-of-the-art refrigeration, storage, and sanitation—yet the ice cream is still mixed by hand rather than by automated equipment. With an eye toward future growth, Graeter's is refining its information system to provide managers with all the details they need to make timely decisions in today's fast-paced business environment.

Graeter's competition ranges from small, local businesses to international giants such as Unilever, which owns Ben & Jerry's, and Nestle, which owns Haagen-Dazs. Throughout the economic ups and downs of recent years, Graeter's has continued to expand, and its ice creams are now distributed through 6,200 stores in 43 states. Oprah Winfrey and other celebrities have praised its products in public. But the owners are just as proud of their home-town success. "Graeter's in Cincinnati is synonymous with ice cream," says Bob Graeter. "People will say, 'Let's go get a Graeter's.' "[12]

Questions

1. How have Graeter's owners used the four factors of production to build the business over time?
2. Which of Graeter's stakeholders are most affected by the family's decision to take a long-term view of the business rather than aiming for short-term profit? Explain your answer.
3. Knowing that Graeter's competes with multinational corporations as well as small businesses, would you recommend that Graeter's expand by licensing its brand to a company in another country? Why or why not?

Building a Business Plan: Part 1

A *business plan* is a carefully constructed guide for a person starting a business. The purpose of a well-prepared business plan is to show how practical and attainable the entrepreneur's goals are. It also serves as a concise document that potential investors can examine to see if they would like to invest or assist in financing a new venture. A business plan should include the following 12 components:

- Introduction
- Executive summary
- Benefits to the community
- Company and industry
- Management team
- Manufacturing and operations plan
- Labor force
- Marketing plan
- Financial plan
- Exit strategy
- Critical risks and assumptions
- Appendix

A brief description of each of these sections is provided in Chapter 5 (see also Table 5-3 on page 139).

This is the first of seven exercises that appear at the ends of each of the seven major parts in this textbook. The goal of these exercises is to help you work through the preceding components to create your own business plan. For example, in the exercise for this part, you will make decisions and complete the research that will help you to develop the introduction for your business plan and the benefits to the community that your business will provide. In the exercises for Parts 2 through 6, you will add more components to your plan and eventually build a plan that actually could be used to start a business. The flowchart shown in Figure 3.6 gives an overview of the steps you will be taking to prepare your business plan.

The First Step: Choosing Your Business

One of the first steps for starting your own business is to decide what type of business you want to start. Take some time to think about this decision. Before proceeding, answer the following questions:

- Why did you choose this type of business?
- Why do you think this business will be successful?
- Would you enjoy owning and operating this type of business?

Warning: Do not rush this step. This step often requires much thought, but it is well worth the time and effort. As an added bonus, you are more likely to develop a quality business plan if you really want to open this type of business.

Now that you have decided on a specific type of business, it is time to begin the planning process. The goal for this part is to complete the introduction and benefits-to-the-community components of your business plan.

Before you begin, it is important to note that the business plan is not a document that is written and then set aside. It is a living document that an entrepreneur should refer to continuously in order to ensure that plans are being carried through appropriately. As the entrepreneur begins to execute the plan, he or she should monitor the business environment continuously and make changes to the plan to address any challenges or opportunities that were not foreseen originally.

Throughout this course, you will, of course, be building your knowledge about business. Therefore, it will be appropriate for you to continually revisit parts of the plan that you have already written in order to refine them based on your more comprehensive knowledge. You will find that writing your plan is not a simple matter of starting at the beginning and moving chronologically through to the end. Instead, you probably will find yourself jumping around the various components, making refinements as you go. In fact, the second component—the executive summary—should be written last, but because of its comprehensive nature and its importance to potential investors, it appears after the introduction in the final business plan. By the end of this course, you should be able to put the finishing touches on your plan, making sure that all the parts create a comprehensive and sound whole so that you can present it for evaluation.

The Introduction Component

1.1. Start with the cover page. Provide the business name, street address, telephone number, Web address (if any), name(s) of owner(s) of the business, and the date the plan is issued.

1.2. Next, provide background information on the company and include the general nature of the business: retailing, manufacturing, or service; what your product or service is; what is unique about it; and why you believe that your business will be successful.

FIGURE 3-6 Business Plan

Steps in creating a business plan

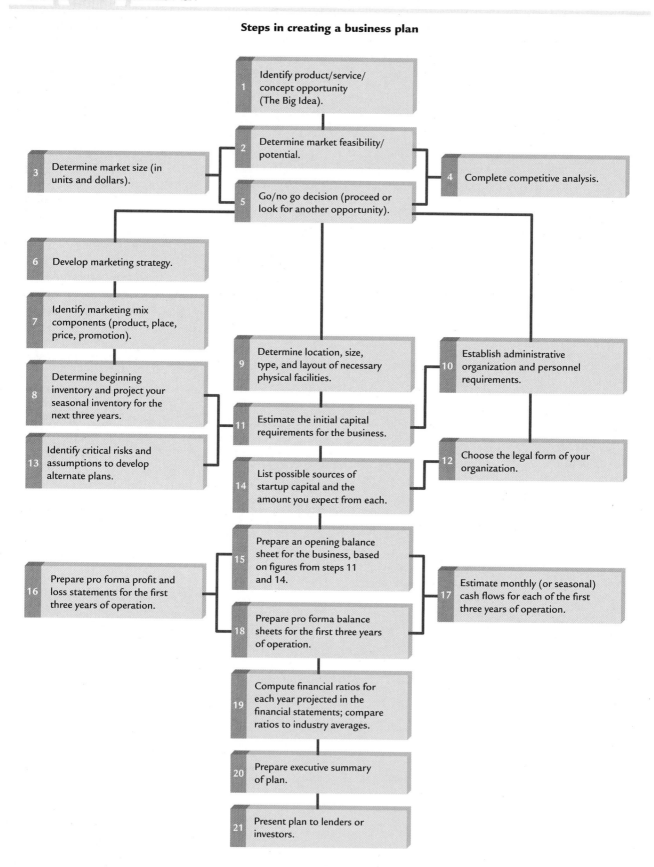

1. Identify product/service/concept opportunity (The Big Idea).

2. Determine market feasibility/potential.

3. Determine market size (in units and dollars).

4. Complete competitive analysis.

5. Go/no go decision (proceed or look for another opportunity).

6. Develop marketing strategy.

7. Identify marketing mix components (product, place, price, promotion).

8. Determine beginning inventory and project your seasonal inventory for the next three years.

9. Determine location, size, type, and layout of necessary physical facilities.

10. Establish administrative organization and personnel requirements.

11. Estimate the initial capital requirements for the business.

12. Choose the legal form of your organization.

13. Identify critical risks and assumptions to develop alternate plans.

14. List possible sources of startup capital and the amount you expect from each.

15. Prepare an opening balance sheet for the business, based on figures from steps 11 and 14.

16. Prepare pro forma profit and loss statements for the first three years of operation.

17. Estimate monthly (or seasonal) cash flows for each of the first three years of operation.

18. Prepare pro forma balance sheets for the first three years of operation.

19. Compute financial ratios for each year projected in the financial statements; compare ratios to industry averages.

20. Prepare executive summary of plan.

21. Present plan to lenders or investors.

Source: Hatten, Timothy, *Small Business Management*, Fifth Edition. Copyright © 2012 Cengage Learning.

1.3. Then include a summary statement of the business's financial needs, if any. You probably will need to revise your financial needs summary after you complete a detailed financial plan later in Part 6.

1.4. Finally, include a statement of confidentiality to keep important information away from potential competitors.

The Benefits-to-the-Community Component

In this section, describe the potential benefits to the community that your business could provide. Chapter 2 in your textbook, "Being Ethical and Socially Responsible," can help you in answering some of these questions. At the very least, address the following issues:

1.5. Describe the number of skilled and nonskilled jobs the business will create, and indicate how purchases of supplies and other materials can help local businesses.

1.6. Next, describe how providing needed goods or services will improve the community and its standard of living.

1.7. Finally, state how your business can develop new technical, management, or leadership skills; offer attractive wages; and provide other types of individual growth.

Review of Business Plan Activities

Read over the information that you have gathered. Because the Building a Business Plan exercises at the end of Parts 2 through 7 are built on the work you do in Part 1, make sure that any weaknesses or problem areas are resolved before continuing. Finally, write a brief statement that summarizes all the information for this part of the business plan.

Endnotes

1. Based on information in "Strong Dollar Dents Coca-Cola's Profits," *New York Times*, October 16, 2012, www.nytimes.com; Leon Stafford, "Coca-Cola to Spend $30 Billion to Grow Globally," *Atlanta Journal-Constitution*, September 9, 2012, www.ajc.com; Melanie Lee, "Exclusive: Coke Adds Billion Dollar Brand from China to Portfolio," *Reuters*, February 1, 2011, www.reuters.com; Lara O'Reilly, "Coke Restructures Global Businesses," *Marketing Week*, July 31, 2012, www.marketingweek.co.uk; www.coca-cola.com.

2. The White House, Office of the Press Secretary, Press Release, August 6, 2002.

3. International Trade Administration website at www.trade.gov/press /press-releases/2013/export-factsheet-february2013-020813.pdf (accessed May 26, 2013).

4. This section draws heavily from the *World Economic Outlook* International Monetary Fund website at www.imf.org/external/pubs/ft /weo/2013/update/01/index.htm (accessed February 5, 2013).

5. Ibid.

6. U.S. Department of Commerce, International Trade Administration, "Jobs Supported by Exports: An Update," March 12, 2012, www.trade .gov/mas/ian/index.asp (accessed February 6, 2013), and The White House Fact Sheet at www.whitehouse.gov/blog/2012/05/30/president (accessed February 6, 2013).

7. The World Trade Organization website at www.wto.org/english/news_e /pres11_e/pres11_e.htm (accessed February 5, 2013).

8. Office of the United States Trade Representative website at www.ustr. gov/tpp (accessed February 4, 2013).

9. The World Trade Organization at www.wto.org/english/news_e/sppl_e /spp1220_htm, (accessed February 6, 2013).

10. Ibid.

11. Sources: Andre Soliani, "Surge," *Bloomberg BusinessWeek*, April 3, 2012, www.businessweek.com; "Invigorated Roussef Shifts Focus to 'Brazil Cost,'" *Reuters*, April 2, 2012, www.reuters.com; Komal Sri-Kumar, "Brazil Should Embrace a Freer Market," *Financial Times*, March 6, 2012, www .ft.com; "Multinationals Choose Brazilian Investment," *Obelisk Investment News*, May 4, 2011, www.obeliskinternational.com.

12. Sources: Based on information from Kimberly L. Jackson, "Graeter's Premium Chocolate Chip Ice Cream Lands at Stop & Shop," *Newark Star-Ledger (NJ)*, April 4, 2012, www.nj.com; "Graeter's Ice Cream Debuts in Bay Area," *Tampa Bay Times (St. Petersburg, FL)*, January 10, 2012, p. 4B; Jim Carper, "Graeter's Runs a Hands-on Ice Cream Plant," *Dairy Foods*, August 2011, pp. 36+; Jim Carper, "The Greater Good," *Dairy Foods*, August 2011, pp. 95+; "Graeter's Unveils New 'Mystery Flavor,'" *Dayton Daily News*, March 29, 2012, www.daytondailynews. com; Bob Driehaus, "A Cincinnati Ice Cream Maker Aims Big," *New York Times*, September 11, 2010, www.nytimes.com; Lucy May, "Graeter's Northern Kentucky Franchisee Puts Stores on the Block," *Business Courier*, August 6, 2010, http://cincinnati.bizjournals.com; www.graeters .com; interviews with company staff and Cengage videos about Graeter's.

© AUREMAR/SHUTTERSTOCK.COM

Choosing a Form of Business Ownership

Why Should You Care?

There's a good chance that during your lifetime you will work for a business or start a business. With this fact in mind, the material in this chapter can help you to understand how and why businesses are organized.

Learning Objectives

Once you complete this chapter, you will be able to:

1 Describe the advantages and disadvantages of sole proprietorships.

2 Explain the different types of partners and the importance of partnership agreements.

3 Describe the advantages and disadvantages of partnerships.

4 Summarize how a corporation is formed.

5 Describe the advantages and disadvantages of a corporation.

6 Examine special types of corporations, including S-corporations, limited-liability companies, and not-for-profit corporations.

7 Discuss the purpose of a joint venture and syndicate.

8 Explain how growth from within and growth through mergers can enable a business to expand.

Berkshire Hathaway Buys and Holds for Long-Term Growth

Berkshire Hathaway, based in Omaha, Nebraska, has purchased an unusual mix of companies over the years, ranging from manufacturers of candies (See's Candies), carpets (Shaw Industries), construction materials (Johns Manville and Acme Brick) and chemicals (Lubrizol) to railroads (Burlington Northern Santa Fe), retailers (Nebraska Furniture Mart, among others), home builders (Clayton Homes), and insurance firms (GEICO, among others). The eclectic list of acquisitions also includes newspapers, apparel firms, private jet rentals, furniture manufacturers, even an ice-cream franchise business. Add it all up, and Berkshire Hathaway owns more than 70 businesses, brings in $143.7 billion in annual revenue, and employs 270,000 people worldwide.

The common thread connecting these acquisitions is Berkshire Hathaway's "buy and hold" approach to growth, which has contributed to its corporate success. Its top executives are always scouting for promising long-term business opportunities in almost any industry. For example, after Warren Buffett, Berkshire Hathaway's long-time CEO, sampled chocolates made by See's Candies in 1971, he became a brand fan and bought the California firm in 1972 for $25 million. Today, See's earns $83 million in profits from $376 million in annual sales—giving the corporate parent a lucrative return on its acquisition investment. This "buy and hold" philosophy applies to every acquisition, large and small. When Berkshire Hathaway acquired more than two dozen newspapers, Buffett told the editors that when he finds businesses worth investing in, he buys them with the intention of keeping them.

Although Berkshire Hathaway has the final say in selecting chief executives, it rarely gets involved in any acquired firm's day-to-day decisions. Instead, it steps back to let its businesses follow their own paths to success and profits. With billions of dollars in cash in the bank, Berkshire Hathaway continues to hunt for other acquisition targets that are well-managed and have long-term profit potential.[1]

Did You Know?

Berkshire Hathaway owns more than 70 companies and rings up annual revenues topping $143 billion.

When Warren Buffett started his first partnership more than 50 years ago, he never dreamed he would wind up putting together a wildly diverse collection of businesses under one corporate umbrella. Today, Berkshire Hathaway—the company profiled in the Inside Business opening case for this chapter—now owns more than 70 different corporations, brings in more than $143 billion in annual revenue, and employees 270,000 people.

It all started when Buffett set up a series of partnerships with family and friends to pool cash for buying big blocks of stock in companies he had researched. Not all of the companies Buffett chose paid off, but many were so successful that Buffett quickly earned a worldwide reputation for his ability to pick just the "right" company. Although Warren Buffett started with partnerships and eventually chose the corporate form of ownership, there are other forms of ownership including sole proprietorships, S-corporations, and limited-liability companies that may meet a business owner's needs. In fact, choosing the right form of ownership is one of the most important decisions a business owner must make.

We begin this chapter by describing the three common forms of business ownership: sole proprietorships, partnerships, and corporations. We discuss how these types of businesses are formed and note the advantages and disadvantages of each. Next, we consider several types of business ownership usually chosen for special purposes, including S-corporations, limited-liability companies (LLCs), not-for-profit corporations, joint ventures, and syndicates. We conclude the chapter with a discussion of how businesses can grow through internal expansion or through mergers with other companies.

SOLE PROPRIETORSHIPS

A **sole proprietorship** is a business that is owned (and usually operated) by one person. Although a few sole proprietorships are large and have many employees, most are small. Sole proprietorship is the simplest form of business ownership and the easiest to start. In most instances, the owner (the *sole* proprietor) simply decides that he or she is in business and begins operations. Some of today's largest corporations, including Walmart, JCPenney, and Procter & Gamble Company, started out as tiny—and in many cases, struggling—sole proprietorships.

Often entrepreneurs with a promising idea choose the sole proprietorship form of ownership. Annie Withey, for example, created a cheddar cheese–flavored popcorn snack food. Annie's popcorn, called Smartfood, became one of the fastest-selling snack foods in U.S. history. After a few years, PepsiCo Inc.'s Frito-Lay division bought the brand for about $15 million. Ms. Withey went on to develop an all-natural white-cheddar macaroni and cheese product. Today even though her firm, Annie's Homegrown, has grown and become part of a larger conglomerate, Annie remains the entrepreneurial heart of the company and still thinks like a sole proprietor.

As you can see in Figure 4-1, there are approximately 23 million nonfarm sole proprietorships in the United States. They account for 72 percent of the country's business firms. Although the most popular form of ownership when compared with partnerships and corporations, they rank last in total sales revenues. As shown in Figure 4-2, sole proprietorships account for about $1.3 trillion, or about 4 percent of total annual sales.

Sole proprietorships are most common in retailing, service, and agriculture. Thus, the clothing boutique, corner grocery, television-repair shop down the street, and small, independent farmers are likely to be sole proprietorships.

Advantages of Sole Proprietorships

Most of the advantages of sole proprietorships arise from the two main characteristics of this form of ownership: simplicity and individual control.

EASE OF START-UP AND CLOSURE Sole proprietorship is the simplest and cheapest way to start a business. A sole proprietorship can be, and most often is, established without the services of an attorney. The legal requirements often are limited to registering the name of the business and obtaining any necessary licenses or permits.

FIGURE 4-1 Relative Percentages of Nonfarm Sole Proprietorships, Partnerships, and Corporations in the United States

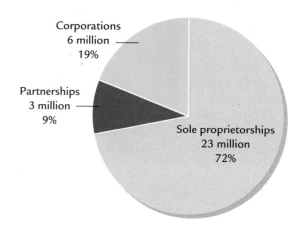

Corporations
6 million
19%

Partnerships
3 million
9%

Sole proprietorships
23 million
72%

Source: "Statistics of Income," The Internal Revenue Service website at www.irs.gov, accessed January 30, 2013.

FIGURE 4-2 Total Sales Receipts of American Businesses

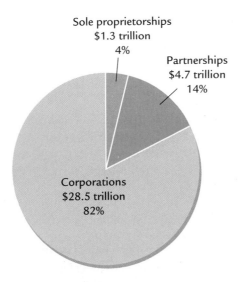

Sole proprietorships
$1.3 trillion
4%

Partnerships
$4.7 trillion
14%

Corporations
$28.5 trillion
82%

Source: "Statistics of Income," The Internal Revenue Service website at www.irs.gov, accessed January 30, 2013.

If the enterprise does not succeed, the firm can be closed as easily as it was opened. Creditors must be paid, of course, but generally, the owner does not have to go through any legal procedure before hanging up an "Out of Business" sign.

PRIDE OF OWNERSHIP A successful sole proprietor is often very proud of her or his accomplishments—and rightfully so. In almost every case, the owner deserves a great deal of credit for solving the day-to-day problems associated with operating a sole proprietorship. Unfortunately, the reverse is also true. When the business fails, it is often the sole proprietor who is to blame.

RETENTION OF ALL PROFITS Because all profits become the personal earnings of the owner, the owner has a strong incentive to succeed. This direct financial reward attracts many entrepreneurs to the sole proprietorship form of business and, if the business succeeds, is a source of great satisfaction.

NO SPECIAL TAXES Profits earned by a sole proprietorship are taxed as the personal income of the owner. As a result, sole proprietors must report certain financial information for the business on their personal income tax returns and make estimated quarterly tax payments to the federal government. Thus, a sole proprietorship does not pay the special state and federal income taxes that corporations pay.

FLEXIBILITY OF BEING YOUR OWN BOSS A sole proprietor is completely free to make decisions about the firm's operations. Without asking or waiting for anyone's approval, a sole proprietor can change a store's hours, move a shop's location, open a new store, or close an old one. And, he or she can make an immediate change in business hours. The manager of a store in

An entrepreneur with a sweet tooth! Hail a taxi anywhere in New York City and tell the driver, "Take me to the best cheesecake in New York." Odds are you will end up at a Junior's Restaurant. Founded in 1950 by Harry Rosen, the restaurant remains a family-owned business today. In this photo, Alan, a member of the Rosen family, displays some of the products that made this restaurant a New York tradition.

a large corporate chain such as Best Buy Company may have to seek the approval of numerous managers and company officials before making such changes.

Disadvantages of Sole Proprietorships

The disadvantages of a sole proprietorship stem from the fact that these businesses are owned by one person. Some capable sole proprietors experience no problems. Individuals who start out with few management skills and little money are most at risk for failure.

UNLIMITED LIABILITY Unlimited liability is a legal concept that holds a business owner personally responsible for all the debts of the business. There is legally no difference between the debts of the business and the debts of the proprietor. If the business fails, or if the business is involved in a lawsuit and loses, the owner's personal property—including savings and other assets—can be seized (and sold if necessary) to pay creditors.

Unlimited liability is perhaps the major factor that tends to discourage would-be entrepreneurs with substantial personal wealth from using the sole proprietor form of business organization.

LACK OF CONTINUITY Legally, the sole proprietor *is* the business. If the owner retires, dies, or is declared legally incompetent, the business essentially ceases to exist. In many cases, however—especially when the business is a profitable enterprise—the owner's heirs take it over and either sell it or continue to operate it. The business also can suffer if the sole proprietor becomes ill and cannot work for an extended period of time. If the owner, for example, has a heart attack, there is often no one who can step in and manage the business. An illness can be devastating if the sole proprietor's personal skills are what determine if the business is a success or a failure.

LACK OF MONEY Banks, suppliers, and other lenders usually are often unwilling to lend large sums of money to sole proprietorships. Only one person—the sole proprietor—can be held responsible for repaying such loans, and the assets of most sole proprietors usually are limited. Moreover, these assets may have been used already as security or collateral for personal borrowing (a home mortgage or car loan) or for short-term credit from suppliers. Lenders also worry about the lack of continuity of sole proprietorships: Who will repay a loan if the sole proprietor dies? Finally, many lenders are concerned about the large number of sole proprietorships that fail—a topic discussed in Chapter 5.

The limited ability to borrow money can prevent a sole proprietorship from growing. It is the main reason that many business owners, when in need of relatively large amounts of capital, change from a sole proprietorship to a partnership or corporate form of ownership.

LIMITED MANAGEMENT SKILLS The sole proprietor is often the sole manager—in addition to being the only salesperson, buyer, accountant, and, on occasion, janitor. Even the most experienced business owner is unlikely to have expertise in all these areas. Unless he or she obtains the necessary expertise by hiring employees, assistants, or consultants, the business can suffer in the areas in which the owner is less knowledgeable. For the many sole proprietors who cannot hire the help they need, there just are not enough hours in the day to do everything that needs to be done.

DIFFICULTY IN HIRING EMPLOYEES The sole proprietor may find it hard to attract and keep competent help. Potential employees may feel that there is no room for advancement in a firm whose owner assumes all managerial responsibilities. And when those who *are* hired are ready to take on added responsibility, they may find that the only way to do so is to quit the sole proprietorship and go to work for a larger firm or start up their own businesses. The lure of higher salaries and increased benefits also may cause existing employees to change jobs.

Beyond the Sole Proprietorship

Like many others, you may decide that the major disadvantage of a sole proprietorship is the limited amount that one person can do in a workday. One way to reduce the effect of this disadvantage (and retain many of the advantages) is to have more than one owner.

PARTNERSHIPS

A person who would not think of starting and running a sole proprietorship business alone may enthusiastically seize the opportunity to form a business partnership. The U.S. Uniform Partnership Act defines a **partnership** as a voluntary association of two or more persons to act as co-owners of a business for profit. For example, in 1990, two young African-American entrepreneurs named Janet Smith and Gary Smith started IVY Planning Group—a company that provides strategic planning and performance measurement for clients. Today, almost 25 years later, the company has evolved into a multimillion-dollar company that has hired a diverse staff of employees and provides cultural diversity training for *Fortune* 1000 firms, large not-for-profit organizations, and government agencies. In recognition of its efforts, IVY Planning Group has been recognized by DiversityBusiness.com as one of the top 50 minority-owned companies. And both Janet Smith and Gary Smith have been named "1 of 50 Influential Minorities in Business" by Minority Business and Professionals Network.[2]

As shown in Figures 4-1 and 4-2, there are approximately 3 million partnerships in the United States, and this type of ownership accounts for about $4.7 trillion in sales receipts each year. Note, however, that this form of ownership is much less common than the sole proprietorship or the corporation. In fact, as Figure 4-1 shows, partnerships represent only about 9 percent of all American businesses. Although there is no legal maximum on the number of partners a partnership may have, most have only two. Regardless of the number of people involved, a partnership often represents a pooling of special managerial skills and talents; at other times, it is the result of a sole proprietor taking on a partner for the purpose of obtaining more capital.

Types of Partners

All partners are not necessarily equal. Some may be active in running the business, whereas others may have a limited role.

GENERAL PARTNERS A **general partner** is a person who assumes full or shared responsibility for operating a business. General partners are active in day-to-day business operations, and each partner can enter into contracts on behalf of the other partners. He or she also assumes unlimited liability for all debts, including debts incurred by any other general partner without his or her knowledge or consent. To avoid future liability, a general partner who withdraws from the partnership must give notice to creditors, customers, and suppliers.

Learning Objective

2 **Explain the different types of partners and the importance of partnership agreements.**

partnership a voluntary association of two or more persons to act as co-owners of a business for profit

general partner a person who assumes full or shared responsibility for operating a business

limited partner a person who invests money in a business but has no management responsibility or liability for losses beyond the amount he or she invested in the partnership

LIMITED PARTNERS A **limited partner** is a person who invests money in a business but who has no management responsibility or liability for losses beyond his or her investment in the partnership. Typically, the general partner or partners collect management fees and receive a percentage of profits. Limited partners receive a portion of profits and tax benefits. Limited partnerships, for example, may be formed to finance real estate, oil and gas, motion picture, and other business ventures.

Because of potential liability problems, special rules apply to limited partnerships. These rules are intended to protect customers and creditors who deal with limited partnerships. For example, prospective partners in a limited partnership must file a formal declaration, usually with the secretary of state, that describes the essential details of the partnership and the liability status of each partner involved in the business. At least one general partner must be responsible for the debts of the limited partnership. Also, some states prohibit the use of the limited partner's name in the partnership's name.

The Partnership Agreement

Articles of partnership refers to an agreement listing and explaining the terms of the partnership. Although both oral and written partnership agreements are legal and can be enforced in the courts, a written agreement has an obvious advantage. It is not subject to lapses of memory.

Figure 4-3 shows a typical partnership agreement. The partnership agreement should state

- Who will make the final decisions
- What each partner's duties will be
- The investment each partner will make
- How much profit or loss each partner receives or is responsible for
- What happens if a partner wants to dissolve the partnership or dies

Although the people involved in a partnership can draft their own agreement, most experts recommend consulting an attorney.

When entering into a partnership agreement, partners would be wise to let a neutral third party—a consultant, an accountant, a lawyer, or a mutual friend—assist with any disputes that might arise.

Concept Check

✓ How does a sole proprietorship differ from a partnership?

✓ Explain the difference between a general partner and a limited partner.

✓ Describe the issues that should be included in a partnership agreement.

Learning Objective

3 **Describe the advantages and disadvantages of partnerships.**

ADVANTAGES AND DISADVANTAGES OF PARTNERSHIPS

When compared to sole proprietorships and corporations, partnerships are the least popular form of business ownership. Still there are situations when forming a partnership makes perfect sense. Before you make a decision to form a partnership, all the people involved should consider both the advantages and disadvantages of a partnership.

Advantages of Partnerships

Partnerships have many advantages. The most important are described as follows.

EASE OF START-UP Partnerships are relatively easy to form. As with a sole proprietorship, the legal requirements often are limited to registering the name of the business and obtaining any necessary licenses or permits. It may not even be necessary to prepare written articles of partnership, although doing so is generally a good idea.

AVAILABILITY OF CAPITAL AND CREDIT Because partners can pool their funds, a partnership usually has more capital available than a sole proprietorship

FIGURE 4-3 Articles of Partnership

The articles of partnership is a written or oral agreement that lists and explains the terms of a partnership.

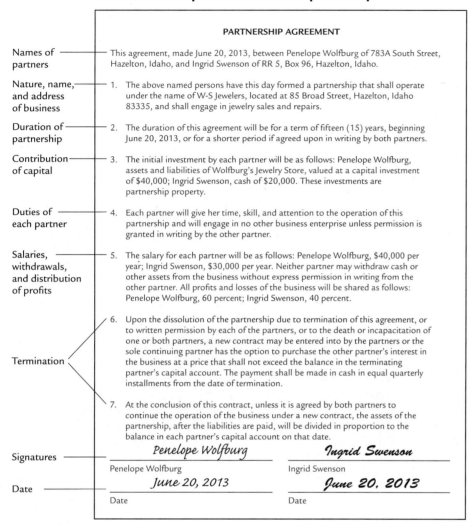

PARTNERSHIP AGREEMENT

Names of partners — This agreement, made June 20, 2013, between Penelope Wolfburg of 783A South Street, Hazelton, Idaho, and Ingrid Swenson of RR 5, Box 96, Hazelton, Idaho.

Nature, name, and address of business — 1. The above named persons have this day formed a partnership that shall operate under the name of W-S Jewelers, located at 85 Broad Street, Hazelton, Idaho 83335, and shall engage in jewelry sales and repairs.

Duration of partnership — 2. The duration of this agreement will be for a term of fifteen (15) years, beginning June 20, 2013, or for a shorter period if agreed upon in writing by both partners.

Contribution of capital — 3. The initial investment by each partner will be as follows: Penelope Wolfburg, assets and liabilities of Wolfburg's Jewelry Store, valued at a capital investment of $40,000; Ingrid Swenson, cash of $20,000. These investments are partnership property.

Duties of each partner — 4. Each partner will give her time, skill, and attention to the operation of this partnership and will engage in no other business enterprise unless permission is granted in writing by the other partner.

Salaries, withdrawals, and distribution of profits — 5. The salary for each partner will be as follows: Penelope Wolfburg, $40,000 per year; Ingrid Swenson, $30,000 per year. Neither partner may withdraw cash or other assets from the business without express permission in writing from the other partner. All profits and losses of the business will be shared as follows: Penelope Wolfburg, 60 percent; Ingrid Swenson, 40 percent.

Termination — 6. Upon the dissolution of the partnership due to termination of this agreement, or to written permission by each of the partners, or to the death or incapacitation of one or both partners, a new contract may be entered into by the partners or the sole continuing partner has the option to purchase the other partner's interest in the business at a price that shall not exceed the balance in the terminating partner's capital account. The payment shall be made in cash in equal quarterly installments from the date of termination.

7. At the conclusion of this contract, unless it is agreed by both partners to continue the operation of the business under a new contract, the assets of the partnership, after the liabilities are paid, will be divided in proportion to the balance in each partner's capital account on that date.

Signatures — *Penelope Wolfburg*   *Ingrid Swenson*

Penelope Wolfburg   Ingrid Swenson

Date — *June 20, 2013*   *June 20, 2013*

Date   Date

Source: Adapted from Goldman and Sigismond, *Cengage Advantage Books: Business Law 8E.* © 2011 Cengage Learning.

does. This additional capital, coupled with the general partners' unlimited liability, may encourage banks and suppliers to extend more credit or approve larger loans to a partnership than to a sole proprietor. This does not mean that partnerships can borrow all the money they need. Many partnerships have found it hard to get long-term financing simply because lenders worry about the possibility of management disagreements and lack of continuity.

PERSONAL INTEREST General partners are very concerned with the operation of the firm—perhaps even more so than sole proprietors. After all, they are responsible for the actions of all other general partners, as well as for their own. The pride of ownership from solving the day-to-day problems of operating a business—with the help of another person(s)—is a strong motivating force and often makes all the people involved in the partnership work harder to become more successful.

COMBINED BUSINESS SKILLS AND KNOWLEDGE Partners often have complementary skills. The weakness of one partner—in manufacturing, for example—may

Two entrepreneurs with one goal. There is a special pride of ownership that takes place when two people are solving problems and working together for the same purpose. Being responsible for what happens to the company—as well as your business partner—can be a motivating force for working that much harder to be successful.

be offset by another partner's strength in that area. Moreover, the ability to discuss important decisions with another concerned individual often relieves some pressure and leads to more effective decision making.

RETENTION OF PROFITS As in a sole proprietorship, all profits belong to the owners of the partnership. The partners share directly in the financial rewards and therefore are highly motivated to do their best to make the firm succeed. As noted, the partnership agreement should state how much profit or loss each partner receives or is responsible for.

NO SPECIAL TAXES Although a partnership pays no income tax, the Internal Revenue Service requires partnerships to file an annual information return that states the names and addresses of all partners involved in the business. The return also must provide information about income and expenses and distributions made to each partner. Then each partner is required to report his or her share of profit (or loss) from the partnership on his or her individual tax return. Ultimately each partner's share of the partnership profit is taxed in the same way a sole proprietor is taxed.

Disadvantages of Partnerships

Although partnerships have many advantages when compared with sole proprietorships and corporations, they also have some disadvantages, which anyone thinking of forming a partnership should consider.

UNLIMITED LIABILITY As we have noted, each *general* partner has unlimited liability for all debts of the business. Each partner is legally and personally responsible for the debts, taxes, and actions of any other partner conducting partnership business, even if that partner did not incur those debts or do anything wrong. General partners thus run the risk of having to use their personal assets to pay creditors. *Limited* partners, however, risk only their original investment.

Today, many states allow partners to form a *limited-liability partnership* (LLP), in which a partner may have limited-liability protection from legal action resulting from the malpractice or negligence of the other partners. Many states that allow LLPs restrict this type of ownership to certain types of professionals such as accountants, architects, attorneys, and similar professionals. (Note the difference between a limited partnership and an LLP. A limited partnership must have at least one general partner that has unlimited liability. On the other hand, all partners in an LLP may have limited liability *for the malpractice and negligence of the other partners*.)

MANAGEMENT DISAGREEMENTS What happens to a partnership if one of the partners brings a spouse or a relative into the business? What happens if a partner wants to withdraw more money from the business? Notice that each of these situations—and for that matter, most of the other problems that can develop in a partnership—involves one partner doing something that disturbs the other partner(s). This human factor is especially important because business partners—with egos, ambitions, and money on the line—are especially susceptible to friction. When partners begin to disagree about decisions, policies, or ethics, distrust may build and get worse as time passes—often to the point where it is impossible to operate the business successfully.

LACK OF CONTINUITY Partnerships are terminated if any one of the general partners dies, withdraws, or is declared legally incompetent. However, the remaining partners can purchase that partner's ownership share. For example, the partnership agreement may permit surviving partners to continue the business after buying a deceased partner's interest from his or her estate. However, if the partnership loses an owner whose specific management or technical skills cannot be replaced, it is not likely to survive.

FROZEN INVESTMENT It is easy to invest money in a partnership, but it is sometimes quite difficult to get it out. This is the case, for example, when remaining partners are unwilling to buy the share of the business that belongs to a partner who retires. To avoid such difficulties, the partnership agreement should include some procedure for buying out a partner.

In some cases, a partner must find someone outside the firm to buy his or her share. How easy or difficult it is to find an outsider depends on how successful the business is and how willing existing partners are to accept a new partner.

Beyond the Partnership

The main advantages of a partnership over a sole proprietorship are increased availability of capital and credit and the combined business skills and knowledge of the partners. However, some of the basic disadvantages of the sole proprietorship also plague the general partnership. A third form of business ownership, the corporation, overcomes many of these disadvantages.

Concept Check

✓ What are the advantages of a partnership?

✓ What are the disadvantages of a partnership?

CORPORATIONS

Learning Objective

4 **Summarize how a corporation is formed.**

Back in 1837, William Procter and James Gamble—two sole proprietors—formed a partnership called Procter & Gamble (P&G) and set out to compete with 14 other soap and candle makers in Cincinnati, Ohio. Then, in 1890, Procter & Gamble incorporated to raise additional capital for expansion that eventually allowed the company to become a global giant. P&G brands serve over 4.6 billion of the 7 billion people in the world today because the corporation operates in 180 countries around the globe.[3] Like many large corporations, P&G's market capitalization is greater than the gross domestic product of many countries. Although this corporation is a corporate giant, the firm's executives and employees believe it also has a responsibility to be an ethical corporate citizen. For example, P&G's purpose statement (or mission) is

> We will provide branded products and services of superior quality and value that improve the lives of the world's consumers, now and for generations to come. As a result, consumers will reward us with leadership sales, profit and value creation, allowing our people, our shareholders and the communities in which we live and work to prosper.[4]

While not all sole proprietorships and partnerships become corporations, there are reasons why business owners choose the corporate form of ownership. Let's begin with a definition of a corporation. Perhaps the best definition of a corporation was given by Chief Justice John Marshall in a famous Supreme Court decision in 1819. A corporation, he said, "is an artificial person, invisible, intangible, and existing only in contemplation of the law." In other words, a **corporation** (sometimes referred to as a *regular* or *C-corporation*) is an artificial person created by law, with most of the legal rights of a real person. These include

- The right to start and operate a business
- The right to buy or sell property
- The right to borrow money
- The right to sue or be sued
- The right to enter into binding contracts

Unlike a real person, however, a corporation exists only on paper. There are approximately 6 million corporations in the United States. They comprise about 19 percent of all businesses, but they account for 82 percent of sales revenues (see Figures 4-1 and 4-2).

corporation an artificial person created by law with most of the legal rights of a real person, including the rights to start and operate a business, to buy or sell property, to borrow money, to sue or be sued, and to enter into binding contracts

Corporate Ownership

The shares of ownership of a corporation are called **stock**. The people who own a corporation's stock—and thus own part of the corporation—are called **stockholders**. Once a corporation has been formed, it may sell its stock to individuals or other companies that want to invest in the corporation. It also may issue stock as a reward to key employees or as a return to investors in place of cash payments.

A **closed corporation** is a corporation whose stock is owned by relatively few people and is not sold to the general public. As an example, Mars—the company famous for M&Ms, Snickers, Dove, Milky Way, Twix, and other chocolate candy—is a privately held, family-owned, closed corporation. Although many people think that a closed corporation is a small company, there are exceptions. Mars, for example, has annual sales of more than $30 billion, employs more than 70,000 associates worldwide, and operates in over 70 different countries.[5]

An **open corporation** is one whose stock can be bought and sold by any individual. Examples of open corporations include General Electric, Microsoft, Apple, and Sony.

Procter & Gamble: Once a sole proprietorship, then a partnership, and now a very large corporation. Although one of the largest corporations in the world, P&G was started when two sole proprietors formed a partnership to sell soap and candles. Today the corporation's product line has expanded and it now operates in 180 different countries around the globe.

stock the shares of ownership of a corporation

stockholder a person who owns a corporation's stock

closed corporation a corporation whose stock is owned by relatively few people and is not sold to the general public

open corporation a corporation whose stock can be bought and sold by any individual

Forming a Corporation

Although you may think that incorporating a business guarantees success, it does not. There is no special magic about placing the word *Incorporated* or the abbreviation *Inc.* after the name of a business. Unfortunately, like sole proprietorships or partnerships, corporations can go broke. The decision to incorporate a business, therefore, should be made only after carefully considering whether the corporate form of ownership suits your needs better than the sole proprietorship or partnership forms.

If you decide that the corporate form is the best form of organization for you, most experts recommend that you begin the incorporation process by consulting a lawyer to be sure that all legal requirements are met. While it may be possible to incorporate a business without legal help, it is well to keep in mind the old saying, "A man who acts as his own attorney has a fool for a client." Table 4-1 lists some aspects of starting and running a business that may require legal help.

TABLE 4-1 Ten Aspects of Business That May Require Legal Help

1. Choosing either the sole proprietorship, partnership, corporate, or some special form of ownership
2. Constructing a partnership agreement
3. Incorporating a business
4. Registering a corporation's stock
5. Obtaining a trademark, patent, or copyright
6. Filing for licenses or permits at the local, state, and federal levels
7. Purchasing an existing business or real estate
8. Creating valid contracts
9. Hiring employees and independent contractors
10. Extending credit and collecting debts

© CENGAGE LEARNING 2015

WHERE TO INCORPORATE A business is allowed to incorporate in any state that it chooses. Most small- and medium-sized businesses are incorporated in the state where they do the most business. The founders of larger corporations or of those that will do business nationwide often compare the benefits that various states provide to corporations. The decision on where to incorporate usually is based on two factors: (1) the cost of incorporating in one state compared with the cost in another state and (2) the advantages and disadvantages of each state's corporate laws and tax structure. Some states are more hospitable than others, and some offer fewer restrictions, lower taxes, and other benefits to attract new firms. Delaware, Nevada, and Wyoming are often chosen by corporations that do business in more than one state because of their corporation-friendly laws and pro-business climate.[6]

An incorporated business is called a **domestic corporation** in the state in which it is incorporated. In all other states where it does business, it is called a **foreign corporation**. Sears Holdings Corporation, the parent company of Sears and Kmart, is incorporated in Delaware, where it is a domestic corporation. In the remaining 49 states, Sears is a foreign corporation. Sears must register in all states where it does business and also pay taxes and annual fees to each state. A corporation chartered by a foreign government and conducting business in the United States is an **alien corporation**. Volkswagen AG and Sony Corporation are examples of alien corporations.

THE CORPORATE CHARTER Once a home state has been chosen, the incorporator(s) submits *articles of incorporation* to the secretary of state. When the articles of incorporation are approved, they become a contract between a corporation and the state in which the state recognizes the formation of the artificial person that is the corporation. Usually, the articles of incorporation include the following information:

- The firm's name and address
- The incorporators' names and addresses
- The purpose of the corporation
- The maximum amount of stock and types of stock to be issued
- The rights and privileges of stockholders
- The length of time the corporation is to exist

To help you to decide if the corporate form of organization is the right choice, you may want to visit the library for more information on the incorporation process. You can also use an Internet search engine and enter the term "business incorporation" for useful websites. In addition, before making a decision to organize your business as a corporation, you may want to consider two additional areas: stockholders' rights and the importance of the organizational meeting.

STOCKHOLDERS' RIGHTS There are two basic types of stock. Owners of **common stock** may vote on corporate matters. Generally, an owner of common stock has one vote for each share owned. However, any claims of common-stock owners on profits, dividends, and assets of the corporation are paid after the claims of others. The owners of **preferred stock** usually have no voting rights, but their claims on dividends are paid before those of common-stock owners. Although large corporations may issue both common and preferred stock, generally small corporations issue only common stock.

Perhaps the most important right of owners of both common and preferred stock is to share in the profit earned by the corporation through the payment of dividends. A **dividend** is a distribution of earnings to the stockholders of a corporation.

domestic corporation a corporation in the state in which it is incorporated

foreign corporation a corporation in any state in which it does business except the one in which it is incorporated

alien corporation a corporation chartered by a foreign government and conducting business in the United States

common stock stock owned by individuals or firms who may vote on corporate matters but whose claims on profits and assets are subordinate to the claims of others

preferred stock stock owned by individuals or firms who usually do not have voting rights but whose claims on dividends are paid before those of common-stock owners

dividend a distribution of earnings to the stockholders of a corporation

Personal Apps

Are you a stockholder?

AP IMAGES/KEVIN P. CASEY

Even if you own a single share of common stock, you're legally a part owner of the corporation. You're entitled to receive any dividends paid to shareholders and you can vote on important matters such as electing the board of directors. Your vote is counted—and it counts.

proxy a legal form listing issues to be decided at a stockholders' meeting and enabling stockholders to transfer their voting rights to some other individual or individuals

board of directors the top governing body of a corporation, the members of which are elected by the stockholders

Other rights include receiving information about the corporation, voting on changes to the corporate charter, and attending the corporation's annual stockholders' meeting, where they may exercise their right to vote.

Because common stockholders usually live all over the nation, very few actually may attend a corporation's annual meeting. Instead, they vote by proxy. A **proxy** is a legal form listing issues to be decided at a stockholders' meeting and enabling stockholders to transfer their voting rights to some other individual or individuals. The stockholder can register a vote and transfer voting rights simply by signing and returning the form. Today, most corporations also allow stockholders to exercise their right to vote by proxy by accessing the Internet or using a toll-free phone number.

ORGANIZATIONAL MEETING As the last step in forming a corporation, the incorporators and original stockholders meet to adopt corporate bylaws and elect their first board of directors. (Later, directors will be elected or reelected at the corporation's annual meetings by the firm's stockholders.) The board members are directly responsible to the stockholders for the way they operate the firm.

Corporate Structure

The organizational structure of most corporations is more complicated than that of a sole proprietorship or partnership. In a corporation, both the board of directors and the corporate officers are involved in management.

BOARD OF DIRECTORS As an artificial person, a corporation can act only through its directors, who represent the corporation's stockholders. The **board of directors** is the top governing body of a corporation and is elected by the stockholders. In theory, then, the stockholders are able to control the activities of the entire corporation through its directors because they are the group that elects the board of directors (see Figure 4-4).

Board members can be chosen from within the corporation or from outside it. *Note:* For a small corporation, only one director is required in many states although you can choose to have more. Directors who are elected from within the corporation are usually its top managers—the president and

Free pizza! It helps if a corporation has a CEO that believes in the firm's products. In this photo, John Schnatter, founder, chairman of the board, and CEO of Papa John's Pizza, is sharing some of the firm's famous pizza with Super Bowl fans.

AP IMAGES/TOM STRICKLAND

FIGURE 4-4 Hierarchy of Corporate Structure

Stockholders exercise a great deal of influence through their right to elect the board of directors.

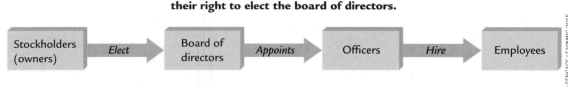

Stockholders (owners) → *Elect* → Board of directors → *Appoints* → Officers → *Hire* → Employees

© CENGAGE LEARNING 2015

Ethical Success or Failure?

Do We Need More Women in the Board Room?

Half of the world is female, yet only 16 percent of the directors on the boards of *Fortune* 500 U.S. corporations are women—and more than 20 percent of those corporations have no women directors. By comparison, Norway has the world's highest percentage of women directors (more than 30 percent), followed by Sweden (more than 25 percent). Then again, Norway's laws require that 40 percent of director's seats on corporate boards be reserved for women. Spain and France have also set quotas for women directors on corporate boards.

Should more women be serving on U.S. corporate boards? From a business perspective, women directors tend to be in tune with the views of female customers who are responsible for 75 percent of all buying decisions. And, women board members are also more in tune with employees and managers. In many cases, women handle negotiations differently than men do, their careers

follow slightly different paths, and their leadership styles may differ, as well. All these differences can be strengths as boards grapple with internal and external issues.

On the other hand, few women have risen to the top management ranks of U.S. corporations, which means that boards must widen their search to find women directors. Also, boards scouting for directors generally look for the best candidates with top-notch skills, education, and achievements, putting much less weight on gender. Should U.S. corporations take deliberate steps to bring more women into the board room?

Sources: Based on information in Heather R. Huhman "Five Lessons from Female Board Members," *Forbes*, July 5, 2012, www.forbes.com; "Too Many Suits," *Economist*, November 26, 2011, pp. 11–14; "Still Lonely at the Top," *Economist*, July 23, 2011, pp. 61–62; Judy B. Rosener, "The 'Terrible Truth' About Women On Corporate Boards," *Forbes*, June 7, 2011, www.forbes.com.

---

executive vice presidents, for example. Those elected from outside the corporation generally are experienced managers or entrepreneurs with proven leadership ability and/or specific talents the organization seems to need. In smaller corporations, majority stockholders usually serve as board members.

The major responsibilities of the board of directors are to set company goals and develop general plans (or strategies) for meeting those goals. The board also is responsible for the firm's overall operation and appointing corporate officers.

CORPORATE OFFICERS **Corporate officers** are appointed by the board of directors. Although a small corporation may not have all of the following officers, the chairman of the board, president, executive vice presidents, corporate secretary, and treasurer are all corporate officers. They help the board to make plans, carry out strategies established by the board, hire employees, and manage day-to-day business activities. Periodically (usually each month), they report to the board of directors. And at the annual meeting, the directors report to the stockholders.

ADVANTAGES AND DISADVANTAGES OF CORPORATIONS

Back in 2000, Manny Ruiz decided that it was time to start his own company. With the help of a team of media specialists, he founded Hispanic PR Wire. Today, Hispanic PR Wire is the real thing and has established itself as the nation's premier news distribution service reaching U.S. Hispanic media and opinion leaders.[7] Mr. Ruiz chose to incorporate this business because it provided a number of advantages that other forms of business ownership did not offer. Typical advantages include limited liability, ease of raising capital, ease of transfer of ownership, perpetual life, and specialized management.

> ## Concept Check
>
> ✓ Explain the difference between an open corporation and a closed corporation.
>
> ✓ How is a domestic corporation different from a foreign corporation and an alien corporation?
>
> ✓ Outline the incorporation process, and describe the basic corporate structure.
>
> ✓ What rights do stockholders have?

Learning Objective

5 **Describe the advantages and disadvantages of a corporation.**

corporate officers the chairman of the board, president, executive vice presidents, corporate secretary, treasurer, and any other top executive appointed by the board of directors

Advantages of Corporations

limited liability a feature of corporate ownership that limits each owner's financial liability to the amount of money that he or she has paid for the corporation's stock

LIMITED LIABILITY One of the most attractive features of corporate ownership is **limited liability**. With few exceptions, each owner's financial liability is limited to the amount of money he or she has paid for the corporation's stock. This feature arises from the fact that the corporation is itself a legal person, separate from its owners. If a corporation fails or is involved in a lawsuit and loses, creditors have a claim only on the corporation's assets. Because it overcomes the problem of unlimited liability connected with sole proprietorships and general partnerships, limited liability is one of the chief reasons why entrepreneurs often choose the corporate form of organization.

EASE OF RAISING CAPITAL The corporation is one of the most effective forms of business ownership for raising capital. Like sole proprietorships and partnerships, corporations can borrow from lending institutions. However, they also can raise additional sums of money by selling stock. Individuals are more willing to invest in corporations than in other forms of business because of limited liability, and they can generally sell their stock easily—hopefully for a profit.

EASE OF TRANSFER OF OWNERSHIP Accessing a brokerage firm website or a telephone call to a stockbroker is all that is required to put most stock up for sale. Willing buyers are available for most stocks at the market price. Ownership is transferred when the sale is made, and practically no restrictions apply to the sale and purchase of stock issued by an open corporation.

PERPETUAL LIFE Since it is essentially a legal "person," a corporation exists independently of its owners and survives them. The withdrawal, death, or incompetence of a key executive or owner does not cause the corporation to be terminated. Sears, Roebuck and Co. was originally founded in 1893 and is one of the nation's largest retailing corporations, even though its original co-founders, Richard Sears and Alvah Roebuck, have been dead for decades.

SPECIALIZED MANAGEMENT Typically, corporations are able to recruit more skilled, knowledgeable, and talented managers than proprietorships and partnerships. This is so because they pay bigger salaries, offer excellent employee benefits, and are large enough to offer considerable opportunity for advancement. Within the corporate structure, administration, human resources, finance, marketing, and operations are placed in the charge of experts in these fields.

BLOOMBERG/GETTY IMAGES

Now you can buy not only Michael Kors clothing, but also stock in the company. For a company like Michael Kors, the ability to sell stock to the public is an excellent way to raise capital that can be used to fund expansion and other business activities. Information on the reasons why investors purchase stocks and how to evaluate stock investments is provided in Appendix A—Understanding Personal Finances and Investments.

Disadvantages of Corporations

Like its advantages, many of a corporation's disadvantages stem from its legal definition as an artificial person or legal entity. The most serious disadvantages are described in the following text. (See Table 4-2 for a comparison of some of the advantages and disadvantages of a sole proprietorship, general partnership, and corporation.)

DIFFICULTY AND EXPENSE OF FORMATION Forming a corporation can be a relatively complex and costly process. The use of an attorney is usually necessary to complete the legal forms that are submitted to the secretary of state. Application fees, attorney's fees, registration costs associated with selling stock, and other organizational costs can amount to thousands of dollars for even a medium-sized corporation. The costs of incorporating, in terms of both time and money, discourage many owners of smaller businesses from forming corporations.

GOVERNMENT REGULATION AND INCREASED PAPERWORK A corporation must meet various government standards before it can sell its stock to the public. Then it must file many reports on its business operations and finances with local, state, and federal governments. In addition, the corporation must make periodic reports to its stockholders. To prepare all the necessary reports, even small corporations often need the help of an attorney, certified public accountant, and other professionals on a regular basis. In addition, a corporation's activities are restricted by law to those spelled out in its charter.

CONFLICT WITHIN THE CORPORATION Because a large corporation may employ thousands of employees, some conflict is inevitable. For example, the pressure to increase sales revenue, reduce expenses, and increase profits often leads to increased stress and tension for both managers and employees. This is especially true when a corporation operates in a competitive industry, attempts to develop and market new products, or must downsize the workforce to reduce employee salary expense during an economic crisis.

DOUBLE TAXATION Corporations must pay a tax on their profits. In addition, stockholders must pay a personal income tax on

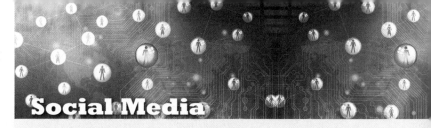

Social Media

Going Social with SCORE

© ANNETTE SCHAFF/SHUTTERSTOCK.COM

As "Counselors to America's Small Business," SCORE (formerly known as the Service Corps of Retired Executives) offers five ways for entrepreneurs to go social with peers and experts:

- *Facebook* Score's Facebook page (www.facebook.com /SCOREFans) is a hub for Q&A about starting a business.

- *YouTube* On SCORE's YouTube channel (www.youtube.com /SCORESmallBusiness), business owners can view and comment on brief videos highlighting tips for business success.

- *Blog* The SCORE blog (http://blog.score.org/) features timely articles about vital aspects of business ownership and operations.

- *Twitter* In 140 characters or less, SCORE mentors offer business advice and links to more info via Twitter (http://twitter.com /SCOREMentors).

- *Pinterest* Score's Pinterest page (http://pinterest.com /scorementors) features small business success stories, news, tips, and more.

TABLE 4-2 Some Advantages and Disadvantages of a Sole Proprietorship, Partnership, and Corporation

	Sole Proprietorship	General Partnership	Regular C-Corporation
Protecting against liability for debts	Difficult	Difficult	Easy
Raising money	Difficult	Difficult	Easy
Ownership transfer	Difficult	Difficult	Easy
Preserving continuity	Difficult	Difficult	Easy
Government regulations	Few	Few	Many
Formation	Easy	Easy	Difficult
Income taxation	Once	Once	Twice

© CENGAGE LEARNING 2015

profits received as dividends. Corporate profits thus are taxed twice—once as corporate income and a second time as the personal income of stockholders. *Note:* Both the S-corporation and the limited-liability company (LLC) discussed in the next section eliminate the disadvantage of double taxation because they are taxed like a partnership.

LACK OF SECRECY Because open corporations are required to submit detailed reports to government agencies and to stockholders, they cannot keep all of their operations confidential. Competitors can study these corporate reports and then use the information to compete more effectively. In effect, every public corporation has to share some of its secrets with its competitors.

SPECIAL TYPES OF BUSINESS OWNERSHIP

Learning Objective

6 Examine special types of corporations, including S-corporations, limited-liability companies, and not-for-profit corporations.

In addition to the sole proprietorship, partnership, and the regular corporate form of organization, some entrepreneurs choose other forms of organization that meet their special needs. Additional organizational options include S-corporations, LLCs, and not-for-profit corporations.

S-Corporations

S-corporation a corporation that is taxed as though it were a partnership

If a corporation meets certain requirements, its directors may apply to the Internal Revenue Service for status as an S-corporation. An **S-corporation** is a corporation that is taxed as though it were a partnership. In other words, the corporation's income is taxed only as the personal income of its stockholders. Corporate profits or losses "pass through" the business and are reported on the owners' personal income tax returns.

To qualify for the special status of an S-corporation, a firm must meet the following criteria:[8]

1. No more than 100 stockholders are allowed.
2. Stockholders must be individuals, estates, or certain trusts.
3. There can be only one class of outstanding stock.
4. The firm must be a domestic corporation eligible to file for S-corporation status.
5. There can be no partnerships, corporations, or nonresident-alien stockholders.
6. All stockholders must agree to the decision to form an S-corporation.

Becoming an S-corporation can be an effective way to avoid double taxation while retaining the corporation's legal benefit of limited liability.

Limited-Liability Companies

limited-liability company (LLC) a form of business ownership that combines the benefits of a corporation and a partnership while avoiding some of the restrictions and disadvantages of those forms of ownership

A new form of ownership called a limited-liability company is recognized in all 50 states—although each state's laws may differ. A **limited-liability company (LLC)** is a form of business ownership that combines the benefits of a corporation and a partnership while avoiding some of the restrictions and disadvantages of those forms of ownership. Chief advantages of an LLC are as follows:

1. Like a sole proprietorship or partnership, an LLC enjoys pass-through taxation. This means that owners report their share of profits or losses in the company on their individual tax returns and avoid the double taxation imposed on most corporations. LLCs with at least two members are taxed like a partnership. LLCs with just one member are taxed like a sole proprietorship. LLCs can even elect to be taxed as a corporation or S-corporation if there are benefits to offset the corporate double taxation and other restrictions.
2. Like a corporation, it provides limited-liability protection for acts and debts of the LLC. An LLC thus extends the concept of personal-asset protection to small business owners.

3. The LLC type of organization provides more management flexibility and fewer restrictions when compared with corporations. A corporation, for example, is required to hold annual meetings and record meeting minutes; an LLC is not.

Although many experts believe that the LLC is nothing more than a variation of the S-corporation, there is a difference. An LLC is not restricted to 100 stockholders—a common drawback of the S-corporation. Although the owners of an LLC may file the required articles of organization in any state, most choose to file in their home state—the state where they do most of their business.

Even though most LLCs are small- to medium-sized businesses, an LLC doesn't have to be small. American Girl Brands—an LLC that sells dolls, clothing, furniture, books, and magazines for the popular American Girl product lines—chose the LLC type of business ownership because it provided limited liability for investors and avoided some of the restrictions and disadvantages of other forms of business ownership.

For help in understanding the differences between a regular corporation, S-corporation, and an LLC, see Table 4-3.

Edible Arrangements: A limited-liability company. A limited-liability company doesn't have to be small. Edible Arrangements has over 1,100 stores around the world and is ranked as one of America's top 5,000 fastest growing private companies. It chose the limited-liability form of ownership to avoid some of the restrictions and disadvantages of other forms of business ownership.

Not-for-Profit Corporations

A **not-for-profit corporation** (sometimes referred to as *non-profit*) is a corporation organized to provide a social, educational, religious, or other service rather than to earn a profit. Various charities, museums, private schools, colleges, and charitable organizations are organized in this way, primarily to ensure limited liability.

While the process used to organize a not-for-profit corporation is similar to the process used to create a regular corporation, each state does have different laws. Once approved by state authorities, not-for-profit corporations must meet specific Internal Revenue Service guidelines in order to obtain tax-exempt status.

Today, there is a renewed interest in not-for-profits because these organizations are formed to improve communities and change lives. For example, Habitat for Humanity is a not-for-profit corporation and was formed to provide homes for qualified lower

not-for-profit corporation a corporation organized to provide a social, educational, religious, or other service rather than to earn a profit

TABLE 4-3 Some Advantages and Disadvantages of a Regular Corporation, S-Corporation, and Limited-Liability Company

	Regular C-Corporation	S-Corporation	Limited-Liability Company
Double taxation	Yes	No	No
Limited liability and personal asset protection	Yes	Yes	Yes
Management flexibility	No	No	Yes
Restrictions on the number of owners/stockholders	No	Yes	No
Internal Revenue Service tax regulations	Many	Many	Fewer

© CENGAGE LEARNING 2015

Concept Check

✓ Explain the difference between an S-corporation and a limited-liability company.

✓ How does a regular (C) corporation differ from a not-for-profit corporation?

income people who cannot afford housing. Even though this corporation may receive more money than it spends, any surplus funds are "reinvested" in building activities to provide low-cost housing to qualified individuals.

Many not-for-profit corporations operate in much the same way as for-profit businesses. Employees of not-for-profit businesses are responsible for making sure the organization achieves its goals and objectives, ensuring accountability for finances and donations, and monitoring activities to improve the performance of both paid employees and volunteers. If you are interested in a business career, don't rule out the non-profit sector. You might consider volunteering in a local not-for-profit organization to see if you enjoy this type of challenge.

Learning Objective

7 Discuss the purpose of a joint venture and syndicate.

JOINT VENTURES AND SYNDICATES

Today, two additional types of business organizations—joint ventures and syndicates—are used for special purposes. Each of these forms of organization is unique when compared with more traditional forms of business ownership.

Joint Ventures

joint venture an agreement between two or more groups to form a business entity in order to achieve a specific goal or to operate for a specific period of time

A **joint venture** is an agreement between two or more groups to form a business entity in order to achieve a specific goal or to operate for a specific period of time. Both the scope of the joint venture and the liabilities of the people or businesses involved usually are limited to one project. Once the goal is reached, the period of time elapses, or the project is completed, the joint venture is dissolved.

Corporations, as well as individuals, may enter into joint ventures. Major oil producers often have formed a number of joint ventures to share the extremely high cost of exploring for offshore petroleum deposits. And many U.S. companies are forming joint ventures with foreign firms in order to enter new markets around the globe. For example, Walmart has joined forces with India's Bharti Enterprises to establish wholesale cash-and-carry stores that sell directly to local retailers, manufacturers, and farmers in different cities and towns in India. Plans are for each store to offer an assortment of food and nonfood items at competitive wholesale prices, allowing retailers and small business owners to lower their cost of operation. By 2012, the Bharti–Walmart joint venture had opened 14 cash-and-carry stores and employed over 4,000 associates.[9]

Syndicates

syndicate a temporary association of individuals or firms organized to perform a specific task that requires a large amount of capital

A **syndicate** is a temporary association of individuals or firms organized to perform a specific task that requires a large amount of capital. The syndicate is formed because no one person or firm is willing to put up the entire amount required for the undertaking. Like a joint venture, a syndicate is dissolved as soon as its purpose has been accomplished.

Syndicates are used most commonly to underwrite large insurance policies, loans, and investments. To share the risk of default, banks have formed syndicates to provide loans to developing countries. Stock brokerage firms usually join together in the same way to market a new issue of stock. In May 2012 and after years of anticipation in the investment world, Facebook sold stock to investors. Facebook—the world's leading social media website—raised $16 billion with the help of a syndicate of Wall Street firms, including Bank of America, JPMorgan Chase & Co., Morgan Stanley, and Goldman Sachs.[10] This initial public offering, often referred to as an IPO, is one of the largest in recent history. (An *initial public offering* is the term used to describe the first time a corporation sells stock to the general public.)

Concept Check

✓ In your own words, define a joint venture and a syndicate.

✓ In what ways are joint ventures and syndicates alike? In what ways do they differ?

CORPORATE GROWTH

Learning Objective

8 Explain how growth from within and growth through mergers can enable a business to expand.

Growth seems to be a basic characteristic of business. One reason for seeking growth has to do with profit: A larger firm generally has greater sales revenue and thus greater profit. Another reason is that in a growing economy, a business that does not grow is actually shrinking relative to the economy. A third reason is that business growth is a means by which some executives boost their power, prestige, and reputation.

Growth poses new problems and requires additional resources that first must be available and then must be used effectively. The main ingredient in growth is capital—and as we have noted, capital is most readily available to corporations.

Growth from Within

Most corporations grow by expanding their present operations. Some introduce and sell new but related products. Others expand the sale of present products to new geographic markets or to new groups of consumers in geographic markets already served. Although Walmart was started by Sam Walton in 1962 with one discount store, today Walmart has over 10,000 stores in the United States and 26 other countries and has long-range plans for expanding into additional international markets.[11]

Growth from within, especially when carefully planned and controlled, can have relatively little adverse effect on a firm. For the most part, the firm continues to do what it has been doing, but on a larger scale. For instance, Larry Ellison, co-founder and CEO of Oracle Corporation of Redwood Shores, California, built the firm's annual revenues up from a mere $282 million in 1988 to approximately $37 billion today.[12] Much of this growth has taken place over the last 20 years as Oracle capitalized on its global leadership in information management software.

Growth Through Mergers and Acquisitions

Another way a firm can grow is by purchasing another company. The purchase of one corporation by another is called a **merger**. An *acquisition* is essentially the same thing as a merger, but the term usually is used in reference to a large corporation's purchases of other corporations. Although most mergers and acquisitions are friendly, hostile takeovers also occur. A **hostile takeover** is a situation in which the management and board of directors of a firm targeted for acquisition disapprove of the merger.

When a merger or acquisition becomes hostile, a corporate raider—another company or a wealthy investor—may make a tender offer or start a proxy fight to gain control of the target company. A **tender offer** is an offer to purchase the stock of a firm targeted for acquisition at a price just high enough to tempt stockholders to sell their shares. Corporate raiders also may initiate a proxy fight. A **proxy fight** is a technique used to gather enough stockholder votes to control a targeted company.

If the corporate raider is successful and takes over the targeted company, existing management usually is replaced. Faced with this probability, existing management may take specific actions, sometimes referred to as "poison pills," "shark repellents," or "porcupine provisions," to maintain control of the firm and avoid the hostile takeover. Whether mergers are friendly or hostile, they are generally classified as *horizontal, vertical,* or *conglomerate* (see Figure 4-5).

merger the purchase of one corporation by another

hostile takeover a situation in which the management and board of directors of a firm targeted for acquisition disapprove of the merger

tender offer an offer to purchase the stock of a firm targeted for acquisition at a price just high enough to tempt stockholders to sell their shares

proxy fight a technique used to gather enough stockholder votes to control a targeted company

One more airline merger. The proposed merger between American Airlines and U.S. Airways would create one of the largest airlines in the world. While the mega-merger could be good for both companies, consumer advocates worry the merger could result in less competition among airlines, fewer flights to some markets, *and* higher ticket prices for customers.

FIGURE 4-5 Three Types of Growth by Merger

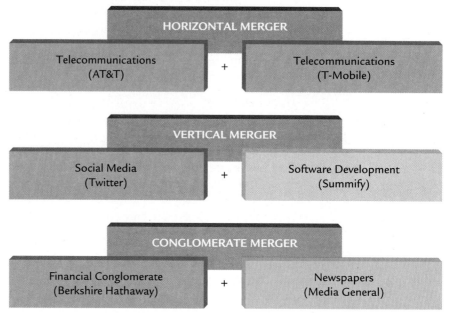

Today, mergers are classified as horizontal, vertical, or conglomerate.

HORIZONTAL MERGER

| Telecommunications (AT&T) | + | Telecommunications (T-Mobile) |

VERTICAL MERGER

| Social Media (Twitter) | + | Software Development (Summify) |

CONGLOMERATE MERGER

| Financial Conglomerate (Berkshire Hathaway) | + | Newspapers (Media General) |

© CENGAGE LEARNING 2015

HORIZONTAL MERGERS A *horizontal merger* is a merger between firms that make and sell similar products or services in similar markets. The proposed merger between AT&T and T-Mobile was an example of a horizontal merger because both firms provide cell phone service to their customers. This type of merger tends to reduce the number of firms in an industry—and thus may reduce competition. As a result most horizontal mergers are reviewed carefully by federal agencies before they are approved in order to protect competition in the marketplace. In fact, the AT&T merger with T-Mobile was effectively blocked when the U.S. Department of Justice filed a law suit to block the merger. According to the Department of Justice, the main reason behind the government's legal action was to protect the competitive environment and the consumers' right to choose. Rather than fight the government's attempt to block the merger, AT&T withdrew its offer to acquire T-Mobile. For more information about the government's actions to block the AT&T merger with T-Mobile, read the Video Case on page 125.

VERTICAL MERGERS A *vertical merger* is a merger between firms that operate at different but related levels in the production and marketing of a product. Generally, one of the merging firms is either a supplier or a customer of the other. A vertical merger occurred when social media giant Twitter acquired Summify. At the time of the 2012 merger, Summify, based in Vancouver, was a start-up technology company in the process of building the next generation of newsreader software that had a unique approach to summarizing the most important information from social media feeds from Google, Facebook, and Twitter. Rather than develop its own software to summarize the most important information, Twitter simply purchased the Summify company.[13]

CONGLOMERATE MERGERS A *conglomerate* merger takes place between firms in completely different industries. A conglomerate merger occurred when financial conglomerate Berkshire Hathaway acquired Media General Corporation. While both companies were recognized as successful companies that have a history of increasing sales revenues and profits, they operate in different industries. Berkshire Hathaway, led by its CEO Warren Buffett, has a long history of acquiring firms that have great financial potential. Media General, on the other hand, is a smaller company with its main business interests in 63 daily and weekly newspapers in the southeastern part of the United States.[14] The Berkshire Hathaway–Media General merger was friendly because it was beneficial for both firms. (Note: For more information on the Berkshire Hathaway Corporation and its merger activities, review the Inside Business opening case for this chapter.)

Merger and Acquisition Trends for the Future

Economists, financial analysts, corporate managers, and stockholders still hotly debate whether mergers and acquisitions are good for the economy—or for individual companies—in the long run. Takeover advocates argue that for companies that have been taken over, the purchasers have been able to make the company more profitable and productive by installing a new top-management team, by reducing expenses, and by forcing the company to concentrate on one main business.

Takeover opponents argue that takeovers do nothing to enhance corporate profitability or productivity. These critics argue that the only people who benefit from takeovers are investment bankers, brokerage firms, and takeover "artists," who receive financial rewards by manipulating corporations rather than by producing tangible products or services.

While there have always been mergers and acquisitions, the current economy has changed the dynamics of how and why firms merge. Most experts now predict that mergers and acquisitions after the economic crisis will be the result of cash-rich companies looking to acquire businesses that will enhance their position in the marketplace. Analysts also anticipate more mergers that involve companies or investors from other countries. Regardless of the companies involved or where the companies are from, future mergers and acquisitions will be driven by solid business logic and the desire to compete in the international marketplace.

Whether they are sole proprietorships, partnerships, corporations, or some other form of business ownership, most U.S. businesses are small. In the next chapter, we focus on these small businesses. We examine, among other things, the meaning of the word *small* as it applies to business and the place of small business in the American economy.

Concept Check

✓ What happens when a firm makes a decision to grow from within?

✓ What is a hostile takeover? How is it related to a tender offer and a proxy fight?

✓ Explain the three types of mergers.

✓ Describe the current merger trends and how they affect the businesses involved and their stockholders.

Looking for Success? *Get Flashcards, Quizzes, Games, Crosswords, and more @ www.cengagebrain.com.*

Summary

1 Describe the advantages and disadvantages of sole proprietorships.

In a sole proprietorship, all business profits become the property of the owner, but the owner is also personally responsible for all business debts. A successful sole proprietorship can be a great source of pride for the owner. When comparing different types of business ownership, the sole proprietorship is the simplest form of business to enter, control, and leave. It also pays no special taxes. Perhaps for these reasons, 72 percent of all American business firms are sole proprietorships. Sole proprietorships nevertheless have disadvantages, such as unlimited liability and limits on one person's ability to borrow or to be an expert in all fields. As a result, this form of ownership accounts for only 4 percent of total revenues when compared with partnerships and corporations.

2 Explain the different types of partners and the importance of partnership agreements.

Like sole proprietors, general partners are responsible for running the business and for all business debts. Limited partners receive a share of the profit in return for investing in the business. However, they are not responsible for business debts beyond the amount they have invested. Regardless of the type of partnership, it is always a good idea to have a written agreement (or articles of partnership) setting forth the terms of a partnership. When entering a partnership, partners would be wise to let a neutral third party assist with any disputes that might arise.

3 Describe the advantages and disadvantages of partnerships.

Although partnership eliminates some of the disadvantages of sole proprietorship, it is the least popular of the major forms of business ownership. The major advantages of a partnership include ease of start-up, availability of capital and credit, personal interest, combined skills and knowledge, retention of profits, and possible tax advantages. The effects of management disagreements are one of the major disadvantages of a partnership. Other disadvantages include unlimited liability (in a general partnership), lack of continuity, and frozen investment. By forming a limited partnership, the disadvantage of unlimited liability may be eliminated for the limited partner(s). This same disadvantage may be eliminated for partners that form a LLP. Of course, special requirements must be met if partners form either the limited partnership or the LLP.

4 Summarize how a corporation is formed.

A corporation is an artificial person created by law, with most of the legal rights of a real person, including the right to start and operate a business, to buy or sell property, to borrow money, to be sued or sue, and to enter into contracts. With the corporate form of ownership, stock can be sold to individuals to raise capital. The people who own a corporation's common or preferred stock are called stockholders. Stockholders are entitled to receive any dividends paid by the corporation, and common stockholders can vote either in person or by proxy. Generally, corporations are classified as closed corporations (few stockholders) or open corporations (many stockholders).

The process of forming a corporation is called incorporation. Most experts believe that the services of a lawyer are necessary when making decisions about where to incorporate and about obtaining a corporate charter, issuing stock, holding an organizational meeting, and all other legal details involved in incorporation. In theory, stockholders are able to control the activities of the corporation because they elect the board of directors who appoint the corporate officers.

5 Describe the advantages and disadvantages of a corporation.

Perhaps the major advantage of the corporate form is limited liability—stockholders are not liable for the corporation's debts beyond the amount they paid for its stock. Other important advantages include ease of raising capital, ease of transfer of ownership, perpetual life, and specialized management. A major disadvantage of a large corporation is double taxation: All profits are taxed once as corporate income and again as personal income because stockholders must pay a personal income tax on the profits they receive as dividends. Other disadvantages include difficulty and expense of formation, government regulation, conflict within the corporation, and lack of secrecy.

6 Examine special types of corporations, including S-corporations, limited-liability companies, and not-for-profit corporations.

S-corporations are corporations that are taxed as though they were partnerships but that enjoy the benefit of limited liability. To qualify as an S-corporation, a number of criteria must be met. An LLC is a form of business ownership that provides limited liability and has fewer restrictions when compared to a regular corporation or an S-corporation. LLCs with at least two members are taxed like a partnership and thus avoid the double taxation imposed on most corporations. LLCs with just one member are taxed like a sole proprietorship. When compared with a regular corporation or an S-corporation, an LLC is more flexible. Not-for-profit corporations are formed to provide social services and to improve communities and change lives rather than to earn profits.

7 Discuss the purpose of a joint venture and syndicate.

Two additional forms of business ownership—the joint venture and a syndicate—are used by their owners to meet special needs. A joint venture is formed when two or more groups form a business entity in order to achieve a specific goal or to operate for a specific period of time. Once the goal is reached, the period of time elapses, or the project is completed, the joint venture is dissolved. A syndicate is a temporary association of individuals or firms organized to perform a specific task that requires large amounts of capital. Like a joint venture, a syndicate is dissolved as soon as its purpose has been accomplished.

8 Explain how growth from within and growth through mergers can enable a business to expand.

A corporation may grow by expanding its present operations or through a merger or an acquisition. Although most mergers are friendly, hostile takeovers also occur. A hostile takeover is a situation in which the management and board of directors of a firm targeted for acquisition disapprove of the merger. Mergers generally are classified as horizontal, vertical, or conglomerate.

While economists, financial analysts, corporate managers, and stockholders debate the merits of mergers, some trends should be noted. First, experts predict that future mergers will be the result of cash-rich companies looking to acquire businesses that will enhance their position in the marketplace. Second, more mergers are likely to involve foreign companies or investors. Third, mergers will be driven by business logic and the desire to compete in the international marketplace.

Key Terms

You should now be able to define and give an example relevant to each of the following terms:

sole proprietorship (102)	closed corporation (110)	proxy (112)	joint venture (118)
unlimited liability (104)	open corporation (110)	board of directors (112)	syndicate (118)
partnership (105)	domestic corporation (111)	corporate officers (113)	merger (119)
general partner (105)	foreign corporation (111)	limited liability (114)	hostile takeover (119)
limited partner (106)	alien corporation (111)	S-corporation (116)	tender offer (119)
corporation (109)	common stock (111)	limited-liability company	proxy fight (119)
stock (110)	preferred stock (111)	(LLC) (116)	
stockholder (110)	dividend (111)	not-for-profit corporation (117)	

Discussion Questions

1. If you were to start a business, which ownership form would you choose? What factors might affect your choice?
2. Why might an investor choose to become a partner in a limited partnership instead of purchasing the stock of an open corporation?
3. Discuss the following statement: "Corporations are not really run by their owners."
4. What kinds of services do not-for-profit corporations provide? Would a career in a not-for-profit corporation appeal to you?
5. Is growth a good thing for all firms? How does management know when a firm is ready to grow?

Test Yourself

Matching Questions

1. _____ It is an association of two or more business owners.
2. _____ A distribution of earnings to the stockholders of a corporation.
3. _____ This type of ownership is the simplest type of business to start.
4. _____ A person who invests only money in a partnership.
5. _____ The concept of being personally responsible for all debts of a business.
6. _____ A business entity or artificial being with most of the legal rights of a person.
7. _____ A legal document that describes the purpose of the corporation.
8. _____ An offer to purchase the stock of a firm targeted for acquisition.

9. _____ A temporary association of individuals or firms organized to perform a specific task that requires a large amount of capital.
10. _____ A company chartered in a foreign country doing business in the United States.

    a. alien corporation
    b. corporate charter
    c. syndicate
    d. tender offer
    e. vertical venture
    f. limited partner
    g. voluntary association
    h. corporation
    i. dividend
    j. partnership
    k. sole proprietorship
    l. unlimited liability

True False Questions

11. **T F** Unlimited liability is an advantage of a sole proprietorship.
12. **T F** Preferred stockholders elect the board of directors that manage the day-to-day business activities of a corporation.
13. **T F** A conglomerate merger takes place between firms in completely different industries.
14. **T F** A limited partner is responsible for any debts of the partnership, regardless of whether he or she was directly involved in the transaction that created the debt.

15. **T F** The articles of partnership is a written contract describing the terms of a partnership.

16. **T F** Compared to a corporation, a partnership is more difficult and expensive to establish.

17. **T F** The S-corporation form of organization allows a corporation to avoid double taxation.

18. **T F** Corporate officers are elected by the firm's stockholders.

19. **T F** The board of directors is directly responsible to the stockholders.

20. **T F** The amount paid for stock is the most a shareholder can lose in the corporate form of ownership.

Multiple-Choice Questions

21. _____ During college, Elyssa Wood earned extra money by using her culinary skills to cater special parties. After graduation, she decided to turn her part-time job into a full-time business that she plans to expand in the future. In the meantime, she wants to maintain complete control of the business. She will most likely organize the business as a
    a. master limited partnership.
    b. corporation.
    c. general partnership.
    d. sole proprietorship.
    e. cooperative.

22. _____ Which of the following is not an advantage of a corporate form of ownership?
    a. It is easier to raise capital.
    b. Ownership can be transferred easily and quickly.
    c. The death of an owner does not terminate the corporation.
    d. Profits are taxed twice.
    e. The liability of the owners is limited.

23. _____ A corporation incorporated in Texas doing business in New York is known in
    a. New York as a domestic corporation.
    b. Texas as a foreign corporation.
    c. Texas as a domestic corporation.
    d. New York as an alien corporation.
    e. The firm cannot do business in New York.

24. _____ PepsiCo acquired Pizza Hut. What type of merger was this?
    a. Limited
    b. Syndicated
    c. Joint venture
    d. Horizontal
    e. Vertical

25. _____ J. R. Imax, a financial investor, wants to control the Simex Company. So far he has been unsuccessful in purchasing enough stock to give him control. To reach his goal, which technique should he use to gather enough stockholder votes to control the company?
    a. Poison pill
    b. Liability takeover
    c. Merger
    d. Acquisition
    e. Proxy fight

26. _____ A corporation whose stock is owned by relative few people is called a(n)
    a. limited corporation.
    b. open corporation.
    c. closed corporation.
    d. domestic corporation.
    e. friendly corporation.

27. _____ When two business firms need large sums of money to finance a major project, they are likely to establish a
    a. closed corporation.
    b. syndicate.
    c. new sole proprietorship business.
    d. legal tender corporation.
    e. conglomerate venture.

28. _____ The ability to combine skills and knowledge is an advantage of a
    a. partnership.
    b. sole proprietorship.
    c. limited venture.
    d. an enterprise venture.
    e. a horizontal business.

29. _____ One of the advantages of an LLC is that owners have _____ liability.
    a. unlimited
    b. restricted
    c. special
    d. limited
    e. taxable

30. _____ Unlimited liability means
    a. there is no limit on the amount an owner can borrow.
    b. creditors will absorb any loss from nonpayment of debt.
    c. the business can borrow money for any type of purchase.
    d. the owner is responsible for all business debts.
    e. stockholders can borrow money from the business.

Answers to the Test Yourself questions appear at the end of the book on page TY-1

Video Case

AT&T and T-Mobile: What Went Wrong with Their Merger?

When it tried to buy T-Mobile for $39 billion in 2011, AT&T went so far as to offer the company a "break up" fee of $3 billion in cash plus assets valued at $1 billion if the deal fell through. Why was AT&T so determined to purchase T-Mobile? AT&T was no. 2 in the wireless phone-service market. T-Mobile was no. 4. By merging, they would have become the nation's largest wireless provider, surpassing Verizon. The deal would also have given AT&T access to the spectrum (airwaves) T-Mobile owned but couldn't afford to upgrade to 4G (state-of-the-art, fourth-generation technology).

Executives at the companies said that in addition to creating jobs, the merger would result in fewer dropped calls and faster connection times for customers. The merged company would also be able to immediately expand wireless service to rural areas that lacked it. "AT&T will immediately gain cell sites equivalent to what would have taken on average five years to build without the transaction," the two companies said in their merger announcement. The announcement also referred to a government report that showed that despite many mergers in the industry over the past decade, the price of wireless service had declined.

Investors cheered when they heard about the merger. However, many consumers, the Department of Justice, and the Federal Communications Commission (FCC) were wary of the deal. The merged company would have controlled nearly half of the market. The only remaining big players in the industry would have been Verizon and Sprint. Some industry experts thought Sprint might get forced out of the market because it held the least market share. They also believed few new companies would enter the market. Competing against a combined AT&T and T-Mobile would make it too difficult.

What would the merger have meant for consumers? Dan Gillmor, the director of the Knight Center for Digital Media Entrepreneurship at Arizona State University, said he thought the deal would be bad for consumers. They would have fewer wireless providers to choose from, Gillmor said. He also predicted consumers could end up paying higher prices. "T-Mobile is the only company that's now competing seriously on price," he explained.

Researchers at the magazine *Consumer Reports* also concluded that T-Mobile charged less than many of its competitors for different types of plans. What firm would keep AT&T and its prices in check if it were to swallow up T-Mobile? Another issue was that a number of surveys had found that AT&T's service quality was uneven. Would it get worse following the merger? Or better?

As you learned earlier in the chapter, the Department of Justice ultimately filed a lawsuit to block the merger. "The combination of AT&T and T-Mobile would result in tens of millions of consumers all across the United States facing higher prices, fewer choices, and lower-quality products for mobile wireless services," said Department of Justice Deputy Attorney General James M. Cole. And even though AT&T and T-Mobile claimed the merger would produce more jobs, an investigation by the FCC came to a different conclusion. The internal records of the two companies showed that the firms planned to lay off personnel by combining duplicate functions in their organizations such as their sales, management, and customer service departments. The FCC also disputed the companies' claim that the merger would immediately expand wireless service to rural areas. Why? Because T-Mobile serviced mostly urban areas—not rural ones.

Acquiring T-Mobile became such an upward battle that AT&T eventually abandoned the effort and paid T-Mobile the $4 billion breakup fee. A few months later, T-Mobile announced it was spending $4 billion to expand and upgrade its network to 4G.[15]

Questions

1. Did the Department of Justice make the right decision when it blocked the merger of T-Mobile and AT&T? Why or why not?
2. What do you think the pros and cons of acquiring a competing company are? Create a list of each.
3. Name some other examples of horizontal, vertical, and conglomerate mergers you're aware of. Considering the impact of mergers on competition, what are the advantages and disadvantages of each type of merger?

Building Skills for Career Success

1. Social Media Exercise

Not-for-profit organizations have used social media to redefine how they can get funding for their missions. There are even a few that exist totally online. Check out www .donorschoose.org and www.kiva.org. Both of these depend on crowds (called crowdfunding) to either fund educational projects (Donors Choose) or lend money to support projects all over the world (Kiva) using the microfinancing model.

a. Take a minute to explore these sites and view some of the projects up for funding. How are these projects organized? Do you think these models are effective? Why or why not?

b. Both Donors Choose and Kiva are not-for-profits; do you think these models are useful for "for-profit" businesses? Why or why not?

2. Building Team Skills

Suppose that you have decided to quit your job as an insurance adjuster and open a bakery. Your business is now growing, and you have decided to add a full line of catering services. This means more work and responsibility. You will need someone to help you, but you are undecided about what to do. Should you hire an employee or find a partner? If you add a partner, what type of decisions should be made to create a partnership agreement?

Assignment

1. In a group, discuss the following questions:
   a. What are the advantages and disadvantages of adding a partner versus hiring an employee?
   b. Assume that you have decided to form a partnership. What articles should be included in a partnership agreement?
   c. How would you go about finding a partner?
2. As a group, prepare an articles-of-partnership agreement. Be prepared to discuss the pros and cons of your group's agreement with other groups from your class, as well as to examine their agreements.
3. Summarize your group's answers to these questions, and present them to your class.

3. Researching Different Careers

Many people spend their entire lives working in jobs that they do not enjoy. Why is this so? Often, it is because they have taken the first job they were offered without giving it much thought. How can you avoid having this happen to you? First, you should determine your "personal profile" by identifying and analyzing your own strengths, weaknesses, things you enjoy, and things you dislike. Second, you should identify the types of jobs that fit your profile. Third, you should identify and research the companies that offer those jobs.

Assignment

a. Take two sheets of paper and draw a line down the middle of each sheet, forming two columns on each page. Label column 1 "Things I Enjoy or Like to Do," column 2 "Things I Do Not Like Doing," column 3 "My Strengths," and column 4 "My Weaknesses."
b. Record data in each column over a period of at least one week. You may find it helpful to have a relative or friend give you input.
c. Summarize the data, and write a profile of yourself.
d. Take your profile to a career counselor at your college or to the public library and ask for help in identifying jobs that fit your profile. Your college may offer testing to assess your skills and personality. The Internet is another resource.
e. Research the companies that offer the types of jobs that fit your profile.
f. Write a report on your findings.

Endnotes

1. Based on information in Jim Maxwell, "Buffett's Winning Attitude: Bullish on Newspapers," *Bristol Herald Courier (Bristol, Virginia)*, October 21, 2012, www.tricities.com; Daniel Roberts, "The Secrets of See's Candies," *Fortune*, August 22, 2012, http://management.fortune.cnn.com; "Fortune 500 #7, Berkshire Hathaway," *Fortune*, May 21, 2012, http://money.conn.com/magazines/fortune/fortune500; Michael J De La. Merced, "Buffett Talks Succession and Taxes at Berkshire Annual Meeting," *New York Times*, May 5, 2012, www.nytimes.com.
2. The IVY Planning Group website at www.ivygroupllc.com (accessed January 12, 2013).
3. The Procter & Gamble website at www.pg.com (accessed January 13, 2013).
4. Ibid.
5. The Mars Corporate website at www.mars.com (accessed January 13, 2013).
6. The My New Company website at www.mynewcompany.com (accessed January 13, 2013).
7. The Hispanic PR Wire website at www.hispanicprwire.com (accessed January 14, 2013).
8. The Internal Revenue Service website at www.irs.gov (accessed January 13, 2013).
9. The Walmart Corporate website at www.walmartstores.com (accessed November 25, 2011).
10. "Facebook, Banks Sued Over Pre-IPO Analyst Calls," The Reuters website at www.reuters.com (accessed May 23, 2012).
11. The Walmart Corporate website at www.walmartstores.com (accessed January 13, 2013).
12. The Oracle website at www.oracle.com (accessed January 17, 2013).
13. "Twitter Acquires Social Media Feed Condenser Summify," The Tech World website at www.techworld.com (accessed January 20, 2012).
14. The Media General, Inc. website at www.mediageneral.com (accessed May 17, 2012).
15. Based on information from Brad Reed, AT&T and T-Mobile Again Remind Us of "Why We Should Grateful Their Merger Collapsed," BGR website, August 23, 2012, http:bgr.com; "AT&T T-Mobile Deal Dropped after Fierce Government Backlash," The Huffington Post, December 20, 2011, www.huffingtonpost.com; Amy Schatz and Greg Bensinger, "FCC Blasts AT&T Deal," *Wall Street Journal*, November 30, 2011; http://online.wsj.com; David Goldman, "DOJ Files Antitrust Suit to Block AT&T Merger with T-Mobile," *CNNMoney*, August 31, 2011, http://money.cnn.com; Russ Wiles, "AT&T Merger with T-Mobile May Cut Competition," *Arizona Republic*, March 11, 2011, www.azcentral.com/arizonarepublic.

© MONKEY BUSINESS IMAGES/SHUTTERSTOCK.COM

Small Business, Entrepreneurship, and Franchises

Learning Objectives

Once you complete this chapter, you will be able to:

1 Define what a small business is and recognize the fields in which small businesses are concentrated.

2 Identify the people who start small businesses and the reasons why some succeed and many fail.

3 Assess the contributions of small businesses to our economy.

4 Describe the advantages and disadvantages of operating a small business.

5 Explain how the Small Business Administration helps small businesses.

6 Explain the concept and types of franchising.

7 Analyze the growth of franchising and its advantages and disadvantages.

Why Should You Care?

America's small businesses drive the U.S. economy. Small businesses represent 99.7 percent of all employer firms, and there is a good probability that you will work for a small business or perhaps even start your own business. This chapter can help you to become a good employee or a successful entrepreneur.

Dunkin' Brands Helps Franchisees Brew up Sales

Massachusetts-based Dunkin' Brands (www.dunkinbrands.com) is in the middle of a growth spurt that will bring thousands of new Dunkin' Donuts coffee shops and Baskin-Robbins ice-cream shops under the control of local entrepreneurs worldwide. As a franchisor, Dunkin' Brands works with entrepreneurs who want to own their own business backed by the advantages of a well-known brand and proven methods of operation. Currently, franchisees operate a total of nearly 17,000 Dunkin' Donuts and Baskin-Robbins stores and, in all, ring up global revenues of $8.3 billion each year.

Baskin-Robbins, famous for its wide variety of ice-cream flavors, is especially strong outside the United States. Franchisees have signed to launch new shops across Asia and in other regions where economic growth is boosting personal income. Meanwhile, Dunkin' Donuts has an aggressive growth strategy for increasing the number of U.S. franchised stores to 15,000 by 2030. Brewing up this level of expansion means building on its track record of success in the Eastern states, where Dunkin' Donuts has long been popular, to help franchisees open shops in the Western states, where the brand has been less visible—until now.

Westward expansion will put Dunkin' Donuts into some areas dominated by powerful rivals like Starbucks (which doesn't offer franchises) as well as independent coffee shops that have already carved out a loyal customer base. To give franchise owners even more competitive strength, Dunkin' Donuts has stepped up its introduction of new menu items, including non-breakfast foods and beverages to attract customers throughout the day. It's also increased efficiency through cutting-edge technology that streamlines customer transactions and store operations procedures. Finally, the company is giving the Dunkin' Donuts brand a bigger boost nationwide through advertising, social media, online promotions, mobile communications, and marketing alliances with major sports teams.[1]

Did You Know?

Dunkin' Donuts has 10,000 franchised locations worldwide and its sister company, Baskin-Robbins, has nearly 7,000 franchised locations worldwide.

Most businesses start small and those that survive usually stay small. However, they provide a solid foundation for our economy—as employers, as suppliers and purchasers of goods and services, and as taxpayers.

In this chapter, we do not take small businesses for granted. Instead, we look closely at this important business sector—beginning with a definition of small business, a description of industries that often attract small businesses, and a profile of some of the people who start small businesses. Next, we consider the importance of small businesses in our economy. We also present the advantages and disadvantages of smallness in business. We then describe services provided by the Small Business Administration, a government agency formed to assist owners and managers of small businesses. We conclude the chapter with a discussion of the pros and cons of franchising, an approach to small-business ownership that has become very popular in the last 55 years.

Learning Objective

1 Define what a small business is and recognize the fields in which small businesses are concentrated.

small business one that is independently owned and operated for profit and is not dominant in its field

SMALL BUSINESS: A PROFILE

The Small Business Administration (SBA) defines a **small business** as "one which is independently owned and operated for profit and is not dominant in its field." How small must a firm be not to dominate its field? That depends on the particular industry it is in. The SBA has developed the following specific "smallness" guidelines for the various industries, as shown in Table 5-1.[2] The SBA periodically revises and simplifies its small-business size regulations.

Annual sales in millions of dollars may not seem very small. However, for many firms, profit is only a small percentage of total sales. Thus, a firm may earn only $50,000 or $60,000 on yearly sales of $1 million—and that is small in comparison

TABLE 5-1 Industry Group–Size Standards

Small-business size standards are usually stated in number of employees or average annual sales. In the United States, 99.7 percent of all businesses are considered small.

Industry Group	Size Standard
Manufacturing, mining industries	500 employees
Wholesale trade	100 employees
Agriculture	$750,000
Retail trade	$7 million
General and heavy construction (except dredging)	$33.5 million
Dredging	$20 million
Special trade contractors	$14 million
Travel agencies	$3.5 million (commissions and other income)
Business and personal services except	$7 million
• Architectural, engineering, surveying, and mapping services	$4.5 million
• Dry cleaning and carpet cleaning services	$4.5 million

Source: www.sbaonline.sba.gov/contractingopportunities/owners/basics/what (accessed June 5, 2013).

with the profits earned by most medium-sized and large firms. Moreover, most small firms have annual sales well below the maximum limits in the SBA guidelines.

Small businesses are very important to the U.S. economy. For example, small businesses

- represent 99.7 percent of all employer firms;
- employ about half of all private sector employees;
- pay 43 percent of total U.S. private payroll;
- have generated 64 percent of net new jobs over the past 18 years;
- create more than half of the nonfarm private GDP;
- hire 43 percent of high-tech workers (scientists, engineers, computer programmers, and others);
- are 52 percent home-based and 2 percent franchises;
- made up 97.5 percent of all identified exporters and produced 31 percent of export value; and
- produced 16.5 times more patents per employee than large patenting firms.[3]

The Small-Business Sector

In the United States, it typically takes less than a week and $600 to establish a business as a legal entity. The steps include registering the name of the business, applying for tax IDs, and setting up unemployment and workers' compensation insurance. In Japan, however, a typical entrepreneur spends more than $3,500 and 31 days to follow 11 different procedures.

A surprising number of Americans take advantage of their freedom to start a business. There are, in fact, about 27.9 million businesses in this country. Only just 18,500 of these employ more than 500 workers—enough to be considered large.

Interest in owning or starting a small business has never been greater than it is today. During the last decade, the number of small businesses in the United States has increased 49 percent. For the last few years, new-business formation in the United States has broken successive records, except during the 2001–2002 and 2008 recessions.

Have you worked for a small business?

Sometime in your career, you're likely to have a job in a small business. You might work in a store, in a service business, or in production. If you're thinking of starting your own business, be sure to watch how these entrepreneurs manage their companies.

© CANDYBOX IMAGES/SHUTTERSTOCK.COM

Recently, 533,945 new businesses were incorporated. Furthermore, part-time entrepreneurs have increased fivefold in recent years; they now account for one-third of all small businesses.[4]

According to a recent study, 69 percent of new businesses survive at least two years, about 50 percent survive at least five years, and 31 percent survive at least ten years.[5] The primary reason for these failures is mismanagement resulting from a lack of business know-how. The makeup of the small-business sector thus is constantly changing. Despite the high failure rate, many small businesses succeed modestly. Some, like Apple Computer, Inc., are extremely successful—to the point where they can no longer be considered small. Taken together, small businesses are also responsible for providing a high percentage of the jobs in the United States. According to some estimates, the figure is well over 50 percent.

Industries That Attract Small Businesses

Some industries, such as auto manufacturing, require huge investments in machinery and equipment. Businesses in such industries are big from the day they are started—if an entrepreneur or group of entrepreneurs can gather the capital required to start one.

By contrast, a number of other industries require only a low initial investment and some special skills or knowledge. It is these industries that tend to attract new businesses. Growing industries, such as outpatient-care facilities, are attractive because of their profit potential. However, knowledgeable entrepreneurs choose areas with which they are familiar, and these are most often the more established industries.

Small enterprise spans the gamut from corner newspaper vending to the development of optical fibers. The owners of small businesses sell gasoline, flowers, and coffee to go. They publish magazines, haul freight, teach languages, and program computers. They make wines, movies, and high-fashion clothes. They build new homes and restore old ones. They fix appliances, recycle metals, and sell used cars. They drive cabs and fly planes. They make us well when we are ill, and they sell us the products of corporate giants. In fact, 74 percent of real estate, rental, and leasing industries; 61 percent of the businesses in the leisure and hospitality services; and 86 percent of the construction industries are dominated by small businesses. The various kinds of businesses generally fall into three broad categories of industry: distribution, service, and production.

DISTRIBUTION INDUSTRIES This category includes retailing, wholesaling, transportation, and communications—industries concerned with the movement of goods from producers to consumers. Distribution industries account for approximately 33 percent of all small businesses. Of these, almost three-quarters are involved in retailing, that is, the sale of goods directly to consumers. Clothing and jewelry stores, pet shops, bookstores, and grocery stores, for example, are all retailing firms. Slightly less than one-quarter of the small distribution firms are wholesalers. Wholesalers purchase products in quantity from manufacturers and then resell them to retailers.

SERVICE INDUSTRIES This category accounts for more than 48 percent of all small businesses. Of these, about three-quarters provide such nonfinancial services as medical and dental care; watch, shoe, and TV repairs; haircutting and styling; restaurant meals; and dry cleaning. About 8 percent of the small service firms offer financial services, such as accounting, insurance, real estate, and investment counseling. An increasing number of self-employed Americans are running service businesses from home.

Concept Check

✓ What information would you need to determine whether a particular business is small according to SBA guidelines?

✓ Which two areas of business generally attract the most small business? Why are these areas attractive to small business?

✓ Distinguish among service industries, distribution industries, and production industries

PRODUCTION INDUSTRIES This last category includes the construction, mining, and manufacturing industries. Only about 19 percent of all small businesses are in this group, mainly because these industries require relatively large initial investments. Small firms that do venture into production generally make parts and subassemblies for larger manufacturing firms or supply special skills to larger construction firms.

THE PEOPLE IN SMALL BUSINESSES: THE ENTREPRENEURS

Learning Objective

2 Identify the people who start small businesses and the reasons why some succeed and many fail.

The entrepreneurial spirit is alive and well in the United States. One study revealed that the U.S. population is quite entrepreneurial when compared with those of other countries. More than 70 percent of Americans would prefer being an entrepreneur to working for someone else. This compares with 46 percent of adults in Western Europe and 58 percent of adults in Canada. Another study on entrepreneurial activity found that of 36 countries studied, the United States was in the top third in entrepreneurial activity and was the leader when compared with Japan, Canada, and Western Europe.[6]

Small businesses typically are managed by the people who started and own them. Most of these people have held jobs with other firms and still could be so employed if they wanted. Yet owners of small businesses would rather take the risk of starting and operating their own firms, even if the money they make is less than the salaries they otherwise might earn.

Researchers have suggested a variety of personal factors as reasons why people go into business for themselves. These are discussed next.

Characteristics of Entrepreneurs

Entrepreneurial spirit is the desire to create a new business. For example, Nikki Olyai always knew that she wanted to create and develop her own business. Her father, a successful businessman in Iran, was her role model. She came to the United States at the age of 17 and lived with a host family in Salem, Oregon, attending high school there. Undergraduate and graduate degrees in computer science led her to start Innovision Technologies while she held two other jobs to keep the business going and took care of her four-year-old son. Recently, Nikki Olyai's business was honored by the Women's Business Enterprise National Council's "Salute to Women's Business Enterprises" as one of 11 top successful firms. For three consecutive years, her firm was selected as a "Future 50 of Greater Detroit Company."

Other Personal Factors

Other personal factors in small-business success include

- independence;
- a desire to determine one's own destiny;
- a willingness to find and accept a challenge;
- family background (in particular, researchers think that people whose families have been in business, successfully or not, are most apt to start and run their own businesses); and
- age (those who start their own businesses also tend to cluster around certain ages—more than 70 percent are between 24 and 44 years of age; see Figure 5-1).

AP IMAGES/NATI HARNIK

Meet Sam Altman, co-founder and CEO of Loopt. In 2004, Altman co-founded a location-based social networking mobile application when he was a sophomore majoring in computer science at Stanford University. *BusinessWeek* named him one of the "Best Young Entrepreneurs in Technology" and *Inc.* magazine ranked him number 4 among the top 30 entrepreneurs under the age of 30. In 2012, prepaid money card issuer Green Dot Corp. agreed to acquire Loopt Inc. for $43.4 million.

FIGURE 5-1 How Old Is the Average Entrepreneur?

People in all age groups become entrepreneurs, but more than 70 percent are between 25 and 44 years of age.

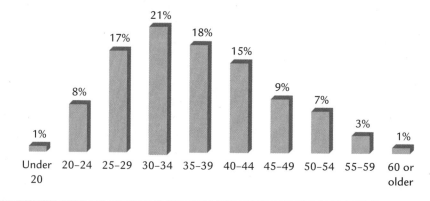

Under 20	20–24	25–29	30–34	35–39	40–44	45–49	50–54	55–59	60 or older
1%	8%	17%	21%	18%	15%	9%	7%	3%	1%

Source: Data developed and provided by the National Federation of Independent Business Foundation and sponsored by the American Express Travel Related Services Company, Inc.

Motivation

There must be some motivation to start a business. A person may decide that he or she simply has "had enough" of working and earning a profit for someone else. Another may lose his or her job for some reason and decide to start the business he or she has always wanted rather than to seek another job. Still another person may have an idea for a new product or a new way to sell an existing product. Or the opportunity to go into business may arise suddenly, perhaps as a result of a hobby. For example, Cheryl Strand started baking and decorating cakes from her home while working full time as a word processor at Clemson University. Her cakes became so popular that she soon found herself working through her lunch breaks and late into the night to meet customer demand.

Victor "Beau" Shell, a child entrepreneur. This 9-year old boy co-owns and operates a small ice cream truck business in Athens, Georgia. In 2013, Shell celebrated his first anniversary and joined the Athens Area Chamber of Commerce. His mother says, "He is a natural business owner. I am so proud of his entrepreneurial spirit."

AP IMAGES/RICHARD HAMM

Women as Small-Business Owners

According to the latest 2013 data available from the SBA

- Women are 51 percent of the U.S. population, and according to the SBA, they owned at least 30 percent of all small businesses in 2012.
- Women already own 66 percent of the home-based businesses in this country, and the number of men in home-based businesses is growing rapidly.
- About 7.8 million women-owned businesses in the United States provide almost 7.6 million jobs and generate $1.2 trillion in sales.
- Women-owned businesses in the United States have proven that they are more successful; more than 40 percent have been in business for 12 years or more.
- Women-owned businesses are financially sound and credit-worthy, and their risk of failure is lower than average.
- Compared to other working women, self-employed women are older, better educated, and have more managerial experience.

- Just over one-half of small businesses are home based, and 91 percent have no employees. About 60 percent of home-based businesses are in service industries, 16 percent in construction, 14 percent in retail trade, and the rest in manufacturing, finance, transportation, communications, wholesaling, and other industries.[7]

Teenagers as Small-Business Owners

High-tech teen entrepreneurship is definitely exploding. "There's not a period in history where we've seen such a plethora of young entrepreneurs," comments Nancy F. Koehn, associate professor of business administration at Harvard Business School. Still, teen entrepreneurs face unique pressures in juggling their schoolwork, their social life, and their high-tech workload. Some ultimately quit school, whereas others quit or cut back on their business activities. Consider Brian Hendricks at Winston Churchill High School in Potomac, Maryland. He is the founder of StartUpPc and VB Solutions, Inc. StartUpPc, founded in 2001, sells custom-built computers and computer services for home users, home offices, small businesses, and students. Brian's services include design, installation of systems, training, networking, and on-site technical support. A year later, Brian founded VB Solutions, Inc., which develops and customizes websites and message boards. The firm sets up advertising contracts and counsels website owners on site improvements. The company has designed corporate ID kits, logos, and websites for clients from all over the world. Brian learned at a very young age that working for yourself is one of the best jobs available. According to Brian, a young entrepreneur must possess "the five P's of entrepreneurship"—planning, persistence, patience, people, and profit. Brian knows what it takes to be a successful entrepreneur. His accolades include Junior Achievement's "National Youth Entrepreneur of the Year" and SBA's "Young Entrepreneur of the Year" awards.[8]

In some people, the motivation to start a business develops slowly as they gain the knowledge and ability required for success as a business owner. Knowledge and ability—especially, management ability—are probably the most important factors involved. A new firm is very much built around the entrepreneur. The owner must be able to manage the firm's finances, its personnel (if there are any employees), and its day-to-day operations. He or she must handle sales, advertising, purchasing, pricing, and a variety of other business functions. The knowledge and ability to do so are acquired most often through experience working for other firms in the same area of business.

Why Some Entrepreneurs and Small Businesses Fail

Small businesses are prone to failure. Capital, management, and planning are the key ingredients in the survival of a small business, as well as the most common reasons for failure. Businesses can experience a number of money-related problems. It may take

TABLE 5-2 U.S. Business Start-ups, Closures, and Bankruptcies

	New	Closures	Bankruptcies
2011	781,000	752,000	47,806
2010	781,000	752,000	56,282
2009	518,500	680,716	60,837
2008	597,074	641,400	43,546
2007	668,395	592,410	28,322
2006	670,058	599,333	19,695
2005	644,122	565,745	39,201

NA = Not available.

Source: U.S. Small Business Administration, Office of Advocacy, *Small Business Economy 2012*, www.sba.gov/advocacy/849/6282 (accessed June 5, 2013).

several years before a business begins to show a profit. Entrepreneurs need to have not only the capital to open a business but also the money to operate it in its possibly lengthy start-up phase. One cash flow obstacle often leads to others. Moreover, a series of cash flow predicaments usually ends in a business failure. This scenario is played out all too often by small and not-so-small start-up Internet firms that fail to meet their financial backers' expectations and so are denied a second wave of investment dollars to continue their drive to establish a profitable online firm. According to Maureen Borzacchiello, co-owner of Creative Display Solutions, a trade show products company, "Big businesses such as Bear Stearns, Fannie Mae and Freddie Mac, and AIG can get bailouts, but small-business owners are on their own when times are tough and credit is tight."

Many entrepreneurs lack the management skills required to run a business. Money, time, personnel, and inventory all need to be managed effectively if a small business is to succeed. Starting a small business requires much more than optimism and a good idea.

Success and expansion sometimes lead to problems. Frequently, entrepreneurs with successful small businesses make the mistake of overexpansion. Fast growth often results in dramatic changes in a business. Thus, the entrepreneur must plan carefully and adjust competently to new and potentially disruptive situations.

Every day, and in every part of the country, people open new businesses. For example, 781,000 new businesses recently opened their doors. At the same time, however, 752,000 businesses closed their business and 47,806 businesses declared bankruptcy (see Table 5-2).[9] Although many fail, others represent well-conceived ideas developed by entrepreneurs who have the expertise, resources, and determination to make their businesses succeed. As these well-prepared entrepreneurs pursue their individual goals, our society benefits in many ways from their work and creativity. Billion-dollar companies such as Apple Computer, McDonald's Corporation, and Procter & Gamble are all examples of small businesses that expanded into industry giants.

Concept Check

✓ What kinds of factors encourage certain people to start new businesses?

✓ What are the major causes of small-business failure? Do these causes also apply to larger businesses?

Learning Objective

3 Assess the contributions of small businesses to our economy.

THE IMPORTANCE OF SMALL BUSINESSES IN OUR ECONOMY

This country's economic history abounds with stories of ambitious men and women who turned their ideas into business dynasties. The Ford Motor Company started as a one-man operation with an innovative method for industrial production. L.L.Bean, Inc., can trace its beginnings to a basement shop in Freeport, Maine. Both Xerox and Polaroid began as small firms with a better way to do a job. Indeed, every year since 1963, the president of the United States has proclaimed National Small Business Week to recognize the contributions of small businesses to the economic well-being of America.

Providing Technical Innovation

Invention and innovation are part of the foundations of our economy. The increases in productivity that have characterized the past 200 years of our history are all rooted in one principal source: new ways to do a job with less effort for less money. Studies show that the incidence of innovation among small-business workers is significantly higher than among workers in large businesses. Small firms produce two-and-a-half times as many innovations as large firms relative to the number of persons employed. In fact, small firms employ 43 percent of all high-tech workers such as scientists, engineers, and computer specialists. No wonder small firms produce 16 to 17 times more patents per employee than large patenting firms.

Consider Waymon Armstrong, the owner of a small business that uses computer simulations to help government and other clients prepare for and respond to natural disasters, medical emergencies, and combat. In presenting the 2010 National Small Business Person of the Year award, Karen Mills, Administrator of the U.S. Small Business Administration, said, "Waymon Armstrong is a perfect example of the innovation, inspiration, and determination that exemplify America's most successful entrepreneurs. He believed in his brainchild to the point where he deferred his own salary for three years to keep it afloat. When layoffs loomed for his staff after 9/11, their loyalty and belief in the company was so great that they were willing to work without pay for four months.

"Waymon's commitment to his employees and to his business—Engineering & Computer Simulations, Inc.—demonstrates the qualities that make small businesses such a powerful force for job creation in the American economy and in their local communities," said Mills. "It's the same qualities that will lead us to economic recovery. We are especially proud that his company benefited from two grants under SBA's Small Business Innovation and Research Program."[10]

According to the U.S. Office of Management and Budget, more than half the major technological advances of the 20th century originated with individual inventors and small companies. Even just a sampling of those innovations is remarkable:

- Air-conditioning
- Airplane
- Automatic transmission
- FM radio
- Heart valve
- Helicopter
- Instant camera
- Insulin
- Jet engine
- Penicillin
- Personal computer
- Power steering

Perhaps even more remarkable—and important—is that many of these inventions sparked major new U.S. industries or contributed to an established industry by adding some valuable service.

MICHAEL BRYANT/NEWSCOM

Providing technical innovation. Lutron Electronics invented a dimmer switch for CFL lighting; Allure energy has integrated home energy management with entertainment; Blu Homes took some cues from the "Transformers" franchise to build high-tech prefab homes; and Tremont Electric has built a wearable kinetic energy generator.

Providing Employment

Small firms traditionally have added more than their proportional share of new jobs to the economy. Seven out of the ten industries that added the most new jobs were small-business-dominated industries. Small businesses creating the most new jobs recently included business services, leisure and hospitality services, and special trade contractors. Small firms hire a larger proportion of employees who are younger workers, older workers, women, or workers who prefer to work part time.

Furthermore, small businesses provide 67 percent of workers with their first jobs and initial on-the-job training in basic skills. According to the SBA, small businesses represent 99.7 percent of all employers, employ more than 50 percent of the private workforce, and provide about two-thirds of the net new jobs added to our economy.[11] Small businesses thus contribute significantly to solving unemployment problems.

Providing Competition

Small businesses challenge larger, established firms in many ways, causing them to become more efficient and more responsive to consumer needs. A small business cannot, of course, compete with a large firm in all respects. However, a number of small firms, each competing in its own particular area and its own particular way, together have the desired competitive effect. Thus, several small janitorial companies together add up to reasonable competition for the no-longer-small ServiceMaster.

Filling Needs of Society and Other Businesses

Small firms also provide a variety of goods and services to each other and to much larger firms. Sears, Roebuck & Co. purchases merchandise from approximately 12,000 suppliers—and most of them are small businesses. General Motors relies on more than 32,000 companies for parts and supplies and depends on more than 11,000 independent dealers to sell its automobiles and trucks. Large firms generally buy parts and assemblies from smaller firms for one very good reason: It is less expensive than manufacturing the parts in their own factories. This lower cost eventually is reflected in the price that consumers pay for their products.

It is clear that small businesses are a vital part of our economy and that, as consumers and as members of the labor force, we all benefit enormously from their existence. Now let us look at the situation from the viewpoint of the owners of small businesses.

Learning Objective

4 Describe the advantages and disadvantages of operating a small business.

THE PROS AND CONS OF SMALLNESS

Do most owners of small businesses dream that their firms will grow into giant corporations—managed by professionals—while they serve only on the board of directors? Or would they rather stay small, in a firm where they have the opportunity (and the responsibility) to do everything that needs to be done? The answers depend on the personal characteristics and motivations of the individual owners. For many, the advantages of remaining small far outweigh the disadvantages.

Advantages of Small Business

Small-business owners with limited resources often must struggle to enter competitive new markets. They also have to deal with increasing international competition. However, they enjoy several unique advantages.

PERSONAL RELATIONSHIPS WITH CUSTOMERS AND EMPLOYEES For those who like dealing with people, small business is the place to be. The owners of retail shops get to know many of their customers by name and deal with them on a personal basis. Through such relationships, small-business owners often become involved in the social, cultural, and political life of the community.

Relationships between owner-managers and employees also tend to be closer in smaller businesses. In many cases, the owner is a friend and counselor as well as the boss.

These personal relationships provide an important business advantage. The personal service small businesses offer to customers is a major competitive weapon—one that larger firms try to match but often cannot. In addition, close relationships with employees often help the small-business owner to keep effective workers who might earn more with a larger firm.

ABILITY TO ADAPT TO CHANGE Being his or her own boss, the owner-manager of a small business does not need anyone's permission to adapt to change.

Getting personal. For those who like dealing with people, small business is the place to be. Here a business owner provides personalized service to a happy customer.

An owner may add or discontinue merchandise or services, change store hours, and experiment with various price strategies in response to changes in market conditions. And through personal relationships with customers, the owners of small businesses quickly become aware of changes in people's needs and interests, as well as in the activities of competing firms.

SIMPLIFIED RECORD KEEPING Many small firms need only a simple set of records. Record keeping might consist of a checkbook, a cash-receipts journal in which to record all sales, and a cash-disbursements journal in which to record all amounts paid out. Obviously, enough records must be kept to allow for producing and filing accurate tax returns.

INDEPENDENCE Small-business owners do not have to punch in and out, bid for vacation times, take orders from superiors, or worry about being fired or laid off. They are the masters of their own destinies—at least with regard to employment. For many people, this is the prime advantage of owning a small business.

OTHER ADVANTAGES According to the SBA, the most profitable companies in the United States are small firms that have been in business for more than ten years and employ fewer than 20 people. Small-business owners also enjoy all the advantages of sole proprietorships, which were discussed in Chapter 4. These include being able to keep all profits, the ease and low cost of going into business and (if necessary) going out of business, and being able to keep business information secret.

Disadvantages of Small Business

Personal contacts with customers, closer relationships with employees, being one's own boss, less cumbersome record-keeping chores, and independence are the bright side of small business. In contrast, the dark side reflects problems unique to these firms.

RISK OF FAILURE As we have noted, small businesses (especially new ones) run a heavy risk of going out of business—about 50 percent survive at least five years. Older, well-established small firms can be hit hard by a business recession mainly because they do not have the financial resources to weather an extended difficult period.

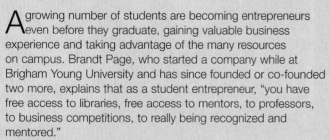

Students by Day, Entrepreneurs by Night

A growing number of students are becoming entrepreneurs even before they graduate, gaining valuable business experience and taking advantage of the many resources on campus. Brandt Page, who started a company while at Brigham Young University and has since founded or co-founded two more, explains that as a student entrepreneur, "you have free access to libraries, free access to mentors, to professors, to business competitions, to really being recognized and mentored."

Corinne Prevot had already earned $8,000 from her ski apparel business, Skida, before she entered college. After taking an entrepreneurship course as a freshman at Middlebury College, she rethought her approach to business. She researched competitors, looked at distribution, repriced her products, and formalized her branding. Now Skida's yearly sales are more than $100,000, and Prevot is ready to expand.

Partners Noah Chilton, Harry Kelley, Jackson Kroopf, and Misha Epstein like gourmet coffee, so they created a rolling cart to bring their favorite brews to classmates at Vassar through a business they called Tree City. The entrepreneurs buy from growers who use eco-friendly agricultural methods and they discuss good coffee while they brew a fresh cup for each customer. "Part of what we love about coffee is the way it brings people together," Kroopf says.

Sources: Based on information in Rebecca Palmer, "The College of Hard Knocks," *Utah Business*, January 11, 2012, www.utahbusiness.com; Joanna Hamer, "Tree City Serves Up Ethical Coffee, Enticing Conversation," *Miscellany News* (Poughkeepsie, New York), October 25, 2011, www.miscellanynews.com; Helen Coster, "All Star Student Entrepreneurs," *Forbes*, August 3, 2011, www.forbes.com; Brian Nichols, "Know-How for Hire," *New York Times Education Life*, November 6, 2011, p. 34.

business plan a carefully constructed guide for the person starting a business

LIMITED POTENTIAL Small businesses that survive do so with varying degrees of success. Many are simply the means of making a living for the owner and his or her family. The owner may have some technical skill—as a hair stylist or electrician, for example—and may have started a business to put this skill to work. Such a business is unlikely to grow into big business. In addition, employees' potential for advancement is limited.

LIMITED ABILITY TO RAISE CAPITAL Small businesses typically have a limited ability to obtain capital. Figure 5-2 shows that most small-business financing comes out of the owner's pocket. Personal loans from lending institutions provide only about one-fourth of the capital required by small businesses. About 50 percent of all new firms begin with less than $30,000 in total capital, according to Census Bureau and Federal Reserve surveys. In fact, almost 36 percent of new firms begin with less than $20,000, usually provided by the owner or family members and friends.[12] According to the SBA, average capital for starting a new business is $80,000.

Although every person who considers starting a small business should be aware of the hazards and pitfalls we have noted, a well-conceived business plan may help to avoid the risk of failure. The U.S. government is also dedicated to helping small businesses make it. It expresses this aim most actively through the SBA.

The Importance of a Business Plan

Lack of planning can be as deadly as lack of money to a new small business. Planning is important to any business, large or small, and never should be overlooked or taken lightly. A **business plan** is a carefully constructed guide for the person starting a business. Consider it as a tool with three basic purposes: communication, management, and planning. As a communication tool, a business plan serves as a concise document that potential investors can examine to see if they would like to invest or assist in financing a new venture. It shows whether a business has the potential to make a profit. As a management tool, the business plan helps to track, monitor, and evaluate the progress. The business plan is a living document; it is modified as the entrepreneur gains knowledge and experience. It also serves to establish time lines and milestones and allows comparison of growth projections against actual accomplishments. Finally, as a planning tool, the business plan guides a businessperson through the various phases of business. For example, the plan helps to identify obstacles to avoid and to establish alternatives. According to Robert Krummer, Jr., chairman of First Business Bank in Los Angeles, "The business plan is a necessity. If the person who wants to start a small business can't put a business plan together, he or she is in trouble."

Components of a Business Plan

Table 5-3 shows the 12 sections that a business plan should include. Each section is further explained at the end of each of the seven major parts in the text. The goal of each end-of-the-part exercise is to help a businessperson create his or her

FIGURE 5-2 Sources of Capital for Entrepreneurs

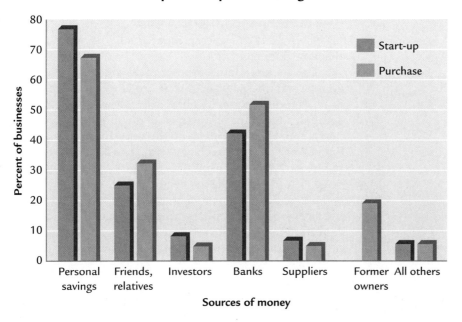

Small businesses get financing from various sources; the most important is personal savings.

Source: Data developed and provided by the National Federation of Independent Business Foundation and sponsored by the American Express Travel Related Services Company, Inc.

TABLE 5-3 Components of a Business Plan

1. *Introduction.* Basic information such as the name, address, and phone number of the business; the date the plan was issued; and a statement of confidentiality to keep important information away from potential competitors.

2. *Executive Summary.* A one- to two-page overview of the entire business plan, including a justification why the business will succeed.

3. *Benefits to the Community.* Information on how the business will have an impact on economic development, community development, and human development.

4. *Company and Industry.* The background of the company, choice of the legal business form, information on the products or services to be offered, and examination of the potential customers, current competitors, and the business's future.

5. *Management Team.* Discussion of skills, talents, and job descriptions of management team, managerial compensation, management training needs, and professional assistance requirements.

6. *Manufacturing and Operations Plan.* Discussion of facilities needed, space requirements, capital equipment, labor force, inventory control, and purchasing requirement.

7. *Labor Force.* Discussion of the quality of skilled workers available and the training, compensation, and motivation of workers.

8. *Marketing Plan.* Discussion of markets, market trends, competition, market share, pricing, promotion, distribution, and service policy.

9. *Financial Plan.* Summary of the investment needed, sales and cash flow forecasts, breakeven analysis, and sources of funding.

10. *Exit Strategy.* Discussion of a succession plan or going public. Who will take over the business?

11. *Critical Risks and Assumptions.* Evaluation of the weaknesses of the business and how the company plans to deal with these and other business problems.

12. *Appendix.* Supplementary information crucial to the plan, such as résumés of owners and principal managers, advertising samples, organization chart, and any related information.

Source: From HATTEN, *Small Business Management*, 5E. © 2012 Cengage Learning.

A business plan is a great idea!

Although writing a business plan won't guarantee your success, it will help you think through many of the issues that can trip up entrepreneurs. And if you work for a big company, you may find yourself writing a kind of business plan for a product or project.

© YEKO PHOTO STUDIO/SHUTTERSTOCK.COM

own business plan. When constructing a business plan, the businessperson should strive to keep it easy to read, uncluttered, and complete. Like other busy executives, officials of financial institutions do not have the time to wade through pages of extraneous data. The business plan should answer the four questions banking officials and investors are most interested in: (1) What exactly is the nature and mission of the new venture? (2) Why is this new enterprise a good idea? (3) What are the businessperson's goals? (4) How much will the new venture cost?

The great amount of time and consideration that should go into creating a business plan probably will end up saving time later. For example, Sharon Burch, who was running a computer software business while earning a degree in business administration, had to write a business plan as part of one of her courses. Burch has said, "I wish I'd taken the class before I started my business. I see a lot of things I could have done differently. But it has helped me since because I've been using the business plan as a guide for my business." Table 5-4 provides a business plan checklist. Accuracy and realistic expectations are crucial to an effective business plan. It is unethical to deceive loan officers, and it is unwise to deceive yourself.

TABLE 5-4 Business Plan Checklist

1. Does the executive summary grab the reader's attention and highlight the major points of the business plan?

2. Does the business-concept section clearly describe the purpose of the business, the customers, the value proposition, and the distribution channel and convey a compelling story?

3. Do the industry and market analyses support acceptance and demand for the business concept in the marketplace and define a first customer in depth?

4. Does the management team plan persuade the reader that the team could implement the business concept successfully? Does it assure the reader that an effective infrastructure is in place to facilitate the goals and operations of the company?

5. Does the product/service plan clearly provide details on the status of the product, the time line for completion, and the intellectual property that will be acquired?

6. Does the operations plan prove that the product or service could be produced and distributed efficiently and effectively?

7. Does the marketing plan successfully demonstrate how the company will create customer awareness in the target market and deliver the benefit to the customer?

8. Does the financial plan convince the reader that the business model is sustainable—that it will provide a superior return on investment for the investor and sufficient cash flow to repay loans to potential lenders?

9. Does the growth plan convince the reader that the company has long-term growth potential and spin-off products and services?

10. Does the contingency and exit-strategy plan convince the reader that the risk associated with this venture can be mediated? Is there an exit strategy in place for investors?

Source: From ALLEN, *Launching New Ventures*, 6E. © 2012 Cengage Learning.

Concept Check

✓ What are the major advantages and disadvantages of smallness in business?

✓ What are the major components of a business plan? Why should an individual develop a business plan?

THE SMALL BUSINESS ADMINISTRATION

Learning Objective

5 Explain how the Small Business Administration helps small businesses.

The **Small Business Administration (SBA)**, created by Congress in 1953, is a governmental agency that assists, counsels, and protects the interests of small businesses in the United States. It helps people get into business and stay in business. The agency provides assistance to owners and managers of prospective, new, and established small businesses. Through more than 1,000 offices and resource centers throughout the nation, the SBA provides both financial assistance and management counseling. Recently, the SBA provided training, technical assistance, and education to more than 3 million small businesses. It helps small firms to bid for and obtain government contracts, and it helps them to prepare to enter foreign markets.

Small Business Administration (SBA) a governmental agency that assists, counsels, and protects the interests of small businesses in the United States

SBA Management Assistance

Statistics show that most failures in small business are related to poor management. For this reason, the SBA places special emphasis on improving the management ability of the owners and managers of small businesses. The SBA's Management Assistance Program is extensive and diversified. It includes free individual counseling, courses, conferences, workshops, and a wide range of publications. Recently, the SBA provided management and technical assistance to nearly 1 million small businesses through its 900 Small Business Development Centers and 13,000 volunteers from the Service Corps of Retired Executives.[13]

MANAGEMENT COURSES AND WORKSHOPS The management courses offered by the SBA cover all the functions, duties, and roles of managers. Instructors may be teachers from local colleges and universities or other professionals, such as management consultants, bankers, lawyers, and accountants. Fees for these courses are quite low. The most popular such course is a general survey of eight to ten different areas of business management. In follow-up studies, businesspeople may concentrate in depth on one or more of these areas depending on their particular strengths and weaknesses. The SBA occasionally offers one-day conferences. These conferences are aimed at keeping owner-managers up-to-date on new management developments, tax laws, and the like. The Small Business Training Network (SBTN) is an online training network consisting of 23 SBA-run courses, workshops, and resources. Some of the most requested courses include Entrepreneurship, Starting and Managing Your Own Business, Developing a Business Plan, Managing the Digital Enterprise, Identify Your Target Market, and Analyze Profitability. Find out more at www.sba.gov/training. Recently, more than 240,000 small-business owners benefited from SBA's free online business courses.

SCORE The **Service Corps of Retired Executives (SCORE)**, Counselors to America's Small Business, created in 1964, is a group of more than 13,000 retired and active businesspeople, including more than 2,000 women who volunteer their services to small businesses through the SBA. The collective experience of SCORE volunteers spans the full range of American enterprise. These volunteers have worked for such notable companies as Eastman Kodak, General Electric, IBM, and Procter & Gamble. Experts in areas of accounting, finance, marketing, engineering, and retailing provide counseling and mentoring to entrepreneurs.

Service Corps of Retired Executives (SCORE) a group of businesspeople who volunteer their services to small businesses through the SBA

A small-business owner who has a particular problem can request free counseling from SCORE. An assigned counselor visits the owner in his or her establishment and, through careful observation, analyzes the business situation and the problem. If the problem is complex, the counselor may call on other volunteer experts to assist. Finally, the counselor offers a plan for solving the problem and helping the owner through the critical period.

Minority-owned businesses. Are you ready to start your business, but don't know where to start or what opportunities are available to minority groups? The SBA provides information on federal government programs and services that help members of the minority groups start their own businesses.

Consider the plight of Elizabeth Halvorsen, a mystery writer from Minneapolis. Her husband had built up the family advertising and graphic arts firm for 17 years when he was called in 1991 to serve in the Persian Gulf War. The only one left behind to run the business was Mrs. Halvorsen, who admittedly had no business experience. Enter SCORE. With a SCORE management expert at her side, she kept the business on track. Recently, SCORE volunteers served more than 523,800 small-business people like Mrs. Halvorsen through its 348 offices. Since its inception, SCORE has assisted more than 10 million small-business people with online and face-to-face small business counseling.[14]

Help for Minority-Owned Small Businesses

Americans who are members of minority groups have had difficulty entering the nation's economic mainstream. Raising money is a nagging problem for minority business owners, who also may lack adequate training. Members of minority groups are, of course, eligible for all SBA programs, but the SBA makes a special effort to assist those minority groups who want to start small businesses or expand existing ones. For example, the Minority Business Development Agency awards grants to develop and increase business opportunities for members of racial and ethnic minorities.

Helping women become entrepreneurs is also a special goal of the SBA. Emily Harrington, one of nine children, was born in Manila, the Philippines. She arrived in the United States in 1972 as a foreign-exchange student. Convinced that there was a market for hard-working, dedicated minorities and women, she launched Qualified Resources, Inc., a professional staffing services firm. *Inc.* magazine selected her firm as one of "America's Fastest Growing Private Companies" just six years later. Harrington credits the SBA with giving her the technical support that made her first loan possible. Finding a SCORE counselor to work directly with her, she refined her business plan until she got a bank loan. Before contacting the SBA, Harrington was turned down for business loans "by all the banks I approached," even though she worked as a manager of loan credit and collection for a bank. Later, Emily Harrington was SBA's winner of the local, regional, and national Small Business Entrepreneurial Success Award for Rhode Island, the New England region, and the nation! For several years in a row, Qualified Resources, Inc., was named one of the fastest growing private companies in Rhode Island. Now with more than 100 Women's Business Centers, entrepreneurs like Harrington can receive training and technical assistance, access to credit and capital, federal contracts, and international markets. The SBA's Online Women's Business Center (www.sba.gov/aboutsba/sbaprograms/onlinewbc/index.html) is a state-of-the-art Internet site to help women expand their businesses. This free, interactive website offers women information about business principles and practices, management techniques, networking, industry news, market research and technology training, online counseling, and hundreds of links to other sites, as well as information about the many SBA services and resources available to them.

small-business institutes (SBIs) groups of senior and graduate students in business administration who provide management counseling to small businesses

SMALL-BUSINESS INSTITUTES small-business institutes (SBIs), created in 1972, are groups of senior and graduate students in business administration who provide management counseling to small businesses. SBIs have been set up on more than 520 college campuses as another way to help business owners. The students work in small groups guided by faculty advisers and SBA management-assistance experts. Like SCORE volunteers, they analyze and help solve the problems of small-business owners at their business establishments.

SMALL-BUSINESS DEVELOPMENT CENTERS small-business development centers (SBDCs) are university-based groups that provide individual counseling and practical training to owners of small businesses. SBDCs draw from the resources of local, state, and federal governments, private businesses, and universities. These groups can provide managerial and technical help, data from research studies, and other types of specialized assistance of value to small businesses. In 2012, there were more than 900 SBDC locations, primarily at colleges and universities, assisting people such as Kathleen DuBois. After scribbling a list of her abilities and the names of potential clients on a napkin in a local restaurant, Kathleen DuBois decided to start her own marketing firm. Beth Thornton launched her engineering firm after a discussion with a colleague in the ladies room of the Marriott. When Richard Shell was laid off after 20 years of service with Nisource (Columbia Gas), he searched the Internet tirelessly before finding the right franchise option. Introduced by mutual friends, Jim Bostic and Denver McMillion quickly connected, built a high level of trust, and combined their diverse professional backgrounds to form a manufacturing company. Although these entrepreneurs took different routes in starting their new businesses in West Virginia, all of them turned to the West Virginia Small Business Development Center for the technical assistance to make their dreams become a reality.

SBA PUBLICATIONS The SBA issues management, marketing, and technical publications dealing with hundreds of topics of interest to present and prospective managers of small firms. Most of these publications are available from the SBA free of charge. Others can be obtained for a small fee from the U.S. Government Printing Office.

SBA Financial Assistance

Small businesses seem to be constantly in need of money. An owner may have enough capital to start and operate the business. But then he or she may require more money to finance increased operations during peak selling seasons, to pay for required pollution control equipment, to finance an expansion, or to mop up after a natural disaster such as a flood or a terrorist attack. For example, the Supplemental Terrorist Activity Relief program has made more than $3.7 billion in loans to 8,202 small businesses harmed or disrupted by the September 11 terrorist attacks. In early 2013, 90 days after Hurricane Sandy hit the Northeast, the SBA guaranteed over $1 billion loans to more than 16,800 businesses, homeowners, and renters.[15] Earlier, the SBA offered economic injury loans to fishing and fishing-dependent small businesses as a result of the Deepwater BP spill that shut down commercial and recreational fishing waters. According to the SBA Administrator, "SBA remains committed to taking every step to help small businesses deal with the financial challenges they are facing as a result of the Deepwater BP oil spill."[16] The SBA offers special financial-assistance programs that cover all these situations. However, its primary financial function is to guarantee loans to eligible businesses.

REGULAR BUSINESS LOANS Most of the SBA's business loans are actually made by private lenders such as banks, but repayment is partially guaranteed by the agency. That is, the SBA may guarantee that it will repay the lender up to 90 percent of the loan if the borrowing firm cannot repay it. Guaranteed loans approved on or after October 1, 2002, may be as large as $2.0 million (this loan limit may be increased in the future). The average size of an SBA-guaranteed business loan is about $300,000, and its average duration is about eight years.

Concept Check

✓ Identify five ways in which the SBA provides management assistance to small businesses.

✓ Identify two ways in which the SBA provides financial assistance to small businesses.

✓ Why does the SBA concentrate on providing management and financial assistance to small business?

✓ What is venture capital? How does the SBA help small businesses to obtain it?

Learning Objective

6 Explain the concept and types of franchising.

SMALL-BUSINESS INVESTMENT COMPANIES Venture capital is money that is invested in small (and sometimes struggling) firms that have the potential to become very successful. In many cases, only a lack of capital keeps these firms from rapid and solid growth. The people who invest in such firms expect that their investments will grow with the firms and become quite profitable.

The popularity of these investments has increased over the past 30 years, but most small firms still have difficulty obtaining venture capital. To help such businesses, the SBA licenses, regulates, and provides financial assistance to **small-business investment companies (SBICs)**.

An SBIC is a privately owned firm that provides venture capital to small enterprises that meet its investment standards. Such firms as America Online, Apple Computer, Costco, Jenny Craig, Federal Express, Compaq Computer, Intel Corporation, Outback Steakhouse, and Staples, Inc., all were financed through SBICs during their initial growth period. More than 300 SBICs are intended to be profit-making organizations. The aid that SBA offers allows them to invest in small businesses that otherwise would not attract venture capital. Since Congress created the program in 1958, SBICs have financed more than 107,000 small businesses for a total of about $60 billion. In 2012, SBICs benefited 1,339 businesses, and 34 percent of these firms were owned by women or other minorities.[17]

We have discussed the importance of the small-business segment of our economy. We have weighed the advantages and drawbacks of operating a small business as compared with a large one. But is there a way to achieve the best of both worlds? Can one preserve one's independence as a business owner and still enjoy some of the benefits of "bigness"? Let's take a close look at franchising.

FRANCHISING

A **franchise** is a license to operate an individually owned business as if it were part of a chain of outlets or stores. Often, the business itself is also called a *franchise*. Among the most familiar franchises are McDonald's, H&R Block, AAMCO Transmissions, GNC (General Nutrition Centers), and Dairy Queen. Many other franchises carry familiar names; this method of doing business has become very popular in the last 55 years or so. It is an attractive means of starting and operating a small business.

What Is Franchising?

Franchising is the actual granting of a franchise. A **franchisor** is an individual or organization granting a franchise. A **franchisee** is a person or organization purchasing a franchise. The franchisor supplies a known and advertised business name, management skills, the required training and materials, and a method of doing business. The franchisee supplies labor and capital, operates the franchised business, and agrees to abide by the provisions of the franchise agreement. Table 5-5 lists the basic franchisee rights and obligations that would be covered in a typical franchise agreement.

Types of Franchising

Franchising arrangements fall into three general categories. In the first approach, a manufacturer authorizes a number of retail stores to sell a certain brand-name item. This type of franchising arrangement, one of the oldest, is prevalent in sales of passenger cars and trucks, farm equipment, shoes, paint, earth-moving equipment, and petroleum. About 90 percent of all gasoline is sold through franchised, independent retail service stations, and franchised dealers handle virtually all sales of new cars and trucks. In the second type of franchising arrangement, a

TABLE 5-5 Basic Rights and Obligations Delineated in a Franchise Agreement

Franchisee rights include:

1. use of trademarks, trade names, and patents of the franchisor;

2. use of the brand image and the design and decor of the premises developed by the franchisor;

3. use of the franchisor's secret methods;

4. use of the franchisor's copyrighted materials;

5. use of recipes, formulae, specifications, processes, and methods of manufacture developed by the franchisor;

6. conducting the franchised business upon or from the agreed premises strictly in accordance with the franchisor's methods and subject to the franchisor's directions;

7. guidelines established by the franchisor regarding exclusive territorial rights; and

8. rights to obtain supplies from nominated suppliers at special prices.

Franchisee obligations include:

1. to carry on the business franchised and no other business upon the approved and nominated premises;

2. to observe certain minimum operating hours;

3. to pay a franchise fee;

4. to follow the accounting system laid down by the franchisor;

5. not to advertise without prior approval of the advertisements by the franchisor;

6. to use and display such point-of-sale advertising materials as the franchisor stipulates;

7. to maintain the premises in good, clean, and sanitary condition and to redecorate when required to do so by the franchisor;

8. to maintain the widest possible insurance coverage;

9. to permit the franchisor's staff to enter the premises to inspect and see if the franchisor's standards are being maintained;

10. to purchase goods or products from the franchisor or his designated suppliers;

11. to train the staff in the franchisor's methods to ensure that they are neatly and appropriately clothed; and

12. not to assign the franchise contract without the franchisor's consent.

Source: Excerpted from the SBA's "Is Franchising for Me?" www.sba.gov (accessed August 26, 2013).

producer licenses distributors to sell a given product to retailers. This arrangement is common in the soft drink industry. Most national manufacturers of soft drink syrups—The Coca-Cola Company, Dr. Pepper/Seven-Up Companies, PepsiCo, Royal Crown Companies, Inc.—franchise independent bottlers who then serve retailers. In a third form of franchising, a franchisor supplies brand names, techniques, or other services instead of a complete product. Although the franchisor may provide certain production and distribution services, its primary role is the careful development and control of marketing strategies. This approach to franchising, which is the most typical today, is used by Avis, Hampton Hotels, 7-Eleven Inc., Anytime Fitness, Denny's Inc., Pizza Hut Inc., McDonald's, and SUBWAY, to name but a few.

Concept Check

✓ Explain the relationships among a franchise, the franchisor, and the franchisee.

✓ Describe the three general categories of franchising arrangements.

Learning Objective

7 Analyze the growth of franchising and its advantages and disadvantages.

THE GROWTH OF FRANCHISING

Franchising, which began in the United States around the time of the Civil War, was used originally by large firms, such as the Singer Sewing Company, to distribute their products. Franchising has been increasing steadily in popularity since the early 1900s, primarily for filling stations and car dealerships; however, this retailing strategy has experienced enormous growth since the mid-1970s. The franchise proliferation generally has paralleled the expansion of the fast-food industry.

Of course, franchising is not limited to fast foods. Hair salons, tanning parlors, and dentists and lawyers are expected to participate in franchising arrangements in growing numbers. Franchised health clubs, pest exterminators, and campgrounds are already widespread, as are franchised tax preparers and travel agencies. The real estate industry also has experienced a rapid increase in franchising.

Also, franchising is attracting more women and minority business owners in the United States than ever before. One reason is that special outreach programs designed to encourage franchisee diversity have developed. Consider Angela Trammel, a young mother of two. She had been laid off from her job at the Marriott after 9/11. Since she was a member of a Curves Fitness Center and liked the concept of empowering women to become physically fit, she began researching the cost of purchasing a Curves franchise and ways to finance the business. "I was online looking for financing, and I linked to Enterprise Development Group in Washington, DC. I knew that they had diverse clients." The cost for the franchise was $19,500, but it took $60,000 to open the doors to her fitness center. "Applying for a loan to start the business was much harder than buying a house," said Trammel. Just three years later, Angela and her husband, Ernest, own three Curves Fitness Centers with 12 employees. Recently, since giving birth to her third child, she has found the financial freedom and flexibility needed to care for her busy family. In fact, within a three-year period, the Trammels grew their annual household income from $80,000 to $250,000.[18] Franchisors such as Wendy's, McDonald's, Burger King, and Church's Chicken all have special corporate programs to attract minority and women franchisees. Just as important, successful women and minority franchisees are willing to get involved by offering advice and guidance to new franchisees.

Getting ad value from your car. Joe McGuinness founded Signs By Tomorrow in 1986. Today, with over 180 locations nationwide, the Columbia, Maryland-based franchise company turns hundreds of autos into rolling billboards each year, much like this one for 1-800-GOT-JUNK. Some companies may compensate your gas costs to use your car.

AP IMAGES/PRNEWSFOTO

Herman Petty, the first African-American McDonald's franchisee, remembers that the company provided a great deal of help while he worked to establish his first units. In turn, Petty traveled to help other black franchisees, and he invited new franchisees to gain hands-on experience in his Chicago restaurants before starting their own establishments. In 1972, Petty also organized a support group, the National Black McDonald's Operators Association, to help black franchisees in other areas. Today, members of this association own nearly 1,300 McDonald's restaurants throughout the United States, South Africa, and the Caribbean with annual sales of more than $2.7 billion. "By staying together, we will realize the dream that our forefathers envisioned: an organization of successful African-American entrepreneurs who did not forget their humble beginnings," says Roland G. Parrish, the McDonald's franchisee who leads the group.

Dual-branded franchises, in which two franchisors offer their products together, are a new small-business trend. For example, in 1993, pleased with the success of its first co-branded restaurant with Texaco in Beebe, Arkansas, McDonald's now has more than 400 co-branded restaurants in the United States. Also, an agreement between franchisors Doctor's Associates, Inc., and TCBY Enterprises, Inc., now allows franchisees to sell SUBWAY sandwiches and TCBY yogurt in the same establishment.

Are Franchises Successful?

Franchising is designed to provide a tested formula for success, along with ongoing advice and training. The success rate for businesses owned and operated by franchisees is significantly higher than the success rate for other independently owned small businesses. In a recent nationwide Gallup poll of 944 franchise owners, 94 percent of franchisees indicated that they were very or somewhat successful, only 5 percent believed that they were very unsuccessful or somewhat unsuccessful, and 1 percent did not know. Despite these impressive statistics, franchising is not a guarantee of success for either franchisees or franchisors. Too rapid expansion, inadequate capital or management skills, and a host of other problems can cause failure for both franchisee and franchisor. Thus, for example, the Dizzy Dean's Beef and Burger franchise is no longer in business. Timothy Bates, a Wayne State University economist, warns, "Despite the hype that franchising is the safest way to go when starting a new business, the research just doesn't bear that out." Just consider Boston Chicken, which once had more than 1,200 restaurants before declaring bankruptcy in 1998.

Advantages of Franchising

Franchising plays a vital role in our economy and soon may become the dominant form of retailing. Why? Because franchising offers advantages to both the franchisor and the franchisee.

TO THE FRANCHISOR The franchisor gains fast and well-controlled distribution of its products without incurring the high cost of constructing and operating its own outlets. The franchisor thus has more capital available to expand production and to use for advertising. At the same time, it can ensure, through the franchise agreement, that outlets are maintained and operated according to its own standards.

The franchisor also benefits from the fact that the franchisee—a sole proprietor in most cases—is likely to be very highly motivated to succeed. The success of the franchise means more sales, which translate into higher royalties for the franchisor.

TO THE FRANCHISEE The franchisee gets the opportunity to start a business with limited capital and to make use of the business experience of others. Moreover, an outlet with a nationally advertised name, such as RadioShack, McDonald's, or Century 21, has guaranteed customers as soon as it opens.

If business problems arise, the franchisor gives the franchisee guidance and advice. This counseling is primarily responsible for the very high degree of success enjoyed by franchises. In most cases, the franchisee does not pay for such help.

The franchisee also receives materials to use in local advertising and can take part in national promotional campaigns sponsored by the franchisor. McDonald's and its franchisees, for example, constitute one of the nation's top 20 purchasers of advertising. Finally, the franchisee may be able to minimize the cost of advertising, supplies, and various business necessities by purchasing them in cooperation with other franchisees.

The growth of franchising. Franchising is designed to provide a tested formula for success, along with ongoing advice and training. The franchisor, such as Wendy's or Burger King, supplies a known and advertised business name, management skills, the required training and materials, and a method of doing business. Franchising, however, is not a guarantee of success for either franchisees or franchisors.

Disadvantages of Franchising

The main disadvantage of franchising affects the franchisee, and it arises because the franchisor retains a great deal of control. The franchisor's contract can dictate every aspect of the business: decor, design of employee uniforms, types of signs, and all the details of business operations. All Burger King French fries taste the same because all Burger King franchisees have to make them the same way.

Contract disputes are the cause of many lawsuits. For example, Rekha Gabhawala, a Dunkin' Donuts franchisee in Milwaukee, alleged that the franchisor was forcing her out of business so that the company could profit by reselling the downtown franchise to someone else; the company, on the other hand, alleged that Gabhawala breached the contract by not running the business according to company standards. In another case, Dunkin' Donuts sued Chris Romanias, its franchisee in Pennsylvania, alleging that Romanias intentionally underreported gross sales to the company. Romanias, on the other hand, alleged that Dunkin' Donuts, Inc., breached the contract because it failed to provide assistance in operating the franchise. Other franchisees claim that contracts are unfairly tilted toward the franchisors. Yet others have charged that they lost their franchise and investment because their franchisor would not approve the sale of the business when they found a buyer.

To arbitrate disputes between franchisors and franchisees, the National Franchise Mediation Program was established in 1993 by 30 member firms, including Burger King Corporation, McDonald's Corporation, and Wendy's International, Inc. Negotiators have since resolved numerous cases through mediation. Recently, Carl's Jr. brought in one of its largest franchisees to help set its system straight, making most franchisees happy for the first time in years. The program also helped PepsiCo settle a long-term contract dispute and renegotiate its franchise agreements.

Because disagreements between franchisors and franchisees have increased in recent years, many franchisees have been demanding government regulation of franchising. In 1997, to avoid government regulation, some of the largest franchisors proposed a new self-policing plan to the Federal Trade Commission.

Franchise holders pay for their security, usually with a one-time franchise fee and continuing royalty and advertising fees, collected as a percentage of sales. A SUBWAY franchisee pays an initial franchise fee of $15,000 and an annual fee of 8 percent of gross sales. In some fields, franchise agreements are not uniform. One franchisee may pay more than another for the same services.

Even success can cause problems. Sometimes a franchise is so successful that the franchisor opens its own outlet nearby, in direct competition—although franchisees

may fight back. For example, a court recently ruled that Burger King could not enter into direct competition with the franchisee because the contract was not specific on the issue. A spokesperson for one franchisor contends that the company "gives no geographical protection" to its franchise holders and thus is free to move in on them. Franchise operators work hard. They often put in 10- and 12-hour days, six days a week. The International Franchise Association advises prospective franchise purchasers to investigate before investing and to approach buying a franchise cautiously. Franchises vary widely in approach as well as in products. Some, such as Dunkin' Donuts and Baskin-Robbins, demand long hours. Others, such as Great Clips and SportClips hair salons, are more appropriate for those who do not want to spend many hours at their stores.

GLOBAL PERSPECTIVES IN SMALL BUSINESS

For small American businesses, the world is becoming smaller. National and international economies are growing more and more interdependent as political leadership and national economic directions change and trade barriers diminish or disappear. Globalization and instant worldwide communications are rapidly shrinking distances at the same time that they are expanding business opportunities. According to a recent study, the Internet is increasingly important to small-business strategic thinking, with more than 50 percent of those surveyed indicating that the Internet represented their most favored strategy for growth. This was more than double the next-favored choice, strategic alliances reflecting the opportunity to reach both global and domestic customers. The Internet and online payment systems enable even very small businesses to serve international customers. In fact, technology now gives small businesses the leverage and power to reach markets that were once limited solely to large corporations. According to the U.S. Commercial Service, "More than 70 percent of the world's purchasing power is outside of the United States and over the next five years, 85 percent of the world's economic growth will be overseas."[19]

The SBA offers help to the nation's small-business owners who want to enter the world markets. The SBA's efforts include counseling small firms on how and where to market overseas, matching U.S. small-business executives with potential overseas customers, and helping exporters to secure financing. The agency brings small U.S. firms into direct contact with potential overseas buyers and partners. The SBA International Trade Loan program provides guarantees of up to $5 million in loans to small-business owners. These loans help small firms in expanding or developing new export markets. The U.S. Commercial Service, a Commerce Department division, aids small- and medium-sized businesses in selling overseas. The division's global network includes more than 100 offices in the United States and 151 others in 75 countries around the world.[20]

Consider Daniel J. Nanigian, president of Nanmac Corporation in Framingham, Massachusetts. This company manufactures temperature sensors used in a wide range of industrial applications. With an export strategy aimed at growing revenues in diverse foreign markets including China, the Nanmac Corporation experienced explosive growth in 2009. The company nearly doubled its sales from $2.7 million in 2008 to $5.1 million in 2009. The company's international sales, at $300,000 in 2004, reached $700,000 in 2009 and $1.7 million in 2010. Its administrative, sales, and manufacturing employees have increased by 80 percent.

The company has a strong presence in China and is expanding in other markets, as well, including Latin America, Singapore, and Russia. Under Nanigian's guidance, the company has developed creative solutions and partnerships to help maximize its presence internationally. As part of its China strategy, Nanmac partners with distributors, recruits European and in-country sales representatives, uses a localized Chinese website, and relies for advice on the export assistance programs of the Massachusetts Small Business Development Center Network's Massachusetts Export Center. The strategy, along with travel to China to conduct technical training seminars and attend trade shows and technical conferences, has helped to grow Nanmac's Chinese client list from 1 in 2003 to more than 30 accounts today. Mr. Nanigian received SBA's Small Business Exporter of the Year Award.[21]

International trade will become more important to small-business owners as they face unique challenges in the new century. Small businesses, which are expected to remain the dominant form of organization in this country, must be prepared to adapt to significant demographic and economic changes in the world marketplace.

This chapter ends our discussion of American business today. From here on, we shall be looking closely at various aspects of business operations. We begin, in the next chapter, with a discussion of management—what management is, what managers do, and how they work to coordinate the basic economic resources within a business organization.

Concept Check

✓ What does the franchisor receive in a franchising agreement? What does the franchisee receive? What does each provide?

✓ Cite one major benefit of franchising for the franchisor. Cite one major benefit of franchising for the franchisee.

✓ How does the SBA help small business-owners who want to enter the world markets?

Summary

1 **Define what a small business is and recognize the fields in which small businesses are concentrated.**

A small business is one that is independently owned and operated for profit and is not dominant in its field. There are about 27.9 million businesses in this country, and 99.7 percent of them are small businesses. Small businesses employ more than half the nation's workforce. About 69 percent of small businesses survive at least two years and about 50 percent survive at least five years. More than half of all small businesses are in retailing and services.

2 **Identify the people who start small businesses and the reasons why some succeed and many fail.**

Such personal characteristics as independence, desire to create a new enterprise, and willingness to accept a challenge may encourage individuals to start small businesses. Various external circumstances, such as special expertise or even the loss of a job, also can supply the motivation to strike out on one's own. Poor planning and lack of capital and management experience are the major causes of small-business failures.

3 **Assess the contributions of small businesses to our economy.**

Small businesses have been responsible for a wide variety of inventions and innovations, some of which have given rise to new industries. Historically, small businesses have created the bulk of the nation's new jobs. Further, they have mounted effective competition to larger firms. They provide things that society needs, act as suppliers to larger firms, and serve as customers of other businesses, both large and small.

4 **Describe the advantages and disadvantages of operating a small business.**

The advantages of smallness in business include the opportunity to establish personal relationships with customers and employees, the ability to adapt to changes quickly, independence, and simplified record keeping. The major disadvantages are the high risk of failure, the limited potential for growth, and the limited ability to raise capital.

5 **Explain how the Small Business Administration helps small businesses.**

The Small Business Administration (SBA) was created in 1953 to assist and counsel the nation's millions of small-business owners. The SBA offers management courses and workshops; managerial help, including one-to-one counseling through SCORE; various publications; and financial assistance through guaranteed loans and SBICs. It places special emphasis on aid to minority-owned businesses, including those owned by women.

6 **Explain the concept and types of franchising.**

A franchise is a license to operate an individually owned business as though it were part of a chain. The franchisor provides a known business name, management skills, a method of doing business, and the training and required materials. The franchisee contributes labor and capital, operates the franchised business, and agrees to abide by the provisions of the franchise agreement. There are three major categories of franchise agreements.

7 **Analyze the growth of franchising and its advantages and disadvantages.**

Franchising has grown tremendously since the mid-1970s. The franchisor's major advantage in franchising is fast and well-controlled distribution of products with minimal capital outlay. In return, the franchisee has the opportunity to open a business with limited capital, to make use of the business experience of others, and to sell to an existing clientele. For this, the franchisee usually must pay both an initial franchise fee and a continuing royalty based on sales. He or she also must follow the dictates of the franchise with regard to operation of the business.

Worldwide business opportunities are expanding for small businesses. The SBA assists small-business owners in penetrating foreign markets. The next century will present unique challenges and opportunities for small-business owners.

Key Terms

You should now be able to define and give an example relevant to each of the following terms:

small business (128)
business plan (138)
Small Business
    Administration (SBA)
    (141)

Service Corps of Retired
    Executives (SCORE)
    (141)
small-business institutes
    (SBIs) (142)

small-business development
    centers (SBDCs) (143)
venture capital (144)
small-business investment
    companies (SBICs) (144)

franchise (144)
franchising (144)
franchisor (144)
franchisee (144)

Discussion Questions

1. Most people who start small businesses are aware of the high failure rate and the reasons for it. Why, then, do some take no steps to protect their firms from failure? What steps should they take?
2. Are the so-called advantages of small business really advantages? Wouldn't every small-business owner like his or her business to grow into a large firm?
3. Do average citizens benefit from the activities of the SBA, or is the SBA just another way to spend our tax money?
4. Would you rather own your own business independently or become a franchisee? Why?

Test Yourself

Matching Questions

1. _____ A carefully constructed guide for the person starting a business.
2. _____ A group of retired and active business people who volunteer their services to small businesses through the SBA.
3. _____ A government agency that assists, counsels, and protects the interests of small businesses in the United States.
4. _____ Money that is invested in small (and sometimes struggling) firms that have the potential to become very successful.
5. _____ Group of senior and graduate students in business administration who provide management counseling to small businesses.
6. _____ A business that is independently owned and operated for profit and is not dominant in its field.
7. _____ A person or organization purchasing a franchise.

8. _____ A license to operate an individually owned business as though it were a part of a chain of outlets or stores.
9. _____ The actual granting of a franchise.
10. _____ An individual or organization granting a franchise.

a. venture capital
b. franchisee
c. joint venture
d. Small-Business Institutes (SBIs)
e. SCORE
f. small business
g. franchise
h. strategic alliance
i. business plan
j. franchising
k. SBA
l. franchisor

True False Questions

11. **T F** The SBA has defined a small business as one independently owned, operated for profit, and not dominant in its field.
12. **T F** The various types of businesses attracting small business are generally grouped into service industries, distribution industries, and financial industries.
13. **T F** Small businesses are generally managed by professional managers.
14. **T F** Small firms have traditionally added more than their proportional share of new jobs to the economy.
15. **T F** Economically, the U.S government is not concerned with whether or not small businesses make it.
16. **T F** SCORE is a group of active business executives offering their services to small businesses for a fee.
17. **T F** A small-business investment company (SBIC) is a government agency that provides venture capital to small enterprises.

18. **T F** The purchaser of a franchise is called the franchisor.

19. **T F** An agreement between two franchisors in which the two franchisors offer their products together is called double franchising.

20. **T F** International trade will become more important to small-business owners in the new century.

Multiple-Choice Questions

21. _____ What is the primary reason that so many new businesses fail?
    a. Owner does not work hard enough
    b. Mismanagement resulting from lack of business know-how
    c. Low employee quality for new businesses
    d. Lack of brand-name recognition
    e. Inability to compete with well-established brand names

22. _____ Businesses such as flower shops, restaurants, bed and breakfasts, and automobile repair are good candidates for entrepreneurs because they
    a. do not require any skills.
    b. are the most likely to succeed.
    c. can obtain financing easily.
    d. require no special equipment.
    e. have a relatively low initial investment.

23. _____ An individual's desire to create a new business is referred to as
    a. the entrepreneurial spirit.
    b. the desire for ownership.
    c. self-determination.
    d. self-evaluation.
    e. the *laissez-faire* spirit.

24. _____ What is a common mistake that small-business owners make when their businesses begin growing?
    a. They sell more goods and services.
    b. They put too much money in advertising.
    c. They move beyond their local area.
    d. They over-expand without proper planning.
    e. They invest too much of their own money.

25. _____ The fact that insulin and power steering both originated with individual inventors and small companies is testimony to the power of small businesses as providers of
    a. employment.
    b. competition.
    c. technical innovation.
    d. capital.
    e. quality products.

26. _____ In her small retail shop, Jocelyn knows most of her best customers by name and knows their preferences in clothing and shoes. This demonstrates which advantage of a small business?
    a. Ability to adapt to change
    b. Independence from customer's desires
    c. Simplified record keeping
    d. Personal relationships with customers
    e. Small customer base

27. _____ Shonta started a graphic design firm a year ago. The business has done well, but it needs a lot more equipment, computers, and employees to continue expanding. Shonta thinks she can get all the money she will need from her bank. What advice might you give to her?
    a. She is right—the bank is likely to lend her as much as she needs because banks primarily focus on supporting small businesses.
    b. She is crazy—banks do not lend money to small businesses but only to well-known, well-established organizations.
    c. She should sell her business immediately before it fails because most small businesses fail during the first five years.
    d. She should not accept any new clients so that she can end the need to add additional equipment and employees.
    e. She should consider alternative sources of financing because banks provide only a portion of the total capital to small businesses.

28. _____ Volunteers for SCORE are
    a. mostly university business professors.
    b. active executives from large corporations.
    c. generally either lawyers or accountants.
    d. graduate business students working on projects.
    e. retired and active businesspeople from different industries.

29. _____ An individual or organization granting a license to operate an individually owned business as though it were part of a chain of outlets or stores is a(n)
    a. franchise.
    b. franchisor.
    c. franchisee.
    d. venture capitalist.
    e. entrepreneur.

30. _____ Manju asks for your advice in opening a new business. She plans to provide tax-related services to individuals and small-business owners in her community. Of course, she wants an attractive means of starting and operating her business with a reasonable hope of succeeding in it. What will be your advice?
    a. Start your own independent business.
    b. Form a partnership with a CPA.
    c. Consider purchasing a franchise.
    d. Forget about opening the business because it is too risky.
    e. First secure a loan from the Small Business Administration.

Answers to the Test Yourself questions appear at the end of the book on page TY-1.

Video Case

From Two Men and a Truck to 220 Franchises and 1,400 Trucks

Two Men and a Truck (www.twomenandatruck.com) began in the 1980s as a way for brothers Brig and Jon Sorber to make money while in high school. They started with one old pickup truck, placed a newspaper ad promoting their moving services in and around Lansing, Michigan, and charged $25 per hour to transport household goods. Their mother Mary Ellen Sheets created the hand-drawn logo of stick-figure men inside a truck, which has been part of the company's business identity since the beginning.

When the brothers left for college, their mother took over to keep the moving business on the move. Demand was so strong, in fact, that Sheets decided to buy a larger used truck for $350, hire two more men, and undertake even larger moving jobs. During school breaks, the brothers came home and earned extra spending money by climbing into one of the trucks and helping homeowners move.

Two Men and a Truck continued to attract so many customers that Sheets finally quit her job to operate the business as a full-time entrepreneur. In 1985, she hired more people, purchased a new truck, and set a tone of superior customer service embodied by the "Grandma Rule"—treat every customer with the same care and respect you would show your own grandmother. Within two years, Two Men and a Truck had earned its first profit, which Sheets donated to community charities. This was only the first of many efforts driven by the entrepreneur's core value of taking care of people—the community as well as the customers.

One day, Sheets was part of a panel about entrepreneurship and met a woman who had successfully franchised her business. With this woman's encouragement, Sheets looked into the idea of franchising Two Men and a Truck. She asked her daughter Melanie Bergeron to join the family business as head of the franchising division. Thanks to a grant, Bergeron was able to learn about franchising through weekly consultations with experts at the accounting firm of Deloitte & Touche. Two Men and a Truck started to offer franchises and as its aggressive growth continued, Bergeron's brothers returned to work in the family business a few years later.

Over time, each family member has found ways to apply his or her own strengths to the challenges and opportunities faced by the company, and to function effectively as business partners when they're all in the office dealing with a problem. Today, Brig Sorber is the CEO, Jon Sorber is the executive vice president, and Melanie Bergeron serves as chair of Two Men and a Truck. Looking ahead, the company has a structured succession plan in place for an orderly transition if the next generation chooses to become part of the business. Alicia Sorber, Brig's daughter, is already involved, working for a franchisee and learning from her father's experiences and ideas.

Two Men and a Truck now has 220 franchisees and 1,400 trucks across the United States and is expanding into Europe. The company's annual revenue is $275 million and it handles more than 400,000 moves every year. Franchisees have adopted the company's credo of caring, using their trucks and employees for the benefit of local causes. For example, some have moved boxes of donated food from collection points to food banks for distribution to needy families. Others have delivered cleaning supplies, food, and personal care items to areas hit hard by natural disasters. No matter what cause they support, local franchisees show how Two Men and a Truck cares for its communities as well as its customers.[22]

Questions

1. Which advantages of small business helped Mary Ellen Sheets establish and grow Two Men and a Truck?
2. Which disadvantages of small business did Two Men and a Truck have to overcome? If you had been part of the business at the start, what suggestions would you have offered for overcoming these issues?
3. Do you think it's a good idea for Two Men and a Truck to offer franchises outside of North America? Why or why not? What kinds of questions would international franchisees be likely to ask the company?

Building Skills for Career Success

1. Social Media Exercise

American Express's "Open Forum" is a website that is designed for small-business owners (www.openforum.com). Do a search using a search engine like Google or Bing and you will also find its presence on Tumblr and Pinterest. Take a look at the Open Forum website and answer the following questions.

1. What questions can Open Forum answer for business owners?
2. Develop a list of five issues or topics that you feel illustrates how American Express does an effective job of presenting information on this website.

2. Building Team Skills

A business plan is a written statement that documents the nature of a business and how that business intends to achieve its goals. Although entrepreneurs should prepare a business plan *before* starting a business, the plan also serves as an effective guide later on. The plan should concisely describe the business's mission, the amount of capital it requires, its target market, competition, resources, production plan, marketing plan, organizational plan, assessment of risk, and financial plan.

Assignment

1. Working in a team of four students, identify a company in your community that would benefit from using a business plan, or create a scenario in which a hypothetical entrepreneur wants to start a business.
2. Using the resources of the library or the Internet and/or interviews with business owners, write a business plan incorporating the information in Table 5-3.
3. Present your business plan to the class.

3. Researching Different Careers

Many people dream of opening and operating their own businesses. Are you one of them? To be successful, entrepreneurs must have certain characteristics; their profiles generally differ from those of people who work for someone else. Do you know which personal characteristics make some entrepreneurs succeed and others fail? Do you fit the successful entrepreneur's profile? What is your potential for opening and operating a successful small business?

Assignment

1. Use the resources of the library or the Internet to establish what a successful entrepreneur's profile is and to determine whether your personal characteristics fit that profile. Internet addresses that can help you are www.smartbiz.com/sbs/arts/ieb1.html and www.sba.gov (see "Start your Business" and "FAQ"). These sites have quizzes online that can help you to assess your personal characteristics. The SBA also has helpful brochures.
2. Interview several small-business owners. Ask them to describe the characteristics they think are necessary for being a successful entrepreneur.
3. Using your findings, write a report that includes the following:
   a. A profile of a successful small-business owner
   b. A comparison of your personal characteristics with the profile of the successful entrepreneur
   c. A discussion of your potential as a successful small-business owner

Running a Business
Part 2

Graeter's: A Fourth-Generation Family Business

Independent and family-owned for more than 140 years, Graeter's has successfully made the transition from a 19th-century mom-and-pop ice cream business to a 21st-century corporation with three manufacturing facilities, dozens of ice cream shops, and hundreds of employees. Much of the company's success over the years has been due to the family's strong and enduring entrepreneurial spirit.

Small Business, Big Ambitions

The road to small-business success started with co-founder Louis Charles Graeter, who developed the startup's first flavors, insisted on only the finest ingredients, and made all his ice cream by hand in small batches to ensure freshness and quality. After his death, his wife and co-founder Regina maintained the same high level of quality as she led the company through three decades of aggressive growth. Her great-grandson, CEO Richard Graeter II, says that "without her strength, fortitude, and foresight, there would be no Graeter's ice cream today."

Richard, Bob, and Chip, great-grandsons of the founders, are the fourth generation to own and operate Graeter's. They grew up in the business, and now they share responsibility for the firm's day-to-day management and for determining its future direction. Bob worked his way up to vice president of operations, starting with a management position in one of the Graeter's ice-cream shops. Chip, currently vice president of retail operations, handled all kinds of jobs in Graeter's stores as a teenager. He uses this first-hand knowledge of customer relations to fine-tune every store function.

Richard Graeter became the company's CEO in 2007. "Even though I have the title of CEO, in a family business titles don't mean a whole lot," he comments. "The functions that I am doing now as CEO, I was doing as executive vice president for years . . . It really was and remains a partnership with my two cousins . . . Our fathers brought us into the business at an early age . . . I think most important is we saw our fathers and their dedication and the fact that, you know, they came home later, they came home tired, they got up early and went to work before we ever got up to go to school in the morning, and you see that dedication and appreciate that—that is what keeps your business going."

Graeter continues, "It can be challenging to work with your family. My father and I didn't always see things the same way. But on the other hand, there is a lot of strength in the family relationship . . . we certainly had struggles, and family businesses do struggle, especially with transition . . . but we found people to help us, including lawyers, accountants, and a family-business psychologist."

Growing Beyond Cincinnati

To expand beyond Cincinnati without diverting resources from the existing stores and factory, the third generation of Graeter's family owners decided to license a handful of franchise operators. One franchise operation was so successful that it even opened its own factory. A few years ago, however, the fourth generation switched gears on growth and repurchased all the stores of its last remaining franchisee. "When you think about Graeter's," says the CEO, "the core of Graeter's is the quality of the product. You can't franchise your core. So by franchising our manufacturing, that created substantial risk for the organization, because the customer doesn't know that it is a franchise. . . . They know it is Graeter's. . . . You really have to rely on the intention and goodwill of the individual franchisees to make the product the way you would make it, and that is not an easy thing to guarantee."

After working with consultants to carefully analyze the situation and evaluate alternative paths to future growth, the founder's great-grandsons decided against further franchising. Instead, they pursued nationwide distribution through a large network of grocery stores and supermarket chains. They also built a new facility to increase production capacity and hired experienced executives to help manage the expanded business.

As a private company, Graeter's can take actions like these without worrying about the reaction of the stock market. Specifically, Graeter's is an S-corporation, which allows it limited-liability protection coupled with the benefit of not being taxed as a corporation. Instead, the three owners—who are the stockholders—pay only personal income taxes on the corporation's profits. In the event of significant legal or tax code changes, Graeter's owners do have the option of choosing a different form of corporate organization.[23]

Questions

1. Graeter's current management team bought the business from their parents, who did not have a formal succession plan in place to indicate who would do what. Do you think the current team should have such a plan specifying who is to step into the business, when, and with what responsibilities? Why or why not?

2. Graeter's hired management consultants to help improve its training procedures and expand distribution. "I think my cousins and I all have come to realize we can't do it alone," says the CEO. Why do you think the management team made this decision? Does the involvement of outside consultants move Graeter's further from its roots as a family business?

3. Do you agree with Graeter's decision to stop franchising? Explain your answer.

Building a Business Plan: Part 2

After reading Part 2, "Business Ownership and Entrepreneurship," you should be ready to tackle the company and industry component of your business plan. In this section, you will provide information about the background of the company, choice of the legal business form, information on the product or services to be offered, and descriptions of potential customers, current competitors, and the business's future. This chapter and the previous chapter (Chapter 4) in your textbook, "Choosing a Form of Business Ownership," and Chapter 5, "Small Business, Entrepreneurship, and Franchises," can help you to answer some of the questions in this part of the business plan.

The Company and Industry Component

The company and industry analysis should include the answers to at least the following questions:

2.1. What is the legal form of your business? Is your business a sole proprietorship, a partnership, or a corporation?

2.2. What licenses or permits will you need, if any?

2.3. Is your business a new independent business, a takeover, an expansion, or a franchise?

2.4. If you are dealing with an existing business, how did your company get to the point where it is today?

2.5. What does your business do, and how does it satisfy customers' needs?

2.6. How did you choose and develop the products or services to be sold, and how are they different from those currently on the market?

2.7. What industry do you operate in, and what are the industry-wide trends?

2.8. Who are the major competitors in your industry?

2.9. Have any businesses recently entered or exited? Why did they leave?

2.10. Why will your business be profitable, and what are your growth opportunities?

2.11. Does any part of your business involve e-business?

Review of Business Plan Activities

Make sure to check the information you have collected, make any changes, and correct any weaknesses before beginning Part 3. *Reminder:* Review the answers to questions in the preceding part to make sure that all your answers are consistent throughout the business plan. Finally, write a summary statement that incorporates all the information for this part of the business plan.

Endnotes

1. Based on information in Leslie Patton, "Seattle's Best to Take on Dunkin' with Drive-Throughs," *Bloomberg*, November 14, 2012, www.bloomberg.com; Jenn Abelson and Todd Wallack, "Dunkin' Donuts Lays Claim to 'Best Coffee in America' Trademark," *Boston Globe*, October 4, 2012, www.bostonglobe.com; Lisa Baertlein, "Dunkin' Brands Raises 2012 View as Competition Brews," *Reuters*, October 25, 2012, www.reuters.com.

2. U.S. Small Business Administration website at www.sbaonline.sba.gov/contractingopportunities/owners/basic/what (accessed June 5, 2013).

3. U.S. Small Business Administration, Office of Advocacy, *Frequently Asked Questions*, updated September 2012, www.sba.gov/advo (accessed June 5, 2013).

4. Ibid.

5. Ibid.

6. Thomas A. Garrett, "Entrepreneurs Thrive in America," *Bridges*, Federal Reserve Bank of St. Louis, Spring 2005, 2.

7. U.S. Small Business Administration, Office of Advocacy, *Frequently Asked Questions*, updated September 2012, www.sba.gov/advo (accessed February 8, 2013), and the SBA website at sba.gov/about-sba-services/7367/432861 (accessed June 5, 2013).

8. U.S. Small Business Administration, *News Release*, Number 05–53, September 13, 2005, www.sba.gov/teens/brian_hendricks.html (accessed February 8, 2013).

9. U.S. Small Business Administration, Office of Advocacy, *Frequently Asked Questions*, updated September 2012, www.sba.gov/advo (accessed June 5, 2013).

10. SBA Press Release, "Computer Simulation Company from Florida Is National Small Business of the Year," May 25, 2010, www.sba.gov/news (accessed March 15, 2012).

11. U.S. Small Business Administration, Office of Advocacy, *Frequently Asked Questions*, September 2012, www.sba.gov/advo (accessed June 5, 2013).

12. Timothy S. Hatten, *Small Business Management: Entrepreneurship and Beyond*, 5th ed., Copyright © 2012 by Cengage Learning. Reprinted with permission.

13. SCORE website at www.score.org/about-score (accessed February 8, 2013).

14. SCORE website at score.org (accessed February 8, 2013).

15. The SBA website at www.sba.gov (accessed February 8, 2013).

16. U.S. Small Business Administration, *News Release*, Release Number 10–33, May 26, 2010, www.sba.gov/news (accessed March 18, 2012).

17. SBIC Program Overview, website at http://archive.sba.gov/idc/groups/public/documents/sba_program_office/inv_sbic; Small Business

18. Investor Alliance website at www.nabic.org (accessed March 23, 2012); sba.gov/INV (accessed February 8, 2013) and the SBA website at sba.gov/content/sbc-program-overview-0 (accessed February 8, 2013).

18. Cindy Elmore, "Putting the Power into the Hands of Small Business Owners," *Marketwise*, Federal Reserve Bank of Richmond, Issue II, 2005, 13.

19. U.S. Commercial Service, U.S. Department of Commerce 2011 Annual Report, accessed at trade.gov/cs/cs_annualreport12.pdf (accessed February 9, 2013).

20. SBA Press Release 12-12, "SBA Announces a New Partnership to Connect Small Businesses With Corporate Supply Chains," March 22, 2012, www.sba.gov/news (accessed March 23, 2012); and International Trade website at www.trade.gov/CS/ (accessed March 23, 2012); and trade.gov/cs/cs_annualreport12.pdf (accessed February 9, 2013).

21. SBA Press Release, "SBA 2010 Small Business Exporter of the Year," www.sba.gov/news (accessed March 20, 2012); and NANMAC Corporation website at http://nanmac.com/press-sba.html (accessed February 9, 2013).

22. Sources: Based on information in Joe Boomgaard, "Mother Knows Best: Mary Ellen Sheets Helps Foster Culture for Two Men and a Truck Moving Company," *MiBiz (Grand Rapids, Michigan)*, May 13, 2012, www.mibiz.com; "Janelle Dowley Distinction: President and Franchisee of Two Men and a Truck," *Palm Beach Post (Florida)*, February 20, 2012, p. 2D; "In the Classroom: ABC Academy, Two Men and a Truck Join Forces in Thanksgiving Food Collection," *Michigan Live*, November 19, 2012, www.mlive.com; J. Patrick Pepper, "Woodhaven: From Downriver to Sandy's Downtrodden, a Special Delivery," *News Herald (Downriver, Michigan)*, November 16, 2012, www.thenewsherald.com; www.twomenandatruck.com.

23. Sources: Based on information from Kimberly L. Jackson, "Graeter's Premium Chocolate Chip Ice Cream Lands at Stop & Shop," *Newark Star-Ledger (NJ)*, April 4, 2012, www.nj.com; "Graeter's Ice Cream Debuts in Bay Area," *Tampa Bay Times (St. Petersburg, FL)*, January 10, 2012, p. 4B; Jim Carper, "Graeter's Runs a Hands-on Ice Cream Plant," *Dairy Foods*, August 2011, pp. 36+; Jim Carper, "The Greater Good," *Dairy Foods*, August 2011, pp. 95+; "Graeter's Unveils New 'Mystery Flavor,'" *Dayton Daily News*, March 29, 2012, www.daytondailynews.com; Bob Driehaus, "A Cincinnati Ice Cream Maker Aims Big," *New York Times*, September 11, 2010, www.nytimes.com; Lucy May, "Graeter's Northern Kentucky Franchisee Puts Stores on the Block," *Business Courier*, August 6, 2010, http://cincinnati.bizjournals.com; www.graeters.com; interviews with company staff and Cengage videos about Graeter's.

© PRESSMASTER/SHUTTERSTOCK.COM

Understanding the Management Process

Learning Objectives

Once you complete this chapter, you will be able to:

1 Define what management is.

2 Describe the four basic management functions: planning, organizing, leading and motivating, and controlling.

3 Distinguish among the various kinds of managers in terms of both level and area of management.

4 Identify the key management skills of successful managers.

5 Explain the different types of leadership.

6 Discuss the steps in the managerial decision-making process.

7 Describe how organizations benefit from total quality management.

Why Should You Care?

Most of the people who read this chapter will advance upward and become managers. Thus an overview of the field of management is essential.

Amazon's Customer First Philosophy

Ever since the online retailer Amazon.com (www.amazon.com) opened its virtual doors in 1995, founder and CEO Jeff Bezos has put long-term customer satisfaction at the top of his list when planning for the future. Amazon.com is an Internet success story, graduating from a scrappy, garage-based startup to a well-managed retail power player and a trusted provider of information services. Its mission is to "be earth's most customer centric company." When executives face a decision about creating a new product or buying a business, the first question they ask is whether it will be good for Amazon's customers. If not, they don't move ahead.

Bezos is known for his big-picture view of business and his long-range planning expertise. He looks ahead five to seven years and has the patience to give innovations enough time to establish themselves. For example, when Amazon introduced the Kindle e-book reader in 2007, digital books were not yet mainstream. By making the Kindle easy to use and pricing it lower than competing products, Amazon attracted millions of buyers. Then, after Apple launched the iPad in 2010, Amazon responded with a popularly priced tablet version of the Kindle. By this time, people were routinely downloading books, movies, music, and other content.

Despite the Kindle's enormous success, the product line itself is not profitable—all according to plan. Bezos wants Amazon to profit when customers *use* their Kindles, not when they buy their Kindles. In fact, customers with a Kindle read four times as many books as before they bought the Kindle, and they continue buying printed books while buying digital books as well, which means Amazon benefits in the long run.

Looking ahead to Amazon's e-commerce future, Bezos has acquired a firm that makes robots to move merchandise inside order fulfillment centers. The robots aren't intended to displace employees, but to make them more productive as Amazon opens new facilities to keep up with the orders its customers will place next month, next year, and beyond.[1]

Did You Know?

Amazon rings up more than $48 billion in annual revenue from retailing and information services.

The leadership employed at Amazon, which creates the company's unique culture, illustrates that management can be one of the most exciting and rewarding professions available today. Depending on its size, a firm may employ a number of specialized managers who are responsible for particular areas of management, such as marketing, finance, and operations. That same organization also includes managers at several levels within the firm. In this chapter, we define *management* and describe the four basic management functions of planning, organizing, leading and motivating, and controlling. Then we focus on the types of managers with respect to levels of responsibility and areas of expertise. Next, we focus on the skills of effective managers and the different roles managers must play. We examine several styles of leadership and explore the process by which managers make decisions. We also describe how total quality management can improve customer satisfaction.

Learning Objective

1 **Define what management is.**

management the process of coordinating people and other resources to achieve the goals of an organization

WHAT IS MANAGEMENT?

Management is the process of coordinating people and other resources to achieve the goals of an organization. As we saw in Chapter 1, most organizations make use of four kinds of resources: material, human, financial, and informational (see Figure 6-1).

Material resources are the tangible, physical resources an organization uses. For example, General Motors uses steel, glass, and fiberglass to produce cars and trucks on complex machine-driven assembly lines. A college or university uses books, classroom buildings, desks, and computers to educate students. And the Mayo Clinic uses operating room equipment, diagnostic machines, and laboratory tests to provide health care.

Perhaps the most important resources of any organization are its *human resources*—people. In fact, some firms live by the philosophy that employees are their most important assets. Some managers believe that the way employees are developed and managed has more impact on an organization than other vital components such as marketing, financial decisions, production, or technology. Research supports this belief. It shows that prioritizing human resources and working to ensure that employees are happy can greatly affect productivity and customer relationships. For example, taking steps to put employees in a good mood early in the day can positively impact company performance.[2]

Financial resources are the funds an organization uses to meet its obligations to investors and creditors. A 7-Eleven convenience store obtains money from customers at the checkout counter and uses a portion to pay its suppliers. Your college obtains money in the form of tuition, income from endowments, and state and federal grants. It uses the money to pay bills, insurance premiums, and salaries.

Increasingly, organizations are finding that they cannot afford to ignore *information*. External environmental conditions—the economy, consumer markets, technology, politics, and cultural forces—are all changing so rapidly that a business must adapt to survive. To adapt to change, the business must gather information about competitors and changes to the industry in order to learn from the failures and successes of others.

It is important to realize that the four types of resources described earlier are only general categories. Within each category are hundreds or thousands of more specific resources. It is this complex mix of specific resources—which varies between companies and industries—that managers must coordinate to produce goods and services.

Another way to look at management is in terms of the different functions managers perform, which are planning, organizing, leading and motivating employees, and controlling. We look at each of these management functions in the next section.

Concept Check

✓ What is management?

✓ What are the four kinds of resources?

FIGURE 6-1 The Four Main Resources of Management

Managers coordinate an organization's resources to achieve the organization's goals.

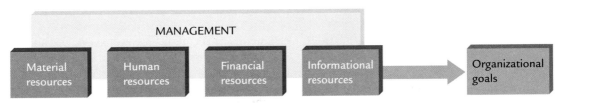

MANAGEMENT

Material resources → Human resources → Financial resources → Informational resources → Organizational goals

© CENGAGE LEARNING 2015

Learning Objective

2 Describe the four basic management functions: planning, organizing, leading and motivating, and controlling.

BASIC MANAGEMENT FUNCTIONS

After years of declining profits and the near destruction of the auto industry in the wake of the recent economic crisis, Ford analyzed its situation and restructured to respond to changes in the industry and cut costs. This plan involved hiring new managers, including a new Chief Operating Officer. It also physically restructured by closing plants in Europe, moving manufacturing operations closer to major markets such as Brazil, and adding new car models adapted to the needs of growing target markets.[3]

Management functions do not occur according to some rigid, preset timetable. Managers do not plan in January, organize in February, lead and motivate in March, and control in April. At any given time, managers may engage in a number of functions simultaneously. However, each function tends to lead naturally to others. Figure 6-2 provides a visual framework for a more detailed discussion of the four basic management functions. How well managers perform these key functions determines whether a business is successful.

Planning

planning establishing organizational goals and deciding how to accomplish them

mission a statement of the basic purpose that makes an organization different from others

strategic planning process the establishment of an organization's major goals and objectives and the allocation of resources to achieve them

goal an end result that an organization is expected to achieve over a one- to ten-year period

objective a specific statement detailing what an organization intends to accomplish over a shorter period of time

Planning, in its simplest form, is establishing organizational goals and deciding how to accomplish them. It is often referred to as the "first" management function because all other management functions depend on planning. Organizations such as Twitter, Amazon, and Facebook base the planning process on a mission statement.

An organization's **mission** is a statement of the basic purpose that makes that organization different from others. Starbucks mission statement, for example, is "to inspire and nurture the human spirit—one person, one cup, and one neighborhood at a time." Amazon.com's mission is "to be earth's most customer-centric company; to build a place where people can come to find and discover anything they might want to buy online." Facebook's mission statement is "to give people the power to share and make the world more open and connected."[4] Once a mission has been stated, the next step is to engage in strategic planning.

STRATEGIC PLANNING PROCESS The **strategic planning process** involves establishing an organization's major goals and objectives and allocating resources to achieve them. Top management is responsible for strategic planning, although customers, products, competitors, and company resources all factor into the process.

In today's rapidly changing business environment, constant internal or external changes may necessitate changes in a company's goals, mission, or strategy. The timeline for strategic plans is generally one to two years, but can be much longer. Strategic plans should be flexible and include action items, such as outlining how plans will be implemented.

ESTABLISHING GOALS AND OBJECTIVES A **goal** is an end result that an organization is expected to achieve over a one- to ten-year period. An **objective** is a specific statement detailing what the organization intends to accomplish over a shorter period of time.

Goals and objectives can involve a variety of factors, such as sales, company growth, costs, customer satisfaction, and employee morale. Whereas a small manufacturer may focus primarily on sales objectives for the next six months, a large firm may be more interested in goals that will impact the firm for several years. While many

Human Resources. Superior human resources management can set a firm apart. Do you have a great business plan or product? A competitor can easily copy both. Great employees, however, are much harder to duplicate. That's why being able to attract, train, and retain talented workers can give a firm a competitive advantage over its rivals.

© KONSTANTIN CHAGIN/SHUTTERSTOCK.COM

FIGURE 6-2 The Management Process

Note that management is not a step-by-step procedure but a process with a feedback loop that represents a flow.

Planning → Organizing → Leading and motivating → Controlling

Review and modify

© CENGAGE LEARNING 2015

retailers have scaled back in recent years, Starbucks has set ambitious growth targets through opening new stores and acquiring new businesses, such as the Evolution Fresh juice chain, La Boulange bakery, and the Teavana tea chain. The company aims to open around 1,000 new stores annually, to achieve 20,000 global outlets within the next few years.[5] Finally, goals are set at every level of an organization. Every member of an organization—the president of the company, the head of a department, and an operating employee at the lowest level—has a set of goals that he or she hopes to achieve.

It is likely that some conflicts will arise among levels within the organization, but goals must be made consistent across an organization. A production department, for example, may have a goal of minimizing costs. One way to do this is to produce only one type of product and limited customer service. Marketing may have a goal of maximizing sales, which might be achieved by offering a wide range of products and options. As part of goal-setting, the manager responsible for *both* departments must strike a balance between conflicting goals. This balancing process is called *optimization*.

The optimization of conflicting goals requires insight and ability. Faced with the marketing-versus-production conflict just described, most managers would find a middle ground through offering a moderately diverse product line featuring only the most popular products. Such a compromise would be best for the whole organization.

SWOT ANALYSIS SWOT analysis is the identification and evaluation of a firm's strengths, weaknesses, opportunities, and threats. Strengths and weaknesses are internal factors that affect a company's capabilities. Strengths refer to a firm's favorable characteristics and core competencies. **Core competencies** are approaches and processes that a company performs well that may give it an advantage over its competitors. These core competencies may help the firm attract financial and human resources that increase the firm's capacity to produce products that satisfy customers. Weaknesses refer to internal limitations a company faces in developing or implementing plans. At times, managers have difficulty identifying and understanding the negative effects of weaknesses in their organizations.

External opportunities and threats exist independently of the firm. Opportunities refer to favorable conditions in the environment that could benefit the organization if properly exploited. Threats, on the other hand, are conditions or barriers that may prevent the firm from reaching its objectives. Opportunities and threats can stem

---

General Motors Mission Statement

"G.M. is a multinational corporation engaged in socially responsible operations, worldwide. It is dedicated to provide products and services of such quality that our customers will receive superior value while our employees and business partners will share in our success and our stock-holders will receive a sustained superior return on their investment."

General Motors

© KURHAN/SHUTTERSTOCK

What is your organization's purpose? How is it different than other organizations? Those are the questions a firm's mission statement like the one shown here should answer. Mission statements are meant for multiple audiences, including a company's customers, investors, the general public, and employees. Most firms familiarize their personnel with their mission statements so they know what's expected of them and what they should strive for.

SWOT analysis the identification and evaluation of a firm's strengths, weaknesses, opportunities, and threats

core competencies approaches and processes that a company performs well that may give it an advantage over its competitors

Are you ready to be a manager? Start now to inventory your personal and professional strengths, weaknesses, opportunities, and threats so you can identify areas for improvement and prepare for future success.

- *What are your strengths?* Think about the skills, training, and experiences that successful managers need. For example, are you a top-notch communicator? Do you have excellent technical skills? Do you know how to get along with people at all levels? Are you following developments in your industry and in the business world?

- *What are your weaknesses?* Are your skills and training up to date? Do you know how to make a good impression with potential employers? Do you have the enthusiasm, commitment, confidence, and patience you need for success in management? Are you ready for more responsibility? How can you acquire the education or experience you need for your chosen field?

- *What opportunities do you see?* Are businesses looking for the capabilities, education, and job experience that you count among your strengths? Are you involved in volunteer activities, hobbies, or internships that help you develop your management capabilities? Can your personal or professional contacts provide ideas or guidance about moving into management?

- *What threats might affect you?* What unfavorable trends might affect your ability to advance into management? Which developments in the business world are likely to be most challenging to you as a manager? What steps can you take today to be ready for tomorrow's threats and opportunities?

Sources: Based on information in Ron Ashkenas, "The Case for Growing Your Own Senior Leaders," *Harvard Business Review Blog Network*, October 30, 2012, http://blogs.hbr.org; Michael Mink, "Develop and Maximize Strengths to Lead Effectively," *Investor's Business Daily*, October 2, 2012, http://news.investors.com; Peter Whitehead, "A Tough Test of Leadership Ability," *Financial Times*, March 29, 2012, p. 1; Glenn Llopis, "Five Most Effective Ways to Invest in Your Career," *Forbes*, October 22, 2012, www.forbes.com.

from many sources within the business environment. Because environmental factors vary between firms and industries, threats for some firms may be opportunities for others. Examples of strengths, weaknesses, opportunities, and threats are shown in Figure 6-3.

TYPES OF PLANS Once goals and objectives have been set for the organization, managers must develop plans for achieving them. A **plan** is an outline of the actions by which an organization intends to accomplish its goals and objectives. The organization develops several types of plans, as shown in Figure 6-4.

An organization's **strategic plan** is its broadest plan, developed as a guide during the strategic planning process for major policy setting and decision making. Strategic plans are set by the board of directors and top management and are generally designed to achieve the organization's long-term goals. Thus, a firm's strategic plan defines what business the company is in or wants to be in and the kind of company it is or wants to be. After decades of being one of the dominant video game companies in the world, Nintendo faces stiff competition from free or low-cost games, such as Angry Birds, that can be played on smartphones and tablets. Sharply sagging sales prompted the company to revise its strategic plan to focus more on product innovation and adapting to the new ways users play games. Its Wii U console, for example, combines aspects of an iPad with traditional gaming controls.[6]

In addition to strategic plans, most organizations also employ several narrower kinds of plans. A **tactical plan** is a smaller scale plan developed to implement a strategy. Most tactical plans cover a one- to three-year period. If a strategic plan will take five years to complete, the firm may develop five tactical plans, one covering each year. Tactical plans may be updated periodically as dictated by conditions and experience. Their more limited scope permits them to be changed more easily than strategies. As part of its tactical plan to improve revenue, Best Buy's CEO is fighting slumping sales with a reinvention effort called "Renew Blue." This plan involves more emphasis on online sales through bestbuy.com and improving distribution so that stores do not run out of popular items.[7]

An **operational plan** is a type of plan designed to implement tactical plans. Operational plans are usually established for one year or less and deal with how to accomplish the organization's specific objectives.

Regardless of how hard managers try, sometimes business activities do not go as planned. Today, most corporations also develop contingency plans along with strategies, tactical plans, and operational plans. A **contingency plan** is a plan that outlines alternative courses of action that may be taken if an organization's other plans are disrupted or become ineffective. As the European Union struggles with debt, fiscal austerity measures, and Greece's possible exit from the Euro zone,

plan an outline of the actions by which an organization intends to accomplish its goals and objectives

strategic plan an organization's broadest plan, developed as a guide for major policy setting and decision making

tactical plan a smaller scale plan developed to implement a strategy

operational plan a type of plan designed to implement tactical plans

FIGURE 6-3 Elements and Examples of SWOT Analysis

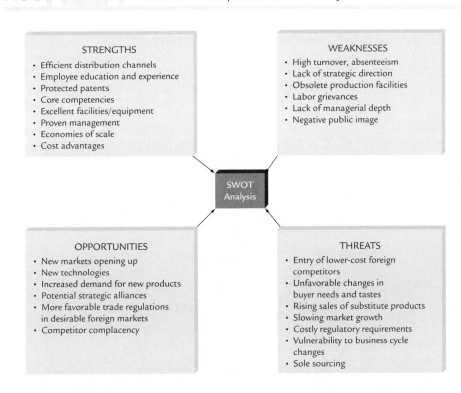

STRENGTHS
- Efficient distribution channels
- Employee education and experience
- Protected patents
- Core competencies
- Excellent facilities/equipment
- Proven management
- Economies of scale
- Cost advantages

WEAKNESSES
- High turnover, absenteeism
- Lack of strategic direction
- Obsolete production facilities
- Labor grievances
- Lack of managerial depth
- Negative public image

SWOT Analysis

OPPORTUNITIES
- New markets opening up
- New technologies
- Increased demand for new products
- Potential strategic alliances
- More favorable trade regulations in desirable foreign markets
- Competitor complacency

THREATS
- Entry of lower-cost foreign competitors
- Unfavorable changes in buyer needs and tastes
- Rising sales of substitute products
- Slowing market growth
- Costly regulatory requirements
- Vulnerability to business cycle changes
- Sole sourcing

© CENGAGE LEARNING 2015

companies have developed contingency plans to ensure that production continues, distribution is unaffected, and workers are paid. Most companies have plans for different scenarios.[8]

Organizing the Enterprise

After goal-setting and planning, the manager's second major function is organization. **Organizing** is the grouping of resources and activities to accomplish some end result in an efficient and effective manner. Consider the case of an inventor who creates a new product and goes into business to sell it. At first, the inventor will do everything on his or her own—purchase raw materials, make the product, advertise it, sell it, and keep business records. Eventually, as business grows, the inventor will need help. To begin with, he or she might hire a professional sales representative and a part-time bookkeeper. Later, it also might be necessary to hire sales staff, people to assist with production, and an accountant. As the inventor hires new personnel, he or she must decide what each person will do, to whom each person will report, and how each person can best take part in the organization's activities. We discuss these and other facets of the organizing function in much more detail in Chapter 7.

Leading and Motivating

The leading and motivating function is concerned with an organization's human resources. Specifically, **leading** is the process of influencing people to work toward a common goal. **Motivating** is the process of providing reasons for

contingency plan a plan that outlines alternative courses of action that may be taken if an organization's other plans are disrupted or become ineffective

organizing the grouping of resources and activities to accomplish some end result in an efficient and effective manner

leading the process of influencing people to work toward a common goal

motivating the process of providing reasons for people to work in the best interests of an organization

C.W. GRIFFIN/MCT/LANDOV

Tearing down the walls at Burger King. Burger King's top-level executives no longer have closed door offices, and employees no longer work in cubicles. The new physical arrangement facilitates better communication and collaboration among employees at all levels.

FIGURE 6-4 Types of Plans

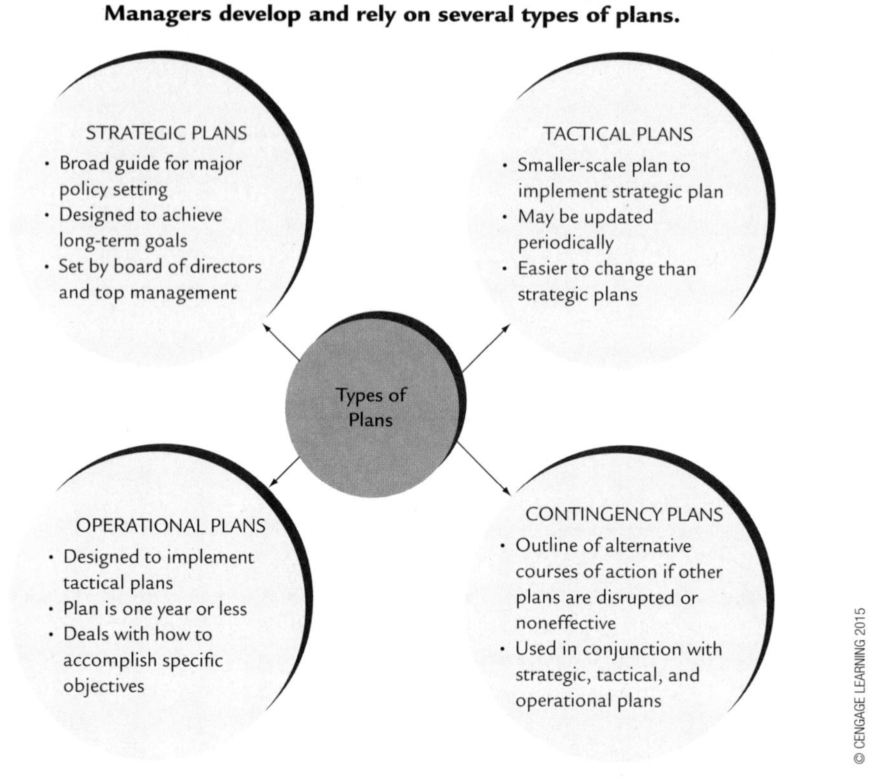

Managers develop and rely on several types of plans.

STRATEGIC PLANS
- Broad guide for major policy setting
- Designed to achieve long-term goals
- Set by board of directors and top management

TACTICAL PLANS
- Smaller-scale plan to implement strategic plan
- May be updated periodically
- Easier to change than strategic plans

Types of Plans

OPERATIONAL PLANS
- Designed to implement tactical plans
- Plan is one year or less
- Deals with how to accomplish specific objectives

CONTINGENCY PLANS
- Outline of alternative courses of action if other plans are disrupted or noneffective
- Used in conjunction with strategic, tactical, and operational plans

© CENGAGE LEARNING 2015

directing the combined processes of leading and motivating

people to work in the best interests of an organization. Together, leading and motivating are often referred to as **directing**.

Leading and motivating are critical activities because of the importance of an organization's human resources. Obviously, different people do things for different reasons—that is, they have different *motivations*. Some are interested primarily in earning as much money as they can. Others may be spurred on by opportunities to get promoted. Part of a manager's job, then, is to determine what factors motivate workers and to try to provide those incentives to encourage effective performance. Many people choose to work at Amazon because it is the largest online retailer, worth over $100 billion, and they want to be part of a major international company with tremendous market share. Jeff Bezos, CEO of Amazon, is the top CEO in America and has guided Amazon to success through his model leadership. While other companies pay more (no executive earns over $175,000), he motivates his employees through keeping the workplace fast-paced and exciting, providing benefits like restricted stock options, and maintaining a tight focus on customer satisfaction and needs.[9] A lot of research has been done on both motivation and leadership. As you will see in Chapter 10, research on motivation has yielded very useful information. However, research on leadership has been less successful. Despite decades of study, no one has discovered a general set of personal traits or characteristics that makes a good leader. Later in this chapter, we discuss leadership in more detail.

Controlling Ongoing Activities

controlling the process of evaluating and regulating ongoing activities to ensure that goals are achieved

Controlling is the process of evaluating and regulating ongoing activities to ensure that goals are achieved. Honeywell Aerospace, for example, makes employee and product safety a priority goal. Because of the intricacy of its products, the company

FIGURE 6-5 The Control Function

The control function includes three steps: setting standards, measuring actual performance, and taking corrective action.

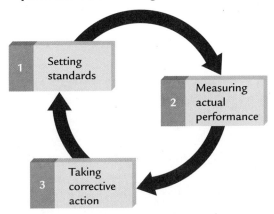

© CENGAGE LEARNING 2015

upholds rigorous quality standards in their design, manufacture, and distribution through the application of its Honeywell Quality Value program.

The control function includes three steps (see Figure 6-5). The first is *setting standards* against which performance can be compared. The second is *measuring actual performance* and comparing it with the standard. The third is *taking corrective action* as necessary. Notice that the control function is circular in nature. The steps in the control function must be repeated periodically until the goal is achieved. For example, suppose that Southwest Airlines establishes a goal of increasing profits by 12 percent. Southwest's management will monitor its profit on a monthly basis to ensure success. After three months, if profit has increased by 3 percent, management may assume that plans are effective. In this case, no action will likely be taken. However, if profit has increased only 1 percent, some corrective action will be needed to get the firm on track. The action that is required depends on the reason for the less-than-expected increase.

Concept Check

✓ Why is planning sometimes referred to as the "first" management function?

✓ What is a plan? Differentiate between the major types of plans.

✓ What kind of motivations do different employees have?

✓ What are the three steps of controlling?

KINDS OF MANAGERS

Managers can be classified in two ways: according to their level within an organization and according to their area of management. In this section, we use both perspectives to explore the various types of managers.

Levels of Management

For the moment, think of an organization as a three-story structure (as illustrated in Figure 6-6). Each story corresponds to one of the three general levels of management: top managers, middle managers, and first-line managers.

TOP MANAGERS A **top manager** is an upper-level executive who guides and controls an organization's overall fortunes. Top managers represent the smallest of the three groups. In terms of planning, they are generally responsible for developing the organization's mission. They also determine the firm's strategy. It takes years of hard work, long hours, and perseverance, talent, and no small share of good luck to reach the ranks of top management in large companies. Common job titles associated with top managers are president, vice president, chief executive officer (CEO), and chief operating officer (COO).

Learning Objective

3 **Distinguish among the various kinds of managers in terms of both level and area of management.**

top manager an upper-level executive who guides and controls the overall fortunes of an organization

FIGURE 6-6 Management Levels Found in Most Companies

**The coordinated effort of all three levels of managers
is required to implement the goals of any company.**

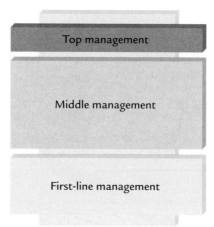

© CENGAGE LEARNING 2015

middle manager a manager who implements the strategy and major policies developed by top management

first-line manager a manager who coordinates and supervises the activities of operating employees

financial manager a manager who is primarily responsible for an organization's financial resources

operations manager a manager who manages the systems that convert resources into goods and services

MIDDLE MANAGERS Middle managers make up the largest group of managers in most organizations. A **middle manager** is a manager who implements the strategy and major policies developed by top management. Middle managers develop tactical and operational plans, and they coordinate and supervise the activities of first-line managers. Titles at the middle-management level include division manager, department head, plant manager, and operations manager.

FIRST-LINE MANAGERS A **first-line manager** is a manager who coordinates and supervises the activities of operating employees. First-line managers spend most of their time working with and motivating their employees, answering questions, and solving day-to-day problems. Most first-line managers are former operating employees who were promoted into management. Many of today's middle and top managers began their careers on this first management level. Common titles for first-line managers include office manager, supervisor, and foreman.

Areas of Management Specialization

Organizational structure can also be divided into areas of management specialization (see Figure 6-7). The most common areas are finance, operations, marketing, human resources, and administration. Depending on its mission, goals, and objectives, an organization may include other areas as well—research and development (R&D), for example.

FINANCIAL MANAGERS A **financial manager** is primarily responsible for an organization's financial resources. Accounting and investment are specialized areas within financial management. Because financing

AP IMAGES/MARK LENNIHAN

A top manager's out-of-this-world business strategy. At the age of 16, Richard Branson, the CEO and founder of the Virgin Group, started his first business venture: a magazine called *The Student*. Today, the Virgin Group consists of over 400 companies, including Virgin Telecommunications, Virgin Radio, Virgin Cola, Virgin Wine, Virgin Spa, Virgin Airlines—and the list goes on. In the near future, Virgin Galactic, one of Branson's newest companies, aims to launch paying customers into space.

FIGURE 6-7 Areas of Management Specialization

Other areas may have to be added, depending on the nature of the firm and the industry.

| Finance | Operations | Marketing | Human resources | Administration | Others (e.g., research and development) |

© CENGAGE LEARNING 2015

affects the operation of the entire firm, many CEOs and presidents of large companies are people who were first trained as financial managers.

OPERATIONS MANAGERS An **operations manager** manages the systems that convert resources into goods and services. Traditionally, operations management has been equated with manufacturing—the production of goods. However, in recent years, many of the techniques and procedures of operations management have been applied to the production of services and to a variety of nonbusiness activities. As with financial management, operations management has produced a large percentage of today's company CEOs and presidents.

MARKETING MANAGERS A **marketing manager** is responsible for facilitating the exchange of products between an organization and its customers or clients. Specific areas within marketing are marketing research, product management, advertising, promotion, sales, and distribution. A sizable number of today's company presidents have risen from marketing management.

HUMAN RESOURCES MANAGERS A **human resources manager** is charged with managing an organization's human resources programs. He or she engages in human resources planning, designs systems for hiring, training, and evaluating the performance of employees, and ensures that the organization follows government regulations concerning employment practices. There are many technological tools to help human resources managers. For example, Workday, Inc. produces a suite of software and tools for human resources departments, including a program to streamline the recruiting and hiring process and tools that help HR managers collect and process information.

ADMINISTRATIVE MANAGERS An **administrative manager** (also called a *general manager*) is not associated with any specific functional area, but provides overall administrative guidance and leadership. A hospital administrator is an example of an administrative manager. He or she does not specialize in operations, finance, marketing, or human resources management but instead coordinates the activities of specialized managers in all these areas. In many respects, most top managers are really administrative managers.

Whatever their level and specialization in the organization, successful managers generally exhibit certain key skills and are able to play a variety of managerial roles. However, as we shall see, some skills are likely to be more critical at one level of management than at another.

marketing manager a manager who is responsible for facilitating the exchange of products between an organization and its customers or clients

human resources manager a person charged with managing an organization's human resources programs

administrative manager a manager who is not associated with any specific functional area but who provides overall administrative guidance and leadership

Concept Check

✓ Describe the three levels of management.

✓ Identify the various areas of management specialization, and describe the responsibilities of each.

© AUREMAR/SHUTTERSTOCK.COM

Harnessing the cooperation of an organization's specialized managers. Imagine the managers of different departments as a team of horses. If they—and their employees—don't all work together and pull in the same direction, the organization won't get to the destination it's trying to reach.

KEY SKILLS OF SUCCESSFUL MANAGERS

As shown in Figure 6-8, managers need a variety of skills, including conceptual, analytic, interpersonal, technical, and communication skills.

Conceptual Skills

conceptual skills the ability to think in abstract terms

Conceptual skills involve the ability to think in abstract terms. Conceptual skills allow a manager to see the "big picture" and understand how the various parts of an organization or idea can fit together. Jack Dorsey, creator of Twitter, is a master at seeing large trends and developing products that address needs. In 2009, he created a product called Square, which lets small businesses run credit transactions using their smartphones. Even Starbucks is on board. Square handles all credit and debit card transactions at its 7,000 stores.[10] Conceptual skills are useful in a wide range of situations, including the optimization of goals described earlier.

Analytic Skills

analytic skills the ability to identify problems correctly, generate reasonable alternatives, and select the "best" alternatives to solve problems

interpersonal skills the ability to deal effectively with other people

technical skills specific skills needed to accomplish a specialized activity

communication skills the ability to speak, listen, and write effectively

Employers expect managers to use **analytic skills** to identify problems correctly, generate reasonable alternatives, and select the "best" alternatives to solve problems. Top-level managers especially need these skills because they must discern the important issues from the less important ones, as well as recognize the underlying reasons for different situations. Managers who use these skills not only address a situation but also correct the initial event or problem that caused it to occur. Thus, these skills are vital to running a business efficiently and logically.

FIGURE 6-8 Key Skills of Successful Managers

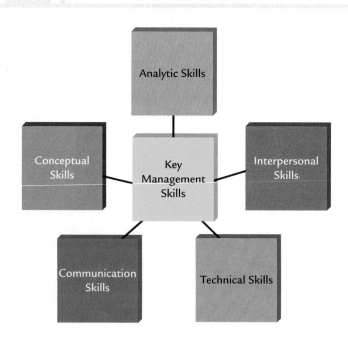

© CENGAGE LEARNING 2015

Concept Check

✓ What are the key skills that successful managers should have?

✓ For each skill, provide two reasons why a successful manager should have that skill.

Interpersonal Skills

Interpersonal skills involve the ability to deal effectively with other people, both inside and outside an organization. Examples of interpersonal skills are the ability to relate to people, understand their needs and motives, and show genuine compassion. After the incoming chief was ousted for having an improper relationship with a subordinate, Lockheed Martin chose Marillyn Hewson as its new CEO. Hewson was selected not only for her dedicated performance and competence, but also for her strong interpersonal skills and humility. Employees appreciate her willingness to listen to them. Her polite and gracious personality is also a strength in an industry that regularly interacts with the government.[11]

Technical Skills

Technical skills involve specific skills needed to accomplish a specialized activity. For example, engineers and machinists need technical skills to do their jobs. First-line managers (and, to a lesser extent, middle managers) need to understand the technical skills relevant to the activities they manage in order to train subordinates, answer questions, and provide guidance, even though the managers may not perform the technical tasks themselves. In general, top managers do not rely on technical skills as heavily as managers at other levels. Still, understanding the technical side of a business is an aid to effective management at every level.

Communication Skills

Communication skills, both oral and written, involve the ability to speak, listen, and write effectively. Managers need both oral and written communication skills. Because a large part of a manager's day is spent conversing with others, the ability to speak *and* listen is critical. Oral communication skills are used when a manager makes sales presentations, conducts interviews, and holds press conferences. Written communication skills are important because a manager's ability to prepare letters, e-mails, memos, sales reports, and other written documents may spell the difference between success and failure. Computers, smartphones, and other high-tech devices make communication in today's businesses easier and faster. To manage an organization effectively and to stay informed, it is very important that managers understand how to use and maximize the potential of digital communication devices.

Social Media

CEO Dilemma: To Blog or Not to Blog?

At the advertising agency Saatchi & Saatchi, the hotel company Marriott International, and the online retailer Zappos.com, the chief executive officer is also the chief blogger. CEOs who blog not only share ideas with customers, employees, and the public, but also encourage dialogue, build relationships, and add a personal touch to corporate communication. Yet most CEOs don't blog, because of time constraints, legal issues, or the potential for misunderstanding. Should blogging be a high priority for CEOs?

Saatchi & Saatchi's CEO blogs frequently on a wide range of topics, from creativity and pop culture to leadership and global business. See the blog at http://krconnect.blogspot.com.

COURTESY OF KR CONNECT

© BLEND IMAGES/SHUTTERSTOCK.COM

How good are your managerial skills? To be successful, managers must master and simultaneously utilize a number of skills. These include technical skills that aid with specialized work, conceptual skills that foster abstract thinking, and interpersonal skills to help manage and motivate their employees. Which of these skills will you need to work on as you build your career?

leadership the ability to influence others

autocratic leadership task-oriented leadership style in which workers are told what to do and how to accomplish it without having a say in the decision-making process

participative leadership leadership style in which all members of a team are involved in identifying essential goals and developing strategies to reach those goals

entrepreneurial leadership personality-based leadership style in which the manager seeks to inspire workers with a vision of what can be accomplished to benefit all stakeholders

LEADERSHIP

Leadership has been defined broadly as the ability to influence others. Leadership is different from management in that a leader strives for voluntary cooperation, whereas a manager may have to depend on coercion to change employee behavior.

Formal and Informal Leadership

Some experts make distinctions between formal leadership and informal leadership. Formal leaders have legitimate power of position. They have *authority* within an organization to influence others to work toward the organization's objectives. Informal leaders usually have no such authority and may or may not exert their influence in support of the organization. Both formal and informal leaders make use of several kinds of power, including the ability to grant rewards or impose punishments, the possession of expert knowledge, and personal attraction or charisma. Informal leaders who identify with the organization's goals are a valuable asset to any organization. However, a business can be greatly hampered by informal leaders who turn work groups against management.

Styles of Leadership

For many years, finding a consensus on the most important leadership traits was difficult. Leadership was viewed as a combination of personality traits, such as self-confidence, concern for people, intelligence, and dependability. In recent years, the emphasis has been on styles of leadership. Several styles have emerged, including *autocratic*, *participative*, and *entrepreneurial*.

Autocratic leadership is very task-oriented. Decisions are made unilaterally, with little concern for employee opinions. Employees are told exactly what is expected from them and given specific guidelines, rules, and regulations on how to achieve their tasks.

Participative leadership is common in today's business organizations. Participative leaders consult workers before making decisions. This helps workers understand which goals are important and fosters a sense of ownership and commitment to reach them. Participative leaders can be classified into three groups: consultative, consensus, and democratic. *Consultative leaders* discuss issues with workers but retain the final authority for decision making. *Consensus leaders* seek input from almost all workers and make final decisions based on their support. *Democratic leaders* give final authority to the group. They collect opinions and base their decisions on the vote of the group. New Belgium Brewing frequently appears on lists of best places to work in part because of the company's "high involvement, ownership culture" and participative leader, CEO Kim Jordan. She encourages employees to own stock and make important business decisions.[12] Communication is open up and down the hierarchy. Coaching, collaborating, and negotiating are important skills for participative leaders.

Entrepreneurial leadership is personality dependent. Although each entrepreneur is different, this leadership style is generally task-oriented, driven, charismatic, and enthusiastic.[13] The entrepreneurial personality tends to take initiative, be visionary, and be forward-looking. Their enthusiasm energizes and inspires employees. Entrepreneurial leaders tend to be very invested in their businesses, working long hours to ensure

Personal Apps

Who do you admire?

Think of a leader you admire—someone in the business world or an entertainer raising awareness for a social cause, for example. Why does this person inspire you or make you want to take action? What can you learn from his or her leadership that will help you become a leader in *your* life?

AP IMAGES/MARK LENNIHAN

success. They may not understand why their employees do not have the same level of passion for their work. Hamdi Ulukaya, President and CEO of yogurt company Chobani, was recognized by Ernst & Young as a top entrepreneur. He beat out thousands of others for this distinction through his tireless commitment to the success of the company and its mission, delivering a high-quality product, and focusing on developing loyal customers.[14]

A CEO who leads by example. Bill Gates's leadership style and technological know-how have helped him foster an environment at Microsoft in which top-notch products can be created. Gates's leadership style includes dimensions of both autocratic and participative leadership.

Which Leadership Style Is the Best?

Today, most management experts agree that no "best" managerial leadership style exists. Each of the styles described—autocratic, participative, and entrepreneurial—has advantages and disadvantages. For example, participative leadership can motivate employees to work effectively because they have a sense of ownership in decision making. However, the decision-making process in participative leadership takes time that subordinates could be devoting to the work itself.

Although hundreds of research studies have been conducted to prove which leadership style is best, there are no definite conclusions. Each of the leadership styles can be highly effective in the right situation. The *most* effective style depends on the right balance between interaction among employees, characteristics of the work situation, and the manager's personality.

Concept Check

✓ Describe the major leadership styles.

✓ Which one is best?

MANAGERIAL DECISION MAKING

Decision making is the act of choosing one alternative from a set of alternatives.[15] In ordinary situations, decisions are made casually and informally. We encounter a problem, mull it over, settle on a solution, and go on. Managers, however, require a more systematic method for solving complex problems. As shown in Figure 6-9, managerial decision-making process involves four steps: (1) identifying the problem or opportunity, (2) generating alternatives, (3) selecting an alternative, and (4) implementing and evaluating the solution.

Learning Objective

6 Discuss the steps in the managerial decision-making process.

decision making the act of choosing one alternative from a set of alternatives

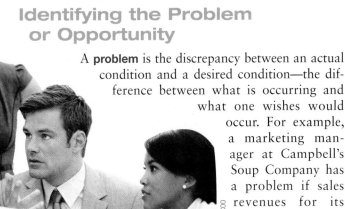

Identifying the Problem or Opportunity

A **problem** is the discrepancy between an actual condition and a desired condition—the difference between what is occurring and what one wishes would occur. For example, a marketing manager at Campbell's Soup Company has a problem if sales revenues for its Pepperidge Farm Goldfish crackers are declining (the actual condition). To solve this problem,

problem the discrepancy between an actual condition and a desired condition

FIGURE 6-9 Major Steps in the Managerial Decision-Making Process

Managers require a systematic method
for solving problems in a variety of situations.

Identifying the problem or opportunity → Generating alternatives → Selecting an alternative → Implementing and evaluating the solution

© CENGAGE LEARNING 2015

the marketing manager must take steps to increase sales revenues (desired condition). Most people consider a problem to be "negative," but a problem also can be "positive." Some problems can be viewed as "opportunities."

Although accurate identification of a problem is essential before it can be solved or turned into an opportunity, this stage of decision making creates many difficulties for managers. Sometimes managers' preconceptions of the problem prevent them from seeing the actual situation. They produce an answer before the proper question has been asked, leading him or her to focus on insignificant issues. Also, managers may mistakenly analyze problems in terms of symptoms rather than underlying causes.

Effective managers learn to look ahead so that they are prepared when decisions must be made. They clarify situations and examine the causes of problems, asking whether the presence or absence of certain variables alters a situation. Finally, they consider how individual behaviors and values affect the way problems or opportunities are defined.

Generating Alternatives

After a problem has been defined, the next task is to generate alternatives. The more important the decision, the more attention must be devoted to this stage. Managers should be open to fresh, innovative ideas as well as obvious answers.

Certain techniques can aid in the generation of creative alternatives. Brainstorming, commonly used in group discussions, encourages participants to produce many new ideas. During brainstorming, other group members are not permitted to criticize or ridicule. Another approach, developed by the U.S. Navy, is called "Blast! Then Refine." Group members tackle a recurring problem by erasing all previous solutions and procedures. The group then re-evaluates its original objectives, modifies them if necessary, and devises new solutions. Other techniques—including trial and error—are also useful in this stage of decision making.

Selecting an Alternative

Final decisions are influenced by a number of considerations, including financial constraints, human and informational resources, time limits, legal obstacles, and political factors. Managers must select the alternative that will be most effective and practical. When publishing giant, Meredith Corporation (*Family Circle* and *Every Day with Rachel Ray*), acquired *Eating Well* magazine, managers had to decide what focus it would have. For example, it could emphasize comfort food or health food. After analyzing the alternatives and the competition, managers decided to focus on healthy meals on a shoestring, a choice that has paid off.[16]

At times, two or more alternatives or some combination of alternatives will be equally appropriate. Managers may choose solutions to problems on several levels. The word *satisfice* describes solutions that are only adequate and not ideal. When lacking time or information, managers often make decisions that "satisfice." Whenever possible, managers should try to investigate alternatives carefully and select the ideal solution.

Implementing and Evaluating the Solution

Implementation of a decision requires time, planning, preparation of personnel, and evaluation of results. Managers usually deal with unforeseen consequences even when they have carefully considered the alternatives.

The final step in managerial decision making entails evaluating a decision's effectiveness. If the alternative that was chosen removes the difference between the actual condition and the desired condition, the decision is considered effective. If the problem still exists, managers may select one of the following choices:

- Decide to give the chosen alternative more time to work.
- Adopt a different alternative.
- Start the problem identification process all over again.

Managers should be aware that failure to evaluate decisions adequately may have negative consequences.

MANAGING TOTAL QUALITY

The management of quality is a high priority in many organizations today. Major reasons for a greater focus on quality include foreign competition, more demanding customers who have the ability to comparison shop online, and poor financial performance resulting from reduced market shares and higher costs. Over the last few years, several U.S. firms have lost the dominant competitive positions they had held for decades.

Total quality management is a much broader concept than just controlling the quality of the product itself (which is discussed in Chapter 8). **Total quality management (TQM)** is the coordination of efforts directed at improving customer satisfaction, increasing employee participation, strengthening supplier partnerships, and facilitating an organizational atmosphere of continuous quality improvement. For TQM programs to be effective, management must address each of the following components:

- *Customer satisfaction.* Ways to improve include producing higher-quality products, providing better customer service, and showing customers that the company cares.
- *Employee participation.* This can be increased by allowing employees to contribute to decisions, develop self-managed work teams, and assume responsibility for improving the quality of their work.
- *Strengthening supplier partnerships.* Developing good working relationships with suppliers can ensure that the right supplies and materials will be delivered on time at lower costs.
- *Continuous quality improvement.* A program based on continuous improvement has proven to be the most effective long-term approach.

One tool that is used for TQM is called benchmarking. **Benchmarking** is the process of evaluating the products, processes, or management practices of another organization for the purpose of improving quality. The benchmark should be superior in safety, customer service, productivity, innovation, or in some other way.

For example, competitors' products might be disassembled and evaluated, or wage and benefit plans might be surveyed to measure compensation packages against the labor market. The four basic steps of benchmarking are identifying

total quality management (TQM) the coordination of efforts directed at improving customer satisfaction, increasing employee participation, strengthening supplier partnerships, and facilitating an organizational atmosphere of continuous quality improvement

benchmarking a process used to evaluate the products, processes, or management practices of another organization that is superior in some way in order to improve quality

Learning Objective

7 Describe how organizations benefit from total quality management.

Total Quality Management. Prior to the 1970s, products "Made in Japan" were often considered shoddy. Not anymore. Toyota Motor Company, the maker of Lexus, worked hard to change that image by pioneering the use of total quality management practices. As a part of its total quality management practices, Toyota meticulously inspects its products and continuously strives to improve them.

objectives, forming a benchmarking team, collecting and analyzing data, and acting on the results. Best practices may be discovered in any industry or organization.

Although many factors influence the effectiveness of a TQM program, two issues are crucial. First, top management must make a strong commitment to a TQM program by treating quality improvement as a top priority and giving it frequent attention. Firms that establish a TQM program but then focus on other priorities will find that their quality-improvement initiatives will fail. Second, management must coordinate the specific elements of a TQM program so that they work in harmony with each other.

Although not all U.S. companies have TQM programs, they provide many benefits. Overall financial benefits include lower operating costs, higher return on sales and on investments, and an improved ability to use premium pricing rather than competitive pricing. Firms that do not implement TQM are sometimes afraid that the costs of doing so will be prohibitive. While implementing TQM can be high initially, the savings from preventing future problems and integrating systems usually make up for the expense. The long-term costs of not implementing TQM can involve damage to a company's reputation and lost productivity and time spent fixing mistakes after they have happened.[17]

Looking for Success? *Get Flashcards, Quizzes, Games, Crosswords and more at @ www.cengagebrain.com.*

Summary

1 Define what management is.

Management is the process of coordinating people and other resources to achieve an organization's goals. Managers are concerned with four types of resources—material, human, financial, and informational.

2 Describe the four basic management functions: planning, organizing, leading and motivating, and controlling.

Managers perform four basic functions, which do not occur according to a rigid, preset timetable. At any time, managers may engage in a number of functions simultaneously. However, each function tends to lead naturally to the next. Managers engage in planning—determining where the firm should be going and how best to get there. One method of planning that can be used is SWOT analysis, which identifies and evaluates a firm's strengths, weaknesses, opportunities, and threats. Three types of plans, from the broadest to the most specific, are strategic, tactical, and operational. Managers also organize resources and activities to accomplish results in an efficient and effective manner, and they lead and motivate others to work in the best interests of the organization. In addition, managers control ongoing activities to keep the organization on course. There are three steps in the control function: setting standards, measuring actual performance, and taking corrective action.

3 Distinguish among the various kinds of managers in terms of both level and area of management.

Managers—or management positions—may be classified from two different perspectives. From the perspective of level within the organization, there are top managers, who control the organization as a whole, middle managers, who implement strategies and major policies, and first-line managers, who supervise the activities of operating employees. From the viewpoint of area of management, managers most often deal with the areas of finance, operations, marketing, human resources, and administration.

4 Identify the key management skills of successful managers.

Managers need a variety of skills in order to run a successful and efficient business. Conceptual skills are used to think in abstract terms or see the "big picture." Analytic skills are used to identify problems correctly, generate reasonable alternatives, and select the "best" alternatives to solve problems. Interpersonal skills are used to deal effectively with other people, both inside and outside an organization. Technical skills are needed to accomplish a specialized activity, whether they are used to actually do the task or to train and assist employees. Communication skills are used to speak, listen, and write effectively.

5 Explain the different types of leadership.

Managers' effectiveness often depends on their styles of leadership—that is, their ability to influence others, either formally or informally. Autocratic leaders are very task oriented; they tell their employees exactly what is expected from them and give them specific instructions on how to do their assigned tasks. Participative leaders consult their employees before making decisions and can be classified into three groups: consultative, consensus, and democratic. Entrepreneurial leaders are different depending on their personalities, but they are generally enthusiastic and passionate about their work and tend to take the initiative.

6 Discuss the steps in the managerial decision-making process.

Decision making, an integral part of a manager's work, is the process of developing a set of possible alternative solutions to a problem and choosing one alternative from among the set. Managerial decision making involves four steps: Managers must accurately identify problems, generate several possible solutions, choose the solution that will be most effective under the circumstances, and implement and evaluate the chosen course of action.

7 Describe how organizations benefit from total quality management.

Total quality management (TQM) is the coordination of efforts directed at improving customer satisfaction, increasing employee participation, strengthening supplier partnerships, and facilitating an organizational atmosphere of continuous quality improvement. Another tool used for TQM is benchmarking, which involves comparing and evaluating the products, processes, or management practices of another organization that is superior in some way in order to improve quality. The five basic steps in benchmarking are identifying objectives, forming a benchmarking team, collecting data, analyzing data, and acting on the results. To have an effective TQM program, top management must make a strong, sustained commitment to the effort and must be able to coordinate all the program's elements so that they work in harmony. Benefits of TQM include lower operating costs, higher return on sales and on investment, and an improved ability to use premium pricing rather than competitive pricing.

Key Terms

You should now be able to define and give an example relevant to each of the following terms:

management (160)
planning (162)
mission (162)
strategic planning process (162)
goal (162)
objective (162)
SWOT analysis (163)
core competencies (163)
plan (164)
strategic plan (164)

tactical plan (164)
operational plan (164)
contingency plan (165)
organizing (165)
leading (165)
motivating (165)
directing (166)
controlling (166)
top manager (167)
middle manager (168)
first-line manager (168)

financial manager (168)
operations manager (168)
marketing manager (169)
human resources manager (169)
administrative manager (169)
conceptual skills (170)
analytic skills (170)
interpersonal skills (170)
technical skills (170)

communication skills (170)
leadership (172)
autocratic leadership (172)
participative leadership (172)
entrepreneurial leadership (172)
decision making (173)
problem (173)
total quality management (TQM) (175)
benchmarking (175)

Discussion Questions

1. Define the word *manager* without using the word *management* in your definition.
2. Does a healthy firm (one that is doing well) have to worry about effective management? Explain.
3. What might be the mission of a neighborhood restaurant? Of the Salvation Army? What might be reasonable objectives for these organizations?
4. What are the major elements of SWOT analysis?
5. How do a strategic plan, a tactical plan, and an operational plan differ? What do they all have in common?
6. Why are leadership and motivation necessary in a business in which people are paid for their work?
7. Compare and contrast the major styles of leadership.

8. According to this chapter, the leadership style that is most effective depends on interaction among the employees, characteristics of the work situation, and the manager's personality. Do you agree or disagree? Explain your answer.

9. What are the major benefits of a total quality management program?

10. Do you think that people are really as important to an organization as this chapter seems to indicate?

11. Discuss what happens during each of the four steps of the managerial decision-making process.

12. As you learned in this chapter, managers often work long hours at a hectic pace. Would this type of career appeal to you? Explain.

Test Yourself

Matching Questions

1. _____ The process of accomplishing objectives through people.

2. _____ The process of establishing an organization's goals and objectives.

3. _____ Its purpose is to implement a strategy.

4. _____ Its purpose is to outline alternative courses of action.

5. _____ The process of influencing people to work.

6. _____ It is a combination of leading and motivating.

7. _____ A vast amount of time is spent motivating employees.

8. _____ Specific skills needed to work a computer.

9. _____ The ability to influence others.

10. _____ Improving customer satisfaction and increasing employee participation are two objectives of this process.

   a. conceptual skills
   b. contingency plan
   c. directing
   d. first-line manager
   e. leadership
   f. leading
   g. management
   h. operations manager
   i. strategic planning
   j. tactical plan
   k. technical skills
   l. total quality management (TQM)

True False Questions

11. **T F** Management functions occur according to a rigid, preset timetable.

12. **T F** As managers carry out their functions, the first step is to control, the second to organize, and the third to plan.

13. **T F** An organization's mission is the means by which it fulfills its purpose.

14. **T F** SWOT analysis is the identification and evaluation of a firm's strengths and weaknesses and external opportunities

15. **T F** Operational plans aimed at increasing sales would include specific advertising activities.

16. **T F** Measuring actual performance is the first step in the control process.

17. **T F** Top managers rely on technical skills more than managers at other levels.

18. **T F** A democratic leader makes all the decisions and tells subordinates what to do.

19. **T F** Brainstorming is a common technique used to generate alternatives in solving problems.

20. **T F** Implementation of a decision requires time, planning, preparation of personnel, and evaluation of results.

Multiple-Choice Questions

21. _____ The process of developing a set of goals and committing an organization to them is called
   a. organizing.
   b. planning.
   c. motivating.
   d. controlling.
   e. directing.

22. _____ Grouping resources and activities to accomplish some goal is called
   a. motivating.
   b. directing.
   c. leading.
   d. planning.
   e. organizing.

23. _____ Acme Houseware established a goal to increase its sales by 20 percent in the next year. To ensure that the firm reaches its goal, the sales reports are monitored on a weekly basis. When sales show a slight decline, the sales manager takes actions to correct the problem. Which management function is the manager using?
    a. Leading
    b. Controlling
    c. Directing
    d. Organizing
    e. Planning

24. _____ Who is responsible for developing a firm's mission?
    a. Top managers
    b. First-level managers
    c. Operations managers
    d. Middle managers
    e. Supervisors

25. _____ The chief executive officer of Southwest Airlines provides the company with leadership and overall guidance and is responsible for developing its mission and establishing its goals. Which area of management is being used?
    a. Human resources
    b. Operations
    c. Financial
    d. Administrative
    e. Marketing

26. _____ This manager is responsible for facilitating the exchange of products between an organization and its customers or clients.
    a. Human resources manager
    b. Marketing manager
    c. Operations manager
    d. Financial manager
    e. Administrative manager

27. _____ These types of skills allow a manager to see the "big picture" and understand how the various parts of an organization or idea can fit together.
    a. Interpersonal skills
    b. Conceptual skills
    c. Technical skills
    d. Communication skills
    e. Analytical skills

28. _____ Because a large part of the manager's day is spent conversing with others, it is important for the managers to have
    a. conceptual skills.
    b. analytical skills.
    c. technical skills.
    d. communication skills.
    e. interpersonal skills

29. _____ Which leadership style is task-oriented, driven, charismatic, and enthusiastic?
    a. Autocratic leadership
    b. Participative leadership
    c. Entrepreneurial leadership
    d. Democratic leadership

30. _____ Which of the following statements is correct about TQM?
    a. Top management must make a strong commitment to a TQM program by treating quality improvement as a top priority.
    b. Employees should be aware of TQM movement, not necessarily involved in it.
    c. Managers need to ask for input occasionally in order to practice TQM.
    d. The top administration should appear to be interested in TQM.
    e. In order for TQM to function effectively, you need a lot of resources.

Answers to the Test Yourself questions appear at the end of the book on page TY-1.

Video Case
L.L.Bean Relies on Its Core Values and Effective Leadership

L.L.Bean's first product was a waterproof boot, designed by Maine outdoorsman Leon Leonwood Bean, who promised complete customer satisfaction. One hundred pairs were sold—and 90 pairs were returned because of a defect. Bean refunded the customers' money and went to work perfecting the product, now one of the most popular in the firm's long and successful history.

L.L.Bean began in 1912 as a tiny mail-order company and has grown to include 14 retail stores in ten states, an online store, and a popular catalog showcasing many of the company's 20,000 items, including high-quality clothing, accessories, outdoor gear, luggage, linens, and furniture. It

is still privately owned and family run and has had just three presidents in its history—L.L.Bean himself, his grandson Leon Gorman, and now Chris McCormick, the first nonfamily member to lead the firm. New England is the core of L.L.Bean's market, and its selling cycle accelerates sharply every year around the winter holidays. Headquartered in Freeport, Maine, near its original store, the company reports annual sales of over $1.5 billion.

Managers at L.L.Bean today have many opportunities for using their planning, organizing, leading, and controlling skills. During the preholiday selling season, for instance, temporary workers hired to handle the increased workload bring the regular staff of about 4,600 to almost double its size, so managers have to reorganize the teams of 25 to 30 front-line employees who work in the call centers. Regular employees not currently in leadership positions are asked to head the teams of temps, ensuring they have an experienced person to help them develop their skills and perform to expectations. This organizing strategy works so well that many temps return year after year.

Planning skills come to the fore when top management decides when and where to open new retail stores, whether to expand the number of outlet stores offering discontinued items and overstocks, and how much to invest in ensuring that L.L.Bean buildings meet the highest standards of environmental stewardship. One recent strategic planning project resulted in the creation of a new clothing and accessories collection called L.L.Bean Signature, featuring updated versions of classic items from the company's 100-year heritage.

With respect to the control function, managers assess employee performance with a continuous evaluation process. Corporate-level goals are broken down to the level of the individual store and employee. If something isn't on track, the supervisor is expected to let the employee know and help figure out a solution. However, control at L.L.Bean is not entirely a top-down process. Employees are encouraged to develop their own personal goals, such as learning a new skill or gaining a better appreciation of the way L.L.Bean makes business decisions. Managers help them find ways to meet these personal objectives as well, through a temporary reassignment within the firm or participation in a special company project.

L.L.Bean has a strong collaborative work culture in which it is equally important to work through your supervisor, your co-workers, and your subordinates. That means everyone is a leader to some extent. Formal management candidates are asked to demonstrate both analytical and interpersonal skills and to model the company's six core values: outdoor heritage, integrity, service, respect, perseverance, and safe and healthy living. In the early days of the company, L.L.Bean lived above the store and would come downstairs in the middle of the night to help a customer who rang the bell. "A customer is the most important person ever in this office—in person or by mail," he was fond of saying. So, true to his beliefs, leadership style continues to revolve around serving the customer's needs. As one L.L.Bean manager said, the company is all about salespeople and customer service representatives so that they can better serve customers.[18]

Questions

1. What style of leadership do you think most L.L.Bean managers probably employ?
2. To produce hot water in L.L.Bean's flagship store, the company recently installed a solar hot water system that will offset almost 11,000 pounds of carbon dioxide emissions every year. Suggest some of the questions the company's managers might have asked at each level of planning (strategic, tactical, operational, and contingency) for this project.
3. Which managerial role or roles do you think the leaders of L.L.Bean's temp teams fill?

Building Skills for Career Success

1. Social Media Exercise

Crowdsourcing is a set of principles, processes, and platforms to get things done that includes putting out an open call to a group and managing the responses and output. Crowdsourcing can be like outsourcing in a bigger way because instead of contracting to one known entity, you are putting a call out to a bigger group, often a global online community, to either get many to participate or to find the person you need by casting a much wider net.

There are crowdsourcing companies that perform specific types of work such as translations (MyGengo, Smartling), transcription (CastingWords), keyword marketing (Trada), even design and marketing work (Prova, 99Designs, CrowdSpring). Each company operates differently. In the case of transcription or translation, you give work to a company like CastingWords or MyGengo, and they in turn put the job out to their "crowd" of workers from around the world. They are like the middleman to helping you get the work done, and their distributed workforce can be less costly to them so they pass on their savings to your organization.

1. Check out a few of these crowdsourcing companies. What are your thoughts? Do you think they are effective? Why or why not?
2. Which type of leadership is most likely to include the use of crowdsourcing?
3. Can you think of other areas in businesses that can benefit from the use of crowdsourcing? What are they?

2. Building Team Skills

Over the past few years, an increasing number of employees, stockholders, and customers have demanded to know more about their companies. As a result, more companies have been taking the time to analyze their operations and to prepare mission statements that focus on the purpose of the company. The mission statement is becoming a critical planning tool for successful companies. To make effective decisions, employees must understand the purpose of their company.

Assignment

1. Divide into teams and write a mission statement for one of the following types of businesses:

   Food service, restaurant
   Banking
   Airline
   Auto repair
   Cabinet manufacturing

2. Discuss your mission statement with other teams. How did the other teams interpret the purpose of your company? What is the mission statement saying about the company?

3. Write a one-page report on what you learned about developing mission statements.

3. Researching Different Careers

A successful career requires planning. Without a plan, or roadmap, you will find it very difficult, if not impossible, to reach your desired career destination. The first step in planning is to establish your career goal. You then must set objectives and develop plans for accomplishing those objectives. This kind of planning takes time, but it will pay off later.

Assignment

Complete the following statements:

1. My career objective is to
   *
   *
   *
   *

This statement should encapsulate what you want to accomplish over the long run. It may include the type of job you want and the type of business or industry you want to work in. Examples include the following:

* My career goal is to work as a top manager in the food industry.
* My career goal is to supervise aircraft mechanics.
* My career goal is to win the top achievement award in the advertising industry.

2. My career objectives are to
   *
   *
   *
   *

Objectives are benchmarks along the route to a career destination. They are more specific than a career goal. A statement about a career objective should specify what you want to accomplish, when you will complete it, and any other details that will serve as criteria against which you can measure your progress. Examples include the following:

* My objective is to enroll in a management course at Main College in the spring semester 2014.
* My objective is to earn an A in the management course at Main College in the spring semester 2014.
* My objective is to be promoted to supervisor by January 1, 2016.
* My objective is to prepare a status report by September 30 covering the last quarter's activities by asking Charlie in Quality Control to teach me the procedures.

3. Exchange your goal and objectives statements with another class member. Can your partner interpret your objectives correctly? Are the objectives concise and complete? Do they include criteria against which you can measure your progress? If not, discuss the problem and rewrite the objective.

Endnotes

1. Based on information in "Kindle Fire HD and Paperwhite Sales Make Amazon No Profit", *BBC News,* October 11, 2012, www.bbc.co.uk; Erika Andersen, "The Shift that Will Save Your Business—and 3 Ways to Make It Happen," *Forbes,* October 29, 2012, www.forbes.com; John Letzing, "Amazon Adds that Robotic Touch," *Wall Street Journal,* March 20, 2012, www.wsj.com; James B. Stewart, "Amazon Says Long Term and Means It," *New York Times,* December 16, 2011, www.nytimes .com; www.amazon.com.

2. Nancy Rothbard. "Put on a Happy Face, Seriously," *Wall Street Journal,* October 24, 2011, http://online.wsj.com/article/SB100014240529702033 8880457661294373851 6996.html.

3. Mike Ramsey, "Ford Names COO, Revamps Regional Chiefs," *Wall Street Journal,* November 1, 2012, http://online.wsj.com/article/SB1000 14240529702048463045780925421 02235974.html; Mike Ramsey, "Ford Pledges New Focus in South America," *Wall Street Journal,* November 14, 2012, http://online.wsj.com/article/SB10001424127887324556304578 119193988515894.html.

4. Twitter, https://twitter.com/ (accessed November 17, 2012); Amazon.com, http://phx.corporate-ir.net/phoenix.zhtml?c=97664& p=irol-faq#14296 (accessed November 17, 2012); Facebook, https:// www.facebook.com/facebook?v=info (accessed November 17, 2012).

5. Lisa Jennings, "Starbucks to Accelerate Growth in 2013," *Nation's Restaurant News,* November 2, 2012, http://nrn.com/news/starbucks -accelerate-growth-2013.

6. Nick Wingfield, "Nintendo Confronts a Changed Video Game World," *New York Times,* November 24, 2012, http://www.nytimes .com/2012/11/25/technology/nintendos-wii-u-takes-aim-at-a-changed -video-game-world.html.

7. Ann Zimmerman and Joan E. Solsman, "Best Buy's Turnaround Plan Models Unlikely Set of Retailers," *Wall Street Journal,* November 15, 2012, http://online.wsj.com/article/SB1000142412788732455630457811 9321442547426.html.

8. Nelson D. Schwartz, "U.S. Companies Brace for an Exit From the Euro by Greece," *New York Times,* September 2, 2012, http://www.nytimes .com/2012/09/03/business/economy/us-companies-prepare-in-case -greece-exits-euro.html.

9. Adam Lashinsky, "Amazon's Jeff Bezos: The ultimate disrupter," *Fortune,* November 16, 2012, http://management.fortune.cnn .com/2012/11/16/jeff-bezos-amazon/.

10. Seth Stevenson, "Simplicity and Order for All," *Wall Street Journal,* October 26, 2012, http://online.wsj.com/article/SB100014240529702044 2590457807264069124604.html.

11. Christopher Drew, "Lockheed's Incoming Chief Forced Out Over Ethics Violation," *New York Times*, November 9, 2012, http://www .nytimes.com/2012/11/10/business/lockheed-citing-ethics-violation -says-incoming-chief-has-quit.html; Loren Thompson, "Lockheed's New CEO is the Right Mix of Tough and Sensible," *Forbes*, November 13, 2012, http://www.forbes.com/sites/lorenthompson/ 2012/11/13/lockheed-martins-new-ceo-is-the-right-mix-of-tough -and-sensible/.

12. Bryan Simpson, "New Belgium Brewing: How Intangibles Keep Employees Coming Back for More," *Sustainable Brands*, July 2012, http://www.sustainablebrands.com/news_and_views/jul2012/new

-belgium-brewing-how-intangibles-keep-employees-coming -back-more.

13. Andrew J. Dubrin, *Leadership: Research Findings, Practice and Skills*, 7th ed. (Mason, OH: South-Western/Cengage Learning, 2013).

14. Anthony Volastro, "Who is the Entrepreneur of the Year?" *CNBC*, November 26, 2012, http://www.cnbc.com/id/49967727.

15. Ricky Griffin, *Management*, 11th ed. (Mason, OH: South-Western Cengage, 2012), 7.

16. Christine Haughney, "A Sale Gives a Magazine on Healthy Eating a New Lease on Life," *New York Times*, October 21, 2012, http://www.nytimes .com/2012/10/22/business/media/eating-well-magazines-new-lease-on -life.html.

17. Martin Murray, "Total Quality Management (TQM)," http://logistics .about.com/od/qualityinthesupplychain/a/TQM.htm (accessed March 23, 2012).

18. Based on information on the company website www.llbean.com (accessed January 20, 2011); company news release, "L.L.Bean Installs a Solar Hot Water System to Its Flagship Store in Freeport," www .llbean.com, June 15, 2010; interviews with L.L.Bean employees, and the video, "L.L.Bean Relies on Its Core Values and Effective Leadership."

Creating a Flexible Organization

Learning Objectives

Once you complete this chapter, you will be able to:

1 Understand what an organization is and identify its characteristics.

2 Explain why job specialization is important.

3 Identify the various bases for departmentalization.

4 Explain how decentralization follows from delegation.

5 Understand how the span of management describes an organization.

6 Describe the four basic forms of organizational structure.

7 Describe the effects of corporate culture.

8 Understand how committees and task forces are used.

9 Explain the functions of the informal organization and the grapevine in a business.

Why Should You Care?

To operate a successful business, those in charge must create an organization that operates efficiently and is able to attract employees.

Autonomy Fosters Innovation and Success at W.L. Gore

At W.L. Gore & Associates (www.gore.com), the Delaware-based multinational firm best known for its durable Gore-Tex water-shedding fabric, CEO Terri Kelly is among the few employees with an official job title. The 55-year-old company operates in 30 nations and rings up $3 billion in annual revenue from its portfolio of 1,000 products, ranging from specialized fibers and turbine filters to fiber optic cables and pharmaceutical hoses. Every one of Gore's 10,000 employees (called "associates") is responsible for defining his or her own responsibilities, and because everyone is a part-owner, all have a real stake in the company's long-term success.

Rather than reporting to a manager and referring decisions to higher levels, associates form teams on their own and make decisions with the input of anyone in the organization with the relevant knowledge and expertise. This unconventional "lattice" structure encourages internal communication, commitment, cooperation, and creativity. Coming to agreement on a major decision takes more time at Gore than in traditionally structured organizations. However, because associates are involved every step of the way and healthy debate is part of the process, their ideas and contributions improve the end result.

When new associates are hired, they work with a sponsor to learn how to be effective within the lattice organization and how to chart a rewarding career path. Turnover is low because associates thrive on the challenges, opportunities, experimentation, and teamwork. Even during the recent economic downturn, Gore continued to expand and build on the technological breakthroughs pioneered by its talented and motivated associates.

Thanks to its innovative organization and positive workplace environment, Gore has been named numerous times to *Fortune's* annual list of "100 Best Companies to Work For." Associates have the freedom to develop their capabilities, authority to make things happen through teamwork, and individual accountability for a job well done.[1]

Did You Know?

W.L. Gore employs 10,000 people and rings up $3 billion in annual sales from more than 1,000 products.

To survive and to grow, companies such as W.L. Gore must constantly look for ways to improve their methods of doing business. Managers at W.L. Gore, like those at many organizations, maintain an organizational structure that best achieves company goals and creates products that foster long-term customer relationships.

When firms are organized, or reorganized, the focus is sometimes on achieving low operating costs. Other firms, such as Nike, emphasize providing high-quality products to ensure customer satisfaction. The issue of a firm's organizational structure is important because it can influence performance.

We begin this chapter by examining the business organization—what it is and how it functions in today's business environment. Next, we focus one by one on five characteristics that shape an organization's structure. We discuss job specialization within a company, the grouping of jobs into manageable units or departments, the delegation of power from management to workers, the span of management, and establishment of a chain of command. Then we step back for

ANDREY POPOV/PHOTOS.COM

an overall view of organizational structure, describe the effects of corporate culture, and focus in on how committees and task forces are used. Finally, we look at the network of social interactions—the informal organization—that operates within the formal business structure.

WHAT IS AN ORGANIZATION?

We used the term *organization* throughout Chapter 6 without really defining it, mainly because its everyday meaning is close to its business meaning. Here, however, let us agree that an **organization** is a group of two or more people working together to achieve a common set of goals. A neighborhood dry cleaner owned and operated by a husband-and-wife team is an organization. IBM and Home Depot, which employ thousands of workers worldwide, are also organizations. Although each corporation's organizational structure is more complex than the dry-cleaning establishment, all must be organized to achieve their goals.

An inventor who goes into business to produce and market a new invention hires people, decides what each will do, determines who will report to whom, and so on. These activities are the essence of organizing, or creating, the organization. An organization chart helps to illustrate the shape of an organization.

Developing Organization Charts

An **organization chart** is a diagram that represents the positions and relationships within an organization. An example of an organization chart is shown in Figure 7-1. Each rectangle represents a particular position or person in the organization. At the top is the president, next are the vice presidents, and so on. The solid vertical lines connecting each level of the hierarchy indicate who is in the chain of command. The **chain of command** is the line of authority that extends from the highest to the lowest levels of the organization. You can see that each vice president reports directly to the president. Similarly, the plant managers, regional sales managers, and accounting department manager report to the vice presidents. An organization's chain of command can be short or long. A small local restaurant may have a very short chain of command consisting of the owner at the top and employees below. Large multinational corporations, on the other hand, may have very long chains of command. No matter what the length of the chain of command, organizations must ensure that communication along the chain is clear. Not everyone who works for an organization is part of the direct chain of command. In the chart these positions are represented by broken lines, as you can see with the directors of legal services, public affairs, and human resources. Instead, they hold *advisory*, or *staff*, positions. This difference will be examined later in the chapter when we discuss line-and-staff positions.

Most smaller organizations find organization charts useful. They clarify positions and relationships for everyone in the organization, and they help managers to track growth and change in the organizational structure. However, many large organizations, such as ExxonMobil, Kellogg's, and Procter & Gamble, do not maintain complete, detailed charts. There are two reasons for this. First, it is difficult to chart even a few dozen positions accurately, much less the thousands that characterize larger firms. Second, larger organizations are almost always changing parts of their structure. An organization chart would be outdated before it was completed. Increasingly, technology can help even large and complicated organizations implement up-to-date organization charts.

Major Considerations for Organizing a Business

When a firm is started, management must decide how to organize the firm. These decisions focus on job design, departmentalization, delegation, span of management, and chain of command. In the next several sections, we discuss major issues associated with these dimensions.

organization a group of two or more people working together to achieve a common set of goals

organization chart a diagram that represents the positions and relationships within an organization

chain of command the line of authority that extends from the highest to the lowest levels of an organization

Concept Check

✓ How do large and small organizations use organizational charts differently?

✓ Identify the major considerations when organizing a business.

FIGURE 7-1 A Typical Corporate Organization Chart

A Company's organization chart represents the positions and relationships within the organization and shows the managerial chains of command.

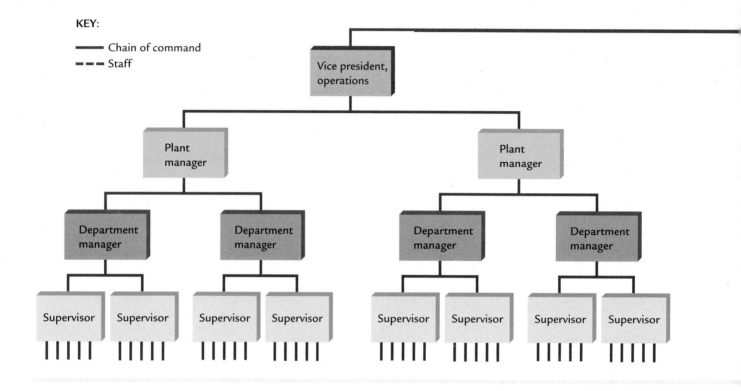

KEY:

—— Chain of command
--- Staff

JOB DESIGN

Learning Objective

2 Explain why job specialization is important.

In Chapter 1, we defined *specialization* as the separation of a manufacturing process into distinct tasks and the assignment of different tasks to different people. Here we are extending that concept to *all* the activities performed within an organization.

Job Specialization

job specialization the separation of all organizational activities into distinct tasks and the assignment of different tasks to different people

Job specialization is the separation of all organizational activities into distinct tasks and the assignment of different tasks to different people. Adam Smith, the 18th-century economist whose theories gave rise to capitalism, was the first to emphasize the power of specialization in his book, *The Wealth of Nations*. According to Smith, the various tasks in a particular pin factory were arranged so that one worker drew the wire for the pins, another straightened the wire, a third

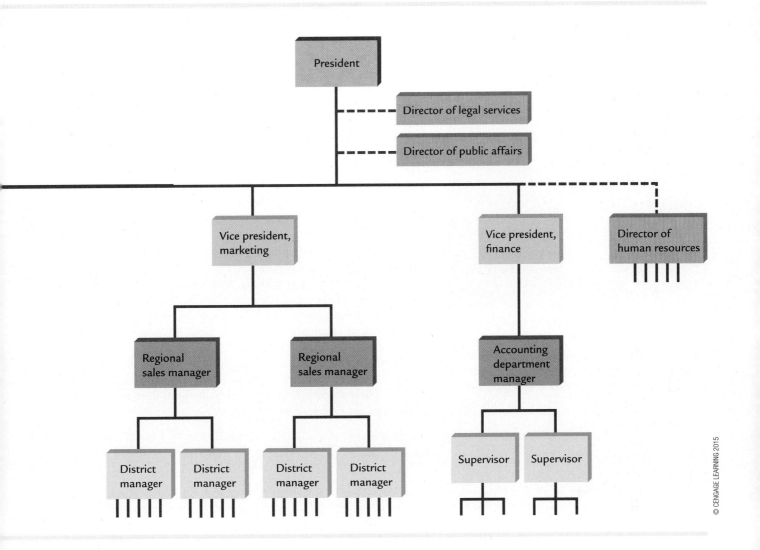

cut it, a fourth ground the point, and a fifth attached the head. Smith claimed that 10 men were able to produce 48,000 pins per day. Before specialization, they could produce only 200 pins per day because each worker had to perform all five tasks!

The Rationale for Specialization

For a number of reasons, some job specialization is necessary in every organization because the "job" of most organizations is too large for one person to handle. In a firm such as Ford Motor Company, thousands of people are needed to manufacture automobiles. Others are needed to sell the cars, control the firm's finances, and so on.

Second, when a worker has to learn one specific, highly specialized task, that individual can learn it quickly and perform it efficiently. Third, a worker repeating the same job does not lose time changing operations, as the pin workers did when producing complete pins. Fourth, the more specialized the job, the easier it is to

Concept Check

✓ What are the positive and negative effects of specialization?

✓ What are three ways to reduce the negative effects of specialization?

design specialized equipment. And finally, the more specialized the job, the easier the job training.

Alternatives to Job Specialization

Unfortunately, specialization can have negative consequences. The most significant drawback is the boredom and dissatisfaction employees may feel when repeating the same job. Bored employees may be absent from work frequently, not put much effort into their work, and even sabotage the company's efforts to produce quality products.

To combat these problems, managers often turn to job rotation. **Job rotation** is the systematic shifting of employees from one job to another. For example, a worker may be assigned a different job every week for a four-week period and then return to the first job in the fifth week. Job rotation provides a variety of tasks so that workers are less likely to become bored and dissatisfied. Intel, for instance, encourages job rotation as a means of sharing ideas, perspectives, and best practices across the company. Job rotation helps workers stay interested in their jobs, develop new skills, and identify new roles where they may want to focus their energies in the future. According to the Society for Human Resource Management, around 38 percent of employers offer some kind of cross-training for their workers.[2]

Two other approaches—job enlargement and job enrichment—also can provide solutions to the problems caused by job specialization. These topics, along with other methods used to motivate employees, are discussed in Chapter 10.

Specialization has its drawbacks. This employee has a specialized job that includes cutting out leather components that will be used to produce handbags. Specialization is efficient for the firm, but it can leave employees bored and dissatisfied. What do you think a firm can do to offset these problems?

© OLAF SPEIER/SHUTTERSTOCK.COM

DEPARTMENTALIZATION

After jobs are designed, they must be grouped together into "working units," or departments. This process is called **departmentalization**, which is the process of grouping jobs into manageable units. Today, the most common bases for organizing a business into effective departments are by function, by product, by location, and by customer.

By Function

Departmentalization by function groups jobs that relate to the same organizational activity. Under this scheme, all marketing personnel are grouped together in the marketing department, all production personnel in the production department, and so on.

Most smaller and newer organizations departmentalize by function. Supervision is simplified because everyone is involved in the same activities and coordination is easy. The disadvantages of this method of grouping jobs are that it can lead to slow decision making and it tends to emphasize the department over the organization as a whole.

By Product

Departmentalization by product groups activities related to a particular good or service. This approach is used often by older and larger firms that produce and sell a variety of products. Each department handles its own marketing, production, financial management, and human resources activities.

Departmentalization by product makes decision making easier and provides for the integration of all activities associated with each product. However, it causes some duplication of specialized activities—such as finance—between departments. Moreover, the emphasis is placed on the product rather than on the whole organization.

By Location

Departmentalization by location groups activities according to the defined geographic area in which they are performed. Departmental areas may range from whole countries (for international firms) to regions within countries (for national firms) to areas of several city blocks (for police departments organized into precincts). For example, Ford has divisions for the Americas, Europe, Asia Pacific and Africa, and China. Departmentalization by location allows the organization to respond readily to the unique demands or requirements of different locations. Nevertheless, a large administrative staff and an elaborate control system may be needed to coordinate operations across many locations.

By Customer

Departmentalization by customer groups activities according to the needs of various customer populations. The advantage of this approach is that it allows the firm to deal efficiently with unique customers or customer groups. The biggest drawback is that a larger-than-usual administrative staff is needed.

How is your school organized? These call center employees are organized by their function. Some businesses are organized by more than their functions, though. For example, if your university has more than one campus, they are organized by location but also by function such as by their business, social sciences, and math departments. Your school also might be organized by customer such as by undergraduate, graduate, and continuing education students.

Combinations of Bases

Many organizations use a combination of departmentalization bases. PepsiCo, for instance, is divided by product and location. It has product divisions such as Beverages, Frito-Lay, Quaker, and Latin American Foods, as well as divisions based on location such as Asia, Europe, the Middle East, and Africa.[3]

Take a moment to examine Figure 7-2. Notice that departmentalization by customer is used to organize New-Wave Fashions, Inc., into three major divisions: Men's,

departmentalization by location grouping activities according to the defined geographic area in which they are performed

departmentalization by customer grouping activities according to the needs of various customer populations

Concept Check

✓ What are the four most common bases for departmentalization?

✓ Give an example of each.

FIGURE 7-2 Multibase Departmentalization for New-Wave Fashions, Inc.

Most firms use more than one basis for departmentalization to improve efficiency and to avoid overlapping positions.

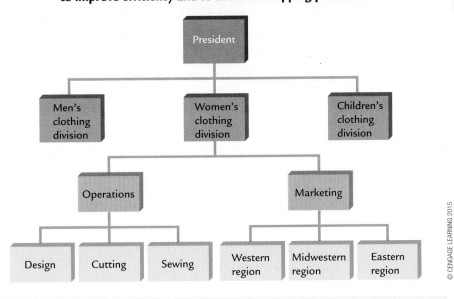

Women's, and Children's clothing. Then functional departmentalization is used to distinguish the firm's production and marketing activities. Finally, location is used to organize the firm's marketing efforts.

Learning Objective

4 Explain how decentralization follows from delegation.

delegation assigning part of a manager's work and power to other workers

responsibility the duty to do a job or perform a task

authority the power, within an organization, to accomplish an assigned job or task

accountability the obligation of a worker to accomplish an assigned job or task

decentralized organization an organization in which management consciously attempts to spread authority widely in the lower levels of the organization

centralized organization an organization that systematically works to concentrate authority at the upper levels of the organization

DELEGATION, DECENTRALIZATION, AND CENTRALIZATION

The third major step in the organizing process is to distribute power in the organization. **Delegation** assigns work and power to other workers. The degree of centralization or decentralization of authority is determined by the overall pattern of delegation within the organization.

Delegation of Authority

Because no manager can do everything, delegation is vital to completion of a manager's work. Delegation is also important in developing the skills and abilities of subordinates. It allows those who are being groomed for higher-level positions to play increasingly important roles in decision making.

STEPS IN DELEGATION The delegation process generally involves three steps (see Figure 7-3). First, the manager must *assign responsibility*. **Responsibility** is the duty to do a job or perform a task. In most job settings, a manager simply gives the worker a job to do. Typical job assignments might range from preparing a report on the status of a new quality control program to being put in charge of a task force. Second, the manager must *grant authority*. **Authority** is the power, within the organization, to accomplish an assigned job or task. This might include the power to obtain specific information, order supplies, authorize relevant expenditures, or make certain decisions. Finally, the manager must *create accountability*. **Accountability** is the obligation of a worker to accomplish an assigned job or task.

FIGURE 7-3 Steps in the Delegation Process

To be successful, a manager must learn how to delegate. No one can do everything alone.

THE DELEGATION PROCESS

© CENGAGE LEARNING 2015

Note that accountability is created but it cannot be delegated. Suppose that you are an operations manager for Target and are responsible for performing a specific task. You, in turn, delegate this task to someone else. You nonetheless remain accountable to your immediate supervisor for getting the task done properly. If the other person fails to complete the assignment, you—not the person to whom you delegated the task—will be held accountable.

BARRIERS TO DELEGATION For several reasons, managers may be unwilling to delegate work. This may be because the manager does not trust the employee to complete the task, or because the manager fears the employee will perform exceptionally and attract the notice of higher level managers. Finally, some managers do not delegate because they are disorganized and they are not able to plan and assign work effectively.

Decentralization of Authority

The pattern of delegation throughout an organization determines the extent to which that organization is decentralized or centralized. In a **decentralized organization**, management consciously attempts to spread authority widely across various organization levels. A **centralized organization**, on the other hand, systematically works to concentrate authority at the upper levels. For example, shipping companies like UPS, tend to be centralized, with shipping dispatches coordinated by upper management. Large organizations may have characteristics of both decentralized and centralized organizations. Random House and Penguin Books merged to become the largest consumer book publishing house in the world. Yet, the merged company hopes to maintain the flexibility and creativity of a smaller and more decentralized company while taking advantage of the benefits of large scale.[4]

A number of factors can influence the extent to which a firm is decentralized. One is the external environment in which the firm operates. The more complex and unpredictable this environment, the more likely it is that top management will let lower-level managers make important decisions because lower-level managers are closer to the problems. Another factor is the nature of the decision itself. The riskier or more important the decisions that have to be made, the greater the tendency to centralize decision making. A third factor is the abilities

Entrepreneurial Success

Successful Leaders Are Successful Delegators

Starting a business? This is a good time to learn to delegate, because as the business grows, you'll need help getting everything done. Lifelong entrepreneur Sir Richard Branson, who heads the Virgin Group, realized the importance of delegation early in his business career. He found that by hiring enthusiastic, capable employees to handle his fledgling firm's daily operations, he would have more time to focus on strategy and on problem solving. Branson also gave his employees the flexibility to develop their own skills and contribute their own ideas to improve the business, making delegation a win–win for all.

Another tip for effective delegation: Understand which tasks must be done and which must be done by *you,* and divide the work accordingly. Although somebody has to buy office supplies, it doesn't necessarily have to be added to your to-do list. On the other hand, you may not want to delegate a few small or unimportant tasks that give you satisfaction, as long as you don't allow them to take up too much of your day.

Finally, agree on specific goals, set deadlines, and communicate regularly after you delegate—and then resist the impulse to manage too closely. You can be supportive and provide guidance without hovering over an employee's shoulder or undermining the employee's authority. Unless a major problem arises, step back and allow the assigned person to assume responsibility instead of rushing in to take charge before you're needed.

Sources: Based on information in Erica Quin-Easter, "From Entrepreneur to Manager: Managing for Growth," *Bangor Daily News (Maine)*, October 11, 2012, www.bangordailynews.com; "Richard Branson on the Art of Delegation," *Entrepreneur*, July 19, 2011, www.entrepreneur.com; Jeffrey R. Cornwall, "When Starting a Business, Delegate, Delegate, Delegate," *Christian Science Monitor*, March 14, 2012, www.csmonitor.com; Adelaide Lancaster, "Get the Job You Love: An Entrepreneur's Guide to Delegating," *Forbes*, May 15, 2012, www.forbes.com.

Delegate, delegate, delegate. The industrialist Andrew Carnegie once said, "No person will make a great business who wants to do it all himself or get all the credit." Delegating gives employees different tasks to do, which can enrich and enlarge their jobs. It also enables both employees and their superiors to learn new skills required for higher-level positions.

Concept Check

✓ Identify and describe the three steps in the delegation process.

✓ Differentiate decentralized organization and centralized organization.

Learning Objective

5 **Understand how the span of management describes an organization.**

span of management (or span of control) the number of workers who report directly to one manager

of lower-level managers. If these managers do not have strong decision-making skills, top managers will be reluctant to decentralize. Finally, a firm that has practiced centralization or decentralization is likely to maintain that same posture in the future.

In principle, neither decentralization nor centralization is right. What works for one organization may or may not work for another. Every organization must assess its own situation and choose the level of centralization or decentralization that will work best.

THE SPAN OF MANAGEMENT

The fourth major step in organizing a business is establishing the **span of management (or span of control)**, which is the number of workers who report directly to one manager. Hundreds of years of research has shown that there is no perfect ratio of subordinates to managers. More recently, theorists have focused on the width of the span of management. This issue is complicated because the span of management may change by department within the same organization. A highly mechanized factory where all operations are standardized may allow for a wide span of management. An advertising agency, where new problems and opportunities arise every day and where teamwork is a constant necessity, will have a much narrower span of management.

Wide and Narrow Spans of Management

A *wide* span of management exists when a manager has a larger number of subordinates. A *narrow* span exists when the manager has only a few subordinates. Several factors determine the span that is best for a particular manager (see Figure 7-4). Generally, the span of management may be wide when (1) the manager and the subordinates are very competent, (2) the organization has a well-established set of

FIGURE 7-4 The Span of Management

Several criteria determine whether a firm uses a wide span of management, in which a number of workers report to one manager, or a narrow span, in which a manager supervises only a few workers.

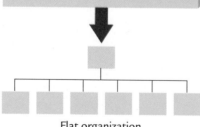

WIDE SPAN
- High level of competence in managers and workers
- Standard operating procedures
- Few new problems

NARROW SPAN
- Physical dispersion of subordinates
- Manager has additional tasks
- High level of interaction required between manager and workers
- High frequency of new problems

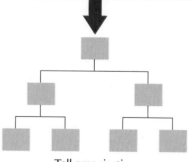

Flat organization

Tall organization

© CENGAGE LEARNING 2015

standard operating procedures, and (3) few new problems are expected to arise. The span should be narrow when (1) workers are physically located far from one another, (2) the manager has much work to do in addition to supervising workers, (3) a great deal of interaction is required between supervisor and workers, and (4) new problems arise frequently.

Organizational Height

The span of management has an obvious impact on relations between managers and workers. It has a more subtle, but equally important, impact on the height of the organization. **Organizational height** is the number of layers, or levels, of management in a firm. The span of management plays a direct role in determining the height of the organization (see Figure 7-4). If the span of management is wide, fewer levels are needed, and the organization is *flat*. If the span of management is narrow, more levels are needed, and the resulting organization is *tall*.

In a tall organization, administrative costs are higher because more managers are needed. Communication may become distorted because information has to pass up and down through more levels. When companies are cutting costs, one option is to decrease organizational height in order to reduce related administrative expenses. For example, in the wake of fallout from the 2008 financial crisis and stricter rules on risky forms of investing, major Swiss bank UBS laid off 10,000 employees (15 percent of staff) and scrapped its risky fixed income business. These steps were meant to simplify the company's structure and help it return to its roots as a private banker.[5] Although flat organizations avoid these problems, their managers may perform more administrative duties simply because there are fewer managers. Wide spans of management also may require managers to spend considerably more time supervising and working with subordinates.

Narrow versus wide spans of management: Which is better? The manager on the right side of the photo supervises only a handful of employees. Consequently, he has a narrow span of management. Companies are constantly searching for the ideal number of employees their supervisors should manage.

organizational height the number of layers, or levels, of management in a firm

Concept Check

✓ Describe the two spans of management.

✓ What are problems associated with each one?

FORMS OF ORGANIZATIONAL STRUCTURE

Up to this point, we have focused our attention on the major characteristics of organizational structure. In many ways, this is like discussing the parts of a jigsaw puzzle one by one. It is now time to put the puzzle together. We will next discuss four basic forms of organizational structure: line, line-and-staff, matrix, and network.

The Line Structure

The simplest and oldest form of organizational structure is the **line structure**, in which the chain of command goes directly from person to person throughout the organization. Thus, a straight line could be drawn down through the levels of management, from the chief executive down to the lowest level in the organization. In a small retail store, for example, an hourly employee might report to an assistant manager, who reports to a store manager, who reports to the owner.

Managers within a line structure, called **line managers**, make decisions and give orders to subordinates to achieve the organization's goals. A line structure's simplicity and clear chain of command allow line managers to make decisions quickly with direct accountability because the decision maker only has one supervisor to report to.

The downside of a line structure is that line managers are responsible for many activities, and therefore must have a wide range of knowledge about all of them. While this may not be a problem for small organizations with a lower volume of

Learning Objective

6 Describe the four basic forms of organizational structure.

line structure an organizational structure in which the chain of command goes directly from person to person throughout the organization

line managers a position in which a person makes decisions and gives orders to subordinates to achieve the organization's goals

line-and-staff structure an organizational structure that utilizes the chain of command from a line structure in combination with the assistance of staff managers

staff managers a position created to provide support, advice, and expertise within an organization

activities, in a larger organization, activities are more numerous and complex, thus making it more difficult for line managers to fully understand what they are in charge of. Therefore, line managers in a larger organization would have a hard time making an educated decision without expert advice from outside sources. As a result, line structures are not very effective in medium- or large-sized organizations, but are very popular in small organizations.

The Line-and-Staff Structure

A **line-and-staff structure** not only utilizes the chain of command from a line structure but also provides line managers with specialists, called staff managers. Therefore, this structure works much better for medium- and large-sized organizations than line management alone. **Staff managers** provide support, advice, and expertise to line managers, thus eliminating the major drawback of line structures. Staff managers are not part of the chain of command like line managers are, but they do have authority over their assistants (see Figure 7-5).

Both line and staff managers are needed for effective management, but the two positions differ in important ways. Most importantly, line managers have *line authority*, which means that they can make decisions and issue directives relating to the organization's goals. Staff managers seldom have this kind of authority. Instead, they usually have either advisory authority or functional authority. *Advisory authority* is the expectation that line managers will consult the appropriate staff manager when

FIGURE 7-5 Line and Staff Managers

A line manager has direct responsibility for achieving the company's goals and is in the direct chain of command. A staff manager supports and advises the line managers.

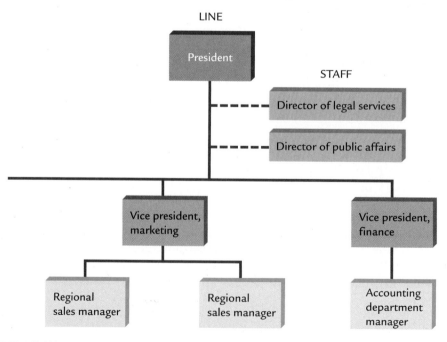

making decisions. *Functional authority* is a stronger form. It is the authority of staff managers to make decisions and issue directives about their areas of expertise. For example, a legal adviser for Nike can decide whether to retain a particular clause in a contract but not product pricing.

Staff managers in a line-and-staff structure tend to have more access to information than line managers. This means that line managers must rely on the staff managers for information. This is usually not an issue, unless the staff manager makes a wrong decision and there is no one else to catch his or her mistake.[6] For a variety of reasons, conflict between line managers and staff managers is fairly common in business. Staff managers often have more formal education and sometimes are younger (and perhaps more ambitious) than line managers. Line managers may perceive staff managers as a threat to their own authority and thus may resent them. For their part, staff managers may become annoyed or angry if their expert recommendations are not adopted by line management.

Fortunately, there are several ways to minimize the likelihood of such conflict. One way is to integrate line and staff managers into one team. Another is to ensure that the areas of responsibility of line and staff managers are clearly defined. Finally, line and staff managers both can be held accountable for the results of their activities.

Line-and-staff organization structure. Ronald McDonald occupies a staff position and does not have direct authority over other employees at McDonald's. The other individuals shown here occupy line positions and do have direct authority over some of the other McDonald's employees.

The Matrix Structure

The **matrix structure** combines vertical and horizontal lines of authority, forming a matrix shape in the organizational chart. The matrix structure occurs when product departmentalization is superimposed on a functionally departmentalized organization. In a matrix organization, authority flows both down and across and individuals report to more than one superior at the same time.

To understand the structure of a matrix organization, consider the usual functional arrangement, with people working in departments such as engineering, finance, and marketing. Now suppose that we assign people from these departments to a special group that is working on a new project as a team—a cross-functional team. A **cross-functional team** consists of individuals with varying specialties, expertise, and skills that are brought together to achieve a common task. Frequently, cross-functional teams are charged with the responsibility of developing new products. The manager in charge of a team is usually called a *project manager*. Any individual who is working with the team reports to *both* the project manager and the individual's superior in the functional department (see Figure 7-6).

Cross-functional team projects may be temporary, in which case the team is disbanded once the mission is accomplished, or they may be permanent. As the world becomes more connected, many companies require managers to have had cross-functional team experience. Major corporations such as GE, Whirlpool, Procter & Gamble all utilize the diverse viewpoints that come out of cross-functional teams.

These teams often are empowered to make major decisions. When a cross-functional team is employed, prospective team members may receive special training because effective teamwork can require different skills. For cross-functional teams to be successful, team members must be given specific information on the job each performs. The team must also develop a sense of cohesiveness and maintain good communications among its members.

Matrix structures offer advantages over other organizational forms, added flexibility probably being the most obvious one. The matrix structure also can increase productivity, raise morale, and nurture creativity and innovation. In addition, employees experience personal development through doing a variety of jobs.

matrix structure an organizational structure that combines vertical and horizontal lines of authority, usually by superimposing product departmentalization on a functionally departmentalized organization

cross-functional team a team of individuals with varying specialties, expertise, and skills that are brought together to achieve a common task

FIGURE 7-6 A Matrix Structure

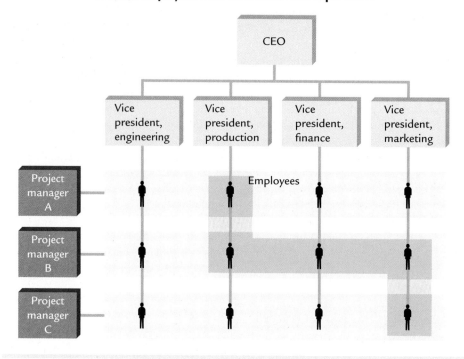

A matrix is usually the result of combining product departmentalization with function departmentalization. It is a complex structure in which employees have more than one supervisor.

CEO

Vice president, engineering

Vice president, production

Vice president, finance

Vice president, marketing

Project manager A

Project manager B

Project manager C

Employees

Source: Ricky W. Griffin, *Management*, 11th ed. Copyright © 2012 by South-Western/Cengage Learning, Mason, OH. Adapted with permission.

The matrix structure also has disadvantages. Having employees report to more than one supervisor can cause confusion about who is in charge. Like committees, teams may take longer to resolve problems and issues than individuals working alone. Other difficulties include personality clashes, poor communication, undefined individual roles, unclear responsibilities, and difficulties in finding ways to reward individual and team performance simultaneously. Because more managers and support staff may be needed, a matrix structure may be more expensive to maintain.

The Network Structure

network structure an organizational structure in which administration is the primary function, and most other functions are contracted out to other firms

In a **network structure** (sometimes called a *virtual organization*), administration is the primary function performed, and other functions such as engineering, production, marketing, and finance are contracted out to other organizations. Frequently, a network organization does not manufacture the products it sells. This type of organization has a few permanent employees consisting of top management and hourly clerical workers. Leased facilities and equipment, as well as temporary workers, are increased or decreased as the organization's needs change. Thus, there is limited formal structure associated with a network organization.

An obvious strength of a network structure is flexibility that allows the organization to adjust quickly to changes. Network structures consist of a lot of teams working together, rather than relying on one centralized leader. This also means that network structures may be more likely to survive if an important leader or member leaves because there is no power vacuum left at the top.[7] Some of the challenges faced by managers in network-structured organizations include controlling the quality of work performed by other organizations, low morale and high turnover among hourly workers, and a lack of a clear hierarchy.

CORPORATE CULTURE

Learning Objective

7 **Describe the effects of corporate culture.**

corporate culture the inner rites, rituals, heroes, and values of a firm

Most managers function within a corporate culture. A **corporate culture** is generally defined as the inner rites, rituals, heroes, and values of a firm. An organization's culture has a powerful influence on how employees think and act. It also can determine public perception of the organization.

Corporate culture generally is thought to have a very strong influence on a firm's performance over time. Hence, it is useful to be able to assess a firm's corporate culture. Common indicators include the physical setting (building or office layouts), what the company says about its corporate culture (in advertising or news releases), how the company greets guests (formal or informal reception areas), and how employees spend their time (working alone in an office or working with others).

Goffee and Jones identified four distinct types of corporate cultures (see Figure 7-7). One is called the *networked culture*, characterized by a base of trust and friendship among employees, a strong commitment to the organization, and an informal environment. A small nonprofit organization may seek to build a networked culture where employees look out for each other and believe strongly in the organizational mission. Building a networked culture in such an organization is important because employees may have to work long hours for relatively little pay, and a strong sense of community and commitment helps to keep productivity high and turnover low.

The phrase *mercenary culture* may have a negative connotation, but it also involves a high degree of passion, energy, sense of purpose, and excitement for one's work. Large banks and investment firms often have mercenary cultures because the environment is fast-paced, the stakes are high, and winning is important. This kind of culture can be very stressful for an employee with an incompatible personality. The term *mercenary* does not imply that employees are motivated to work only for the money, although financial gain does play a role. In this culture, employees are very intense, focused, and determined to win. For example, years after the 2008 economic crisis, Barclays, a major financial company, is still being criticized by regulators for its mercenary culture. Accusations include excessive risk-taking culture and encouraging employees to win by any means.[8]

FIGURE 7-7 Types of Corporate Cultures

Which corporate culture would you choose?

Sociability ↑ High		
Networked Culture • Extrovert energized by relationships • Tolerant of ambiguities and have low needs for structure • Can spot politics and act to stop "negative" politics • Consider yourself easygoing, affable, and loyal to others	**Communal Culture** • You consider yourself passionate • Strong need to identify with something bigger than yourself • You enjoy being in teams • Prepared to make sacrifices for the greater good
Fragmented Culture • Are a reflective and self-contained introvert • Have a high autonomy drive and strong desire to work independently • Have a strong sense of self	**Mercenary Culture** • Goal-oriented and have an obsessive desire to complete tasks • Thrive on competitive energy • Keep "relationships" out of work—develop them

Source: "Types of Corporate Culture," in Rob Goffee and Gareth Jones, *The Character of a Corporation* (New York: HarperCollins, 1998). Copyright © 1998 by Rob Goffee and Gareth Jones. Permission granted by Rob Goffee and Gareth Jones.

Dell Restructures to Jump-Start Innovation

With more than $60 billion in global revenue from computers, cloud computing, and other high-tech offerings, Dell is hardly a scrappy startup. To recapture market share and create the hot new products of tomorrow, the Texas-based company is decentralizing to encourage speedier innovation. As an example, it maintains a separate research-and-development group in Silicon Valley to identify, develop, and market new offerings in networking and other technologies.

As another example, one of Dell's business units—located just eight miles from headquarters—comes up with its own designs for data storage centers. The business acts like a firm founded in somebody's garage, rather than one of many units in a multinational corporation's portfolio. In fact, one of its engineers actually built a piece of equipment in his garage when the unit was young. The head of this unit says "you need a crayon drawing on a napkin," not layers of bureaucracy and strict guidelines, to fuel entrepreneurial innovation. In just five years, this unit has blossomed into a $1 billion business with 500 employees—and more growth is on the horizon.

Restructuring to nurture innovation doesn't guarantee a product hit, as Dell knows from its unsuccessful first experience with a separate smartphone division. Still, decentralization is giving Dell an opportunity to recapture the nimble, innovative spirit of its early days.

Sources: Based on information in Shara Tibken, "Dell Plans to Expand Silicon Valley Staff for R&D," *Marketwatch*, January 31, 2012, http://marketwatch.com/story/dell-plans-to-expand-silicon-valley-staff-for-rd-2012-01-31; Christopher Calnan, "Dell to Up Staff in Santa Clara, Calif.," *Austin Business Journal*, January 31, 2011, http://bizjournals.com/austin/news/2012/01/31/dell-to-up-staff-in-santa-clara-calif.html; Anne VanderMey, "Dell Gets in Touch with Its Inner Entrepreneur," *Fortune*, December 12, 2011, p. 58.

Corporate Culture. Corporate culture can influence an employee's attitudes toward fitness and health. Some organizations have gyms and complimentary healthy snacks such as fruit.

In the *fragmented culture*, employees do not become friends, and they work "at" the organization, not "for" it. Employees have a high degree of autonomy, flexibility, and equality.

The *communal culture* combines the positive traits of the networked culture and the mercenary culture—those of friendship, commitment, high focus on performance, and high energy. People's lives revolve around the product in this culture, and success by anyone in the organization is celebrated by all.[9]

Some experts believe that cultural change is needed when a company's environment changes, such as when the industry becomes more competitive, the company's performance is mediocre, or when the company is growing. It is not uncommon that companies feel they must adjust their culture in order to attract top talent. For example, many companies have formally come out in favor of same-sex marriage, including General Mills, Alcoa, and Aetna. Having a nondiscriminatory culture is seen as important for maintaining a strong workforce for many corporations.[10]

Organizations in the future will look quite different, as technology allows more to be done in small, flexible work groups that are coordinated by computers and held together by strong corporate cultures. Businesses operating in fast-changing industries will require leadership that supports trust and risk taking. Creating a culture of trust in an organization can lead to increases in growth, profit, productivity, and job satisfaction. A culture of trust can help an organization to retain the best people, inspire customer loyalty, develop new markets, and increase creativity.

Another area where corporate culture plays a vital role is the integration of two or more companies. Business leaders often cite the role of corporate cultures in the integration process as one of the primary factors affecting the success of a merger or acquisition. Experts note that corporate culture is a way of conducting business both within the company and externally. If two merging companies do not address differences in corporate culture, they are setting themselves up for missed opportunities and possibly failure.

Concept Check

✓ What is corporate culture?

✓ Explain the four types of corporate cultures.

COMMITTEES AND TASK FORCES

Today, business firms use several types of committees that affect organizational structure. An **ad hoc committee** is created for a specific short-term purpose, such as reviewing the firm's employee benefits plan. Once its work is finished, the ad hoc committee disbands. A **standing committee** is a relatively permanent committee charged with performing a recurring task. A firm might establish a budget review committee, for example, to review departmental budget requests on an ongoing basis. Finally, a **task force** is a committee established to investigate a major problem or pending decision. A firm contemplating a merger with another company might form a task force to assess the pros and cons of the merger.

Committees offer some advantages over individual action. Their several members are able to bring information and knowledge to the task at hand. Furthermore, committees tend to make more accurate decisions and to transmit their results through the organization more effectively. However, committee deliberations take longer than individual actions. In addition, unnecessary compromise may take place within the committee, or the opposite may occur, as one person dominates (and thus negates) the committee process.

Learning Objective

8 **Understand how committees and task forces are used.**

ad hoc committee a committee created for a specific short-term purpose

standing committee a relatively permanent committee charged with performing some recurring task

task force a committee established to investigate a major problem or pending decision

Concept Check

✔ What is the difference between a committee and a task force?

✔ What are the advantages and disadvantages of using committees?

THE INFORMAL ORGANIZATION AND THE GRAPEVINE

So far, we have discussed the organization as a formal structure consisting of interrelated positions. This is the organization that is shown on an organization chart. There is another kind of organization, however, that does not appear on any chart. We define this **informal organization** as the pattern of behavior and interaction that stems from personal rather than official relationships. Embedded within every informal organization are informal groups and the notorious grapevine.

An **informal group** is created by the group members themselves to accomplish goals that may or may not be relevant to the organization. Workers may create an informal group to go bowling, form a union, get a particular manager fired or transferred, or meet for lunch. The group may last for several years or a few hours.

Learning Objective

9 **Explain the functions of the informal organization and the grapevine in a business.**

informal organization the pattern of behavior and interaction that stems from personal rather than official relationships

informal group a group created by the members themselves to accomplish goals that may or may not be relevant to an organization

There is power in numbers. It's common for employees to befriend one another and form informal groups within an organization. The groups provide their members with camaraderie and information, but can create both challenges and benefits for the organization.

BLOOMBERG/GETTY IMAGES

Concept Check

✔ In what ways can informal groups affect a business?

✔ How is the grapevine used in a business organization?

Informal groups can be powerful forces in organizations. They can restrict output, or they can help managers through tight spots. They can cause disagreement and conflict, or they can help to boost morale and job satisfaction. They have the power to improve or worsen employee performance and productivity. Clearly, managers should be aware of informal groups and determine how to utilize them.

The **grapevine** is the informal communications network within an organization. It is completely separate from—and sometimes much faster than—the organization's formal channels of communication. Formal communications usually follow a path that parallels the organizational chain of command. Information can be transmitted through the grapevine in any direction—up, down, diagonally, or horizontally across the organizational structure. Subordinates may pass information to their bosses, an executive may relay something to a maintenance worker, or there may be an exchange of information between people who work in totally unrelated departments. Information gleaned from the grapevine can run the gamut from the latest management decisions to gossip.

How should managers treat the grapevine? Certainly, it would be a mistake to try to eliminate it. People working together, day in and day out, are bound to communicate. A more rational approach is to recognize its existence. For example, managers should respond promptly and aggressively to inaccurate grapevine information to minimize the damage that such misinformation might do. Moreover, the grapevine can come in handy when managers are on the receiving end of important communications from the informal organization.

In the next chapter, we apply these and other management concepts to an extremely important business function: the production of goods and services.

Summary

1 Understand what an organization is and identify its characteristics.

An organization is a group of two or more people working together to achieve a common set of goals. The relationships among positions within an organization can be illustrated by means of an organization chart. Five elements—job design, departmentalization, delegation, span of management, and chain of command—help to determine what an organization chart and the organization itself look like.

2 Explain why job specialization is important.

Job specialization is the separation of all the activities within an organization into smaller components and the assignment of those different components to different people. Several factors combine to make specialization a useful technique for designing jobs, but high levels of specialization may cause employee dissatisfaction and boredom. One technique for overcoming these problems is job rotation.

3 Identify the various bases for departmentalization.

Departmentalization is the grouping of jobs into manageable units. Typical bases for departmentalization are by function, product, location, or customer. Because each of these bases provides particular advantages, most firms—especially larger ones—use a combination of different bases to address different organizational situations.

4 Explain how decentralization follows from delegation.

Delegation is giving part of a manager's work to other workers. It involves the following three steps: (1) assigning responsibility, (2) granting authority, and (3) creating accountability. A decentralized firm is one that delegates as much power as possible to people in the lower management levels. In a centralized firm, on the other hand, power is retained at the upper levels.

5 Understand how the span of management describes an organization.

The span of management is the number of workers who report directly to a manager. Spans generally are characterized as wide (many workers per manager) or narrow (few workers per manager). Wide spans generally result in flat organizations (few layers of management); narrow spans generally result in tall organizations (many layers of management).

6 Describe the four basic forms of organizational structure.

There are four basic forms of organizational structure. The line structure is the oldest and simplest structure, in which the chain of command moves in a straight line from person to person down through the levels of management. The line-and-staff structure is similar to the line structure, but adds specialists called staff managers to assist the line managers in decision making. The line structure works most efficiently for smaller organizations, whereas the line-and-staff structure is used by medium- and large-sized organizations. The matrix structure may be depicted as product departmentalization superimposed on functional departmentalization. With the matrix structure, an employee on a cross-functional team reports to both the project manager and the individual's supervisor in a functional department. In an organization with a network structure, the primary function performed internally is administration, and other functions are contracted out to other firms.

7 Describe the effects of corporate culture.

Corporate culture has both internal and external effects on an organization. An organization's culture can influence the way employees think and act, and it can also determine the public's perception of the organization. Corporate culture can affect a firm's performance over time, either negatively or positively. Creating a culture of trust, for example, can lead to increased growth, profits, productivity, and job satisfaction, while retaining the best employees, inspiring customer loyalty, developing new markets, and increasing creativity. In addition, when two or more companies undergo the integration process, their different or similar corporate cultures can affect the success of a merger or acquisition.

8 Understand how committees and task forces are used.

Committees and task forces are used to develop organizational structure within an organization. An ad hoc committee is created for a specific short-term purpose, whereas a standing committee is relatively permanent. A task force is created to investigate a major problem or pending decision.

9 Explain the functions of the informal organization and the grapevine in a business.

Informal groups are created by group members to accomplish goals that may or may not be relevant to the organization, and they can be very powerful forces. The grapevine—the informal communications network within an organization—can be used to transmit information (important or gossip) through an organization much faster than through the formal communication network. Information transmitted through the grapevine can go in any direction across the organizational structure, skipping up or down levels of management and even across departments.

Key Terms

You should now be able to define and give an example relevant to each of the following terms:

Discussion Questions

1. In what way do organization charts create a picture of an organization?
2. What determines the degree of specialization within an organization?
3. Describe how job rotation can be used to combat the problems caused by job specialization.
4. Why do most firms employ a combination of departmentalization bases?
5. What three steps are involved in delegation? Explain each.
6. How does a firm's top management influence its degree of centralization?
7. How is organization height related to the span of management?
8. Contrast line-and-staff and matrix forms of organizational structure.
9. How does the corporate culture of a local Best Buy store compare to that of a local McDonald's?
10. Which kinds of firms probably would operate most effectively as centralized firms? As decentralized firms?
11. How do decisions concerning span of management and the use of committees affect organizational structure?

Test Yourself

Matching Questions

1. _____ Line of authority from the highest to lowest levels.
2. _____ Two or more people working toward a common goal.
3. _____ Grouping jobs into manageable units.
4. _____ Assigns part of the manager's work to others.
5. _____ The power to accomplish an assigned task.
6. _____ The duty to do a job or perform a task.
7. _____ Combines vertical and horizontal lines of authority.
8. _____ Charged with the responsibility of developing new products.
9. _____ An informal communications network.
10. _____ Committee that investigates major problems or pending decisions.

a. ad hoc committee
b. authority
c. chain of command
d. cross-functional team
e. delegation
f. departmentalization
g. grapevine
h. matrix structure
i. network structure
j. organization
k. responsibility
l. task force
m. span of management

True False Questions

11. **T F** A benefit of specialization is improved efficiency and increased productivity.
12. **T F** Job rotation involves assigning an employee more tasks and greater control.
13. **T F** The power to make decisions is granted through authority.
14. **T F** Accountability is created, not delegated.
15. **T F** The span of management should be wide when a great deal of interaction is required between the supervisor and worker.
16. **T F** Line positions support staff positions in decision making.
17. **T F** Many firms find that by using matrix organization, the motivation level is lowered, and personal growth of employees is limited.
18. **T F** In the mercenary culture, employees work "at" the organization, not "for" it.
19. **T F** Creating a culture of trust can lead to decreased productivity and job satisfaction.
20. **T F** Ad hoc committees can be used effectively to review a firm's employee benefits plan.

Multiple-Choice Questions

21. _____ The process of dividing work to be done by an entire organization into separate parts and assigning the parts to positions within the organization is called _____

a. departmentalization.
b. delegation.
c. job design.
d. specialization.
e. organizing.

22. _____ Who was the first to recognize the power of specialization?
   a. Karl Marx
   b. Max Weber
   c. John Kenneth Galbraith
   d. Adam Smith
   e. Thomas Friedman

23. _____ ABC Distributors is reorganizing to better control costs. The company decided to group hospitals, schools, and churches together into one department. Which departmentalization base is the company using?
   a. Location
   b. Function
   c. Employees
   d. Product
   e. Customer

24. _____ Older and larger firms that produce and sell a variety of products tend to organize by _____
   a. location.
   b. product.
   c. customer.
   d. function.
   e. executive decisions.

25. _____ A supervisor assigned to Wendy, the most proficient employee in the accounting department, a project on cost control that was due in three weeks. For Wendy to be accountable for the project, what must Wendy be given?
   a. Responsibility
   b. Power
   c. Authority
   d. Training
   e. Control

26. _____ Many managers are reluctant to delegate. Which one of the following is not one of the reasons they are reluctant to do so?
   a. They want to be sure that the work gets done.
   b. They fear that workers will do the work well and attract the approving notice of higher-level managers.

   c. They are so disorganized that they simply are not able to plan and assign work.
   d. Most managers are workaholics.
   e. Most subordinates are reluctant to accept delegated tasks.

27. _____ A narrow span of management works best when _____
   a. subordinates are located close together.
   b. the manager has few responsibilities outside of supervision.
   c. little interaction is required between the manager and the worker.
   d. new problems arise frequently.
   e. few problems arise on a daily basis.

28. _____ A relatively permanent committee charged with performing some recurring task is called _____
   a. an ad hoc committee.
   b. a standing committee.
   c. a task force.
   d. a managerial committee.
   e. a permanent committee.

29. _____ A committee is organized to review applications for scholarships. The group will award two scholarships to recent high school graduates. What type of committee would work best?
   a. Ad hoc committee
   b. Task force
   c. Liaison committee
   d. Standing committee
   e. Self-managed team

30. _____ In order to best handle the grapevine, managers should _____
   a. try to eliminate it.
   b. respond slowly to inaccurate information.
   c. respond aggressively to accurate information.
   d. recognize its existence.
   e. reprimand employees who pass on important information.

Answers to the Test Yourself questions appear at the end of the book on page TY-1.

Video Case
Zappos Wants to Make Customers (and Employees) Happy

Zappos (www.zappos.com) doesn't want to simply satisfy its customers—it wants to make them happy, a major reason for its success as an Internet retailer. Founded in 1999 to sell shoes online, the business soon earned a reputation for delivering personalized, responsive customer service. Top executives didn't pressure call-center employees (known internally as members of the Customer Loyalty Team) to follow a script or end conversations quickly. In fact, they encouraged employees to stay on the phone as long as needed to answer customers' questions, discuss merchandise, add a little chit-chat, and provide a "wow" shopping experience. Delighted customers would tell their friends and click or call back for more "wow" the next time they're in the market for new shoes.

By 2009, when it was purchased by the pioneering web giant Amazon, Las Vegas-based Zappos was beginning to branch out into clothing, handbags, and other merchandise. Today, with annual sales surpassing $1 billion, the website features outerwear, beauty products, sporting goods, and many other items, as well as shoes and clothing for the whole family. In addition, the company has established an Insights division to help other companies understand and adapt the unique corporate culture that has given Zappos a vital competitive edge in the dynamic world of e-commerce.

Zappos is so famous for its upbeat, can-do culture—not to mention the many opportunities for advancement available in a fast-growing firm—that it attracts 55,000 job applications every year. During interviews, managers ask offbeat questions such as, "On a scale of one to ten, how weird are you?" The purpose is to determine whether an applicant has the personality and temperament to fit into a corporate culture where fun, change, teamwork, creativity, transparency, and personal growth are highly valued. All newly hired employees have to sign a statement confirming that they understand these core values and are committed to applying them on the job.

Delivering superior service with a virtual smile requires careful behind-the-scenes coordination. Every Zappos employee is responsible for performing specific tasks, supported by regular training plus optional courses to build new skills. Because so many orders come in by phone, the entire workforce (including the CEO) receives a month of call-center training, along with a week of training in the warehouse, to get a first-hand taste of the challenges of customer contact and order fulfillment.

In line with the corporate culture, Zappos provides the tools and the opportunities for employees to become the best they can be. For example, employees are invited to meet with an on-site life coach for assistance in setting and meeting both personal and professional goals. They can sign up to shadow a manager or employee elsewhere in the organization as a way to explore new career possibilities. Work hard, play hard is the rule at Zappos, where holiday parties, picnics, parades, and other special events bring employees together for a bit of fun. These are only some of the ways that Zappos makes the workplace a "Wow" experience for its workforce.

To keep the organization running smoothly, Zappos holds an "all hands" meeting every three months. Videotaped and available online for repeat viewing, these meetings update everyone on the latest departmental and company news, serve as team-building events, and keep employees excited and inspired about working at Zappos. In addition, the firm monitors key performance statistics and posts them at headquarters to inform employees about what's happening to the business, day by day.

Now Zappos is taking on a leadership role in Las Vegas, using its new headquarters in the former city hall as the corporate linchpin in an ambitious plan to revitalize the downtown area. Will Zappos succeed in making its community as happy as its employees and customers?[11]

Questions

1. Do you think Zappos is a decentralized or centralized organization? Do you think it should change? Explain your answer.
2. Of the four types of corporate culture, which most closely describes the culture of Zappos? What are the implications for the organization and for managers and employees?
3. What effect are quarterly meetings and daily posting of performance statistics likely to have on the grapevine inside Zappos?

Building Skills for Career Success

1. Social Media Exercise

Zappos has a reputation for being customer-centered, meaning it embraces the notion that customers come first. One of the ways that it allows employees to communicate with customers is through its blog www.zapposinsights.com/blog.

1. Take a look at this blog. What can you tell about the corporate culture of Zappos?
2. How do they approach customer service? Do you think it works? Why or why not?

2. Building Team Skills

An organization chart is a diagram showing how employees and tasks are grouped and how the lines of communication and authority flow within an organization. These charts can look very different depending on a number of factors, including the nature and size of the business, the way it is departmentalized, its patterns of delegating authority, and its span of management.

Assignment

1. Working in a team, use the following information to draw an organization chart: The KDS Design Center works closely with two home-construction companies, ACME Homebuilders and Highmass. KDS's role is to help customers select materials for their new homes and to ensure that their selections are communicated accurately to the builders. The company is also a retailer of wallpaper, blinds, and drapery. The retail department, the ACME Homebuilders accounts, and the Highmass accounts make up KDS's

three departments. The company has the following positions: president, executive vice president, managers, two appointment coordinators, two ACME Homebuilders coordinators, two Highmass coordinators, two consultants/designers for the Amex and Highmass accounts, 15 retail positions, and four payroll and billing personnel.

2. After your team has drawn the organization chart, discuss the following:
   a. What type of organizational structure does your chart depict? Is it a bureaucratic, matrix, cluster, or network structure? Why?
   b. How does KDS use departmentalization?
   c. To what extent is authority in the company centralized or decentralized?
   d. What is the span of management within KDS?
   e. Which positions are line positions and which are staff? Why?

3. Prepare a three-page report summarizing what the chart revealed about relationships and tasks at the KDS Design Center and what your team learned about the value of organization charts. Include your chart in your report.

3. Researching Different Careers

In the past, company loyalty and the ability to assume increasing job responsibility usually ensured advancement within an organization. While the reasons for seeking advancement (the desire for a better-paying position, more prestige, and job satisfaction) have not changed, the qualifications for career advancement have. In today's business environment, climbing the corporate ladder requires packaging and marketing yourself. To be promoted within your company or to be considered for employment with another company, it is wise to improve your skills continually. By taking workshops and seminars or enrolling in community college courses, you can keep up with the changing technology in your industry.

Networking with people in your business or community can help you to find a new job. Most jobs are filled through personal contacts, proving that who you know can be important.

A list of your accomplishments on the job can reveal your strengths and weaknesses. Setting goals for improvement helps to increase your self-confidence.

Be sure to recognize the signs of job dissatisfaction. If you are feeling unhappy in your job, it may be time to move to another position or company.

Assignment

Are you prepared to climb the corporate ladder? Do a self-assessment by analyzing the following areas and summarize the results in a two-page report.

1. Skills
   - What are your most valuable skills?
   - What skills do you lack?
   - Describe your plan for acquiring new skills and improving your existing skills.
2. Networking
   - How effective are you at using a mentor?
   - Are you a member of a professional organization?
   - In which community, civic, or church groups are you participating?
   - Whom have you added to your contact list in the last six weeks?
3. Accomplishments
   - What achievements have you reached in your job?
   - What would you like to accomplish? What will it take for you to reach your goal?
4. Promotion or new job
   - What is your likelihood for getting a promotion?
   - Are you ready for a change? What are you doing or willing to do to find another job?

Endnotes

1. Based on information in Robert Safian, "Terry Kelly, The 'Un-CEO' of W.L. Gore, on How to Deal with Chaos: Grow Up," *Fast Company,* October 29, 2012. www.fastcompany.com; Gary Hamel, "W.L. Gore: Lessons from a Management Revolutionary, Part 1," *Wall Street Journal*, March 18, 2010, www.wsj.com; Gary Hamel, "W.L. Gore: Lessons from a Management Revolutionary, Part 2," *Wall Street Journal*, April 2, 2010, www.wsj.com.
2. Jennifer Alsever, "Job Swaps: Are They for You?" *Fortune*, October 29, 2012, http://management.fortune.cnn.com/2012/10/24/job-swaps/.
3. PepsiCo Corporate Profile, www.pepsico.com/Investors/Corporate-Profile.html (accessed November 17, 2012).
4. Eric Pfanner and Any Chozick, "Random House and Penguin Merger Creates Global Giant," *New York Times*, October 29, 2012, http://www.nytimes.com/2012/10/30/business/global/random-house-and-penguin-to-be-combined.html.
5. "Francesco Guerrera, "UBS Tells Why it Cut off a Limb," *Wall Street Journal*, November 12, 2012, http://online.wsj.com/article/SB10001424127887323894704578114863817976002.html.
6. Dana Griffin, "Disadvantages of a Line & Staff Organization Structure," *Small Business*, http://smallbusiness.chron.com/disadvantages-line-staff-organization-structure-2762.html (accessed November 17, 2012).
7. John Kotter, "Can Your Organization Handle Losing a Leader?" *Forbes*, March 21, 2012, www.forbes.com/sites/johnkotter/2012/03/21/can-your-organization-handle-losing-a-leader/.
8. Peter J. Henning, "A Triple Whammy for Barclays," *New York Times*, November 5, 2012, http://dealbook.nytimes.com/2012/11/05/a-triple-whammy-for-barclays/.
9. Rob Goffee and Gareth Jones, "The Character of a Corporation: How Your Company's Culture Can Make or Break Your Business," *Jones Harper Business*, December 2003, 182.
10. Leslie Kwoh, "To Snag Top Talent, Companies Come out For Gay Rights," *New York Times*, November 13, 2012, http://blogs.wsj.com/atwork/2012/11/13/to-snag-top-talent-companies-come-out-for-gay-rights/.
11. Sources: Based on information in Rhymer Rigby, "The Benefits of Workplace Levity," *Financial Times,* December 19, 2012, www.ft.com; Carmine Gallo, "America's Happiest Employee," *Forbes*, December 26, 2012, www.forbes.com; Mig Pascual, "Zappos: 5 Out-of-the-Box Ideas for Keeping Employees Engaged," *U.S. News & World Report*, October 30, 2012, http://money.usnews.com; Lisa V. Gillespie, "Workplace Culture: Targeting Soft Skills Yields Hard Returns for Employers," *Employee Benefit News,* April 15, 2012, p. 18; Priya de Langen, "The Right Fit at Zappos," *HRM Asia*, January 5, 2012, www.hrmasia.com; www.zappos.com; Cengage "Zappos" video; www.zappos.com.

Chapter

8

Producing Quality Goods and Services

Why Should You Care?

Think for a moment about the products and services you bought in the past week. Those products and services could not be produced if it weren't for the production activities described in this chapter and that means consumers like you would not be able to purchase the products and services they need or want.

Learning Objectives

Once you complete this chapter, you will be able to:

1 Explain the nature of production.

2 Outline how the conversion process transforms raw materials, labor, and other resources into finished goods or services.

3 Understand the importance of service businesses to consumers, other business firms, and the nation's economy.

4 Describe how research and development leads to new products and services.

5 Discuss the components involved in planning the production process.

6 Explain how purchasing, inventory control, scheduling, and quality control affect production.

7 Summarize how technology can make American firms more productive and competitive in the global marketplace.

Intel Invests in State-of-the-Art Production

How do you create gigantic state-of-the-art production facilities to make products that get tinier and more sophisticated day by day? That's only one of the manufacturing challenges facing California-based Intel (www.intel.com), which has $54 billion in sales revenues and 82,500 employees worldwide. Intel is a pioneer of the microprocessor, the chips that now provide computing power in laptops, servers, smartphones, even cars. Three-quarters of its products come from company factories in Arizona, New Mexico, Oregon, and Massachusetts. Intel also operates factories in China, Ireland, and Israel.

Intel begins its research on new chips a decade in advance, identifying the kinds of products that will need new chips and planning to pack more processing capability into each chip. Engineers and manufacturing experts work together to perfect the new chip design and fine-tune its production at one of the Oregon plants. Following a "copy exactly" strategy, Intel then duplicates the production process at its other factories, to ensure high chip quality, minimize mistakes, and meet market demand.

Every year, Intel spends more than $10 billion to build or expand plants, overhaul the production process, and install cutting-edge equipment to boost efficiency. While some chipmakers partner with outside manufacturers to keep costs down, Intel sees its investment in production as vital to maintaining its competitive edge. Given the fast pace of technological change, Intel needs to be able to switch to an innovative product or process quickly—which it can do because it owns its manufacturing facilities.

The newly opened Intel factory in Hillsboro, Oregon, cost $3 billion and is 60 percent larger than the massive Intel facility next door. Another giant Intel chip plant in Arizona cost $5 billion to build. This extra space gives Intel more flexibility in adapting to future needs and using the latest tools and technology. No one knows what the best-selling chip of 2020 will be, but Intel stands ready to design and produce it.[1]

Did You Know?

Intel invests more than $10 billion every year to build new production facilities and upgrade existing facilities and equipment.

Back in 1968, two scientists, Robert Noyce and Gordon Moore, founded Intel with a vision for semiconductor memory products. Their efforts to develop and manufacture the world's first microprocessor paid off, and today Intel—the company profiled in the Inside Business feature for this chapter—is one of the world's largest and most important chip manufacturers. Now, the company is making a real difference because without the chips the company manufacturers, many of the electronic products and gadgets we often take for granted could not be produced. And while the products you buy may not have the Intel logo on the actual product, Intel chips may be inside making everything work the way it is supposed to work. Looking ahead, the company's chips and technology products will be even more important as new products require more processing capability for the next generation of technology products. In fact, that's why Intel invest billions of dollars each year to research new chips and build or expand plants in order to make sure it has the capacity to produce the chips that are needed years in the future. Today, Intel is an excellent example of what this chapter's content—the production of quality goods and services—is all about.

We begin this chapter with an overview of operations management—the activities required to produce goods and services that meet the needs of customers. In this section, we also discuss the role of manufacturing in the U.S. economy, competition in the global marketplace, and careers in operations management. Next, we describe the conversion process that makes production possible and also note the growing role of services in our economy. Then we examine more closely three important aspects of operations management: developing ideas for new products, planning for production, and effectively controlling operations after production has begun. We close the chapter with a look at the productivity trends and the ways that manufacturing can be improved through the use of technology.

operations management all the activities required to produce goods and services

WHAT IS PRODUCTION?

Have you ever wondered where a new pair of Levi's jeans comes from? Or an Apple iPad Mini, or a Uniroyal tire for your car? Even factory service on a Maytag clothes dryer would be impossible if it weren't for the activities described in this chapter. In fact, these products and services and millions of others like them would not exist if it weren't for production activities.

Let's begin this chapter by reviewing what an operating manager does. In Chapter 6, we described an *operations manager* as a person who manages the systems that convert resources into goods and services. This area of management is usually referred to as **operations management**, which consists of all the activities required to produce goods and services.

To produce a product or service successfully, a business must perform a number of specific activities. For example, suppose that Toyota (the parent company of Lexus automobiles) has an idea for a new, sport version of the Lexus GS 350 that will cost approximately $50,000. Marketing research must determine not only if customers are willing to pay the price for this product but also what special features they want. Then Toyota's operations managers must turn the idea into reality.

Toyota's managers cannot just push the "start button" and immediately begin producing the new automobile. As you will see, planning takes place both *before* anything is produced and *during* the production process.

Managers also must concern themselves with the control of operations to ensure that the organization's goals are achieved. For a product such as the Lexus GS 350, control of operations involves a number of important issues, including product quality, performance standards, the amount of inventory of both raw materials and finished products, and production costs.

We discuss each of the major activities of operations management later in this chapter. First, however, let's take a closer look at American manufacturers and how they compete in the global marketplace.

How American Manufacturers Compete in the Global Marketplace

After World War II, the United States became the most productive country in the world. For almost 30 years, until the late 1970s, its leadership was never threatened. By then, however, manufacturers in Japan, Germany, Taiwan, Korea, Singapore, Sweden, and other industrialized nations were offering U.S. firms increasing competition. Now the Chinese are manufacturing everything from sophisticated electronic equipment and automobiles to less expensive everyday items. And yet, in the face of increasing competition, there is both good and bad news for U.S. manufacturers. First the bad news.

THE BAD NEWS FOR MANUFACTURERS The number of Americans employed in the manufacturing sector has decreased. Currently, approximately 12 million U.S. workers are employed in manufacturing jobs—down from just over 19 million back in 1979.[2] While there are many additional factors, three major factors explain why employment in this economic sector has declined.

- Many of the manufacturing jobs that were lost were outsourced to low-wage workers in nations where there are few labor and environmental regulations.
- It costs about 20 percent more to manufacture goods in the United States than it does anywhere else in the world.[3]

AP IMAGES/APPLE

Why is the product in this photo important? While it may be hard to tell at this stage of production, the product at this work station is one of the most successful products in recent history—the Apple iPhone. On the left, the man in the yellow coat is Apple CEO Tim Cook who is talking with lab technicians that produce the product in this Chinese factory.

- The number of unemployed factory workers increased during the recent economic crisis because of decreased consumer demand for manufactured goods.

As a result, manufacturing accounts for only about 9 percent of the current workforce.[4] Since 1979, 7 million jobs have been lost, and many of those jobs aren't coming back.

THE GOOD NEWS FOR MANUFACTURERS The United States remains one of the largest manufacturing countries in the world. While some people would argue that "Made in America" doesn't mean what it used to mean, consider the following:

- U.S. manufacturers produce approximately 18 percent of total global manufacturing output.[5]
- Every year, manufacturing contributes about 12 percent of the gross domestic product and approximately $2 trillion to the U.S. economy.[6]
- Manufacturing exports are nearly 60 percent of all U.S. exports.[7]
- Between now and 2018, it is anticipated that there will be 2 million job openings for skilled workers in manufacturing.[8]
- For every new manufacturing job created, there are another three new jobs created in the supply chain, the trucking industry, and other related areas of the economy.[9]

As a result, the manufacturing sector is still a very important part of the U.S. economy. Although the number of manufacturing jobs has declined, productivity has increased. At least two very important factors account for increases in productivity: First, innovation—finding a better way to produce products—is the key factor that has enabled American manufacturers to compete in the global marketplace. Second, today's workers in the manufacturing sector are highly skilled in order to operate sophisticated equipment. Simply put, Americans are making more goods, but with fewer employees.

Even more good news is that many American manufacturers that outsourced work to factories in foreign nations are once again beginning to manufacture goods in the United States. For our purposes, the term **reshoring** (sometimes referred to as onshoring or insourcing) describes a situation where U.S. manufacturers bring manufacturing jobs back to the United States. For example, General Electric, Ford, Apple, Caterpillar, Honda, Intel, and Master Lock and many other U.S. firms are involved in reshoring. The primary reasons why U.S. firms are "coming back home" include increasing labor costs in foreign nations, higher shipping costs, significant quality and safety issues, faster product development when goods are produced in the United States, and federal and state subsidies to encourage manufactures to produce products in the United States.

Although there are many challenges facing U.S. manufacturers, experts predict that there could be a significant resurgence for manufacturers that can meet current

reshoring a situation in which U.S. manufacturers bring manufacturing jobs back to the United States

---

Entrepreneurial Success

Profit from Demand for "Made in America"

Quality goods made in America are increasingly in demand worldwide, a trend that's boosting sales and profits for entrepreneurial manufacturers. Cabot Hosiery Mills, located in Vermont, was struggling to compete with overseas producers of socks when the founder and his son had a flash of insight. Rather than continue to make everyday socks, they believed Cabot had the experience and expertise to design and manufacture high-performance socks for the high end of the market. After some experimentation, they came up with Darn Tough socks: durable, well-cushioned, and backed by a lifetime replacement guarantee. Now Cabot sells 4 million Darn Tough socks every year. Although only a few hundred pairs have ever been returned, Cabot examines each one carefully for clues to making Darn Tough even tougher.

Watermark Designs, a manufacturer in Brooklyn, New York, has earned a global reputation for stylish, hand-crafted plumbing fixtures. Because Watermark's designers are based in the factory, they can consult with production managers while they develop a new product, and then have a prototype made or refined within days. For quality control purposes, workers test every faucet before it's shipped to Michigan, Manitoba, Macau, or beyond.

A growing number of U.S. stores, markets, and websites are devoted to made-in-America products, giving manufacturers more opportunities to reach new customers and demonstrate their quality credentials. Entrepreneurs are showcasing everything from boots to bicycles, explaining where their raw materials come from and highlighting the quality and care built into every product.

Sources: Based on information in Jim Dwyer, "In Manufacturing Shift, Made in U.S. but Sold in China," *New York Times*, September 20, 2012, www.nytimes.com; Emanuella Grinberg, "Made in America Markets Create Communities of Like-Minded Consumers," *CNN*, November 5, 2012, www.cnn.com; Jim Motavalli, "To Make Socks in Vermont, You Have to Be Darn Tough," *Success*, September 2011, p. 42.

and future challenges. The bottom line: The global marketplace has never been more competitive and successful U.S. firms will focus on the following:

1. Meeting the needs of customers and improving product quality.
2. Motivating employees to cooperate with management and improve productivity.
3. Reducing costs by selecting suppliers that offer higher quality raw materials and components at reasonable prices.
4. Using computer-aided and flexible manufacturing systems that allow a higher degree of customization.
5. Improving control procedures to help ensure lower manufacturing costs.
6. Using green manufacturing to conserve natural resources and sustain the planet.

For most firms, competing in the global marketplace is not only profitable but also an essential activity that requires the cooperation of everyone within the organization.

Careers in Operations Management

Although it is hard to provide information about specific career opportunities in operations management, some generalizations do apply to this management area. A basic understanding of mass production and the difference between an analytical process and a synthetic process is essential. **Mass production** is a manufacturing process that lowers the cost required to produce a large number of identical or similar products over a long period of time. An **analytical process** breaks raw materials into different component parts. For example, a barrel of crude oil refined by Marathon Oil Corporation—a Texas-based oil and energy exploration company—can be broken down into gasoline, oil, lubricants, and many other petroleum by-products. A **synthetic process** is just the opposite of the analytical one; it combines raw materials or components to create a finished product. Black & Decker uses a synthetic process when it combines plastic, steel, rechargeable batteries, and other components to produce a cordless drill.

Once you understand that operations managers are responsible for producing tangible goods or services that customers want, you must determine how you fit into the production process. Today's successful operations managers must:

1. Be able to motivate and lead people.
2. Understand how technology can make a manufacturer more productive.
3. Appreciate the control processes that help lower production costs and improve product quality.
4. Understand the relationship between the customer, the marketing of a product, and the production of a product.

If operations management seems like an area you might be interested in, why not do more career exploration?

Learning Objective

2 **Outline how the conversion process transforms raw materials, labor, and other resources into finished goods or services.**

utility the ability of a good or service to satisfy a human need

form utility utility created by people converting raw materials, finances, and information into finished products

THE CONVERSION PROCESS

The purpose of manufacturing or a service business is to provide utility to customers. **Utility** is the ability of a good or service to satisfy a human need. Although there are four types of utilities—form, place, time, and possession—operations management focuses primarily on form utility. **Form utility** is created by people converting raw materials, finances, and information into finished products. The other types of utility—place, time, and possession—are discussed in Chapter 11.

But how does the conversion take place? How does Kellogg's convert corn, sugar, salt, and other ingredients; money from previous sales and stockholders' investments; production workers and managers; and economic and marketing forecasts into Frosted Flakes cereal products? How does H&R Block employ more than 100,000 tax preparers and convert retail locations, computers and software, and advertising and promotion into tax services for its clients. They do so through the

---

mass production a manufacturing process that lowers the cost required to produce a large number of identical or similar products over a long period of time

analytical process a process in operations management in which raw materials are broken into different component parts

synthetic process a process in operations management in which raw materials or components are combined to create a finished product

Concept Check

✓ List the major activities in operations management.

✓ What steps have U.S. firms taken to regain a competitive edge in the global marketplace?

✓ What is the difference between an analytical and a synthetic manufacturing process? Give an example of each type of process.

use of a conversion process like the one illustrated in Figure 8-1. As indicated by our H&R Block example, the conversion process can be used to produce services.

Manufacturing Using a Conversion Process

The conversion of resources into products and services can be described in several ways. We limit our discussion here to three: the focus or major resource used in the conversion process, its magnitude of change, and the number of production processes employed.

FOCUS By the *focus* of a conversion process, we mean the resource or resources that make up the major or most important *input*. The resources are financial, material, information, and people—the same resources discussed in Chapters 1 and 6. For a bank such as Citibank, financial resources are the major resource. A chemical and energy company such as Chevron concentrates on material resources. Your college or university is concerned primarily with information. And temporary employment services, such as Manpower, focus on the use of human resources.

MAGNITUDE OF CHANGE The *magnitude* of a conversion process is the degree to which the resources are physically changed. At one extreme lie such processes as the one by which the Glad Products Company produces Glad® Cling Wrap. Various chemicals in liquid or powder form are combined to produce long, thin sheets of plastic Glad Cling Wrap. Here, the original resources are totally unrecognizable in the finished product. At the other extreme, Southwest Airlines produces no physical change in its original resources. The airline simply provides a service and transports people from one place to another.

NUMBER OF PRODUCTION PROCESSES A single firm may employ one production process or many. In general, larger firms that make a variety of products use multiple production processes. For example, GE

What does it take to make a home? It is often said that a home must have people in order to be a real home. And yet, a lot of different materials—concrete, lumber, sheet rock, flooring, roofing, etc. must be combined to produce the finished product—a home that people can live in.

FIGURE 8-1 The Conversion Process

The conversion process converts ideas and resources into useful goods and services.

PRODUCTION INPUTS
- Concept or idea for a new good or service
- Human, financial, material, and informational resources

CONVERSION
- Plan necessary production activities to create a good or service
- Design the good or service
- Execute the plan to produce the good or service
- Evaluate the quality of the good or service
- Improve the good or service based on evaluation
- Redesign the good or service if necessary

OUTPUTS
- Completed good or service

© CENGAGE LEARNING 2015

Concept Check

✓ Explain how utility is related to form utility.

✓ In terms of focus, magnitude of change, and number, characterize the production processes used by a local pizza parlor, a dry-cleaning establishment, and an automobile repair shop.

Learning Objective

3 **Understand the importance of service businesses to consumers, other business firms, and the nation's economy.**

service economy an economy in which more effort is devoted to the production of services than to the production of goods

manufactures some of its own products, buys other merchandise from suppliers, and operates multiple divisions including a finance division, a lighting division, an appliance division, a healthcare division, and other divisions responsible for the products and services that customers associate with the GE name. Smaller firms, by contrast, may use one production process. For example, Texas-based Advanced Cast Stone, Inc., manufactures one basic product: building materials made from concrete.

THE INCREASING IMPORTANCE OF SERVICES

The application of the basic principles of operations management to the production of services has coincided with a dramatic growth in the number and diversity of service businesses. In 1900, only 28 percent of American workers were employed in service firms. By 1950, this figure had grown to 40 percent, and by the beginning of 2013, it had risen to 87 percent.[10] In fact, the American economy is now characterized as a service economy (see Figure 8-2). A **service economy** is one in which more effort is devoted to the production of services than to the production of goods.

Planning Quality Services

Today, the managers of restaurants, laundries, real estate agencies, banks, movie theaters, airlines, travel bureaus, and other service firms have realized that they can benefit from the experience of manufacturers. And while service firms are different from manufacturing firms, both types of businesses must complete many of the same activities in order to be successful. For example, as illustrated in the middle section of Figure 8-1, service businesses must plan, design, execute, evaluate, improve, and redesign their services in order to provide the services that their customers want.

For a service firm, planning often begins with determining who the customer is and what needs the customer has. After customer needs are identified, the next step for successful service firms is to develop a plan that will enable the firm to deliver the services that their customers want or need. For example, a swimming pool repair business must develop a business plan that includes a process for hiring and training qualified employees, obtaining necessary parts and supplies, marketing the

FIGURE 8-2 Service Industries

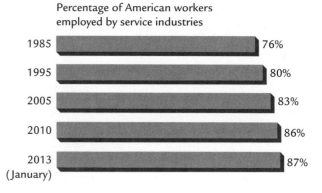

The growth of service firms has increased so dramatically that we now live in what is referred to as a service economy.

Percentage of American workers employed by service industries

Year	Percentage
1985	76%
1995	80%
2005	83%
2010	86%
2013 (January)	87%

Source: U.S. Bureau of Labor Statistics website, www.bls.gov (accessed February 15, 2013).

firm's services, and creating management and accounting systems to control the firm's activities. Once the firm provides a service to a customer, successful firms evaluate their operating systems and measure customer satisfaction. And if necessary, redesign their operating systems and their services to improve the customer's experience.

Evaluating the Quality of a Firm's Services

The production of services is very different from the production of manufactured goods in the following five ways:

1. When compared to manufactured goods, customers are much more involved in obtaining the service they want or need.
2. Services are consumed immediately and, unlike manufactured goods, cannot be stored. For example, a hair stylist cannot store completed haircuts.
3. Services are provided when and where the customer desires the service. In many cases, customers will not travel as far to obtain a service.
4. Services are usually labor-intensive because the human resource is often the most important resource used in the production of services.
5. Services are intangible, and it is therefore more difficult to evaluate customer satisfaction.[11]

Compared with manufacturers, service firms often listen more carefully to customers and respond more quickly to the market's changing needs. For example, Maggiano's Little Italy restaurant is a chain of eating establishments owned by Brinker International. In order to continuously improve customer service, the restaurant encourages diners to complete online surveys that prompt diners to evaluate the food, atmosphere, service, and other variables. The information from the surveys is then used to fine-tune the way Maggiano's meets its customers' needs.

In addition, many service firms are now using social media to build relationships with their customers. Coldwell Banker, one of the largest real estate companies in the United States sponsors an Internet blog that can be used not only to provide information about the current housing market, but also as a method to encourage comments and questions from customers.

Now that we understand something about the production process that is used to transform resources into goods and services, we can consider three major activities involved in operations management: research and development, planning for production, and operations control.

Concept Check

✓ How is the production of services similar to the production of manufactured goods?

✓ How is the production of services different from the production of manufactured goods?

✓ How can service firms measure customer satisfaction?

WHERE DO NEW PRODUCTS AND SERVICES COME FROM?

No firm can produce a product or service until it has an idea. Both Apple's iPad Mini and Ford's Electric Focus automobile began as an idea and as a result of a company's research and development activities.

Research and Development

How did we get the Apple iPad Mini or the Electric Ford Focus automobile? We got them as a result of people working with new ideas that developed into useful products. These activities generally are referred to as research and development. For our purposes, **research and development (R&D)** involves a set of activities intended to identify new ideas that have the potential to result in new goods and services.

Today, business firms use three general types of R&D activities. *Basic research* consists of activities aimed at uncovering new knowledge. The goal of basic research is scientific advancement, without regard for its potential use in the development of goods and services. *Applied research*, in contrast, consists

Learning Objective

4 Describe how research and development leads to new products and services.

research and development (R&D) a set of activities intended to identify new ideas that have the potential to result in new goods and services

of activities geared toward discovering new knowledge with some potential use. *Development and implementation* involves research activities undertaken specifically to put new or existing knowledge to use in producing goods and services. For many companies, R&D is a very important part of their business operations. The 3M company, for example, has always been known for its development and implementation research activities. Currently, 3M employs 7,900 researchers worldwide and has invested more than $7 billion over the last five years to develop new products designed to make people's lives easier and safer.[12]

Product Extension and Refinement

If a firm sells only one product or service, when customers quit buying the product or service, the firm will die. To stay in business, the firm must, at the very least, find ways to refine or extend the want-satisfying capability of its product or service. Consider television sets. Since they were introduced in the late 1930s, television sets have been constantly *refined* so that they now provide clearer, sharper pictures with less dial adjusting. During the same time, television sets also were *extended*. There are basic flat-screen televisions without added features, and many others that include DVD or Blu-Ray players and Apps that can be used to access the Internet. The latest development—high-definition television—has already become the standard.

For most firms, extension and refinement are expected results of their research, development, and implementation activities. Each refinement or extension results in an essentially "new" product whose sales make up for the declining sales of a product that was introduced earlier. When consumers were introduced to the original five varieties of Campbell's Soup, they discovered that these soups were of the highest quality,

Concept Check

✓ Describe how research and development leads to new products.

✓ What is the difference between basic research, applied research, and development and implementation?

✓ Explain why product extension and refinement are important.

There are no guarantees when developing new products and services! Although a firm's research and development activities can make the difference between success and failure, developing new products and services is not a perfect science. In fact, the search for new products and services that have the potential to be successful often begins in the laboratory where scientists work to turn ideas into actual products.

as well as inexpensive, and the soups were an instant success. Although one of the most successful companies at the beginning of the 1900s, Campbell's had to continue to innovate, refine, and extend its product line. For example, many consumers in the United States live in what is called an on-the-go society. To meet this need, Campbell's Soup has developed ready-to-serve products that can be popped into a microwave at work or school.

HOW DO MANAGERS PLAN PRODUCTION?

Learning Objective

5 Discuss the components involved in planning the production process.

Only a few of the many ideas for new products ever reach the production stage. For those ideas that do, however, the next step is planning for production. Once a new idea for a product or service has been identified, planning for production involves three different phases: design planning, facilities planning, and operational planning (see Figure 8-3).

Design Planning

When the R&D staff at Samsung recommended to top management that the firm manufacture and market a "Smart Fridge" with a touch screen, Wi-Fi connectivity, and apps that allow consumers to update their calendars, leave notes to family members, or even provide recipe suggestions, the company could not simply swing into production the next day. Instead, a great deal of time and energy had to be invested in determining what the new refrigerator would look like, where and how it would be produced, and what options would be included. These decisions are a part of design planning. **Design planning** is the development of a plan for converting an idea into an actual product or service. The major decisions involved in design planning deal with product line, required capacity, and use of technology.

design planning the development of a plan for converting an idea into an actual product or service

PRODUCT LINE A **product line** is a group of similar products that differ only in relatively minor characteristics. During the design-planning stage, a manufacturer like Samsung must determine how many different models to produce and what major options to offer. Likewise, a restaurant chain such as Pizza Hut must decide how many menu items to offer.

product line a group of similar products that differ only in relatively minor characteristics

FIGURE 8-3 Planning for Production

Once research and development identifies an idea that meets customer needs, three additional steps are used to convert the idea to an actual good or service.

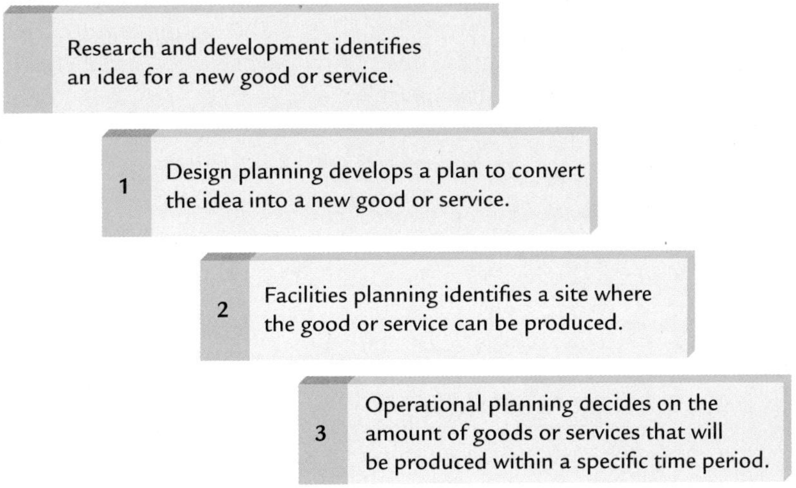

Research and development identifies an idea for a new good or service.

1 Design planning develops a plan to convert the idea into a new good or service.

2 Facilities planning identifies a site where the good or service can be produced.

3 Operational planning decides on the amount of goods or services that will be produced within a specific time period.

© CENGAGE LEARNING 2015

Question: Why do people buy Apple products? Answer: One "big" reason why people buy Apple products is the firm's research and development efforts to design products that actually work. Although many people often underestimate the importance of product design, even small details can make a big difference—especially when selling products in the very competitive technology industry.

An important issue in deciding on the product line is to balance customer preferences and production requirements. Typically, marketing personnel want a "long" product line that offers customers many options. Because a long product line with more options gives customers greater choice, it is easier to sell products that meet the needs of individual customers. On the other hand, production personnel generally want a "short" product line with fewer options because products are easier to produce.

Once the product line has been determined, each distinct product within the product line must be designed. **Product design** is the process of creating a set of specifications from which a product can be produced. For example, product engineers for Samsung must make sure that their new "Smart Fridge" keeps food frozen in the freezer compartment. At the same time, they must make sure that lettuce and tomatoes do not freeze in the crisper section of the refrigerator. The need for a complete product design is fairly obvious; products that work cannot be manufactured without it. But services should be designed carefully as well—and *for the same reason.*

product design the process of creating a set of specifications from which a product can be produced

capacity the amount of products or services that an organization can produce in a given time

REQUIRED PRODUCTION CAPACITY Capacity is the amount of products or services that an organization can produce in a given period of time. (For example, the capacity of a Panasonic assembly plant might be 1.3 million high-definition televisions per year.) Operations managers—again working with the firm's marketing managers—must determine the required capacity. This, in turn, determines the size of the production facility. If the facility is built with too much capacity, valuable resources (plant, equipment, and money) will lie idle. If the facility offers insufficient capacity, additional capacity may have to be added later when it is much more expensive than in the initial building stage.

Capacity means about the same thing to service businesses. For example, the capacity of a restaurant such as the Hard Rock Cafe in Nashville, Tennessee, is the number of customers it can serve at one time.

labor-intensive technology a process in which people must do most of the work

capital-intensive technology a process in which machines and equipment do most of the work

USE OF TECHNOLOGY During the design-planning stage, management must determine the degree to which *automation* and *technology* will be used to produce a product or service. Here, there is a trade-off between high initial costs and low operating costs (for automation) and low initial costs and high operating costs (for human labor). Ultimately, management must choose between a labor-intensive technology and a capital-intensive technology. A **labor-intensive technology** is a process in which people must do most of the work. Housecleaning services and the New York Yankees baseball team, for example, are labor-intensive. A **capital-intensive technology** is a process in which machines and equipment do most of the work. A Sony automated assembly plant is capital intensive because there are fewer workers that operate automated machinery.

Site Selection and Facilities Planning

Generally, a business will choose to produce a new product in an existing factory as long as (1) the existing factory has enough capacity to handle customer demand for both the new product and established products and (2) the cost of refurbishing an existing factory is less than the cost of building a new one.

After exploring the capacity of existing factories, management may decide to build a new production facility. In determining where to locate production facilities, management must consider a number of variables, including the following:

- Locations of major customers and suppliers.
- Availability and cost of skilled and unskilled labor.

- Quality of life for employees and management in the proposed location.
- The cost of land and building costs.
- Local and state taxes, environmental regulations, and zoning laws.
- The amount of financial support and subsidies, if any, offered by local and state governments.
- Special requirements, such as great amounts of energy or water used in the production process.

Before making a final decision about where a proposed plant will be located and how it will be organized, two other factors—human resources and plant layout—should be examined.

HUMAN RESOURCES Several issues involved in site selection and facilities planning fall within the province of human resources managers. When Nestlé built its new 900,000-square-foot production facility to make liquid Nesquik® and Coffee-Mate® products in Anderson, Indiana, human resources managers were involved to make sure the necessary managers and employees needed to staff the plant were available. And when a company decides to build a new facility in a foreign country, again human resources managers are involved. For example, suppose that a U.S. firm like AT&T wants to lower labor costs by importing products from China. It has two choices. It can build its own manufacturing facility in a foreign country or it can outsource production to local firms. In either case, human resources become involved in the decision. If the decision is made to build its own plant, human resources managers will have to recruit managers and employees with the appropriate skills who are willing to relocate to a foreign country, develop training programs for local Chinese workers, or both. On the other hand, if the decision is made to outsource production to local suppliers, human resources managers must make sure that local suppliers are complying with the U.S. company's human rights policies and with all applicable national and local wage and hour laws.

PLANT LAYOUT Plant layout is the arrangement of machinery, equipment, and personnel within a production facility. Three general types of plant layout are used (see Figure 8-4).

The *process layout* is used when different operations are required for creating small batches of different products or working on different parts of a product. The plant is arranged so that each operation is performed in its own particular area. An auto repair facility at a local automobile dealership provides an example of a process layout. The various operations may be engine repair, bodywork, wheel alignment, and safety inspection. If you take your Lincoln Navigator for a wheel alignment, your car "visits" only the area where alignments are performed.

A *product layout* (sometimes referred to as an *assembly line*) is used when all products undergo the same operations in the same sequence. Workstations are arranged to match the sequence of operations, and work flows from station to station.

Sustain the Planet

Saving Energy—And the Environment

The industrial sector uses approximately 40% of the world's total delivered energy, so it's fertile ground for energy optimization efforts. By working with their customers on energy resource management and reducing emissions and waste, Rockwell Automation, a manufacturer of industrial automation control and information solutions, is helping make their customers' operations cleaner, more energy efficient, and more competitive. In short, they're showing their customers ways they can save money and energy while saving the environment. Take a closer look at how Rockwell is helping their customers meet their lean objectives while still meeting their green objectives at www.rockwellautomation.com.

Sources: "Sustainable Production," The Rockwell Automation website at www.rockwellautomation.com, accessed February 15, 2013; Presher, A. (August 8, 2011), "Energy Optimization as Productivity Enhancer," *DesignNews*. Retrieved from www.designnews.com/document.asp?doc_id=231868; "Rockwell Automation named to Dow Jones Sustainability North America Index," *ReliablePlant*, retrieved February 22, 2012 from www.reliableplant.com/Read/26680/Rockwell-Automation-sustainability-index.

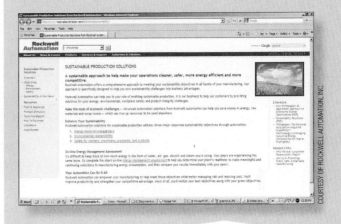

COURTESY OF ROCKWELL AUTOMATION, INC.

plant layout the arrangement of machinery, equipment, and personnel within a production facility

FIGURE 8-4 Facilities Planning

The process layout is used when small batches of different products are created or when working on different parts of a product. The product layout (assembly line) is used when all products undergo the same operations in the same sequence. The fixed-position layout is used in producing a product too large to move.

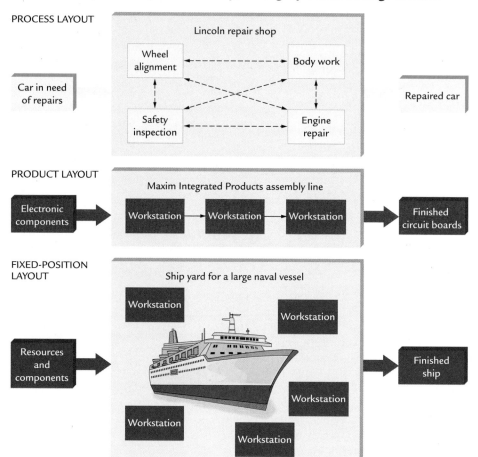

PROCESS LAYOUT

Lincoln repair shop

Car in need of repairs

Wheel alignment — Body work — Safety inspection — Engine repair

Repaired car

PRODUCT LAYOUT

Maxim Integrated Products assembly line

Electronic components → Workstation → Workstation → Workstation → Finished circuit boards

FIXED-POSITION LAYOUT

Ship yard for a large naval vessel

Resources and components → Workstation ... Workstation → Finished ship

© CENGAGE LEARNING 2015

A big product! The British Royal Navy's aircraft carrier HMS Queen Elizabeth was constructed using a fixed-position layout. To see how large the ship is, compare its size with the people at the bottom of this photo. When a product is this large, it is easier to move people, machinery, and parts to where they are needed instead of moving the ship.

CHRIS ISON/PA PHOTOS/LANDOV

An assembly line is the best example of a product layout. For example, California-based Maxim Integrated Products, Inc., uses a product layout to manufacture components for consumer and business electronic products. A *fixed-position layout* is used when a very large product is produced. Shipbuilders apply this method because of the difficulty of moving a large product such as an ocean liner. The product remains stationary, and people and machines are moved as needed to assemble the product.

Operational Planning

The objective of operational planning is to decide on the amount of products or services each facility will produce during a specific period of time. Four steps are required.

STEP 1: SELECTING A PLANNING HORIZON A **planning horizon** is simply the time period during which an operational plan will be in effect. A common planning horizon for production plans is one year. Then, before each year is up, management must plan for the next. A planning horizon of one year generally is long enough to average out seasonal increases and decreases in sales. At the same time, it is short enough for planners to adjust production to accommodate long-range sales trends.

Fruit tarts that taste as good as they look. For just a moment, assume you are the production manager of a large bakery that must produce thousands of fruit tarts each week. What would your factory look like? How could plant layout improve your firm's productivity? How would you manage human resources, purchasing, and quality control? All good questions that should be answered before a single fruit tart is produced.

STEP 2: ESTIMATING MARKET DEMAND The *market demand* for a product is the quantity that customers will purchase at the going price. This quantity must be estimated for the time period covered by the planning horizon. Sales projections developed by marketing managers are the basis for market-demand estimates.

planning horizon the period during which an operational plan will be in effect

STEP 3: COMPARING MARKET DEMAND WITH CAPACITY The third step in operational planning is to compare the estimated market demand with the facility's capacity to satisfy that demand. (Remember that capacity is the amount of products or services that an organization can produce in a given time period.) One of three outcomes may result: Demand may exceed capacity, capacity may exceed demand, or capacity and demand may be equal. If they are equal, the facility should be operated at full capacity. However, if market demand and capacity are not equal, adjustments may be necessary.

STEP 4: ADJUSTING PRODUCTS OR SERVICES TO MEET DEMAND The biggest reason for changes to a firm's production schedule is changes in the amount of products or services that a company sells to its customers. For example, Indiana-based Berry Plastics produces all kinds of plastic products. One particularly successful product line for Berry Plastics is drink cups that can be screen-printed to promote a company or its products or services.[13] If Berry Plastics obtains a large contract to provide promotional cups to a large fast-food chain such as Whataburger or McDonald's, the company may need to work three shifts a day, seven days a week, until the contract is fulfilled. Unfortunately, the reverse is also true. If the company's sales force does not generate new sales, there may be only enough work for the employees on one shift.

When market demand exceeds capacity, several options are available to a firm. Production of products or services may be increased by operating the facility overtime with existing personnel or by starting a second or third work shift. For manufacturers, another response is to subcontract or outsource a portion of the work to other manufacturers. If the excess demand is likely to be permanent, the firm may expand the current facility or build another facility.

Concept Check

✓ What are the major elements of design planning?

✓ Define capacity. Why is it important for a manufacturing business or a service business?

✓ What factors should be considered when selecting a site for a new manufacturing facility?

✓ What is the objective of operational planning? What four steps are used to accomplish this objective?

What happens when capacity exceeds market demand? Again, there are several options. To reduce output temporarily, workers may be laid off or the facility may be operated on a shorter-than-normal workweek. To adjust to a permanently decreased demand, management may shift the excess capacity of a manufacturing facility to the production of other goods or services. The most radical adjustment is to eliminate the excess capacity by selling unused manufacturing facilities.

Learning Objective

6 Explain how purchasing, inventory control, scheduling, and quality control affect production.

OPERATIONS CONTROL

We have discussed the development of an idea for a product or service and the planning that translates that idea into the reality. Now we are ready to begin the actual production process. In this section, we examine four important areas of operations control: purchasing, inventory control, scheduling, and quality control (see Figure 8-5).

Purchasing

purchasing all the activities involved in obtaining required materials, supplies, components, and parts from other firms

Purchasing consists of all the activities involved in obtaining required materials, supplies, components (or subassemblies), and parts from other firms. Levi Strauss, for example, must purchase denim cloth, thread, and zippers before it can produce a single pair of jeans.

The objective of purchasing is to ensure that required materials are available when they are needed, in the proper amounts, and at minimum cost. Generally, the company with purchasing needs and suppliers must develop a working relationship built on trust. In addition, many companies believe that purchasing is one area where they can promote diversity. For example, AT&T developed a Supplier Diversity Program in 1968. Today, more than 45 years later, goals for the AT&T program include purchasing a total of 21.5 percent of all products and services from minorities, women, and disabled veteran business enterprises.[14]

Purchasing personnel should constantly be on the lookout for new or backup suppliers, even when their needs are being met by their present suppliers, because problems such as strikes and equipment breakdowns can cut off the flow of purchased materials from a primary supplier at any time.

The choice of suppliers should result from careful analysis of a number of factors. The following are especially critical:

- *Price.* Comparing prices offered by different suppliers is always an essential part of selecting a supplier.
- *Quality.* Purchasing specialists always try to buy materials at a level of quality in keeping with the type of product being manufactured. The lowest acceptable quality is usually specified by product designers.
- *Reliability.* An agreement to purchase high-quality materials at a low price is the purchaser's dream. However, the dream becomes a nightmare if the supplier does not deliver.

FIGURE 8-5 Four Aspects of Operations Control

Implementing the operations control system in any business requires the effective use of purchasing, inventory control, scheduling, and quality control.

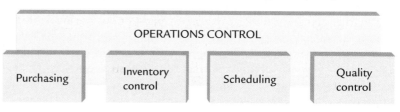

© CENGAGE LEARNING 2015

- *Credit terms.* Purchasing specialists should determine if the supplier demands immediate payment or will extend credit.
- *Shipping costs.* The question of who pays the shipping costs should be answered before any supplier is chosen.

Inventory Control

Can you imagine what would happen if a Coca-Cola manufacturing plant ran out of the company's familiar red-and-white aluminum cans? It would be impossible to complete the manufacturing process and ship the cases of Coke to retailers. Management would be forced to shut the assembly line down until the next shipment of cans arrived from a supplier. The simple fact is that shutdowns are expensive because costs such as wages, rent, utilities, insurance, and other expenses still must be paid.

Operations managers are concerned with three types of inventories. A *raw-materials inventory* consists of materials that will become part of the product during the production process. The *work-in-process inventory* consists of partially completed products. The *finished-goods inventory* consists of completed goods. Each type of inventory also has a *holding cost*, or storage cost, and a *stock-out cost*, the cost of running out of inventory. **Inventory control** is the process of managing inventories in such a way as to minimize inventory costs, including both holding costs and potential stock-out costs.

Today, computer systems are being used to keep track of inventories and alert managers to impending stock-outs. One of the most sophisticated methods of inventory control used today is materials requirements planning. **Materials requirements planning (MRP)** is a computerized system that integrates production planning and inventory control. One of the great advantages of an MRP system is its ability to juggle delivery schedules and lead times effectively. For a complex product such as an automobile with 4,000 or more individual parts, it is virtually impossible for individual managers to oversee the hundreds of parts that go into the finished product. However, a manager using an MRP system can arrange both order and delivery schedules so that materials, parts, and supplies arrive when they are needed.

Because large firms can incur huge inventory costs, much attention has been devoted to inventory control. The just-in-time system being used by some businesses is one result of all this attention. A **just-in-time inventory system** is designed to ensure that materials or supplies arrive at a facility just when they are needed so that storage and holding costs are minimized. For example, managers using a just-in-time inventory system at a Toyota assembly plant determine the number of automobiles that will be assembled in a specified time period. Then Toyota purchasing personnel order just the parts needed to produce those automobiles. In turn, suppliers deliver the parts in time or when they are needed on the assembly line.

Without proper inventory control, it is impossible for operations managers to schedule the work required to produce goods and services that can be sold to customers.

Scheduling

Scheduling is the process of ensuring that materials and other resources are at the right place at the right time. The materials and resources may be moved from a warehouse to the workstations, they may move from station to station along an assembly line, or they may arrive at workstations "just in time" to be made part of the work-in-process there.

inventory control the process of managing inventories in such a way as to minimize inventory costs, including both holding costs and potential stock-out costs

materials requirements planning (MRP) a computerized system that integrates production planning and inventory control

just-in-time inventory system a system designed to ensure that materials or supplies arrive at a facility just when they are needed so that storage and holding costs are minimized

scheduling the process of ensuring that materials and other resources are at the right place at the right time

© SPFLAUM/SHUTTERSTOCK.COM

Tracking inventory can be a tedious, but necessary chore. For a wholesaler or retailer, running out of inventory means a business has nothing to sell. For a manufacturer, no inventory can lead to shutting down a production facility and no finished products. In either case, no inventory equals no sales and can lead to no profits.

As our definition implies, both place and time are important to scheduling. The *routing* of materials is the sequence of workstations that the materials will follow. Assume that Drexel Heritage—one of America's largest and oldest furniture manufacturers—is scheduling production of an oval coffee table made from cherry wood. Operations managers route the needed materials (wood, screws, packaging materials, etc.) through a series of individual workstations along an assembly line. At each workstation, a specific task is performed, and then the partially finished coffee table moves to the next workstation. When routing materials, operations managers are especially concerned with the sequence of each step of the production process. For the coffee table, the top and legs must be cut to specifications before the wood is finished. (If the wood were finished before being cut, the finish would be ruined, and the coffee table would have to be stained again.)

When scheduling production, managers also are concerned with timing. The *timing* function specifies when the materials will arrive at each station and how long they will remain there. For the cherry coffee table, it may take workers 30 minutes to cut the table top and legs and another 30 minutes to drill the holes and assemble the table. Before packaging the coffee table for shipment, it must be finished with cherry stain and allowed to dry. This last step may take as long as three days depending on weather conditions and humidity.

Regardless of whether the finished product requires a simple or complex production process, operations managers are responsible for monitoring schedules—called *follow-up*—to ensure that the work flows according to the schedule.

Quality Control

Over the years, more and more managers have realized that quality is an essential "ingredient" of the good or service being produced. This view of quality provides several benefits. The number of defects decreases, which causes profits to increase. Furthermore, making products or completing services right the first time reduces many of the rejects and much of the rework.

As mentioned earlier in this chapter, American business firms that compete in the very competitive global marketplace have taken another look at the importance of improving quality. Today, there is even a national quality award. The **Malcolm Baldrige National Quality Award** is given by the President of the United States to organizations judged to be outstanding in specific managerial tasks that lead to improved quality for both products and services. Past winners include Mesa Products, Ritz-Carlton Hotels, Boeing Aerospace, Motorola, Nestlé Purina Petcare, Cargill Corn Milling North America, and Richland Community College (part of the Dallas Community College District), among many others. All Baldrige winners have one factor in common: They use quality control to improve their firm's products or services.

Quality control is the process of ensuring that goods and services are produced in accordance with design specifications. The major objective of quality control is to see that the organization lives up to the standards it has set for itself on quality. Some firms, such as Mercedes-Benz, have built their reputations on quality. Other firms adopt a strategy of emphasizing lower prices along with reasonable (but not particularly high) quality. Today, many firms use the techniques described in Table 8-1 to gather information and statistics that can be used to improve the quality of a firm's products or services.

Although the techniques described in Table 8-1 can provide information and statistics, it is people who must act on the information and make changes to improve the production process. And the firm's employees are often the most important component needed to improve quality.

Quality matters! In this photo, an employee inspects a custom-made shoe to make sure small details like the quality of leather and stitching meet the company's design specifications. Products that are not within design specifications and don't pass inspection are removed from production.

TABLE 8-1 Four Widely Used Techniques to Improve the Quality of a Firm's Products.

Technique	Description
Benchmarking	A process of comparing the way a firm produces products or services to the methods used by organizations known to be leaders in an industry in order to determine the "best practices" that can be used to improve quality.
Continuous Improvement	Continuous improvement is a never-ending effort to eliminate problems and improve quality. Often this method involves many small changes or steps designed to improve the production process on an ongoing basis.
Statistical Process Control (SPC)	Sampling to obtain data that are plotted on control charts and graphs to see if the production process is operating as it should and to pinpoint problem areas.
Statistical Quality Control (SQC)	A detailed set of specific statistical techniques used to monitor all aspects of the production process to ensure that both work-in-process and finished products meet the firm's quality standards.

IMPROVING QUALITY THROUGH EMPLOYEE PARTICIPATION One of the first steps needed to improve quality is employee participation. Simply put: Successful firms encourage employees to accept full responsibility for the quality of their work. When Toyota, once the role model for world-class manufacturing, faced a quality crisis, the company announced a quality-improvement plan based on its famous "Toyota Way." One tenet of the Toyota Way is the need to solve problems at their source, which allows factory workers to stop the production line if necessary to address a problem. Another tenet that enabled Toyota to resolve quality problems was the use of quality circles designated to deal with difficulties as they arise. A **quality circle** is a team of employees who meet on company time to solve problems of product quality. Quality circles have also been used successfully in companies such as IBM, Northrop Grumman Corporation, Lockheed Martin, and GE.

Increased effort is also being devoted to **inspection**, which is the examination of the quality of work-in-process. Employees perform inspections at various times during production. Purchased materials may be inspected when they arrive at the production facility. Subassemblies and manufactured parts may be inspected before they become part of a finished product. In addition, finished goods may be inspected before they are shipped to customers. Items that are within design specifications continue on their way. Those that are not within design specifications are removed from production.

Total quality management (TQM) can also be used to improve quality of a firm's products or services. As noted in Chapter 6, a TQM program coordinates the efforts directed at improving customer satisfaction, increasing employee participation, strengthening supplier partnerships, and facilitating an organizational atmosphere of continuous quality improvement. Firms such as American Express, AT&T, Motorola, and Hewlett-Packard all have used TQM to improve product quality and, ultimately, customer satisfaction.

Another technique that businesses may use to improve not only quality but also overall performance is Six Sigma. **Six Sigma** is a disciplined approach that relies on statistical data and improved methods to eliminate defects for a firm's products and services. Although many experts agree that Six Sigma is similar to TQM, Six Sigma often has more top-level support, much more teamwork, and a new corporate attitude or culture.[15] The companies that developed, refined, and have the most experience with Six Sigma are Motorola, GE, Ford, and Honeywell. Although each of these companies is a corporate giant, the underlying principles of Six Sigma can be used by any firm, regardless of size.

WORLD QUALITY STANDARDS: ISO 9000 AND ISO 14000 Without a common standard of quality, customers may be at the mercy of manufacturers and vendors. As the number of companies competing in the global marketplace

quality circle a team of employees who meet on company time to solve problems of product quality

inspection the examination of the quality of work-in-process

Six Sigma a disciplined approach that relies on statistical data and improved methods to eliminate defects for a firm's products and services

Nobody likes complaints!

You don't want to buy a shoddy product, and any company you work for doesn't want to gain a reputation for poor quality. That's why strict quality control is so important.

International Organization for Standardization (ISO) a network of national standards institutes and similar organizations from over 160 different countries that is charged with developing standards for quality products and services that are traded throughout the globe

Concept Check

✓ Why is selecting a supplier important? What factors should be considered when selecting a supplier?

✓ What costs must be balanced and minimized through inventory control?

✓ Explain in what sense scheduling is a control function of operations managers.

✓ How can a business firm improve the quality of its products or services?

has increased, so has the seriousness of this problem. To deal with the problem of standardization, the International Organization for Standardization, a nongovernmental organization with headquarters in Geneva, Switzerland, was created. The **International Organization for Standardization (ISO)** is a network of national standards institutes and similar organizations from over 160 different countries that is charged with developing standards for quality products and services that are traded throughout the globe. According to the organization,

> ISO's work makes a positive difference to the world we live in. ISO standards add value to all types of business operations. They contribute to making the development, manufacturing and supply of products and services more efficient, safer and cleaner. They make trade between countries easier and fairer. ISO standards also serve to safeguard consumers and users of products and services in general, as well as making their lives simpler.[16]

Standardization is achieved through consensus agreements between national delegations representing all the economic stakeholders—suppliers, customers, and often governments. The member organization for the United States is the American National Standards Institute located in Washington, D.C.

Although certification is not a legal requirement to conduct business globally, the organization's member countries have approved the ISO standards. In fact, ISO standards are so prevalent around the globe that many customers refuse to do business with noncertified companies. As an added bonus, companies completing the certification process often discover new, cost-efficient ways to improve their existing quality-control programs.

In 1987, the panel published ISO 9000 (*iso* is Greek for "equal"), which sets the guidelines for quality management procedures that manufacturers and service providers must use to receive certification. Certification by independent auditors and laboratory testing services serves as evidence that a company meets the standards for quality control procedures in design, production processes, and product testing.

As a continuation of this standardization process, the ISO has developed many different standards for businesses that provide goods and services to customers around the globe. For example, the ISO 14000 is a family of international standards for incorporating environmental concerns into operations and product standards. ISO standards are also updated periodically. For example, ISO 9001:2008 includes important clarifications and addresses issues of compatibility with ISO's other quality standards.

Production Planning: A Summary

In this chapter, the activities that firms use to produce products and services have been described. And yet, it is often hard to determine how the individual activities fit together in a logical sequence. Now, toward the end of the chapter, it may help to look at a table to see how all of the "pieces of the puzzle" fit together. At the top of Table 8-2, planning for production begins with research and development, design planning, site selection and facilities planning, and operational planning—all topics described in this chapter. In the middle of Table 8-2, activities that were described in the Operations Control section (purchasing, inventory control, scheduling, and quality control) are summarized. The goal of all the planning activities in the top section and operations control activities in the middle section is to create and produce a successful product or service. Of course, the steps for planning production and operations control should always be evaluated to determine if the firm's activities can be improved in order to meet the needs of its customers and to increase the firm's productivity.

TABLE 8-2 Production Planning: A Summary

Both planning for production and operations control are necessary if a firm is to produce a successful product or service.

The Process Begins with Planning for Production
1. *Research and Development* identifies ideas for a product or service.
2. *Design Planning* develops a plan for producing a product or service.
3. *Site Selection and Facilities Planning* identifies a production site, a plant layout, and if human resources are available.
4. *Operational Planning* decides on the amount of products or services that will be produced.

Then Four Operations Control Steps Are Used to Produce a Product or Service
1. *Purchasing* obtains required materials, supplies, and parts from other firms.
2. *Inventory Control* ensures that materials, supplies, and parts are available when needed.
3. *Scheduling* ensures that materials and other resources are at the right place and at the right time in the production process.
4. *Quality Control* determines if the firm has lived up to the standards it has set for itself on the quality of its products or services.

The End Result: A Successful Product or Service

© CENGAGE LEARNING 2015

IMPROVING PRODUCTIVITY WITH TECHNOLOGY

Learning Objective

7 Summarize how technology can make American firms more productive and competitive in the global marketplace.

No coverage of operations management would be complete without a discussion of productivity and technology. Productivity concerns all managers, but it is especially important to operations managers, the people who must oversee the creation of a firm's goods or services. In Chapter 1, *productivity* was defined as the average level of output per worker per hour. Hence, if each worker at plant A produces 75 units per day and each worker at plant B produces only 70 units per day, the workers at plant A are more productive. If one bank teller serves 25 customers per hour and another serves 28 per hour, the second teller is more productive.

Productivity Trends

For U.S. businesses, overall productivity growth for output per hour averaged 4.2 percent for the period 1979–2011.[17] More specifically, 2011 output per hour for U.S. firms increased 2 percent.[18] (*Note:* At the time of publication, 2011 was the last year that complete statistics were available.) While the 2 percent increase in output per hour in 2011 was lower when compared with our average productivity growth, 11 other nations that the U.S. Bureau Labor Statistics tracks each year had larger growth in productivity than the United States—as illustrated in Figure 8-6.[19]

Improving Productivity Growth

Many U.S. firms are using a number of techniques to improve productivity. For example, a large number of business firms are adopting the concept of lean manufacturing. **Lean manufacturing** is a concept built on the idea of eliminating waste from all of the activities required to produce a product or service. Benefits of lean manufacturing include a reduction in the amount of resources required to produce a product or service, more efficient use of employee time, improved quality, and

lean manufacturing a concept built on the idea of eliminating waste from all of the activities required to produce a product or service

FIGURE 8-6 Productivity Growth Rates

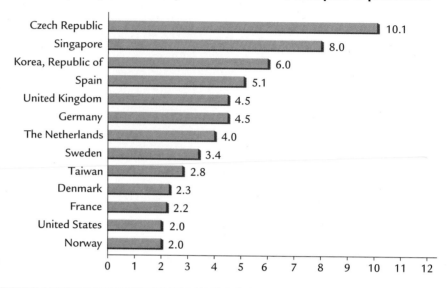

This graph identifies nations with the largest increase in output per hour in 2011—the last year that complete results were available prior to publication.

Nation	Rate
Czech Republic	10.1
Singapore	8.0
Korea, Republic of	6.0
Spain	5.1
United Kingdom	4.5
Germany	4.5
The Netherlands	4.0
Sweden	3.4
Taiwan	2.8
Denmark	2.3
France	2.2
United States	2.0
Norway	2.0

Source: Based on information in "International Comparisons of Manufacturing Productivity and Unit Labor Cost Trends, 2011," The Bureau of Labor Statistics website at www.bls.gov (accessed December 6, 2012).

increased profits. In addition to lean manufacturing, several other factors must be considered if U.S. firms are going to increase productivity *and* their ability to compete in the global marketplace. For example:

- The United States must stabilize its economy so that firms will invest more money in new facilities, equipment, technology, and employee training.
- Managers and executives must cooperate with employees to increase employee motivation and participation in the workplace.
- All government policies must be examined to ensure that unreasonable regulations that may be hindering productivity growth are eliminated.
- Successful techniques that have been used in manufacturing firms must be used to increase productivity in the service industry.
- Increased use of automation, robotics, and computer manufacturing systems must be used to lower production costs.
- There must be more emphasis on satisfying the customer's needs with quality goods and services.

Finally, innovation and research and development efforts to create new products and services must be increased in order for U.S. firms to compete in the global marketplace.

The Impact of Automation, Robotics, and Computers on Productivity

automation the total or near-total use of machines to do work

Automation is the total or near-total use of machines to do work. The rapid increase in automated procedures has been made possible by the microprocessor, a silicon chip that led to the production of desktop computers for businesses, homes, and schools. In factories, microprocessors are used in robotics and in computer manufacturing systems.

Robotics Robotics is the use of programmable machines to perform a variety of tasks by manipulating materials and tools. Robots work quickly, accurately, and steadily. For example, Illumina, Inc., a San Diego company, sells robotic equipment that performs medical laboratory tests. As an added bonus, Illumina's robotic equipment can work 24 hours a day at much lower costs than if human lab workers performed the same tests.[20]

Robots are especially effective in tedious, repetitive assembly-line jobs, as well as in handling hazardous materials. Lincoln Electric, for example, provides robotic arc welders that eliminate the hot, dirty job of welding, which is key to many manufacturing tasks. As an added bonus, robotic arc welders are often quicker and are more precise than old-fashioned welding machines.

Robots are also useful as artificial "eyes" that can check the quality of products as they are being processed on assembly lines. To date, the automotive industry has made the most extensive use of robotics, but robots also have been used to mine coal, inspect the inner surfaces of pipes, assemble computer components, provide certain kinds of patient care in hospitals, and clean and guard buildings at night.

© NATALIYA HORA/SHUTTERSTOCK.COM

Robotics can be a manufacturer's best friend. One of the first industries to use robotics to increase the number of products produced and improve employee productivity was the automobile industry. In this photo, robotics is used to move the right side of a sport utility vehicle (SUV) from one workstation on an assembly line to the next station.

robotics the use of programmable machines to perform a variety of tasks by manipulating materials and tools

COMPUTER MANUFACTURING SYSTEMS People are quick to point out how computers have changed their everyday lives, but most people do not realize the impact computers have had on manufacturing. In simple terms, the factory of the future has already arrived. For most manufacturers, the changeover began with the use of computer-aided design and computer-aided manufacturing. **Computer-aided design (CAD)** is the use of computers to aid in the development of products. Ford speeds up car design, Canon designs new photocopiers, and American Greetings creates new birthday cards by using CAD.

Computer-aided manufacturing (CAM) is the use of computers to plan and control manufacturing processes. A well-designed CAM system allows manufacturers to become much more productive. Not only are a greater number of products produced, but speed and quality also increase. Using CAM systems, Toyota produces automobiles, Hasbro manufactures toys, and Apple Computer creates electronic products.

If you are thinking that the next logical step is to combine the CAD and CAM computer systems, you are right. Today, the most successful manufacturers use CAD and CAM together to form a computer-integrated manufacturing system. Specifically, **computer-integrated manufacturing (CIM)** is a computer system that not only helps to design products but also controls the machinery needed to produce the finished product. For example, Fifth & Pacific Companies (formerly Liz Claiborne) uses CIM to design clothing, to establish patterns for new fashions, and then to cut the cloth needed to produce the finished product. Other advantages of using CIM include improved flexibility, more efficient scheduling, and higher product quality—all factors that make a production facility more competitive in today's global economy.

computer-aided design (CAD) the use of computers to aid in the development of products

computer-aided manufacturing (CAM) the use of computers to plan and control manufacturing processes

computer-integrated manufacturing (CIM) a computer system that not only helps to design products but also controls the machinery needed to produce the finished product

FLEXIBLE MANUFACTURING SYSTEMS Manufacturers have known for a number of years that the mass-production and traditional assembly lines used to manufacture products present a number of problems. For example, although traditional assembly lines turn out extremely large numbers of identical products economically, the system requires expensive, time-consuming retooling of equipment whenever a new product is to be manufactured. This type of manufacturing is often referred to as a continuous process. **Continuous process** is a manufacturing process in which a firm produces the same product(s) over a long period of time. Now it is possible to use flexible manufacturing systems to solve such problems. A **flexible manufacturing system (FMS)** combines electronic machines and CIM in a single production system. Instead of having to spend large amounts of time and effort to retool the traditional mechanical equipment on an assembly line for each new product, an FMS is rearranged simply by reprogramming electronic machines. Because FMSs require less time and expense to reprogram than traditional systems, manufacturers can produce smaller batches of a variety of products without raising the production cost. Flexible manufacturing is sometimes referred to as an intermittent process. An **intermittent process** is a manufacturing process in which a firm's manufacturing machines and equipment are changed to produce different products.

© ISTOCKPHOTO.COM/PHOTOVIDEOSTOCK

continuous process a manufacturing process in which a firm produces the same product(s) over a long period of time

flexible manufacturing system (FMS) a single production system that combines electronic machines and CIM

intermittent process a manufacturing process in which a firm's manufacturing machines and equipment are changed to produce different products

For most manufacturers, the driving force behind FMSs is the customer. In fact, the term *customer-driven production* is often used to describe a manufacturing system that is driven by customer needs and what customers want to buy. For example, advanced software and a flexible manufacturing system have enabled Dell Computer to change to a more customer-driven manufacturing process. Although the costs of designing and installing an FMS such as this are high, the electronic equipment is used more frequently and efficiently than the machinery on a traditional assembly line.

Sustainability and Technological Displacement

In Chapter 1, *sustainability* was defined as creating and maintaining the conditions under which humans and nature can exist in productive harmony while fulfilling the social, economic, and other requirements of present and future generations. While sustainability affects all aspects of a nation, its people, and the economy, the concept is especially important for manufacturers and service providers. Because of the amount of resources required to produce goods and services, these businesses must conserve resources whenever possible. As an added bonus, efforts to reduce waste and sustain the planet can often improve a firm's bottom-line profit amount.

Today, many countries around the globe produce goods and services and compete with U.S. manufacturers. And yet, U.S. producers are known for quality and innovation—especially for products that are more expensive or more complicated to manufacture. As a result, most experts agree that, because U.S. manufacturers will continue to innovate, workers who have manufacturing jobs will be highly skilled and can work with the automated and computer-aided manufacturing systems. Those that don't possess high-tech skills will be dispensable and unemployed. Many workers will be faced with the choice of retraining for new jobs or seeking jobs in other sectors of the economy. Government, business, and education will have to cooperate to prepare workers for new roles in an automated workplace.

The next chapter discusses many of the issues caused by technological displacement. In addition, a number of major components of human resources management are described, and we see how managers use various reward systems to boost motivation, productivity, and morale.

Concept Check

✓ How might productivity be measured in a restaurant? In a department store? In a public school system?

✓ How can robotics, computer manufacturing systems, and flexible manufacturing systems help a manufacturer to produce products?

Summary

1 Explain the nature of production.

Operations management consists of all the activities that managers engage in to create goods and services. Operations are as relevant to service organizations as to manufacturing firms. Today, U.S. companies are forced to compete in an ever-smaller world to meet the needs of more-demanding customers. As a result, U.S. manufacturers have used innovation to improve productivity. Because of innovation, fewer workers are needed, but those workers who are needed possess the skills to use automation and technology. In an attempt to regain a competitive edge, manufacturers have taken another look at the importance of improving quality and meeting the needs of their customers. They also have used new techniques to motivate employees, reduced costs, used computer-aided and flexible manufacturing systems, improved control procedures, and used green manufacturing. Competing in the global economy is not only profitable but also an essential activity that requires the cooperation of everyone within an organization. A number of career options are available for employees in operations management.

2 Outline how the conversion process transforms raw materials, labor, and other resources into finished goods or services.

A business transforms resources into goods and services in order to provide utility to customers. Utility is the ability of a good or service to satisfy a human need. Form utility is created by people converting raw materials, finances, and information into finished products. Conversion processes vary in terms of the major resources used to produce goods and services (focus), the degree to which resources are changed (magnitude of change), and the number of production processes that a business uses.

3 Understand the importance of service businesses to consumers, other business firms, and the nation's economy.

The application of the basic principles of operations management to the production of services has coincided with the growth and importance of service businesses in the United States. Today 87 percent of American workers are employed in the service industry. In fact, the American economy is now characterized as a service economy. For a service firm, planning often begins with determining who the customer is and what needs the customer has. After customer needs are identified the next step is to develop a plan that will enable the firm to deliver the services that their customers want or need. Although it is often more difficult to measure customer satisfaction, today's successful service firms work hard at providing the services customers want. For example, compared with manufacturers, service firms often listen more carefully to customers and respond more quickly to the market's changing needs.

4 Describe how research and development leads to new products and services.

Operations management often begins with product research and development and often referred to as R&D. The results of R&D may be entirely new products or services or extensions and refinements of existing products or services. R&D activities are classified as basic research (aimed at uncovering new knowledge), applied research (discovering new knowledge with some potential use), and development and implementation (using new or existing knowledge to produce goods and services). If a firm sells only one product or provides only one service, when customers quit buying the product or service, the firm will die. To stay in business, the firm must, at the very least, find ways to refine or extend the want-satisfying capability of its product or service.

5 Discuss the components involved in planning the production process.

Planning for production involves three major phases: design planning, site selection and facilities planning, and operational planning. First, design planning is undertaken to address questions related to the product line, required production capacity, and the use of technology. Then production facilities, human resources, and plant layout must be considered. Operational planning focuses on the use of production facilities and resources. The steps for operational planning include (1) selecting a planning horizon, (2) estimating market demand, (3) comparing market demand with capacity, and (4) adjusting production of products or services to meet demand.

6 Explain how purchasing, inventory control, scheduling, and quality control affect production.

The major areas of operations control are purchasing, inventory control, scheduling, and quality control.

Purchasing involves selecting suppliers. The choice of suppliers should result from careful analysis of a number of factors, including price, quality, reliability, credit terms, and shipping costs. Inventory control is the management of stocks of raw materials, work-in-process, and finished goods to minimize the total inventory cost. Scheduling ensures that materials and other resources are at the right place at the right time. Quality control guarantees that products and services are produced in accordance with design specifications. The major objective of quality control is to see that the organization lives up to the standards it has set for itself on quality. A number of different activities including quality circles, inspection, total quality management, and six sigma can be used to encourage employee participation and to improve quality.

7 **Summarize how technology can make American firms more productive and competitive in the global marketplace.**

Productivity is the average level of output per worker per hour. From 1979 to 2011, U.S. productivity growth averaged a 4.2 percent increase. More specifically, productivity in 2011 increased 2 percent. Although a 2 percent increase was lower when compared to our average productivity growth over the 1979 to 2011 time period, 11 other nations that the U.S. Bureau of Labor Statistics tracks each year had larger growth in productivity than the United States. Several factors must be considered if U.S. firms are going to increase productivity and their ability to compete in the global marketplace.

Automation, the total or near-total use of machines to do work, has for some years been changing the way work is done in factories. A growing number of industries are using programmable machines called robots. Computer-aided design, computer-aided manufacturing, and computer-integrated manufacturing use computers to help design and manufacture products. A flexible manufacturing system (FMS) combines electronic machines and CIM to produce smaller batches of products more efficiently than on the traditional assembly line. Instead of having to spend vast amounts of time and effort to retool the traditional mechanical equipment on an assembly line for each new product, an FMS is rearranged simply by reprogramming electronic machines. An FMS is sometimes referred to as an intermittent process.

Key Terms

You should now be able to define and give an example relevant to each of the following terms:

operations management (208)
reshoring (209)
mass production (210)
analytical process (210)
synthetic process (210)
utility (210)
form utility (210)
service economy (212)
research and development (R&D) (213)
design planning (215)
product line (215)

product design (216)
capacity (216)
labor-intensive technology (216)
capital-intensive technology (216)
plant layout (217)
planning horizon (219)
purchasing (220)
inventory control (221)
materials requirements planning (MRP) (221)

just-in-time inventory system (221)
scheduling (221)
Malcolm Baldrige National Quality Award (222)
quality control (222)
quality circle (223)
inspection (223)
Six Sigma (223)
International Organization for Standardization (ISO) (224)
lean manufacturing (225)
automation (226)

robotics (227)
computer-aided design (CAD) (227)
computer-aided manufacturing (CAM) (227)
computer-integrated manufacturing (CIM) (227)
continuous process (228)
flexible manufacturing system (FMS) (228)
intermittent process (228)

Discussion Questions

1. Why would Rubbermaid—a successful U.S. company—need to expand and sell its products to customers in foreign countries?
2. What steps have U.S. firms taken to regain a competitive edge in the global marketplace?
3. Do certain kinds of firms need to stress particular areas of operations management? Explain.
4. Is it really necessary for service firms to engage in research and development? In planning for production and operations control?
5. How are the four areas of operations control interrelated?
6. Is operations management relevant to nonbusiness organizations such as colleges and hospitals? Why or why not?

Test Yourself

Matching Questions

1. _____ It is a plan for converting a product idea into an actual product or service.

2. _____ Raw materials are broken into different components.

3. _____ Its focus is minimizing holding costs and potential stock-out costs.

4. _____ It is created by people converting materials, finances and information into finished goods.

5. _____ A manufacturing process in which a firm's manufacturing machines and equipment are changed to produce different products.

6. _____ Work is accomplished mostly by equipment.

7. _____ Input from workers is used to improve the workplace.

8. _____ The average level of output per worker per hour.

9. _____ Computers are the main tool used in the development of products.

10. _____ The time period during which an operational plan will be in effect.

    a. analytical process
    b. capital-intensive technology
    c. product line
    d. computer-aided design
    e. design planning
    f. form utility
    g. inventory control
    h. plant layout
    i. planning horizon
    j. productivity
    k. quality circle
    l. intermittent process

True False Questions

11. **T** **F** Capacity is the degree to which input resources are physically changed by the conversion process.

12. **T** **F** Reshoring is sometimes referred to as onshoring or insourcing.

13. **T** **F** Operations management is the process of creating a set of specifications from which the product can be produced.

14. **T** **F** A purchasing agent need not worry about a tiny difference in price when a large quantity is being bought.

15. **T** **F** A synthetic process combines raw materials or components to create a finished product.

16. **T** **F** When work stations are arranged to match the sequence of operations, a process layout is being used.

17. **T** **F** Work-in-process inventories are raw materials and supplies waiting to be processed.

18. **T** **F** The purpose of research and development is to identify new ideas that have the potential to result in new goods and services.

19. **T** **F** For a food-processing plant such as Kraft Foods, capacity refers to the number of employees working on an assembly line.

20. **T** **F** Labor-intensive technology is accompanied by low initial costs and high operating costs.

Multiple-Choice Questions

21. _____ One worker in Department A produces 45 units of work per day on a computer, whereas a co-worker produces only 40 units of work per day on a computer. Since the first worker produces more units, that worker has a
    a. lower capacity to use technology.
    b. higher productivity rate.
    c. desire to help the co-worker.
    d. computer-integrated system.
    e. computer-aided system

22. _____ Services differ from the production of manufactured goods in all ways except that services
    a. are consumed immediately and cannot be stored.
    b. aren't as important as manufactured products to the U.S. economy.
    c. are provided when and where the customer desires the service.
    d. are usually labor-intensive.
    e. are intangible, and it's more difficult to evaluate customer service.

23. _____ The goal of basic research is to
    a. uncover new knowledge without regard for its potential use.
    b. discover new knowledge with regard for potential use in development.
    c. discover knowledge for potential use.
    d. put new or existing knowledge to use.
    e. combine ideas.

24. _____ Two important components of scheduling are
    a. lead time and planning.
    b. designing and arranging.
    c. monitoring and controlling.
    d. place and time.
    e. logistics and flow.

25. _____ A common planning horizon for production activities is
   a. one day.
   b. a week.
   c. a month.
   d. six months.
   e. one year.

26. _____ A _____ manufacturing system combines electronic machines and computer-integrated manufacturing in a single-production system.
   a. continuous
   b. analytic
   c. synthetic
   d. flexible
   e. automation

27. _____ The process of acquiring materials, supplies, components, and parts from other firms is known as
   a. acquisition.
   b. planning.
   c. purchasing.
   d. inventory requisition.
   e. materials requirements planning.

28. _____ Procter & Gamble uses _____ production to produce household products.
   a. efficient order
   b. demand
   c. supply order
   d. mass
   e. effective

29. _____ If a good or service satisfies a human need, it has
   a. form.
   b. value.
   c. focus.
   d. magnitude.
   e. utility.

30. _____ The American economy is now characterized as a(n) _____ economy.
   a. civilized
   b. stagnant
   c. service
   d. bureaucratic
   e. industrialized

Answers to the Test Yourself questions appear at the end of the book on page TY-1.

Video Case
Chobani Gives the World a Taste for Greek Yogurt

Entrepreneur Hamdi Ulukaya, founder of fast-growing Chobani, needed less than five years to transform a defunct yogurt factory in rural South Edmeston, New York into the U.S. capitol of Greek yogurt production. He came up with the idea of making Greek yogurt in the United States in 2005, when he bought the factory with the help of a Small Business Administration loan from its former owner, Kraft Foods. Ulukaya spent the next 18 months experimenting with recipes while upgrading the factory, arranging a steady supply of milk and other fresh ingredients, and working out the details of what the yogurt cup would look like.

By 2007, Ulukaya had perfected his recipe and was churning out the first cases of Chobani yogurt for an ever-larger list of supermarket customers. His Greek yogurt, thicker and tangier than traditional yogurts, took the industry by storm. Ulukaya originally projected that Chobani would break even if it produced 20,000 cases of yogurt every week. By 2009, the company was getting weekly orders for 200,000 cases—ten times the founder's estimate.

Suddenly, Chobani's Greek yogurt wasn't a tiny, niche product that multinational competitors like Dannon and Yoplait could ignore. Although Ulukaya considered enlarging the factory to accommodate weekly production capacity of 400,000 cases, he decided on the much more ambitious strategy of planning for weekly production capacity of 1 million cases. This huge expansion required new equipment and an around-the-clock production schedule. At the newly enlarged plant, employees would operate machines for 10 hours, followed by a cleaning period of 4 hours to ensure product purity.

By 2012, Chobani was ringing up $1 billion in annual sales throughout North America, and the South Edmeston factory was turning out 12 million yogurt cups every day, making it the country's center of Greek yogurt production. However, Chobani was having difficulty obtaining sufficient quantities of fresh milk to further boost production in the New York plant. Whereas one cup of regular yogurt is made from one cup of milk, one cup of Greek yogurt requires three cups of milk. Ulukaya's $450 million solution to the challenge of milk availability: Build a cavernous new production facility in Twin Falls, Idaho, where Chobani can draw on an abundant local supply of milk. This plant opened in December, 2012, with a weekly production capacity of more than 2 million cases of yogurt. It serves Western states, while the original New York plant ships to Eastern states.

Even as Chobani gears up for higher production and higher market share in North America, it's also getting ready for growth halfway around the world. Ulukaya purchased a dairy near Melbourne, Australia, and invested millions of dollars to upgrade and expand yogurt production at the site. From this facility, Chobani will serve Australia and export its popular Greek yogurt to new markets in Asia. In addition, it maintains a sales office in Europe to support expansion on the continent.

Today, Chobani—a company that didn't even exist a decade ago—dominates the U.S. market for Greek yogurt. It has expanded its product line to include Greek yogurt for children and various sizes and flavors of Greek yogurt for adults. Not long ago, Ulukaya opened a specialty yogurt shop in a trendy part of New York City. New flavor combinations that prove especially popular there may soon be transferred to the production lines in New York, Idaho, and beyond.[21]

Questions

1. Do you agree with Ulukaya's decision to open a production facility in Idaho instead of buying milk and trucking it to Chobani's New York plant? In addition to the cost of transporting the milk, are there other factors that might have influenced Ulukaya's decision to build a second plant?

2. What can Chobani do to gauge market demand for Greek yogurt and for particular flavors and products in its own product line? Identify at least three specific ideas.

3. Chobani's equipment runs for 10 hours and must be idle for four hours while being cleaned. Its plants operate day and night, all week long. What are the implications for the company's purchasing, inventory control, scheduling, and quality control functions?

Building Skills for Career Success

1. Social Media Exercise

Starbucks has taken an innovative approach to improving their products and the customer experience in their stores. Their entire purpose is to create a "third place" beyond home and work where people can congregate and socialize (while having a nice cup of coffee). To engage customers, they created a website called My Starbucks Idea (http://mystarbucksidea.com) that allows customers to post their ideas and then allows customers to also vote on them.

1. Visit the http://mystarbucksidea.com site. Do you have an idea for Starbucks? If so, post it. Do you have a feeling about one of the current ideas? If so, then vote for it.

2. Do you think this is an effective way to gain customer ideas for new products? Why or why not?

3. Can you think of other ways that corporate executives at Starbucks can gauge customer interest in their products and in-store experience using social media?

2. Building Team Skills

Suppose that you are planning to build a house in the country. It will be a brick, one-story structure of approximately 2,000 square feet, centrally heated and cooled. It will have three bedrooms, two bathrooms, a family room, a dining room, a kitchen with a breakfast nook, a study, a utility room, an entry foyer, a two-car garage, a covered patio, and a fireplace. Appliances will operate on electricity and propane fuel. You have received approval and can be connected to the cooperative water system at any time. Public sewerage services are not available; therefore, you must rely on a septic system. You want to know how long it will take to build the house.

Assignment

1. In a group, identify the major activities involved in the project and sequence them in the proper order.

2. Estimate the time required for each activity.

3. Present your list of activities to the class and ask for comments and suggestions.

3. Researching Different Careers

Because service businesses are now such a dominant part of our economy, job seekers sometimes overlook the employment opportunities available in production. Two positions often found in manufacturing and production are quality-control inspector and purchasing agent.

Assignment

1. Using the *Occupational Outlook Handbook* at your local library or on the Internet (http://stats.bls.gov/oco /home.htm), find the following information for the jobs of quality-control inspector and purchasing agent:

   Nature of work, including main activities and responsibilities
   Job outlook
   Earnings
   Training, qualifications, and advancement.

2. Look for other production jobs that may interest you and compile the same sort of information about them.

3. Summarize in a two-page report the key things you learned about jobs in production.

Running a Business

Part 3

Graeter's Grows Through Good Management, Organization, and Quality

Graeter's began as a tiny Cincinnati business and now enjoys a national reputation for the quality of its premium ice cream. Even though the $30 million company recently opened a new factory to support its expansion plans, it still clings fiercely to its original small-batch production method for making creamy ice cream from fresh ingredients. CEO Richard Graeter emphasizes that profits are important, but "staying true to who you are and investing in your business is what makes sure that your business is going to be here tomorrow." That's why Graeter's still makes all of its ice cream by hand, ensuring that the texture and taste meet its high standards batch after batch, year after year.

More than a Family Affair

Graeter's top-management team includes the CEO and his two cousins, Bob and Chip Graeter. As vice president of operations, Bob is responsible for manufacturing, as well as for developing new products and finding suppliers to provide ingredients such as fresh fruits, cream, eggs, and chocolates. His brother Chip oversees all of the company's ice cream shops. Rounding out the management team is a chief operating officer, a controller, a vice president of sales and marketing, and a candy production manager.

"Every major decision, we make on a consensus basis," Richard says, describing the equal partnership among the three family members. "That doesn't mean we don't have a different point of view from time to time, but . . . we learn to see each other's view and discuss, debate, and get down to a decision that all of us support. The other thing that we have learned to do, something that is a little different than our parents' generation [did], is bring in outside people into the . . . executive level of the management team. . . . We now work with a couple of consultants to help us plan our strategy to look for a new vision, to develop training programs . . . all those systems that big companies have." Managers stay in close contact with employees at all levels and don't hesitate to ask for their input when solving problems and making decisions.

Inside the Org Chart

Graeter's formalized its organization structure over the years as it opened more stores and expanded beyond Cincinnati.

Today, the store managers report to a group manager, who in turn reports to the vice president of retail operations. At the company's recently opened 28,000 square foot production facility, employees in each of three shifts are supervised by a shift manager, who reports to the vice president of operations. The first and third shifts are responsible for ice cream production, while the second shift is in charge of cleaning and sanitizing the facility.

Because so many Graeter's stores are located miles from headquarters, two managers "shop" each store every month, checking on quality and service. These management visits are supplemented by two monthly visits from "mystery shoppers" who buy ice cream on different days, observing what employees are doing and taking note of what else is happening in the store. Their written reports give Graeter's top managers another view of the business, this time from the customer's perspective.

What's the plan?

Change has come quickly to Graeter's, not all of it anticipated. The company was constructing its second factory to support the drive for nationwide distribution when an unexpected opportunity arose: to buy out the last franchise company operating Graeter's retail stores and take over its factory as well. The management team jumped at the chance. "A few months ago our strategy was just operate one plant," says Richard. "Now our strategy is, adapt to the opportunity that came along . . . we are operating three plants. The goal is to keep all of your assets deployed productively, so if we have these three plants, what is the most we can do out of those plants to be generating product and profit? One example would be supplying restaurants in other cities, which we really weren't considering originally because our new plant was really geared for pints, but if we have this excess capacity, the smart thing to do is figure out what we can do with that."

The newest Graeter's facility, on Regina Graeter Way in Cincinnati, was built to produce as much as 1 million gallons of ice cream per year, although the current annual output is about 625,000 gallons. Many steps, such as putting lids on

© ISTOCKPHOTO.COM/LIVIO

packages and moving them into refrigerated storage, are handled by automated equipment. Yet all of the ice cream is still made in small batches and by hand. Experienced technicians wield a paddle to gradually mix in ingredients such as molten chocolate, which have been pasteurized on the premises to comply with government regulations. Once the ice cream reaches the right temperature and texture, another employee hand-packs it into individual packages, which are then automatically capped, stamped with a date code, sealed, and whisked away to be kept cold until being loaded onto trucks for delivery to supermarket customers. Ice cream samples from every shift's output are tested to ensure purity and quality.

Graeter's sets weekly and monthly sales goals for its stores, based on each unit's location and other factors that affect demand. If a store doesn't meet its goals, the group manager acts quickly to find out why and help the store get back on track. As the company explores the possibility of opening Graeter's stores as far away as Los Angeles and New York, the management team is planning carefully and assessing the potential challenges and advantages of coast-to-coast operations.[22]

Questions

1. Based on this case and the two previous Graeter's cases, what are the company's most important strengths? Can you identify any weaknesses that might affect its ability to grow?

2. How would you describe the departmentalization and the organizational structure at Graeter's? Do you think Graeter's is centralized or decentralized, and what are the implications for its plans for growth?

3. The newest Graeter's plant can produce far more ice cream than is needed today. The company also makes ice cream at its original plant and at the plant formerly owned by a franchisee. What are the implications for Graeter's strategy and for its operational planning?

Building a Business Plan: Part 3

Now you should be ready to provide evidence that you have a management team with the necessary skills and experience to execute your business plan successfully. Only a competent management team can transform your vision into a successful business. You also should be able to describe your manufacturing and operations plans. The three chapters in Part 3 of your textbook, "Understanding the Management Process," "Creating a Flexible Organization," and "Producing Quality Goods and Services," should help you in answering some of the questions in this part of the business plan.

The Management Team Component

The management team component should include the answers to at least the following questions:

3.1. How is your team balanced in technical, conceptual, interpersonal, and other special skills needed in your business?

3.2. What will be your style of leadership?

3.3. How will your company be structured? Include a statement of the philosophy of management and company culture.

3.4. What are the key management positions, compensation, and key policies?

3.5. Include a job description for each management position and specify who will fill that position. *Note:* Prepare an organization chart and provide the résumé of each key manager for the appendix.

3.6. What other professionals, such as a lawyer, an insurance agent, a banker, and a certified public accountant, will you need for assistance?

The Manufacturing and Operations Plan Component

If you are in a manufacturing business, now is a good time to describe your manufacturing and operations plans, space requirements, equipment, labor force, inventory control, and purchasing requirements. Even if you are in a service-oriented business, many of these questions still may apply.

The manufacturing and operations plan component should include the answers to at least the following questions:

3.7. What are the advantages and disadvantages of your planned location in terms of

- Wage rates
- Unionization
- Labor pool
- Proximity to customers and suppliers
- Types of transportation available
- Tax rates
- Utility costs
- Zoning requirements

3.8. What facilities does your business require? Prepare a floor plan for the appendix. Will you rent, lease, or purchase the facilities?

3.9. Will you make or purchase component parts to be assembled into the finished product? Make sure to justify your "make-or-buy" decision.

3.10. Who are your potential subcontractors and suppliers?

3.11. How will you control quality, inventory, and production? How will you measure your progress?

3.12. Is there a sufficient quantity of adequately skilled people in the local labor force to meet your needs?

Review of Business Plan Activities

Be sure to go over the information you have gathered. Check for any weaknesses and resolve them before beginning Part 4. Also, review all the answers to the questions in Parts 1, 2, and 3 to be certain that they are consistent throughout the entire business plan. Finally, write a brief statement that summarizes all the information for this part of the business plan.

Endnotes

1. Based on information in Noel Randewich, "Insight: As Chip Plants Get Pricey, U.S. Risks Losing Edge," *Reuters,* May 1, 2012, www.reuters.com; Shara Tibken, "Nissan to Use Intel Chips for 'Infotainment,'" *Wall Street Journal,* April 6, 2012, www.wsj.com; "Intel's Ivy Bridge Launch Shows Company's Manufacturing Muscle," *eWeek,* April 23, 2012, www.eweek.com; Mike Rogoway, "Intel Goes Big to Get Small," *Oregonian,* May 28, 2011, www.oregonlive.com; www.intel.com.

2. The Bureau of Labor Statistics website at www.bls.gov (accessed February 14, 2013).

3. Tom Raum, "Obama Call for Manufacturing Revival a Tough Goal," the Yahoo! Finance website at http://finance.yahoo.com (accessed February 10, 2012).

4. The Bureau of Labor Statistics website at www.bls.gov (accessed February 14, 2013).

5. Daniel J. Meckstroth, PH.D., "Is China the Largest Manufacturer in the World?" The Manufacturers Alliance for Production and Innovation website at www.mapi.net, accessed January 31, 2012.

6. Mary Ellen Berry, "Manufacturing's Heavy Lifting within the U.S. Economy, Forbes, January 13, 2012, website at www.forbes.com.

7. "Secretary Bryson Discusses the Future of U.S. Manufacturing at MIT," The Department of Commerce website at www.commerce.gov (accessed May 9, 2012).

8. "Obama Seeks to Increase Partnerships between Community Colleges, Industry to Train New Workers," *Washington Post,* February 13, 2012, website at www.washingtonpost.com.

9. Zackary Roth and Daniel Gross, "President Obama Touts 'Onshoring': Is Made in America Back?" the Yahoo! Finance website at http://finance.yahoo.com (accessed February 15, 2012).

10. The Bureau of Labor Statistics website at www.bls.gov (accessed February 15, 2013).

11. Robert Kreitner and Carlene Cassidy, *Management*, 12th ed. (Mason, OH: Cengage Learning, 2013).

12. The 3M Corporation website at www.3m.com (accessed February 15, 2013).

13. The Berry Plastics Corporation website at www.berryplastics.com (accessed February 16, 2013).

14. The AT&T Supplier website at www.attsuppliers.com (accessed February 15, 2013).

15. "What Makes Six Sigma Work," The iSixSigma website at www.isixsigma.com (accessed February 16, 2013).

16. The International Organization of Standardization (ISO) website at www.iso.org (accessed February 15, 2013).

17. The Bureau of Labor Statistics website at www.bls.gov (accessed February 17, 2013).

18. Ibid.

19. Ibid.

20. The Illumina, Inc., website at www.illumina.com (accessed February 17, 2013).

21. Sources: Based on information in Bryan Gruley, "How a Turkish Immigrant Made a Billion Dollars in Eight Years Selling . . . Yogurt," *Bloomberg Businessweek,* February 4, 2013, pp. 60–64; Andrew Grossman, "Yogurt Boom Leaves Dairy Farmers Behind," *Wall Street Journal*, June 26, 2012, www.wsj.com; Bill Roberts, "Twin Falls Welcomes New Chobani Yogurt Plant," *Idaho Statesman*, December 17, 2012, www.idahostatesman.com; Mark Astley, "What to Expect in 2013," *Dairy Reporter*, January 9, 2013, www.dairyreporter.com; Meghan Walsh, "Chobani Takes Gold in the Yogurt Aisle," *Bloomberg Businessweek*, July 31, 2012, www.businessweek.com.

22. Sources: Based on information from the Graeter's website at www.graeters.com, accessed February 17, 2013; Kimberly L. Jackson, "Graeter's Premium Chocolate Chip Ice Cream Lands at Stop & Shop," *Newark Star-Ledger (NJ),* April 4, 2012, www.nj.com; "Graeter's Ice Cream Debuts in Bay Area," *Tampa Bay Times (St. Petersburg, FL),* January 10, 2012, p. 4B; Jim Carper, "Graeter's Runs a Hands-on Ice Cream Plant," *Dairy Foods*, August 2011, pp. 36+; Jim Carper, "The Greater Good," *Dairy Foods*, August 2011, pp. 95+; "Graeter's Unveils New 'Mystery Flavor,'" *Dayton Daily News*, March 29, 2012, www.daytondailynews.com; Bob Driehaus, "A Cincinnati Ice Cream Maker Aims Big," *New York Times*, September 11, 2010, www.nytimes.com; Lucy May, "Graeter's Northern Kentucky Franchisee Puts Stores on the Block," *Business Courier*, August 6, 2010, http://cincinnati.bizjournals.com; interviews with company staff and Cengage videos about Graeter's.

Attracting and Retaining the Best Employees

Why Should You Care?

Being able to understand how to attract and keep the right people is crucial. Also, you can better understand about your own interactions with your co-workers.

Learning Objectives

Once you complete this chapter, you will be able to:

1 Describe the major components of human resources management.

2 Identify the steps in human resources planning.

3 Describe cultural diversity and understand some of the challenges and opportunities associated with it.

4 Explain the objectives and uses of job analysis.

5 Describe the processes of recruiting, employee selection, and orientation.

6 Discuss the primary elements of employee compensation and benefits.

7 Explain the purposes and techniques of employee training and development.

8 Discuss performance appraisal techniques and performance feedback.

9 Outline the major legislation affecting human resources management.

Google Grows Through People Power

Two million people apply to work at Google (www.google.com) every year, but only a tiny fraction are selected by this well-known pioneer of Internet search technology. Incorporated in 1998, Google is headquartered in California's Silicon Valley and earns most of its $38 billion in annual revenue from the sale of online advertising. Over the years, the company has developed or acquired a wide range of high-tech offerings, from YouTube (online videos) and Chrome (web browser) to Google Maps (maps and directions) and Google Wallet (mobile payments). Now the teenaged Google is poised for even more aggressive growth—and it's out to hire the best and brightest employees to supercharge its long-term success.

Google has hundreds of recruiters reaching out to college graduates and experienced professionals alike, looking for top-notch talent and team players to fill specific job openings. Although the company doesn't administer personality or skills tests, it does put candidates through an intensive series of interviews to determine whether they have the aptitude, attitude, and initiative to be effective within Google's famously fast-paced and creative culture. With an eye toward the future, the company sometimes makes job offers to outstanding candidates, hires them, and *then* creates appropriate positions. This not only boosts Google's brainpower, it keeps candidates away from competitors.

Along with top salaries, Google employees enjoy generous benefits and on-site extras such as free meals and fitness facilities. Dogs are welcome in many Google offices, a plus for pet owners. Googlers (employees) are encouraged to spend up to 20 percent of their time on projects they choose. The company offers hundreds of courses to develop the management and technical skills of its employees and also provides special coaching for promising up-and-comers. No wonder Google regularly appears on *Fortune* magazine's annual list of the best 100 U.S. companies to work for.[1]

Did You Know?

Google employs 33,000 people in 40 countries, and with aggressive growth in mind, it plans to hire thousands more every year.

Google recruits some of the most skilled people in the tech industry and retains and keeps them satisfied by offering good compensation and unusual benefits. We begin our study of human resources management (HRM) with an overview of how businesses acquire, maintain, and develop human resources. After listing the steps by which firms match their human resources needs with the supply available, we explore several dimensions of cultural diversity. Then we examine the concept of job analysis. Next, we focus on how a firm's recruiting, selection, and orientation procedures impact a firm's success in acquiring employees. We describe forms of employee compensation, which can impact employee loyalty and productivity. Then we discuss methods of employee training, management development, and performance appraisal. Finally, we consider legislation that affects HRM practices.

HUMAN RESOURCES MANAGEMENT: AN OVERVIEW

Human resources, the people who work within an organization, are the most important and valuable resource for a business. Without them, a firm would cease to function. Organizations will expend a great deal of effort to acquire and utilize human resources fully. This effort is known as *human resources management*, or *staffing* and *personnel management*.

Human resources management (HRM) consists of all the activities involved in acquiring, maintaining, and developing an organization's human resources. HRM begins with acquisition—getting people to work for the organization. The acquisition process can be very competitive, particularly for skilled employees and in

Learning Objective

1 Describe the major components of human resources management.

human resources management (HRM) all the activities involved in acquiring, maintaining, and developing an organization's human resources

How many skills do you have?

The more skills you develop, the more valuable you are to any employer. Do your own personal skills inventory before you write a résumé or interview for a job. Then you'll be prepared to explain the special skills you can bring to an employer.

The power of people. Many firms believe their employees are their most important assets. However, unlike other assets such as machinery, capital, and products, employees can choose to leave an organization. Carefully designing compensation and reward packages can help a firm attract and retain valuable employees.

fields where demand for workers exceed supply. Next, steps must be taken to retain these valuable resources. (After all, they are the only business resources that can voluntarily leave an organization.) Finally, human resources should be developed to their full capacity.

HRM Activities

Each of the three phases of HRM—acquiring, maintaining, and developing human resources—consists of related actions. Acquisition, for example, includes planning, and the various activities that lead to hiring new personnel. Altogether this phase of HRM includes five separate activities:

- *Human resources planning*—determining the firm's future human resources needs
- *Job analysis*—determining the exact nature of the positions
- *Recruiting*—attracting people to apply for positions
- *Selection*—choosing and hiring the most qualified applicants
- *Orientation*—acquainting new employees with the firm

Maintaining human resources consists primarily of encouraging employees to remain with the firm and to work effectively by using a variety of HRM programs, including the following:

- *Employee relations*—increasing employee job satisfaction through satisfaction surveys, employee communication programs, exit interviews, and fair treatment
- *Compensation*—rewarding employee effort through monetary payments
- *Benefits*—providing rewards to ensure employee well-being

The development phase of HRM is concerned with improving employees' skills and expanding their capabilities. The two important activities of this phase are:

- *Training and development*—teaching employees new skills and new jobs, and more effective ways of performing their present jobs

- *Performance appraisal*—assessing employees' current and potential performance levels

We will discuss each of these activities in more detail later in the chapter.

Responsibility for HRM

In general, HRM is a shared responsibility of line managers and staff HRM specialists. In very small organizations, the owner handles all or most HRM activities. As a firm grows in size, a human resources manager generally is hired to take over some staff responsibilities. In very large firms such as Disney, HRM activities tend to be highly specialized, with separate groups for compensation, benefits, training and development, and other staff activities. GE, for example, has divisions and offices all over the world. Because of the size and complexity of the organization, GE has hundreds of HR managers to cover different geographic areas and departments within the firm.

Specific HRM activities are assigned to those in the best position to perform them. Human resources planning and job analysis usually are carried out by staff specialists with input from line managers. Similarly, staff experts handle recruiting and selection, although line managers are involved in hiring decisions. Staff specialists devise orientation programs that are carried out by both staff specialists and line managers. Compensation systems (including benefits) most often are developed and administered by the HRM staff. However, line managers recommend pay increases and promotions. Training and development activities are the joint responsibility of staff and line managers. Performance appraisal is the job of the line manager, although HRM personnel design the firm's appraisal system in many organizations.

Concept Check

✓ What are the three phases of human resource management?

✓ Identify the activities associated with each phase.

✓ How does the responsibility of HRM change with the size of a firm?

HUMAN RESOURCES PLANNING

Learning Objective

2 **Identify the steps in human resources planning.**

Human resources planning is the development of strategies to meet a firm's future human resources needs. The organization's overall strategic plan is the starting point of the process. From this, human resource planners can forecast future demand for human resources. Next, the planners must determine whether the needed human resources will be available. Finally, they have to take steps to match supply with demand.

human resources planning the development of strategies to meet a firm's future human resources needs

Forecasting Human Resources Demand

Planners should base human resource demand forecasts on all relevant information available. The firm's overall strategic plan will provide information about future business ventures, new products, and projected expansions or contractions of specific product lines. Information on past staffing levels, evolving technologies, industry staffing practices, and projected economic trends also can be helpful. Technological advances are creating new opportunities in forecasting and planning for human resources demand. A survey released by Deloitte Consulting found that new technologies such as social media, cloud computing, and analytics have increased the speed of doing business, which enhances the importance of international growth and strong leadership in organizations. Firms must hire HR talent fluent in new technologies in order to take advantage of opportunities and be aware of threats.[2]

HRM managers use forecasting information to determine both the number of employees required and their qualifications. Planners use a wide range of methods to predict specific personnel needs. For example, a simple method projects personnel requirements to increase or decrease in the same proportion as sales revenue. Thus, a 30 percent increase in projected sales volume over the next two years results in a forecasted personnel increase of 30 percent for the same period. (This method can be applied to specific positions and to the workforce in general. It is not, however, a very precise forecasting method.) At the other end of the spectrum are complex computer programs that perform HRM activities, such as forecasting future human resources requirements, using algorithms and demographic data.

Forecasting Human Resources Supply

A forecast of human resource supply must take into account both the present workforce and any changes that may occur within it. For example, suppose that planners project that in five years a firm that currently employs 100 engineers will need to employ 200 engineers. Forecasting is not as simple as planning to hire 100 additional engineers. Some of the firm's current engineers will leave, move to other jobs within the firm, or be promoted. Thus, planners may project the supply of current engineers in five years at 87, which means that the firm will have to hire a total of

113 new engineers. When forecasting supply, planners should also account for the organization's existing employees to determine who can be retrained to perform required tasks.

Two useful techniques for forecasting human resources supply are the replacement chart and the skills inventory. A **replacement chart** is a list of key personnel and their possible replacements within a firm. It is important to maintain this chart to ensure that top-management positions can be filled quickly in the event of an unexpected death, resignation, or retirement. Some firms provide additional training for employees who might eventually replace top managers.

A **skills inventory** is a searchable database containing information on the skills and experience of all present employees, which can be mined to find candidates to fill available positions. For a special project, a manager may be seeking a current employee with specific information technology skills, at least six years of experience, and fluency in French. The skills inventory can quickly identify qualified employees. Skill-assessment tests, which provide the information in a skills inventory, can be administered internally or by outside vendors. Some companies, such as Halogen Software, offer customizable skills assessment and training software that allows firms to examine skills more expertly without contracting with an outside provider.

Matching Supply with Demand

Once they have forecasted the supply and demand for personnel, HR planners can devise a course of action for matching one with the other. When demand is predicted to be greater than supply, they must make plans to recruit new employees. The timing of recruitment efforts depends on the types of positions to be filled. Suppose that we expect to open another plant in five years that will need a plant manager and 25 maintenance workers, along with additional support staff. We can wait to recruit maintenance personnel. However, because the job of a plant manager is so critical, we may begin the process to fill that position immediately.

When the supply of employees is predicted to be greater than demand, the firm must take steps to reduce the size of its workforce. When the oversupply is expected to be temporary, some employees may be *laid off*—dismissed from the workforce until they are needed again.

Perhaps the most humane method for making personnel cutbacks is through attrition. *Attrition* is the normal reduction in the workforce that occurs when employees leave a firm. The U.S. Postal Service, in order to become leaner and more competitive with other delivery services, aims to cut its 650,000-person workforce by 100,000 in upcoming years, mostly by attrition as people retire or find other jobs. Most stakeholders believe this is a necessary move as the USPS runs a $1 billion-a-month deficit and customer numbers are low.[3]

Early retirement is another option. Under early retirement, people who are within a few years of retirement are permitted to retire ahead of schedule with full benefits. Depending on the age makeup of the workforce, this may or may not reduce the staff enough.

As a last resort, unnecessary employees are sometimes simply *fired*. However, because of its negative

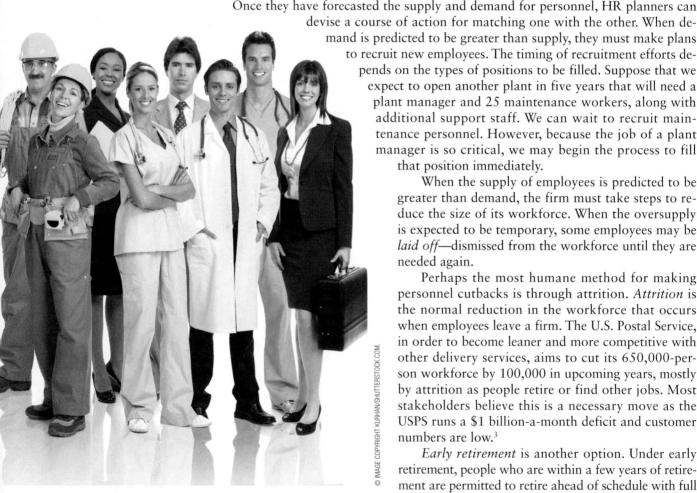

The demand for labor versus its supply: A balancing act. The supply and demand for employees with different skills is constantly shifting. In some industries, qualified workers are plentiful. In others, they are hard to find, even when the nation's unemployment rate is high.

© IMAGE COPYRIGHT KURHAN/SHUTTERSTOCK.COM.

impact, this method generally is used only when absolutely necessary. In order to regain profitability, Canadian Pacific Railway used a combination of attrition, early retirements, and firings to reduce the size of its workforce by 4,500 people.[4]

CULTURAL DIVERSITY IN HUMAN RESOURCES

Learning Objective

3 Describe cultural diversity and understand some of the challenges and opportunities associated with it.

Today's workforce is highly diverse, with employees bringing a wide variety of beliefs, expectations, and behavioral norms to the workplace. Managers must be sensitive to and aware of these differences. For instance, European businesspeople may offer a kiss on the cheek as a greeting. Latin Americans tend to stand closer to people with whom they are talking than North Americans prefer. Without cultural sensitivity, a job applicant who will not make eye contact during an interview may be rejected for being unapproachable, when, according to his or her culture, he or she was just being polite.

A large number of women, minorities, and immigrants have entered the U.S. workforce in recent decades. It is estimated that women make up about 47 percent of the U.S. workforce; African Americans and Hispanics each make up about 12 and 15 percent of U.S. workers, respectively.[5] Women now account for the majority of workers in the financial, education, and health services industries. They make up 52 percent of management positions in the United States.[6]

Cultural (or workplace) diversity refers to the differences among people in a workforce owing to race, ethnicity, and gender. Increasing cultural diversity is forcing managers to learn to supervise and motivate people who have a broad range of value systems. In addition to cultural diversity, other changes have taken place as well. The high proportion of women in the workforce, combined with a new emphasis on participative parenting by men, has brought many family-related issues to the workplace. Today's more educated employees also want greater independence and flexibility, leading to improved quality of life.

cultural (workplace) diversity differences among people in a workforce owing to race, ethnicity, and gender

Although cultural diversity presents a challenge, managers should view it as an opportunity rather than a limitation. When managed properly, cultural diversity can result in a stronger organization. Table 9-1 shows several benefits that creative management of cultural diversity can offer, such as cost advantages and being in a better

Striving for Success

What Does a Chief Diversity Officer Do?

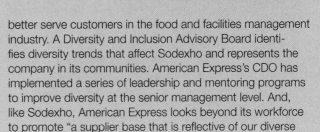

Hundreds of America's largest corporations have named a chief diversity officer (CDO) to enhance diversity recruiting and training initiatives. But what, exactly, does a CDO do? At Ingersoll Rand, the CDO has implemented a leadership training program for women employees and started internal networking groups for women, military veterans, and African Americans, aiming to increase innovation and support global growth. In addition to training, the CDO of Caesars Entertainment, which runs hotels and casinos, forms "Diverse by Design" teams to tackle difficult challenges. He picks employees from different cultural, geographical, demographic, and professional backgrounds to bring new insights and perspectives to solving each problem.

At Sodexho, the CDO is applying diversity principles to its suppliers as well as to its workforce, so the company can better serve customers in the food and facilities management industry. A Diversity and Inclusion Advisory Board identifies diversity trends that affect Sodexho and represents the company in its communities. American Express's CDO has implemented a series of leadership and mentoring programs to improve diversity at the senior management level. And, like Sodexho, American Express looks beyond its workforce to promote "a supplier base that is reflective of our diverse customer base, employees, and shareholders."

Sources: Based on information in Leslie Kwoh, "Firms Hail New Chiefs (of Diversity)," *Wall Street Journal*, January 5, 2012, http://online.wsj.com/article/SB10001424052 9702038995045771292617328845778.html; Eric Baca, Mariana Gutierrez Briones, and Jorge Ferraez, "From the Mouths of the Leaders: Conversations with Four Chief Diversity Officers," *Latino Leaders*, December 2011, pp. 24; Todd Henneman, "Making the Pieces Fit," *Workforce Management*, August 1, 2011, p. 12.

TABLE 9-1 Advantages of Cultural Diversity

Economic Measure	Description
Cost	The cost of poorly integrating workers increases with diversity. However, companies that handle diversity well can create cost advantages over those that do a poor job. Companies can also reduce costs by hiring culturally sensitive and trained workers.
Resource acquisition	Companies develop reputations as being favorable or unfavorable employers for women and ethnic minorities. Those with the best reputations will attract and retain the best personnel.
Marketing edge	For multinational organizations, the insight and cultural sensitivity that comes from an international perspective should improve marketing efforts. The same rationale applies to marketing subpopulations domestically.
Flexibility	Culturally diverse employees often are open to a wider array of positions within a company and are more likely to move up the corporate ladder rapidly.
Creativity	Diversity of perspectives and less emphasis on conformity to norms of the past should improve the level of creativity.
Problem solving	Differences within decision making and problem-solving groups potentially produce better decisions through a wider range of perspectives and more thorough critical analysis of issues.
Bilingual skills	Cultural diversity in the workplace is valuable in the global marketplace. Employees with knowledge about another country and can communicate in that language can prevent embarrassing mistakes due to a lack of cultural sophistication. Thus, many companies seek job applicants with a background in cultures in which the company does business.

Sources: Adapted from Taylor H. Cox and Stacy Blake, "Managing Cultural Diversity: Implications for Organizational Competitiveness," *Academy of Management Executive* 5(3):46, 1991; Ricky Griffin and Gregory Moorhead, *Organizational Behavior* (Mason, OH: South-Western/Cengage Learning, 2010), 40; and Richard L. Daft, *Management* (Mason, OH: South-Western/Cengage Learning, 2011), 348–349.

Concept Check

✓ What is cultural diversity in an organization?

✓ What are some of the benefits and challenges of cultural diversity in an organization?

Why hiring a diverse group of employees can benefit your business. Organizations that hire diverse types of employees benefit from their different skills and life experiences. The different points of view of these workers can help a firm find new opportunities and ways of doing things. In addition, diverse employees often have a greater understanding of diverse customers and the goods and services they prefer.

position to attract and retain quality employees. A culturally diverse organization may gain a marketing edge because it understands different cultures and languages. Proper guidance and management of diversity in an organization also can improve creativity. People who embrace cultural diversity frequently are more flexible in the types of positions they will accept and are more comfortable working with diverse co-workers.

Because cultural diversity creates challenges along with advantages, it is important for an organization's employees to understand it. To accomplish this goal, numerous U.S. firms have trained their managers to respect and manage diversity. Diversity training programs may include recruiting minorities, training minorities to be managers, training managers to view diversity positively, teaching English as a second language, and facilitating support groups for immigrants. Many companies recognize the importance of in-depth diversity training programs. International companies are continuously expanding their business and therefore need to meld a cohesive workforce from a labor pool whose demographics are constantly growing more diverse.

A diversity program will be successful only if it is systematic, is ongoing, and has a strong, sustained commitment from top leadership. A recent study shows that diversity training produces positive shifts in workplace attitudes and behaviors, especially when it focuses on the group most resistant to diversity training, which is white male managers.[7] No matter whether a group is resistant to it, cultural diversity is here to stay. Its impact on organizations is widespread and will continue to grow. Management must learn to overcome the obstacles and capitalize on the advantages associated with culturally diverse human resources.

JOB ANALYSIS

A manager needs to understand the nature of a job before he or she can find the right person to do it. It would make no sense to hire new people without knowing why.

Job analysis is a systematic procedure for studying positions to determine their various elements and requirements. Consider a clerk—in a large corporation, there may be 50 kinds of clerk positions, which may all differ in terms of activities performed, the level of proficiency required for each activity, and the set of qualifications demanded. These distinctions are the focus of job analysis.

The job analysis for a particular position typically consists of two parts—a job description and a job specification. A **job description** is a list of the elements that make up a particular job. It includes the duties to be performed, the working conditions, the responsibilities, and the tools and equipment that must be used on the job (see Figure 9-1).

A **job specification** is a list of the qualifications required to perform a particular job, such as certain skills, abilities, education, and experience. In addition to requiring certain experience, some companies also list personality characteristics in job specifications. ManPower Group, a staffing agency, recommends including personality characteristics a candidate well-suited to the job is likely to possess as a way to find candidates that satisfy the outcomes an employer desires when hiring.[8]

The job analysis is not only the basis for recruiting and selecting new employees, it is also used in other areas of HRM, including evaluation and the determination of equitable compensation levels.

Learning Objective

4 Explain the objectives and uses of job analysis.

job analysis a systematic procedure for studying jobs to determine their various elements and requirements

job description a list of the elements that make up a particular job

job specification a list of the qualifications required to perform a particular job

Concept Check

✓ What is job analysis?

✓ What is job specification?

✓ How can it be used to hire the right person for the job?

FIGURE 9-1 Job Description and Job Specification

This job description explains the job of sales coordinator and lists the responsibilities of the position. The job specification is contained in the last paragraph.

SOUTH-WESTERN
JOB DESCRIPTION

TITLE:	Georgia Sales Coordinator	DATE:	3/26/12
DEPARTMENT:	College, Sales	GRADE:	12
REPORTS TO:	Regional Manager	EXEMPT/NONEXEMPT:	Exempt

BRIEF SUMMARY:
Supervise one other Georgia-based sales representative to gain supervisory experience. Captain the four members of the outside sales rep team that are assigned to territories consisting of colleges and universities in Georgia. Oversee, coordinate, advise, and make decisions regarding Georgia sales activities. Based upon broad contact with customers across the state and communication with administrators of schools, the person will make recommendations regarding issues specific to the needs of higher education in the state of Georgia such as distance learning, conversion to the semester system, potential statewide adoptions, and faculty training.

PRINCIPAL ACCOUNTABILITIES:
1. Supervises/manages/trains one other Atlanta-based sales rep.
2. Advises two other sales reps regarding the Georgia schools in their territories.
3. Increases overall sales in Georgia as well as his or her individual sales territory.
4. Assists regional manager in planning and coordinating regional meetings and Atlanta conferences.
5. Initiates a dialogue with campus administrators, particularly in the areas of the semester conversion, distance learning, and faculty development.

DIMENSIONS:
This position will have one direct report in addition to the leadership role played within the region. Revenue most directly impacted will be within the individually assigned territory, the supervised territory, and the overall sales for the state of Georgia.

KNOWLEDGE AND SKILLS:
Must have displayed a history of consistently outstanding sales in personal territory. Must demonstrate clear teamwork and leadership skills and be willing to extend beyond the individual territory goals. Should have a clear understanding of the company's systems and product offerings in order to train and lead other sales representatives. Must have the communication skills and presence to communicate articulately with higher education administrators and to serve as a bridge between the company and higher education in the state.

© CENGAGE LEARNING 2015

Learning Objective

5 Describe the processes
of recruiting, employee
selection, and orientation.

RECRUITING, SELECTION, AND ORIENTATION

In an organization with jobs waiting to be filled, HRM personnel need to (1) find candidates and (2) match the right candidate with each position. Three activities are involved: recruiting, selection, and new employee orientation.

Recruiting

recruiting the process of attracting qualified job applicants

Recruiting is the process of attracting qualified job applicants. Because it is a vital link in a costly process (the cost of hiring an employee can be several thousand dollars), recruiting needs to be systematic. One goal of recruiters is to attract the "right number" of applicants, which is enough to allow a good match between applicants and open positions but not so many that matching requires a lot of time and effort. For example, if there are five open positions and five applicants, the firm has no choice. It must hire all five applicants (qualified or not). At the other extreme, if several hundred job seekers apply for the five positions, HRM personnel will spend weeks processing applications.

Recruiters may seek applicants outside the firm, within the firm, or both. The source used depends on the nature of the position, the situation within the firm, and sometimes the firm's established or traditional recruitment policies.

external recruiting the attempt to attract job applicants from outside an organization

EXTERNAL RECRUITING **External recruiting** is the attempt to attract job applicants from outside an organization. External recruiting may include activities on college campuses and open houses, soliciting recommendations from present employees, posting in newspapers, employment agencies, and online. The Internet is a popular medium for searching and recruiting for positions. Social networking sites like LinkedIn and even Twitter match employers with potential employees. Online job sites help potential employees search for positions by criteria such as location, industry, or pay.

Clearly, it is best to match the recruiting means with the kind of applicant being sought. Technology is helping organizations with this matching process. Facebook, which is popular with many demographic segments, features a job recruiting app. The Social Jobs Partnership combines information from five different recruiting organizations in a centralized board that features nearly 2 million postings. Fifty percent of employers already use Facebook in job searches, making this app a convenient innovation for recruiters.[9]

internal recruiting considering present employees as applicants for available positions

External recruiting has advantages and disadvantages. A primary advantage is that it brings people into a firm who have new perspectives and varied business backgrounds. Some firms prefer to hire recruits directly out of college because they believe that these candidates will be easier to train to fit with the corporate culture and the needs of the company. An additional benefit of hiring younger talent is that they tend to be more technologically savvy than their older counterparts, a characteristic that is highly desirable in today's workplace. A disadvantage of external recruiting is that it is often expensive, especially if private employment agencies must be used. External recruiting also may provoke resentment among present employees who wish to advance within the company.

Don't just search the classified ads to find a job. Potential employees are recruited in a variety of ways. Companies often keep statistics on their recruiting sources so they can determine which methods are the most effective for finding good employees.

INTERNAL RECRUITING **Internal recruiting** involves considering present employees as applicants for available positions. Generally, current employees

© FENG YU/SHUTTERSTOCK.COM

are considered for *promotion* to higher-level positions. However, employees may be considered for *transfer* from one position to another at the same level.

Promoting from within provides strong motivation for current employees and helps the firm to retain quality personnel. The practice of *job posting*, or informing current employees of upcoming openings, is practiced by many different firms. It may be a company policy or required by union contract. The primary disadvantage of internal recruiting is that promoting a current employee leaves another position open. Not only does the firm still incur recruiting and selection costs, but it also must train two employees instead of one.

In many situations it may be impossible to recruit internally. For example, no current employee is qualified to fill a new position, or the firm may be growing so rapidly that there is no time to reassign positions that open as a result of promotion or transfer.

Selection

Selection is the process of gathering information about applicants for a position and using that information to choose the most appropriate applicant. Note the use of the word *appropriate*. In selection, the idea is not to hire the person with the *most* qualifications but rather the applicant who is *most appropriate*. Line managers responsible for the position select applicants. However, HRM personnel usually help by developing a pool of applicants and by expediting their assessment. Common means of obtaining information about applicants' qualifications are employment applications, interviews, references, assessment centers, and online on social networking sites like LinkedIn and Facebook.

selection the process of gathering information about applicants for a position and then using that information to choose the most appropriate applicant

EMPLOYMENT APPLICATIONS An employment application is useful for collecting factual information on a candidate's education, work experience, and personal history (see Figure 9-2). The data from applications are used for two purposes: to identify applicants who are worthy of further scrutiny and to familiarize interviewers with applicant backgrounds. Online applications are common, which help to streamline the process and improve data gathering capabilities for the firm. In fact, paper applications are becoming rare.

Many job candidates submit résumés, and some firms require them. A *résumé* is a one- or two-page summary of the candidate's background and qualifications. It may include a description of the type of job the applicant is seeking. A résumé may be sent to a firm to request consideration for available jobs, or it may be submitted along with an employment application.

To improve the usefulness of information, HRM specialists ask current employees about experiences and characteristics that relate to their current jobs. These factors are included on the applications and may be weighted more heavily when evaluating new applicants' qualifications.

EMPLOYMENT TESTS Tests administered to job candidates usually focus on aptitudes, skills, abilities, or knowledge relevant to the job. Such tests (basic computer skills tests, for example) help an employer gauge how well the applicant will perform the job. Companies may use general intelligence or personality tests, but these are seldom helpful in predicting performance. Many organizations of

FIGURE 9-2 Typical Employment Application

Employers use applications to collect factual information on a candidate's education, work experience, and personal history.

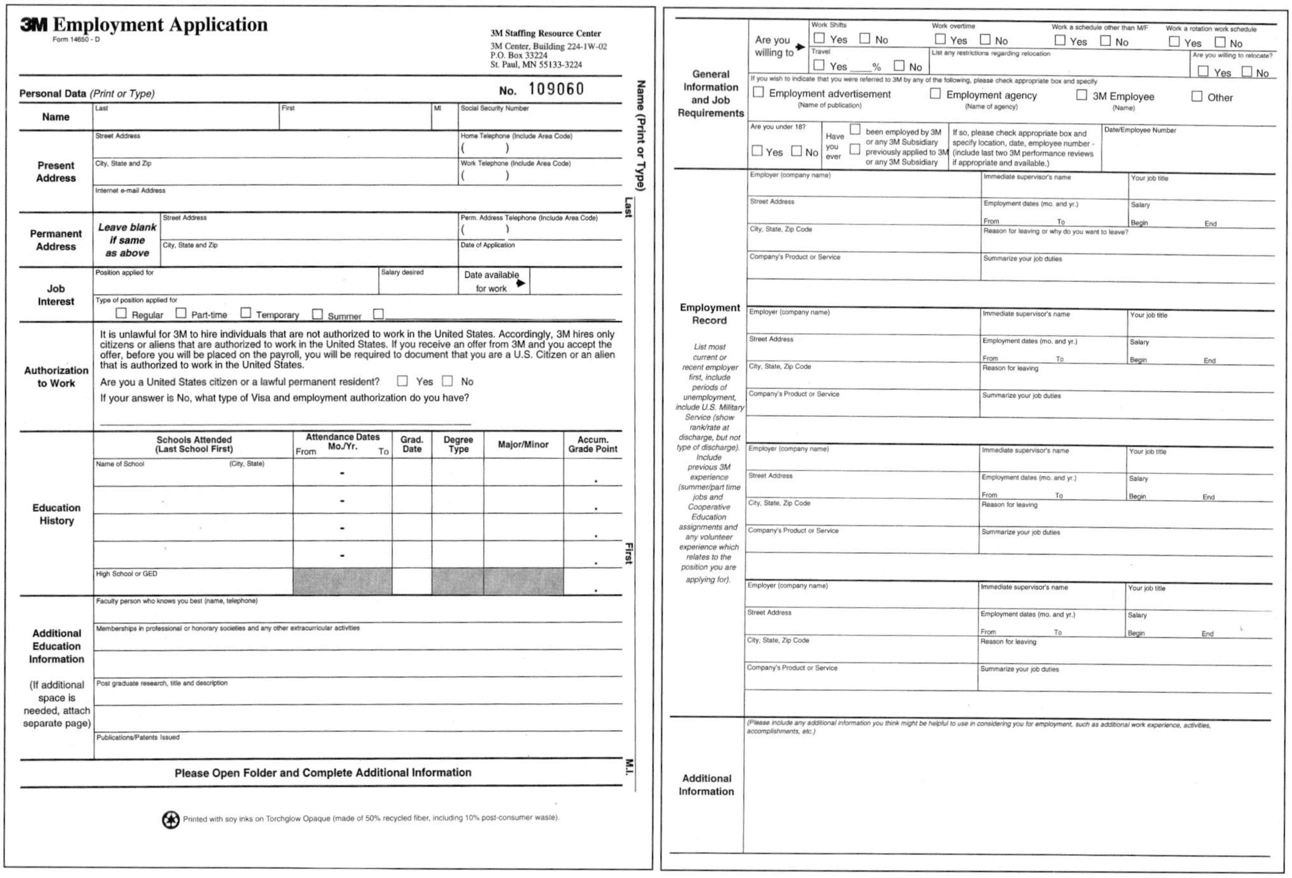

3M Employment Application
Form 14650 - D

3M Staffing Resource Center
3M Center, Building 224-1W-02
P.O. Box 33224
St. Paul, MN 55133-3224

Personal Data (Print or Type) — No. 109060

Name: Last | First | MI | Social Security Number

Present Address: Street Address | Home Telephone (Include Area Code) ( ) | City, State and Zip | Work Telephone (Include Area Code) ( ) | Internet e-mail Address

Permanent Address: *Leave blank if same as above* | Street Address | Perm. Address Telephone (Include Area Code) ( ) | City, State and Zip | Date of Application

Job Interest: Position applied for | Salary desired | Date available for work | Type of position applied for: ☐ Regular ☐ Part-time ☐ Temporary ☐ Summer ☐

Authorization to Work: It is unlawful for 3M to hire individuals that are not authorized to work in the United States. Accordingly, 3M hires only citizens or aliens that are authorized to work in the United States. If you receive an offer from 3M and you accept the offer, before you will be placed on the payroll, you will be required to document that you are a U.S. Citizen or an alien that is authorized to work in the United States.
Are you a United States citizen or a lawful permanent resident? ☐ Yes ☐ No
If your answer is No, what type of Visa and employment authorization do you have?

Education History:

Schools Attended (Last School First)	Attendance Dates Mo./Yr. From	To	Grad. Date	Degree Type	Major/Minor	Accum. Grade Point
Name of School (City, State)	-					.
	-					.
	-					.
	-					.
High School or GED						.

Additional Education Information (If additional space is needed, attach separate page): Faculty person who knows you best (name, telephone) | Memberships in professional or honorary societies and any other extracurricular activities | Post graduate research, title and description | Publications/Patents Issued

Name (Print or Type) Last First M.I.

Please Open Folder and Complete Additional Information

Printed with soy inks on Torchglow Opaque (made of 50% recycled fiber, including 10% post-consumer waste).

General Information and Job Requirements:
Are you willing to → Work Shifts ☐ Yes ☐ No | Work overtime ☐ Yes ☐ No | Work a schedule other than M/F ☐ Yes ☐ No | Work a rotation work schedule ☐ Yes ☐ No
Travel ☐ Yes ___% ☐ No | List any restrictions regarding relocation | Are you willing to relocate? ☐ Yes ☐ No
If you wish to indicate that you were referred to 3M by any of the following, please check appropriate box and specify
☐ Employment advertisement (Name of publication) ☐ Employment agency (Name of agency) ☐ 3M Employee (Name) ☐ Other
Are you under 18? ☐ Yes ☐ No | Have you ever ☐ been employed by 3M or any 3M Subsidiary ☐ previously applied to 3M or any 3M Subsidiary | If so, please check appropriate box and specify location, date, employee number - (include last two 3M performance reviews if appropriate and available.) | Date/Employee Number

Employment Record (*List most current or recent employer first, include periods of unemployment, include U.S. Military Service (show rank/rate at discharge, but not type of discharge). Include previous 3M experience (summer/part time jobs and Cooperative Education assignments and any volunteer experience which relates to the position you are applying for).*)
Employer (company name) | Immediate supervisor's name | Your job title
Street Address | Employment dates (mo. and yr.) From To | Salary Begin End
City, State, Zip Code | Reason for leaving or why do you want to leave?
Company's Product or Service | Summarize your job duties

Employer (company name) | Immediate supervisor's name | Your job title
Street Address | Employment dates (mo. and yr.) From To | Salary Begin End
City, State, Zip Code | Reason for leaving
Company's Product or Service | Summarize your job duties

Employer (company name) | Immediate supervisor's name | Your job title
Street Address | Employment dates (mo. and yr.) From To | Salary Begin End
City, State, Zip Code | Reason for leaving
Company's Product or Service | Summarize your job duties

Employer (company name) | Immediate supervisor's name | Your job title
Street Address | Employment dates (mo. and yr.) From To | Salary Begin End
City, State, Zip Code | Reason for leaving
Company's Product or Service | Summarize your job duties

Additional Information: *(Please include any additional information you think might be helpful to use in considering you for employment, such as additional work experience, activities, accomplishments, etc.)*

Source: Courtesy of 3M.

all sizes use predictive behavior tests, which have become more affordable with improved technology.

INTERVIEWS The interview is perhaps the most widely used selection technique because it provides an opportunity for applicants and the firm to learn more about one another. Job candidates are interviewed by at least one member of the HRM staff and by the person for whom they will be working. Candidates for higher-level jobs may meet with a department head or vice president over several interviews.

Interviewers may pose problems to test the candidate's abilities, probe employment history, and learn something about the candidate's attitudes and motivation. The candidate has a chance to find out more about the job and potential co-workers. They also provide an opportunity to test the personality fit of a candidate with the organizational culture. Many organizations now conduct interviews remotely using services such as Skype or gotomeeting.com, only flying in the most promising candidates for face-to-face meetings.

Unfortunately, interviewing may be the stage at which discrimination begins. For example, suppose that a female applicant mentions that she is the mother of small children. Her interviewer may assume that she will be resistant to job-related travel. In addition, interviewers may be unduly influenced by such

Concept Check

- ✓ What are the differences between internal and external recruiting?
- ✓ Under what conditions are each one of them used?
- ✓ Identify and briefly describe the types of practices and tools that are used in the selection process.

factors as appearance. They may also ask different questions of different applicants so that it becomes impossible to compare candidates' qualifications objectively.

Some of these problems can be solved through better interviewer training and using structured interviews. In a *structured interview*, the interviewer asks only a prepared set of job-related questions. The firm also may consider using several different interviewers for each applicant, but this can be costly.

REFERENCES A job candidate generally is asked to furnish the names of references—people who can verify background information and provide personal evaluations. Naturally, applicants tend to list only references who are likely to say good things. Thus, personal evaluations obtained from references may not be of much value. However, references are often contacted to verify such information as previous job responsibilities and the reason an applicant left a former job. In many cases, online social networking has changed the order in which employers receive information. Employers can peruse LinkedIn accounts, for example, to see reviews and recommendations before even interviewing a candidate.

ASSESSMENT CENTERS An assessment center is used primarily to select current employees for promotion to higher-level positions. Typically, a group of employees is sent to the center for a few days. While there, they participate in activities designed to simulate the management environment and to predict managerial effectiveness. Trained observers make recommendations regarding promotion possibilities. The expense of this technique limits its use.

Orientation

Once all information about job candidates has been collected and analyzed, the company extends a job offer. If it is accepted, the candidate becomes an employee.

Soon after a candidate joins a firm, he or she goes through the firm's orientation program. **Orientation** is the process of acquainting new employees with an organization. Orientation topics range from the location of the company cafeteria to career paths within the firm. The orientation itself may range widely from a half-hour informal presentation to an elaborate program involving dozens of people and lasting several days or weeks.

© GOODLUZ/SHUTTERSTOCK.COM

A job interview is similar to a first date. Like a date, interviews can occur in a variety of locations and through several formats. The purpose is to give the candidate and the company the opportunity to find out about each other. Can you think of any other selection methods that benefit *both* parties in the recruiting process?

orientation the process of acquainting new employees with an organization

COMPENSATION AND BENEFITS

An effective employee reward system must (1) enable employees to satisfy basic needs, (2) provide rewards comparable with those offered by other firms, (3) be distributed fairly within the organization, and (4) recognize that different people have different needs.

A firm's compensation system can be structured to meet the first three of these requirements. The fourth is more difficult because it must account for many variables. Most firms offer a number of benefits that, taken together, generally help to provide for employees' varying needs.

Compensation Decisions

Compensation is the payment employees receive in return for their labor. Its importance to employees is obvious. Because compensation can account for a significant percentage of a firm's operating costs, it is also an important consideration for

Learning Objective

6 Discuss the primary elements of employee compensation and benefits.

compensation the payment employees receive in return for their labor

compensation system the policies and strategies that determine employee compensation

management. For example, health care services have the highest ratio of salaries to operating expenses—salaries account for 54 percent of operating costs.[10] Therefore, the firm's **compensation system**, the policies and strategies that determine employee compensation, must be designed carefully to provide for employees' needs while keeping labor costs within reasonable limits. For most firms, designing an effective compensation system requires three separate management decisions—wage level, wage structure, and individual wages.

WAGE LEVEL Management first must position the firm's general pay level relative to pay levels of comparable firms. Most firms choose a level near the industry average. However, a firm that is not in good financial shape may pay less than average, and large, prosperous organizations may pay more than average.

wage survey a collection of data on prevailing wage rates within an industry or a geographic area

To determine the average pay for a job, the firm may use wage surveys. A **wage survey** is a collection of data on prevailing wage rates within an industry or a geographic area. Such surveys are compiled by industry associations, local governments, personnel associations, and (occasionally) individual firms.

WAGE STRUCTURE Next, management must decide on relative pay levels for all the positions within the firm. The result of this set of decisions is called the firm's *wage structure*.

job evaluation the process of determining the relative worth of the various jobs within a firm

The wage structure almost always is developed on the basis of a job evaluation. **Job evaluation** is the process of determining the relative worth of the various jobs within a firm. Most observers probably would agree that a secretary should make more money than a custodian, but how much more?

A number of techniques may be used to evaluate jobs. The simplest is to rank all the jobs within the firm according to value. A more frequently used method is based on the job analysis. Points are allocated to each element and job requirement. For example, "college degree required" might be worth 50 points, whereas a job requiring only a high school diploma would only receive 25 points. The more points allocated, the more important the job is presumed to be (and the higher its level in the firm's wage structure).

INDIVIDUAL WAGES Finally, the company must determine the specific payments individual employees will receive. Consider the case of two secretaries. Job evaluation was used to determine the level of secretarial pay, but suppose that one secretary has 15 years of experience and can type 80 words per minute accurately while the other has two years of experience and can type only 55 words per minute. In most firms, a wage range would be established (maybe $8.50 to $12.50 per hour) to reflect the range of experience and abilities, with the more qualified secretary receiving the higher wage.

Two wage decisions come into play here. First, the employee's initial rate must be established. It is based on experience, other qualifications, and expected performance. Later, the employee may be given pay increases based on seniority and performance.

Comparable Worth

comparable worth a concept that seeks equal compensation for jobs requiring about the same level of education, training, and skills

It is an established fact that women in the workforce are paid less than men, in spite of measures and legislation to counter this phenomenon. **Comparable worth** is a concept that seeks equal compensation for jobs that require equivalent levels of education, training, and skill. In recent decades, many states have taken steps to ensure that all workers have equal pay for comparable worth, but the issue is contentious. Critics argue that inflating salaries artificially for female-dominated occupations encourages women to keep these jobs rather than seek out higher-paying jobs. Addressing pay inequality is complicated. Studies have shown that, even after controlling for educational attainment and profession, wage gaps persist between men and women.[11] However, another study found that women are generally less likely than men to negotiate their salaries, but they can narrow the wage gap when told the salary is negotiable.[12]

Types of Compensation

Compensation can take a variety of forms. Most forms fall into the following categories: hourly wage, weekly or monthly salary, commissions, incentive payments, lump-sum salary increases, and profit sharing.

HOURLY WAGE An **hourly wage** is a specific amount of money paid for each hour worked. People who earn wages are paid their hourly wage for the first 40 hours worked in any week. Anything in excess of 40 hours is overtime, for which they are paid one-and-one-half times their hourly wage. Workers in retail and fast-food chains, on assembly lines, and in clerical positions usually are paid an hourly wage.

WEEKLY OR MONTHLY SALARY A **salary** is a specific amount of money paid for an employee's work during a set calendar period, regardless of the actual number of hours worked. Salaried employees receive no overtime pay, but they do not lose pay when they work less than 40 hours per week. Most professional and managerial positions are salaried.

COMMISSIONS A **commission** is a payment that is a percentage of sales revenue. Sales representatives and sales managers often are paid entirely through commissions or a combination of commissions and salary.

INCENTIVE PAYMENTS An **incentive payment** is in addition to wages, salary, or commissions. Incentive payments are rewards for outstanding job performance. They may be distributed to all or only select employees. Some firms distribute incentive payments to all employees annually. The size of the payment depends on the firm's earnings and, at times, on the particular employee's length of service with the firm. Firms sometimes offer incentives to employees who exceed specific sales or production goals, a practice called *gain sharing*.

Some organizations reward outstanding workers individually through *merit pay*. This pay-for-performance approach allows management to control labor costs while encouraging employees to work more efficiently.

LUMP-SUM SALARY INCREASES In traditional reward systems, an annual pay increase is spread evenly across each paycheck that year. However, some companies offer a **lump-sum salary increase**. This gives the employee the option of taking the entire pay raise in one lump sum. The employee then draws his or her "regular" pay for the rest of the year. The lump-sum payment typically is treated as an interest-free loan that must be repaid if the employee leaves the firm during the year.

PROFIT-SHARING **Profit-sharing** is the distribution of a percentage of a firm's profit among its employees. The idea is to motivate employees to work effectively by giving them a stake in the company's financial success. For example, every year since 1938 Hormel Foods Corporation has distributed its profits to employees in the form of dividends at the beginning of the winter holiday season. The higher the profits, the higher the dividends employees earn.[13]

Employee Benefits

An **employee benefit** is a reward in addition to regular compensation that is provided indirectly to employees. Employee benefits consist mainly of services (such as insurance) that are paid for partially or totally by employers, and employee expenses (such as college tuition) that employers reimburse. Currently,

Personal Apps

Focus on what you can offer!

When you're applying for a new job, wait to ask about benefits until you've been offered the position. During your first interview, stay focused on the company and how you can be an asset in this position, not on the benefits or compensation.

hourly wage a specific amount of money paid for each hour of work

salary a specific amount of money paid for an employee's work during a set calendar period, regardless of the actual number of hours worked

commission a payment that is a percentage of sales revenue

incentive payment a payment in addition to wages, salary, or commissions

lump-sum salary increase an entire pay raise taken in one lump sum

profit-sharing the distribution of a percentage of a firm's profit among its employees

employee benefit a reward in addition to regular compensation that is provided indirectly to employees

Benefits

Bonuses

Health Insurance

Pension

Stocks

© STUART MILES/SHUTTERSTOCK.COM

What job benefits are crucial to you? The benefits companies provide vary widely. Large companies are often able to offer employees more benefits than small ones. However, in small firms, employees are more likely to do a broader range of tasks and advance to higher positions more quickly.

flexible benefit plan compensation plan whereby an employee receives a predetermined amount of benefit dollars to spend on a package of benefits he or she has selected to meet individual needs

Concept Check

✓ Identify the major compensation decisions that HRM managers make.

✓ What are the different forms of compensation?

✓ What are the major types of employee benefits?

✓ How do flexible benefit plans work?

Learning Objective

7 **Explain the purposes and techniques of employee training and development.**

the average cost of these benefits is 30 percent of an employee's total compensation.[14] Thus, a person who receives a salary of $35,000 really receives total compensation of $50,000, once $15,000 in benefits (30 percent of $50,000) is factored in.

TYPES OF BENEFITS Employee benefits take a variety of forms. *Pay for time not worked* covers such absences as vacation, holidays, and sick leave. *Insurance packages* may include health, life, and dental insurance for employees and their families. Some firms pay the entire cost of the insurance package, and others share the cost with the employee. The costs of *pension and retirement programs* also may be borne entirely by the firm or shared with the employee.

Some benefits are required by law. For example, employers must maintain *workers' compensation insurance*, which pays medical bills for injuries that occur on the job and provides income for employees who are disabled by job-related injuries. Employers must also pay for *unemployment insurance* and contribute to each employee's federal *Social Security* account.

Other benefits employers may provide include tuition-reimbursement plans, credit unions, child-care services, company cafeterias, exercise rooms, and broad employee stock-option plans. Some companies offer special benefits to U.S. military reservists who are called up for active duty.

Increasingly, companies offer unusual benefits to attract the best employees. Google is famous for its unusual perks, such as having bowling alleys on-site and free food at all times of the day. More recently, Apple gave in to employee demands for better benefits. The company now offers such perks as paid sabbaticals if employees want to take time to pursue other projects and valuable stock options.[15]

FLEXIBLE BENEFIT PLANS Through a **flexible benefit plan**, an employee receives a predetermined amount of benefit dollars and may allocate those dollars to various categories of benefits in the way that best fits his or her needs. Some flexible benefit plans offer a broad array of benefit options, including health care, dental care, life insurance, accidental death and dismemberment coverage for the worker and dependents, long-term disability coverage, vacation benefits, retirement savings, and dependent-care benefits. Other firms offer limited options, primarily in health and life insurance and retirement plans.

Although the cost of administering flexible plans is high, a number of organizations, including Phillips Corporation and Coca-Cola, have implemented this option. Because employees' needs are so diverse, flexible plans help firms to offer benefit packages that more specifically meet their employees' needs. Flexible plans can, in the long run, help a company to contain costs because a specified amount is allocated to cover the benefits of each employee. Furthermore, organizations that offer flexible plans with many choices may be perceived as being employee-friendly. Thus, they are in a better position to attract and retain qualified employees.

TRAINING AND DEVELOPMENT

Training and development are extremely important at Verizon, which ranks first on *Training* magazine's "Top 125" list. Verizon has made the list for 11 consecutive years, distinguishing itself through its effectiveness and efficiency, number of training hours logged by employees, and survey results. Employees log more than 9 million training hours annually, which utilize a range of technologies, such as podcasts and blogs. The company offers over 14,000 courses to employees to ensure that they continue their professional development.[16] Many top managers believe that the financial and human resources invested in training and development are well worth it.

Both training and development are aimed at improving employees' skills and abilities. However, the two are usually differentiated as employee training or management development. **Employee training** is the process of teaching operations and technical employees how to do their present jobs more effectively and efficiently. **Management development** is the process of preparing managers and other professionals to assume increased responsibility in both present and future positions. Thus, training and development differ in who is being taught and the purpose of the teaching. However, both are necessary for personal and organizational growth. Companies that hope to stay competitive typically make huge commitments to employee training and development. Developing an effective training program involves analyzing needs, determining the best methods, and developing an evaluation system to gauge effectiveness. Some employers require workers to attain certifications targeted to their field to help them gain and maintain the specific skills they need. There are many different employee training methods, including Internet-based training. Internet training is growing in popularity as it can result in significant cost, travel, and time savings.

Analysis of Training Needs

When thinking about developing a training program, managers first must determine if training is actually needed and, if so, what types of training needs exist. Training needs can vary considerably. For example, some employees may need to improve their technical skills, while others need training on organizational procedures. Training also may focus on business ethics, product information, or customer service. Because training is expensive, it is critical that the correct training needs be identified. Employers may find that sometimes employees need motivation more than they need training.

Training and Development Methods

A number of methods are available for employee training and management development. Most of these methods can be applied to both training and management development.

Nuts About Southwest

Southwest Airlines employees celebrated the company's entrance into the Atlanta market with a Flash Mob, which they posted on the company blog and YouTube. The blog, Nuts About Southwest, was launched in 2006, well before many companies were blogging. The company's Facebook and Twitter accounts were created in 2007. Southwest has had a significant social media presence even though a formal social media policy, with clearly communicated social media guidelines, was not put in place until 2010. The following URL links to Twitter, Facebook, Flickr, LinkedIn, YouTube, and other social media. According to the website, the core blogging team of 30 comprises employees, customers, and business partners.

www.blogsouthwest.com

See also the following sites:

www.facebook.com/Southwest   The Facebook page contains live streaming content, posts promotions and special fares, and builds community through interaction between Southwest employees and customers.

http://twitter.com/southwestair   This site encourages one-on-one interaction with current and future customers.

www.flickr.com/groups/southwestairlines   This site encourages anyone to share photos which are randomly fed into the blog and share videos through YouTube at www.youtube.com/nutsaboutsouthwest

employee training the process of teaching operations and technical employees how to do their present jobs more effectively and efficiently

management development the process of preparing managers and other professionals to assume increased responsibility in both present and future positions

© ADAM GREGOR/SHUTTERSTOCK.COM

- *On-the-job methods.* The trainee learns by doing the work under the supervision of an experienced employee.
- *Simulations.* The work situation is simulated in a separate area so that learning takes place away from the day-to-day pressures of work.
- *Classroom teaching and lectures.*
- *Conferences and seminars.* Experts and learners come together to discuss problems and exchange ideas.
- *Role-playing.* Participants act out others' roles in order to better understand them (primarily a management development tool).

What job training methods have you experienced, and how effective were they?
Organizations train employees using a variety of methods and locations. Depending on the type of business, the training may take just a few hours or more than a year.

Evaluation of Training and Development

Training and development are expensive because the training itself can be costly and employees are not working at full productivity while they are receiving training, costing the firm further revenue. To ensure that training and development are as cost-effective as possible, the managers responsible should evaluate the company's efforts periodically.

In order to set benchmarks and gauge program effectiveness, managers should develop measurable objectives before the training starts. For example, a measurable object would be that, after receiving training, a new employee will be able to produce a report using a specified format and be able to correctly identify 20 critical terms related to the field. The results of training evaluations should be made known to all those involved in the program—including trainees and upper management. For trainees, the results of evaluations can enhance motivation and learning. For upper management, the results may be the basis for making decisions about the training program itself.

Learning Objective

8 Discuss performance appraisal techniques and performance feedback.

performance appraisal the evaluation of employees' current and potential levels of performance to allow managers to make objective human resources decisions

PERFORMANCE APPRAISAL

Performance appraisal is the evaluation of employees' current and potential levels of performance to allow managers to make unbiased human resources decisions. The process has three main objectives. First, managers use performance appraisals to let workers know how well they are doing and how they can improve in the future. Second, a performance appraisal provides an effective basis for distributing rewards, such as pay raises and promotions. Third, performance appraisal helps the organization monitor its employee selection, training, and development activities. If large numbers of employees continually perform below expectations, the firm may need to revise its selection process or strengthen its training and development activities. Most performance appraisal processes include a written document. An example appears in Figure 9-3.

Common Evaluation Techniques

The techniques and methods for appraising employee performance are either objective or judgmental in nature.

OBJECTIVE METHODS Objective appraisal methods use some measurable quantity as the basis for assessing performance. Units of output, dollar volume of sales, number of defective products, and number of insurance claims processed are

FIGURE 9-3 Performance Appraisal

3M **Contribution and Development Summary**
FORM 37450 - B

Employee Name	Employee Number	Job Title
Department		Location
Coach/Supervisor(s) Name(s)		Review Period From : To :

Major Job Responsibilities

Goals/Expectations	Contributions/Results

Contribution (To be completed by coach/supervisor)

☐ Good Level of Contribution for this year   ☐ Exceptional Level of Contribution for this year

☐ Unsatisfactory Level of Contribution for this year

page 3

Development Summary

Areas of Strength	Development Priorities

Career Interests

Next job	Longer Range

Current Mobility

☐ 0 - Currently Unable to Relocate   ☐ 3 - Position Within O.U.S. Area (ex: Europe, Asia)

☐ 1 - Position In Home Country Only (Use if Home Country is Outside U.S.)   ☐ 4 - Position In U.S.

☐ 2 - Position Within O.U.S. Region (e: Nordic, SEA...)   ☐ 5 - Position Anywhere In The World

Development

☐ W - Well placed. Development plans achievable in current role for at least the next year   ☐ X - Not well placed. Action required to resolve placement issues.

☐ C - Ready now for a move to a different job for career broadening experience   **Comments on Development**

☐ I - Ready now for a move to a different job involving increased responsibility

Employee Comments

Coach/Supervisor Comments	Other Supervisor (if applicable) and/or Reviewer

Signatures

Coach/Supervisor	Date	Other Coach/Supervisor or Reviewer	Date
Employee			Date

page 4

Source: Courtesy of 3M.

all objective, measurable quantities. Thus, an employee who processes an average of 26 insurance claims per week is given a higher evaluation than one whose average is 19 claims per week.

Such objective measures may require adjustment depending on the work environment. Suppose that the first of our insurance claims processors works in New York City and the second works in rural Iowa. Both must visit each client because they are processing homeowners' insurance claims. The difference in their average weekly output may be entirely because of the long distances the Iowan must travel to visit clients. In this case, the two workers may very well be equally competent and motivated. Thus, a manager must take into account circumstances that may be hidden by a purely statistical measurement.

JUDGMENTAL METHODS Judgmental appraisal methods are used much more frequently than objective methods. They require that the manager judge or estimate the employee's performance level. These methods are based on employee ranking or rating scales. When ranking is used, the manager ranks subordinates from best to worst. This approach has drawbacks, including the lack of an absolute standard. Use of rating scales is the most popular judgmental appraisal technique. A *rating scale* consists of a number of statements, on which each employee is rated based on the degree to which the statement applies. For example, one statement might be, "This employee always does high-quality work." The supervisor would

Performance feedback can help employees progress within an organization. A business usually evaluates its employees on an annual basis, but sometimes it does so quarterly and even monthly, especially when they are newly hired. Performance reviews that gather feedback about an employee from his or her peers, subordinates, and supervisors can help the person get a realistic view of his or her strengths and weaknesses.

give the employee a rating, from 5 down to 1, corresponding to gradations ranging from "strongly agree" to "strongly disagree." The ratings on all the statements are added to obtain the employee's total evaluation.

AVOIDING APPRAISAL ERRORS Managers must be cautious if they are to avoid making mistakes when appraising employees. It is common to overuse one portion of an evaluation instrument, thus risking overemphasizing or underemphasizing issues. A manager must guard against allowing an employee's poor performance on one activity to influence his or her judgment of that subordinate's work on other activities. Similarly, putting too much weight on recent performance can distort an employee's evaluation. For example, if the employee is being rated on performance over the last year, a manager should not permit last month's disappointing performance to overshadow the quality of the work done in the first 11 months of the year. Finally, a manager must guard against discrimination on the basis of race, age, gender, religion, national origin, or sexual orientation.

Performance Feedback

No matter which appraisal technique is used, managers should discuss the results with the employee soon after completion. The manager should explain the basis for present rewards and should let the employee know what he or she can do to improve. The information provided to an employee in such discussions is called *performance feedback*, and the process is known as a *performance feedback interview*.

There are three major approaches to performance feedback interviews: tell-and-sell, tell-and-listen, and problem solving. In a *tell-and-sell* feedback interview, the superior tells the employee how good or bad the employee's performance has been and attempts to persuade the employee to accept the evaluation. Because the employee has no input into the evaluation, the tell-and-sell interview can lead to defensiveness, resentment, and frustration on the part of the subordinate.

With the *tell-and-listen* approach, the supervisor tells the employee what the employee has done right and wrong and then gives him or her a chance to respond. The subordinate may simply be given an opportunity to react to the supervisor's statements or may be permitted to offer a full self-appraisal.

In the *problem-solving* approach, employees evaluate their own performance and set their own goals for future performance. The supervisor is more a colleague than a judge and offers comments and advice in a noncritical manner while mutually agreeing with the employee on goals for improvement. This is the method most likely to result in employee commitment to the established goals.

To avoid some of the problems associated with the tell-and-sell interview, supervisors sometimes use a mixed approach. The mixed interview uses the tell-and-sell approach to communicate administrative decisions and the problem-solving approach to discuss employee-development issues and future performance goals.

Another approach that has become popular is called a *360-degree evaluation*. A 360-degree evaluation collects anonymous reviews about an employee from his or her peers, subordinates, and supervisors and compiles them into a feedback report for the employee. Companies that invest significant resources in employee-development efforts are especially likely to use 360-degree evaluations.

An employee should not be given a feedback report without first having a one-on-one meeting with his or her supervisor. To ensure effective implementation, upper-level management should adopt this approach first and coach managers on how to use the feedback to achieve positive performance and behavioral outcomes.

Many managers find it difficult to discuss negative appraisals, leading them to ignore performance feedback. However, it is important for employees to be informed of how they can improve. Employers should emphasize employee strengths when delivering a negative appraisal. Without feedback, an employee may be unaware of his or her weaknesses and they will never be addressed. Only through tactful, honest communication can the results of an appraisal be fully used.

Concept Check

✓ What are the main objectives of performance appraisal?

✓ What methods are used?

✓ Describe the three approaches to performance feedback interviews.

THE LEGAL ENVIRONMENT OF HRM

Learning Objective

9 Outline the major legislation affecting human resources management.

Legislation regarding HRM practices has been passed mainly to protect the rights of employees, to promote job safety, and to eliminate discrimination in the workplace. The major federal laws affecting HRM are described in Table 9-2.

National Labor Relations Act and Labor–Management Relations Act

These laws are concerned with dealings between business firms and labor unions. This general area is, in concept, a part of HRM. However, because of its importance, it is often treated as a separate set of activities.

Fair Labor Standards Act

This act, passed in 1938 and amended many times since, applies primarily to wages. It established minimum wages and overtime pay rates. Many managers and other professionals, however, are exempt from this law. Salaried employees seldom get overtime when they work more than 40 hours a week.

Equal Pay Act

Passed in 1963, this law overlaps somewhat with Title VII of the Civil Rights Act (see next section). The Equal Pay Act specifies that men and women who are doing equal jobs must be paid the same wage. Equal jobs are ones that demand equivalent effort, skill, and responsibility and are performed under the same conditions. Discrepancies in pay are legal if they can be attributed to differences in seniority, qualifications, or performance. In spite of having this law on the books for more than half a century, women and men are not treated equally in the workplace. For example, there are only 20 female CEOs of *Fortune* 500 companies, and women still earn 18 percent less than men.[17]

Civil Rights Acts

Title VII of the Civil Rights Act of 1964 forbids organizations with 15 or more employees to discriminate in employee selection and retention on the basis of sex, race, color, religion, or national origin. The purpose of Title VII is to ensure that employers make personnel decisions on the basis of employee qualifications only. As a result of this act, discrimination in employment (especially against African Americans) has been reduced in this country.

A person who believes that he or she has been discriminated against can file a complaint with the EEOC. If it finds that the person has, in fact, been the victim of discrimination, the commission can take legal action on his or her behalf.

The Civil Rights Act of 1991 facilitates an employee's suing and collecting punitive damages for sexual discrimination. Discriminatory promotion and termination decisions as well as on-the-job issues, such as sexual harassment, are covered by this act.

TABLE 9-2 Federal Legislation Affecting Human Resources Management

Law	Purpose
National Labor Relations Act (1935)	Established a collective-bargaining process in labor–management relations and the National Labor Relations Board (NLRB).
Fair Labor Standards Act (1938)	Established a minimum wage and an overtime pay rate for employees working more than 40 hours per week.
Labor–Management Relations Act (1947)	Provides a balance between union power and management power, also known as the Taft–Hartley Act.
Equal Pay Act (1963)	Specifies that men and women who do equal jobs must be paid the same wage.
Title VII of the Civil Rights Act (1964)	Prohibits discrimination in employment practices based on sex, race, color, religion, or national origin.
Age Discrimination in Employment Act (1967–1986)	Prohibits personnel practices that discriminate against people aged 40 years and older. The 1986 amendment eliminated a mandatory retirement age.
Occupational Safety and Health Act (1970)	Regulates the degree to which employees can be exposed to hazardous substances and specifies the safety equipment that the employer must provide.
Employment Retirement Income Security Act (1974)	Regulates company retirement programs and provides a federal insurance program for retirement plans that go bankrupt.
Worker Adjustment and Retraining Notification (WARN) Act (1988)	Requires employers to give employees 60 days notice regarding plant closure or layoff of 50 or more employees.
Americans with Disabilities Act (1990)	Prohibits discrimination against qualified individuals with disabilities in all employment practices, including job-application procedures, hiring, firing, advancement, compensation, training, and other terms, conditions, and privileges of employment.
Civil Rights Act (1991)	Empowers employees to sue employers for sexual discrimination and collect punitive damages.
Family and Medical Leave Act (1993)	Requires an organization with 50 or more employees to provide up to 12 weeks of leave without pay on the birth (or adoption) of an employee's child or if an employee or his or her spouse, child, or parent is seriously ill.
Affordable Care Act (2010)	Requires an organization with 50 or more employees to make health insurance available to employees or pay an assessment and gives employees the right to buy health insurance from another provider if an organization's health insurance is too expensive.

© CENGAGE LEARNING 2015

Age Discrimination in Employment Act

The general purpose of this act, which was passed in 1967 and amended in 1986, is the same as that of Title VII—to eliminate discrimination. However, as the name implies, the Age Discrimination in Employment Act is concerned with discrimination based on age. It outlaws personnel practices that discriminate against people aged 40 years or older in companies with 20 or more employees. Also outlawed are company policies that specify a mandatory retirement age. Employers must base employment decisions on ability, not on a number.

Occupational Safety and Health Act

Passed in 1970, this act is concerned with issues of employee health and safety. For example, the act regulates the degree to which employees can be exposed to hazardous substances. It also specifies the safety equipment that the employer must provide.

The Occupational Safety and Health Administration (OSHA) was created to enforce this act. Inspectors from OSHA investigate employee complaints regarding unsafe working conditions. They also make spot checks on companies operating in particularly hazardous industries, such as chemicals and mining, to ensure compliance with the law. A firm found to be in violation of federal standards can

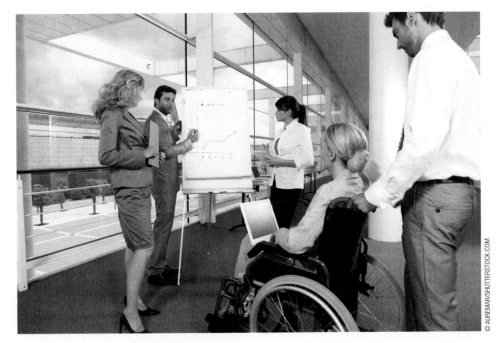

Focus on what employees and job candidates can do—not what they can't. The American Disabilities Act (ADA) requires businesses to make reasonable accommodations for applicants and employees with disabilities. The law is not the only reason why firms should hire and retain the disabled. Studies have shown that firms that do so experience positive business outcomes. Many manual and electronic devices are available today that can help the disabled work safely and productively. Something as small as slightly redesigning workstations can make it possible for people of all abilities to work in many jobs.

be heavily fined or shut down. Nonetheless, many people feel that issuing OSHA violations is not enough to protect workers from harm.

Employee Retirement Income Security Act

This act was passed in 1974 to protect the retirement benefits of employees. It does not require that firms provide a retirement plan. However, it does specify that if a retirement plan is provided, it must be managed in such a way that the interests of employees are protected. It also provides federal insurance for retirement plans that go bankrupt.

Affirmative Action

Affirmative action is not one act, but a series of executive orders issued by the President of the United States. It applies to all employers with 50 or more employees holding federal contracts in excess of $50,000. It prescribes that such employers (1) actively encourage job applications from members of minority groups and (2) hire qualified employees from minority groups who are not fully represented in their organizations. Many firms that do not hold government contracts voluntarily take part in affirmative action.

Americans with Disabilities Act

The Americans with Disabilities Act (ADA) prohibits discrimination against qualified individuals with disabilities in all employment practices—including job-application procedures, hiring, firing, advancement, compensation, training, and other terms and conditions of employment. All private employers and government agencies with 15 or more employees are covered by the ADA. Defining who is a qualified individual with a disability is, of course, difficult. Depending on how *qualified individual with a disability* is interpreted, more than 50 million Americans can be included under this law.[18] It also mandates that all businesses that serve the public must make their facilities accessible to people with disabilities.

    The ADA not only protects individuals with obvious physical disabilities, but also safeguards those with less visible conditions such as heart disease, diabetes,

Concept Check

✓ How is the National Labor Relations Act different from the Fair Labor Standards Act?

✓ How does the Civil Rights Act influence the selection and promotion of employees?

✓ What is the Occupational Safety and Health Act?

✓ What is the purpose of the Americans with Disabilities Act?

epilepsy, cancer, AIDS, and mental illnesses. Because of this law, many organizations no longer require job applicants to pass physical examinations as a condition of employment.

Employers are required to provide disabled employees with reasonable accommodation. *Reasonable accommodation* is any modification or adjustment to a job or work environment that will enable a qualified employee with a disability to perform a central job function, such as making existing facilities accessible to and usable by wheelchair-bound individuals. Reasonable accommodation also might mean restructuring a job, modifying work schedules, acquiring or modifying equipment, providing qualified readers or interpreters, or changing training programs.

Looking for Success? *Get Flashcards, Quizzes, Games, Crosswords, and more @ www.cengagebrain.com.*

Summary

1 Describe the major components of human resources management.

Human resources management (HRM) is the set of activities involved in acquiring, maintaining, and developing an organization's human resources. Responsibility for HRM is shared by specialized staff and line managers. HRM activities include human resources planning, job analysis, recruitment, selection, orientation, compensation, benefits, training and development, and performance appraisal.

2 Identify the steps in human resources planning.

Human resources planning consists of forecasting the human resources that a firm will need and planning a course of action to match supply with demand. Layoffs, attrition, early retirement, and (as a last resort) firing are ways to reduce the size of the workforce when needed. Supply is increased through hiring.

3 Describe cultural diversity and understand some of the challenges and opportunities associated with it.

Cultural diversity refers to the differences among people in a workforce owing to race, ethnicity, and gender. With an increasing number of women, minorities, and immigrants in the U.S. workforce, management is faced with challenges and competitive advantages. Some organizations have implemented diversity-related training programs to make the most of cultural diversity. With proper guidance and management, a culturally diverse organization can prove beneficial to all involved.

4 Explain the objectives and uses of job analysis.

Job analysis provides a job description and a job specification for each position within a firm. A job description is a list of the elements that make up a particular job. A job specification is a list of qualifications required to perform a job. Job analysis is used in evaluation and in the determination of compensation levels and serves as the basis for recruiting and selecting new employees.

5 Describe the processes of recruiting, employee selection, and orientation.

Recruiting is the process of attracting qualified job applicants. Candidates for open positions may be recruited from within or outside a firm. In the selection process, information about candidates is obtained from applications, résumés, tests, interviews, references, assessment centers, even online social networking sites. This information is used to select the most appropriate candidate for the job. Newly hired employees will then go through an orientation program to learn about the firm and the specifics of the job.

6 Discuss the primary elements of employee compensation and benefits.

Compensation is the payment employees receive in return for their labor. In developing a system for paying employees, management must decide on the firm's general wage level (relative to other firms), the wage structure within the firm, and individual wages. Wage surveys and job analyses are useful in making these decisions. Employees may be paid hourly wages, salaries, or commissions. They also may receive incentive payments, lump-sum salary increases, and profit-sharing payments. Employee benefits, which are nonmonetary rewards to employees, add about 30 percent to the cost of compensation.

7 Explain the purposes and techniques of employee training and development.

Employee-training and management-development programs enhance the ability of employees to contribute to a firm. When developing a training program, the company should analyze training needs and then select training methods. Because training is expensive, an organization should periodically evaluate the effectiveness of its training programs.

8 Discuss performance appraisal techniques and performance feedback.

Performance appraisal, or evaluation, is used to provide employees with performance feedback, to serve as a basis for distributing rewards, and to monitor selection and training activities. Both objective and judgmental appraisal techniques are used. Their results are communicated to employees through three performance feedback approaches: tell-and-sell, tell-and-listen, and problem solving.

9 Outline the major legislation affecting human resources management.

A number of laws have been passed that affect HRM practices and that protect the rights and safety of employees. Some of these are the National Labor Relations Act of 1935, the Labor–Management Relations Act of 1947, the Fair Labor Standards Act of 1938, the Equal Pay Act of 1963, Title VII of the Civil Rights Act of 1964, the Age Discrimination in Employment Acts of 1967 and 1986, the Occupational Safety and Health Act of 1970, the Employment Retirement Income Security Act of 1974, the Worker Adjustment and Retraining Notification Act of 1988, the Americans with Disabilities Act of 1990, the Civil Rights Act of 1991, and the Family and Medical Leave Act of 1993.

Key Terms

You should now be able to define and give an example relevant to each of the following terms:

human resources management (HRM) (239)	job description (245)	wage survey (250)	profit-sharing (251)
human resources planning (241)	job specification (245)	job evaluation (250)	employee benefit (251)
replacement chart (242)	recruiting (246)	comparable worth (250)	flexible benefit plan (252)
skills inventory (242)	external recruiting (246)	hourly wage (251)	employee training (253)
cultural (workplace) diversity (243)	internal recruiting (246)	salary (251)	management development (253)
job analysis (245)	selection (247)	commission (251)	performance appraisal (254)
	orientation (249)	incentive payment (251)	
	compensation (249)	lump-sum salary increase (251)	
	compensation system (250)		

Discussion Questions

1. In general, on what basis is responsibility for HRM divided between line and staff managers?
2. How is a forecast of human resources demand related to a firm's organizational planning?
3. How do human resources managers go about matching a firm's supply of workers with demand?
4. What are the major challenges and benefits associated with a culturally diverse workforce?
5. What are the advantages and disadvantages of external recruiting? Of internal recruiting?
6. How is a job analysis used in the process of job evaluation?
7. Suppose that you have just opened a new Ford sales showroom and repair shop. Which of your employees would be paid wages, which would receive salaries, and which would receive commissions?
8. Why is it so important to provide feedback after a performance appraisal?
9. How accurately can managers plan for future human resources needs?
10. Are employee benefits really necessary? Why?
11. As a manager, what actions would you take if an operations employee with six years of experience on the job refused ongoing training and ignored performance feedback?
12. Why are there so many laws relating to HRM practices?
13. Of the laws discussed in the text, which are the most important, in your opinion?

Test Yourself

Matching Questions

1. _____ Jobs are studied to determine specific tasks.

2. _____ People are acquired, maintained, and developed for the firm.

3. _____ Personal qualifications required in a job are described.

4. _____ Potential applicants are made aware of available positions.

5. _____ The reward employees receive for their labor.

6. _____ The process for teaching employees to do their jobs more efficiently.

7. _____ An employee's work performance is evaluated.

8. _____ Gain sharing is an example.

9. _____ It seeks equal compensation for similar jobs.

10. _____ Employees may choose from a variety of benefit options.

a. comparable worth
b. compensation
c. employee training
d. flexible benefit plan
e. human resources management
f. incentive payment
g. wage survey
h. job analysis
i. job specification
j. performance appraisal
k. recruiting
l. profit sharing

True False Questions

11. **T F** Staffing, personnel management, and human resources management are synonymous terms.

12. **T F** Attrition is the process of acquiring information on applicants.

13. **T F** Recruiting is an activity of human resources acquisition.

14. **T F** The selection process matches the right candidate with each job.

15. **T F** The most widely used selection technique is the employment test.

16. **T F** In a structured interview, the interviewer uses a prepared set of questions.

17. **T F** Employee benefits, such as vacation and sick leave, are required by law.

18. **T F** Transfers involve moving employees into higher-level positions.

19. **T F** The purpose of Title VII is to ensure that employers make personnel decisions on the basis of employee qualifications.

20. **T F** The Employee Retirement Income Security Act requires firms to provide a retirement plan for their employees.

Multiple-Choice Questions

21. _____ Human resources planning requires the following steps except
    a. using the firm's strategic plan.
    b. forecasting the firm's future demand.
    c. determining availability of human resources.
    d. acquiring funds for implementation.
    e. matching supply with demand.

22. _____ Which of the following is least likely to be the responsibility of a line manager?
    a. Developing a compensation system
    b. Implementing an orientation program
    c. Job analysis
    d. Recommending a promotion
    e. Hiring employees

23. _____ Melinda walked into First National Bank to pick up an application for an administrative assistant position. When she asked about the duties and working conditions, the busy receptionist handed her a job
    a. description.
    b. inventory.
    c. analysis.
    d. orientation.
    e. specification.

24. _____ Companies develop reputations as being favorable or unfavorable prospective employers for women and ethnic minorities. Based on this understanding or company reputation, what advantage do companies that have a good record for managing diversity have over others?
    a. Resource acquisition
    b. Flexibility
    c. Bilingual skills
    d. Cost saving
    e. Creativity

25. _____ Which of the following is the term used to describe a process of "recruiting minorities, training minorities to be managers, training managers to view diversity positively, and teaching English as a second language"?
   a. Problem solving
   b. Flexibility
   c. Resource acquisition
   d. Diversity training programs
   e. Acquiring bilingual skills

26. _____ A one-page summary of an applicant's qualifications is known as a(n) _____
   a. application form.
   b. data sheet.
   c. summary sheet.
   d. resume.
   e. qualification sheet.

27. _____ Which of the following is the best way to describe "employee-development training"?
   a. Attracting the best people to apply for positions
   b. Using satisfaction surveys and employee communication programs
   c. Recruiting experienced employees from other firms
   d. Providing rewards to ensure employee well-being
   e. Improving employees' skills and expanding their capabilities

28. _____ Which of the following is a good example of the "judgmental method" of evaluation?
   a. Each employee is rated on the degree to which the statement applies.
   b. The number of insurance claims processed is evaluated.

   c. The units of output per employee are calculated.
   d. An employee's dollar volume of sales per week is assessed.
   e. The number of defective products an employee produces, on average, is counted.

29. _____ Required retirement before age 70 was outlawed in the
   a. Age Discrimination in Employment Act.
   b. Equal Pay Act.
   c. Fair Labor Standards Act.
   d. Employee Retirement Income Security Act.
   e. Civil Rights Act.

30. _____ Larry was hurt while playing football in his senior year in high school. Since then, he has been confined to a wheelchair. After receiving his college diploma, he applied for a supervision job in a local warehouse. Under ADA, the employer must provide reasonable accommodation for disabled employees. Which activity will not legally cover Larry?
   a. Providing adequate home medical care
   b. Making existing facilities accessible
   c. Modifying work schedules
   d. Providing qualified readers
   e. Changing examinations

Answers to the Test Yourself questions appear at the end of the book on page TY-2.

Video Case
The Container Store Hires Great Employees to Sell Empty Boxes

Empty boxes are big business for the Container Store (www.containerstore.com), headquartered just outside Dallas in Coppell, Texas. Founded in 1978, the company has grown to 57 stores nationwide and $700 million in annual revenue by specializing in storage products for home and office. From stacking bins and spice racks to trash cans and toy caddies, the Container Store sells a variety of functional, stylish storage solutions for every situation.

Kip Tindell, co-founder and CEO, attributes the company's decades-long success to the high caliber of its employees. "When you're selling empty boxes, you'd better have great people," he explains. Tindell's philosophy that "one great person equals three good people" has become the cornerstone of the Container Store's approach to recruiting, hiring, training, and retaining employees. To attract and keep

enthusiastic people who enjoy working with customers, the company pays above-average wages—much higher than the typical retailer. It also offers numerous benefits, including medical coverage, generous discounts on store merchandise, paid vacation time, and even pet insurance.

Not surprisingly, hundreds of people apply for every job opening. The Container Store requires as many as nine interviews before managers make a decision about which "great" candidate to select. Only 3 percent of the people who apply to work for the company wind up being hired. Once they're hired, new employees enter a training program to gain the skills they need for on-the-job success. All full-time employees receive more than 260 hours of intensive training during their first 12 months. Part-time workers receive 150 hours of training during the first year. The purpose is to improve employees' product knowledge, teach them how to assess customers' storage needs, and provide the techniques and tools they need to suggest creative solutions for each individual's needs. The training also covers professional development topics to prepare employees for future career advancement.

Although retailers usually experience high turnover, the Container Store's turnover is exceptionally low, because it is so selective in hiring, rewards its employees well for performance, and provides a satisfying work environment. During the recent recession, when many employers were forced to cut costs through layoffs, the CEO reassured his employees that they didn't have to worry about being laid off. Rather than reduce its workforce, the company cut back slightly on some benefits and found other ways to lower expenses during the financial crunch. When the economy turned around and profits began to rise, the Container Store restored employee benefits to their former levels. It also embarked on its most aggressive expansion ever, opening six new stores in a single year and hiring hundreds of employees to fill the newly created sales positions.

The Container Store's no-layoff policy is only one way it proves how much it values its employees. Following the principle "communication is leadership," the retailer practices transparency, allowing employees access to most types of information except specific details about what individuals are paid. Not only do employees have the information they need to do their jobs, they can get a big picture overview of the company and its challenges and accomplishments. Thanks to its reputation for putting employees first, the Container Store has been named many times to *Fortune* magazine's annual list of 100 best companies to work for in America.[19]

Questions

1. What effect does low turnover have on the Container Store's ability to forecast human resources supply and match supply with demand?
2. Do you agree with the Container Store's decision to allow employees access to all kinds of company information except individual compensation? Explain your answer.
3. If you were interviewing applicants for a sales position at the Container Store, what questions would you ask, and why?

Building Skills for Career Success

1. Social Media Exercise

LinkedIn (www.linkedin.com) is the largest and best-known social network for professionals. Many of you are probably already familiar with it.

1. Do you have a profile? If not, you might want to consider developing one because many companies recruit from LinkedIn and it can be a great tool for professional networking.
2. If you already have a profile, think about how you might improve it. Do you participate in discussion groups? Have you reached out and connected to people in industries where you want to work?

2. Building Team Skills

The New Therapy Company is soliciting a contract to provide five nursing homes with physical, occupational, speech, and respiratory therapy. The therapists will rotate among the five nursing homes. The therapists have not yet been hired, but the nursing homes expect them to be fully trained and ready to go to work in three months. The previous therapy company lost its contract because of high staff turnover owing to employee "burnout" (a common problem in this field), high costs, and low-quality care. The nursing homes want a plan specifying how the New Therapy Company will meet staffing needs, keep costs low, and provide high-quality care.

Assignment

1. Working in a group, discuss how the New Therapy Company can meet the deadline and still ensure a high quality of care. Also discuss the following:
   a. How many of each type of therapist will the company need?
   b. How will it prevent therapists from burning out?
   c. How can it retain experienced staff and still limit costs?
   d. Are promotions available for staff? What does the career ladder look like?
   e. How will the company manage therapists at five different locations? How will it keep in touch with them (computer, voice mail, or monthly meetings)? Would it make more sense to have therapists work permanently at each location rather than rotate among them?
   f. How will the company justify the travel costs? What other expenses might it expect?
2. Prepare a plan for the New Therapy Company to present to the nursing homes.

3. Researching Different Careers

A résumé provides a summary of your skills, abilities, and achievements. It also may include a description of the type of job you want. An effective résumé clearly communicates your career objectives, your experience and qualifications, and shows that you have given serious thought to your career.

Assignment

1. Prepare a résumé for a job that you want using the information in Appendix A (see text website).
   a. Determine your skills and decide which are important for this particular job.
   b. Decide which format—chronological or functional—will be most effective in presenting your skills and experience.
   c. Keep the résumé to one page, if possible (no more than two pages). (Note that portfolio items may be attached for certain jobs, such as artwork.)
2. Have several people review the résumé for accuracy.
3. Ask your instructor to comment on your résumé.

Endnotes

1. Based on information in Joseph Walker, "School's in Session at Google," *Wall Street Journal*, July 5, 2012, www.wsj.com; Nancy M. Davis, "Google's Top Recruiter," *HR Magazine*, July 2012, p. 40; Anne Vander-Mey, "Inside Google's Recruiting Machine," *Fortune*, February 24, 2012, http://tech.fortune.cnn.com; Mike Swift, "The Opposite of Evil: Google Named Best Place to Work in America," *San Jose Mercury News*, January 19, 2012, www.mercurynews.com; www.google.com.

2. "Human Capital Trends 2012: Leap Ahead," Deloitte, http://www.deloitte.com/view/en_US/us/Services/consulting/human-capital/human-capital-trends-2012/index.htm, accessed November 23, 2012.

3. Editorial, "Reforming the Postal Service," *The New York Times*, March 1, 2012,www.nytimes.com/2012/03/01/opinion/reforming-the-postal-service.html.

4. Robert Gillies, "Canadian Pacific Railway to Eliminate 4,500 Jobs," ABC News, December 5, 2012, http://abcnews.go.com/International/wireStory/canadian-pacific-railway-eliminate-4500-jobs-17878985#.UMNsRXdRXE0.

5. U.S. Department of Labor, Bureau of Labor Statistics,http://bls.gov/cps/accessed November 23, 2012.

6. Women in the Labor Force: A Data Book, U.S. Department of Labor, Bureau of Labor Statistics, December 2011,http://bls.gov/cps/wlf-databook-2011.pdf, accessed November 23, 2012.

7. Lisa Quast, "For a More Inclusive Workplace, Train Men First, Specifically White Male Managers," *Forbes*, August 27, 2012, http://www.forbes.com/sites/lisaquast/2012/08/27/for-a-more-inclusive-workplace-train-men-specifically-white-male-employees/, accessed December 15, 2012.

8. Chana R. Shoenberger, "Help Wanted . . . but in a Whole New Way," *Wall Street Journal*, October 29, 2012, http://online.wsj.com/article/SB10000872396390444426404577646041283872130.html.

9. Donna Tam, "Recruiters Post 1.7 Million Jobs on New Facebook Jobs Board," CNET, November 14, 2012, http://news.cnet.com/8301-1023_3-57549764-93/recruiters-post-1.7-million-jobs-on-new-facebook-jobs-board/.

10. "Salaries as a percentage of operating cost," Society for Human Resource Management, November 1, 2008, www.shrm.org/Research/Articles/Articles/Pages/MetricoftheMonthSalariesasPercentageofOperatingExpense.aspx, accessed December 8, 2012.

11. Korva Coleman, "Equal Pay for Equal Work: Not Even College Helps Women," Capital Public Radio, October 24, 2012, http://www.capradio.org/news/npr/story?storyid=163536890.

12. Ben Popkin, "Women likely to earn more when told they can negotiate," *Today*, November 9, 2012, http://lifeinc.today.com/_news/2012/11/09/14996561-women-likely-to-earn-more-when-told-they-can-negotiate.

13. Press release, "Hormel Announces Increase to 47th Consecutive Annual Dividend,"http://www.hormelfoods.com/Newsroom/Press-Releases/2012/11/20121120-01, accessed November 23, 2012.

14. "Employment Cost Statistics," U.S. Department of Labor, Bureau of Labor Statistics, September 2012, http://www.bls.gov/news.release/eci.nr0.htm, accessed November 23, 2012.

15. Jessica E. Lessin, "Apple Gives into Employee Perks," *Wall Street Journal*, November 12, 2012, http://online.wsj.com/article/SB10001424127887324073504578115071154910456.html.

16. News release, "Verizon's Employee Training Programs Ranked Tops in the U.S.," *Verizon*, February 17, 2012, http://newscenter.verizon.com/press-releases/verizon/2012/verizons-employee-training.html, accessed December 8, 2012.

17. Colleen Leahey, Update: Fortune 500 Women CEOs Hits Record 20, *Fortune*, July 18, 2012, http://postcards.blogs.fortune.cnn.com/2012/07/18/fortune-500-women-ceos-2/; Eduardo Porter, "Motherhood Still a Cause of Pay Inequality," *New York Times*, June 12, 2012, http://www.nytimes.com/2012/06/13/business/economy/motherhood-still-a-cause-of-pay-inequality.html.

18. ADA Update: A Primer for Small Businesses, U.S. Department of Justice, Civil Rights Division, www.ada.gov/regs2010/smallbusiness/smallbusprimer2010.htm#whoiscovered, accessed November 24, 2012.

19. Based on information in Jason Heid, "Breakfast with Kip Tindell of The Container Store," *D Magazine*, November 2012, www.dmagazine.com; Steven R. Thompson, "Container Store Uses Personal Approach in New Strategy," *Dallas Business Journal*, April 27, 2012, www.bizjournals.com; Brooke Baker, "No. 1, Small Companies: The Container Store," *Indianapolis Star*, April 7, 2012, www.indystar.com; Caitlin Keating, "No Layoffs—Ever!" *Fortune*, January 20, 2012, http://money.cnn.com; Cengage "Container Store" video; www.containerstore.com.

© KURHAN/SHUTTERSTOCK.COM

Motivating and Satisfying Employees and Teams

Why Should You Care?

As you move up into management positions or operate your own business, you will need to understand what motivates others in an organization.

Learning Objectives

Once you complete this chapter, you will be able to:

1 Explain what motivation is.

2 Understand some major historical perspectives on motivation.

3 Describe three contemporary views of motivation: equity theory, expectancy theory, and goal-setting theory.

4 Explain several techniques for increasing employee motivation.

5 Understand the types, development, and uses of teams.

Satisfied Employees Help Create Satisfied Customers at American Express

How does a global company provide responsive service to 97 million customers from Memphis to Milan to Mumbai and beyond? That's the challenge facing American Express (www.americanexpress.com), the New York–based global financial services firm with 62,500 employees worldwide and $30 billion in annual revenues. Every year, customers use their American Express cards to buy $822 billion worth of goods and services. The company also works with a global network of stores, restaurants, and other businesses that accept its cards for purchases.

The key to offering personalized around-the-clock assistance, all around the world, is to have a knowledgeable, committed workforce that's ready and willing to help customers who visit branch offices in 130 countries or get in touch by phone, e-mail, or online. In fact, human resources are a key strength at American Express. The company, which regularly appears on *Fortune* magazine's list of best U.S. companies to work for, is highly selective about who it recruits—and it works hard to keep its employees and managers motivated and satisfied.

Although many companies save money by training employees to keep calls short and stick to a script when conversing with customers, American Express does the opposite. Employees are empowered to listen carefully, use their creativity to resolve problems, and suggest appropriate products as needed for each customer's situation. This approach keeps employees involved in their work and adds an important personal touch to every customer contact.

To help employees balance their professional and personal lives, American Express allows some employees to share full-time job positions or work more hours per day for a shorter workweek. A growing number of employees work from home, connecting with customers and colleagues via phone and technology. Internal surveys confirm that this flexibility helps keep turnover very low. In any given year, only 7 percent of American Express's full-time employees choose to leave. So satisfied is the workforce that 16 percent of U.S. employees have remained with American Express for 20 years or more.[1]

Did You Know?

American Express's worldwide workforce of 62,500 serves 97 million cardholders 24 hours a day, 7 days a week.

To achieve its goals, any organization—be it American Express, Google, or a local convenience store—must be sure that its employees have more than the right raw materials, adequate facilities, and equipment that works. The organization also must ensure that its employees are *motivated*. A high level of employee motivation derives from effective management practices.

In this chapter, after first explaining what motivation is, we present several studies and views of motivation that have influenced management practices over the years: Taylor's ideas of scientific management, Mayo's Hawthorne Studies, Maslow's hierarchy of needs, Herzberg's motivation–hygiene theory, McGregor's Theory X and Theory Y, Ouchi's Theory Z, and reinforcement theory. Then, turning our attention to contemporary theory, we examine equity, expectancy, and goal-setting theories. Finally, we discuss specific techniques managers can use to foster employee motivation and satisfaction.

WHAT IS MOTIVATION?

A *motive* is something that causes a person to act. A successful athlete is said to be "highly motivated." A student who avoids work is said to be "unmotivated." We define **motivation** as the individual internal process that energizes, directs, and sustains behavior. It is the personal "force" that causes you or me to act in a particular way. For example, although job rotation may increase your job satisfaction and your enthusiasm for your work so that you devote more energy to it, it may not have the same impact on me.

Learning Objective

1 Explain what motivation is.

motivation the individual internal process that energizes, directs, and sustains behavior; the personal "force" that causes you or me to behave in a particular way

Morale is an employee's attitude or feelings about the job, about superiors, and about the firm itself. To achieve organizational goals effectively, employees need more than the right raw materials, adequate facilities, and efficient equipment. High morale results mainly from the satisfaction of needs on the job or as a result of doing the job. One need that might be satisfied on the job is the need *to be recognized* as an important contributor to the organization. A need satisfied as a result of the job is the need for *financial security*. High morale leads to dedication, loyalty, and a desire to do the job well. Low morale, however, can lead to shoddy work, absenteeism, and high turnover rates as employees leave to seek more satisfying jobs with other firms. Turnover can be very costly. To minimize it, companies may try to create work environments that increase employee satisfaction. One obvious indicator of satisfaction at a specific organization is whether employees report that they like working there and whether other people want to work there. In a recent list of *Fortune* magazine's "Top 100 Companies to Work For," the top ten best companies to work for were Google, Boston Consulting Group, SAS, Wegmans Food Markets, Edward Jones, Netapp, Camden Property Trust, REI Recreational Equipment, CHG Healthcare Services, and Quicken Loans.[2] Motivation, morale, and the satisfaction of employees' needs are highly intertwined considerations. Their relationships to business success and productivity have been the subject of much study since the end of the 19th century. We continue our discussion of motivation by outlining some landmarks of the early research.

HISTORICAL PERSPECTIVES ON MOTIVATION

Researchers often begin a study with a fairly narrow goal in mind, usually to test a specific hypothesis. After they develop an understanding of their subject, however, they realize that their research has broader applications. This is exactly what happened when early research into productivity grew into the study of employee motivation.

Scientific Management

Toward the end of the 19th century, Frederick W. Taylor, an American mechanical engineer, became interested in improving the efficiency of individual workers. This interest, which stemmed from his own experiences in manufacturing plants, eventually led to the development of **scientific management**, the application of scientific principles to management of work and workers.

One of Taylor's first jobs was with the Midvale Steel Company in Philadelphia, where he developed a strong distaste for waste and inefficiency. While there, he observed a practice he dubbed "soldiering." Workers "soldiered," or worked slowly, because they feared that if they worked faster, they would run out of work and lose

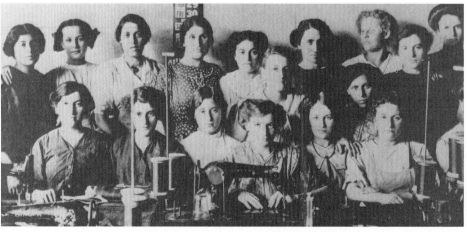

their jobs. Taylor realized that workers could get away with this because managers had no idea what productivity levels *should* be.

After Midvale, Taylor spent several years at Bethlehem Steel. While there, he made his most significant contribution to the field of motivation. He suggested that each job be broken down into separate tasks. Then management should determine (1) the best way to perform each task and (2) the job output to expect when employees performed the tasks properly. Next, management should choose the best person for each job and train that person in doing the job properly. Finally, management should monitor workers to ensure that jobs were performed as planned.

Taylor also developed the idea that most people work only to earn money. He therefore reasoned that pay should be tied directly to output. The more a person produces, the more he or she should be paid. This gave rise to the **piece-rate system**, under which employees are paid a certain amount for each unit of output they produce. Under Taylor's piece-rate system, each employee is assigned an output quota. If they exceed the quota, they receive a higher per unit rate for all work produced (see Figure 10-1). Today, the piece-rate system is still used by some manufacturers and by farmers who grow crops that are harvested by farm laborers.

When Taylor's system was put into practice at Bethlehem Steel, the results were dramatic. Average earnings per day for steel handlers rose from $1.15 to $1.88. (Do not let the low wages obscure the fact that this was an increase of more than 61 percent!) The average amount of steel handled per day increased from 16 to 57 tons.

Taylor's revolutionary ideas had a profound impact on management practice. However, his view of motivation was soon recognized as overly simplistic and narrow. It is true that most people expect to be paid for their work, but it is also true that people work for a variety of reasons other than pay. Therefore, simply increasing a person's pay may not increase that person's motivation or productivity.

piece-rate system a compensation system under which employees are paid a certain amount for each unit of output they produce

The Hawthorne Studies

Between 1927 and 1932, Elton Mayo, an Australian sociologist and organizational theorist, conducted two experiments at the Hawthorne plant of the Western Electric Company in Chicago. The original objective of these studies, now referred to as the *Hawthorne Studies*, was to determine the effects of the work environment on employee productivity.

The first set of experiments tested the effect of lighting levels on productivity. One group of workers was subjected to varying lighting, while a second was not. To the amazement of the researchers, productivity increased for both groups.

FIGURE 10-1 Taylor's Piece-Rate System

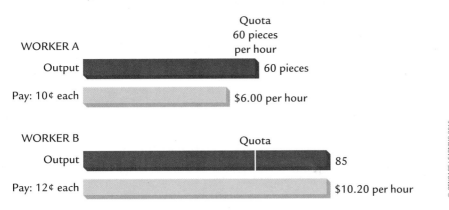

Workers who exceeded their quotas were rewarded with a higher rate per piece for all the pieces they produced.

WORKER A — Quota 60 pieces per hour
Output: 60 pieces
Pay: 10¢ each: $6.00 per hour

WORKER B — Quota
Output: 85
Pay: 12¢ each: $10.20 per hour

© CENGAGE LEARNING 2015

For the group whose lighting was varied, productivity remained high until the light was reduced to the level of moonlight!

The second set of experiments focused on the effectiveness of the piece-rate system in increasing the output of groups of workers. Researchers expected that output would increase because faster workers would put pressure on slower workers to produce more. Again, the results were not as expected. Output remained constant irrespective of the "standard" rates management set.

When faced with unexpected outcomes, the researchers concluded that *human factors* were responsible for the results. In the lighting experiments, researchers had given both groups of workers a *sense of involvement* in their jobs merely by asking them to participate in the research. These workers—perhaps for the first time—felt as though they were an important part of the organization. The level of light did not matter. In the piece-rate experiments, each group of workers informally set the acceptable rate of output for the group. To gain or retain the *social acceptance* of the group, each worker felt pressure to produce at the same rate as the group pace.

The Hawthorne Studies showed that such human factors are at least as important to motivation as pay rates. From these and other studies, the *human relations movement* in management was born. Its premise was simple: Employees who are happy and satisfied with their work are motivated to perform better. Hence, management is best served by providing a work environment that maximizes employee satisfaction.

Maslow's Hierarchy of Needs

Abraham Maslow, an American psychologist whose best-known works were published in the 1960s and 1970s, developed a theory of motivation based on a hierarchy of needs. A **need** is a personal requirement. Maslow assumed that humans are "wanting" beings who seek to fulfill a variety of needs, which he argued can be arranged from most basic to most complex in a sequence now known as **Maslow's hierarchy of needs** (see Figure 10-2).

At the bottom of the pyramid are **physiological needs**, the things we require to survive. They include food and water, clothing, shelter, and sleep. In the employment context, these needs usually are satisfied through adequate wages.

At the next level are **safety needs**, the things we require for physical and emotional security. Safety needs may be satisfied through job stability, health insurance, pension plans, and safe working conditions. The rising costs of health care in today's work environment threatens some workers' sense of safety. Many firms are switching to more

need a personal requirement

Maslow's hierarchy of needs a sequence of human needs in the order of their importance

physiological needs the things we require for survival

safety needs the things we require for physical and emotional security

FIGURE 10-2 Maslow's Hierarchy of Needs

Psychologist Abraham Maslow believed that people act to fulfill five categories of needs.

Self-actualization needs

Esteem needs

Social needs

Safety needs

Physiological needs

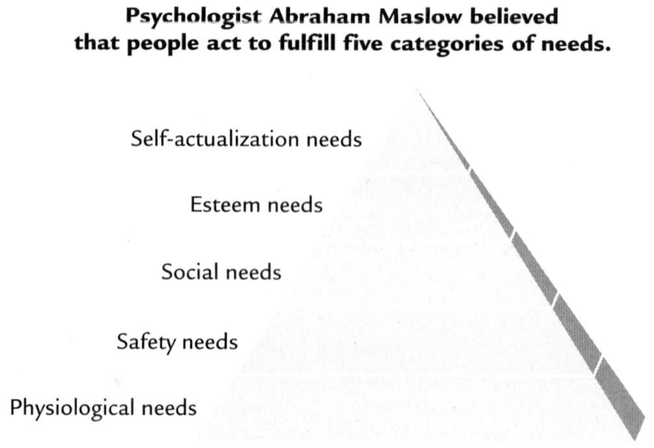

© CENGAGE LEARNING 2015

part-time workers for low-wage positions in order to avoid health insurance costs and fees. Under new law, large employers must provide health insurance to those who work more than 30 hours per week, or risk paying a fine. The move might backfire as employees seek to satisfy their safety needs at more secure jobs.[3]

Next are the **social needs**, the human requirements for love and affection and a sense of belonging. These needs are fulfilled in the workplace through the work environment and the informal organization and outside of the workplace by family and friends. Many employers offer their workers flexible scheduling options in order to improve their quality of lives, which includes time for family and friends. Employees who have flexible work schedules are more likely to be able to attend family events or to socialize. Employers can satisfy workers' social needs, which can improve productivity by making them happier, by doing things like leaving cookies in the break room or holding motivational meetings to foster a team spirit.[4]

At the level of **esteem needs**, we require respect and recognition from others and a sense of our own accomplishment and worth (self-esteem). These needs may be satisfied through personal accomplishment, promotion to positions with greater responsibility, various honors and awards, and other forms of recognition.

At the top of the hierarchy are the **self-actualization needs**, which are the need to grow, develop, and become all that we are capable of being. These are the most difficult needs to satisfy, and the means of satisfying them tend to vary with the individual. For some people, learning a new skill, starting a new career after retirement, or trying to become the best at some endeavor may be the way to realize self-actualization.

Maslow suggested that people work up the hierarchy, satisfying their physiological needs before safety needs, for example. However, needs at one level do not have to be satisfied completely before needs at the next higher level come into play. People can also move up and down the hierarchy. For example, if a person loses a good job, he may find himself trying to satisfy safety needs when he only recently had focused on social needs.

Maslow's hierarchy of needs provides a guide for management and a useful way of viewing employee motivation. By and large, American business has been able to satisfy workers' basic needs, but the higher-order needs present more of a challenge. The means of satisfying these needs varies from one employee to another.

social needs the human requirements for love and affection and a sense of belonging

esteem needs our need for respect, recognition, and a sense of our own accomplishment and worth

self-actualization needs the need to grow and develop and to become all that we are capable of being

Herzberg's Motivation–Hygiene Theory

Frederick Herzberg, an American psychologist, interviewed approximately 200 accountants and engineers in Pittsburgh in the 1950s to develop his theory of motivation. He asked them to think of a time when they had felt especially good about their jobs and their work and to describe the factor or factors that had caused them to feel that way. Next, he asked them about a time when they had felt especially bad about their work. He was surprised to find that feeling good and feeling bad resulted from entirely different factors. That is, low pay may make a particular person feel bad, but high pay does not necessarily make that same person feel good.

motivation–hygiene theory the idea that satisfaction and dissatisfaction are separate and distinct dimensions

SATISFACTION AND DISSATISFACTION Before Herzberg's interviews, the general assumption was that employee satisfaction and dissatisfaction lay at opposite ends of the same scale. However, Herzberg's interviews convinced him that satisfaction and dissatisfaction are different dimensions altogether. In other words, the opposite of satisfaction is not dissatisfaction. The idea that satisfaction and dissatisfaction are separate and distinct dimensions is referred to as the **motivation–hygiene theory** (see Figure 10-3).

What satisfies employees? Companies sometimes use travel awards as incentives for better employee performance. According to the motivation–hygiene theory, when an incentive for higher performance is not provided, is that a dissatisfier?

FIGURE 10-3 Herzberg's Motivation–Hygiene Theory

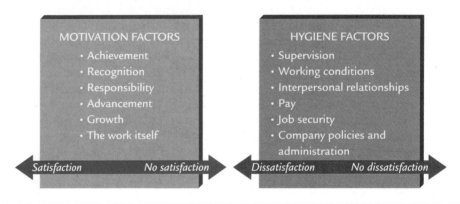

Herzberg's theory takes into account that there are different dimensions to job satisfaction and dissatisfaction and that these factors do not overlap.

MOTIVATION FACTORS
- Achievement
- Recognition
- Responsibility
- Advancement
- Growth
- The work itself

Satisfaction   *No satisfaction*

HYGIENE FACTORS
- Supervision
- Working conditions
- Interpersonal relationships
- Pay
- Job security
- Company policies and administration

Dissatisfaction   *No dissatisfaction*

© CENGAGE LEARNING 2015

motivation factors job factors that increase motivation, although their absence does not necessarily result in dissatisfaction

hygiene factors job factors that reduce dissatisfaction when present to an acceptable degree but that do not necessarily result in high levels of motivation

The job factors that Herzberg found most frequently associated with satisfaction were achievement, recognition, responsibility, advancement, growth, and the work itself. These factors generally are referred to as **motivation factors** because their presence increases motivation. However, their absence does not necessarily result in dissatisfaction. When motivation factors are present, they act as *satisfiers*.

Dissatisfaction, on the other hand, is caused by job factors such as supervision, working conditions, interpersonal relationships, pay, job security, company policies, and administration. These factors, called **hygiene factors**, reduce dissatisfaction when they are present to an acceptable degree. However, they do not necessarily result in high levels of motivation. When hygiene factors are absent, they act as *dissatisfiers*.

USING HERZBERG'S MOTIVATION–HYGIENE THEORY Herzberg provides explicit guidelines for using the motivation–hygiene theory of employee motivation. He suggests that the hygiene factors must be present to ensure that a worker can function comfortably. He warns, however, that a state of *no dissatisfaction* cannot exist. In any situation, people always will be dissatisfied with something.

According to Herzberg, managers should utilize hygiene factors to make the work environment as positive as possible, but should expect only short-term improvements in motivation. Managers must focus instead on providing those satisfiers that will enhance motivation and long-term effort.

We should note that employee pay has proven to have more effect than Herzberg's theory indicates. He suggests that pay provides only short-term, not true, motivation. Yet, in many organizations, pay is a form of recognition and reward for achievement—and recognition and achievement are both motivation factors. The effect of pay may

© ISTOCKPHOTO.COM/LISAFX

depend on how it is distributed. If a pay increase does not depend on performance (as in across-the-board or cost-of-living raises), it may not motivate people. However, if pay is increased as a form of recognition (as in bonuses or incentives), it can play a role in motivating employees to higher performance.

Theory X and Theory Y

The concepts of Theory X and Theory Y were advanced by Douglas McGregor, an American business professor, in his book, *The Human Side of Enterprise*, in 1967. They represent opposing sets of assumptions that underlie management's attitudes and beliefs regarding workers' behavior.

Theory X is a concept of employee motivation generally consistent with Taylor's ideas about scientific management. Theory X is based on the following assumptions:

1. People dislike work and try to avoid it.
2. Because people dislike work, managers must coerce, control, and frequently threaten employees to achieve organizational goals.
3. People generally must be led because they have little ambition and will not seek responsibility; they are concerned mainly about security.

The logical outcome of such assumptions will be a highly controlled work environment—one in which managers make all the decisions and employees take all the orders.

On the other hand, **Theory Y** is a concept of employee motivation generally consistent with the ideas of the human relations movement. Theory Y is based on the following assumptions:

1. People do not naturally dislike work. In fact, work is an important part of all of our lives.
2. People will work toward goals to which they are committed.
3. People become committed to goals when it is clear that accomplishing the goals will bring personal rewards.
4. People often seek out and willingly accept responsibility.
5. Employees have the potential to help accomplish organizational goals.
6. Organizations generally do not make full use of their human resources.

Obviously, Theory Y is much more positive than Theory X. McGregor argued that most managers behave in accordance with Theory X, but he maintained that Theory Y is more appropriate and effective as a guide for managerial action (see Table 10-1).

The human relations movement and Theories X and Y increased managers' awareness of the importance of social factors in the workplace during the second half of the 20th century. However, human motivation is a complex and dynamic process to which there is no simple key. It is clear from decades of research that neither money nor social factors alone can provide the answer.

Theory X a concept of employee motivation generally consistent with Taylor's scientific management; assumes that employees dislike work and will function only in a highly controlled work environment

Theory Y a concept of employee motivation generally consistent with the ideas of the human relations movement; assumes responsibility and work toward organizational goals, and by doing so they also achieve personal rewards

TABLE 10-1 Theory X and Theory Y Contrasted

Area	Theory X	Theory Y
Attitude toward work	Dislike	Involvement
Control systems	External	Internal
Supervision	Direct	Indirect
Level of commitment	Low	High
Employee potential	Ignored	Identified
Use of human resources	Limited	Not limited

© CENGAGE LEARNING 2015

Theory Z

William Ouchi, currently a management professor at UCLA, studied business practices in American and Japanese firms as discussed in his book, *Theory Z: How American Management Can Meet the Japanese Challenge*. He concluded that different types of management systems dominate in these two countries. In Japan, Ouchi found what he calls *type J* firms. They are characterized by lifetime employment, collective (or group) decision making, collective responsibility for the outcomes of decisions, slow evaluation and promotion, implied control mechanisms, nonspecialized career paths, and a holistic concern for employees as people.

American industry is dominated by what Ouchi calls *type A* firms, which follow a different pattern. They emphasize short-term employment, individual decision making, individual responsibility for the outcomes of decisions, rapid evaluation and promotion, explicit control mechanisms, specialized career paths, and a segmented concern for employees only as employees.

A few very successful American firms represent a blend of the type J and type A patterns. These firms, called *type Z* organizations, emphasize long-term employment, collective decision making, individual responsibility for the outcomes of decisions, slow evaluation and promotion, informal control along with some formalized measures, moderately specialized career paths, and a holistic concern for employees.

Ouchi's **Theory Z** posits that some middle ground between his type A and type J practices is best for American business (see Figure 10-4). A major part of Theory Z emphasizes on participative decision making. The focus is on "we" rather than on "us versus them." Theory Z employees and managers view the organization as a family. This participative spirit fosters cooperation and encourages the dissemination of information and organizational values.

Reinforcement Theory

Reinforcement theory is based on the premise that people will repeat behavior that is rewarded and will cease behavior that is punished. A *reinforcement* is an action that follows directly from a particular behavior. It may be a pay raise after a particularly large sale to a new customer or a reprimand for coming late to work.

Reinforcements can take a variety of forms and can be used in a number of ways. A *positive reinforcement* is one that strengthens desired behavior by providing

---

Theory Z the belief that some middle ground between type A and type J practices is best for American business

reinforcement theory a theory of motivation based on the premise that rewarded behavior is likely to be repeated, whereas punished behavior is less likely to recur

Concept Check

✓ What are the major elements of Taylor's "scientific management"?

✓ What were Elton Mayo's conclusions from the Hawthorne Studies?

✓ What are the different levels in Maslow's hierarchy of needs?

✓ What are the major elements of Herzberg's motivation–hygiene theory?

✓ What are the underlying assumptions of Theory X and Theory Y?

FIGURE 10-4 The Features of Theory Z

The best aspects of Japanese and American management theories combine to form the nucleus of Theory Z.

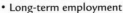

TYPE J FIRMS (Japanese)	TYPE Z FIRMS (Best choice for American firms)	TYPE A FIRMS (American)
• Lifetime employment	• Long-term employment	• Short-term employment
• Collective decision making	• Collective decision making	• Individual decision making
• Collective responsibility	• Individual responsibility	• Individual responsibility
• Slow promotion	• Slow promotion	• Rapid promotion
• Implied control mechanisms	• Informal control	• Explicit control mechanisms
• Nonspecialized career paths	• Moderately specialized career paths	• Specialized career paths
• Holistic concern for employees	• Holistic concern for employees	• Segmented concern for employees

a reward, such as praise or recognition from supervisors for a job done well. A reward increases (strengthens) their willingness to perform well in the future. A *negative reinforcement* strengthens desired behavior by eliminating an undesirable task or situation. Suppose that a machine shop must be cleaned thoroughly every month—a dirty, miserable task. During a month when the workers do a less-than-satisfactory job, the boss requires them to clean the factory themselves, rather than bringing in the usual private maintenance service. The employees will be motivated to work harder the next month to avoid the unpleasant cleanup duty.

Punishment is a consequence of undesirable behavior. Common forms of punishment used in organizations include reprimands, reduced pay, disciplinary layoffs, and termination (firing). Punishment often does more harm than good by creating a negative work environment, fostering worker hostility, and encouraging employees to engage in undesirable behaviors behind the backs of supervisors.

Managers who rely on *extinction* hope to eliminate undesirable behavior by not responding to it with the hope that the behavior will eventually go "extinct." Suppose, for example, that an employee writes memo after memo to his or her manager about insignificant events. If the manager does not respond to any of these memos, the employee probably will stop writing them, and the behavior will stop.

The effectiveness of reinforcement depends on which type is used and how it is timed. Some situations lend themselves to the use of more than one approach. Generally, positive reinforcement is considered the most effective with most employees, and it is recommended when the manager has a choice.

Continual reinforcement can become tedious for both managers and employees, especially when the same behavior is being reinforced over and over again in the same way. At the start, it may be necessary to reinforce a desired behavior every time it occurs. Generally, once a desirable behavior has been more or less established, only occasional reinforcement will be needed.

CONTEMPORARY VIEWS ON MOTIVATION

Maslow's hierarchy of needs and Herzberg's motivation–hygiene theory are popular and widely known theories of motivation. Each takes a broader view than the narrow focus of scientific management and Theories X and Y. However, they do have a weakness: each attempts to specify *what* motivates people, but neither explains *why* or *how* motivation develops or is sustained over time. More recently, managers have explored three other models that take a more dynamic view of motivation. These are equity theory, expectancy theory, and goal-setting theory.

Learning Objective

3 Describe three contemporary views of motivation: equity theory, expectancy theory, and goal-setting theory.

Equity Theory

The **equity theory** of motivation is based on the premise that people are motivated to obtain and preserve equitable treatment for themselves. As used here, *equity* is the distribution of rewards in direct proportion to each employee's contribution to the organization. Everyone need not receive the same rewards, but the rewards should be in accordance with individual contributions.

According to this theory, we conceive of equity in the following way. First, we develop our own input-to-outcome ratio. *Inputs* are the time, effort, skills, education, experience, and so on that we contribute to the organization. *Outcomes* are the rewards we get from the organization, such as pay, benefits, recognition,

equity theory a theory of motivation based on the premise that people are motivated to obtain and preserve equitable treatment for themselves

The Gamification of Motivation

Gamification—adapting elements of video games to challenge and reward employees—is changing the way businesses motivate employees. Target, for example, lets cashiers compete against each other for bragging rights about who delivers the speediest checkout service. Employees at LiveOps, which provides call-center software, earn badges and other intangible rewards playing an ongoing virtual game that encourages friendly competition while sharpening work skills. The game is so popular that 75 percent of LiveOps employees play at least twice a month, and employee performance has improved, as well.

IBM has created a number of games that only employees can play, some directly related to work situations and others indirectly related. In one game, employees try to improve the efficiency of systems that keep a virtual city running. Chuck Hamilton, who leads IBM's virtual learning department, says these games help far-flung employees feel more connected to each other and the company.

The U.K. Department of Work and Pensions has a Web-browser game called Idea Street that rewards employees for submitting and fine-tuning ideas for higher effectiveness and efficiency. Employees earn points when they send in an idea, comment on ideas submitted by others, or sign up to implement someone else's idea. A leader board tracks the highest-ranked players—and the department expects to save $30 million by implementing the top ideas.

Sources: Based on information in Fiona Graham, "What If You Got Paid to Play Games at Work?" *BBC News*, February 28, 2012, http://bbc.co.uk/news/business-17160118; Rachel Emma Silverman, "Latest Game Theory: Mixing Work and Play," *Wall Street Journal*, October 10, 2011, http://online.wsj.com/article/SB10001424052970204294504576615371783795248.html; Kenrick Vezina, "Using Games to Get Employees Thinking," *MIT Technology Review*, August 17, 2011, http://technologyreview.com/business/38191/.

expectancy theory a model of motivation based on the assumption that motivation depends on how much we want something and on how likely we think we are to get it

and promotions. Next, we compare this ratio to what we perceive as the input-to-outcome ratio for some other person. It might be a co-worker, a friend who works for another firm, or even an average of all the people in our organization. This person is called the *comparison other*. Note that the important consideration is that we believe our perception to be correct, whether or not it is.

If the two ratios are roughly the same, we feel that the organization is treating us equitably. In this case, we are motivated to leave things as they are. However, if our ratio is the higher of the two, we feel under-rewarded and are motivated to make changes. We may (1) decrease our own inputs by not working as hard, (2) try to increase our outcome by asking for a raise in pay, (3) try to get the comparison other to increase some inputs or receive decreased outcomes, (4) leave the work situation, or (5) conduct a new comparison with a different comparison other.

Equity theory is most relevant to pay as an outcome. Because pay is a very real measure of a person's worth to an organization, comparisons involving pay are a natural part of organizational life. Managers can try to avoid problems arising from inequity by making sure that rewards are distributed on the basis of performance and that everyone clearly understands the basis for his or her own pay.

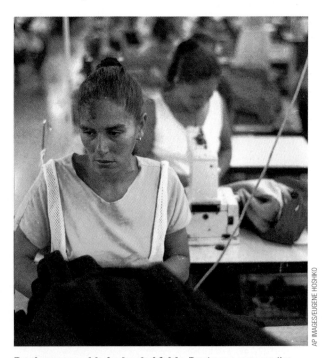

AP IMAGES/EUGENE HOSHIKO

Employees want to be treated fairly. Employees compare the amount of effort they put into their jobs and the outcomes they get to that of their co-workers. This is the idea behind equity theory. At sweatshops such as this one, though, all employees are treated unfairly. Does equity theory come into play in this instance?

Expectancy Theory

Expectancy theory, developed by Victor Vroom, a Canadian business professor, is a very complex model of motivation based on a simple assumption. According to expectancy theory, motivation depends on how much we want something and on how likely we think we are to get it (see Figure 10-5). Consider, for example, the case of three sales representatives who are candidates for promotion to

FIGURE 10-5 Expectancy Theory

Vroom's theory is based on the idea that motivation depends on how much people want something and on how likely they think they are to get it.

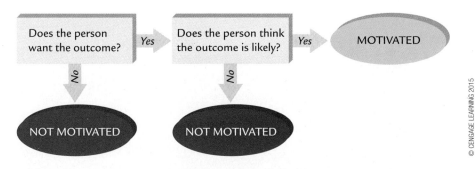

© CENGAGE LEARNING 2015

one sales manager's job. Bill has had a very good sales year and always gets positive performance evaluations. However, he is not sure that he wants the job because it involves travel, long working hours, and stress and pressure. Paul wants the job badly, but does not think he has much chance of getting it. He has had a terrible sales year and gets only mediocre performance evaluations from his present boss. Susan wants the job as much as Paul, and she thinks that she has a pretty good shot. Her sales have improved this past year, and her evaluations are the best in the company.

Expectancy theory would predict that Bill and Paul are not very motivated to seek the promotion. Bill does not really want it, and Paul does not think that he has much of a chance of getting it. Susan, however, is very motivated to seek the promotion because she wants it and thinks that she can get it.

Expectancy theory is complex because each action we take is likely to lead to several outcomes, some of which we want and others we do not. For example, a person who works hard and puts in many extra hours may get a pay raise, be promoted, and gain valuable new job skills. However, that person also may be forced to spend less time with his or her family and to cut back on social activities.

For one person, the promotion may be paramount, the pay raise and new skills fairly important, and the loss of family and social life of negligible importance. For someone else, the family and social life may be most important, the pay raise of moderate importance, the new skills unimportant, and the promotion undesirable because of the additional hours it would require. The first person would be motivated to work hard and put in the extra hours, whereas the second person would not be motivated at all to do so. In other words, it is the bundle of outcomes combined with the individual's perception of each outcome's importance that determines motivation.

Expectancy theory is difficult to apply, but it does provide several useful guidelines for managers. It suggests that managers must recognize that (1) employees work for a variety of reasons, (2) these reasons, or expected outcomes, may change over time, and (3) it is necessary to show employees how they can attain the outcomes they desire.

Goal-Setting Theory

Goal-setting theory states that employees are motivated to achieve goals that they and their managers establish together. The goal should be very specific, moderately difficult, and one that the employee will be committed to achieve.[5] Rewards should be tied directly to goal achievement. Using goal-setting theory, a manager can design rewards that fit employee needs, clarify expectations, maintain equity, and provide reinforcement. For example, a manager might discover that one of her employees is very motivated by the occasional day off. Therefore, the manager and the employee may work out a plan that involves a free day as a reward after he completes a project

goal-setting theory a theory of motivation suggesting that employees are motivated to achieve goals that they and their managers establish together

What do employees want?

That's what their managers need to determine. Different employees are motivated by different rewards. Figuring out which rewards motivate each employee is a key step in goal setting.

© IMAGEGAMI/SHUTTERSTOCK.COM

Concept Check

✓ What is equity theory?

✓ How do managers use it in order to decide the pay structure of employees?

✓ What is expectancy theory and how is it different from goal-setting theory?

Learning Objective

4 **Explain several techniques for increasing employee motivation.**

management by objectives (MBO) a motivation technique in which managers and employees collaborate in setting goals

satisfactorily and ahead of schedule, as long as he is up-to-date in his other work. This theory takes into account the goal the employee has to achieve and the rewards that will accrue if the goal is accomplished.

KEY MOTIVATION TECHNIQUES

Today, it takes more than a generous salary to motivate employees. Increasingly, companies are trying to provide motivation by satisfying employees' less-tangible needs. Businesses may use simple, low- or no-cost, or complex and expensive approaches to motivation. In this section, we discuss several specific techniques that help managers to boost employee motivation and job satisfaction.

Management by Objectives

Management by objectives (MBO) is a motivation technique in which managers and employees collaborate in setting goals. The primary purpose of MBO is to clarify the roles employees are expected to play in reaching the organization's goals.

MBO increases employee motivation by empowering them with an active role in goal-setting and performance evaluation. Most MBO programs consist of a series of five steps. The first step in setting up an MBO program is to secure the acceptance of top management. It is essential that top managers endorse and participate in the program if others in the firm are to accept it. This also provides a natural starting point for educating employees about the purposes and mechanics of MBO.

In the second step, top management and other parties must establish preliminary goals that reflect a firm's mission and strategy. The intent of an MBO program is to have these goals filter down through the organization.

The third step is the heart of MBO. It consists of three smaller steps:

1. The manager explains to each employee that he or she has accepted certain goals for the organization, or a group within the organization, and asks the individual to think about how he or she can help to achieve these goals.
2. The manager later meets with each employee individually. Together they establish individual goals for the employee. Whenever possible, the goals should be measurable and should specify the time frame for completion (usually one year).
3. The manager and the employee decide what resources the employee will need to accomplish his or her goals.

As the fourth step, the manager and employees meet periodically to review each employee's progress. They may agree to modify certain goals during these meetings if circumstances have changed. For example, a sales representative accepted a goal of increasing sales by 20 percent. However, an aggressive competitor has since entered the marketplace, making this goal unattainable. In light of this circumstance, the goal is revised down to 10 or 15 percent.

The fifth step in the MBO process is evaluation. At the end of the designated time period, the manager and each employee meet again to determine which of the individual's goals were met and which were not, and why. The employee's reward (in the form of a pay raise, praise, or promotion) is based primarily on the degree of goal attainment.

As with every other management method, MBO has advantages and disadvantages. MBO can motivate employees by involving them actively in the life of the firm. The collaboration on goal setting and performance appraisal improves communication and makes employees feel that they are an important part of the organization. Periodic progress reviews also enhance quality control within an organization. Shortcomings of MBO are that it must have the support of top management, it can result in a lot of paperwork, and managers may not like to work out goals with subordinates.

Job Enrichment

Job enrichment is a method of motivating employees by providing them with variety in their tasks while giving them some responsibility for, and control over, their jobs. At the same time, employees gain new skills and acquire a broader perspective about how their individual work contributes to the goals of the organization. Earlier in this chapter, we noted that Herzberg's motivation–hygiene theory is one rationale for the use of job enrichment. That is, the added responsibility and control that job enrichment confers on employees increases their satisfaction and motivation. For example, engineers at Google get to spend 20 percent of their time at work on projects of their choosing.[6] This type of enrichment can motivate employees and result in benefits for the company. At times, **job enlargement**, expanding a worker's assignments to include additional but similar tasks, can lead to job enrichment. Job enlargement might mean that a worker on an assembly line who used to connect three wires to components moving down the line now connects five wires. Unfortunately, the added tasks often are just as routine as those the worker performed before the change and may not be an effective motivator over the long term.

Whereas job enlargement does not really change the routine and monotonous nature of jobs, job enrichment does. Job enrichment results in increased sense of employee responsibility, increased control over how the job is performed, and new tasks. Job enrichment gives workers more authority and assigns tasks in complete, natural units (rather than breaking it down into the smallest possible task). Employees frequently are given fresh and challenging job assignments. By blending more planning and decision making into jobs, enrichment gives work more depth and complexity.

Job redesign is a type of job enrichment in which work is restructured in ways that cultivate the worker–job match. Job redesign can be achieved by combining tasks, forming work groups, or establishing closer customer relationships. Employees often are more motivated when

job enrichment a motivation technique that provides employees with more variety and responsibility in their jobs

job enlargement expanding a worker's assignments to include additional but similar tasks

job redesign a type of job enrichment in which work is restructured to cultivate the worker–job match

Job enlargement versus job enrichment. It's no secret. Doing the same task over and over at your job is boring. Being able to do a variety of tasks helps. Having more responsibility over how you do your job is even better.

jobs are combined because the increased variety of tasks presents a more rewarding challenge. Depending on the form it takes, job redesign can give employees a stronger sense of belonging to a team, a clearer image of how their work contributes to the organization as a whole, and a more personal investment in the satisfaction of clients. Furthermore, a job redesign that carefully matches worker to job can prevent stress-related injuries. Employees may play an active role in redesigning their jobs to their liking. If an employee recognizes an opportunity at work to rework his or her job in such a way as to improve efficiency or productivity, he or she may want to approach a superior with the idea. Redesigning a position based around organizational needs may help improve employee satisfaction and reduce employee turnover—all while improving efficiency at the firm.[7]

Job enrichment works best with employees who want more challenging work. Employees must desire personal growth and have the skills and knowledge to perform more complex tasks. Lack of self-confidence, fear of failure, and distrust of management's intentions are likely to lead to ineffective performance on enriched jobs. Some workers prefer routine jobs because they find them satisfying. Job enrichment would not be appealing for these individuals. Companies that use job enrichment as an alternative to specialization also face extra expenses, such as the cost of retraining.

Behavior Modification

behavior modification a systematic program of reinforcement to encourage desirable behavior

Behavior modification is a systematic program of reinforcement to encourage desirable behavior. Behavior modification involves both rewards to encourage desirable actions and punishments to discourage undesirable actions. Rewards, such as compliments and expressions of appreciation, tend to be much more effective behavior modifiers than punishments, such as reprimands and scorn.

When applied to management, behavior modification strives to encourage desirable organizational behavior. This technique begins with identifying and measuring a *target behavior*—the behavior that is to be changed (e.g., low production levels or a high rate of absenteeism). Next, managers provide positive reinforcement in the form of a reward when employees exhibit the *desired behavior* (e.g., increased production or less absenteeism). The reward might be praise or a more tangible form of recognition, such as a gift, meal, or trip. For example, Apple offers Corporate Gifts and Rewards Program to give companies the ability to reward their staff or very loyal customers with iPods, iPhones, iPads, Mac computers, or iTunes gift cards. Finally, the levels of the target behavior are measured again to determine whether the desired changes have been achieved. If the target behavior has not changed significantly in the desired direction, the reward system must be changed to one that is likely to be more effective. The key is to devise effective rewards that will not only modify employees' behavior in desired ways, but also motivate them. To this end, experts suggest that management should reward quality, loyalty, and productivity.

Flextime

flextime a system in which employees set their own work hours within employer-determined limits

Flextime is a system in which employees set their own work hours within certain limits determined by employers. Typically, the firm establishes two bands of time: the *core time*, when all employees must be at work, and the *flexible time*, when employees may choose whether to be at work. The only condition is that every employee must work a total of eight hours each day. For example, the hours between 9 and 11 a.m. and 1 and 3 p.m. might be core times, and the hours between 6 and 9 a.m., 11 a.m. and 1 p.m., and 3 and 6 p.m. might be flexible times. This would give employees the option of coming in early and getting off early, coming in later and leaving later, or taking a long lunch break. But flextime also ensures that everyone is present at certain times, when conferences with supervisors and department meetings can be scheduled. Another type of flextime allows employees to work a 40-hour work week in four days instead of five. Offering flextime can be a low-cost way for a firm to show an employee that it cares about his or her well-being through offering a better work–life balance.[8]

The needs and lifestyles of today's workforce are changing. Dual-income families make up a much larger share of the workforce than ever before, and women are one of its fastest-growing sectors. A growing number of employees are responsible for the care of elderly relatives. Recognizing that these changes increase the demand for family time during the normal work day, many employers are offering flexible work schedules to help employees to manage their time better and increase employee motivation and job satisfaction. However, two common problems associated with using flextime are (1) supervisors sometimes find their jobs complicated by having employees who come and go at different times and (2) employees without flextime sometimes resent co-workers who have it.

However, while most people still work standard 40-hour weeks, flexible schedules are becoming much more common and easier to manage as improvements in technology allow people to stay connected, no matter where they are or what time it is. Medical and health, education and training, administrative jobs, and accounting are all likely to offer flexible schedule options. For example, the accounting firm Ernst & Young, offers flextime as a reward for working in an intense industry that requires long hours during busy times. In order to offset the 60- or 70-hour workweeks during tax season, it allows their employees to work three-day weeks or take extended breaks during the summer. Its flexible work policies have landed Ernst & Young on *Working Mother* magazine's "100 Best Companies" list for 16 years in a row.[9] Flex policies like this help to reduce employee burnout and keep turnover low in what can be a stressful industry.

Part-Time Work and Job Sharing

Part-time work is permanent employment in which individuals work less than a standard work week. The specific number of hours worked varies, but part-time jobs are structured so that all responsibilities can be completed in the number of hours an employee works. Part-time work is of special interest to parents who want more time with their children. While some firms are famous for offering part-time workers benefits, such as Starbucks, REI, and Barnes & Noble, most do not offer this perk. In fact, more companies are switching to part-time workers in order to cut back on the rising cost of offering benefits. Some companies even use high-tech software that models demand so that employers can predict exactly how many workers are needed at any given time, further reducing the length of shifts and numbers of workers needed.[10]

part-time work permanent employment in which individuals work less than a standard work week

job sharing an arrangement whereby two people share one full-time position

Job sharing (sometimes referred to as *work sharing*) is an arrangement whereby two people share one full-time position. One job sharer may work from 8 a.m. to noon, and the other from 1 to 5 p.m., or they may alternate workdays. Job sharing is different than part-time work because two people share one single position, which is generally more skilled than a part-time position would be. Job sharing can be difficult to orchestrate at the beginning, but may contribute to greater job satisfaction and ease in creating work–life balance. Job sharing can actually lead people to be more productive, as they know that their time at work is limited and that someone else is directly depending on the quality of their work. This arrangement may be especially appealing to parents who wish to maintain a professional position while also making time for children.[11] Job sharing combines the security of a full-time position with the flexibility of a part-time one. For firms, job sharing provides a unique

AP IMAGES/DAMIAN DOVARGANES

Part-time pay, full-time benefits. Many employees want to work part-time but can't afford not to have benefits such as health insurance. Companies known for hiring part-time employees with full benefits include UPS, REI, Land's End, Starbucks, and Barnes & Noble.

Sustain the Planet

Cash for Conservation?

Is money a motivator? If you work at Genentech, you might just be able to earn cash rewards for "going green." In an effort to help preserve the environment, Genentech's employee commuter program helps its employees save time and money by sharing rides to work and using carpool lanes while they earn cash rewards. The program pays employees $4 per day for not driving to work alone or $4 per passenger per day for the drivers of carpools and vanpools. The company also offers free bus service, pre-tax transportation payroll deductions, and a company subsidy for commuting expenses, all designed to help employees avoid stress and traffic and protect the environment.

www.gene.com/gene/careers/gride.html

telecommuting working at home all the time or for a portion of the work week

empowerment making employees more involved in their jobs by increasing their participation in decision making

opportunity to attract highly skilled employees who are not available on a full-time basis. In addition, companies can save on benefits expenses and avoid the disruptions of employee turnover. For employees, opting for the flexibility of job sharing may mean giving up some of the benefits, such as health insurance, received for full-time work. Job sharing is difficult if tasks are not easily divisible or if two people do not work or communicate well with one another.

Telecommuting

A growing number of companies allow **telecommuting**, working at home all the time or for a portion of the work week. Technology such as e-mail, cloud computing, smart phones, laptops, tablets, video conferencing, and overnight couriers all make working at home easier and more convenient than ever before. Working at home means that individuals can set their own hours and have more time with their families. A Cisco study reports that a full 45 percent of the U.S. workforce has a position that is suitable for telecommuting at least part of the time. A survey by the software company Wrike reveals that 83 percent of workers do some work from home each day.[12]

A growing body of research indicates that telecommuters are actually more effective than their in-office counterparts. This is because remote workers feel pressured to counter any perception that they do not work as hard. Remote workers try harder to connect, use technological tools more effectively, and use time more efficiently.[13]

In addition to increased productivity, companies that allow occasional telecommuting have lower real estate and travel expenses, improved morale, and the flexibility to access larger labor pools. Telecommuting also reduces fossil fuel emissions from putting fewer cars on the road. By having fewer employees commuting to work, the Reason Public Policy Institute estimates that approximately 350 lives are saved per year. Of all the companies that give employees the option to telecommute or work from home, Cisco is ranked number one with 90 percent of its employees classified as "regular" telecommuters.[14]

Among the disadvantages of telecommuting are feelings of isolation, putting in long hours, and being distracted by family or household responsibilities. The stigma also remains, in spite of evidence to the contrary, that telecommuters are less productive than office-based staff. In addition, some supervisors have difficulty monitoring productivity of remote workers.

Employee Empowerment

Many companies are increasing employee motivation and satisfaction through the use of empowerment. **Empowerment** means making employees more involved in their jobs and in the operations of the organization by increasing their participation in decision making. With empowerment, control no longer flows exclusively from the top level of the organization downward. Empowered employees have a voice in what they do and how and when they do it. In some organizations, employees' input is restricted to individual choices, such as when to take breaks. In other companies, their responsibilities may encompass more far-reaching issues. Successful companies treat their employees like assets, empowering them to fully utilize their talents and shift responsibilities with the firm's needs. Technology clearly plays a role in empowering employees, but does so creating an open and safe workplace

Office space—at home. Many companies are finding it cost-effective to allow employees to work at home. Working at home means that Nancy Allor can spend more time with her daughter Carrie. Telecommuting arrangements such as this can be a win-win situation for both employees and their firms.

where employees feel like they can speak up and are heard. Allowing employees access to information, such as reports, performance data, and communications, can empower them and make them feel more satisfied with their jobs.

For empowerment to work effectively, management must be involved. Managers should set expectations, communicate standards, institute periodic evaluations, and guarantee follow-up. If effectively implemented, empowerment can lead to increased job satisfaction, improved job performance, higher self-esteem, and increased organizational commitment. Obstacles to empowerment include resistance on the part of management, distrust of management on the part of workers, inadequate training of employees, and poor communication between levels of the organization.

Employee Ownership

Some organizations have discovered that an effective technique for motivating employees is **employee ownership**—that is, employees own the company they work for by virtue of being stockholders. Employee-owned businesses directly reward employees for success. When the company enjoys increased sales or lower costs, employees benefit directly. The National Center for Employee Ownership, an organization that studies employee-owned American businesses, reports that employee stock ownership plans (ESOPs) provide considerable employee incentive and increase employee involvement and commitment. In the United States today, an estimated 10.3 million employees participate in 10,900 ESOPs and stock bonus plans.[15]

As a means to motivate executives and managers to feel invested in the company as they work long days, some firms provide stock options as part of the employee compensation package. An option is simply the right to buy shares of the firm within a prescribed time at a set price. If the firm does well and its stock price rises past the set price (presumably because of all the work being done by the employee), the employee can exercise the option and sell the stock to cash in on the company's success. However, not all companies choose to engage in ESOPs because they can be complex and expensive for the firm. This is particularly true of smaller organizations that may not have the means to manage such a program.

employee ownership a situation in which employees own the company they work for by virtue of being stockholders

Concept Check

✓ What are the five steps of most MBO programs?

✓ How can companies use job enrichment as a method for motivating employees?

✓ What is behavior modification and how is it used in organizations?

✓ What benefits does a company receive when using flextime, job sharing, and telecommuting?

✓ How do employee ownership and employee empowerment help in increasing employee motivation and satisfaction?

TEAMS AND TEAMWORK

The concepts of teams and teamwork may be most commonly associated with sports, but they are also integral parts of business organizations. This organizational structure is popular because it encourages employees to participate more fully in business decisions. The growing number of companies organizing their workforces into teams reflects an effort to increase employee productivity and creativity because team members are working on specific goals and are given greater autonomy. This leads to greater job satisfaction as employees feel more involved in the management process.[16]

What Is a Team?

team two or more workers operating as a coordinated unit to accomplish a specific task or goal

In a business organization, a **team** is two or more workers operating as a coordinated unit to accomplish a specific task or goal.[17] A team may be assigned any number of tasks or goals, from development of a new product to selling that product. A team can also be created to identify or solve a problem that an organization is experiencing. Teamwork may seem like a simple concept, but teams are a microcosm of the organization and any complications in the work environment will affect the team. It is important to take into account the different work and communication styles and personalities of team members in order to create a productive team.[18]

Types of Teams

problem-solving team a team of knowledgeable employees brought together to tackle a specific problem

self-managed teams groups of employees with the authority and skills to manage themselves

cross-functional team a team of individuals with varying specialties, expertise, and skills that are brought together to achieve a common task

Businesses may have several types of teams to achieve different purposes, including problem-solving teams, self-managed teams, cross-functional teams, and virtual teams.

PROBLEM-SOLVING TEAMS The most common type of team in business organizations is the **problem-solving team**. It is generally used temporarily in order to bring knowledgeable employees together to tackle a specific problem. Once the problem is solved, the team typically is disbanded.

SELF-MANAGED WORK TEAMS **Self-managed teams** are groups of employees with the authority and skills to manage themselves. Experts suggest that workers on self-managed teams are more motivated and satisfied because they have greater task variety and job control. On many work teams, members are cross-trained to perform everyone else's jobs and rotate through all the jobs for which the team is responsible. In a traditional business structure, management is responsible for hiring and firing employees, establishing budgets, purchasing supplies, conducting performance reviews, and taking corrective action. When self-managed teams are in place, they take over some or all of these management functions. The major advantages and disadvantages of self-managed teams are mentioned in Figure 10-6.

CROSS-FUNCTIONAL TEAMS Traditionally, businesses have organized employees into departments based on a common function or specialty. However, increasingly, business organizations are faced with projects that require a diversity of skills from multiple departments. A **cross-functional team** consists of individuals with varying specialties, expertise, and skills that are brought together to achieve a common task.

© CARLOSSELLER/SHUTTERSTOCK.COM

Using technology to close time and space and get more done. Skype, e-mail, and other electronic methods are allowing employees continents away from one another to work together effectively. Being able to hire the best employees from all around the globe to work virtually with one another can give a firm a competitive advantage. Virtual teams located in different time zones and on different continents can also enable a company to work on important projects 24-7.

FIGURE 10-6 Advantages and Disadvantages of Self-Managed Teams

While self-managed teams provide advantages, managers must recognize their disadvantages.

ADVANTAGES	DISADVANTAGES
• Boosts employee morale	• Additional training costs
• Increases productivity	• Teams may be disorganized
• Aids innovation	• Conflicts may arise
• Reduces employee boredom	• Leadership role may be unclear

© CENGAGE LEARNING 2015

For example, a purchasing agent might create a cross-functional team to gain insight into useful purchases for the company. This structure avoids departmental separation and allows greater efficiency when there is a single goal. Although cross-functional teams are not necessarily self-managed, most self-managed teams are cross-functional. Cross-functional teams can also be cross-divisional. Ideally, a cross-functional team consists of a group of people with complementary skill sets and perspectives to enable the group to solve problems effectively and efficiently. The Internet and digital tools have helped strengthen the communication abilities of cross-functional teams. Increasingly, the ability to work in cross-functional teams is an important skill as the world becomes more interconnected and businesses must adapt quickly to change.

VIRTUAL TEAMS Teams do not even have to be geographically close, thanks to sophisticated communications technology. A **virtual team** consists of members who are geographically dispersed but communicate electronically. In fact, team members may never meet in person but rely solely on e-mail, teleconferences, faxes, voice mail, and other technological interactions. In the global business environment, virtual teams connect employees located anywhere in the world on a common task. However, distance and the lack of face-to-face interactions can make working on virtual teams difficult. Clear communication is very important, especially among team members who have never met in person. E-mail communications, for example, are easily misinterpreted. Team members must be aware of and employ individuals' preferred communication strategies to ensure that virtual teams are productive.[19]

virtual team a team consisting of members who are geographically dispersed but communicate electronically

Go team, go! More companies today are using team-building exercises to help their employees figure out how to work better with one another. Sprint uses team-building exercises, such as whitewater rafting, for this purpose as well as to raise money for charities.

© AMMIT/SHUTTERSTOCK.COM

FIGURE 10-7 Stages of Team Development

Developing and Using Effective Teams

It takes time for team members to establish individual roles, relationships, and duties in order to become an effective team. As a team matures, it passes through five stages of development, as shown in Figure 10-7.

When attempting to develop teams, managers must understand that multiple stages are generally required.

FORMING The team is new. Members get to know each other.

STORMING The team may be volatile. Goals and objectives are developed.

NORMING The team stabilizes. Roles and duties are accepted and recognized.

PERFORMING The team is dynamic. Everyone makes a focused effort to accomplish goals.

ADJOURNING The team is finished. The goals have been accomplished and the team is disbanded.

FORMING In the first stage, *forming*, team members are introduced to one another and begin to develop a social dynamic. The members of the team are unsure about how to relate to one another, what behaviors are acceptable, and what the ground rules are for the team. Through group member interaction over time, team members become more comfortable and a group dynamic emerges.

STORMING During the storming stage, the interaction may be volatile and the team may lack unity. This is the stage at which goals and objectives begin to develop. Team members will brainstorm to develop ideas and plans and establish a broad-ranging agenda. It is important for team members to grow comfortable with each other so that they can contribute openly. It is unlikely that a team leader has come forth by this stage, although an informal leader may emerge. The success or failure of the ideas in the storming stage determines how long the team will take to reach the next stage.

NORMING After storming and the first burst of activity, the team begins to stabilize during the *norming* stage. Each person's role within the group begins to solidify, and members recognize the roles of others. A sense of unity grows during this stage. If it has not occurred already, an identified leader will emerge. The group may remain somewhat in flux during norming, and may even regress back to the storming stage if any conflict, especially over the leadership role, occurs.

PERFORMING The fourth stage, *performing*, is when the team achieves its full potential, finally focusing on the assigned task. This stage may take a long time to develop, as team development issues can be complicated. The members of the team finally work in harmony under the established roles to accomplish the necessary goals.

ADJOURNING In the final stage, *adjourning*, the team is disbanded because the project is complete. Team members may be reassigned to other teams or tasks. This stage will not occur if the team is placed together for a task with no specific date of completion. For example, a marketing team may continue to develop promotional efforts for a store even after a specific promotional task has been accomplished.

Roles Within a Team

Within any team, each member has a role to play in helping the team attain its objectives. Each of these roles adds important dimensions to team member interactions. The group member who pushes the team toward achieving goals and objectives plays the *task-specialist role* by concentrating fully on the assigned task. In a cross-functional team, this might be the person with the most expertise relating to the current task. The *socioemotional* role is played by the individual who supports and encourages the emotional needs of the other members, placing the team members' personal needs above the task at hand. Although this may sound like an unimportant role, the socioemotional member's dedication to team cohesiveness leads to greater unity and higher productivity. Some team members play a *dual role*, which is a combination of the socioemotional and task-specialist roles. The team leader might not always play this dual role, but the team is likely to be most successful when he or she does. Sometimes an individual assumes the *nonparticipant role*. This role behavior is characterized by a person who does not contribute to accomplishing the task and does not provide favorable input with respect to team members' socioemotional needs. He or she is obviously not a desirable team member to have.

Team Cohesiveness

Developing a unit from a diverse group of personalities, specialties, backgrounds, and work styles can be challenging and complicated. In a cohesive team, the members get along and are able to accomplish their tasks effectively. Team cohesiveness is affected by different factors, internal and external to the team. To assure cohesiveness, the ideal team size is generally 5 to 12. Anything larger and relationship development becomes too complicated. Anything smaller and the group may be excessively burdened and tasks may not get completed. Jeff Bezos, CEO of Amazon, famously believes that the team is too large if it takes more than two small pizzas to feed them.[20] One of the most reliable ways to build cohesiveness within a team is through competition with other teams. When two teams are competing for a single prize or recognition, they are forced to become more goal-oriented and to put aside conflict. A favorable appraisal from an outsider may strengthen team cohesiveness. Because the team is being praised as a group, team members recognize their contribution as a unit. Teams are also more successful when goals have been agreed upon beforehand. A team that is clear about its objective will be able to focus on accomplishing it. Frequent interaction also builds team cohesiveness through increasing familiarity.

Personal Apps

Is your team virtual?

The prevalence of technology in all of our lives has helped to make the world a smaller place. Friends, family, and co-workers are never more than a text message, e-mail, or Skype conversation away. Virtual teams also rely on these and other technologies to stay in touch.

Team Conflict and How to Resolve It

Conflict occurs when a disagreement arises between two or more team members. Conflict traditionally has been viewed as negative, but it is unavoidable. If handled properly conflict can improve a team. For example, if two team members disagree about a proposition, both will spend extra time analyzing the situation closely to determine the best decision. As long as conflict is handled in a respectful and professional manner, it can improve the quality of work produced. However, if conflict turns hostile and affects the work environment, then steps must be taken to arrive at a compromise. Compromises can be difficult because neither party ends up getting everything he or she wants. The best solution is a middle-ground alternative in which each party is satisfied to some degree. Conflict must be acknowledged before it can be dealt with or used in a constructive manner. Ignoring conflict may cause it to simmer or grow, disrupting team progress.

Benefits and Limitations of Teams

Teamwork can be key to reducing turnover and costs and increasing productivity, customer service, and product quality. There is also evidence that working in teams leads to higher levels of job satisfaction among employees and a harmonious work environment. Thus, an increasingly large number of companies use teams as a valuable element of their organizational structures. However, the process of organizing teams can be stressful and time consuming, and there is no guarantee that the team will develop effectively. If a team lacks cohesiveness and is unable to resolve conflict, the company may experience lower productivity.

Concept Check

✓ What are the major types of teams?

✓ Highlight some differences between cross-functional teams and virtual teams.

✓ Identify and describe the stages of team development.

✓ How can team conflict be reduced?

✓ What are some of the benefits and limitations of a team?

Summary

1 Explain what motivation is.

Motivation is the individual internal process that energizes, directs, and sustains behavior. Motivation is affected by employee morale—that is, the employee's feelings about the job, superiors, and the firm itself. Motivation, morale, and job satisfaction are closely related.

2 Understand some major historical perspectives on motivation.

One of the first approaches to employee motivation was Frederick Taylor's scientific management, the application of scientific principles to the management of work and workers. Taylor believed that employees work only for money and that they must be closely supervised. This thinking led to the piece-rate system, under which employees are paid a certain amount for each unit they produce.

The Hawthorne Studies attempted to determine the effects of the work environment on productivity. Results of these studies indicated that human factors affect productivity more than physical aspects of the workplace do.

Maslow's hierarchy of needs suggests that people are motivated by five sets of needs. In ascending order of complexity, these motivators are physiological, safety, social, esteem, and self-actualization needs. People are motivated by the most basic set of needs that remains unfulfilled. As needs at one level are satisfied, people try to satisfy needs at the next level.

Frederick Herzberg found that job satisfaction and dissatisfaction are influenced by two distinct sets of factors. Motivation factors, including recognition and responsibility, affect an employee's degree of satisfaction, but their absence does not necessarily cause dissatisfaction. Hygiene factors, including pay and working conditions, affect an employee's degree of dissatisfaction but do not affect satisfaction.

Theory X is a concept of motivation that assumes that employees dislike work and will function effectively only in a highly controlled environment. Thus, to achieve an organization's goals, managers must coerce, control, and threaten employees. This theory generally is consistent with Taylor's ideas of scientific management. Theory Y is more in keeping with the results of the Hawthorne Studies and the human relations movement. It suggests that employees can be motivated to behave as responsible members of the organization.

Theory Z emphasizes long-term employment, collective decision making, individual responsibility for the outcomes of decisions, informal control, and a holistic concern for employees.

Reinforcement theory is based on the idea that people will repeat behavior that is rewarded and will avoid behavior that is punished.

3 Describe three contemporary views of motivation: equity theory, expectancy theory, and goal-setting theory.

Equity theory maintains that people are motivated to obtain and preserve equitable treatment for themselves. Expectancy theory suggests that our motivation depends on how much we want something and how likely we think we are to get it. Goal-setting theory suggests that employees are motivated to achieve a goal that they and their managers establish together.

4 Explain several techniques for increasing employee motivation.

Management by objectives (MBO) is a motivation technique in which managers and employees collaborate in setting goals. MBO motivates employees by involving them directly in their jobs and in the organization as a whole. Job enrichment seeks to motivate employees by varying their tasks and giving them more responsibility for and control over their jobs. Job enlargement, expanding a worker's assignments to include additional tasks, is one aspect of job enrichment. Job redesign is a type of job enrichment in which work is restructured to improve the worker–job match.

Behavior modification uses reinforcement to encourage desirable behavior. Rewards for productivity, quality, and loyalty change employees' behavior in desirable ways and increase motivation.

Allowing employees to work flexible hours is another way to build motivation and job satisfaction. Flextime is a system of work scheduling that allows workers to set their own schedules, as long as they fall within the limits established by employers. Part-time work is permanent employment in which individuals work less than a standard work week. Job sharing is an arrangement whereby two people share one full-time position. Telecommuting allows employees to work at home for all or part of the work week. All of these work arrangements give employees more time outside the workplace to deal with family responsibilities or to enjoy free time.

Employee empowerment, self-managed work teams, and employee ownership are also techniques that boost employee motivation. Empowerment increases employees' involvement in their jobs by increasing their decision-making authority. Self-managed work teams are groups of employees with the authority and skills to manage themselves. When employees participate in ownership programs, such as employee stock ownership plans (ESOPs), they have more incentive to make the company succeed and therefore work more effectively.

5 Understand the types, development, and uses of teams.

A large number of companies use teams to increase their employees' productivity. In a business organization, a team is a group of workers functioning together as a unit to complete a common goal or purpose.

There are several types of teams that function in specific ways to achieve different purposes. A problem-solving team is a team of knowledgeable employees brought together to tackle a specific problem. Self-managed work teams involve groups of employees with the authority and skills to manage themselves. A cross-functional team is a team of individuals with varying specialties, expertise, and skills. A virtual team is a team consisting of members who are geographically dispersed and communicate electronically.

The five stages of team development are forming, storming, norming, performing, and adjourning. As a team develops, it becomes more productive and unified in order to achieve its assigned objective and goals. The four roles within teams are task specialist, socio-emotional, dual, and nonparticipative. Each of these roles plays a specific part in the team's interaction. For a team to be successful, members must learn how to resolve and manage conflict so that the team can work cohesively to accomplish goals.

Key Terms

You should now be able to define and give an example relevant to each of the following terms:

motivation (267)
morale (268)
scientific management (268)
piece-rate system (269)
need (270)
Maslow's hierarchy of needs (270)
physiological needs (270)
safety needs (270)
social needs (271)

esteem needs (271)
self-actualization needs (271)
motivation–hygiene theory (271)
motivation factors (272)
hygiene factors (272)
Theory X (273)
Theory Y (273)
Theory Z (274)
reinforcement theory (274)

equity theory (275)
expectancy theory (276)
goal-setting theory (277)
management by objectives (MBO) (278)
job enrichment (279)
job enlargement (279)
job redesign (279)
behavior modification (280)
flextime (280)

part-time work (281)
job sharing (281)
telecommuting (282)
empowerment (282)
employee ownership (283)
team (284)
problem-solving team (284)
self-managed teams (284)
cross-functional team (284)
virtual team (285)

Discussion Questions

1. How did the results of the Hawthorne Studies influence researchers' thinking about employee motivation?
2. What are the five levels of needs in Maslow's hierarchy? How are a person's needs related to motivation?
3. What are the two dimensions in Herzberg's theory? What kinds of elements affect each dimension?
4. According to equity theory, how does an employee determine whether he or she is being treated equitably?
5. According to expectancy theory, what two variables determine motivation?
6. Describe the steps involved in the MBO process.

7. What are the objectives of the MBO? What do you think might be its disadvantage?
8. How does employee participation increase motivation?
9. Identify and describe the major types of teams.
10. What are the major benefits and limitations associated with the use of self-managed teams?
11. Explain the major stages of team development.
12. What combination of motivational techniques do you think would result in the best overall motivation and reward system?
13. In what ways are team cohesiveness and team conflict related?

Test Yourself

Matching Questions

1. _____ A force that causes people to behave in a particular way

2. _____ Based on an assumption that people dislike work.

3. _____ Employees believe they will receive the rewards.

4. _____ When not provided, they become dissatisfiers.

5. _____ Needs that can be met by health care benefits.

6. _____ Promotions and rewards can fulfill these needs.

7. _____ Behavior that is rewarded is likely to be repeated.

8. _____ Employees become more involved in the decision-making process.

9. _____ Employees are given more variety and responsibility in their jobs.

10. _____ Groups that have more task variety and greater job control.

    a. virtual team
    b. empowerment
    c. esteem needs
    d. expectancy theory
    e. hygiene factors
    f. job enrichment
    g. motivation
    h. reinforcement theory
    i. self-managed teams
    j. safety needs
    k. Theory X
    l. morale

True False Questions

11. **T   F** Giving employee recognition builds employee morale.

12. **T   F** Frederick W. Taylor made his most significant contribution to management practice by his involvement with the Hawthorne Studies.

13. **T   F** The Hawthorne Studies concluded that human factors were responsible for the outcomes of the experiments.

14. **T   F** Maslow's higher-level needs are the easiest to satisfy.

15. **T   F** Self-actualization needs are the most basic needs that Maslow discovered.

16. **T   F** Herzberg's theory suggests that pay is a strong motivator.

17. **T   F** Theory X is a set of assumptions that are consistent with the human relations movement.

18. **T   F** According to the expectancy theory, motivation depends on how much we want something and how likely we think we are to get it.

19. **T   F** MBO is an inflexible system that requires all goals to be met; if not, the employee is fired.

20. **T   F** A systematic program of reinforcement that encourages desirable behavior is called behavior modification.

Multiple-Choice Questions

21. _____ If Delta Airlines ticket agents discovered that they were being paid a lot less per ticket sold than United Airlines ticket agents, we might expect the Delta ticket agents to _____
    a. increase their sales so that they will make as much as their United peers.
    b. think their outcome-to-input ratios are lower than those of the United ticket agents.
    c. have as a group very different personal needs than United ticket agents.
    d. be very satisfied because they work for a great airline.
    e. feel that rewards are being distributed fairly and equitably.

22. _____ Randi Wood wants to become the best manager in the firm. She takes every available opportunity to learn new skills and improve her knowledge about management. Which need is Randi attempting to satisfy?
    a. Social
    b. Esteem
    c. Self-actualization
    d. Physiological
    e. Safety

23. _____ The idea that satisfaction and dissatisfaction are separate and distinct dimensions comes from which of the following theories?
    a. Frederick Herzberg's motivation–hygiene theory
    b. Maslow's hierarchy of needs
    c. Frederick Taylor's scientific management
    d. Reinforcement theory
    e. Hawthorne Studies

24. _____ Herzberg cited _____ as a cause of dissatisfaction.
    a. working conditions
    b. promotions
    c. pay for special projects
    d. rewards
    e. challenging work

25. _____ According to Theory Y, which type of behavior would a supervisor expect from an employee?
   a. Delegate most of the work to others
   b. Avoid working too hard
   c. Spend time discussing job security
   d. Ask to leave early several times a month
   e. Seek opportunities to learn new skills

26. _____ Developing an input-to-output ratio is the basis of the _____ theory.
   a. equity
   b. expectancy
   c. reward
   d. reinforcement
   e. quality circle

27. _____ Expectancy theory is difficult to apply, but it does provide several useful guidelines for managers. One such outcome that managers must realize is that _____
   a. everyone expects the same things.
   b. employees expect to be financially rewarded for hard work.
   c. employees work for a variety of reasons.
   d. most employees tend to be unreasonable in their expectations.
   e. managers need to use the authoritarian style to get tasks accomplished.

28. _____ Which of the following is a motivation technique that provides employees with more variety and responsibility in their jobs?
   a. Job rotation
   b. Job enrichment
   c. Job redesign
   d. Job enlargement
   e. Job analysis

29. _____ What stage of a team is usually slow to develop and occurs when the team begins to focus strongly on the assigned task and away from team-development issues?
   a. Norming
   b. Storming
   c. Performing
   d. Adjourning
   e. Unifying

30. _____ The group member who pushes forward toward goals and places the objective first is playing the

   _____
   a. task-specialist role.
   b. socioemotional role.
   c. nonparticipant role.
   d. dual role.
   e. aggressor role.

Answers to the Test Yourself questions appear at the end of the book on page TY-2.

Video Case
Putting the Focus on People at the Fruit Guys

People are as important as profits to Chris Mittelstaedt, founder and CEO of the Fruit Guys (http://fruitguys.com). Remembering the downside of some earlier on-the-job experiences, such as not being asked to help solve problems, Mittelstaedt resolved to make employee empowerment and collaborative teamwork top priorities when he started his own business. Today, his Fruit Guys business rings up $10 million in annual sales and employs dozens of people in the San Francisco area and beyond.

Mittelstaedt's path to entrepreneurial success grew out of a need to make a change in his professional life when his wife was expecting their first child. He was unhappy at a temporary job and thinking about possible ideas for a new business of his own. In speaking with friends and family, Mittelstaedt realized that many office workers who snack on junk food might prefer something healthier if it was conveniently at hand. This led to the concept of selling weekly deliveries of fresh, ripe fruit to companies so their employees would have healthy snacks at work. Mittelstaedt named his new company the Fruit Guys and began making the rounds of corporate headquarters to sign up customers. He also

connected with local growers who could provide a steady supply of apples, oranges, and other fruits in season.

As the business grew, Mittelstaedt had to hire employees to sort, package, and deliver fruits to his expanding customer base, as well as hiring employees to handle billing, human resources, and other functions. This is where his background working for other firms came into play: As the head of a small business, he wanted to motivate his employees the way he wished his managers had motivated him, by treating them fairly, showing respect for their capabilities as individuals and team members, and inviting their input as valued members of the organization. "People like to be part of something bigger than themselves," he says. The same is true for suppliers, which is why he pays growers fair prices and offers support to help them profit from what they produce.

Although the company has had its ups and downs over the years, Mittelstaedt has remained true to his principles of building positive relationships with customers, employees, and suppliers. Rather than setting one employee against each other in a race for advancement, the entrepreneur looks for win-win ways to develop the talents of everyone on the team.

He emphasizes each employee's vital role in the company's overall success, expecting them to reach out to colleagues for coordination purposes as well as to take responsibility for completing their assigned tasks. Recognizing that employees have their own goals and dreams, Mittelstaedt encourages everyone to make the most of opportunities for participation, learning, communication, and expanded responsibilities at the Fruit Guys.

These days, Mittelstaedt's company has a healthy roster of regular customers that includes high-tech firms, law firms, accounting firms, manufacturers, and even public schools. But no matter how big the Fruit Guys gets, the founder is determined to maintain the healthy corporate culture that shows respect for the individual, fosters involvement, and fuels committed teamwork.[21]

Questions

1. When Chris Mittelstaedt says, "People like to be part of something bigger than themselves," what are the implications for employee motivation?
2. Why would an accounting firm spend money week after week for deliveries of fresh fruit for its employees? Explain your answer in terms of the motivation concepts in this chapter.
3. What other techniques would you suggest Mittelstaedt use to motivate his employees, and why?

Building Skills for Career Success

1. Social Media Exercise

Infosys is a successful software company with nearly 150,000 employees. Social media is integral to its strategy and communications approach. The company uses social media to engage younger employees in these processes and to empower them. In order to do this, the company created STRAP Surround as a social platform to engage employees and allow executives to teach. It contains blogs, discussion forums, an in-house version of YouTube for video sharing, and a range of physical activities and games. The system has provided a mountain of data on its workforce for executives to process.

Here is one example. Employees participated in a series of live events related to a strategy execution topic. These events resulted in tens of thousands of ideas shared via social media. Through these events, management discovered some new things about the effectiveness of different communications media. For example, social media was most effective for structured questions, such as those asking about technologies for future growth, digital consumer behavior, and health care. Moderators made sure to thank participants and the information gathered was passed along to managers. Some employees who provided particularly useful answers were chosen to become team members.[22]

1. Do you think social media is an effective way to engage employees who are in large organizations? Why or why not?
2. Do you think social media would work well in smaller companies? Why or why not?
3. Do you think that using social media changes the corporate culture and the way in which teams communicate for the better or worse? Explain your answer.

2. Building Team Skills

Empowerment makes workers feel more involved in their jobs and the operations of the organization by involving them in decision making. However, empowerment is a tool that is used inconsistently in different workplaces. If you worked in a position that did not empower you, would you want it? How do you envision empowerment looking in the workplace?

Assignment

Form small groups of three or four. Each member of the group should think about the last time you had a complaint that you brought to a company's attention. Perhaps you purchased an item that quickly malfunctioned, you wanted to exchange a pair of pants for a larger size, or you were not happy with the service you received at an auto body shop.

1. Who helped you address the problem? Was the salesperson empowered to give you a refund or an exchange? Or did the employee have to call in a manager?
2. Every group member should share their experiences with one another.
3. Discuss the following among your group:
   a. From the perspective of upper management, what are the pros and cons of empowering workers to take care of problems?
   b. What about from the perspective of the employees?
   c. How did your experiences as customers change, depending on how empowered the workers were? Did you prefer dealing with the employee or the manager?

3. Researching Different Careers

Because a manager's job varies from department to department within firms, as well as among firms, it is virtually impossible to write a generic description of a manager's job. If you are contemplating becoming a manager, you may find it helpful to shadow several managers to learn firsthand what they do.

Assignment

1. Make an appointment with managers in three firms, preferably firms of different sizes. When you make the appointments, request a tour of the facilities.

2. Ask the managers the following questions:
   a. What do you do in your job?
   b. What do you like most and least about your job? Why?
   c. What skills do you need in your job?
   d. How much education does your job require?
   e. What advice do you have for someone thinking about pursuing a career in management?

3. Summarize your findings in a two-page report. Include answers to these questions:
   a. Is management a realistic field of study for you? Why?
   b. What might be a better career choice? Why?

Running a Business
Part 4

At Graeter's, Tenure Is "a Proud Number"

Although you might think working for an ice-cream company would be motivating under almost any circumstances, Graeter's doesn't take its employees' commitment for granted. Including full-time and part-time seasonal workers, the company employs about 800 people in three production facilities and dozens of ice-cream shops. Teenagers who take a summer job at a Graeter's shop often return to help out during the winter holidays and then come back to work the following summer, and the summer after that. Production employees tend to remain with the company for long periods, as well, and Graeter's is relying on their experience and expertise as it expands its national distribution and opens new stores far from the Cincinnati base.

Professional Procedures with Personal Touches

Over the last few years, Graeter's has benefitted from tightening up some of its long-standing human resource management (HRM) procedures, including those for hiring and evaluating employees. David Blink, the company's controller, explains: "We hire based on potential . . . . We are looking for people who are conscientious about their work, who do a good job, who show up every day. We are a fun place to work . . . . We have turnover based on seasonal work only because we hire a lot of college kids [and] high school kids" to work during the summer months. Managers begin recruiting during the spring so that each store is fully staffed in advance of the peak ice-cream buying season. The company also accepts job applications through its website.

When filling job openings at its three factories, Graeter's looks for people with baking industry skills. On the job, employees and managers alike wear name badges that show the number of years they have worked for the firm, "and that is a proud number," says Blink. Graeter's adds a personal touch by celebrating employees' birthdays and milestones such as 25 years of service with the firm.

According to a consultant who works with top management, goals and measurement systems weren't strongly emphasized in the company's early days. "If [employees] came in and they made ice cream, if they made enough for the week, for the day, that was enough," he says. These days, however, Graeter's sets specific production and store goals so that all employees know what is expected of them. It also has measurement systems in place to track progress toward

© ISTOCKPHOTO.COM/UUNIO

those goals. "We have defined the behaviors that are acceptable and not acceptable within the company," the consultant continues, "We communicate that. We teach and educate people." At the retail level, Graeter's training focuses on how employees can make the in-store experience engaging, fun, and memorable for customers.

In the factory, higher production goals have given newly empowered employees achievements to boast about on the slogan T-shirts they wear. The workforce is eager to submit suggestions for improvement, and morale is high. The company also offers advancement opportunities for employees who are ready to take on more responsibility. Graeter's low rate of turnover indicates that employees feel involved with the firm and the work they do. In fact, some employees spend their entire working careers with Graeter's and eventually retire from the firm.

Benefits That Pay

The benefits package for managers and full-time employees is competitive. Graeter's offers profit sharing, and it has made a profit year after year. It also has a 401(k) retirement plan that matches employees' contributions, plus a rolling allowance for paid time-off that is separate from paid vacations and holidays, and is based on the employee's tenure with the firm. Other benefits include medical, life, and disability insurance. Store employees wear uniforms (paid for by the company) and receive a 25 percent discount when they buy Graeter's products. All managers and employees receive the training they need to be effective in their positions and to develop their professional skills.

"You Can't Do It Alone"

The management team has grown as the company moves forward with its aggressive nationwide expansion plans. CEO Richard Graeter, a great-grandson of the company's founders, believes in recruiting outstanding people, compensating

them well, and giving them the autonomy they need to get things done. "In the last few months," he notes, "I have hired a vice president of sales and marketing . . . [and] we hired a vice president of finance, basically a CFO [chief financial officer] because we are big enough to support that . . . Identifying the gaps in your executive team and your talent pool, and going out and finding people to fill those gaps, is probably one of my most critical functions in addition to looking out to define the strategic direction of the company. I've got some wonderful people on the team now, and they are really helping us make the jump from a small business to a medium-sized business . . . People at that level, you've got to pay them well. It's worth it, though . . . They can command the kind of salary they do because they bring the talent you need to navigate the waters."

"You can't do it alone," Richard concludes. "That is the other thing that I think my cousins and I all have come to realize; we can't do it alone. Our fathers and aunt and the folks that came before them . . . they did it all, from figuring out where to build the next store to hanging up the laundry at the end of the day." Now, to achieve the fast-growing company's ambitious goals, he's found that "you need to rely on talent that is beyond just you."[23]

Questions

1. Imagine that you're a human resources manager for Graeter's. If you were writing the job specification for an entry-level, part-time employee who will serve customers in one of the scoop shops, what qualifications would you include, and why?

2. Food production facilities like the three Graeter's factories must comply with strict regulations to ensure purity and safety. What kinds of teams might Graeter's use in these facilities, and for what specific purposes?

3. Graeter's is currently a non-union company. How might the experience of working there change if a union were to be introduced?

Building a Business Plan: Part 4

In this section of your business plan, you will expand on the type and quantity of employees that will be required to operate the business. Your human resources requirements are determined by the type of business and by the size and scale of your operation. From the preceding section, you should have a good idea of how many people you will need. Part 4 of your textbook, "Human Resources," especially Chapters 9 and 10, should help you in answering some of the questions in this part of the business plan.

The Human Resources Component

To ensure successful performance by employees, you must inform workers of their specific job requirements. Employees must know what is expected of the job, and they are entitled to expect regular feedback on their work. It is vital to have a formal job description and job specification for every position in your business. Also, you should establish procedures for evaluating performance.

The labor force component should include the answers to at least the following questions:

4.1. How many employees will you require, and what qualifications should they have—including skills, experience, and knowledge? How many jobs will be full-time? Part-time?

4.2. Will you have written job descriptions for each position?

4.3. Have you prepared a job application form? Do you know what can legally be included in it?

4.4. What criteria will you use in selecting employees?

4.5. Have you made plans for the orientation process?

4.6. Who will do the training?

4.7. What can you afford to pay in wages and salaries? Is this in line with the going rate in your region and industry?

4.8. Who will evaluate your employees?

4.9. Will you delegate any authority to employees?

4.10. Have you developed a set of disciplinary rules?

4.11. Do you plan to interview employees when they resign?

Review of Business Plan Activities

Remember that your employees are the company's most valuable and important resource. Therefore, make sure that you expend a great deal of effort to acquire and make full use of this resource. Check and resolve any issues in this component of your business plan before beginning Part 5. Again, make sure that your answers to the questions in each part are consistent with the entire business plan. Finally, write a brief statement that summarizes all the information for this part of the business plan.

Endnotes

1. Based on information in Kathleen Koster, "From the Ground Up," *Employee Benefit News*, October 1, 2012, p. 32; Geoff Colvin, "AmEx Customer Service in Action," *Fortune*, April 19, 2012, http://management.fortune.cnn.com; Johanna Jainchill, "Amex Transitioning Travel Counselors to Home-Based Network," *Travel Weekly*, April 2, 2012, p. 8; "100 Best Companies to Work For: #60, American Express," *Fortune*, February 6, 2012, http://money.cnn.com; www.americanexpress.com.

2. "2012 Top 100 Best Companies to Work For," February 6, 2012, *Fortune*, http://money.cnn.com/magazines/fortune/best-companies/2012/full_list/, accessed November 28, 2012.

3. Julie Jargon, Louise Radnofsky, and Alexandra Berzon, "Health Care Law Spurs a Shift to Part-Time Workers," *Wall Street Journal*, November 4, 2012, http://online.wsj.com/article/SB100014240529702047071045780949417090478334.html.

4. Nancy Rothbard, "Put on a Happy Face. No, Seriously," *Wall Street Journal*, October 24, 2012, http://online.wsj.com/article/SB1000142405297020338880457661294373851699.html, accessed November 28, 2012; Jessica Pryce-Jones, "Five Ways to Be Productive and Happy at Work," *Wall Street Journal*, November 25, 2012, http://blogs.wsj.com/source/2012/11/25/five-ways-to-be-happy-and-productive-at-work/.

5. Ricky W. Griffin, *Fundamentals of Management*, 6th ed. (Mason, OH: South-Western/Cengage Learning, 2012), 303–305.

6. "The Engineer's Life at Google," Google Jobs, www.google.com/jobs/lifeatgoogle/englife/index.html, accessed November 29, 2012.

7. John Baldoni, "Your Next Job May Be Staring You in the Face," CBS Money Watch, March 6, 2012, www.cbsnews.com/8301-500395_162-57390281/your-next-job-may-be-staring-you-in-the-face/, accessed November 29, 2012.

8. Robert Matuson, "Low-Cost Ways to Show Employees They're Highly Valued," *Fast Company*, March 7, 2012, www.fastcompany.com/1822943/low-cost-ways-to-show-your-employees-they-are-highly-valued?partner=gnews, accessed November 29, 2012.

9. "2012 100 Best Companies," *Working Mother*, http://www.workingmother.com/best-company-list/129110, accessed November 29, 2012.

10. Steven Greenhouse, "A Part-Time Life, as Hours Shrink and Shift," *New York Times*, October 27, 2012, http://www.nytimes.com/2012/10/28/business/a-part-time-life-as-hours-shrink-and-shift-for-american-workers.html.

11. Lisa Gates, "Yes You Can Negotiate a Job Share Without Taking a Pay Cut," *Forbes*, January 24, 2012, http://www.forbes.com/sites/shenegotiates/2012/01/24/yes-you-can-negotiate-a-job-share-without-taking-a-pay-cut/, accessed December 22, 2012.

12. Dan Schawbel, "The Rise of the Remote Worker, or How to Work from Home Without Getting Fired," *Time*, March 13, 2012, http://moneyland.time.com/2012/03/13/the-rise-of-the-remote-worker-or-how-to-work-from-home-without-getting-fired/; "Connected World Technology Report, 2011," Cisco, http://www.cisco.com/en/US/netsol/ns1120/index.html, accessed November 29, 2012.

13. Scott Edinger, "Why Remote Workers Are More (Yes, More) Engaged," *Harvard Business Review Blog*, August 24, 2012, http://blogs.hbr.org/cs/2012/08/are_you_taking_your_people_for.html?awid=6449339475255159080-3271.

14. http://money.cnn.com/magazines/fortune/best-companies/2012/benefits/telecommuting.html, February 6, 2012 issue, accessed November 29, 2012.

15. "A Brief Overview of Employee Ownership," December, 2011, http://www.nceo.org/articles/employee-ownership-esop-united-states, accessed November 29, 2012.

16. Ricky W. Griffin, *Fundamentals of Management* (Mason, OH: South-Western/Cengage Learning, 2012), 396.

17. Richard L. Doft, *Management* (Mason, OH: South-Western/Cengage Learning, 2012), 510.

18. Chana R. Shoenberger, "How to Get People to Work Together," *Wall Street Journal*, September 7, 2012, http://blogs.wsj.com/atwork/2012/09/07/how-to-get-people-to-work-together.

19. Max Nisen, "You Need to Really Know Every Person to Make a Virtual Team Work," *Business Insider*, November 29, 2012, http://www.businessinsider.com/how-to-boost-morale-in-a-virtual-workplace-2012-11.

20. George Anders, "Jeff Bezos Reveals His Number 1 Leadership Secret," *Forbes*, April 4, 2012, http://www.forbes.com/forbes/2012/0423/ceo-compensation-12-amazon-technology-jeff-bezos-gets-it.html, accessed November 30, 2012.

21. Based on information in Chris Mittelstaedt, "5 Employee Morale Killers," *Inc.*, March 16, 2012, www.inc.com; Chris Mittelstaedt, "Is This Your Employees' Idea of Service?" *Inc.*, June 19, 2012, www.inc.com; Stacy Finz, "Fruit Guys Thrives on Adaptability, Realistic Goals," *San Francisco Chronicle*, February 12, 2012, www.sfgate.com; Cengage "Fruit Guys" video; http://fruitguys.com.

22. Vanessa DiMauro and Adam Zawel (2012), "Social Media for Strategy-Focused Organizations," *Balanced Scorecard Report: The Strategy Execution Source*, January–February, 14,3.

23. Based on information from Kimberly L. Jackson, "Graeter's Premium Chocolate Chip Ice Cream Lands at Stop & Shop," *Newark Star-Ledger (NJ)*, April 4, 2012, www.nj.com; "Graeter's Ice Cream Debuts in Bay Area," *Tampa Bay Times (St. Petersburg, FL)*, January 10, 2012, p. 4B; Jim Carper, "Graeter's Runs a Hands-on Ice Cream Plant," *Dairy Foods*, August 2011, pp. 36+; Jim Carper, "The Greater Good," *Dairy Foods*, August 2011, pp. 95+; "Graeter's Unveils New 'Mystery Flavor,'" *Dayton Daily News*, March 29, 2012, www.daytondailynews.com; Bob Driehaus, "A Cincinnati Ice Cream Maker Aims Big," *New York Times*, September 11, 2010, www.nytimes.com; Lucy May, "Graeter's Northern Kentucky Franchisee Puts Stores on the Block," *Business Courier*, August 6, 2010, http://cincinnati.bizjournals.com; www.graeters.com; interviews with company staff and Cengage videos about Graeter's.

Building Customer Relationships Through Effective Marketing

Learning Objectives

Once you complete this chapter, you will be able to:

1 Understand the meaning of *marketing* and the importance of management of customer relationships.

2 Explain how marketing adds value by creating several forms of utility.

3 Trace the development of the marketing concept and understand how it is implemented.

4 Understand what markets are and how they are classified.

5 Understand the two major components of a marketing strategy—target market and marketing mix.

6 Explain how the marketing environment affects strategic market planning.

7 Understand the major components of a marketing plan.

8 Describe how market measurement and sales forecasting are used.

9 Distinguish between a marketing information system and marketing research.

10 Identify the major steps in the consumer buying decision process and the sets of factors that may influence this process.

Why Should You Care?

Marketers are concerned about building long-term customer relationships. To develop competitive product offerings, business people must identify acceptable target customer groups and understand their behaviors.

Volkswagen: Eternally Trying to be the "People's Car"

From Bentley luxury cars and Beetle compact cars to Ducati motorcycles and Scania buses, Volkswagen (www.vw.com) has accelerated worldwide sales by having a brand and vehicle for nearly every market and customer. Headquartered in Wolfsburg, Germany, Volkswagen already sells more than 8 million cars, motorcycles, and trucks every year. By 2018, its goal to become the global leader by selling more than 10 million vehicles per year, including 800,000 in the U.S. market alone.

Volkswagen uses its expertise in engineering and design to create features and styling that meet the needs of local customers in its target markets, at a profit. The Volkswagen Golf, with a peppy engine for city driving and a convenient hatchback, is Europe's best-selling car. Audi's upscale cars are increasingly popular among higher-income buyers and carry a sizable profit margin, as well. Bentley's luxury cars have status-symbol appeal, while Porsche is a favorite among sports-car buffs and Bugatti's race-car heritage gives it a unique image. Sleek Italian styling and powerful motors set Ducati bikes apart from their competitors. Skoda has made its mark with affordability, scoring significant sales gains in Russia, India,

and China. And, reflecting the company's sustainability agenda, a number of Volkswagen models are available with diesel engines or hybrid gas-electric engines for a greener environment and higher fuel efficiency.

When Volkswagen's marketing experts prepare their yearly plans, they take a particularly close look at economic forces, which are a major influence on vehicle purchasing. For example, the recent debt crisis and recession put the brakes on vehicle purchasing in Europe. On the other hand, economic expansion in China fueled purchases of Volkswagen's cars in that key market, opening new opportunities for capturing market share. Finally, competition is a critical factor, with both General Motors and Toyota presenting strong challenges to Volkswagen's race to the top of the industry. Can Volkswagen accelerate its marketing success year after year to achieve its long-term goals?[1]

Did You Know?

Volkswagen sells 8 million vehicles worldwide per year and aims to become the global market leader by 2018.

Numerous organizations, like Volkswagen, use marketing efforts to alert customers to their range of products that seek to satisfy customer demand and create value. Understanding customers' needs and wants are crucial to providing the products that satisfy customers. Although marketing encompasses a diverse set of decisions and activities, it always begins and ends with the customer. The American Marketing Association defines **marketing** as "The activity, set of institutions, and processes for creating, communicating, delivering, and exchanging offerings that have value for customers, clients, partners, and society at large."[2] The marketing process involves eight major functions and numerous related activities, all of which are essential to the marketing process (see Table 11-1).

In this chapter, we examine how marketing activities add value to products. We trace the evolution of the marketing concept and describe how organizations practice it. Next, our focus shifts to market classifications and marketing strategy. We analyze the four elements of a marketing mix and discuss uncontrollable factors in the marketing environment. Then we examine the major components of a marketing plan. We consider tools for strategic market planning, including market measurement, sales forecasts, marketing information systems, and marketing research. Finally, we look at the forces that influence consumer and organizational buying behavior.

marketing the activity, set of institutions, and processes for creating, communicating, delivering, and exchanging offerings that have value for customers, clients, partners, and society at large

relationship marketing establishing long-term, mutually satisfying buyer–seller relationships

Learning Objective

1 Understand the meaning of *marketing* and the importance of management of customer relationships.

MANAGING CUSTOMER RELATIONSHIPS

Without marketing relationships with customers businesses would not be successful. Therefore, maintaining positive relationships with customers is an important goal for marketers. The term **relationship marketing** refers to "marketing decisions and activities focused on achieving long-term, satisfying relationships with customers." Relationship

TABLE 11-1 Eight Major Marketing Functions

Exchange functions: All companies—manufacturers, wholesalers, and retailers—buy and sell to market their merchandise.
1. **Buying** includes obtaining raw materials to make products, knowing how much merchandise to keep on hand, and selecting suppliers.
2. **Selling** creates possession utility by transferring the title of a product from seller to customer.
Physical distribution functions: These functions involve the flow of goods from producers to customers. Transportation and storage provide time utility and place utility and require careful management of inventory.
3. **Transporting** involves selecting a mode of transport that provides an acceptable delivery schedule at an acceptable price.
4. **Storing** goods is often necessary to sell them at the best selling time.
Facilitating functions: These functions help the other functions to take place.
5. **Financing** helps at all stages of marketing. To buy raw materials, manufacturers often borrow from banks or receive credit from suppliers. Wholesalers may be financed by manufacturers, and retailers may receive financing from the wholesaler or manufacturer. Finally, retailers often provide financing to customers.
6. **Standardization** sets uniform specifications for products or services. Grading classifies products by size and quality, usually through a sorting process. Together, standardization and grading facilitate production, transportation, storage, and selling.
7. **Risk taking**—even though competent management and insurance can minimize risks—is a constant reality of marketing because of such losses as bad-debt expense, obsolescence of products, theft by employees, and product-liability lawsuits.
8. **Gathering** market information is necessary for making all marketing decisions.

© CENGAGE LEARNING 2015

marketing deepens and reinforces the buyer's trust in the company, which, as the customer's loyalty grows, increases a company's understanding of the customer's needs and desires. Successful marketers respond to customers' needs and strive to increase value to buyers continually over time. Eventually, this interaction becomes a solid relationship that fosters cooperation and mutual trust. The Internet has expanded and improved relationship marketing options for many firms by making targeted communication faster, cheaper, and easier. Digital technologies allow firms to connect to consumers and have a dialogue with them in real time. This not only improves the speed at which firms can innovate, but consumers are satisfied because they feel the firm is listening to them.

To build long-term customer relationships, marketers are increasingly turning to marketing research and information technology. **Customer relationship management (CRM)** focuses on using information about customers to create marketing strategies that develop and sustain desirable customer relationships. By increasing customer value over time, organizations try to retain and increase long-term profitability through customer loyalty. Because CRM is such an important part of creating and building customer loyalty, many companies offer high-tech products aimed at helping firms to identify good customers and to manage relations with them over the long-term. The accessibility of technology has contributed to a more even playing field for firms of all sizes.

Managing customer relationships requires identifying patterns of buying behavior and using this information to focus on the most promising and profitable customers. Companies must be sensitive to customers' requirements and desires and

customer relationship management (CRM) using information about customers to create marketing strategies that develop and sustain desirable customer relationships

© IQONCEPT/SHUTTERSTOCK.COM

Developing long-term customer relationships. Many companies spend a considerable amount of money on marketing programs to develop and maintain long-term relationships with their customers—especially the valuable ones. Often it's more profitable to retain these customers by offering them big rewards than attracting new customers who may never develop the same loyalty.

Ethical Success or Failure?

The Customer Is Always Right—or Not

Is the customer *always* right? When customers return a broken product to Kohler, which makes kitchen and bathroom fixtures, the company nearly always offers a replacement, to maintain good customer relations. Still, "there are times you've got to say 'no,'" explains a Kohler warranty expert, such as when a product is undamaged or has been abused. Entrepreneur Lauren Thorp, who owns the e-commerce company Umba Box, says, "While the customer is 'always' right, sometimes you just have to fire a customer." When Thorp has tried everything to resolve a complaint and realizes that the customer will be dissatisfied no matter what, she returns her attention to the rest of her customers, who she says are "the reason for my success."

What about customers who hurt other customers? On Black Friday, at the start of the Christmas gift-buying season, some customers waiting for bargains have started

fights or broken store fixtures. What about customers who abuse marketers' policies? Costco traditionally offered a money-back guarantee on everything. A few years ago, however, the retailer noticed that some customers were returning older televisions, receiving refunds, and then buying newer models at lower prices. To stop these practices, Costco now offers a 90-day return policy on electronics and invites customers to call a toll-free hotline for technical assistance.

Sources: Based on information in Leslie Bradshaw, "Lauren Thorp on Taking the Plunge," *Forbes*, March 6, 2012, www.forbes.com; "Warranty Success Stories," *Warranty Week*, March 1, 2012, www.warrantyweek.com; Laarni A. Ragaza, "Costco Laptops and Desktops for the Holidays," *PC Magazine*, November 19, 2010, www.pcmag.com; Nick Carbone, "Black and Blue Friday," *Time*, November 26, 2011, www.time.com; www.costco.com.

---

customer lifetime value a measure of a customer's worth (sales minus costs) to a business over one's lifetime

establish communication to build customers' trust and loyalty. In some instances, it may be more profitable for a company to focus on satisfying a valuable existing customer than to attempt to attract a new one who may never develop the same level of loyalty. This involves determining how much the customer will spend over his or her lifetime. The **customer lifetime value** (CLV) is a measure of a customer's worth (sales minus costs) to a business during one's lifetime.[3] CLV also includes the intangible benefits of retaining lifetime-value customers, such as their ability to provide feedback to a company and refer new customers of similar value, but these are important considerations as well. The amount of money a company is willing to spend to retain such customers is also a factor. In general, when marketers focus on customers chosen for their lifetime value, they earn higher profits in future periods than when they focus on customers selected for other reasons.[4] Thanks to technological innovations and improved research, it is a fairly straightforward task to calculate CLV. In fact, businesses can utilize reliable free online tools to calculate CLV, including one created by the Harvard Business School.[5] Because the loss of a potential lifetime customer can result in lower profits, managing customer relationships has become a major focus of marketers.

Concept Check

✓ How can technology help to build long-term customer relationships?

✓ What are the benefits of retaining customers?

Learning Objective

2 Explain how marketing adds value by creating several forms of utility.

utility the ability of a good or service to satisfy a human need

form utility utility created by converting production inputs into finished products

place utility utility created by making a product available at a location where customers wish to purchase it

UTILITY: THE VALUE ADDED BY MARKETING

Utility is the ability of a good or service to satisfy a human need. The latest iPad, Nike Zoom running shoes, or Mercedes Benz luxury car all satisfy human needs. Thus, each possesses utility. There are four kinds of utility.

Form utility is created by converting production inputs into finished products. Marketing efforts may influence form utility indirectly because the data gathered as part of marketing research are frequently used to determine the size, shape, and features of a product.

The three kinds of utility that are created directly by marketing are place, time, and possession utility. **Place utility** is created by making a product available at a location where customers wish to purchase it. A pair of shoes is given place utility when it is shipped from a factory to a department store.

Time utility is created by making a product available when customers wish to purchase it. For example, Halloween costumes may be manufactured in April but not displayed until September, when consumers start buying them. By storing the costumes until there is a demand, the manufacturer or retailer provides time utility.

Possession utility is created by transferring title (or ownership) of a product to a buyer. For a product as simple as a pair of shoes, ownership usually is transferred by means of a sales slip or receipt. For such products as automobiles and homes, the transfer of title is a more complex process. Along with the title to products, the seller transfers the right to use that product (see Figure 11-1).

Place, time, and possession utility have real value in terms of both money and convenience. This value is created and added to goods and services through a wide variety of marketing activities—from research indicating what customers want to product warranties ensuring that customers get what they pay for. Overall, these marketing activities account for about half of every dollar spent by consumers. When they are part of an integrated marketing program that delivers maximum utility to the customer, many would agree that they are worth the cost.

Place, time, and possession utility are only the most fundamental applications of marketing activities. In recent years, marketing activities have been influenced by a broad business philosophy known as the *marketing concept*.

Putting products at the customer's fingertips. Firms try to provide customers with products whenever and wherever they need them.

time utility utility created by making a product available when customers wish to purchase it

possession utility utility created by transferring title (or ownership) of a product to a buyer

Concept Check

✓ Explain the four kinds of utility.

✓ Provide an example of each.

FIGURE 11-1 Types of Utility

Form utility is created by the production process, but marketing creates place, time, and possession utility.

Wanted:
One pair of size 8 shoes in Duluth, immediately. Will pay $50.

	CAN SATISFY THE NEED WITH:	BUT CANNOT SATISFY THE NEED WITH:
Form utility	Size 8 shoes	Size 10 shoes
Place utility	Size 8 shoes in Duluth	Size 8 shoes in Los Angeles
Time utility	Size 8 shoes in Duluth available now	Size 8 shoes in Duluth available next month
Possession utility	Size 8 shoes in Duluth available now for $50	Size 8 shoes in Duluth available now for $80

Learning Objective

3 Trace the development of the marketing concept and understand how it is implemented.

marketing concept a business philosophy that a firm should provide goods and services that satisfy customers' needs through a coordinated set of activities that allow the firm to achieve its objectives

THE MARKETING CONCEPT

The **marketing concept** is a business philosophy that a firm should provide goods and services that satisfy customers' needs through a coordinated set of activities that allow the firm to achieve its objectives. Initially, the firm communicates with potential customers to assess their product needs. Then, the firm develops a good or service to satisfy those needs. Finally, the firm continues to seek ways to provide customer satisfaction. This process is an application of the marketing concept or marketing orientation. For example, in order to satisfy the demands of an increasingly young and tech-savvy target market, Univision, a leader in Spanish-language television, has launched a major rebranding campaign to attract market share away from rivals. The campaign includes logo refreshes for the parent company and subsidiaries, new production agreements for developing edgier content, and new distribution agreements—all with the aim of attracting new customers and satisfying the wants and needs of the market.[6]

Evolution of the Marketing Concept

From the start of the Industrial Revolution until the early 20th century, business effort was directed mainly toward the production of goods. Consumer demand for manufactured products was so great that manufacturers could almost bank on selling everything they produced. Business had a strong *production orientation*, which placed a strong emphasis on increased output and production efficiency. Marketing was limited to taking orders and distributing finished goods.

In the 1920s, production caught up with and began to exceed demand. Producers had to direct their efforts toward selling goods rather than just producing them. This new *sales orientation* was characterized by increased advertising, enlarged sales forces, and, occasionally, high-pressure selling techniques. Manufacturers produced the goods they expected consumers to want, and marketing consisted primarily of promoting products through personal selling and advertising, taking orders, and delivering goods.

During the 1950s, however, businesspeople started to realize that even enormous advertising expenditures and proven sales techniques were not sufficient to gain a competitive edge. It was then that business managers recognized that they were not primarily producers or sellers, but were in the business of satisfying customers' needs. Marketers realized that the best approach was to adopt a customer orientation—in other words, the organization had to first determine what customers need and then develop goods and services to fill those particular needs (see Table 11-2).

© JOHNKWAN/DREAMSTIME.COM

Tell us what you *really* think. Customer satisfaction is a major element of the marketing concept. Many businesses attempt to measure customer satisfaction through surveys. Surveys can be conducted in a variety of ways: in-person, by mail or fax, or online. Online surveys have made it very inexpensive for firms to gather customer feedback.

TABLE 11-2 Evolution of Customer Orientation

Business managers recognized that they were not primarily producers or sellers, but were in the business of satisfying customers' wants.		
Production Orientation	**Sales Orientation**	**Customer Orientation**
Take orders	Increase advertising	Determine customer needs
Distribute goods	Enlarge sales force	Develop products to fill these needs
	Intensify sales techniques	Achieve the organization's goals

© CENGAGE LEARNING 2015

All functional areas—research and development, production, finance, human resources, and, of course, marketing—play a role in providing customer satisfaction.

Implementing the Marketing Concept

To implement the marketing concept, a firm first must obtain information about its present and potential customers. The firm must determine not only what customers' needs are, but also how well these needs are satisfied by products currently in the market—both its own products and those of competitors. It must ascertain how its products might be improved and what opinions customers have about the firm and its marketing efforts.

The firm then must use this information to pinpoint the specific needs and potential customers toward which it will direct its marketing activities and resources. Next, the firm must mobilize its marketing resources to (1) provide a product that will satisfy its customers, (2) price the product at a level that is acceptable to buyers and will yield a profit, (3) promote the product so that potential customers will be aware of its existence and its ability to satisfy their needs, and (4) ensure that the product is distributed so that it is available to customers where and when it is needed.

Finally, the firm must again obtain marketing information—this time regarding the effectiveness of its efforts. Can the product be improved? Is it being promoted properly? Is it being distributed efficiently? Is the price too high or too low? The firm must be ready to modify any or all of its marketing activities based on information about its customers and competitors. For example, Toys "R" Us modified its marketing activities in China after conducting research on local preferences, including a demand for educational toys. The information helped the retailer to develop a strategy for distribution in China, which represents a large new market. Without modifying marketing activities, the retailer would have met with failure in a country where encouraging childhood play is still not common.[7]

MARKETS AND THEIR CLASSIFICATION

A **market** is a group of individuals or organizations, or both, that need products in a given category and that have the ability, willingness, and authority to purchase them. Markets are broadly classified as consumer or business-to-business and marketing efforts vary depending on the intended market. Marketers should understand the general characteristics of these two groups.

Consumer markets consist of purchasers and/or household members who intend to consume or benefit from the purchased products and who do not buy products to make profits. *Business-to-business markets*, also called *industrial markets*, are grouped broadly into producer, reseller, governmental, and institutional categories. These markets purchase specific kinds of products for use in making other products for resale or for day-to-day operations. *Producer markets* consist of individuals and business organizations that buy certain products to use in the manufacture of other products. *Reseller markets* consist of intermediaries, such as wholesalers and retailers, who buy finished products and sell them for a profit. *Governmental markets* consist of federal, state, county, and local governments. They buy goods and services

Personal Apps

Think about the purchases you've made this year.

From books and beverages to movies and music, you are part of the consumer market. You want these products and you also have the ability, authority, and money to buy them.

© WILLIAM PERUGINI/SHUTTERSTOCK.COM

Concept Check

✓ Identify the major components of the marketing concept.

✓ How did the customer orientation evolve?

✓ What steps are involved when implementing the marketing concept?

Learning Objective

4 **Understand what markets are and how they are classified.**

market a group of individuals or organizations, or both, that need products in a given category and that have the ability, willingness, and authority to purchases them

to maintain internal operations and to provide citizens with such products as highways, education, water, energy, and national defense. Governmental purchases total billions of dollars each year. *Institutional markets* include churches, not-for-profit private schools and hospitals, civic clubs, fraternities and sororities, charitable organizations, and foundations. Their goals are different from the typical business goals of profit, market share, or return on investment.

Learning Objective

5 Understand the two major components of a marketing strategy—target market and marketing mix.

marketing strategy a plan that will enable an organization to make the best use of its resources and advantages to meet its objectives

marketing mix a combination of product, price, distribution, and promotion developed to satisfy a particular target market

DEVELOPING MARKETING STRATEGIES

A **marketing strategy** is a plan that will enable an organization to make the best use of its resources and advantages to meet its objectives. A marketing strategy consists of (1) the selection and analysis of a target market and (2) the creation and maintenance of an appropriate **marketing mix**, a combination of product, price, distribution, and promotion developed to satisfy a particular target market.

Target Market Selection and Evaluation

A **target market** is a group of individuals or organizations, or both, for which a firm develops and maintains a marketing mix suitable for the specific needs and preferences of that group. In selecting a target market, marketing managers examine potential markets for their possible effects on the firm's sales, costs, and profits. The managers attempt to determine whether the organization has the resources to produce a marketing mix that meets the needs of a particular target market and whether satisfying these needs is consistent with the firm's overall objectives. They also analyze the strengths and number of competitors already marketing to the target market. A target market can range in size from millions of people to only a few, depending on the product and the marketer's objectives. Zipcar is a car-sharing company that targets people who either live in cities and do not want to own a car, or those who cannot afford a car or only need one occasionally. Its target market treats cars as something that is needed to get around, not as a status symbol.[8] On the other hand, Rolls-Royce targets its automobiles toward a small, very exclusive market: wealthy people who want the ultimate in prestige in an automobile. Some companies target multiple markets with different products, prices, distribution systems, and promotion for each one. For example, some high-end clothing designers target multiple markets through developing affordable lines distributed at mass market retail outlets, such as Target, Kmart, and Walmart. This strategy allows designers to reach customers with varying needs and levels of disposable income. For example, Target has partnered with such high-end designers as Jason Wu, Rodarte, and Prabal Gurung, and department stores like Neiman Marcus to offer affordable versions of high-end products. The strategy has introduced the normally elite brands to a much larger market, as well as giving Target a stylish image.[9]

LAB SERIES SKINCARE FOR MEN

NEW
10 SKIN-PERFECTING BENEFITS IN ONE AMAZING FORMULA

LAB SERIES SKINCARE FOR MEN
BB TINTED MOISTURIZER SPF 35
Baume Hydratant Teinté SPF 35
TREAT

PERFECTED FOR MEN
NEW BB TINTED MOISTURIZER SPF 35

96% SAW EVEN SKIN TONE IMMEDIATELY   **94%** SAW AN IMMEDIATE REDUCTION IN THE APPEARANCE OF PORES

HIGH TECH. HIGH PERFORMANCE. SKINCARE FOR MEN. ONLY.
Buy now at labseries.co.uk

IMAGE COURTESY OF THE ADVERTISING ARCHIVES

Reaching the right market segments. The market for moisturizers is segmented based on gender. Some skin care products are aimed at women, while others, such as the LAB Series, are aimed at men. There are very few brands of moisturizers that are aimed at both men and women.

UNDIFFERENTIATED APPROACH A company that designs a single marketing mix and directs it at the entire market for a particular product is using an **undifferentiated approach** (see Figure 11-2). This approach assumes that individual customers in the target market

FIGURE 11-2 General Approaches for Selecting Target Markets

The undifferentiated approach assumes that individual customers have similar needs and that most customers can be satisfied with a single marketing mix. When customers' needs vary, the market segmentation approach—either concentrated or differentiated—should be used.

target market a group of individuals or organizations, or both, for which a firm develops and maintains a marketing mix suitable for the specific needs and preferences of that group

undifferentiated approach directing a single marketing mix at the entire market for a particular product

UNDIFFERENTIATED APPROACH

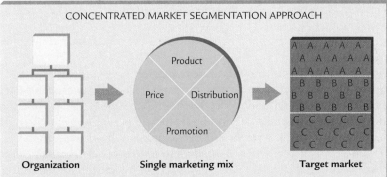

CONCENTRATED MARKET SEGMENTATION APPROACH

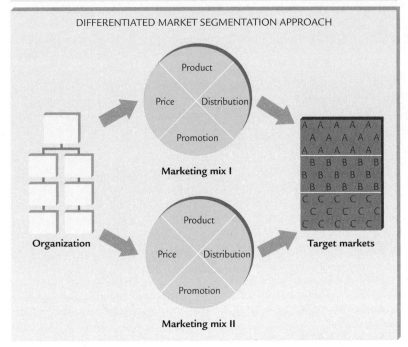

DIFFERENTIATED MARKET SEGMENTATION APPROACH

NOTE: The letters in each target market represent potential customers. Customers that have the same letters have similar characteristics and similar product needs.

Source: William M. Pride and O. C. Ferrell, *Marketing: Concepts and Strategies*, 17th ed. (Mason, OH: South-Western/Cengage Learning, 2014). Adapted with permission.

for a specific kind of product have similar needs and that the organization can satisfy most customers with a single marketing mix, which consists of one type of product with little or no variation, one price, one promotional program aimed at everyone, and one distribution system to reach all customers in the total market. Products that can be marketed successfully with the undifferentiated approach include staple food items, such as sugar and salt, and some produce. An undifferentiated approach is useful in only a limited number of situations because buyers have varying needs for most product categories, which requires the market segmentation approach.

MARKET SEGMENTATION APPROACH Market segmentation is required because different consumers have different needs. A firm that markets 40-foot yachts would not direct its marketing effort toward every person in the total boat market, for instance, because not all boat buyers have the same needs. Marketing efforts directed at the wrong target market are wasted.

Instead, the firm should direct its attention toward a particular portion, or segment, of the total market for boats. A **market segment** is a group of individuals or organizations within a market that shares one or more common characteristics. The process of dividing a market into segments is called **market segmentation**. As shown in Figure 11-2, there are two market segmentation approaches: concentrated and differentiated. When an organization uses *concentrated* market segmentation, a single marketing mix is directed at a single market segment. If *differentiated* market segmentation is used, multiple marketing mixes are focused on multiple market segments.

In our boat example, one common characteristic, or *basis*, for segmentation might be end use of a boat. The firm would be interested primarily in the market segment whose uses for a boat could lead to the purchase of a 40-foot yacht. Other bases for segmentation might be income or geographic location. Variables can affect the type of boat an individual might purchase. When choosing a basis for segmentation, it is important to select a characteristic that relates to differences in customers' needs for a product. The yacht producer, for example, would not use religion to segment the boat market because people's needs for boats do not vary based on religion.

market segment a group of individuals or organizations within a market that share one or more common characteristics

market segmentation the process of dividing a market into segments and directing a marketing mix at a particular segment or segments rather than at the total market

Two pens, two different concentrated targeting strategies. Mont Blanc pens, which are expensive, and Bic pens, which are not, are marketed using a concentrated targeting strategy. Each one is aimed at a different market segment. They do not compete for the same customers. Which do you buy and why?

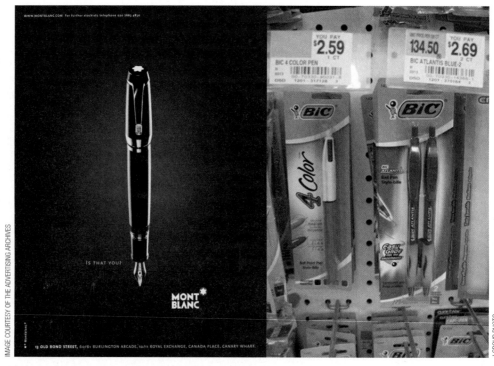

TABLE 11-3 Common Bases of Market Segmentation

Demographic	Psychographic	Geographic	Behavioristic
Age	Personality attributes	Region	Volume usage
Gender	Motives	Urban, suburban, rural	End use
Race	Lifestyles	Market density	Benefit expectations
Ethnicity		Climate	Brand loyalty
Income		Terrain	Price sensitivity
Education		City size	
Occupation		County size	
Family size		State size	
Family life cycle			
Religion			
Social class			

Source: William M. Pride and O. C. Ferrell, *Marketing: Concepts and Strategies*, 17th ed. (Mason, OH: South-Western/Cengage Learning, 2014). Adapted with permission.

Marketers use a wide variety of segmentation bases. Those most commonly applied to consumer markets are shown in Table 11-3. Each may be used as a single basis for market segmentation or in combination with other bases. Top-Toy, a Toys "R" Us licensee in Sweden, has turned traditional toy market segmentation on its head by choosing to segment toys by age only. It releases gender-neutral catalogs that market dolls and toy cars, for example, to girls and boys equally. Marketers are responding to the cultural trend toward total gender equality in Sweden.[10]

Creating a Marketing Mix

A business firm controls four important elements of marketing that it combines in a way that reaches the firm's target market. These are the *product* itself, the *price* of the product, the means chosen for its *distribution*, and the *promotion* of the product. When combined, these four elements form a marketing mix (see Figure 11-3). As part of restructuring to regain profitability, clothing retailer Abercrombie & Fitch (A&F) completely reconfigured its marketing mix. The company reduced production time for new clothing and limited its stock of inventory to deliver trendy clothes more quickly to stores. A&F focuses advertisements and promotions on teenagers and international markets, and has changed distribution networks through closing underperforming U.S. stores and expanding overseas. It is now directly competing with successful low-cost clothing retailers like Forever 21 and Zara.[11]

A firm can vary its marketing mix by changing any one or more of the ingredients. Thus, a firm may use one marketing mix to reach one target market and another marketing mix to reach a different target market. For example, most automakers produce several different types and models of vehicles and aim them at different market segments based on the potential customers' age, income, and other factors.

IMAGE COURTESY OF THE ADVERTISING ARCHIVES

Developing the right marketing mix. Firms have little control over the marketing environment. However, they *can* control the marketing mixes for their products—that is, the nature of the products themselves and how they are priced, distributed, and promoted. Marketers at Pepsi Co. have developed a specific marketing mix for Diet Pepsi. Who do you think the product is aimed at?

FIGURE 11-3 The Marketing Mix and the Marketing Environment

The marketing mix consists of elements that the firm controls—product, price, distribution, and promotion. The firm generally has no control over forces in the marketing environment.

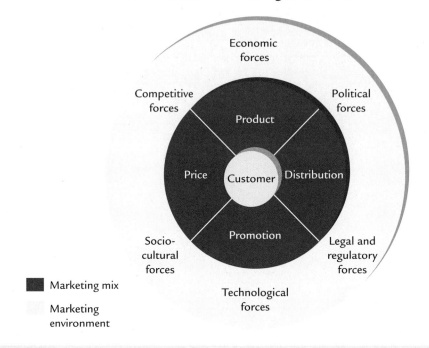

Source: William M. Pride and O. C. Ferrell, *Marketing: Concepts and Strategies*, 17th ed. (Mason, OH: South-Western/Cengage Learning, 2014). Adapted with permission.

The *product* ingredient of the marketing mix includes decisions about the product's design, brand name, packaging, and warranties. When McDonald's decides on brand names, package designs, sizes of orders, flavors of sauces, and recipes, these choices are all part of the product ingredient.

The *pricing* ingredient is concerned with both base prices and discounts. Pricing decisions are intended to achieve particular goals, such as to maximize profit or to make room for new models. The rebates offered by automobile manufacturers are a pricing strategy developed to boost low auto sales.

The *distribution* ingredient involves not only transportation and storage, but also selecting intermediaries. How many levels of intermediaries is ideal in the distribution of a product? Should the product be distributed as widely as possible or should distribution be restricted to specialized outlets? Companies will likely have to alter the distribution ingredient over time. For example, as customers' consumption habits shift, publishers have had to alter how they distribute books. Harper-Collins recently shut down its last U.S. book warehouse—a sign of the increasing popularity of digital books and the changing landscape of publishing. HarperCollins will save money on distribution by subcontracting its print distribution to a partner as it focuses more on electronic book formats.[12]

The *promotion* ingredient focuses on providing information to target markets. The major forms of promotion are advertising, personal selling, sales promotion, and public relations. Careful planning and implementation of promotional tools is crucial to ensure their effectiveness. Distribution and promotion are discussed in more detail in Chapter 13.

These ingredients of the marketing mix are controllable elements. A firm can vary each of them to suit its organizational and marketing goals and target market needs. As we extend our discussion of marketing strategy, we will see that the marketing environment includes a number of *uncontrollable* elements as well.

Concept Check

✓ What are the major components of a marketing strategy?

✓ Describe the major approaches used in target market selection.

✓ Identify the four elements of the marketing mix.

MARKETING STRATEGY AND THE MARKETING ENVIRONMENT

The marketing mix consists of elements that a firm controls and uses to reach its target market. The firm also has control of organizational resources, such as finances and data, which can be utilized to accomplish marketing goals and refine the marketing mix. All of a firm's marketing activities can be affected by external forces, which are generally uncontrollable. As Figure 11-3 illustrates, the following forces make up the external *marketing environment*:

- *Economic forces*—the effects of economic conditions on customers' ability and willingness to buy
- *Sociocultural forces*—influences in a society and its culture that result in changes in attitudes, beliefs, norms, customs, and lifestyles
- *Political forces*—influences that arise through the actions of political figures
- *Competitive forces*—the actions of competitors, who are in the process of implementing their own marketing plans
- *Legal and regulatory forces*—laws that protect consumers and competition and government regulations that affect marketing
- *Technological forces*—technological changes that can create new marketing opportunities or cause products to become obsolete rapidly

These forces influence decisions about marketing mix ingredients. Changes in the environment can impact existing marketing strategies. In addition, changes in environmental forces may lead to abrupt shifts in customers' needs. Consider the effect technological forces have had on printed newspapers. Years ago, very few people would have predicted that consumers would one day read their news on a computer or their phone. Yet many people now do exactly that.

Concept Check

✔ Describe the environmental forces that affect a firm's marketing decision and activities

✔ How are marketing decisions affected by environmental forces?

DEVELOPING A MARKETING PLAN

A **marketing plan** is a written document that specifies an organization's resources, objectives, marketing strategy, and implementation and control efforts to be used in marketing a specific product or product group. The marketing plan describes the firm's current position or situation, establishes marketing objectives for the product, and specifies how the organization will attempt to achieve these objectives. Marketing plans vary with respect to the time period involved. Short-range plans are for one year or less, medium-range plans cover from over one year to five years, and long-range plans cover periods of more than five years.

Although time-consuming, developing a clear, well-written marketing plan is important. The plan helps establish a unified vision for an organization and is used for communication among the firm's employees. It covers responsibilities, tasks, and schedules for implementation, specifies how resources are to be allocated to achieve marketing objectives, and helps marketing managers monitor and evaluate the performance of the marketing strategy. Because the forces of the marketing environment are subject to change, marketing plans have to be updated frequently. Marriot

marketing plan a written document that specifies an organization's resources, objectives, strategy, and implementation and control efforts to be used in marketing a specific product or product group

© ISTOCKPHOTO.COM/YMGERMAN

TABLE 11-4 Components of the Marketing Plan

Plan Component	Component Summary	Highlights
Executive summary	One- to two-page synopsis of the entire marketing plan	
Environmental analysis	Information about the company's current situation with respect to the marketing environment	1. Assessment of marketing environment factors 2. Assessment of target market(s) 3. Assessment of current marketing objectives and performance
SWOT analysis	Assessment of the organization's strengths, weaknesses, opportunities, and threats	1. Strengths 2. Weaknesses 3. Opportunities 4. Threats
Marketing objectives	Specification of the firm's marketing objectives	Qualitative measures of what is to be accomplished
Marketing strategies	Outline of how the firm will achieve its objectives	1. Target market(s) 2. Marketing mix
Marketing implementation	Outline of how the firm will implement its marketing strategies	1. Marketing organization 2. Activities and responsibilities 3. Implementation timetable
Evaluation and control	Explanation of how the firm will measure and evaluate the results of the implemented plan	1. Performance standards 2. Financial controls 3. Monitoring procedures (audits)

Source: William M. Pride and O. C. Ferrell, *Marketing: Concepts and Strategies*, 17th ed. (Mason, OH: South-Western/Cengage Learning, 2014). Reprinted with permission.

Concept Check

✓ What are the major components of a marketing plan?

✓ Why is developing a well-written marketing plan important?

hotel chain, Springhill Suites, identifies its target audience as more cultured and educated than average. For its new marketing strategy, it hired a photographer and blogger, Ken Kaminesky, to engage in a cross-country road trip looking for American art and artists. He documented his journey via Twitter, Pinterest, Facebook, and Instagram. Art has been an integral factor in Springhill Suite's marketing plan for years, as its target market is art savvy.[13]

The major components of a marketing plan are shown in Table 11-4.

Learning Objective

8 **Describe how market measurement and sales forecasting are used.**

sales forecast an estimate of the amount of a product that an organization expects to sell during a certain period of time based on a specified level of marketing effort

Concept Check

✓ Why is sales forecasting important?

✓ What methods do businesses use to forecast sales?

MARKET MEASUREMENT AND SALES FORECASTING

Measuring the sales potential of specific market segments can help an organization make important decisions. An accurate measure of a market segment can help a firm to determine the feasibility of entering new segments and how best to allocate marketing resources and activities among market segments in which it is already active. All such estimates should identify the relevant time frame. As with marketing plans, these plans may be short-range for periods of less than one year, medium-range for one to five years, or long-range for more than five years. The estimates should also define the geographic boundaries of the forecast, such as a city, county, state, or group of nations. Finally, analysts should indicate whether their estimates are for a specific product item, a product line, or an entire product category.

A **sales forecast** is an estimate of the amount of a product that an organization expects to sell during a certain period of time based on a specified level of marketing effort. Managers may rely on sales forecasts when they purchase raw materials, schedule production, secure financial resources, consider plant or equipment purchases, hire personnel, and plan inventory levels. Because the accuracy of a sales forecast is so important, organizations often use several forecasting methods, including executive judgments, surveys of buyers or sales personnel, time-series analyses, correlation analyses, and market tests. The specific methods used depend on the costs involved, type of product, characteristics of the market, time span of the forecast, purposes for which the forecast is used, stability of historical sales data, availability of the required information, and expertise and experience of forecasters. To assist with complicated predictions, many companies utilize sales forecasting software.

MARKETING INFORMATION

The availability and proper utilization of accurate and timely information are critical to making effective marketing decisions. Thanks to the proliferation of information-gathering technology, marketers have access to a wealth of data. It is accessible through two major channels: a marketing information system or marketing research.

Marketing Information Systems

A **marketing information system** is a system for managing marketing information that is gathered continually from internal and external sources. Most of these systems are computer based because of the large quantities of data the system must accept, store, sort, and retrieve. *Continual* data collection is essential to ensure the most up-to-date information.

In concept, the operation of a marketing information system is simple. Data from a variety of sources are fed into the system. Data from *internal* sources include sales figures, product and marketing costs, inventory levels, and activities of the sales force. Data from *external* sources relate to the organization's suppliers, intermediaries, and customers. It can also come from competitors' marketing activities and economic conditions. All these data are stored and processed by the marketing information system. Marketers then choose the output format most useful for making marketing decisions, such as daily sales reports by territory and product, forecasts of sales or buying trends, and reports on changes in market share for the major brands in a specific industry. Both the information outputs and their form depend on the requirements of the personnel in the organization. It is imperative that marketers have access to and understand how to use the latest technologies in order to maximize the efficiency and effectiveness of marketing information systems.

Marketing Research

Marketing research is the process of systematically gathering, recording, and analyzing data concerning a particular marketing problem. Marketing research is an important step of the marketing process because it involves collecting and analyzing data on what consumers want and need, their consumption habits, trends, and changes in the marketing environment. The Internet has made marketing research easier and cheaper than ever. Online platforms, such as Facebook and Twitter, can help fledgling companies measure market demand and test out product and service ideas from a significant sampling of

Can you hear me now? Would you be interested in having a pre-recruited group of your customers ready and willing to participate in data collection surveys at a moment's notice? If so, you might want to sign up for online software such as PortalPanel, produced by the marketing research company Toluna. Data gathered from good marketing research can be invaluable. Poor quality data can be disastrous and may lead marketers to make the wrong decisions.

a target market for little or no cost. The Internet also offers numerous databases and other sources of valuable information on competitors, target markets, and the marketing environment.[14] When conducting marketing research, businesses commonly use external marketing research companies to do one or more of the steps in Table 11-5. Note that in its advertisement, Toluna is an organization that helps businesses gather information. Toluna maintains a large group of online participants who are willing to respond to surveys quickly. This advertisement encourages businesses to consider using Toluna's research services to assist them when conducting survey-based marketing research.

Table 11-5 outlines a six-step procedure for conducting marketing research. It is particularly well tsuited to test new products, determine various characteristics of consumer markets, and evaluate promotional activities.

Using Technology to Gather and Analyze Marketing Information

Marketers have more access to reliable data and programs for analyzing them than ever before. Technology has allowed even small firms an unprecedented level of access to high-quality data.

A *database* is a collection of information arranged for easy access and retrieval. Using databases, marketers tap into sources such as internal sales reports, newspaper articles, company news releases, government economic reports, and bibliographies. Many marketers use commercial databases, such as LEXIS-NEXIS, to obtain information for marketing decisions. A great deal of information that used to be obtainable only for a high price from companies specializing in producing commercial databases is now available via the Internet. Firms occasionally need to access the broad and in-depth information contained in large commercial databases, such as Dun & Bradsteet's Global Commercial database, with 200 million business records.[15]

Information provided by a single firm on household demographics, purchases, television viewing behavior, and responses

TABLE 11-5 The Six Steps of Marketing Research

1. Define the problem.	The problem is stated clearly and accurately, as it will determine the research issues and approaches, the right questions to ask, and the types of solutions that are acceptable. This is a crucial step that should not be rushed.
2. Make a preliminary investigation.	The preliminary investigation aims to develop a sharper definition of the problem and a set of tentative answers, which are developed by examining internal information and published data and by talking with persons who have experience with the problem. These answers will be tested by further research.
3. Plan the research.	At this stage, researchers know what facts are needed to resolve the identified problem and what facts are available. They make plans on how to gather needed but missing data.
4. Gather factual information.	Once a plan is in place, researchers can collect primary information by mail, interviews, observation, and get secondary information from commercial or government data sources. The choice depends on the plan and the available sources of information.
5. Interpret the information.	Facts by themselves do not always provide a sound solution to a marketing problem. They must be interpreted and analyzed to determine the choices available to management.
6. Reach a conclusion.	Once the data have been evaluated, researchers seek to draw conclusions and make recommendations. These may be obvious or not, depending on intangible factors and whether data used were complete. When there are gaps in the data, it is important for researchers to state this.

© CENGAGE LEARNING 2015

Using Neuroscience for Marketing Research

Marketers are beginning to use neuroscience—studying the brain and the nervous system—to learn more about the inner workings of consumer behavior. For example, when Frito-Lay wanted to dig deeper into consumers' reactions to its Cheetos, it hired a company to measure the brain waves of consumers as they snacked on the cheese puffs. The research showed that consumers enjoyed the messy orange cheese crumbs that Cheetos leave all over their fingers. Based on this research, Frito-Lay has used messy-fingers visuals in its ads and Facebook messages.

The Nabisco cookie brand Chips Ahoy! used insights from neuroscience when redesigning a package. Previous research showed that consumers placed a high value on resealable packaging, so researchers tested different ways to highlight the new design's resealability tab. They also tested package images and, based on response, chose an image featuring chocolate chips "flying" off the cookie.

Magazines are also using neuroscience for marketing research. *New Scientist* magazine measured the brainwaves of readers to understand how they react to cover art. Putting the results into practice, one issue with a specially designed cover enjoyed 12 percent higher newsstand sales compared with the previous year. Also, *Time* magazine is using neuroscience to gauge consumer involvement in the ads that accompany its iPad apps. Although neuroscience won't replace traditional research techniques, it's another tool for collecting data for marketing decisions.

Sources: Based on information in Carmen Nobel, "What Neuroscience Tells Us About Consumer Desire, *Harvard Business School Working Knowledge*, March 26, 2012, http://hbswk.hbs.edu; "Marketing on the Brain," *Marketing*, November 2, 2011, p. 24; Scott Young, "Neuroscience Explains the Emotional Buy," *Brand Packaging*, July 2011, p. 16; Deena Higgs Nenad, "Emotional Marketing," *Editor & Publisher*, January 2011, p. 7.

to promotions such as coupons and free samples is called *single-source data*. Consumers often use multiple devices to view shows and movies, including televisions, smartphones, and computers, making it difficult for companies to track media consumption habits and needs. To solve this problem, Arbitron and comScore joined with major media companies to form the Coalition for Independent Media Measurement (CIMM) to compile accurate single-source data. It represents a step forward in helping marketers track consumer media consumption over multiple devices.[16]

Online information services offer subscribers access to e-mail, websites, downloadable files, news, databases, and research materials. By subscribing to mailing lists, marketers can receive electronic newsletters and participate in online discussions with other network users. This ability to communicate online with customers, suppliers, and employees improves the capability of a firm's marketing information system and helps the company track its customers' changing desires and buying habits.

The *Internet* is a powerful communication medium, linking customers and companies around the world and providing affordable information to companies and customers. *Advertising Age* and Nielsen, for example, both have websites that are highly useful when conducting marketing research. While most Web pages are open to all Internet users, some companies, such as U.S. West and Turner Broadcasting System, also maintain internal Web pages, called *intranets*, which allow employees to access internal data and facilitate communication among departments.

Table 11-6 lists a variety of good resources for secondary information, which is existing information that has been gathered by other organizations. As can be seen in Table 11-6, secondary information can come from a variety of sources, including governments, trade associations, general publications and news outlets, and corporate information.

Many companies also use social media outlets to solicit feedback from customers on their existing or upcoming products. While there is always a risk that customers will give a company or its products bad reviews online, most firms deem the risk worthwhile to conduct the low-cost research they need to be successful. If handled correctly, consumer complaints can be an important source of data on how to improve products and services.

Concept Check

✓ Data from a marketing information system is collected from which internal and external sources?

✓ What are the major reasons for conducting marketing research?

✓ Identify and describe the six steps of the marketing research process.

✓ How does technology facilitate collecting and analyzing marketing information?

TABLE 11-6 Sources of Secondary Information

Government sources	
Economic census	www.census.gov/
Export.gov—country and industry market research	www.export.gov/mrktresearch/index.asp
National Technical Information Services	www.ntis.gov/
Strategis—Canadian trade	http://strategis.ic.gc.ca/
Trade associations and shows	
American Society of Association Executives	www.asaecenter.org/
Directory of Associations	www.marketingsource.com/associations/
Trade Show News Network	www.tsnn.com/
Magazines, newspapers, video, and audio news programming	
Google Video Search	http://www.google.com/videohp?hl=en
Media Jumpstation	www.directcontactpr.com/jumpstation/
Google News Directory	www.google.com/Top/News/
Yahoo! Video Search	http://video.search.yahoo.com/
Corporate information	
The Public Register Online	www.annualreportservice.com/
Bitpipe	www.bitpipe.com/
Business Wire—press releases	www.businesswire.com/
Hoover's Online	www.hoovers.com/
Open Directory Project	http://dmoz.org/
PR Newswire—press releases	www.prnewswire.com/

Source: Adapted from "Data Collection: Low-Cost Secondary Research," KnowThis.com, www.knowthis.com/principles-of-marketing-tutorials/data-collection-low-cost-secondary-research/ (accessed December 26, 2012).

Learning Objective

10 **Identify the major steps in the consumer buying decision process and the sets of factors that may influence this process.**

buying behavior the decisions and actions of people involved in buying and using products

consumer buying behavior the purchasing of products for personal or household use, not for business purposes

business buying behavior the purchasing of products by producers, resellers, governmental units, and institutions

personal income the income an individual receives from all sources *less* the Social Security taxes the individual must pay

TYPES OF BUYING BEHAVIOR

Buying behavior may be defined as the decisions and actions of people involved in buying and using products.[17] **Consumer buying behavior** refers to the purchasing of products for personal or household use, not for business purposes. **Business buying behavior** is the purchasing of products by producers, resellers, governmental units, and institutions. Because a firm's success depends in large part on buyers' reactions to a marketing strategy, it is important to understand buying behavior. Marketing managers are better able to predict customer responses to marketing strategies and to develop a satisfying marketing mix if they are aware of the factors that affect buying behavior.

Consumer Buying Behavior

Consumers' buying behaviors differ for different types of products. For frequently purchased low-cost items, a consumer uses routine response behavior, which involves very little search or decision–making effort. The buyer uses limited decision making for purchases made occasionally, or when more information is needed about an unknown product in a well-known product category. When buying an unfamiliar or expensive item, or one that is seldom purchased, the consumer engages in extended decision making. Consumers have become empowered by information found on the Internet that allows them to compare prices and features and read reviews about products without stepping into a store. In situations where they would have relied on salespeople in the past, consumers now feel informed enough by online research to make purchasing decisions themselves. In this environment, marketing and customer service are increasingly important.[18]

A person deciding on a purchase goes through some or all of the steps shown in Figure 11-4. First, the consumer acknowledges that a problem exists that might be solved by a product or service. Then, the buyer looks for information, which may include brand names, product characteristics, warranties, and other features. Next, the buyer weighs the various alternatives, makes a choice, and acquires the item. In the after-purchase stage, the consumer evaluates the suitability of the product, which will affect future purchases. As Figure 11-4 shows, the buying process is influenced by situational factors (physical surroundings, social surroundings, time, purchase reason, and buyer's mood and condition), psychological factors (perception, motives, learning, attitudes, personality, and lifestyle), and social factors (family, roles, reference groups, online social networks, social class, culture, and subculture).

Consumer buying behavior is also affected by the ability to buy, called one's *buying power*, which is largely determined by income. As every taxpayer knows, not all income is available for spending. For this reason, marketers consider income in three different ways. **Personal income** is the income an individual receives from all sources *less* the Social Security taxes the

Problem recognition. Problem recognition is the first stage of the consumer buying decision process. Sometimes a deodorant advertisement is designed to raise doubts in a consumer's mind as to whether or not his or her deodorant is providing maximum effective protection.

FIGURE 11-4 Consumer Buying Decision Process and Possible Influences on the Process

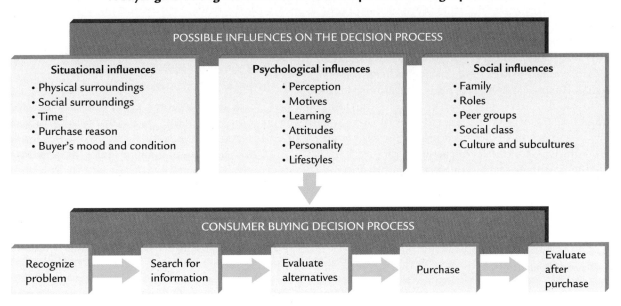

A buyer goes through some or all of these steps when making a purchase.

POSSIBLE INFLUENCES ON THE DECISION PROCESS

Situational influences	Psychological influences	Social influences
• Physical surroundings • Social surroundings • Time • Purchase reason • Buyer's mood and condition	• Perception • Motives • Learning • Attitudes • Personality • Lifestyles	• Family • Roles • Peer groups • Social class • Culture and subcultures

CONSUMER BUYING DECISION PROCESS

Recognize problem → Search for information → Evaluate alternatives → Purchase → Evaluate after purchase

Source: William M. Pride and O. C. Ferrell, *Marketing: Concepts and Strategies*, 17th ed. (Mason, OH: South-Western/Cengage Learning, 2014). Adapted with permission.

disposable income personal income *less* all additional personal taxes

discretionary income disposable income *less* savings and expenditures on food, clothing, and housing

individual must pay. **Disposable income** is personal income *less* all additional personal taxes. These taxes include income, estate, gift, and property taxes levied by local, state, and federal governments. The long-term savings rate for disposable income in the United States is generally about 3 percent, with savings increasing slightly during recessionary times.[19] **Discretionary income** is disposable income *less* savings and expenditures on food, clothing, and housing. Discretionary income is of particular interest to marketers because consumers have the most choice in spending it. Consumers use their discretionary income to purchase a wide variety of items ranging from automobiles and vacations to movies and pet food.

Business Buying Behavior

Business buyers are generally better informed than consumers and consider a product's quality, its price, and the service provided by suppliers. Business purchases can be large, and a committee or a group of people, rather than just one person, often decides on purchases. Committee members must consider the organization's objectives, purchasing policies, resources, and personnel. The process of business buying is different than consumer buying. It occurs through description, inspection, sampling, or negotiation. Because business transactions can be more complicated and orders tend to be larger, obtaining complete and correct information on buyers and sellers is important.

Concept Check

✓ Why is it important to understand buying behavior?

✓ How does a customer's decision-making time vary with the type of product?

✓ What are the five stages of the consumer buying decision process?

✓ What are the possible influences on this process?

✓ What is the difference between disposable income and discretionary income?

Looking for Success? *Get Flashcards, Quizzes, Games, Crosswords, and more @ www.cengagebrain.com.*

Summary

1 **Understand the meaning of *marketing* and the importance of management of customer relationships.**

Marketing is an organizational function and a set of processes for creating, communicating, and delivering value to customers and for managing customer relationships in ways that benefit the organization and its stakeholders. Maintaining positive relationships with customers is crucial. Relationship marketing is establishing long-term, mutually satisfying buyer–seller relationships. Customer relationship management uses information about customers to create marketing strategies that develop and sustain desirable customer relationships. Managing customer relationships requires identifying patterns of buying behavior and focusing on the most profitable customers. Customer lifetime value (CLV) is a combination of purchase frequency, average value of purchases, and brand-switching patterns over the entire span of a customer's relationship with the company.

2 **Explain how marketing adds value by creating several forms of utility.**

Marketing adds value in the form of utility, or the power of a product or service to satisfy a need. It creates place utility by making products available where customers want them, time utility by making products available when customers want them, and possession utility by transferring the ownership of products to buyers.

3 **Trace the development of the marketing concept and understand how it is implemented.**

From the Industrial Revolution until the early 20th century, businesspeople focused on the production of goods. From the 1920s to the 1950s, the emphasis moved to the selling of goods. During the 1950s, businesspeople recognized that their enterprises involved not only producing and selling products, but also satisfying customers' needs. They began to implement the marketing concept, a business philosophy that involves the entire organization in the dual processes of meeting the customers' needs and achieving the organization's goals.

Implementation of the marketing concept begins and ends with customers—first to determine what customers' needs are and then to evaluate how well the firm is meeting these needs.

4 Understand what markets are and how they are classified.

A market consists of people with a need, the ability to buy, and the desire and authority to purchase. Markets are classified as consumer and business-to-business or industrial, which includes producer, reseller, governmental, and institutional markets.

5 Understand the two major components of a marketing strategy— target market and marketing mix.

A marketing strategy is a plan for the best use of an organization's resources to meet its objectives. Developing a marketing strategy involves selecting and analyzing a target market and creating and maintaining a marketing mix that will satisfy the target market. A target market is chosen through the undifferentiated or the market segmentation approach. A market segment is a group of individuals or organizations within a market that have similar characteristics and needs. Businesses that use an undifferentiated approach design a single marketing mix and direct it at the entire market for a particular product. The market segmentation approach directs a marketing mix at a segment of a market.

The four elements of a firm's marketing mix are product, price, distribution, and promotion. The product ingredient includes decisions about the product's design, brand name, packaging, and warranties. The pricing ingredient is concerned with base prices and various types of discounts. Distribution involves not only transportation and storage but also the selection of intermediaries. Promotion focuses on providing information to target markets. The elements of the marketing mix can be varied to suit broad organizational goals, marketing objectives, and target markets.

6 Explain how the marketing environment affects strategic market planning.

To achieve a firm's marketing objectives, marketing-mix strategies must begin with an assessment of the marketing environment, which, in turn, influences decisions about marketing-mix ingredients. Marketing activities are affected by the external forces that make up the marketing environment. These forces include economic, sociocultural, political, competitive, legal and regulatory, and technological forces. Economic forces affect customers' ability and willingness to buy. Sociocultural forces are societal and cultural factors, such as attitudes, beliefs, and lifestyles, that affect customers' buying choices. Political forces and legal and regulatory forces influence marketing planning through laws that protect consumers and regulate competition. Competitive forces involve the actions of competitors. Technological forces can create new marketing opportunities or cause a product to become obsolete.

7 Understand the major components of a marketing plan.

A marketing plan is a written document that specifies an organization's resources, objectives, strategy, and implementation and control efforts to be used in marketing a specific product or product group. The marketing plan describes a firm's current position, establishes marketing objectives, and specifies the methods the organization will use to achieve these objectives. Marketing plans can be short-range for one year or less, medium-range for two to five years, or long-range for periods of more than five years.

8 Describe how market measurement and sales forecasting are used.

Market measurement and sales forecasting are used to estimate sales potential and predict product sales in specific market segments.

9 Distinguish between a marketing information system and marketing research.

Strategies are monitored and evaluated through marketing research and marketing information systems, which store and process internal and external data and produce reports in a form that aids marketing decision making. A marketing information system manages marketing information that is gathered continually from internal and external sources. Marketing research is the process of systematically gathering, recording, and analyzing data concerning a particular marketing problem. Technology is making information for marketing decisions more accessible. Electronic communication tools can be very useful for accumulating accurate and affordable information. Information technologies that are changing the way marketers obtain and use information are databases, online information services, and the Internet. Many companies are using social media to obtain research data and feedback from customers.

10 Identify the major steps in the consumer buying decision process and the sets of factors that may influence this process.

Buying behavior consists of the decisions and actions of people involved in buying and using products. Consumer buying behavior refers to the purchase of products for personal or household use. Organizational buying behavior is the purchase of products by producers, resellers, governments, and institutions. Understanding buying behavior helps marketers predict how buyers will respond to marketing strategies. The consumer buying decision process consists of five steps: recognizing the problem, searching for information, evaluating alternatives, purchasing, and post-purchase evaluation. Factors affecting the consumer buying decision process fall into three categories: situational influences, psychological influences, and social influences.

Key Terms

You should now be able to define and give an example relevant to each of the following terms:

marketing (298)
relationship marketing (298)
customer relationship
    management (CRM) (299)
customer lifetime value (300)
utility (300)
form utility (300)
place utility (300)
time utility (301)

possession utility (301)
marketing concept (302)
market (303)
marketing strategy (304)
marketing mix (304)
target market (305)
undifferentiated
    approach (305)
market segment (306)

market segmentation (306)
marketing plan (309)
sales forecast (310)
marketing information
    system (311)
marketing research (311)
buying behavior (314)
consumer buying
    behavior (314)

business buying
    behavior (314)
personal income (315)
disposable income (316)
discretionary income (316)

Discussion Questions

1. What is relationship marketing?
2. How is a marketing-oriented firm different from a production-oriented firm or a sales-oriented firm?
3. What are the major requirements for a group of individuals and organizations to be a market? How does a consumer market differ from a business-to-business market?
4. What are the major components of a marketing strategy?
5. What is the purpose of market segmentation? What is the relationship between market segmentation and the selection of target markets?
6. Describe the forces in the marketing environment that affect an organization's marketing decisions.

7. What is a marketing plan, and what are its major components?
8. What new information technologies are changing the ways that marketers keep track of business trends and customers?
9. Why do marketers need to understand buying behavior?
10. Is it a good strategy to focus most marketing efforts on the most profitable customers?
11. How might adoption of the marketing concept benefit a firm? How might it benefit the firm's customers?
12. Is marketing information as important to small firms as it is to larger firms? Explain.
13. How does the marketing environment affect a firm's marketing strategy?

Test Yourself

Matching Questions

1. _____ The process of planning and executing the conception, pricing, promotion, and distribution of ideas, goods, and services.
2. _____ A business philosophy that involves satisfying customers' needs, while also achieving a firm's goals.
3. _____ Value is added through converting raw materials into finished goods.
4. _____ The individuals in a market who share common characteristics.
5. _____ Income that is left after savings, food, clothing, and housing are paid.
6. _____ A combination of marketing elements designed to reach a target market.
7. _____ A plan of actions intended to accomplish a marketing goal.

8. _____ The decision-making process that is used when purchasing personal-use items.
9. _____ Marketing activities that focus on a particular group, such as teenagers.
10. _____ The document that establishes the marketing objectives for a product.

a. consumer buying behavior
b. discretionary income
c. form utility
d. possession utility
e. market segment
f. marketing
g. marketing concept
h. customer lifetime value
i. marketing mix
j. marketing plan
k. marketing strategy
l. target market

True False Questions

11. **T** **F** Marketing is a process that adds value to products.

12. **T** **F** Financing and risk taking are physical distribution functions of marketing.

13. **T** **F** The first step in implementing the marketing concept is to provide a product that satisfies customers.

14. **T** **F** Markets are classified as consumer markets or business-to-business markets.

15. **T** **F** The marketing mix is composed of product, price, distribution, and promotion.

16. **T** **F** When Toyota focuses its advertising for the Corolla on the population between the ages of 20 and 34, it is targeting a specific market.

17. **T** **F** The four common bases of market segmentation are demographic, strategic, geographic, and discretionary.

18. **T** **F** Pricing is an uncontrollable element of the marketing environment.

19. **T** **F** Government reports, trade shows, and annual reports can all be good resources for marketing research.

20. **T** **F** Understanding factors that affect buying behavior helps marketing managers to predict consumer responses to marketing strategies and helps to develop a marketing mix.

Multiple-Choice Questions

21. _____ Which major function of marketing is riddled with thefts, obsolescence, and lawsuits?
    a. Risk taking
    b. Standardizing
    c. Financing
    d. Information gathering
    e. Selling

22. _____ When fresh vegetables are shipped to Oklahoma from Mexico, which utility is added?
    a. Form
    b. Place
    c. Price
    d. Possession
    e. Time

23. _____ The sales orientation was predominant during the
    a. late 1800s.
    b. 1920s.
    c. 1940s.
    d. late 1950s.
    e. 1970s.

24. _____ To implement the marketing concept, the firm must mobilize its marketing resources to
    a. price the product at a level that is acceptable to buyers.
    b. provide a product that will not satisfy the firm's objectives.
    c. minimize promotion.
    d. reduce the number of distribution sites.
    e. obtain incorrect marketing information.

25. _____ Women in the market can be classified as
    a. market segmentation.
    b. a marketing mix.
    c. a market segment.
    d. an independent market.
    e. a producer market.

26. _____ What element of the marketing mix provides information to consumers?
    a. Product
    b. Price
    c. Promotion
    d. Distribution
    e. Quality

27. _____ Which element of the marketing mix focuses on transportation, storage, and intermediaries?
    a. Product
    b. Price
    c. Distribution
    d. Promotion
    e. Buying

28. _____ Which environmental force influences change in consumers' attitudes, beliefs, norms, customs, and lifestyles?
    a. Legal, political, and regulatory
    b. Competitive
    c. Technological
    d. Economic
    e. Sociocultural

29. _____ What situational influence can affect the consumer buying process?
    a. They have uses for the products.
    b. They like the convenience that products provide.
    c. They take pride in ownership of products.
    d. They believe that products will enhance their wealth.
    e. All of the above.

30. _____ What type of income is Ramona's $2,450 monthly take-home amount after taxes?
    a. Ordinary
    b. Personal
    c. Disposable
    d. Gross
    e. Discretionary

Answers to the Test Yourself questions appear at the end of the book on page TY-2.

Video Case

Raleigh Wheels Out Steel Bicycle Marketing

From its 19th-century roots as a British bicycle company, Raleigh has developed a worldwide reputation for marketing sturdy, comfortable, steel-frame bicycles. The firm, named for the street in Nottingham, England, where it was originally located, was a trendsetter in designing and manufacturing bicycles. When Raleigh introduced steel-frame bicycles equipped with three-speed gear hubs in 1903, it revolutionized the industry and set off a never-ending race to improve the product's technology. In the pre-auto era, its bicycles became a two-wheeled status symbol for British consumers, and the brand maintained its cachet for decades. Although Raleigh's chopper-style bicycles were hugely popular in the 1970s, international competition and changing consumer tastes have taken a toll during the past few decades.

Now Raleigh markets a wide variety of bicycles to consumers in Europe, Canada, and the United States. Its U.S. division, based in Kent, Washington, has been researching new bicycles for contemporary consumers and developing models that are lighter, faster, and better. Inspired by the European lifestyle and tradition of getting around on bicycles, and its long history in the business, Raleigh is looking to reinvigorate sales and capture a larger share of the $6 billion U.S. bicycle market.

Raleigh's U.S. marketers have been observing the "messenger market," customers who ride bicycles through downtown streets to deliver documents and small packages to businesses and individuals. They have also noted that many everyday bicycle riders dress casually, in T-shirts and jeans, rather than in special racing outfits designed for speed. Targeting consumers who enjoy riding bicycles as a lifestyle, Raleigh's marketers are focusing on this segment's specific needs and preferences as they develop, price, promote, and distribute new models.

In recent years, Raleigh's marketers have stepped up the practice of bringing demonstration fleets to public places where potential buyers can hop on one of the company's bicycles and pedal for a few minutes. The idea is to allow consumers who enjoy bicycling to actually experience the fun feeling of riding a Raleigh. The marketers are also fanning out to visit bicycle races and meet bicyclists in cities and towns across America, encouraging discussions about Raleigh and about bicycling in general and seeking feedback about particular Raleigh products.

Listening to consumers, Raleigh's marketers recognized that many had misperceptions about the weight of steel-frame bicycles. Although steel can be quite heavy, Raleigh's bicycles are solid yet light, nimble, and easy to steer. Those who have been on bicycles with steel frames praise the quality of the ride, saying that steel "has a soul," according to market research.

To stay in touch with its target market, Raleigh is increasingly active in social media. It has several thousand fans who visit its Facebook page to see the latest product concepts and post their own photos and comments about Raleigh bicycles. It also uses Twitter to keep customers informed and answer questions about its bicycles and upcoming demonstration events. The company's main blog communicates the latest news about everything from frame design and new bike colors under consideration to product awards and racing activities. It has a separate blog about both the fun and the challenges of commuting on bicycle, a topic in which its customers are intensely interested because so many do exactly that. By listening to customers and showing that it understands the daily life of its target market, Raleigh is wheeling toward higher sales in a highly competitive marketplace.[20]

Questions for Discussion

1. Is Raleigh using the marketing concept? Explain.
2. What type of approach does Raleigh use to select target markets?
3. Of the four categories of segmentation variables, which is most important to Raleigh's segmentation strategy, and why?

Building Skills for Career Success

1. Social Media Exercise

Building customer relationships through effective marketing

Comcast, the cable and communications provider, was one of the first companies to use Twitter for customer service. Developed by Frank Eliason, the company's first Director of Digital Care, Bill Gerth currently manages the ComcastCares feed on Twitter. Gerth and the Comcast team scan Twitter for complaints about service and contact the customers to see how Comcast can remedy the situation. This has altered the culture of the organization and prompted other companies to utilize Twitter for customer service. Visit the site at Comcastcares on Twitter.

1. After reviewing Comcastcares on Twitter, do you think that this helps with customer service? Why or why not?
2. Do you see other applications for Twitter for a communications giant like Comcast?

2. Building Team Skills

Review the text definitions of *market* and *target market*. Markets can be classified as consumer or industrial. Buyer behavior consists of the decisions and actions of those involved in buying and using products or services. By examining aspects of a company's products, you can determine the company's target market and the characteristics important to members of that target market.

Assignment

1. Working in teams of three to five, identify a company and a few of its most popular products.
2. List and discuss characteristics that customers may find important, including price, quality, brand name, variety of services, salespeople, customer service, special offers, promotional campaign, packaging, convenience of use, convenience of purchase, location, guarantees, store/office decor, and payment terms.
3. Write a description of the company's primary customer (target market).

3. Researching Different Careers

Before interviewing for a job, you should learn all you can about the company to help prepare you to ask meaningful questions during the interview. To find out more about a company, you can conduct market research before you interview.

Assignment

1. Choose at least two local companies for which you might like to work.
2. Contact your local Chamber of Commerce. (The Chamber of Commerce collects information about local businesses and most of its services are free.) Ask for the information you desire.
3. Call the Better Business Bureau in your community (or check online) to determine if there are any complaints against the companies you are researching.
4. Prepare a report summarizing your findings.

Endnotes

1. Based on information in Christoph Rauwald, "Volkswagen Speeds Ahead in China," *Wall Street Journal*, November 13, 2012, www.wsj.com; Christoph Rauwald, "Volkswagen Sees Slowing Demand," *Wall Street Journal*, October 24, 2012, www.wsj.com; Diana T. Kurylko, "VW's 3 Marketing Messages: Engineering, Humor, Price," *Automotive News*, August 27, 2012, p. 22; David Jolly, "Volkswagen Reports Record Profit," *New York Times*, February 24, 2012, www.nytimes.com; www.volkswagen.com.
2. "Definition of Marketing," American Marketing Association, www.marketingpower.com/AboutAMA/Pages/DefinitionofMarketing.aspx, accessed December 1, 2012.
3. V. Kumar, *Customer Lifetime Value* (Hanover, MA: now Publishers, 2008), 5.
4. Rajkumar Venkatesan and V. Kumar, "A Customer Lifetime Value Framework for Customer Selection and Resource Selection and Resource Allocation Strategy," *Journal of Marketing* 68 (October 2004), 106–125.
5. Dennis Price, "How Much Is a Customer REALLY Worth?" *Insider Retailing*, March 18, 2012, www.insideretailing.com.au/IR/IRNews/How-much-is-a-customer-REALLY-worth--4454.aspx, accessed December 24, 2012; Customer Lifetime Value Calculator, http://hbsp.harvard.edu/multimedia/flashtools/cltv/index.html, accessed December 24, 2012.
6. Tanzina Vega, "A Spate of Rebranding for Spanish-Language TV," *New York Times*, December 2, 2012, http://www.nytimes.com/2012/12/03/business/media/a-spate-of-rebranding-for-spanish-language-television.html.
7. Laurie Burkitt and Ann Zimmerman, "Toys 'R' Us Grows in China, With Tiger Moms in Mind," *Wall Street Journal*, November 19, 2012, http://online.wsj.com/article/SB10001424127887323622904578128840637201504.html.
8. "Is Zipcar for Me?," Zipcar, http://www.zipcar.com/is-it, accessed January 26, 2013.
9. "Style," Target, http://www.target.com/c/target-style-ways-to-shop/-/N-568yu#?lnk=lnav_more%20to%20explore_3&intc=805575|null, accessed January 26, 2013.
10. Anna Molin, "In Sweden, Playtime Goes Gender-Neutral for the Holidays," *Wall Street Journal*, November 28, 2012, http://online.wsj.com/article/SB10001424127887324205404578147373422297406.html.
11. Andria Cheng, "Refashioning Perks up Abercrombie," *Wall Street Journal*, November 14, 2012, http://online.wsj.com/article/SB10001424127887324556304578118641486799744.html.
12. Jeffrey A. Trachtenberg, "HarperCollins Closes its Last Warehouses," *Wall Street Journal*, November 5, 2012, http://online.wsj.com/article/SB10001424052970204349404578101283153626900.html.
13. Stuart Elliot, "A Hotel Chain Scouts for Regional Art and Artists," *New York Times*, September 24, 2012, http://www.nytimes.com/2012/09/24/business/media/springhill-suites-makes-art-the-focus-of-a-marketing-plan-campaign-spotlight.html.
14. Kevin Colleran, "Four Low-Cost Ways to Measure Market Demand," *Wall Street Journal*, December 4, 2012, http://blogs.wsj.com/accelerators/2012/12/04/4-easy-ways-to-measure-market-demand/.
15. Dun & Bradstreet, http://www.dnb.com/, accessed December 4, 2012.
16. Stuart Elliot, "Tracking Viewers from TV to Computer to Smartphone," *New York Times*, June 11, 2012, http://mediadecoder.blogs.nytimes.com/2012/06/11/tracking-viewers-from-tv-to-computer-to-smartphone/, accessed December 23, 2012.
17. William M. Pride and O. C. Ferrell, *Foundations of Marketing*, 4th ed. (Mason, OH: South-Western/Cengage Learning, 2011), 128.
18. Christine Crandell, "The New Corporate Power Couple," *Forbes*, February 25, 2012, http://www.forbes.com/sites/christinecrandell/2012/02/25/the-new-corporate-power-couple/, accessed December 24, 2012.
19. Press release, "Personal Income and Outlays, December 2012," U.S. Department of Commerce, Bureau of Economic Analysis, www.bea.gov/newsreleases/national/pi/pinewsrelease.htm.
20. "BRAINy Awards Honor Individuals," *Bicycle Retailer and Industry News*, April 15, 2010, www.bicycleretailer.com/news/newsDetail/3961.html; Francis Lawell, "Raleigh: Cycling to Success?" *Business Review (UK)* (February, 2009), pp. 16ff; "Industry Overview 2008," *National Bicycle Dealers Association*, http://nbda.com/articles/industry-overview-2008-pg34.htm; www.raleigh.co.uk/; www.raleighusa.com.

© PETER J. KOVACS/SHUTTERSTOCK.COM

Chapter 12

Creating and Pricing Products That Satisfy Customers

Why Should You Care?

To be successful, a business person must understand how to develop and manage a mix of appropriate priced products and to change the mix of products as customers' needs change.

Learning Objectives

Once you complete this chapter, you will be able to:

1 Explain what a product is and how products are classified.

2 Discuss the product life-cycle and how it leads to new-product development.

3 Define *product line* and *product mix* and distinguish between the two.

4 Identify the methods available for changing a product mix.

5 Explain the uses and importance of branding, packaging, and labeling.

6 Describe the economic basis of pricing and the means by which sellers can control prices and buyers' perceptions of prices.

7 Identify the major pricing objectives used by businesses.

8 Examine the three major pricing methods that firms employ.

9 Explain the different strategies available to companies for setting prices.

10 Describe three major types of pricing associated with business products.

Thinking Outside the Box at Oreo

Cookie lovers have been twisting, licking, and dunking Oreo cookies (http://brands.nabisco.com/Oreo/) for more than a century. The original Oreo sandwich cookie featured a thin layer of vanilla creme between two crispy chocolate wafers. In recent years, parent company Nabisco has updated the Oreo with an ever-expanding pantry of innovative flavors, colors, sizes, and shapes to please many millions of fans worldwide.

For example, when Nabisco began marketing Oreo cookies in China in 1996, using the same recipe as Oreos sold in North America, it expected an enthusiastic response. However, sales in China were so lackluster for so long that the company wasn't certain it would leave Oreos on the market. Before making a decision about yanking the product, Nabisco conducted in-depth research—and discovered that Chinese consumers found the filling too sweet and the cookies too bitter. Based on the results, the company had to rethink its approach.

After Nabisco's product experts fine-tuned the recipe for local taste buds, Oreo's sales in China began to improve. Then they took another look at the characteristics that made Oreos such an iconic cookie in the U.S. market. Did the cookies have to be chocolate with vanilla filling? Did they have to be round? Soon Nabisco was experimenting with novel fillings like green tea-flavored creme and mango-flavored creme. It created one version of Oreos in a cylindrical straw shape and another in a thin rectangular shape, both suitable for easy dunking. Sales in China skyrocketed, and today Oreos are the country's top-selling cookies.

Now Nabisco has applied this strategy in other key markets. In Argentina, it offers Oreos with a banana-dulce de leche filling. In Indonesia, it offers Oreos with a chocolate-peanut filling. Meanwhile, Nabisco is bringing out new Oreo varieties for its U.S. brand fans. Seasonal products like Halloween cookies with candy-corn filling and winter cookies with red filling give customers even more reasons to buy, twist, lick, and dunk whenever they crave the Oreo experience.[1]

Did You Know?

Oreo has boosted annual revenues to $2 billion worldwide by developing new flavor combinations, shapes, and sizes geared to local tastes.

A **product** like Oreo cookies has everything one receives in an exchange, including all tangible and intangible attributes and expected benefits. In addition to a sweet and satisfying taste, Oreo cookies come in a familiar package marked with an iconic label. The brand also has the intangible benefit of being an American classic, a favorite snack for more than a century. A car includes tangible benefits, such as a warranty and a GPS navigation system, and intangible attributes, such as status and the memories generated from road trips. Developing and managing products effectively, including these tangible and intangible benefits, are crucial to an organization's ability to maintain successful marketing mixes.

A product can be a good, a service, or an idea. A *good* is a real, physical thing that we can touch, such as an Oreo cookie. A *service* is the result of applying human or mechanical effort to a person or thing. A service is a change we pay others to make for us. A real estate agent's services result in a change in the ownership of real property. A barber's services result in a change in your hairstyle. An *idea* may take the form of philosophies, lessons, concepts, or advice. Often ideas are bundled with a good or service. Thus, we might buy a book (a good) that provides ideas on how to lose weight. Alternatively, we might join Weight Watchers for ideas on how to lose weight and for help (service) in doing so.

In this chapter, we first look at the different aspects of products. We examine product classifications and describe the four stages, or life-cycles, through which every product progresses. Next, we illustrate how firms manage products by modifying or deleting existing ones and developing new products. We also discuss branding, packaging, and labeling. Then our focus shifts to pricing. We explain competitive factors that influence sellers' pricing decisions and explore buyers' perceptions of prices. After considering organizational objectives that can be accomplished through pricing, we outline several methods for setting prices. Finally, we describe pricing strategies by which sellers can reach target markets successfully.

product everything one receives in an exchange, including all tangible and intangible attributes and expected benefits; it may be a good, a service, or an idea

consumer product a product purchased to satisfy personal and family needs

business product a product bought for resale, for making other products, or for use in a firm's operations

convenience product a relatively inexpensive, frequently purchased item for which buyers want to exert only minimal effort

shopping product an item for which buyers are willing to expend considerable effort on planning and making the purchase

specialty product an item that possesses one or more unique characteristics for which a significant group of buyers is willing to expend considerable purchasing effort

CLASSIFICATION OF PRODUCTS

Different classes of products are directed at different target markets according to their varying needs and wants. A product's classification largely determines what kinds of distribution, promotion, and pricing are appropriate in marketing it.

Products can be grouped into two general categories: consumer and business (also called *business-to-business* or *industrial products*). A product purchased to satisfy personal and family needs is a **consumer product**. A product bought by a business for resale, for making other products, or for use in a firm's operations is a **business product**. The same item can be both a consumer and a business product, depending on the buyer's end use. Light bulbs are a consumer product when you use them in your home, but are a business product if you purchase them for use in an office.

Consumer Product Classifications

The traditional and most widely accepted system of classifying consumer products consists of three categories: convenience, shopping, and specialty products. These groupings are based primarily on characteristics of buyers' purchasing behavior.

A **convenience product** is a relatively inexpensive, frequently purchased item for which buyers want to exert only minimal effort to procure. Examples include bread, gasoline, newspapers, soft drinks, and chewing gum. The buyer spends little time in planning the purchase of a convenience item or in comparing available brands or sellers.

A **shopping product** is an item for which buyers are willing to expend considerably more effort on planning and purchasing. Shopping products cost more than convenience products and buyers allocate ample time for comparing prices, product features, qualities, services, and warranties between different stores and brands. Appliances, upholstered furniture, men's suits, bicycles, and mobile phones are examples of shopping products. These products are expected to last for a fairly long time and thus are purchased less frequently than convenience items.

A **specialty product** possesses one or more unique characteristics for which a group of buyers is willing to expend considerable purchasing effort. Buyers know exactly what they want and will not accept a substitute. When seeking out specialty products, purchasers do not compare alternatives. Examples include unique sports cars, a rare imported beer, or original artwork.

Ben & Jerry's ice cream is a covenience product. It's an item you are likely to grab off the shelf without much thought as you walk through the frozen-food aisle of a store. By contrast, people may spend considerable amount of time and effort when buying a shopping product, like furniture.

IMAGE COURTESY OF THE ADVERTISING ARCHIVES

PRESOTTO INDUSTRIE MOBILI S.P.A/DDC DOMUS DESIGN COLLECTION

Business Product Classifications

Based on their characteristics and intended uses, business products can be classified into the following categories: raw materials, major equipment, accessory equipment, component parts, process materials, supplies, and services.

A **raw material** is a basic material that becomes part of a physical product. It usually comes from mines, forests, oceans, or recycled solid wastes. Raw materials are generally bought and sold according to grades and specifications.

Major equipment includes large tools and machines used for production purposes. Examples of major equipment are lathes, cranes, and stamping machines. Some major equipment is custom-made for a particular organization, but other items are standardized products that perform one or several tasks for many types of organizations.

Accessory equipment is standardized equipment used in a firm's production or office activities. Examples include hand tools, fax machines, fractional horsepower motors, and calculators. Compared with major equipment, accessory items are usually less expensive and are purchased routinely with less negotiation.

A **component part** becomes part of a physical product and is either a finished item ready for assembly or a product that needs little processing prior to assembly. Although it becomes an element of a larger product, a component part can often be identified easily. Clocks, tires, computer chips, and switches are examples of component parts.

A **process material** is used directly in the production of another product. Unlike a component part, a process material is not readily identifiable in the finished product. Like raw materials, process materials are purchased according to industry standards or to the specifications of the individual purchaser. Examples include industrial glue and food preservatives.

A **supply** facilitates production and operations but does not become part of a finished product. Paper, pencils, oils, and cleaning agents are examples.

A **business service** is an intangible product that an organization uses in its operations. Examples include financial, legal, online, janitorial, and marketing research services. Purchasers must decide whether to provide their own services internally or to hire a contractor from outside the organization.

raw material a basic material that actually becomes part of a physical product; usually comes from mines, forests, oceans, or recycled solid wastes

major equipment large tools and machines used for production purposes

accessory equipment standardized equipment used in a firm's production or office activities

component part an item that becomes part of a physical product and is either a finished item ready for assembly or a product that needs little processing before assembly

process material a material that is used directly in the production of another product but is not readily identifiable in the finished product

Concept Check

✓ Identify the general categories of products.

✓ Describe the classifications of consumer products.

✓ Based on their characteristics, business products can be classified into what categories?

THE PRODUCT LIFE-CYCLE

In a way, products are like people. They are born, they live, and they die. Every product progresses through a **product life-cycle**, a series of stages in which a product's sales revenue and profit increase, reach a peak, and then decline. A firm must be able to launch, modify, and delete products from its offering in response to changes in product life-cycles. Otherwise, the firm's profits will disappear, and the firm will fail. Depending on the product, life-cycle stages vary in length. In this section, we discuss the stages of the life-cycle and how marketers can use this information.

Stages of the Product Life-Cycle

Generally, the product life-cycle is composed of four stages—introduction, growth, maturity, and decline—as shown in Figure 12-1. Some products progress through these stages rapidly, in a few weeks or months, while others can take years. The Koosh Ball, popular in the late 1980s, had a short life-cycle. In contrast, Parker Brothers' Monopoly game, which was introduced nearly a century ago, is still going strong.

INTRODUCTION In the *introduction stage*, customer awareness and acceptance of the product are low. Sales rise gradually as a result of promotion and distribution activities. There are no competitors at this stage. High development and marketing costs result in low profit, or even in a loss, initially. The price can be high as the firm recoups research and development expenses and ramps up production. Customers

Learning Objective

2 Discuss the product life-cycle and how it leads to new-product development.

supply an item that facilitates production and operations but does not become part of a finished product

business service an intangible product that an organization uses in its operations

product life-cycle a series of stages in which a product's sales revenue and profit increase, reach a peak, and then decline

FIGURE 12-1 Product Life-Cycle

The graph shows sales volume and profits during the life-cycle of a product.

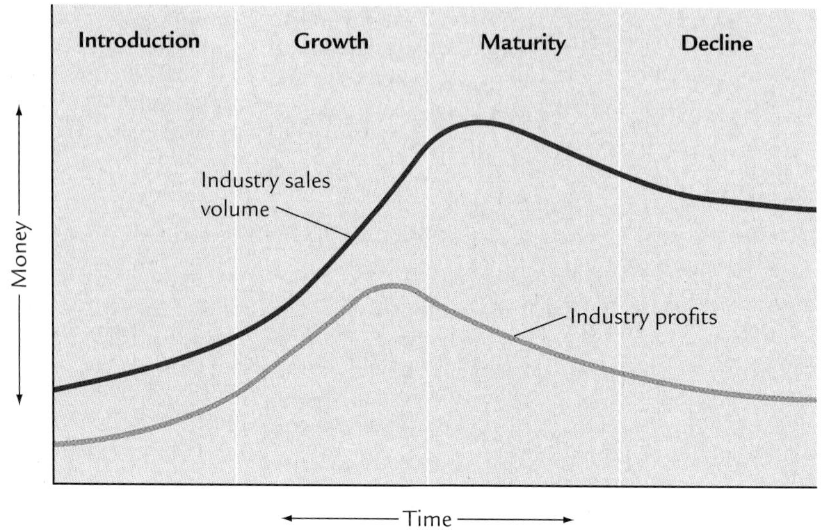

Source: William M. Pride and O. C. Ferrell, *Marketing: Concepts and Strategies*, 17th ed. (Mason, OH: South-Western/Cengage Learning, 2014). Adapted with permission.

are primarily people who want to be at the forefront of owning the new product. The marketing challenge at this stage is to make potential customers aware of the product's existence and its features, benefits, and uses.

A new product is seldom an immediate success. Marketers must monitor early buying patterns and be prepared to modify the product promptly if necessary. The firm should attempt to price the product to attract the market segment that has the greatest desire and ability to purchase it. Plans for distribution and promotion should suit the targeted market segment. All ingredients of the marketing mix may need to be adjusted quickly to maintain sales growth during the introduction stage.

GROWTH In the *growth stage*, sales increase rapidly as consumers gain awareness of the product. Other firms have begun to market competing products. The competition and decreased unit costs (owing to mass production) result in a lower price, which reduces the profit per unit. Industry profits reach a peak and begin to decline during this stage. To meet the needs of the growing market, the originating firm offers modified versions of the product and expands distribution.

Management's goal in the growth stage is to stabilize and strengthen the product's position by encouraging brand loyalty. To beat the competition, the company may further improve the product or expand the product line to appeal to additional market segments. For example, to compete with the dominant Apple iPad in the e-reader category, Amazon and Barnes & Noble both have released e-reader product lines with features aimed at capturing different market segments and gaining market share in the growing industry.

Management also may compete by lowering prices if increased production efficiency has resulted in sufficient savings. As the product becomes more widely accepted, marketers may be able to broaden the network of distributors. Marketers can also emphasize customer service and prompt credit for defective products. During this period, promotional efforts attempt to build brand loyalty among customers.

MATURITY Sales are still increasing at the beginning of the *maturity stage*, but the rate of increase has slowed. Later on, the sales curve peaks and begins to decline, as do industry profits. Product lines are simplified, markets are segmented more carefully, and price competition increases, which forces weaker competitors to leave the industry. Marketers continue to introduce refinements and extensions of the original product to the market.

During a product's maturity stage, its market share may be strengthened by redesigned packaging or style changes. For example, Sabra Foods redesigned its hummus packages and propelled the product to new levels of growth. With a distinctive red lid, Sabra is eye-catching and recognizable on the shelf. Transparent panels allow consumers to see the product, including a fresh garnish of pine nuts and sprinkling of olive oil. Formerly a niche product for Israeli American consumers, the package redesign propelled the company to command a 55 percent market share for hummus and it continues to grow.[2] Redesigned packaging may convince consumers to use the product more often or in new ways.

Pricing strategies are flexible during the maturity stage. Markdowns and price incentives are not uncommon, although price increases may work to offset production and distribution costs. Marketers may offer incentives and assistance of various kinds to dealers to encourage them to support mature products, especially in the face of competition from private-label brands. New promotional efforts and aggressive personal selling may be necessary during this period of intense competition.

DECLINE During the *decline stage*, sales volume decreases sharply and profits continue to fall. The number of competing firms declines, and the only survivors in the marketplace are firms that specialize in marketing the product. Production and marketing costs become the most important determinant of profit.

When a product adds to the success of the overall product line, the company may retain it. Otherwise, management must determine when to eliminate it. A product usually declines because of technological advances or environmental factors, or because consumers have switched to competing brands. Therefore, few changes are made in the product itself during this stage. Instead, management may raise the price to cover costs, reprice to maintain market share, or lower the price to reduce inventory. Management will narrow distribution to the most profitable existing markets. During this period, the company probably will not spend heavily on promotion, although it may use some advertising and sales incentives to slow the product's decline. The company may choose to eliminate less-profitable versions of the product from the product line or may decide to drop the product entirely. For example, to regain ground after significant declines in a very competitive electronics market, HP is aggressively cutting items from unprofitable product lines, including half of its 2,100 laser printers. Having so many products largely similar to one another can be a risk, as they compete for the same consumers.[3]

Personal Apps

Do you have one of these?

Think back to toys that were wildly popular when you were younger. How many do you still see in stores? This shows how quickly some products can pass through the stages of the product life-cycle.

Saying "goodbye" to the pay telephone. The pay telephone is in the decline stage of the product life-cycle. Do you recall seeing one? If so, when and where? You might have a hard time remembering.

Using the Product Life-Cycle

When making marketing strategy decisions, managers must be aware of the life-cycle stage of each product for which they are responsible and to estimate how long the product is expected to remain in that stage. For example, if a product is expected to remain in the maturity stage for a long time, there is no rush to develop a replacement product. A firm risks speeding the decline of an existing product by releasing a replacement before the earlier product has reached the decline stage. Even so, a firm will be willing to take that risk in some cases. In other situations, a company will attempt to extend a product's life-cycle. Extending its life can be an important tool in maintaining a product's profitability. A condiment staple since its introduction more than 140 years ago, Heinz Ketchup has extended its life through packaging innovations, such as squeeze bottles and single-serving containers, releasing different flavors, like balsamic and jalapeño and even experimenting with purple and green-colored ketchup.

PRODUCT LINE AND PRODUCT MIX

A **product line** is a group of similar products that differ only in relatively minor characteristics. Generally, the products within a product line are related to each other in the way they are produced, marketed, or used. Procter & Gamble, for example, manufactures and markets several shampoos, including Prell, Head & Shoulders, and Ivory.

While organizations may start a new product line, many opt to introduce new products within existing product lines. It is less costly than starting a new product line and permits them to apply the experience and knowledge they have acquired to the production and marketing of new products.

An organization's **product mix** consists of all the products the firm offers for sale. For example, Procter & Gamble has nearly 70 brands that fall into one of two product line categories: beauty and grooming and household care, some of which are well-known, such as Gillette and Febreze, and others that are less famous in the United States, such as Lenor and Ariel.[4] Two "dimensions" are often applied to a firm's product mix. The *width* of the mix is the number of product lines it contains. The *depth* of the mix is the average number of individual products within each line. These measures are general—no exact numbers correspond to these categories. Some organizations offer a broad product mix as a means of trying to be competitive in many different categories.

MANAGING THE PRODUCT MIX

Learning Objective

4 Identify the methods available for changing a product mix.

To provide products that satisfy people in a firm's target market or markets and that also achieve the organization's objectives, a marketer must develop, adjust, and maintain an effective product mix. The same product mix is rarely effective for long. As customers' product preferences and attitudes change, their desire for a product may diminish or grow. A firm may also need to alter its product mix to adapt to changes in the competition. For example, a marketer may have to introduce a new product, modify an existing one, or eliminate a product from the mix because one or more competitors have grown more dominant in the market segment. A marketer may also expand the firm's product mix to take advantage of excess marketing and production capacity. For example, General Mills has a wide product mix consisting of many different brands. It frequently expands its product mix by adding new offerings to its different product lines, such as breakfast cereals. The breakfast cereals product line features familiar brands such as Fiber One, Cascadian Farms, and Wheaties. A firm must be careful when altering the product mix that the changes made bring about improvements in the mix. There are three major ways to improve a product mix: change an existing product, delete a product, or develop a new product.

Managing Existing Products

A product mix can be changed by deriving additional products from existing ones. This can be accomplished through product modifications and by line extensions.

PRODUCT MODIFICATIONS **Product modification** refers to changing one or more of a product's characteristics. For this approach to be effective, several conditions must be met. First, the product must be modifiable. Second, existing customers must be able to perceive that a modification has been made, assuming that the modified item is still directed at the same target market. Third, the modification should make the product more consistent with customers' desires so that it provides greater satisfaction. For example, General Motors upgraded the structure and cooling systems in the battery for its Chevrolet Volt hybrid car in order to address some consumer hesitations over the battery's safety. Volt owners were encouraged to bring their vehicles to a dealership to receive the new modified battery. In order to publicize the improvement, GM made widespread announcements regarding the change, including on the National Highway Safety Administration website.[5]

product modification the process of changing one or more of a product's characteristics

Existing products can be altered in three primary ways: in quality, function, and aesthetics. *Quality modifications* are changes that relate to a product's dependability and durability and are usually achieved by alterations in the materials or production process. *Functional modifications* affect a product's versatility, effectiveness, convenience, or safety. They usually require redesign of the product. Typical product categories that have undergone extensive functional modifications include home appliances, office and farm equipment, and consumer electronics. *Aesthetic modifications* change the sensory appeal of a product by altering its taste, texture, sound, smell, or visual characteristics. Because a buyer's purchasing decision is affected by sensory stimuli, an aesthetic modification may impact purchases. Through aesthetic modifications, a firm can differentiate its product from competing brands and gain market share if customers find the modified product more appealing.

AP IMAGES/PAUL SAKUMA

New line extensions help companies like Frito Lay to be more competitive and to maintain or increase their market shares. Frito Lay's first line extension, after its initial introduction of original, was the barbeque flavor. It has since expanded its product mix through its use of product line extensions including such flavors as, Salt & Vinegar, Limon, and Sour Cream & Onion.

line extension development of a new product that is closely related to one or more products in the existing product line but designed specifically to meet somewhat different customer needs

LINE EXTENSIONS A **line extension** is the development of a product closely related to one or more products in the existing product line but designed specifically to meet somewhat different customer needs. Studies show that men now help out more with household chores. Marketers for laundry brand Tide target this segment with Pods, pre-measured capsules of laundry detergent. The detergent inside is the same Tide product, but it is delivered in a different way to satisfy wives who want their husbands to help with chores, but do not trust them to use the correct amount of product.[6]

Many of the so-called new products introduced each year are in fact line extensions. Line extensions are more common than new products because they are a less-expensive, lower-risk alternative for increasing sales. A line extension may focus on a different market segment or be an attempt to increase sales within the same market segment by more precisely satisfying that segment's needs, hopefully taking away market share from competitors.

Deleting Products

product deletion the elimination of one or more products from a product line

To maintain an effective product mix, an organization often has to eliminate some products. This is called **product deletion**. A weak and unprofitable product costs a company time, money, and resources that could be used to modify other products or develop new ones. A weak product's unfavorable image can negatively impact the customer perception and sales of other products sold by the firm.

Most organizations find it difficult to delete a product because of the costs associated with bringing the product to market or for more emotional reasons. Some firms drop weak products only after they have become severe financial burdens. A better approach is to conduct a systematic review of the product's impact on the overall effectiveness of a firm's product mix. Such a review should analyze a product's contribution to a company's sales for a given period and should include estimates of future sales, costs, and profits. This review should help a firm to determine whether changes in the marketing strategy might improve the product's performance.

A product-deletion program can improve a firm's performance. Once a prestige product in many homes, *Encyclopaedia Britannica* stopped issuing print editions for the first time in its 244 years. The latest print version was 32 volumes and cost $1,395. Britannica's online subscription, on the other hand, costs $70 per year, is updated more frequently, and is cheaper for the company to maintain.[7]

Developing New Products

Developing and introducing new products is frequently time consuming, expensive, and risky. Thousands of new products are introduced annually. For most firms, more than half of new products will fail. Even Google, a highly successful company, has a 36 percent failure rate for its products.[8] Although developing new products is risky, failing to introduce new products can be just as hazardous. Successful new products can produce benefits for an organization, including survival, profits, a sustainable competitive advantage, and a favorable public image.

New products are generally grouped into three categories on the basis of their degree of similarity to existing products. *Imitations* are

Fan blades 'chop' the airflow, causing buffeting. The new Dyson fan works differently. An annular jet accelerates the surrounding air and amplifies it fifteen times. There are no blades to chop the air so the airflow is smooth – it cools without the unpleasant buffeting.

Blades cause buffeting.

No blades means no buffeting.

dyson air multiplier
No blades. No buffeting.
Learn more at www.dyson.co.uk
Or experience in-store

Not your grandparents' old fan. You probably won't find a fan like this one in your grandparents' attic. This new type of bladeless fan, developed by Dyson, is called the Air Multiplier. What new-product category do you think the Air Multiplier falls into? Is it an imitation, innovation, or adaptation?

products designed to compete with existing products of other firms. The success of Apple's iPad, for instance, spawned many tablet computer competitors. *Adaptations* are variations of existing products that are intended for an established market. Product refinements and extensions are the adaptations considered most often, although imitative products may also include some refinement and extension. *Innovations* are entirely new products. They may give rise to a new industry or revolutionize an existing one. Innovative products take considerable time, effort, and money to develop. They are by far the riskiest new product to develop and launch and are therefore less common than adaptations and imitations. While other companies market exercise watches and monitors, the larklife is a wristband monitor in a class unto itself. Users wear it and the device monitors exercise, diet, sleep, and other factors and offers coaching on how to maximize health and happiness via an iPhone app.[9] As shown in Figure 12-2, the process of developing a new product consists of seven phases.

IDEA GENERATION Idea generation involves looking for product ideas that will help a firm to achieve its objectives. Although some organizations get their ideas almost by chance, firms trying to maximize product-mix effectiveness develop systematic approaches for generating new-product ideas. Ideas may come from virtually any stakeholder associated with the firm, including managers, researchers, engineers, competitors, advertising agencies, management consultants, private research organizations, customers, salespersons, or top executives. Sometimes, large firms with superior experience and resources may mentor small firms and help them generate ideas to help their businesses grow. Business incubators exist all over the country that pair new businesses with established ones so that the new business can learn about marketing and branding from experts. Goldman Sachs, Walmart, Chase Bank, and Staples have all hosted events and programs to counsel start-ups. Jim Koch of Boston Beer Company, maker of Sam Adams, partners with the small business lender, Accion, for the Brewing the American Dream program, which offers speed coaching sessions and loans to small businesses.[10]

SCREENING During screening, ideas that do not match organizational resources and objectives are rejected. In this phase, a firm's managers consider whether the organization has personnel with the correct expertise to develop and market the proposed product. Management may reject a good idea because the company lacks the necessary skills and abilities to make the product a success. The largest number of product ideas are rejected during the screening phase.

CONCEPT TESTING Concept testing is a phase in which a product idea is presented to a sample of potential buyers through a written or oral description (and perhaps drawings) to determine their attitudes and initial buying intentions. An organization may test one or several concepts when developing a product idea. Concept testing is a low-cost means for an organization to determine consumers' initial reactions to an idea before investing considerable resources in product research and development (R&D). Product development personnel use the results of concept testing to make product attributes and benefits reflect the characteristics and features most important to potential customers. The questions asked vary

FIGURE 12-2 Phases of New-Product Development

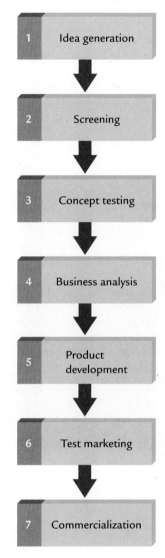

Generally, marketers follow these seven steps to develop a new product.

1. Idea generation
2. Screening
3. Concept testing
4. Business analysis
5. Product development
6. Test marketing
7. Commercialization

Source: William M. Pride and O. C. Ferrell, *Marketing: Concepts and Strategies*, 17th ed. (Mason, OH: South-Western/Cengage Learning, 2014). Adapted with permission.

considerably depending on the type of product idea being tested. The following are typical:

- Which benefits of the proposed product are especially attractive to you?
- Which features are of little or no interest to you?
- What are the primary advantages of the proposed product over the one you currently use?
- If this product were available at an appropriate price, how often would you buy it?
- How could this proposed product be improved?

BUSINESS ANALYSIS Business analysis generates tentative ideas about a potential product's financial performance, including profitability. During this stage, the firm considers how the new product, if it were introduced, would affect the firm's overall sales, costs, and profits. Marketing personnel usually work up preliminary sales and cost projections at this point, with the help of R&D and production managers.

PRODUCT DEVELOPMENT In the product development phase, the company must find out if it is technically feasible to produce the product and if the product can be made at a low enough cost for the company to generate a profit. If a product idea makes it to this point, it is transformed into a working model, or prototype. Often, this step is time consuming and expensive for the organization. If a product moves through this step successfully, then it is ready for test marketing.

TEST MARKETING Test marketing is the limited introduction of a product in several towns or cities that are representative of the intended target market. Its aim is to determine buyers' probable reactions. Marketers experiment with advertising, pricing, and packaging in different test markets and measure the extent of brand awareness, brand switching, and repeat purchases that result from alterations in the marketing mix. Columbus, Ohio, for example, is a popular test market because its demographics are fairly representative of large portions the nation.[11]

COMMERCIALIZATION During commercialization, the organization completes plans for full-scale manufacturing and marketing and prepares project budgets. In the early part of the commercialization phase, marketing management analyzes the results of test marketing to determine necessary changes in the marketing mix. Test marketing may reveal, for example, that marketers must change the product's physical attributes, modify the distribution plan, alter promotional efforts, or change the price. Most new products are marketed in stages, beginning in selected geographic areas and expanding into adjacent areas over a period of time.

Why Do Products Fail?

Despite this rigorous process for developing product ideas, most new products end up as failures. In fact, many well-known companies have produced market failures (see Table 12-1).

Why does a new product fail? Mainly because the product and its marketing program are not planned and tested as thoroughly as they should be. For example,

TABLE 12-1 Examples of Product Failures

Company	Product
Apple	Maps app (2012)
Apple	Newton (1993)
Barbie	Earring Magic Ken (1993)
Coca-Cola	New Coke (1985)
Colgate	Kitchen Entrees (1982)
Ford	Edsel (1957)
Pepsi	Crystal Pepsi (1993)

Source: Adapted from: "25 Biggest Product Flops of All Time," *Daily Finance*, http://www.dailyfinance.com/photos/top-25-biggest-product -flops-of-all-time/ (accessed December 24, 2012); Jillian Berman, "16 Epic Product Fails," Huffington Post, September 28, 2012, http://www .huffingtonpost.com/2012/09/28/company-product-fails_n_1923621.html#slide=1579656.

to save on development costs, a firm may market-test a product before the kinks are worked out, or may not test its entire marketing mix. Or, when problems show up in the testing stage, a firm may try to recover its product development costs by pushing ahead with full-scale marketing anyway. Finally, some firms try to market new products with inadequate financing.

BRANDING, PACKAGING, AND LABELING

Three important features of a product (particularly a consumer product) are its brand, package, and label. These features may be used to associate a product with a successful product line or to distinguish it from existing products. They may be designed to attract customers at the point of sale or to provide information to potential buyers. Because the brand, package, and label are integral elements of the product, they deserve careful attention during product planning.

What Is a Brand?

A **brand** is a name, term, symbol, design, or any combination that identifies a seller's products and distinguishes it from other sellers' products. A **brand name** is the part of a brand that can be spoken. It may include letters, words, numbers, or pronounceable symbols, such as the ampersand in *Procter & Gamble*. A **brand mark**, on the other hand, is the part of a brand that is a symbol or distinctive design, such as the Nike "swoosh." A **trademark** is a brand name or brand mark that is registered with the U.S. Patent and Trademark Office and thus is legally protected from use by anyone except its owner. A **trade name** is the complete and legal name of an organization, such as Pizza Hut or Cengage Learning (the publisher of this text).

Types of Brands

Brands are often classified according to who owns them: manufacturers or stores. A **manufacturer** (or **producer**) **brand**, as the name implies, is a brand that is owned by the manufacturer. Many foods (Kellogg's Frosted Flakes), major appliances (Whirlpool), gasolines (Exxon Mobil), automobiles (Honda), and clothing (Levi's) are sold as manufacturers' brands. Some consumers prefer manufacturer brands because they are usually nationally known, offer consistent quality, and are widely available.

Learning Objective

5 Explain the uses and importance of branding, packaging, and labeling.

brand a name, term, symbol, design, or any combination of these that identifies a seller's products as distinct from those of other sellers

brand name the part of a brand that can be spoken

brand mark the part of a brand that is a symbol or distinctive design

trademark a brand name or brand mark that is registered with the U.S. Patent and Trademark Office and thus is legally protected from use by anyone except its owner

trade name the complete and legal name of an organization

manufacturer (or producer) brand a brand that is owned by a manufacturer

What's your favorite brand?

Do you know exactly what your favorite brand of snack food looks like? Because its logo and packaging are so familiar, you can grab it without examining the other brands on the shelf. That's how recognizable brands save you time.

store (or private) brand a brand that is owned by an individual wholesaler or retailer

generic product (or generic brand) a product with no brand at all

brand loyalty extent to which a customer is favorable toward buying a specific brand

A **store** (or **private**) brand is a brand that is owned by an individual wholesaler or retailer. Among the better-known store brands are Kenmore and Craftsman, both owned by Sears. Owners of store brands claim that they can offer lower prices, earn greater profits, and improve customer loyalty by offering their own brands. Some companies that manufacture private brands also produce their own manufacturer brands. They often find such operations profitable because they can use excess capacity and avoid most marketing costs. Many private-branded grocery products are produced by companies that specialize in making private-label products. Most supermarkets rely heavily on their store brands. According to the Private Label Manufacturer's Association, the popularity and quality of store brands is on the rise, particularly among consumers who seek out good value without sacrificing quality.[12]

Consumer confidence is the most important element in the success of a branded product, whether the brand is owned by a producer or by a retailer. Because branding identifies each product, customers can easily repurchase products that provide satisfaction, performance, and quality. Moreover, they can just as easily avoid or ignore unsatisfactory products. In supermarkets, the products most likely to keep their shelf space are the brands with large market shares and strong customer loyalty.

A **generic product** (sometimes called a **generic brand**) is a product with no brand at all. Its plain package carries only the name of the product—applesauce, peanut butter, or potato chips. Generic products, available in supermarkets since 1977, are sometimes made by the major producers that manufacture name brands.

Benefits of Branding

Both buyers and sellers benefit from branding. Because brands are easily recognizable, they reduce the amount of time buyers spend on shopping, as they can quickly identify the brands they prefer. Choosing particular brands, such as Chanel, Polo, Patagonia, or Nike, can be a way of expressing oneself and identifying with certain lifestyle characteristics and values. Brands also help to reduce the perceived risk of purchase. Finally, customers may receive a psychological reward from owning a brand that symbolizes status. The Lexus brand is an example.

Branding helps a firm to introduce a new product that carries a familiar brand name because buyers already know the brand. Branding aids sellers in their promotional efforts because promotion of each branded product indirectly promotes other products of the same brand. H.J. Heinz, for example, markets many products with the Heinz brand name, such as ketchup, vinegar, gravies, barbecue sauce, and steak sauce.

One chief benefit of branding is the creation of **brand loyalty**, the extent to which a customer is favorable toward buying a specific brand. The stronger the brand loyalty, the greater the likelihood that buyers will consistently choose the brand. There are three levels of brand loyalty: recognition, preference, and insistence. *Brand recognition* is the level of loyalty at which customers are aware that the brand exists and will purchase it if their preferred or familiar brands are unavailable. This is the weakest form of brand loyalty. *Brand preference* is the level of brand

You can easily recognize a manufacturer's brand because it is not sold by just one retailer. This brand was initiated by the manufacturer and is owned and supported by the manufacturer. Gillette razors are sold in many retail stores.

TABLE 12-2 Top Ten Most Valuable Brands in the World

Brand	Brand Value (million $)	Brand	Brand Value (million $)
1. Coca-Cola	77,839	6. GE	43,682
2. IBM	76,568	7. McDonald's	40,062
3. Apple	75,532	8. Intel	39,385
4. Google	69,726	9. Samsung	32,893
5. Microsoft	57,853	10. Toyota	30,280

Source: "Best Global Brands 2012," *Interbrand*, http://www.interbrand.com/en/best-global-brands/2012/Best-Global-Brands-2012.aspx (accessed December 23, 2012).

loyalty at which a customer prefers one brand over competing brands. However, if the preferred brand is unavailable, the customer is willing to substitute another brand. *Brand insistence* is the strongest and least common level of brand loyalty. Brand-insistent customers will not buy substitutes. Apple is a brand known for having brand-insistent customers. Every time Apple releases a new product, customers will stand in line for hours, even days, just to be among the first to purchase it. Brand loyalty in general seems to be declining, partly due to marketers' increased dependence on discounted prices, coupons, and other short-term promotions, and partly because of the enormous array of new products with similar characteristics. It is also easier than ever to comparison shop for products that meet customers, needs at the lowest possible price.

Brand equity is the marketing and financial value associated with a brand's strength in a market. Although difficult to measure, brand equity represents the value of a brand to an organization. The top ten most valuable brands in the world are shown in Table 12-2. The four major factors that contribute to brand equity are brand awareness, brand associations, perceived brand quality, and brand loyalty. Brand awareness leads to brand familiarity—buyers are more likely to select a familiar brand. The symbolic associations of a brand connect it to a personality type or lifestyle. For example, customers associate Michelin tires with protecting family members, Nike products with pushing yourself athletically ("Just Do It"), and Dr Pepper with a unique taste. When consumers are unable to judge for themselves the quality of a product, they may rely on a brand's perceived level of quality. Finally, brand loyalty is a valued element of brand equity because it reduces both a brand's vulnerability to competitors and the need to spend tremendous resources to attract new customers. Loyalty also increases brand visibility and encourages retailers to carry the brand. Sometimes, large firms opt to purchase a well-known brand rather than to compete with it. Facebook, for instance, acquired the popular photo-sharing platform, Instagram, with the intention of minimizing competition and making money off of the service.[13]

brand equity marketing and financial value associated with a brand's strength in a market

Choosing and Protecting a Brand

A number of issues should be considered when selecting a brand name. The name should be easy for customers to say, spell, and recall. Short, one-syllable names such as *Tide* often satisfy this requirement. Words, numbers, and letters can be combined to yield brand names such as Motorola's RAZR V3 phone or BMW's Z4 Roadster. The brand name should suggest, in a positive way, the product's uses, special characteristics, and major benefits, and should be distinctive enough to set it apart from competing brands.

It is important that a firm select a brand that can be protected through registration, reserving it for exclusive use by that firm. Some brands, because of their designs, are infringed on more easily than others. Registration protects trademarks domestically for ten years and can be renewed indefinitely. To protect its exclusive

Social Networking for Success: Small Businesses Turn to Social Media for Effective Marketing

More than 70 percent of small businesses now use Facebook to reach their customers. Twitter, YouTube, and other social media tools are also popular among local firms around the country. Why? Because they're an affordable way to interact with customers, build brand recognition, and reinforce loyalty.

AJ Bombers, a Milwaukee burger restaurant, became a local favorite within a year of its opening, thanks to its crowd-pleasing menu and its social-media activity. The business has earned thousands of Twitter followers, Facebook "likes," and YouTube video views. Most important, AJ Bombers uses social media for two-way conversation, engaging customers and showing the brand's playful personality.

Sources: Donna DeClemente, "Facebook Pages: 4 Strategic Marketing Tips to Engage Fans," *Social Media Today*, February 16, 2011, http://socialmediatoday.com; Dave Folkens, "How Social Media Really Works for Small Business," *Top Rank*, January 20, 2011, www.toprankblog.com; Augie Ray, "World of Mouth and Social Media: A Tale of Two Burger Joints," *Forrester.com*, March 28, 2010, http://blogs.forrester.com/augie_ray.

right to the brand, the company must ensure that the selected brand will not be considered an infringement on any existing brand already registered with the U.S. Patent and Trademark Office. This task may be complicated by the fact that courts determine infringement and base their decisions on whether a brand causes consumers to be confused, mistaken, or deceived about the source of the product. McDonald's is one company that is known for aggressively protecting its trademarks against infringement. It has brought charges against a number of companies with *Mc* names because of concerns that the use of the prefix might give consumers the impression that these companies are associated with or owned by McDonald's.

A firm does not want a brand name to become a generic term that refers to a general product category. Generic terms cannot be legally protected as exclusive brand names. For example, names such as *yo-yo*, *aspirin*, *escalator*, and *thermos*—all exclusively brand names at one time—eventually were declared generic terms that refer to product categories. As such, they can no longer be protected. To ensure that a brand name does not become a generic term, the firm should spell the name with a capital letter and use it as an adjective to modify the name of the general product class, as in Jell-O Brand Gelatin. An organization can deal directly with this problem by advertising that its brand is a trademark and should not be used generically. Firms also can use the registered trademark symbol ® to indicate that the brand is trademarked.

Branding Strategies

The basic branding decision for any firm is how to brand its products. A producer may market its products under its own brands, private brands, or both. A retail store may carry only producer brands, its own brands, or both. Once either type of firm decides to brand, it chooses one of two branding strategies: individual branding or family branding.

individual branding the strategy in which a firm uses a different brand for each of its products

Individual branding is the strategy in which a firm uses a different brand for each of its products. For example, Procter & Gamble uses individual branding for its line of bar soaps, which includes Ivory, Camay, Zest, Safeguard, Coast, and Olay. Individual branding offers two major advantages: a problem with one product will not affect the good name of the firm's other products and the different brands can be directed toward different market segments.

family branding the strategy in which a firm uses the same brand for all or most of its products

Family branding is the strategy in which a firm uses the same brand for all or most of its products. Sony, Dell, IBM, and Xerox use family branding for their product mixes. A major advantage of family branding is that successful promotion for any one item that carries the family brand can help all other products with the same brand name. In addition, a new product has a head-start when its brand name is already known and accepted by customers.

Brand Extensions

A **brand extension** occurs when an organization uses one of its existing brands to brand a new product in a different product category. Iams, a popular maker of dog food, partnered with VPI Pet Insurance to extend its brand into pet insurance. This brand extension was generally well received, as Iams already had a reputation for offering high-quality products to customers who truly care about their pets. Many considered it a smart move because pet insurance is an industry that is relatively free of major, established competitors, thus, Iams can develop strong market share.[14] A brand extension should not be confused with a line extension. A *line extension* refers to using an existing brand on a new product in the same product category, such as a new flavor or new sizes. Pringles engages in line extension when releasing a new flavor, such as its holiday flavors, Cinnamon & Sugar or White Chocolate Peppermint. Marketers must be careful not to extend a brand too many times or extend too far outside the original product category. Either action may weaken the brand.

Packaging

Packaging consists of all the activities involved in developing and providing a container with graphics for a product. The package is a vital part of the product. It can make the product more versatile, safer, or easier to use. Through its shape, size, appearance, and printed message, a package can influence purchasing decisions.

PACKAGING FUNCTIONS Effective packaging is a combination of function and aesthetics. The basic function of packaging materials is to protect the product and maintain its functional form. Fluids such as milk, orange juice, and hair spray need packages that preserve and protect the product inside. Packaging should prevent damage that would affect the product's usefulness and increase costs. Because product tampering has become a problem for marketers of many types of goods, packaging techniques have been developed to counter this danger. Some packages are also designed to foil shoplifting.

Another function of packaging is to offer consumer convenience. For example, individual-serving boxes or plastic bags that contain liquids and do not require refrigeration appeal strongly to parents of small children and to young adults with active lifestyles. The size or shape of a package may relate to the product's storage, convenience of use, or replacement rate. Small, single-serving cans of vegetables, for instance, may prevent waste and make storage easier.

A third function of packaging is to promote a product by communicating its features, uses, benefits, and image. Sometimes a firm develops a reusable package to make its product more desirable. For example, Replenish multi-surface cleaner sells the cleaner concentrate in pods that screw onto the bottom of a spray bottle. Consumers purchase the bottle once, add water, and the pod releases the correct amount of cleaner concentrate. The system saves on plastic and water waste and is cheaper than many competitors' products.[15]

PACKAGE DESIGN CONSIDERATIONS Many factors must be weighed when developing packages. Obviously, one major consideration is cost. Expensive packaging can affect the final cost of a product.

Marketers also must decide whether to package the product in single or multiple units. Multiple-unit packaging can increase demand by increasing the amount of

brand extension using an existing brand to brand a new product in a different product category

packaging all the activities involved in developing and providing a container with graphics for a product

Heinz turns the ketchup bottle on its head.
The original design of the ketchup bottle made it difficult for customers to get the ketchup out. To solve this problem, Heinz put the cap on the bottom of the bottle and made the opening larger. In addition, Heinz made the bottle squeezable.

SUSAN VAN ETTEN

the product available at the point of consumption (in the home, for example). However, multiple-unit packaging does not work for infrequently used products because buyers generally prefer not to have an excess supply or to store products for a long time. However, multiple-unit packaging can make storage and handling easier (as in the case of six-packs used for soft drinks). It can also facilitate special price offers, such as two-for-one sales. Multiple-unit packaging may encourage customers to try a product several times, but it may also backfire and deter them from trying the product if they cannot purchase just one.

Marketers should consider how much consistency is desirable among an organization's package designs. To promote an overall company image, a firm may decide that all packages must be similar or include a distinct design element. This approach, called *family packaging* is often used only for lines of products, as with Campbell's soups, Weight Watchers foods, and Planters nuts. The best policy is sometimes no consistency, especially if a firm's various products are unrelated or aimed at different target markets.

Packages also play an important promotional role. Through verbal and nonverbal symbols, the package informs potential buyers about the product's content, uses, features, advantages, and hazards. Firms can create desirable images and associations by choosing particular colors, designs, shapes, and textures. Many cosmetics manufacturers, for example, design their packages to create impressions of richness, luxury, and exclusivity. The package performs another promotional function when it is designed to be safer or more convenient to use than competitors'.

Packaging also must meet the needs of intermediaries. Wholesalers and retailers consider whether a package is easy to transport, handle, and store. Resellers may refuse to carry certain products if their packages are too cumbersome.

Finally, firms must consider the issue of environmental responsibility when developing packages. Companies must balance consumers' desires for convenience against the need to preserve the environment. Reducing packaging will help with global waste problems because about one-half of all garbage consists of plastic packaging. When deciding on the best packaging for its organic yogurt products, Stonyfield Farm chose lightweight plastic because it costs less to ship and is durable. It partners with Preserve, a company that makes recycled toothbrushes and home goods out of yogurt containers, to reduce packaging waste. Stonyfield Farm encourages recycling at Whole Foods drop-offs.[16]

Labeling

Labeling is the presentation of information on a product or its package. The *label* is the part of a package that contains information, including the brand name and mark, the registered trademark symbol ®, the package size and contents, product claims, directions for use and safety precautions, ingredients, the name and address of the manufacturer, and the Universal Product Code (UPC) symbol, which is used for automated checkout and inventory control.

A number of federal regulations specify information that *must* be included in the labeling for certain products:

- Garments must be labeled with the name of the manufacturer, country of manufacture, fabric content, and cleaning instructions.
- Food labels must contain the most common term for ingredients.
- Any food product for which a nutritional claim is made must have nutrition labeling that follows a standard format.

Concept Check

✓ Describe the major types of brands.

✓ How do brands help customers in product selection? How do brands help companies introduce new products? Explain the three levels of brand loyalty.

✓ Define brand equity and describe the four major factors that contribute toward brand equity. What issues must be considered while choosing a brand name?

✓ What are the major functions of packaging?

- Food product labels must state the number of servings per container, the serving size, the number of calories per serving, the number of calories derived from fat, and the amounts of specific nutrients.
- Non-edible items such as shampoos and detergents must carry safety precautions and instructions for use.

Such regulations are aimed at protecting customers from misleading product claims and the improper (and thus unsafe) use of products. Food manufacturers are not allowed to make misleading health claims about their products.

Labels also may carry the details of written, or express, warranties. An **express warranty** is a written explanation of the producer's responsibilities in the event that a product is found to be defective or otherwise unsatisfactory.

PRICING PRODUCTS

A product is a set of attributes and benefits that has been designed to satisfy its market while earning a profit for its seller. Pricing is an integral part of this equation. Each product has at price at which consumers' desires and expectations are balanced with a firm's need to make a profit. We will now look more closely at how businesses go about determining a product's price.

The Meaning and Use of Price

The **price** of a product is the amount of money a seller is willing to accept in exchange for the product at a given time and under given circumstances. At times, the price results from negotiations between buyer and seller. In many business situations, however, the price is fixed by the seller. Suppose that a seller sets a price of $10 for a product. The seller is saying, "Anyone who wants this product can have it here and now in exchange for $10."

Each interested buyer then makes a personal judgment regarding the product's utility, often in terms of a dollar value. A particular person who feels that he or she will get at least $10 worth of want satisfaction (or value) from the product is likely to buy it. If that person can get more want satisfaction by spending $10 in some other way, he or she will not buy the product.

Price thus serves the function of *allocator*. First, it allocates goods and services among those who are willing and able to buy them. (As we noted in Chapter 1, the answer to the economic question "For whom to produce?" depends primarily on prices.) Second, price allocates financial resources (sales revenue) among producers according to how well they satisfy customers' needs. Third, price helps customers to allocate their own financial resources among various want-satisfying products.

Price and Non-Price Competition

Before a product's price can be set, an organization must determine whether it will compete based on price alone, or on a combination of factors. The choice influences pricing decisions as well as other marketing-mix variables.

Price competition occurs when a seller emphasizes a product's low price and sets a price that equals or beats competitors' prices. To use this approach most effectively, a seller must have the flexibility to change prices often, rapidly, and aggressively in response to competitors'

How low can you go? Price competition is fierce among fast food restaurants. McDonald's launched the first dollar menu in its industry in 2002. It was not long before many of its competitors followed suit with their own value menus.

price changes. Price competition allows a marketer to set prices based on product demand or in response to changes in the firm's finances. Competitors can do likewise, however, which is a major drawback of price competition. If circumstances force a seller to raise prices, competing firms may be able to maintain their lower prices. Some retailers, such as Staples, have taken price competition to a whole new level. They use sophisticated algorithms to instantly alter prices on products offered through their websites based on geography, customer proximity to competitors, buying habits, and other information stored about the customer.[17] The Internet has made it more difficult than ever for sellers to compete on the basis of price, as consumers can quickly and easily conduct comparison-shopping online.

Non-price competition is competition based on factors other than price. It is used most effectively when a seller can make its product stand out through distinctive product quality, customer service, promotion, packaging, or other features. Buyers must be able to perceive these characteristics and consider them desirable. Once customers have chosen a brand for non-price reasons, they may not be as attracted to competing firms and brands. In this way, a seller can build customer loyalty to its brand. A method of non-price competition, **product differentiation**, is the process of developing and promoting differences between one's product and all similar products. Vibram Five Fingers shoes, for example, are sufficiently differentiated from the competition that marketers do not compete on price. The shoes have highly distinct styling and are unlike any other shoe on the market. Modeled on the shape of a foot, including individual toes, they appeal to runners and other athletes who want to protect their feet while having a barefoot experience.[18]

Buyers' Perceptions of Price

In setting prices, managers should consider the price sensitivity of the target market. Members of one market segment may be more influenced by price than members of another. Consumer price sensitivity can also vary between products. For example, buyers may be more sensitive to price when purchasing gasoline than when purchasing running shoes.

Buyers will tolerate a narrow range of prices for certain items and a wider range for others. Consider the varying prices of soft drinks—from 15 cents per ounce at the movies down to 1.5 cents per ounce on sale at the grocery store. Management should be aware of consumers' price limits and the products to which they apply. The firm also should take note of buyers' perceptions of a given product in relation to competing products. A premium price may be appropriate if a product is considered superior to others in its category, or if the product has inspired strong brand loyalty. On the other hand, a lower price may be necessary if buyers have even a slightly negative product perception.

Sometimes buyers equate price and quality. Managers involved in pricing decisions should determine whether this outlook is widespread in the target market. If it is, a higher price may improve a product's image, making it more desirable.

PRICING OBJECTIVES

Before setting prices for a firm's products, management must determine pricing objectives that are in line with organizational and marketing objectives. Of course, one objective of pricing is to make a profit, but this may not be a firm's primary objective. One or more of the following factors may be just as important.

Survival

A firm may have to price its products to survive—either as an organization or as a player in a particular market. This usually means that the firm will cut its price to attract customers, even if it must operate at a loss for a while. Obviously, such a goal cannot be pursued on a long-term basis, for consistent losses would cause the business to fail.

---

non-price competition
competition based on factors other than price

product differentiation the process of developing and promoting differences between one's product and all similar products

Concept Check

✓ What factors must be considered when pricing products?

✓ How does a change in price affect the demand and supply of a product?

✓ Differentiate price competition and non-price competition.

✓ Why is it important to consider the buyer's sensitivity to price when pricing products?

Learning Objective

7 Identify the major pricing objectives used by businesses.

Concept Check

✓ Explain the various types of pricing objectives.

✓ Which ones usually will result in a firm having lower prices?

Profit Maximization

Many firms may state that their goal is to maximize profit, but this goal is impossible to define (and thus impossible to achieve). What, exactly, is the *maximum* profit? How does a firm know when it has been reached? Firms that wish to set profit goals should express them as either specific dollar amounts, or percentage increases, over previous profits.

Target Return on Investment

The *return on investment* (ROI) is the amount earned as a result of a financial investment. Some firms set an annual percentage ROI as a quantifiable means to gauge the success of their pricing goal.

Market-Share Goals

A firm's *market share* is its proportion of total industry sales. Some firms attempt, through pricing, to maintain or increase their market shares. Both U.S. cola giants, Coke and Pepsi, continually try to gain market share through aggressive pricing and other marketing efforts.

Status-Quo Pricing

In pricing their products, some firms are guided by a desire to maintain the status quo. This is especially true in industries that depend on price stability. If such a firm can maintain its profit or market share simply by matching the competition—charging about the same price as competitors for similar products—then it will do so.

LEE HACKER/ALAMY

What does a product's price communicate to you? How buyers perceive a product is often determined by its price. High prices communicate quality and status—which is why the makers of luxury goods such as Rolex watches are often reluctant to sell them at a discount. The producers of these goods don't want to "cheapen" their brands for a quick sales boost because it could hurt the image of these brands.

PRICING METHODS

Once a firm has developed its pricing objectives, it must select a pricing method to reach that goal. Two factors are important to every firm engaged in setting prices. The first is recognition that the market, and not the firm's costs, ultimately determines the price at which a product will sell. The second is awareness that costs and expected sales can be used only to establish a *price floor*, the minimum price at which the firm can sell its product without incurring a loss. In this section, we look at three kinds of pricing methods: cost-based, demand-based, and competition-based pricing.

Cost-Based Pricing

Using the simplest method of pricing, *cost-based pricing*, the seller first determines the total cost of producing (or purchasing) one unit of the product. The seller then adds an amount to cover additional costs (such as insurance or interest) and profit. The amount that is added is called the **markup**. The total of the cost plus the markup is the product's selling price.

A firm's management can calculate markup as a percentage of total costs. Suppose, for example, that the total cost of manufacturing and marketing 1,000 DVD players is $100,000, or $100 per unit. If the manufacturer wants a markup that is 20 percent above costs, the selling price will be $100 plus 20 percent of $100, or $120 per unit.

Markup pricing is easy to apply and is used by many businesses (mostly retailers and wholesalers). However, it has two major flaws. The first is the difficulty of

markup the amount a seller adds to the cost of a product to determine its basic selling price

determining the best markup percentage. If the percentage is too high, the product may be overpriced for its market and too few units will be sold to cover the cost of producing and marketing it. If the markup percentage is too low, the seller forgoes profit it could have earned by assigning a higher price.

The second problem with markup pricing is that it separates pricing from other business functions. The product is priced *after* production quantities are determined, *after* costs are incurred, and almost without regard for the market or the marketing mix. To be most effective, the cost of various business functions should be integrated. *Each* should have an impact on all marketing decisions.

Cost-based pricing can also be calculated through breakeven analysis. For any product, the **breakeven quantity** is the number of units that must be sold for the total revenue (from all units sold) to equal the total cost (of all units sold). **Total revenue** is the total amount received from the sales of a product. We estimate projected total revenue as the selling price multiplied by the number of units sold.

The costs involved in operating a business can be broadly classified as either fixed or variable. A **fixed cost** is a cost incurred no matter how many units of a product are produced or sold. Rent, for example, is a fixed cost because it remains the same whether 1 or 1,000 units are produced. A **variable cost** is a cost that depends on the number of units produced. The cost of fabricating parts for a stereo receiver is a variable cost. The more units produced, the more efficient production will be and the per-unit cost of the parts will go down. The **total cost** of producing a certain number of units is the sum of the fixed costs and the variable costs attributed to those units.

If we assume a particular selling price, we can find the breakeven quantity either graphically or by using a formula. Figure 12-3 graphs the total revenue earned and the total cost incurred by the sale of various quantities of a hypothetical product. With fixed costs of $40,000, variable costs of $60 per unit, and a selling price of $120, the breakeven quantity is 667 units (represented in Figure 12-3 as the intersection of the total revenue and total cost curves). To find the breakeven quantity, first deduct the variable cost from the selling price to determine how much money the sale of one unit contributes toward offsetting fixed costs. Divide that contribution into the total fixed costs to arrive at the breakeven quantity. If the firm sells more than 667 units at $120 each, it will earn a profit. If it sells fewer units, it will suffer a loss.

Demand-Based Pricing

Rather than basing the price of a product on its cost, companies sometimes use a pricing method based on the level of demand for the product: *demand-based pricing*. This method results in a higher price when product demand is strong and a lower price when demand is weak. To use this method, a marketer estimates the amount of a product that customers will demand at different prices and then chooses the price that should generate the highest total revenue. Obviously, the effectiveness of this method depends on the firm's ability to estimate demand accurately.

A firm may favor a demand-based pricing method called *price differentiation* if it wants to use more than one price in the marketing of a specific product. Price differentiation can be based on such considerations as time of the purchase, type of customer, or type of distribution channel. Some popular restaurants use demand-based pricing to ensure a more even flow of customers throughout the day. High-end restaurants, like Le Cirque, utilize the online booking service, Savored, to charge a lower price for the same dinner at 5 pm on a Wednesday, when demand is low, than at 8 pm on a Friday, when demand is high.[19] For price differentiation to work, the company must be able to segment a market on the basis of different strengths of demand. The company must then be able to keep the segments separate enough so that those who buy at lower prices cannot sell to buyers in segments that are charged a higher price. This isolation can be accomplished, for example, by selling

breakeven quantity the number of units that must be sold for the total revenue (from all units sold) to equal the total cost (of all units sold)

total revenue the total amount received from the sales of a product

fixed cost a cost incurred no matter how many units of a product are produced or sold

variable cost a cost that depends on the number of units produced

total cost the sum of the fixed costs and the variable costs attributed to a product

FIGURE 12-3 Breakeven Analysis

Breakeven analysis answers the question: What is the lowest level of production and sales at which a company can break even on a particular product?

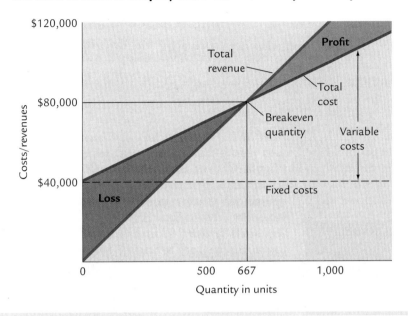

to geographically separated segments. However, the Internet has made price differentiation for products more difficult.

Compared with cost-based pricing, demand-based pricing places a firm in a better position to attain higher profit levels, assuming that buyers value the product at levels sufficiently above the product's cost. To use demand-based pricing, however, management must be able to estimate demand at different price levels, which may be difficult to assess accurately.

Competition-Based Pricing

In using *competition-based pricing*, an organization considers costs and revenue secondary to competitors' prices. The importance of this method increases if competing products are similar and the organization is serving markets in which price is the crucial variable of the marketing strategy. A firm that uses competition-based pricing may choose to sell below competitors' prices, slightly above competitors' prices, or at the same level. The price that your bookstore paid to the publishing company of this text was determined using competition-based pricing. Competition-based pricing can help to attain a pricing objective to increase sales or market share. Competition-based pricing may also be combined with other cost approaches to arrive at a profitable level.

Why you might have paid twice as much for your plane ticket as the person sitting next to you. Airlines use demand-based pricing because the number of passengers that can be put on a specific flight is limited. The sophisticated software the companies use constantly re-price seats based on the number of tickets customers are purchasing at any given time as well as historical data.

Learning Objective

9 Explain the different strate-gies available to companies for setting prices.

PRICING STRATEGIES

A *pricing strategy* is a course of action designed to achieve pricing objectives. The extent to which a business uses any of the following strategies depends on its pricing and marketing objectives, the markets for its products, the degree of product differentiation, the product's life-cycle stage, and other factors. Figure 12-4 is a list of the major types of pricing strategies. We discuss these strategies in the remainder of this section.

New-Product Pricing

The two primary types of new-product pricing strategies are price skimming and penetration pricing. An organization can use either one, or even both, over a period of time.

price skimming the strategy of charging the highest possible price for a product during the introduction stage of its life-cycle

PRICE SKIMMING Some consumers are willing to pay a high price for an innovative product, either because of its novelty or because of the prestige or status that ownership confers. **Price skimming** is the strategy of charging the highest possible price for a product during the introduction stage of its life-cycle. This strategy helps to recover the high costs of R&D quickly. In addition, a skimming policy may hold down demand for the product, which is helpful if the firm's production capacity is limited during the introduction stage. A danger is that a price-skimming strategy may make the product appear more lucrative than it actually is to potential competitors, encouraging more competitors to enter the market.

penetration pricing the strategy of setting a low price for a new product

PENETRATION PRICING At the opposite extreme, **penetration pricing** is the strategy of setting a low price for a new product to build market share quickly. The seller hopes that building a large market share will discourage competitors from entering the market. If the low price stimulates sales, the firm also may be able to order longer production runs, which usually results in lower production costs per unit. A disadvantage of penetration pricing is that it places a firm in a less flexible position on pricing. It is more difficult to raise prices significantly than it is to lower them.

Differential Pricing

An important issue in pricing decisions is whether to use a single price or different prices for the same product. *Differential pricing* means charging different prices to different buyers for the same quality and quantity of product. For differential pricing to be effective, the market must consist of multiple segments with different

FIGURE 12-4 Types of Pricing Strategies

Companies have a variety of pricing strategies available to them.

PRICING STRATEGIES				
New-Product Pricing	**Differential Pricing**	**Psychological Pricing**	**Product-Line Pricing**	**Promotional Pricing**
• Price skimming • Penetration pricing	• Negotiated pricing • Secondary-market pricing • Periodic discounting • Random discounting	• Odd-number pricing • Multiple-unit pricing • Reference pricing • Bundle pricing • Everyday low prices • Customary pricing	• Captive pricing • Premium pricing • Price lining	• Price leaders • Special-event pricing • Comparison discounting

© CENGAGE LEARNING 2015

price sensitivities. When this method is employed, caution should be used to avoid confusing or antagonizing customers. Differential pricing can take several forms, including negotiated pricing, secondary-market pricing, periodic discounting, and random discounting.

NEGOTIATED PRICING Negotiated pricing occurs when the final price is established through bargaining between the seller and the customer. Negotiated pricing occurs at all levels of distribution and is common in a variety of industries. Even when there is a predetermined stated price or a price list, manufacturers, wholesalers, and retailers may negotiate to establish the final sales price. Consumers commonly negotiate prices for houses, cars, and used equipment.

SECONDARY-MARKET PRICING Secondary-market pricing means setting one price for the primary target market and a different price for another market. The price charged in the secondary market is often, but not always, lower. Examples of secondary markets include a geographically isolated domestic market, a market in a foreign country, and a segment willing to purchase a product during off-peak times (such as "early bird" diners at restaurants and off-peak users of mobile phones).

PERIODIC DISCOUNTING Periodic discounting is the temporary reduction of prices on a patterned or systematic basis. For example, many retailers have annual holiday sales, and apparel stores have seasonal sales. From the marketer's point of view, a problem with periodic discounting is that customers can predict when the reductions will occur and may delay their purchases until they can take advantage of the lower prices.

RANDOM DISCOUNTING To alleviate the problem of customers holding off on purchases until a discount period, some organizations employ **random discounting**. That is, they reduce their prices temporarily on a nonsystematic basis. When price reductions of a product occur randomly, current users of that brand are not able to predict when reductions will occur. They therefore will not delay their purchases in anticipation of purchasing the product at a lower price. Marketers also use random discounting to attract new customers.

Psychological Pricing

Psychological pricing strategies encourage purchases based on emotional responses rather than on economically rational ones. These strategies are used primarily for consumer products rather than business products.

ODD-NUMBER PRICING Many retailers believe that consumers respond more positively to odd-number prices such as $4.99 than to whole-dollar prices such as $5. **Odd-number pricing** is the strategy of setting prices using odd numbers that are slightly below whole-dollar amounts. Nine and five are the most popular ending figures for odd-number prices.

MULTIPLE-UNIT PRICING Many retailers (supermarkets in particular) practice **multiple-unit pricing**, setting a single price for two or more units, such as two cans for 99 cents, rather than 50 cents per can. Especially for frequently purchased products, this strategy can increase the amount of an item that is sold. Customers who see the single price and who expect eventually to use more than one unit of the product will purchase multiple units to save money.

REFERENCE PRICING Reference pricing means pricing a product at a moderate level and positioning it next to a more expensive model or brand in the hope that the customer will use the higher price as a reference price (i.e., a comparison price). Because of the comparison, the customer is expected to view the moderate price favorably.

negotiated pricing establishing a final price through bargaining

secondary-market pricing setting one price for the primary target market and a different price for another market

periodic discounting temporary reduction of prices on a patterned or systematic basis

random discounting temporary reduction of prices on an unsystematic basis

odd-number pricing the strategy of setting prices using odd numbers that are slightly below whole-dollar amounts

multiple-unit pricing the strategy of setting a single price for two or more units

reference pricing pricing a product at a moderate level and positioning it next to a more expensive model or brand

BUNDLE PRICING

Bundle pricing is the packaging together of two or more products, usually of a complementary nature, to be sold for a single price. To be attractive to customers, the single price usually is considerably less than the sum of the prices of the individual products. Because the products are complementary, such as shampoo and conditioner, the customer will also find convenience value from purchasing them together. The firm may find bundling to be a valuable strategy because, by bundling slow-moving products with more popular ones, an organization can stimulate sales and increase revenues. Selling products as a package rather than individually also may result in cost savings for the organization. It is common for telecommunications providers to sell service bundles of cable, Internet, and phone service for one price.

EVERYDAY LOW PRICES (EDLPS)

To reduce or eliminate frequent short-term price reductions, some organizations use an approach referred to as **everyday low prices (EDLPs)**. When EDLPs are used, a marketer sets a low price for its products on a consistent basis, rather than setting high prices and frequently discounting them. EDLPs, though not deeply discounted, are set far enough below competitors' prices to make customers feel confident that they are receiving a good deal. EDLPs are employed by retailers such as Walmart and by manufacturers such as Procter & Gamble. A company that uses EDLPs benefits from reduced promotional costs, reduced losses from frequent markdowns, and more stability in sales. However, customers may not trust the EDLP and assume the deal is merely a marketing gimmick.

CUSTOMARY PRICING

In **customary pricing**, certain goods are priced primarily on the basis of tradition. It is not as common as it once was, but examples of customary, or traditional, prices are those set for candy bars and chewing gum.

Product-Line Pricing

Rather than considering products on an item-by-item basis when determining pricing strategies, some marketers employ product-line pricing. *Product-line pricing* means establishing and adjusting the prices of multiple products within a product line. Product-line pricing can provide marketers with flexibility in price setting. For example, marketers can set prices high so that one product is highly profitable, whereas another has a low price to increase market share.

When marketers employ product-line pricing, they have several strategies from which to choose. These include captive pricing, premium pricing, and price lining.

CAPTIVE PRICING

When **captive pricing** is used, the basic product in a product line is priced low, but the price on the items required to operate or enhance it are higher. Two common examples of captive pricing are razor blades and printer ink. The razor handle and the printer are generally priced quite low, but the razor blades and the printer ink replacement cartridges are usually very expensive.

PREMIUM PRICING **Premium pricing** occurs when the highest-quality product or the most-versatile version of similar products in a product line is assigned the highest price. Other products in the line are priced to appeal to more price-sensitive shoppers, or to those seeking product-specific features. Marketers that employ premium pricing often realize a significant portion of profits from the premium-priced products. Examples of product categories in which premium pricing is common are small kitchen appliances, beer, ice cream, and television cable service.

premium pricing pricing the highest-quality or most-versatile products higher than other models in the product line

PRICE LINING **Price lining** is the strategy of selling goods only at certain predetermined prices that reflect definite price breaks. For example, a shop may sell men's ties only at $22 and $37. This strategy is used in clothing and accessory stores. It eliminates minor price differences from the buying decision—both for customers and for managers who buy merchandise to sell in these stores.

price lining the strategy of selling goods only at certain predetermined prices that reflect definite price breaks

Promotional Pricing

Price, as an ingredient in the marketing mix, often is coordinated with promotions. The two variables sometimes are so interrelated that the pricing policy is promotion-oriented. Examples of promotional pricing include price leaders, special-event pricing, and comparison discounting.

PRICE LEADERS Sometimes' a firm prices a few products below the usual markup, near cost, or below cost, which results in **price leaders**. This type of pricing is used most often in supermarkets and restaurants to attract customers by giving them especially low prices on a few items. Management hopes that customers will purchase regularly priced items as well, which will offset the reduced revenues from the price leaders.

price leaders products priced below the usual markup, near cost, or below cost

SPECIAL-EVENT PRICING To increase sales volume, many organizations coordinate price with advertising or sales promotions for seasonal or special occasions. **Special-event pricing** involves advertised sales or price cutting linked to a holiday, season, or event. If the pricing objective is survival, then special sales events may be designed to generate the necessary operating capital.

special-event pricing advertised sales or price cutting linked to a holiday, season, or event

COMPARISON DISCOUNTING **Comparison discounting** sets the price of a product at a specific level and compares it with a higher price. The higher price may be the product's previous price, the price of a competing brand, the product's price at another retail outlet, or a manufacturer's suggested retail price. Comparison discounting can significantly impact customers' decisions. Because this pricing strategy can lead to deceptive pricing practices, the Federal Trade Commission has established guidelines for comparison discounting. If the higher price against which the comparison is made is the price formerly charged for the product, sellers must have made the previous price available to customers for a reasonable period of time. If sellers present the higher price as the one charged by other retailers in the same trade area, they must be able to demonstrate the veracity of the claim. When they present the higher price as the manufacturer's suggested retail price, then the higher price must be similar to the price at which a reasonable proportion of the product was sold.

comparison discounting setting a price at a specific level and comparing it with a higher price

Concept Check

✓ Identify the five categories of pricing strategies.

✓ Describe two specific pricing strategies in each category.

PRICING BUSINESS PRODUCTS

Learning Objective

10 Describe three major types of pricing associated with business products.

Many of the pricing issues discussed thus far in this chapter deal with pricing in general. However, setting prices for business products is different from setting prices for consumer products because of factors such as the size of purchases, transportation considerations, and geographic issues. We examine three types of pricing associated with business products: geographic pricing, transfer pricing, and discounting.

Geographic Pricing

Geographic pricing strategies deal with delivery costs. The pricing strategy that requires the buyer to pay the delivery costs is called *FOB origin pricing*. It stands for "free on board at the point of origin," which means that the price does not include freight charges. Thus the buyer must pay the transportation costs from the seller's warehouse to the buyer's place of business. *FOB destination* indicates that the price does include freight charges, and thus the seller pays these charges.

Transfer Pricing

transfer pricing prices charged in sales between an organization's units

When one unit in an organization sells a product to another unit, **transfer pricing** occurs. The price is determined by calculating the cost of the product. A transfer price can vary depending on the types of costs included in the calculations. The choice of the costs to include depends on the company's management strategy and the nature of the units' interactions. An organization also must ensure that transfer pricing is fair to all units involved in the purchases.

Discounting

discount a deduction from the price of an item

A **discount** is a deduction from an item's price. Producers and sellers offer a wide variety of discounts to their customers, including trade, quantity, cash, and seasonal discounts and allowances. *Trade discounts* are taken off the list prices that are offered to marketing intermediaries, or middlemen. *Quantity discounts* are discounts given to customers who buy in large quantities, which makes seller's per-unit selling cost lower for larger purchases. *Cash discounts* are offered for prompt payment. A seller may offer a discount of "2/10, net 30," meaning that the buyer receives a 2 percent discount if the first payment occurs within ten days and is paid in full within 30 days. A *seasonal discount* is a price reduction to buyers who purchase out of season. This discount encourages off-season sales and ensures steady production throughout the year. An *allowance* is a reduction in price to achieve a desired goal. Trade-in allowances, for example, are price reductions granted for turning in used equipment when purchasing new equipment. Table 12-3 describes some of the reasons for using these discounting techniques and some examples.

Concept Check

✓ Describe the three types of pricing associated with business products.

✓ Differentiate between FOB origin and FOB destination pricing.

✓ Explain the five types of discounts for business products.

TABLE 12-3 Discounts Used for Business Markets

Type	Reasons for Use	Examples
Trade (functional)	To attract and maintain effective resellers by compensating them for performing certain functions, such as transportation, warehousing, selling, and providing credit.	A college bookstore pays about one-third less for a new textbook than the retail price.
Quantity	To encourage customers to buy large quantities when making purchases and, in the case of cumulative discounts, to encourage customer loyalty.	Companies that serve business markets offer a 2 percent discount if an account is paid within ten days.
Seasonal	To allow a marketer to use resources more efficiently by stimulating sales during off-peak periods.	Hotels offer companies deeply discounted accommodations for holding large meetings or conventions there during off-peak months.
Allowance	In the case of a trade-in allowance, to assist the buyer in making the purchase and potentially earn a profit on the resale of used equipment. In the case of a promotional allowance, to ensure that dealers participate in advertising and sales support programs.	A farm equipment dealer takes a farmer's used tractor as a trade-in on a new one. Nabisco pays a promotional allowance to a supermarket for setting up and maintaining a large end-of-aisle display for a two-week period.

Source: Adapted from William M. Pride and O. C. Ferrell, *Foundations of Marketing* (Mason, OH: South-Western/Cengage Learning, 2013), 358.

Summary

1 Explain what a product is and how products are classified.

A product is everything one receives in an exchange, including all attributes and expected benefits. The product may be a manufactured item, a service, an idea, or a combination.

Products are classified according to their ultimate use. Classification affects a product's distribution, promotion, and pricing. Consumer goods, which include convenience, shopping, and specialty products, are purchased to satisfy personal and family needs. Business products are purchased for resale, in making other products, or for use in a firm's operations. Business products can be classified as raw materials, major equipment, accessory equipment, component parts, process materials, supplies, and services.

2 Discuss the product life-cycle and how it leads to new-product development.

Every product moves through a series of four stages—introduction, growth, maturity, and decline—which together form the product life-cycle. As the product progresses through these stages, its sales and profitability increase, peak, and decline. Marketers keep track of the life-cycle stage of products in order to estimate when a new product should be introduced to replace a declining one.

3 Define *product line* and *product mix* and distinguish between the two.

A product line is a group of similar products marketed by a firm. They are related to each other in the way they are produced, marketed, and consumed. The firm's product mix includes all the products it offers for sale. The width of a mix is the number of product lines it contains. The depth of the mix is the average number of individual products within each line.

4 Identify the methods available for changing a product mix.

Customer satisfaction and organizational objectives require marketers to develop, adjust, and maintain an effective product mix. Marketers may improve a product mix by changing existing products, deleting products, and developing new products.

New products are developed through a series of seven steps. The first step, idea generation, involves developing a pool of product ideas. Screening, the second step, removes from consideration those product ideas that do not match organizational goals or resources. Concept testing, the third step, is a phase in which a sample of potential buyers is exposed to a proposed product through a written or oral description in order to determine their initial reactions and buying intentions. The fourth step, business analysis, generates information about potential sales, costs, and profits. During the development step, the product idea is transformed into mock-ups and prototypes to determine if product production is technically feasible and can be produced at reasonable costs. Test marketing is an actual launch of the product in selected cities chosen for their representativeness of target markets. Finally, during commercialization, plans for full-scale production and marketing are refined and implemented. Most product failures result from inadequate product planning and development.

5 Explain the uses and importance of branding, packaging, and labeling.

A brand is a name, term, symbol, design, or any combination of these that identifies a seller's products as distinct from those of other sellers. Brands can be classified as manufacturer brands, store brands, or generic brands. A firm can choose between two branding strategies—individual or family branding, which are used to associate (or *not* associate) particular products with existing products, producers, or intermediaries. Packaging protects goods, increases consumer convenience, and enhances marketing efforts by communicating product features, uses, benefits, and image. Labeling provides customers with product information, some of which is required by law.

6 Describe the economic basis of pricing and the means by which sellers can control prices and buyers' perceptions of prices.

A product is a set of attributes and benefits that has been designed to satisfy its market while earning a profit for its seller. Each product has at price at which it balances consumers desires and expectations with a firm's need to make a profit. The price of a product is the amount of money a seller is willing to accept in exchange for the product at a given time and under given circumstances. Price thus serves the function of *allocator*. It allocates goods and services among those who are willing and able to buy them. It allocates financial resources among producers according to how well they satisfy customers' needs. Price also helps customers to allocate their own financial resources among products.

Price competition occurs when a seller emphasizes a product's low price and sets a price that equals or beats competitors' prices. To use this approach most effectively, a seller must have the flexibility to change prices often. Price competition allows a marketer to set prices based on demand. The Internet has made it more difficult than ever for sellers to compete on price. Non-price competition is based on factors other than price. It is used most effectively when a seller can make its product stand out from the competition by differentiating product quality, customer service, promotion, packaging, or other features. Buyers must be able to perceive these distinguishing characteristics and consider them desirable. Buyers' perceptions of prices are affected by the importance of the product to them, the range of prices they consider acceptable, their perceptions of competing products, and their association of quality with price.

7 Identify the major pricing objectives used by businesses.

Objectives of pricing include survival, profit maximization, target return on investment, achieving market goals, and maintaining the status quo. Firms sometimes have to price products to survive, which usually requires cutting prices to attract customers. The return on investment (ROI) is the amount earned as a result of the investment in developing and marketing the product. Some firms set an annual percentage ROI as the pricing goal. Other firms use pricing to maintain or increase their market share. In industries in which price stability is important, firms often price their products by charging about the same as competitors.

8 Examine the three major pricing methods that firms employ.

The three major pricing methods are cost-based pricing, demand-based pricing, and competition-based pricing.

When cost-based pricing is employed, a proportion of the cost is added to the total cost to determine the selling price. When demand-based pricing is used, the price will be higher when demand is higher, and the price will be lower when demand is lower. A firm that uses competition-based pricing may choose to price below competitors' prices, at the same level as competitors' prices, or slightly above competitors' prices.

9 Explain the different strategies available to companies for setting prices.

Pricing strategies fall into five categories: new-product pricing, differential pricing, psychological pricing, product-line pricing, and promotional pricing. Price skimming and penetration pricing are two strategies used for pricing new products. Differential pricing can be accomplished through negotiated pricing, secondary-market pricing, periodic discounting, and random discounting. Types of psychological pricing strategies are odd-number pricing, multiple-unit pricing, reference pricing, bundle pricing, everyday low prices, and customary pricing. Product-line pricing can be achieved through captive pricing, premium pricing, and price lining. The major types of promotional pricing are price-leader pricing, special-event pricing, and comparison discounting.

10 Describe three major types of pricing associated with business products.

Setting prices for business products is different from setting prices for consumer products because of several factors, including the size of purchases, transportation considerations, and geographic issues. The three types of pricing associated with business products are geographic pricing, transfer pricing, and discounting.

Key Terms

You should now be able to define and give an example relevant to each of the following terms:

product (323)
consumer product (324)
business product (324)
convenience product (324)
shopping product (324)
specialty product (324)
raw material (325)
major equipment (325)
accessory equipment (325)
component part (325)
process material (325)
supply (325)
business service (325)

product life-cycle (325)
product line (328)
product mix (328)
product modification (329)
line extension (330)
product deletion (330)
brand (333)
brand name (333)
brand mark (333)
trademark (333)
trade name (333)
manufacturer (or producer)
   brand (333)

store (or private) brand (334)
generic product (or brand)
   (334)
brand loyalty (334)
brand equity (335)
individual branding (336)
family branding (336)
brand extension (337)
packaging (337)
labeling (339)
express warranty (339)
price (339)
price competition (339)

non-price competition (340)
product differentiation (340)
markup (341)
breakeven quantity (342)
total revenue (342)
fixed cost (342)
variable cost (342)
total cost (342)
price skimming (344)
penetration pricing (344)
negotiated pricing (345)
secondary-market pricing
   (345)

Discussion Questions

1. What does the purchaser of a product obtain besides the good, service, or idea itself?
2. What major factor determines whether a product is a consumer or a business product?
3. What are the four stages of the product life-cycle? How can a firm determine which stage a particular product is in?
4. Under what conditions does product modification work best?
5. Why do products have to be deleted from a product mix?
6. Why must firms introduce new products?
7. What is the difference between manufacturer brands and store brands? Between family branding and individual branding?
8. What is the difference between a line extension and a brand extension?
9. For what purposes is labeling used?
10. Compare and contrast the characteristics of price and non-price competition.
11. How might buyers' perceptions of price influence pricing decisions?
12. What are the five major categories of pricing strategies? Give at least two examples of specific strategies that fall into each category.
13. Identify and describe the main types of discounts that are used in the pricing of business products.
14. Some firms do not delete products until they become financially threatening. What problems may result from this practice?
15. Under what conditions would a firm be most likely to use non-price competition?
16. Under what conditions would a business most likely decide to employ one of the differential pricing strategies?
17. For what types of products are psychological pricing strategies most likely to be used?

Test Yourself

Matching Questions

1. _____ Quantities of products that producers are willing to sell.
2. _____ Quantities of products that buyers are willing to purchase.
3. _____ Presentation of information on a package.
4. _____ The amount earned for investing.
5. _____ Changes that make a product more dependable.
6. _____ Different prices are set for each market.
7. _____ It represents the value of an organization's brand.
8. _____ Customers who consistently choose specific brands.
9. _____ It is the legal name of an organization.
10. _____ The result of bargaining between seller and buyer.

   a. labeling
   b. supply
   c. demand
   d. product differentiation
   e. return on investment (ROI)
   f. secondary-market pricing
   g. quality product modification
   h. trade name
   i. brand loyalty
   j. brand equity
   k. consumer product
   l. negotiated pricing

True False Questions

11. **T   F**   Taken together, tobacco products, alcoholic beverages, and Del Monte brand fruits are considered a product line.

12. **T   F**   Once established, the same product mix remains effective for as long as the firm chooses to use it.

13. **T   F**   Screening is the first step in new product development.

14. **T   F**   Commercialization is the final stage in the development of a new product development.

15. **T   F**   "Peanut Butter" written on a plain white label is an example of a generic product.

16. **T   F**   Packaging has little influence on buying decisions.

17. **T   F**   Labels may carry details of written, or express, warranties.

18. **T   F**   Product differentiation can make a product more competitive with similar products.

19. **T   F**   Total revenue is the selling price times the number of units sold.

20. **T   F**   The breakeven quantity includes the desired profit level.

Multiple-Choice Questions

21. _____ Western Day was a special day at the office. Janice wanted to dress in the latest western fashion, but she had limited funds. She visited several shops before finding the right outfit. For Janice, what type of product is the clothing?
    a. Specialty product
    b. Major equipment
    c. Industrial product
    d. Shopping product
    e. Convenience product

22. _____ Sales increase gradually as a result of promotion and distribution activities, but initially, high development and marketing costs result in low profit, or even in a loss. This best describes which stage of the product life-cycle?
    a. Maturity
    b. Introduction
    c. Decline
    d. Growth
    e. Steady

23. _____ Product modification makes changes to existing products in three primary ways. They are
    a. screening, testing, and changing.
    b. growth, maturity, and decline.
    c. quality, function, and aesthetics.
    d. quantity, description, and appearance.
    e. product, price, and service.

24. _____ The largest number of new product ideas is rejected during this phase.
    a. Concept testing
    b. Screening
    c. Test marketing
    d. Idea generation
    e. Business analysis

25. _____ The manager of a local restaurant wants to add new desserts to the menu. Customers were asked to complete a survey about what they like to eat. The restaurant is in which stage of the new-product development process?
    a. Test marketing
    b. Product development
    c. Idea generation
    d. Screening
    e. Business analysis

26. _____ A customer who consistently buys Sony televisions whenever he or she needs to replace his or her TV set demonstrates
    a. the importance of trademarks.
    b. the importance of trade names.
    c. the importance of brand awareness.
    d. brand loyalty.
    e. brand equity.

27. _____ Dell, IBM, and Xerox use a strategy that helps promote all their products. This strategy is called
    a. family branding.
    b. generic brands.
    c. store brands.
    d. individual branding.
    e. none of the above.

28. _____ Plastic water bottles, while convenient for customers, are a clear example that manufacturers are not considering _____ when designing packaging.
    a. the needs of intermediaries
    b. the needs of retailers
    c. environmental consciousness
    d. family needs
    e. cost-effectiveness

29. _____ When there is a shortage of citrus fruit, the economic forces of supply and demand would suggest that
    a. price will stay constant.
    b. price will decrease.
    c. price will increase.
    d. price, all things remaining equal, will increase.
    e. it will take a long time before the shortage is felt in the market.

30. _____ Like many other food establishments, Denny's offers a senior citizen's discount. This is an example of
    a. periodic discounting.
    b. random discounting.
    c. differential pricing.
    d. negotiated pricing.
    e. senior market pricing.

Answers to the Test Yourself questions appear at the end of the book on page TY-2.

Video Case
From Artistic Roots, Blu Dot Styles Marketing Strategy

When a trio of college friends with backgrounds in art and architecture started moving into their first apartments in the late 1990s, they were frustrated to find that when it came to furniture, they couldn't afford what they liked and didn't like what they could afford. Fortunately for many future furniture shoppers, however, this frustration led the three to found Blu Dot, a Minneapolis-based furniture design and manufacturing company that has flourished since its founding in 1997.

Blu Dot specializes in the creation of furniture that is attractive, of high quality, and affordable. Its modern, streamlined pieces use off-the-shelf materials and simple manufacturing processes that keep the company's costs and prices down. The company also contracts with suppliers that make industrial rather than consumer products, because these suppliers use more efficient and cost-effective processes and technology. These strategies, plus designs that pack flat and are easy to ship, allow the firm to combine what Maurice Blanks, one of the founders, describes as the affordability of the low end of the market and the craftsmanship of the high end. Anyone can design a $600 or $700 coffee table, Blu Dot believes. It's the $99 one the company is aiming for that's more of a challenge.

The company sells seven product lines—tables, storage, accessories, desks, beds, seating, and shelving. Its pricing strategy for each of these is straightforward. Managers add their fixed and variable costs, plus the markup they believe they'll need to keep the business functioning. They then usually look at what competitors are doing with similar products and try to identify three or four different pieces of pricing information to help them settle on a profitable price. The company also uses some creative pricing strategies to make its margins. For instance, one coffee table in a set might have a higher markup, whereas another has a slightly lower one for more price-conscious customers. Overall, then, the target margins are often met.

Blu Dot thinks of its total product offering as consisting of three interdependent elements: the core product, its supplemental features, and its symbolic or experiential value. Although some customers are attracted by the design aspects of the products, others are more concerned with value. That's one reason the company recently introduced a separate brand, called +oo ("too"), and priced it slightly below the original Blu Dot line. These items have been marketed through Urban Outfitters, and Blu Dot has adjusted the prices over time after seeing how sales progressed. Co-founder John Christakos likens Blu Dot's pricing practice to cooking, in that both are processes that allow for fine-tuning as events develop.

In an interesting recent promotion that flirted with the price of zero, Blu Dot celebrated the opening of its new store in New York's hip SoHo district by leaving 25 brand-new units of its iconic "Real Good Chair," normally priced at $129, on various street corners in the city. Most of the chairs were equipped with GPS devices that allowed the company's marketing agency to trace the chairs to those who "rescued" them and brought them home. The company's website proclaims that all the chairs found good homes, and those "scavengers" who agreed to chat with the firm about its products received a second free chair in thank's.[20]

Questions

1. What challenges does Blu Dot face in selling consumer products (as opposed to business products)?
2. Do you think the product life-cycle is an important marketing concept in developing and managing Blu Dot products? Why or why not?
3. Describe the product mix and the role different product lines play in Blu Dot's marketing strategy.

Building Skills for Career Success

1. Social Media Exercise

Creating and pricing products that satisfy customers

As one of the largest railway companies in the United States, Union Pacific has been around for more than 150 years. Recently, the company held a competition that utilized crowdsourcing. It invited participants to vote on an old steam engine's ideal route to take on the "Union Pacific Great Excursion Adventure."[21] Union Pacific split the voting into several rounds and saw strong support from unexpected locations. Smaller towns like Tuscola, IL, were routinely outpacing big metro markets like Chicago in each round. Sometimes the most passion can come from smaller communities for whom winning would be an important accomplishment. Union Pacific recorded nearly 200,000 votes and more than 100,000 e-mail addresses across the campaign. Based on the success of the first campaign, Union Pacific plans to hold another in the future.

1. Visit the website. You may not have thought that social media would be useful for a railroad. What do you think are the most effective elements of the campaign?
2. What can other companies learn from Union Pacific's utilization of crowdsourcing for marketing and promotion?

2. Building Team Skills

In his book, *The Post-Industrial Society*, Peter Drucker wrote:

> Society, community, and family are all conserving institutions. They try to maintain stability and to prevent, or at least slow down, change. But the organization of the post-capitalist society of organizations is a destabilizer. Because its function is to put knowledge to work—on tools, processes, and products; on work; on knowledge itself—it must be organized for constant change. It must be organized for innovation.

New product development is important in this process of systematically abandoning the past and building a future. Current customers can be sources of ideas for new products and services and ways of improving existing ones.

Assignment

1. Working in teams of five to seven, brainstorm ideas for new products or services for your college.
2. Construct questions to ask currently enrolled students (your customers). Sample questions might include:
   a. Why did you choose this college?
   b. How can this college be improved?
   c. What products or services do you wish were available?
3. Conduct the survey and review the results.
4. Prepare a list of improvements and/or new products or services for your college.

3. Researching Different Careers

Standard & Poor's Industry Surveys, designed for investors, provide insight into various industries and the companies that compete within those industries. The "Basic Analysis" section gives overviews of industry trends and issues. The other sections define some basic industry terms, report the latest revenues and earnings of more than 1,000 companies, and occasionally list major reference books and trade associations.

Assignment

1. Identify an industry in which you might like to work.
2. Find the industry in *Standard & Poor's*. (*Note: Standard & Poor's* uses broad categories of industry. For example, an apparel or home-furnishings store would be included under "Retail" or "Textiles.")
3. Identify the following:
   a. Trends and issues in the industry
   b. Opportunities and/or problems that might arise in the industry in the next five years
   c. Major competitors within the industry (These companies are your potential employers.)
4. Prepare a report of your findings.

Endnotes

1. Based on information in Bruce Einhorn, "There's More to Oreo than Black and White," *Bloomberg Businessweek*, May 3, 2012, www.businessweek.com; Nadia Arumugam, "Oreo Cookie Celebrates 100th Birthday with Sprinkles and World Domination," *Forbes*, March 8, 2012, www.forbes.com; Robert Smith, "Rethinking the Oreo for Chinese Consumers," *National Public Radio*, January 27, 2012, www.npr.org; Victoria Lautman, "Kraft Foods's Brand New World," Chicago *Magazine*, June 2011, www.chicagomag.com; http://brands.nabisco.com/Oreo.
2. Anne Marie Mohan, "Hummus Packaging Propels Sabra's Growth," *Packaging World*, December 4, 2012, http://www.packworld.com/package-design/graphic/hummus-packaging-propels-sabra%E2%80%99s-growth.
3. Ben Worthen "What's Gone Wrong With H-P?" *Wall Street Journal*, November 6, 2012, http://online.wsj.com/article/SB10001424052970204755404578101943429107284.html.
4. Procter & Gamble, http://www.pg.com/en_US/brands/all_brands.shtml, accessed December 24, 2012.
5. Nick Bunkley, "GM to Reinforce Battery in its Hybrid Car, the Volt," *The New York Times*, January 20, 2012, www.nytimes.com/2012/01/06/business/gm-to-reinforce-battery-in-hybrid-car.html.
6. Ellen Byron, "A Truce in the Chore Wars," *Wall Street Journal*, December 4, 2012, http://online.wsj.com/article/SB10001424127887323340190457815750031616293.html.
7. Julie Bosman, "After 244 Years, Encyclopaedia Britannica Stops the Presses," *Wall Street Journal*, March 13, 2012, http://mediadecoder.blogs.nytimes.com/2012/03/13/after-244-years-encyclopaedia-britannica-stops-the-presses/, accessed December 27, 2012.
8. Harrison Weber, "Google Fails 36% of the Time," *The Next Web*, October 17, 2011, http://thenextweb.com/google/2011/10/17/google-fails/, accessed December 23, 2012.
9. Sarah Rottman Epps, "Larklife: My Vote for 2012's Most Innovative Product," *Forbes*, October 8, 2012, http://www.forbes.com/sites/forrester/2012/10/08/larklife-my-vote-for-2012s-most-innovative-product/; Larklife, Lark Technologies, http://www.lark.com/products/larklife/experience, accessed December 23, 2012.
10. Robb Mandelbaum, "Making Small Business a Cause," *New York Times*, November 14, 2012, http://www.nytimes.com/2012/11/15/business/smallbusiness/samuel-adams-brewer-counsels-small-businesses.html.
11. Staff writer, "Columbus, Ohio: Test Market of the U.S.A.," CBA News, March 25, 2012, www.cbsnews.com/8301-505125_162-57404087/columbus-ohio-test-market-of-the-u.s.a/, accessed December 27, 2012.
12. "Store Brands Facts," Private Label Manufacturers Association (PLMA), http://plma.com/storeBrands/factsnew12.html, accessed December 23, 2012; Candace Choi, "Store Brand Groceries Now on Premium Shelves," USA Today, March 25, 2012, www.usatoday.com/money/industries/food/story/2012-03-25/store-brand-groceries/53739828/1, accessed December 23, 2012.
13. Jenna Wortham, "Facebook Responds to Anger Over Proposed Instagram Changes," *New York Times*, December 18, 2012, http://www.nytimes.com/2012/12/19/technology/facebook-responds-to-anger-over-proposed-instagram-changes.html.
14. "Pet Insurance," Iams, www.iams.com/pet-health/pet-insurance, accessed January 25, 2013.

15. Replenish, http://myreplenish.com/, accessed December 24, 2012.

16. "Sustainable Packaging," Stonyfield Farm, http://www.stonyfield.com /healthy-planet/our-practices-farm-table/sustainable-packaging, accessed December 24, 2012.

17. Jennifer Valentino-Devries, Jeremy Singer-Vine, and Ashkan Soltani, "Websites Vary Prices, Deals Based on User Information," *Wall Street Journal,* December 23, 2012, http://online.wsj.com/article/SB1000142 4127887323777204578189391813881534.html; Lindsay Wise, "Online Prices Can Change by the Hour, and by the Shopper," *Kansas City Star,* December 1, 2012, http://www.kansascity.com/2012/12/01/3944160 /online-prices-can-change-by-the.html.

18. Vibram Five Fingers, www.vibramfivefingers.com/index.htm, accessed December 13, 2012.

19. Stephanie Clifford, "When it Comes to Reservations, Time is Money," *New York Times*, September 3, 2012, http://www.nytimes.com /2012/09/05/dining/restaurant-prices-can-vary-by-reservation-time .html.com/news/article.jsp?ymd=20120308&content_id=27106214 &vkey=pr_min&c_id=min.

20. Based on information in bludot.com accessed February 21, 2012; "Stuff," bludot.com (accessed February 21, 2012) and originally published in *Minnesota Monthly*; Carl Alviani, "Taking the Middle Ground: Massive Design for the Masses?" Core 77, http://core77.com /reactor/07.05_mlddleground.asp accessed February 13, 2012; interviews with company personnel and the film, "Blu Dot."

21. Union Pacific's Great Excursion Adventure, http://www.up.com/aboutup /special_trains/steam/great_excursion_adventure/upexcursion/index .html, accessed December 27, 2012.

Chapter 13

Distributing and Promoting Products

Why Should You Care?

Not only is it important to create and maintain a mix of products that satisfies customers but also to make these products available at the *right place* and *time* and to communicate with customers effectively.

Learning Objectives

Once you complete this chapter, you will be able to:

1 Identify the various distribution channels and explain the concept of market coverage.

2 Understand how supply-chain management facilitates partnering among channel members.

3 Discuss the need for wholesalers, describe the services they provide, and identify the major types of wholesalers.

4 Distinguish among the major types of retailers and shopping centers.

5 Explain the five most important physical distribution activities.

6 Explain how integrated marketing communications works to have the maximum impact on the customer.

7 Understand the basic elements of the promotion mix.

8 Explain the three types of advertising and describe the major steps of developing an advertising campaign.

9 Recognize the kinds of salespersons, the steps in the personal-selling process, and the major sales management tasks.

10 Describe sales promotion objectives and methods.

11 Understand the types and uses of public relations.

How Dick's Sporting Goods Captures the Category

Whether they like to swing a golf club, bait a fishing rod, run a marathon, or dunk a basketball, sports lovers can browse a vast array of clothing, shoes, and equipment at Dick's Sporting Goods (www.dickssportinggoods.com). The company began with one small bait and tackle shop in 1948 and today operates more than 500 sporting goods stores in 44 states. It also owns 81 Golf Galaxy specialty stores and has begun testing a new type of store featuring shoes and clothing for running enthusiasts. In all, the company rings up $5.2 billion in annual sales.

A typical 55,000-square-foot Dick's Sporting Goods store has tens of thousands of items on display, with even more merchandise available online. The company has created "store within a store" departments for Nike and Under Armour, with additional "store within a store" departments devoted to groups of products related to an individual sport, such as soccer and baseball. In line with an accelerating trend in retail marketing, Dick's also markets a growing number of products under its own private brand.

Given the competitive nature of retailing, Dick's uses its ScoreCard reward program to reinforce customer loyalty. Shoppers earn points every time they buy in a Dick's store or from the Dick's website and for using the retailer's mobile app. They can also earn points for becoming a fan on Facebook (where it has 1.5 million "likes") and following the retailer on Twitter (joining 88,000 other followers).

Dick's generates excitement about its merchandise by promoting selected products and well-known brands in seasonal catalogs and weekly advertisements. In addition, it uses contests and other promotions to highlight its connection with popular sports. Looking ahead, the firm recently opened its fourth distribution center, a key factor in its long-term growth strategy. Right now, Dick's has the capacity to receive, sort, and ship enough merchandise to support up to 750 stores nationwide—and it aims to have as many as 900 stores by the end of the decade.[1]

Did You Know?

Dick's Sporting Goods began as a tiny bait and tackle shop and now operates more than 500 sporting-goods stores spread across 44 states.

Successful companies, like Dick's Sporting Goods, use a particular approach to distribution and marketing channels that gives them a sustainable competitive advantage. More than two million firms in the United States help to move products from producers to consumers. Store chains such as Dollar General, Starbucks, Sears, and Walmart operate retail outlets where consumers make purchases. Some retailers, such as Avon Products and Amway, send their salespeople to the homes of customers. Other retailers, such as Lands' End and L. L. Bean, sell in stores, online, through catalogs, or a combination of the three. Still others, such as Amazon, sell exclusively online.

In this chapter, we initially examine the various distribution channels through which products move as they progress from producer to ultimate user. Then we discuss marketing intermediaries, wholesalers and retailers, and examine major types of shopping centers. Next, we explore the physical distribution function and the major modes of transportation that are used to move goods. Then we discuss integrated marketing communication and the elements of the promotion mix: advertising, personal selling, sales promotion, and public relations.

distribution channel (or marketing channel) a sequence of marketing organizations that directs a product from the producer to the ultimate user

middleman (or marketing intermediary) a marketing organization that links a producer and user within a marketing channel

DISTRIBUTION CHANNELS AND MARKET COVERAGE

Learning Objective

1 Identify the various distribution channels and explain the concept of market coverage.

A **distribution channel**, or **marketing channel**, is a sequence of marketing organizations that directs a product from the producer to the ultimate user. Every marketing channel begins with the producer and ends with either the consumer or the business user.

A marketing organization that links a producer and user within a marketing channel is called a **middleman**, or **marketing intermediary**. For the most part,

merchant middleman a middleman that actually takes title to products by buying them

functional middleman a middleman that helps in the transfer of ownership of products but does not take title to the products

middlemen are concerned with the transfer of *ownership* of products. A **merchant middleman** (or, more simply, a *merchant*) is a middleman that actually takes title to products by buying them. A **functional middleman** on the other hand, helps in the transfer of ownership of products but does not take title to the products.

Commonly Used Distribution Channels

Different channels of distribution generally are used to move consumer and business products. Figure 13-1 illustrates the most common distribution channels for consumer and business products.

PRODUCER TO CONSUMER This channel, often called the *direct channel*, includes no marketing intermediaries. Practically all services and a few consumer goods are distributed through a direct channel. Examples of marketers that sell goods directly to consumers include Mary Kay Cosmetics and Avon Products.

Producers sell directly to consumers for several reasons. They can better control the quality and price of their products. They do not have to pay (through discounts) for the services of intermediaries. Also, they can maintain closer relationships with customers.

retailer a middleman that buys from producers or other middlemen and sells to consumers

PRODUCER TO RETAILER TO CONSUMER A **retailer** is a middleman that buys from producers or other middlemen and sells to consumers. Producers sell directly to retailers when the retailers are large enough to buy in large quantities. This channel is used most often for products that are bulky, such as furniture and automobiles, for which additional handling would increase selling costs. It is also the usual channel for perishable products, such as fruits and vegetables, and for high-fashion products that must reach the consumer in the shortest possible time.

FIGURE 13-1 Distribution Channels

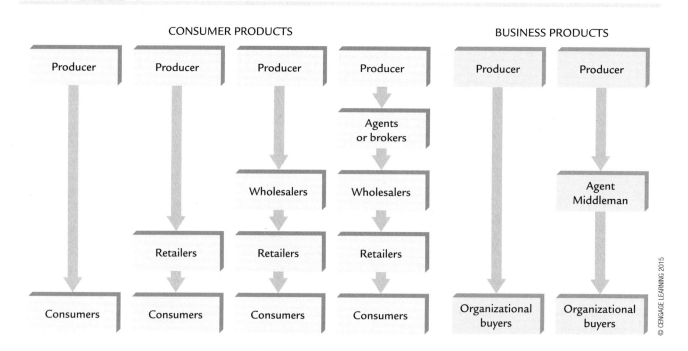

© CENGAGE LEARNING 2015

PRODUCER TO WHOLESALER TO RETAILER TO CONSUMER This channel is known as the *traditional channel* because many consumer goods (especially convenience goods) pass through wholesalers to retailers. A **wholesaler** is a middleman that sells products to other firms. These firms may be retailers, industrial users, or other wholesalers. A producer uses wholesalers when its products are carried by so many retailers that the producer cannot manage and distribute all of them. For example, chewing gum or soda pop manufacturers may use this type of channel.

wholesaler a middleman that sells products to other firms

PRODUCER TO AGENT TO WHOLESALER TO RETAILER TO CONSUMER Producers can use agents to reach wholesalers. Agents are functional middlemen that do not take title to products and that are compensated by commissions paid by producers. Often the products with which agents deal are inexpensive, frequently purchased items. For example, to reach a large number of potential customers, a small manufacturer of gas-powered lawn edgers might choose to use agents to market them to wholesalers. The wholesalers then sell the product to a large network of retailers. This channel is also used for seasonal products (such as Christmas decorations) and by producers that do not have in-house sales forces.

PRODUCER TO ORGANIZATIONAL BUYER In this direct channel, the manufacturer's own sales force sells directly to organizational buyers, or business users. Heavy machinery, airplanes, and major equipment usually are distributed in this way. The very short channel allows the producer to provide customers with expert and timely services, such as delivery, machinery installation, and repairs.

PRODUCER TO AGENT MIDDLEMAN TO ORGANIZATIONAL BUYER Manufacturers use this channel to distribute such items as operating supplies, accessory equipment, small tools, and standardized parts. The agent is an independent intermediary between the producer and the user. Agents generally represent sellers.

USING MULTIPLE CHANNELS Often a manufacturer uses different distribution channels to reach different market segments. For example, candy bars

Concept Check

✓ How do the different types of middlemen link a producer to a user within a marketing channel?

✓ Describe the six distribution channels. Give an example of each.

✓ Explain the three intensities of market coverage. Which types of products are generally associated with each of the different intensity levels (convenience, shopping, or specialty)?

Using multiple marketing channels. Sometimes, companies use multiple marketing channels rather than just one. College textbook publishers often sell their products through multiple marketing channels. This textbook can be purchased directly from the publisher. It can also be purchased at a campus bookstore, or through Amazon.

© 06PHOTO/SHUTTERSTOCK.COM

Got water to drink?

You don't have to be just at a store. Wherever you are—at school, at work, at a ball game, or at a movie—you're likely to see bottled water for sale. So many people buy this item in so many situations that marketers use intensive distribution to make bottled water available just about everywhere.

intensive distribution the use of all available outlets for a product

selective distribution the use of only a portion of the available outlets for a product in each geographic area

exclusive distribution the use of only a single retail outlet for a product in a large geographic area

may be sold through channels containing wholesalers and retailers, as well as channels in which the producer sells them directly through large retailers. Multiple channels are also used to increase sales or to capture a larger share of the market with the goal of selling as much merchandise as possible.

Level of Market Coverage

As with other marketing decisions, producers must analyze all relevant factors when deciding which distribution channels and intermediaries to use. Marketers should weigh the firm's production capabilities and marketing resources, the target market and buying patterns of potential customers, and the product itself. After evaluating these factors, the producer chooses the correct level of *intensity of market coverage*. Then the producer selects channels and intermediaries to implement that coverage.

Intensive distribution is the use of all available outlets for a product. It gives a product the widest possible exposure in the marketplace. The manufacturer saturates the market by selling to any intermediary of good financial standing that is willing to stock and sell the product. For the consumer, intensive distribution means being able to shop at a convenient store and spend minimum time selecting and buying the product. Many convenience goods, including candy, gum, and soft drinks, are distributed intensively.

Selective distribution is the use of only a portion of the available outlets for a product in each geographic area. Manufacturers of goods such as furniture, major home appliances, and clothing typically prefer selective distribution. For instance, you may prefer Hanes brand socks, which are distributed through retailers such as Target and Sears.

Exclusive distribution is the use of only a single retail outlet for a product in a large geographic area. Exclusive distribution usually is limited to prestigious products. It is appropriate, for instance, for specialty goods such as grand pianos, fine china, and expensive jewelry. The producer usually places many requirements (such as inventory levels, sales training, service quality, and warranty procedures) on exclusive dealers. For example, Patek Philippe watches, which may sell for $500,000 or more, are available in only a few select locations.

Learning Objective

2 **Understand how supply-chain management facilitates partnering among channel members.**

supply-chain management long-term partnership among channel members working together to create a distribution system that reduces inefficiencies, costs, and redundancies while creating a competitive advantage and satisfying customers

PARTNERING THROUGH SUPPLY-CHAIN MANAGEMENT

Supply-chain management is a long-term partnership among channel members working together to create a distribution system that reduces inefficiencies, costs, and redundancies while creating a competitive advantage and satisfying customers. Supply-chain management requires cooperation throughout the entire marketing channel, including manufacturing, research, sales, advertising, and shipping. Supply chains focus not only on producers, wholesalers, retailers, and customers, but also on component-parts suppliers, shipping companies, communication companies, and other organizations that participate in product distribution. Suppliers strongly impact what items retail stores carry. This phenomenon, called *category management*, is a common practice for mass merchandisers, supermarkets, and convenience stores. Through category management, the retailer asks a supplier in a particular category how to stock the shelves. Many retailers and suppliers believe this process enhances efficiency.

Traditionally, buyers and sellers have had an adversarial relationship when negotiating purchases. Supply-chain management, however, encourages cooperation in reducing the costs of inventory, transportation, administration, and handling. It also speeds order-cycle times, and increases profits for all channel members. When buyers, sellers, marketing intermediaries, and facilitating agencies work together, customers' needs regarding delivery, scheduling, packaging, and other requirements are better met. Meeting customer needs through a highly innovative, fast, and efficient distribution system helped clothing company, Zara, grow to be the world's largest fashion retailer. Trendy items are produced close to the market so they can be on the shelves quickly, while less trendy items are made where they can be produced most cheaply.[2]

Technology has enhanced the implementation of supply-chain management significantly. Through computerized integrated information sharing, channel members reduce costs and improve customer service. Firms can take advantage of hundreds of electronic trading communities comprised of businesses selling to other businesses, including auctions, exchanges, e-procurement hubs, and multisupplier online catalogs. As many major industries transform their processes, the end result is increased productivity by reducing inventory, shortening cycle time, and reducing wasted human effort.

Concept Check

✓ How does supply-chain management encourage cooperation between buyers and sellers?

✓ How has technology enhanced the implementation of supply-chain management?

MARKETING INTERMEDIARIES: WHOLESALERS

Learning Objective

3 Discuss the need for wholesalers, describe the services they provide, and identify the major types of wholesalers.

Wholesalers are possibly the most misunderstood of marketing intermediaries. Producers sometimes try to cut out wholesalers in favor of dealing directly with retailers or consumers. However, wholesalers increase distribution efficiency. The marketing activities performed by wholesalers *must* be performed by other channel members if wholesalers are eliminated, which means that cutting out wholesalers may not reduce distribution costs.

Wholesalers Provide Services to Retailers and Manufacturers

Wholesalers help retailers by

- Buying in large quantities and selling to retailers in smaller quantities and delivering goods to retailers.
- Stocking in one place the variety of goods that retailers otherwise would have to buy from many producers.
- Providing assistance in other vital areas, including promotion, market information, and financial aid.

Wholesalers help manufacturers by

- Performing functions similar to those provided to retailers.
- Providing a sales force, reducing inventory costs, assuming credit risks, and furnishing market information.

Types of Wholesalers

Wholesalers generally fall into two categories: merchant wholesalers, and agents and brokers. Of these, merchant wholesalers constitute the largest portion. They account for about four-fifths of all wholesale establishments and employees.

OBERHAEUSER/CARO/ALAMY

Wholesalers facilitate trade by connecting manufacturers with retailers.
A general-merchandise wholesaler buys many types of products from a broad range of manufacturers, warehouses the products, and then sells them to retailers. So, instead of having to contact hundreds of different manufacturers to stock their shelves, retailers need to contact only a small number of wholesalers.

merchant wholesaler a middleman that purchases goods in large quantities and sells them to other wholesalers or retailers and to institutional, farm, government, professional, or industrial users

MERCHANT WHOLESALERS A **merchant wholesaler** is a middleman that purchases goods in large quantities and sells them to other wholesalers or retailers and to institutional, farm, government, professional, or industrial users. Merchant wholesalers have the following characteristics:

- They usually operate one or more warehouses at which they receive, take title to, and store goods. These wholesalers are sometimes called *distributors* or *jobbers*.
- Most merchant wholesalers are businesses composed of salespeople, order takers, receiving and shipping clerks, inventory managers, and office personnel.
- The successful merchant wholesaler must analyze available products and market needs. It must be able to adapt the type, variety, and quality of its products to changing market conditions.
- Merchant wholesalers may be classified as full-service or limited-service wholesalers depending on the number of services they provide. A **full-service wholesaler** performs the entire range of wholesaler functions. These functions include delivering goods, supplying warehousing, arranging for credit, supporting promotional activities, and providing general customer assistance.

full-service wholesaler a middleman that performs the entire range of wholesaler functions

general-merchandise wholesaler a middleman that deals in a wide variety of products

limited-line wholesaler a middleman that stocks only a few product lines but carries numerous product items within each line

specialty-line wholesaler a middleman that carries a select group of products within a single line

A full-service wholesaler can be of three different types:

- A **general-merchandise wholesaler** deals in a wide variety of products, such as drugs, hardware, nonperishable foods, cosmetics, detergents, and tobacco.
- A **limited-line wholesaler** stocks only a few product lines but carries numerous product items within each line.
- A **specialty-line wholesaler** carries a select group of products within a single line. Food delicacies, such as shellfish, represent a product handled by this type of wholesaler.

AGENTS AND BROKERS Agents and brokers are functional middlemen. Functional middlemen do not take title to products. They perform a small number of marketing activities and are paid a commission that is a percentage of the sales price.

agent a middleman that expedites exchanges, represents a buyer or a seller, and often is hired permanently on a commission basis

broker a middleman that specializes in a particular commodity, represents either a buyer or a seller, and is likely to be hired on a temporary basis

An **agent** is a middleman that expedites exchanges, represents a buyer or a seller, and often is hired permanently on a commission basis. When agents represent producers, they are known as *sales agents* or *manufacturer's agents*. As long as the products represented do not compete, a sales agent may represent one or several manufacturers on a commission basis. The agent solicits orders for the manufacturers within a specific territory. As a rule, the manufacturers ship the merchandise and bill the customers directly. The manufacturers also set the prices and other conditions of the sales. The sales agent provides immediate entry into a territory, regular calls on customers, selling experience, and a known, predetermined selling expense (a commission that is a percentage of sales revenue).

A **broker** is a middleman that specializes in a particular commodity, represents either a buyer or a seller, and is likely to be hired on a temporary basis. Food brokers which sell grocery products to resellers, are the exception to this rule. They generally have long-term relationships with clients. Brokers may perform only the selling function or both buying and selling using their established contacts and specialized knowledge of their fields.

Concept Check

✓ What services do wholesalers provide to producers and to retailers?

✓ Identify and describe the various types of wholesalers.

Learning Objective

4 **Distinguish among the major types of retailers and shopping centers.**

MARKETING INTERMEDIARIES: RETAILERS

Retailers are the final link between producers and consumers. Retailers may buy from either wholesalers or producers. They can sell goods, services (such as auto repairs or haircuts), or both. Sears, Roebuck & Co. sells consumer goods, financial services, and repair services for home appliances purchased at Sears.

TABLE 13-1 The Ten Largest U.S. Retailers

Rank	Company	Revenues (in millions)	# of Stores
1	Walmart Stores, Inc. (U.S.A.)	$453,976	4,423
2	Kroger	$85,491	3,574
3	Target	$68,466	1,763
4	Costco	$68,233	7,651
5	The Kroger Co. (U.S.A.)	$89,054	425
6	The Home Depot	$70,391	1,963
7	CVS Caremark	$59,786	7,345
8	Lowe's	$50,207	1,712
9	Best Buy	$50,705	1,443
10	Safeway	$41,884	1,453

Source: "2012 Top 100 Retailers" Stores, http://www.stores.org/2012/Top-100-Retailers (accessed January 4, 2013).

independent retailer a firm that operates only one retail outlet

chain retailer a company that operates more than one retail outlet

department store a retail store that (1) employs 25 or more persons and (2) sells at least home furnishings, appliances, family apparel, and household linens and dry goods, each in a different part of the store

The U.S. Census estimates that the United States has about $1.1 million retail establishments.[3] Most retailers are small, with annual revenues well under $1 million. However, some retailers are very large. Table 13-1 lists the ten largest retail organizations in the U.S., their sales revenues, and number of stores.

Types of Retail Stores

One way to classify retailers is by the number of stores owned and operated by the firm.

1. An **independent retailer** is a firm that operates only one retail outlet. Most retailers are independent, one-store operators that generally provide personal service and a convenient location.
2. A **chain retailer** is a company that operates more than one retail outlet. By adding outlets, chain retailers reach new geographic markets. As sales increase, chains usually buy merchandise in larger quantities and thus take advantage of quantity discounts. They also wield more power in their dealings with suppliers. There are many fewer chain retailers than independent retailers.

Another way to classify retail stores is by store size and the kind and number of products carried. We will now take a closer look at store types based on these dimensions.

DEPARTMENT STORES These large retail establishments consist of several sections, or departments, that sell a wide assortment of products. According to the U.S. Census, a **department store** is a retail store that (1) employs 25 or more persons and (2) sells at least home furnishings, appliances, family apparel, and household linens and dry goods, each in a different part of the store. Macy's, Harrods, and Printemps are examples of large, international, department stores. Sears, Roebuck & Co. and JCPenney are also department stores. Traditionally, department stores have been service-oriented. Along with the goods they sell, these retailers provide credit, delivery, personal assistance, liberal return policies, and pleasant shopping atmospheres.

CARLO BEVILACQUA/MARKA/ALAMY

Accessing customers through different types of retailers. When people are asked to name a retailer, they often think of brick-and-mortar establishments like the ones shown in this photo. However, retailing goes on in all kinds of places, including in people's homes and workplaces, online, over the phone and on TV, and even on the streets.

DISCOUNT STORES A **discount store** is a self-service general-merchandise outlet that sells products at lower-than-usual prices. These stores operate on smaller markups and higher merchandise turnover than other retailers and offer minimal customer services. Popular discount stores include Kmart, Walmart, and Dollar General.

WAREHOUSE SHOWROOMS A **warehouse showroom** is a retail facility with five basic characteristics: (1) a large, low-cost building, (2) warehouse materials-handling technology, (3) vertical merchandise displays, (4) a large, on-premises inventory, and (5) minimal service. Some of the best-known showrooms are operated by big furniture retailers. These operations employ few personnel and offer few services. Most customers carry away purchases in the manufacturer's carton, although some warehouse showrooms will deliver for a fee.

CONVENIENCE STORES A **convenience store** is a small food store that sells a limited variety of products but remains open well beyond normal business hours. Because convenience stores are common, most patrons of a particular store live within a mile of it. White Hen Pantry, 7-Eleven, Circle K, and Open Pantry stores, for example, are convenience stores found either regionally or nationally in the U.S. Limited product mixes and higher prices keep convenience stores from threatening the business of other grocery retailers. There are over 148,000 convenience stores in the United States.[4]

SUPERMARKETS A **supermarket** is a large self-service store that sells primarily food and household products. It stocks canned, fresh, frozen, and processed foods, paper products, and cleaning supplies. Supermarkets also may sell such items as housewares, toiletries, toys and games, drugs, stationery, books and magazines, plants and flowers, and a few clothing items. Supermarkets are large-scale operations that emphasize low prices and one-stop shopping for household needs.

SUPERSTORES A **superstore** is a large retail store that carries, not only food and nonfood products ordinarily found in supermarkets, but also additional product lines such as housewares, hardware, small appliances, clothing, personal-care products, garden products, and automotive merchandise. Superstores also provide services, including automotive repair, snack bars and restaurants, photo printing, and banking.

WAREHOUSE CLUBS The **warehouse club** is a large-scale members-only establishment that combines features of cash-and-carry wholesaling with discount retailing. For an annual fee, small retailers or individuals may become members and purchase products at wholesale prices for business use, for resale, or personal use.

Because their product lines are shallow and sales volumes are high, warehouse clubs can offer a broad range of merchandise, including perishable and nonperishable foods, beverages, books, appliances, housewares, automotive parts, hardware, and furniture.

Killing the competition? Or not? Office Depot is an example of a category killer. Category killers aren't likely to annihilate all of the competition though. Small retailers with less product variety and higher prices have found it difficult to compete against category killers. However, small retailers that carry a smaller inventory of products that are different from those stocked by category killers and compete on the basis of service, rather than price, can survive.

TRADITIONAL SPECIALTY STORES A **traditional specialty store** carries a narrow product mix with deep product lines. Traditional specialty stores are sometimes called *limited-line retailers*. If they have depth in one product category, such as baked goods or jewelry, they may be called *single-line retailers*. Specialty stores usually offer deeper product mixes than department stores. They attract customers by emphasizing service, atmosphere, and location. Consumers who are dissatisfied with the impersonal atmosphere of large retailers often find the attention offered by specialty stores appealing. Specialty stores include the Gap, Bath and Body Works, and Foot Locker.

OFF-PRICE RETAILERS An **off-price retailer** is a store that buys manufacturers' seconds, overruns, returns, and off-season merchandise at below-wholesale prices and sells them to consumers at deep discounts. Off-price retailers sell limited lines of national-brand and designer merchandise, usually clothing, shoes, or housewares. Off-price retailers include T.J. Maxx, Burlington Coat Factory, and Nordstrom Rack. Off-price stores charge up to 50 percent less than department stores for comparable merchandise, but offer few customer services. They often include community dressing rooms and central checkout counters. Some off-price retailers have a no-returns, no-exchanges policy.

<aside>**off-price retailer** a store that buys manufacturers' seconds, overruns, returns, and off-season merchandise for resale to consumers at deep discounts</aside>

CATEGORY KILLERS A **category killer** is a very large specialty store that concentrates on a single product line and competes by offering low prices and an enormous number of products. These stores are called *category killers* because they take business away from smaller, higher-cost retail stores. Category killers have increased competition from Internet retailing. The cost of maintaining such large stores can drain a company of its profits. In China, a country previously viewed as a goldmine, large category killers, such as Best Buy, are pulling out completely in an effort to remain profitable. Other major retailers, such as Walmart, are opening fewer and smaller stores.[5]

<aside>**category killer** a very large specialty store that concentrates on a single product line and competes on the basis of low prices and product availability</aside>

Types of Nonstore Selling

Nonstore retailing is selling that does not take place in conventional store facilities. Consumers may purchase products without ever visiting a store. This form of retailing accounts for an increasing percentage of total retail sales. Nonstore retailers use direct selling, direct marketing, and vending machines.

<aside>**nonstore retailing** a type of retailing whereby consumers purchase products without visiting a store</aside>

DIRECT SELLING **Direct selling** is the marketing of products to customers through face-to-face sales presentations at home or in the workplace. Traditionally called *door-to-door selling*, direct selling in the United States began with peddlers more than a century ago and is now a major industry with $28.5 billion in U.S. sales annually.[6] Instead of the door-to-door approach, many companies today—such as Mary Kay, Amway, and Avon—use other approaches. They can identify customers by mail, telephone, the Internet and then set up appointments. Direct selling sometimes involves the "party plan," which can occur in the customer's home or workplace. Direct selling through the party plan requires effective salespeople who identify potential hosts and provide encouragement and incentives for them to organize a gathering. Companies that commonly use the party plan are Tupperware, Stanley Home Products, and Pampered Chef.

<aside>**direct selling** the marketing of products to customers through face-to-face sales presentations at home or in the workplace</aside>

DIRECT MARKETING **Direct marketing** is the use of the telephone, Internet, and nonpersonal media to communicate product and organizational information to customers, who then can purchase products via mail, telephone, or the Internet. Direct marketing is a type of nonstore retailing and can occur through catalog marketing, direct-response marketing, telemarketing, television home shopping, and online.

In **catalog marketing**, an organization provides a catalog from which customers make selections and place orders by mail, telephone, or the Internet. Catalog marketing began in 1872 when Montgomery Ward issued its first catalog to rural families. There are thousands of catalog marketing companies in the U.S., many of which publish online. Some catalog marketers sell products spread over multiple product lines, while others are more specialized. Catalog companies, such as Burpee and Newport

<aside>**direct marketing** the use of the telephone, Internet, and nonpersonal media to introduce products to customers, who then can purchase them via mail, telephone, or the Internet</aside>

<aside>**catalog marketing** a type of marketing in which an organization provides a catalog from which customers make selections and place orders by mail, telephone, or the Internet</aside>

Utilizing multiple retail approaches. Many retailers use multiple marketing strategies to reach potential customers. Crate & Barrel operates over 160 retail stores. It also engages in direct marketing through catalog and online retailing.

SUSAN VAN ETTEN

News, offer considerable depth in only one major product line. The advantages of catalog marketing include efficiency and convenience for customers because they do not have to visit a store. The retailer benefits by being able to locate in remote, low-cost areas, save on expensive store fixtures, and reduce both personal selling and store operating expenses. Disadvantages are that catalog marketing is inflexible, provides limited service, and is most effective for only a selected set of products.

Direct-response marketing occurs when a retailer advertises a product and makes it available through mail, telephone, or online orders. This marketing method has resulted in some products gaining widespread popularity. You may have heard of the Shake Weight, Snuggie, and Magic Bullet—all of which became popular through direct response television marketing campaigns. Direct-response marketing can also be conducted by sending letters, samples, brochures, or booklets to prospects on a mailing list.

direct-response marketing a type of marketing in which a retailer advertises a product and makes it available through mail, telephone, or online orders

telemarketing the performance of marketing-related activities by telephone

Telemarketing is the performance of marketing-related activities by telephone. Some organizations use a prescreened list of prospective clients. Telemarketing has many advantages, such as generating sales leads, improving customer service, speeding up payments on past-due accounts, raising funds for nonprofit organizations, and gathering market data.

However, increasingly restrictive telemarketing laws have made it a less appealing marketing method. In 2003, U.S. Congress implemented a national do-not-call registry, which has more than 200 million numbers on it. The Federal Trade Commission (FTC) enforces violations and companies are subject to fines of up to $16,000 for each call made to numbers on the list. The Federal Communications Commission (FCC) ruled that companies are no longer allowed to call customers using prerecorded marketing calls simply because they had done business in the past. The law also requires that an "opt-out" mechanism be embedded in the call for consumers who do not wish to receive the calls. Companies that are still allowed to make telemarketing phone calls must pay for access to the do-not-call registry and must obtain updated numbers from the registry at least every three days. Certain exceptions do apply to no-call lists. For example, charitable, political, and telephone survey organizations are not restricted by the national registry.[7]

television home shopping a form of selling in which products are presented to television viewers, who can buy them by calling a toll-free number and paying with a credit card

online retailing retailing that makes products available to buyers through computer connections

Television home shopping presents products to television viewers, encouraging them to order through toll-free numbers and pay with credit cards. Home Shopping Network (HSN) originated and popularized this format. Most homes in the U.S. receive at least one home shopping channel.

Online retailing makes products available to buyers through computer connections. Most bricks-and-mortar retailers have websites to sell products, provide information about their company, or distribute coupons. Online retailing is a rapidly growing segment that most retailers view as vital to business. Retailers frequently offer exclusive online sales, or may reward customers who visit their websites with special in-store coupons and other promotions and discounts. Although online retailing represents a major retailing venue, security remains an issue. Some Internet users retain concerns about identity theft and credit-card number theft when shopping online.

automatic vending the use of machines to dispense products

Automatic vending is the use of machines to dispense products. It accounts for less than 2 percent of all retail sales. Automatic vending is one of the most impersonal forms of retailing. Small, standardized, routinely purchased products can be sold in machines because they do not readily spoil and consumers appreciate the convenience. However, vending machines have taken on a cult popularity among some urban-dwelling consumers. Customers can now find a wide variety of products dispensed via vending machine, even high-end items. For example, the Semi-Automatic machine, located in luxury hotels, dispenses $500 watches and $22 eye cream to travelers who forgot items at home. InstyMeds vending machines dispense prescription medications to customers. Fishermen in Pennsylvania can even buy live bait via PA Live Bait Vending.[8]

Types of Shopping Centers

The *planned shopping center* is a self-contained retail facility constructed by independent owners and consisting of various stores. Shopping centers are designed and promoted to serve diverse groups of customers with widely differing needs. The management of a shopping center strives for a coordinated mix of stores, a comfortable atmosphere, adequate parking, pleasant landscaping, and special events to attract customers. The convenience of shopping for most family and household needs in a single location is an important part of shopping-center appeal. A planned shopping center is one of four types: lifestyle, neighborhood, community, or regional.

LIFESTYLE SHOPPING CENTERS A **lifestyle shopping center** is a shopping center that has an open-air configuration and is occupied by upscale national chain specialty stores. The lifestyle shopping center model is popular because it combines shopping with the feel of strolling along Main Street. Some lifestyle shopping centers incorporate activities, sports, and culture into their design in order to encourage customers to shop for longer.[9]

NEIGHBORHOOD SHOPPING CENTERS A **neighborhood shopping center** typically consists of several small convenience and specialty stores. Businesses in neighborhood shopping centers might include small grocery stores, drugstores, gas stations, and fast-food restaurants. These retailers serve consumers who live less than ten minutes away, usually within a two to three-mile radius. Unlike in a lifestyle shopping center, most purchases in the neighborhood shopping center are based on convenience or personal contact. These retailers generally make only limited efforts to coordinate their promotional activities.

COMMUNITY SHOPPING CENTERS A **community shopping center** includes one or two department stores and some specialty stores, along with convenience stores. It attracts consumers from a wider geographic area who will drive longer distances to find products and specialty items unavailable in neighborhood shopping centers. Community shopping centers, which are carefully planned and coordinated, generate traffic with special events such as art exhibits, automobile shows, and sidewalk sales. The management of a community shopping center maintains a mix of tenants so that the center offers wide product mixes and deep product lines.

REGIONAL SHOPPING CENTERS A **regional shopping center** usually has large department stores, numerous specialty stores, restaurants, movie theaters, and sometimes even hotels. It carries a similar mix of merchandise to that available in a downtown shopping district.

Regional shopping centers carefully coordinate management and marketing activities to reach the 150,000 or more customers in their target market. These large centers usually advertise, hold special events, and may even provide transportation for customers. National chain stores can gain leases in regional shopping centers more easily than small independent stores because they are better able to meet the centers' financial requirements.

Personal Apps

Where do you shop?

© STOCKLITE/SHUTTERSTOCK.COM

Thanks to online retailing, you can now buy or rent just about anything with a few clicks of your mouse. With online retailing, the global marketplace is open 24/7. And you can also shop on the go if your cell phone has wireless capabilities.

lifestyle shopping center an open-air-environment shopping center with upscale chain specialty stores

neighborhood shopping center a planned shopping center consisting of several small convenience and specialty stores

community shopping center a planned shopping center that includes one or two department stores and some specialty stores, along with convenience stores

regional shopping center a planned shopping center containing large department stores, numerous specialty stores, restaurants, movie theaters, and sometimes even hotels

Concept Check

✓ Describe the major types of retail stores. Give an example of each.

✓ How does nonstore retailing occur?

✓ What are the four most common types of shopping centers, and what type of store does each typically contain?

The "new" Main Street. Upscale stores and the quaint "Main-Street"-like atmosphere found in small towns a generation ago have made lifestyle shopping centers like this one very popular. No longer are shoppers trapped indoors when they are at malls.

Learning Objective

5 **Explain the five most important physical distribution activities.**

physical distribution all those activities concerned with the efficient movement of products from the producer to the ultimate user

inventory management the process of managing inventories in such a way as to minimize inventory costs, including both holding costs and potential stock-out costs

order processing activities involved in receiving and filling customers' purchase orders

PHYSICAL DISTRIBUTION

Physical distribution is all those activities concerned with the efficient movement of products from the producer to the ultimate user. Physical distribution, therefore, is the movement of the products themselves—both goods and services—through their channels of distribution. It combines several interrelated business functions, the most important of which are inventory management, order processing, warehousing, materials handling, and transportation. Because these functions and their costs are highly interrelated, marketers view physical distribution as an integrated effort that supports other marketing activities. The overall goal of distribution is to get the right product to the right place at the right time and at minimal total cost.

Inventory Management

We define **inventory management** as the process of managing inventories in such a way as to minimize inventory costs, including both holding costs and potential stock-out costs.

Holding costs are the expenses of storing products until they are purchased or shipped to customers. *Stock-out costs* are sales lost when items are not in inventory. Marketers seek to balance these two costs so that the company always has sufficient inventory to satisfy customer demand, but with little surplus because storing unsold products can be very expensive.

Holding costs include the money invested in inventory, the cost of storage space, insurance costs, and inventory taxes. Often even a relatively small reduction in inventory can generate a large increase in available working capital. Sometimes firms discover that risking some stockout costs can be cheaper than having too much inventory. Generally speaking, inventory management software helps companies maintain the correct levels of inventory and know when to place orders.

Order Processing

Order processing consists of activities involved in receiving and filling customers' purchase orders. It may include, not only the means by which customers order products, but also procedures for billing and granting credit.

Fast, efficient order processing can provide a dramatic competitive edge. Those in charge of purchasing goods for intermediaries are especially concerned with their suppliers' promptness and reliability in order processing. To them, promptness and reliability mean minimal inventory costs as well as the ability to order goods when they are needed rather than weeks in advance. The Internet is providing new opportunities for improving services associated with order processing.

Warehousing

Warehousing is the set of activities involved in receiving and storing goods and preparing them for reshipment. Goods are stored to create time utility, meaning they are held until they are needed for use or sale. Warehousing includes the following activities:

- *Receiving goods.* The warehouse accepts delivered goods and assumes responsibility for them.
- *Identifying goods.* Records are made of the quantity of each item received. Items may be marked, coded, or tagged for identification.
- *Sorting goods.* Delivered goods may have to be sorted before being stored.
- *Dispatching goods to storage.* Items must be moved to storage areas, where they can be found later.
- *Holding goods.* The goods are protected in storage until needed.
- *Recalling, picking, and assembling goods.* Items that are to leave the warehouse must be selected from storage and assembled efficiently.
- *Dispatching shipments.* Each shipment is packaged and directed to the proper transport vehicle. Shipping and accounting documents are prepared.

A firm may use its own private warehouses or rent space in public warehouses. A *private warehouse*, owned and operated by a particular firm, can be designed to serve the firm's specific needs. However, the organization must take on the task of financing the facility and determining the best location for it. Generally, only companies that deal in large quantities of goods, such as UPS or Walmart, can justify the expense of private warehouses.

Public warehouses are open to all individuals and firms. Most are located on the outskirts of cities, where rail and truck transportation is easily available. They provide storage facilities, areas for sorting and assembling shipments, and office and display spaces for wholesalers and retailers. Public warehouses also will hold—and issue receipts for—goods used as collateral for borrowed funds.

warehousing the set of activities involved in receiving and storing goods and preparing them for reshipment

Materials Handling

Materials handling is the actual physical handling of goods—in warehouses as well as during transportation. Proper materials-handling procedures and techniques can increase the efficiency and capacity of a firm's warehouse and transportation system, as well as reduce product breakage and spoilage.

Materials handling attempts to reduce the number of times a product is handled. One method is called *unit loading*. Several smaller cartons, barrels, or boxes are combined into a single standard-size load that can be moved efficiently by forklift, conveyer, or truck.

materials handling the actual physical handling of goods, in warehouses as well as during transportation

Transportation

As a part of physical distribution, **transportation** is simply the shipment of products to customers. The greater the distance between seller and purchaser, the more important is the choice of the means of transportation and the particular carrier.

A firm that offers transportation services is called a **carrier**. A *common carrier* is a transportation firm whose services are available to all shippers. Railroads, airlines, and most long-distance trucking firms are common carriers. A *contract carrier* is available for hire by one or several shippers. Contract carriers do not serve the general public and the number of firms they can handle at a time is limited by law. A *private carrier* is owned and operated by the shipper.

transportation the shipment of products to customers

carrier a firm that offers transportation services

A shipper can hire agents called *freight forwarders* to handle transportation. Freight forwarders pick up shipments, ensure that the goods are loaded onto carriers, and assume responsibility for their safe delivery. Freight forwarders have the capacity to group multiple small shipments into one large load, thereby saving smaller firms money by charging them a lower rate.

The six major criteria used for selecting transportation modes are compared in Table 13-2. These six criteria are cost, speed, dependability, load flexibility, accessibility, and frequency.

Obviously, the *cost* of a transportation mode is an important consideration. However, it is not the only one. Higher-cost modes of transportation can convey important benefits. *Speed* is measured by the total time that a carrier possesses the products, including time required for pickup and delivery, handling, and movement between point of origin and destination. Usually there is a direct relationship between cost and speed, meaning faster modes of transportation are more expensive. A transportation mode's *dependability* is determined by its consistency of service. *Load flexibility* is the degree to which a transportation mode can be adapted for moving different kinds of products with varying requirements, such as controlled temperatures or humidity levels. *Accessibility* refers to a transportation mode's ability to move goods over a specific route or network. *Frequency* refers to how frequently a marketer can ship products by a specific transportation mode. Whereas pipelines provide continuous shipments, railroads and waterways follow specific schedules for moving products from one location to another. In Table 13-2, each transportation mode is compared according to these six selection criteria and the percentage of use (ton-miles) for each mode.

RAILROADS Although usage has declined over the years, railroad remains one of the most important modes of transportation in the United States. Rail is also the least expensive mode for many products. Almost all railroads are common carriers, although a few coal-mining companies operate their own lines. Many commodities carried by railroads could not be transported easily by any other means.

TRUCKS The trucking industry consists of common, contract, and private carriers. Trucks are a very popular transportation mode because they have the advantage of being able to move goods to areas not served by railroads. They can handle freight quickly and economically, and they can carry a wide range of shipments. Many shippers favor this mode because it offers door-to-door service, less stringent packaging requirements than ships and airplanes, and flexible delivery schedules. Railroad and truck carriers sometimes team up to provide a form of transportation called *piggyback*, wherein truck trailers are loaded onto railroad flatcars for much of the distance and then pulled by trucks to the final destination.

AIRPLANES Air transport is the fastest, but most expensive, means of transportation. All certified airlines are common carriers. Supplemental or charter lines are contract carriers. Because of the high cost, uneven geographic distribution of airports, and reliance on weather conditions, airlines carry only a tiny fraction of intercity

TABLE 13-2 Characteristics of Transportation Modes

Selection Criteria	Railroads	Trucks	Pipelines	Waterways	Airplanes
Cost	Moderate	High	Low	Very low	Very high
Speed	Average	Fast	Slow	Very slow	Very fast
Dependability	Average	High	High	Average	High
Load flexibility	High	Average	Very low	Very high	Low
Accessibility	High	Very high	Very limited	Limited	Average
Frequency	Low	High	Very high	Very low	Average
Percent of use*	27.8%	32.1%	16.7%	16.3%	0.3%
Products carried	Coal, grain, lumber, heavy equipment, paper and pulp products, chemicals	Clothing, computers, books, groceries and produce, livestock	Oil, processed coal, natural gas, wood chips	Chemicals, bauxite, grain, motor vehicles, agricultural implements	Flowers, food (highly perishable), technical instruments, emergency parts and equipment, overnight mail

*Note: Percent of use values do not add up to 100%. 5% of freight shipments were categorized as Multimodal, and 1.7% were categorized as Other/Unknown.

Source: "Modal Shares of U.S. Freight Shipments by Value, Weight, and Ton-Miles," U.S. Bureau of Transportation Statistics, *National Transportation Statistics* (Washington, DC: U.S. Government Printing Office), http://www.rita.dot.gov/bts/sites/rita.dot.gov.bts/files/publications/freight_shipments_in_america/html/figure_03_table.html (accessed January 4, 2013).

freight. Only high-value, perishable items or goods that are needed immediately usually are shipped by air.

WATERWAYS Cargo ships and barges offer the least expensive, but slowest, form of transportation. They are used mainly for bulky, nonperishable goods such as iron ore, bulk wheat, motor vehicles, and agricultural implements. Of course, shipment by water is limited to cities located on navigable waterways. Many international distributors will combine this mode with a land mode to transport products to their destination.

PIPELINES Pipelines are a highly specialized mode of transportation. They are used primarily to carry petroleum and natural gas. Such products as semiliquid coal and wood chips also can be shipped through pipelines, although their use can be controversial when they cut across animal migratory pathways or spring a leak in remote areas.

WHAT IS INTEGRATED MARKETING COMMUNICATIONS?

Integrated marketing communications is the coordination of promotion efforts to ensure maximal informational and persuasive impact on customers. A major goal of integrated marketing communications is to send a consistent message to customers.

Integrated marketing communications helps organizations coordinate and manage promotions in order to create a consistent message. This approach fosters long-term customer relationships and the efficient use of promotional resources. The concept of integrated marketing communications has been increasingly accepted for several reasons. Mass-media advertising, a very popular promotional method in the

Concept Check

✓ How is inventory management a balancing act between stock-out costs and holding costs?

✓ Explain the seven major warehousing activities.

✓ What is the goal of materials handling?

✓ Describe the major characteristics of the primary transportation modes.

Learning Objective

6 Explain how integrated marketing communications works to have the maximum impact on the customer.

integrated marketing communications coordination of promotion efforts to ensure maximal informational and persuasive impact on customers

Concept Check

✓ What is the major goal of integrated marketing communications?

✓ Why is integrated marketing communications being increasingly accepted?

Learning Objective

7 **Understand the basic elements of the promotion mix.**

promotion communication about an organization and its products that is intended to inform, persuade, or remind target-market members

promotion mix the particular combination of promotion methods a firm uses to reach a target market

advertising a paid nonpersonal message communicated to a select audience through a mass medium

personal selling personal communication aimed at informing customers and persuading them to buy a firm's products

past, is used less today because of its high costs and variable audience sizes. Marketers now take advantage of highly targeted promotional tools, such as cable TV, direct mail, DVDs, the Internet, special-interest magazines, and podcasts. Database marketing allows marketers to be more precise in targeting individual customers.

Because the overall costs of marketing communications are significant, management demands systematic evaluations of communications efforts to ensure that promotional resources are used efficiently. Although the fundamental role of promotion has not changed, the specific communication vehicles employed and the precision with which they are used are evolving.

THE PROMOTION MIX: AN OVERVIEW

Promotion is communication about an organization and its products that is intended to inform, persuade, or remind target-market members. Charities use promotion to inform us of their need for donations, to persuade us to give, and to remind us to do so.

Even the Internal Revenue Service uses promotion (in the form of publicity) to remind us of the April 15 deadline for filing tax returns. The promotion with which we are most familiar—advertising—attempts inform, persuade, or remind us to buy particular products. But advertising is only one aspect of promotion.

A **promotion mix** (sometimes called a *marketing-communications mix*) is the particular combination of promotion methods a firm uses to reach a target market. The makeup of a mix depends on many factors, including the firm's promotional resources and objectives, the nature of the target market, the product characteristics, and the feasibility of the various promotional methods. The four elements of the promotion mix are advertising, personal selling, sales promotion, and public relations, as illustrated in Figure 13-2.

Advertising is a paid nonpersonal message communicated to a select audience through a mass medium. Advertising is flexible and can reach a very large or a small, carefully chosen target group. **Personal selling** is personal communication

FIGURE 13-2 Possible Elements of a Promotion Mix

Depending on the type of product and target market involved, one or more of these ingredients are used in a promotion mix.

Source: William M. Pride and O. C. Ferrell, *Marketing: Concepts and Strategies*, 17th ed. (Mason, OH: South-Western/Cengage Learning, 2014). Adapted with permission.

aimed at informing customers and persuading them to buy a firm's products. It is more expensive to reach a consumer through personal selling than through advertising, but this method provides immediate feedback and often is more persuasive than advertising. **Sales promotion** is the use of activities or materials as direct inducements to customers or salespersons, which can add value to the product and increase the customer's incentive to make a purchase. **Public relations** is a broad set of communication activities used to create and maintain favorable relationships between an organization and various public groups, both internal and external. Public-relations activities are numerous and varied and can be a very effective form of promotion.

While it is possible for a marketer to only use one ingredient of the promotion mix, it is more likely that two, three, or four of these ingredients will be used, depending on the type of product and target market involved.

ADVERTISING

Advertising is a very important element of the promotion mix. U.S. firms currently spend around $155 billion annually on advertising.[10] In this section, we discuss the types of advertising and how to develop an advertising campaign.

Types of Advertising by Purpose

Depending on its purpose and message, advertising may be classified into one of three groups: primary demand, selective demand, or institutional.

PRIMARY-DEMAND ADVERTISING **Primary-demand advertising** is advertising aimed at increasing the demand for all brands of a product within a specific industry. Trade and industry associations, such as The National Pork Producers Council and The California Milk Processor Board, use primary-demand advertising. Due to declining demand the Corn Refiners Association launched a multimedia campaign to downplay news on the negative health impacts of high fructose corn syrup.[11]

SELECTIVE-DEMAND ADVERTISING **Selective-demand (or brand) advertising** is advertising that is used to sell a particular brand of product. It is by far the most common type of advertising, and it accounts for the majority of advertising expenditures.

Selective-demand advertising that aims at persuading consumers to make purchases within a short time is called *immediate-response advertising*. Most local advertising is of this type.

Often local advertisers promote products with immediate appeal. Selective advertising aimed at keeping the public aware of a firm's name or product is called *reminder advertising*.

Comparative advertising compares the sponsored brand with one or more identified competing brands. The association shows the sponsored brand to be as good as or better than the other identified competing brands. Marketers must be careful when using this technique to present information truthfully and not to obscure or distort facts.

ANATOLII BABII/ALAMY

Harnessing the power of social media—or not? Social media allows a business to reach out to customers in a context that is familiar and comfortable to them. Firms attempt to measure the effectiveness of their social media efforts by gathering statistics on the number of followers and fans they have, traffic to their websites, and mentions of their products on social networking sites. Whether or not this type of advertising results in additional sales can be difficult to tell. General Motors pulled its ads off of Facebook after deciding they weren't having much of an impact.

INSTITUTIONAL ADVERTISING **Institutional advertising** is advertising designed to enhance a firm's image or reputation. Some large firms allocate a portion of advertising dollars to build goodwill, rather than to stimulate sales directly. For example, BP launched a campaign highlighting its clean-up efforts and commitment to the Gulf region after the massive Deepwater Horizon oil leak in 2010. The ongoing campaign seeks to restore public confidence in the firm by demonstrating its long-term commitment to the environmental and economic health of the region.[12] A positive public image helps an organization to attract customers, employees, and investors.

Major Steps in Developing an Advertising Campaign

An advertising campaign is developed in several stages, which can vary in the order in which they are implemented. Factors affecting a campaign include the company's resources, products, and target audiences. The development of a campaign in any organization includes the following steps in some form:

1. IDENTIFY AND ANALYZE THE TARGET AUDIENCE The target audience is the group toward which a firm's advertisements are directed. To pinpoint the organization's target audience and develop an effective campaign, marketers analyze various factors, such as the geographic distribution of potential customers, their age, sex, race, income, and education, and their attitudes toward the product, the nature of the competition, and the product's features. It is crucial to correctly identify the target market because all subsequent efforts will fail if not directed at the right audience.

2. DEFINE THE ADVERTISING OBJECTIVES The goals of an advertising campaign should be stated precisely and in quantifiable terms. Objectives should give specific details about the actual and desired position of the company and how it will arrive there, including a timetable for achieving goals. For example, advertising objectives that focus on sales will stress increasing sales by a certain percentage or dollar amount, or expanding the firm's market share by a specific amount.

3. CREATE THE ADVERTISING PLATFORM An advertising platform includes the important selling points, or features, that an advertiser will incorporate into the advertising campaign. These should be features that are lacking in competitors' products and that are important to customers. Although research into what consumers view as important issues is expensive, it is the most productive way to determine what to include in an advertising platform.

4. DETERMINE THE ADVERTISING APPROPRIATION The advertising appropriation is the total amount of money designated for advertising in a given time period. Developing an acceptable advertising appropriation is critical—too little and promotional efforts will not meet demand, too much will waste resources and reduce the funds available for other activities. Advertising appropriations may be based historical or forecasted sales, what competitors spend on advertising, or executive judgment. Companies that spend the most on advertising in the U.S. include Procter & Gamble, General Motors, AT&T, and Verizon Communications.

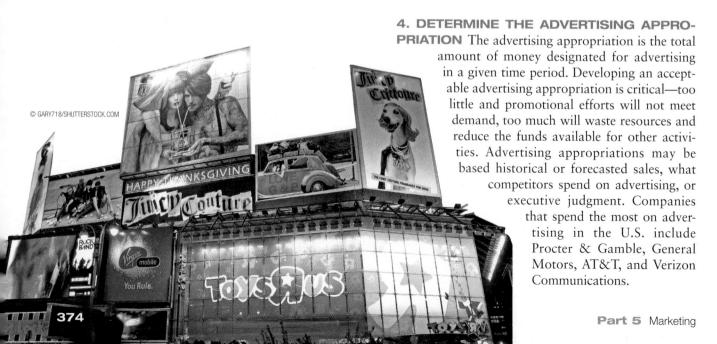

© GARY718/SHUTTERSTOCK.COM

5. DEVELOP THE MEDIA PLAN A media plan outlines a timetable for advertisements and which media will be used. Although cost-effectiveness is not easy to measure, the primary concern of the media planner is to reach the largest proportion of the target audience possible for each dollar spent. Media planners must also consider the location and demographics of the target market, the content of the message, and the characteristics of the audiences reached by various media. The media planner begins with general media decisions, selects subclasses within each medium, and chooses specific media vehicles for the campaign. The advantages and disadvantages of the major media classes are shown in Table 13-3.

6. CREATE THE ADVERTISING MESSAGE The content and form of a message are influenced by the product's features, the characteristics of the target audience, the objectives of the campaign, and the choice of media. An advertiser must consider these factors to choose words and illustrations that will be meaningful and appealing to the target audience. The copy, or words, of an advertisement will vary depending on the media choice, but attempt to engage the audience and move them through attention, interest, desire, and action. Artwork and visuals should complement copy by being visually attractive and communicating an idea quickly.

TABLE 13-3 Advantages and Disadvantages of Major Media Classes

	Advantages	Disadvantages
Television	Reaches large audiences, high frequency available, dual impact of audio and video, highly visible, high prestige, geographic and demographic selectivity, difficult to ignore	Very expensive, highly perishable message, size of audience not guaranteed, amount of prime time limited, lack of selectivity in target market
Direct mail	Little wasted circulation, highly selective, circulation controlled by advertiser, few distractions, personal, stimulates actions, easy to measure performance, hidden from competitors	Very expensive, lacks editorial content to attract readers, often thrown away unread as junk mail, criticized as invasion of privacy, consumers must choose to read the ad
Newspapers	Reaches large audience, purchased to be read, geographic flexibility, short lead time, frequent publication, favorable for cooperative advertising	Not selective for socioeconomic groups or target market, short life, limited reproduction capabilities, large advertising volume limits exposure
Radio	Reaches a large proportion of consumers, mobile and flexible, low relative costs, ad can be changed quickly, high level of geographic and demographic selectivity, encourages use of imagination	Lacks visual imagery, short life of message, listeners' attention limited, market fragmentation, difficult buying procedures, limited media and audience research
Yellow Pages	Wide availability, action and product category oriented, low relative costs, ad frequency and longevity, nonintrusive	Market fragmentation, extremely localized, slow updating, lack of creativity, long lead times, requires large space to be noticed
Magazines	Demographic selectivity, good reproduction, long life, prestige, geographic selectivity when regional issues available	High costs, 30- to 90-day average lead time, high level of competition, limited reach, communicates less frequently
Internet	Immediate response, potential to reach a precisely targeted audience, ability to track customers and build databases, highly interactive medium	Costs of precise targeting can be high, inappropriate ad placement, effects difficult to measure, concerns about security and privacy
Outdoor	Allows for frequent repetition, low cost, message can be placed close to point of sale, geographic selectivity, operable 24 hours a day, high creativity	Message must be short and simple, no demographic selectivity, seldom attracts readers' full attention, criticized as traffic hazard and blight on landscape, much wasted coverage, limited capabilities
Social Media	Target, interact, and connect more personally with customers, receive real-time feedback, direct messages to specific individuals, effectively reach target market/followers	Restricted number of contacts per message because of highly targeted nature, new mediums—unsure of best applications and how to calculate ROI, large time commitment to monitor

Sources: Adapted from William F. Arens, Michael Weigold, and Christian Arens, *Contemporary Advertising* (Burr Ridge, IL: Irwin/McGraw-Hill, 2008); George E. Belch and Michael Belch, *Advertising and Promotion* (Burr Ridge, IL: Irwin/McGraw-Hill, 2009).

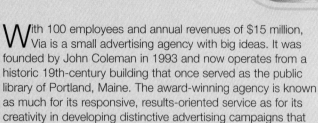

Entrepreneurial Success

Via Ad Agency

With 100 employees and annual revenues of $15 million, Via is a small advertising agency with big ideas. It was founded by John Coleman in 1993 and now operates from a historic 19th-century building that once served as the public library of Portland, Maine. The award-winning agency is known as much for its responsive, results-oriented service as for its creativity in developing distinctive advertising campaigns that help its business clients achieve their promotion objectives.

The chief marketing officer of Samsung Electronics observes that Via's creative experts are good listeners, work collaboratively with clients, and understand the need for measurable results. When Samsung introduced its Galaxy Tab tablet computer, which competes with Apple's iPad, Via was able to crank up a multimedia launch program in only five weeks. Thanks in part to Via's high-performing campaign, Samsung sold more than 1 million Galaxy Tabs in the first three months on the market. Via's expertise and service have attracted a growing roster of clients from different industries, including Unilever ice creams, Macaroni Grill restaurants, Perdue chicken products, and People's United Bank. No wonder *Advertising Age* recently named Via the best small agency of the year.

Sources: Based on information in Emily Maltby, "New Life for an Old Library," *Wall Street Journal*, February 24, 2012, www.wsj.com; Maureen Morrison, "Via Agency Tapped to Handle Perdue's Marketing," *Advertising Age*, November 29, 2011, www .adage.com; Beth Snyder Bulick, "Small Agency of the Year, Gold: Via," *Advertising Age*, August 8, 2011, www.adage.com.; "Via Agency, Baldwin Take Top Honors at Small Agency Awards," *Advertising Age*, July 28, 2011, www.adage.com.

7. EXECUTE THE CAMPAIGN Execution of an advertising campaign requires extensive planning, scheduling, and coordinating because the tasks are carried out by many people and groups and must be completed on time. Production companies, research organizations, media firms, printers, photoengravers, and commercial artists are just a few of the potential contributors to a campaign. Advertising managers must constantly assess the quality of the work and take corrective action when necessary. In some instances, advertisers must make changes in the middle of the campaign to meet objectives.

8. EVALUATE ADVERTISING EFFECTIVENESS A campaign's success should be compared against original objectives at regular intervals before, during, and after campaign launch. An advertiser should be able to track the impact of the campaign on sales and market share, as well as changes in customer attitudes and brand awareness. Data from past and current sales and responses to coupon offers and customer surveys administered by research organizations are some of the ways in which advertising effectiveness can be evaluated. Table 13-4 shows the five advertisers with the most effective campaigns according to the Effie Effectiveness Index, a global ranking system for advertising effectiveness. This ranking takes into account factors such as ROI, sales growth, and brand awareness in relation to money spent on promotional activities.

Advertising Agencies

advertising agency an independent firm that plans, produces, and places advertising for its clients

Advertisers can plan and produce their own advertising with help from in-house media personnel, or they can hire advertising agencies. An **advertising agency** is an independent firm that plans, produces, and places advertising for clients. Many large ad agencies also help with sales promotion and public relations. The cost to a firm can be moderate, especially for large campaigns. It is usually around 15 percent commission. Some firms opt to use a combination of in-house advertising talent and outside specialists.

TABLE 13-4 Most Effective Advertisers

Ranking	Advertiser
1	Unilever
2	Procter & Gamble
3	Nestlé
4	McDonald's
5	PepsiCo

Source: "2012 Effie Effectiveness Index: Overview," http://www.effieindex.com/Pages/Info.aspx?pg=RankingSummary (accessed January 2, 2013).

Social and Legal Considerations in Advertising

Critics of U.S. advertising have two main complaints—that it is wasteful and that it can be deceptive. Although advertising (like any other activity) can be performed inefficiently, evidence shows that it is not wasteful.

- Advertising is the most effective and least expensive means of communicating product information to a large number of individuals and organizations.
- Advertising encourages competition. It thus leads to the development of new and improved products, wider product choices, and lower prices.
- Advertising revenues support mass-communication media—newspapers, magazines, radio, and television, effectively paying for news coverage and entertainment programming.
- Advertising provides job opportunities in fields ranging from sales to film production.

A number of government and private agencies scrutinize advertising for false or misleading claims or offers that might harm consumers. At the national level, the Federal Trade Commission (FTC), the Food and Drug Administration (FDA), and the Federal Communications Commission (FCC) oversee advertising practices. Advertising also may be monitored by state and local agencies, better business bureaus, and industry associations.

Concept Check

✓ Describe the major types of advertising by purpose.

✓ Explain the eight major steps in developing an advertising campaign.

PERSONAL SELLING

Personal selling is the most adaptable of all promotional methods because the person presenting the message can modify it to suit the individual buyer. However, it is also the most expensive method because it involves salespeople communicating with customers one at a time or in small groups. Many selling situations demand the face-to-face contact and adaptability of personal selling. This is especially true of industrial sales, in which a single purchase may amount to millions of dollars. Obviously, sales of that size must be based on carefully planned presentations, personal contact with customers, and thorough negotiations.

Learning Objective

9 Recognize the kinds of salespersons, the steps in the personal-selling process, and the major sales management tasks.

Kinds of Salespersons

Because most businesses employ different salespersons to perform different functions, marketing managers must select the kinds of sales personnel that will be most effective in selling the firm's products. Salespersons may be identified as order getters, order takers, and support personnel. A single individual can, and often does, perform all three functions.

ORDER GETTERS An **order getter** is responsible for what is sometimes called **creative selling**—selling a firm's products to new customers and increasing sales to current customers. An order getter must be able to perceive buyers' needs, supply customers with information about the product, and persuade them to buy it.

ORDER TAKERS An **order taker** handles repeat sales and customer demands to maintain positive relationships. *Inside order takers* receive incoming mail, online, and telephone orders for businesses. Salespersons in retail stores are also inside order takers. *Outside* (or *field*) *order takers* travel to customers. Often the buyer and the field salesperson develop a mutually beneficial relationship of placing, receiving, and delivering orders. Both inside and outside order takers are active salespersons and produce a large proportion of their companies' sales.

SUPPORT PERSONNEL **Sales support personnel** aid in selling but are more involved in locating prospects (likely first-time customers), educating customers,

order getter a salesperson who is responsible for selling a firm's products to new customers and increasing sales to present customers

creative selling selling products to new customers and increasing sales to present customers

order taker a salesperson who handles repeat sales in ways that maintain positive relationships with customers

sales support personnel employees who aid in selling but are more involved in locating prospects, educating customers, building goodwill for the firm, and providing follow-up service

The pros and cons of personal selling. Personal selling is more effective than advertising. It's easy to ignore an advertisement. Saying "no" to a salesperson is much harder. The main drawback of personal selling is that it's expensive, which is why it's generally used to sell high-dollar goods and services.

building goodwill for the firm, and providing follow-up service. The most common categories of support personnel are missionary, trade, and technical salespersons.

A **missionary salesperson**, who usually works for a manufacturer, visits retailers to persuade them to buy the manufacturer's products. If the retailers agree, they buy the products from wholesalers, who are the manufacturer's actual customers.

A **trade salesperson**, who generally works for a food producer or processor, assists customers in promoting products, especially in retail stores. A trade salesperson may obtain additional shelf space for the products, restock shelves, set up displays, and distribute samples. Because trade salespersons usually are order takers as well, they are not strictly support personnel.

A **technical salesperson** assists a company's current customers in technical matters. He or she may explain how to use a product, how it is made, how to install it, or how a system is designed. A technical salesperson should be formally educated in science or engineering.

missionary salesperson
a salesperson—generally employed by a manufacturer—who visits retailers to persuade them to buy the manufacturer's products

trade salesperson
a salesperson—generally employed by a food producer or processor—who assists customers in promoting products, especially in retail stores

technical salesperson
a salesperson who assists a company's current customers in technical matters

Firms usually need to employ sales personnel from several of these categories. Factors that affect which marketing personnel are hired include the number of customers and their characteristics, the product's attributes, complexity, and price, the distribution channels used by the company, and the company's approach to advertising.

The Personal-Selling Process

No two selling situations are exactly alike, and no two salespeople perform their jobs in exactly the same way. Most salespeople, however, follow the six-step procedure illustrated in Figure 13-3.

PROSPECTING The first step in personal selling is to research potential buyers and choose the most likely customers, or prospects. Business associates and customers, public records, telephone and trade-association directories, and company files can all be good sources of new prospects. The salesperson concentrates on those prospects who have the financial resources, willingness, and authority to buy the product.

APPROACHING THE PROSPECT First impressions are often lasting. Therefore, a salesperson's first contact with a prospect is crucial to successful selling. A salesperson should be friendly and knowledgeable about the product, the prospect's needs, and how the product can meet those needs. Those salespeople who demonstrate an understanding of and sensitivity to a customer's situation are more likely to make a good first impression, and make a sale.

MAKING THE PRESENTATION The next step is actual delivery of the sales presentation, which often includes a product demonstration. The salesperson points out the product's features, its benefits, and how it is superior to competitors' merchandise. The salesperson may list other clients (if given permission) during the presentation.

During a demonstration, the salesperson may suggest that the prospect try out the product personally. The demonstration and product trial should underscore specific points made during the presentation.

ANSWERING OBJECTIONS The prospect may raise objections or ask questions at any time during the process. This is the salesperson's chance to eliminate objections that could prevent a sale, to point out additional features, or to mention special services the company offers.

Concept Check

✓ What are the advantages and disadvantages of using personal selling?

✓ Identify the three types of salespersons.

✓ Describe the six steps of the personal-selling process.

CLOSING THE SALE To close the sale, the salesperson asks the prospect to buy the product. This is the critical point in the selling process. Many experienced salespeople utilize a *trial closing*, in which they ask questions before the actual close in a tone that assumes a successful sale. Typical questions are: "When would you want delivery?" and "Do you want the standard model or the one with the special options package?" They allow the salesperson to gauge the likelihood and imminence of a sale.

FOLLOWING UP The salesperson's job does not end with a sale. He or she must follow up to ensure that the product is delivered on time, in the right quantity, and in proper operating condition. During follow-up, the salesperson also makes it clear that he or she is available in case problems develop. Follow-up is essential to the selling process because it leaves a good impression and helps to increase the likelihood of future sales.

Major Sales Management Tasks

A firm's success often hinges on the competent management of its sales force. Although some companies operate efficiently without one, most firms rely on a strong sales force—and the revenue it brings in—for their success.

Sales managers must:

- Set sales objectives in concrete, quantifiable terms and specify a specific period of time and geographic area.
- Adjust the size of the sales force to meet changes in the firm's marketing plan and the marketing environment.
- Attract and hire effective salespersons.
- Develop a training program and decide where, when, how, and for whom to conduct the training.
- Formulate a fair and adequate compensation plan to retain qualified employees.
- Motivate salespersons to keep their productivity high.
- Define sales territories and determine scheduling and routing of the sales force.
- Evaluate the operation holistically, through sales reports, communications with customers, and invoices.

SALES PROMOTION

Sales promotion consists of activities or materials that are direct inducements to customers or salespersons. Receiving a free sample at the supermarket or being invited to join a frequent flier program are examples of sales promotions. Sales promotion techniques can significantly impact sales and are often used to enhance and supplement other promotional methods. Firms have dramatically increased spending on sales promotions as they increase their importance as part of the promotion mix.

Sales Promotion Objectives

Sales promotion activities may be used singly or in combination to achieve one goal or a set of goals. Marketers use sales promotion activities and materials for a number of purposes, including

1. To attract new customers
2. To encourage trial of a new product
3. To invigorate the sales of a mature brand

FIGURE 13-3 The Six Steps of the Personal-Selling Process

Personal selling is not only the most adaptable of all promotional methods but also the most expensive.

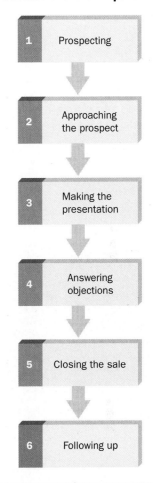

1. Prospecting
2. Approaching the prospect
3. Making the presentation
4. Answering objections
5. Closing the sale
6. Following up

Source: William M. Pride and O. C . Ferrell, *Marketing: Concepts and Strategies*, 17th ed. (Mason, OH: South-Western/Cengage Learning, 2014). Adapted with permission.

Learning Objective

10 **Describe sales promotion objectives and methods.**

4. To boost sales to current customers
5. To reinforce advertising
6. To increase traffic in retail stores
7. To smooth out customer demand
8. To build up reseller inventories
9. To neutralize the competition's promotional efforts
10. To increase the attractiveness of shelf placement and displays

Sales promotion objectives should be consistent with the organization's general goals and with its marketing and promotional objectives.

Sales Promotion Methods

Most sales promotion methods can be classified as promotional techniques for either consumer sales or trade sales.

A **consumer sales promotion method** attracts consumers to particular retail stores and motivates them to purchase certain new or established products. A **trade sales promotion method** encourages wholesalers and retailers to stock and actively promote a manufacturer's product. Incentives such as money, merchandise, marketing assistance, and gifts may provide incentives to resellers to purchase products or support a firm in other ways. Of the combined dollars spent on sales promotion and advertising, about one-half is spent on trade promotions, one-fourth on consumer promotions, and one-fourth on advertising.

Selection of Sales Promotion Methods

Several factors affect a marketer's choice of sales promotion method, including

1. The objectives of the promotional effort
2. Product characteristics—size, weight, cost, durability, uses, features, and hazards
3. Target-market profiles—age, gender, income, location, density, usage rate, and buying patterns
4. Distribution channels and availability of appropriate resellers
5. The competitive and regulatory forces in the environment

REBATES A **rebate** is a return of part of the purchase price of a product. Usually the rebate is offered by the producer to consumers who submit a coupon and a specific proof of purchase. Rebating is a relatively low-cost promotional method, but consumers may not be attracted by it because they view it to be too complicated or time consuming.

COUPONS A **coupon** reduces the retail price of a particular item by a stated amount at the time of purchase. Coupons may be worth anywhere from a few cents to a few dollars. Customers can find coupons in newspapers, magazines, direct mail, and shelf dispensers in stores. Some coupons are precisely targeted at customers. After declining throughout the 1990s, the popularity of coupons has rebounded, largely because consumers can visit coupon websites, and companies send coupons via email to loyal customers. Constant Contact, for instance, offers a Groupon alternative called SaveLocal, with which companies can target customers with specific coupon deals. The service allows businesses to focus on existing customers and provides incentives for those customers to tell others about the deals. This method is a low-cost way of promoting a company's products or services among a customer base that will use and appreciate them.[13]

consumer sales promotion method a sales promotion method designed to attract consumers to particular retail stores and to motivate them to purchase certain new or established products

trade sales promotion method a sales promotion method designed to encourage wholesalers and retailers to stock and actively promote a manufacturer's product

rebate a return of part of the purchase price of a product

coupon reduces the retail price of a particular item by a stated amount at the time of purchase

Do you use coupons? Companies give away coupons to increase the sales of their products and encourage consumers who are unfamiliar with their products to give them a try.

SAMPLES A **sample** is a free product given to customers to encourage trial and purchase. Marketers utilize samples to increase awareness of a product, which can increase sales volume in the early stages of a product's life cycle and improve distribution. Samples may be offered via online coupons, direct mail, or in stores. It is the most expensive sales promotion technique. Established brands, such as cosmetics companies, may use free samples to attract customers and renew interest in a brand. Organizations must consider such factors as seasonal demand for the product, market characteristics, and prior advertising when designing a free sample campaign.

PREMIUMS A **premium** is a gift that a producer offers a customer in return for buying its product. It is used to attract competitors' customers, introduce different sizes of established products, add variety to other promotional efforts, and stimulate consumer loyalty. Creativity is essential when using premiums. To stand out and achieve a significant number of redemptions, the premium must suit the target audience and the brand's image. The premium must also be recognizable and desirable to customers. Premiums are placed on or inside packages and can be distributed through retailers or the mail.

FREQUENT-USER INCENTIVES A **frequent-user incentive** is a program developed to reward customers who engage in repeat (frequent) purchases. Such programs are used commonly by service businesses such as airlines, hotels, and auto rental agencies. Frequent-user incentives foster customer loyalty because the customer is given an additional reason to continue patronizing the company or group of companies.

POINT-OF-PURCHASE DISPLAYS A **point-of-purchase display** is promotional material placed within a retail store. The display is usually located near the product being promoted. It may hold merchandise or information and encouragements to buy the product. Most point-of-purchase displays are prepared and set up by manufacturers and wholesalers.

TRADE SHOWS A **trade show** is an industry-wide exhibit at which many sellers display their products. Some trade shows are organized exclusively for dealers—to permit manufacturers and wholesalers to show their latest lines to retailers. Others are promotions designed to stimulate consumer awareness and interest, such as annual home shows or boat shows.

sample a free product given to customers to encourage trial and purchase

premium a gift that a producer offers a customer in return for buying its product

frequent-user incentive a program developed to reward customers who engage in repeat (frequent) purchases

point-of-purchase display promotional material placed within a retail store

trade show an industry-wide exhibit at which many sellers display their products

Event sponsorships are intended to promote a positive image of a firm. Event sponsorships are a public-relations tool. They are often used in conjunction with advertising, personal selling, and sales promotions.

PCN PHOTOGRAPHY/ALAMY

BUYING ALLOWANCES A **buying allowance** is a temporary price reduction to resellers for purchasing specified quantities of a product. A laundry detergent manufacturer might give retailers $1 for each case of detergent purchased. A buying allowance is an incentive to resellers to handle new products and may stimulate purchase of items in large quantities. A shortcoming of buying allowances is that competitors can counter quickly with their own buying allowances.

COOPERATIVE ADVERTISING **Cooperative advertising** is an arrangement whereby a manufacturer agrees to pay a certain amount of a retailer's media cost for advertising the manufacturer's products. To be reimbursed, a retailer must show proof that the advertisements did appear. Not all retailers take advantage of available cooperative advertising offers, either because they cannot afford to advertise or choose not to.

PUBLIC RELATIONS

As noted earlier, public relations is a broad set of communication activities used to create and maintain favorable relationships between an organization and various public groups, both internal and external. These groups may include customers, employees, stockholders, suppliers, educators, the media, government officials, and society in general.

Types of Public-Relations Tools

Organizations use a variety of public-relations tools to convey messages and to create images. Public-relations professionals prepare written materials such as brochures, newsletters, company magazines, annual reports, and news releases. They also create corporate-identity materials such as logos, business cards, signs, and stationery. Speeches are another public-relations tool.

Another public-relations tool is event sponsorship, in which a company pays for all or part of a special event such as a concert, sports competition, festival, or play. Sponsoring special events is an effective way for organizations to increase brand recognition and receive media coverage, sometimes with relatively little investment. The energy drink brand Red Bull, for example, underscores its reputation for giving consumers energy through sponsoring athletes and teams, acts of daring, and rock concerts. Perhaps most notably, Red Bull sponsored Felix Baumgartner in his mission to be the first man to break the speed of sound during a free fall. Baumgartner caught the attention of the world when he successfully jumped from 128,000 feet, the edge of space—giving Red Bull a lot of attention.[14]

Publicity is an important part of public relations, as it increases public awareness of a firm or brand through mass media communications at no cost to the business. **Publicity** is communication in news-story form about an organization, its products, or both. Organizations use publicity to provide information about products, to announce new product launches, expansions, or research, and to strengthen the company's image. Public-relations personnel sometimes organize events, such as grand openings with prizes and celebrities, to generate news coverage of a company.

The most widely used type of publicity is the **news release**. It is generally one typed page of about 300 words provided by an organization to the media as a form of publicity. The release includes the firm's name, address, phone number, and contact person. A **feature article**, which may run as long as 3,000 words, is usually written for inclusion in a particular publication. For example, a software firm might send an article about its new product to a computer magazine. A **captioned photograph**, a picture accompanied by a brief explanation, is an effective way to illustrate a new or improved product. A **press conference** allows invited media personnel to hear important news announcements and to receive supplementary materials and photographs.

buying allowance a temporary price reduction to resellers for purchasing specified quantities of a product

cooperative advertising an arrangement whereby a manufacturer agrees to pay a certain amount of a retailer's media cost for advertising the manufacturer's products

publicity communication in news-story form about an organization, its products, or both

news release a typed page of about 300 words provide by an organization to the media as a form of publicity

feature article a piece (of up to 3,000 words) prepared by an organization for inclusion in a particular publication

captioned photograph a picture accompanied by a brief explanation

press conference a meeting at which invited media personnel hear important news announcements and receive supplementary textual materials and photographs

Finally, letters to the editor, special newspaper or magazine editorials, and films may be prepared and distributed to appropriate media for possible use in news stories.

Uses of Public Relations

Public relations can be used to promote many things, including people, places, activities, and ideas. Public relations focuses on enhancing the reputation of the total organization by increasing public awareness of a company's products, brands, or activities and by fostering desirable company images, such as that of innovativeness, dependability, or social responsibility. By getting the media to report on a firm's accomplishments, public relations helps a company to maintain public visibility. Effective management of public-relations efforts also can reduce the amount of unfavorable coverage surrounding negative events.

Concept Check

✓ What are the common tools of public relations?

✓ What is publicity, and why do organizations use it?

✓ What are the four common types of publicity?

Looking for Success? *Get Flashcards, Quizzes, Games, Crosswords, and more @ www.cengagebrain.com.*

Summary

1 Identify the various distribution channels and explain the concept of market coverage.

A marketing channel is a sequence of marketing organizations that directs a product from producer to ultimate user. The marketing channel for a particular product is concerned with the transfer of ownership of that product. Merchant middlemen (merchants) actually take title to products, whereas functional middlemen simply aid in the transfer of title.

The channels used for consumer products include the direct channel from producer to consumer, the channel from producer to retailer to consumer, the channel from producer to wholesaler to retailer to consumer, and the channel from producer to agent to wholesaler to retailer to consumer. There are two major channels of industrial products: producer to user and producer to agent middleman to user.

Channels and intermediaries are chosen to implement a given level of market coverage. Intensive distribution is the use of all available outlets for a product, providing the widest market coverage. Selective distribution uses a portion of the available outlets in an area. Exclusive distribution uses only a single retail outlet for a product in a large geographic area.

2 Understand how supply-chain management facilitates partnering among channel members.

Supply-chain management is a long-term partnership among channel members working together to create a distribution system that reduces inefficiencies, costs, and redundancies, while creating a competitive advantage and satisfying customers. Cooperation is required among all channel members, including manufacturing, research, sales, advertising, and shipping. When all channel partners work together, delivery, scheduling, packaging, and other customer requirements are better met. Technology makes supply-chain management easier to implement.

3 Discuss the need for wholesalers, describe the services they provide, and identify the major types of wholesalers.

Wholesalers are intermediaries that purchase from producers or other intermediaries and sell to industrial users, retailers, or other wholesalers. Wholesalers perform many functions in a distribution channel. If they are eliminated, other channel members—such as the producer or retailers—must perform these functions. Wholesalers provide retailers with assistance in promoting products, collecting information and financing. They provide manufacturers with sales assistance, reduce their inventory costs, furnish market information, and extend credit to retailers.

Merchant wholesalers buy and then sell products. Commission merchants and brokers are essentially agents and do not take title to the goods they distribute. Sales branches and offices are owned by the manufacturers and resemble merchant wholesalers and agents, respectively.

4 Distinguish among the major types of retailers and shopping centers.

Retailers are intermediaries that buy from producers or wholesalers and sell to consumers. In-store retailers include department stores, discount stores, warehouse showrooms, convenience stores, supermarkets, super-stores, warehouse clubs, traditional specialty stores, off-price retailers, and category killers. Non store retailers use direct selling, direct marketing, and automatic vending, instead of conventional stores. Types of direct marketing include catalog marketing, direct-response marketing, telemarketing, television home shopping, and online retailing.

There are four major types of shopping centers: lifestyle, neighborhood, community, and regional. Each of these centers has a varying mix of stores and serves geographic areas of different sizes.

5 Explain the five most important physical distribution activities.

Physical distribution consists of activities designed to move products from producers to ultimate users. Its five major functions are inventory management, order processing, warehousing, materials handling, and transportation. These interrelated functions are integrated into marketing efforts.

6 Explain how integrated marketing communications works to have the maximum impact on the customer.

Integrated marketing communications is the coordination of promotion efforts to achieve maximum informational and persuasive impact on customers.

7 Understand the basic elements of the promotion mix.

Promotion is communication about an organization and its products that is intended to inform, persuade, or remind target market members. The major ingredients of a promotion mix are advertising, personal selling, sales promotion, and public relations. The role of promotion is to facilitate exchanges directly or indirectly and to help an organization maintain favorable relationship with groups in the marketing environment.

8 Explain the three types of advertising and describe the major steps of developing an advertising campaign.

Advertising is a paid nonpersonal message communicated to a specific audience through a mass medium. Primary-demand advertising promotes the products of an entire industry rather than just a single brand. Selective-demand advertising promotes a particular brand of product. Institutional advertising is image-building advertising for a firm.

An advertising campaign is developed in several stages. A firm first identifies and analyzes its advertising target. The goals of the campaign must be clearly defined. Then the firm develops the advertising platform and determines the size of advertising budget. The next steps are to develop a media plan, to create the advertising message, and to execute the campaign. Finally, promotion managers must evaluate the effectiveness of the advertising efforts before, during, and/or after the campaign.

9 Recognize the kinds of salespersons, the steps in the personal-selling process, and the major sales management tasks.

Personal selling is personal communication aimed at informing customers and persuading them to buy a firm's products. It is the most adaptable promotional method because the salesperson can modify the message to fit individual buyers. The major types are order getters, order takers, and support personnel. The six steps in the personal-selling process are prospecting, approaching the prospect, making the presentation, answering objections, closing the sale, and following up. Sales managers are involved directly in setting sales force objectives, recruiting, selecting, and training salespersons, compensating and motivating sales personnel, creating sales territories, and evaluating sales performance.

10 Describe sales promotion objectives and methods.

Sales promotion is the use of activities and materials as direct inducements to customers and salespersons. Sales promotions enhance and supplement other promotional methods. Methods of sales promotion include rebates, coupons, samples, premiums, frequent-user incentives, point-of-purchase displays, trade shows, buying allowances, and cooperative advertising.

11 Understand the types and uses of public relations.

Public relations is a broad set of communication activities used to create and maintain favorable relationships between an organization and various public groups, both internal and external. Organizations use a variety of public relations tools to convey messages and create images. Brochures, newsletters, company magazines and annual reports are written public-relations tools. Speeches, event sponsorship, and publicity are other public-relations tools. Publicity is communication in news-story form about an organization, its products, or both. Types of publicity include news releases, feature articles, captioned photographs, and press conferences. Public relations can also be used to promote people, places, activities, and ideas. It can be used to enhance the reputation of an organization and reduce the unfavorable effects of negative events.

Key Terms

You should now be able to define and give an example relevant to each of the following terms:

distribution channel, or marketing channel (357)
middleman (or marketing intermediary) (357)
merchant middleman (358)
functional middleman (358)
retailer (358)
wholesaler (359)
intensive distribution (360)
selective distribution (360)
exclusive distribution (360)
supply-chain management (360)
merchant wholesaler (362)
full-service wholesaler (362)
general-merchandise wholesaler (362)
limited-line wholesaler (362)
specialty-line wholesaler (362)
agent (362)
broker (362)
independent retailer (363)
chain retailer (363)
department store (363)
discount store (364)
warehouse showroom (364)

convenience store (364)
supermarket (364)
superstore (364)
warehouse club (364)
traditional specialty store (364)
off-price retailer (365)
category killer (365)
nonstore retailing (365)
direct selling (365)
direct marketing (365)
catalog marketing (365)
direct-response marketing (366)
telemarketing (366)
television home shopping (366)
online retailing (366)
automatic vending (366)
lifestyle shopping center (367)
neighborhood shopping center (367)
community shopping center (367)
regional shopping center (367)

physical distribution (368)
inventory management (368)
order processing (368)
warehousing (369)
materials handling (369)
transportation (369)
carrier (369)
integrated marketing communications (371)
promotion (372)
promotion mix (372)
advertising (372)
personal selling (372)
sales promotion (373)
public relations (373)
primary-demand advertising (373)
selective-demand (or brand) advertising (374)
institutional advertising (374)
advertising agency (376)
order getter (377)
creative selling (377)
order taker (377)
sales support personnel (377)

missionary salesperson (378)
trade salesperson (378)
technical salesperson (378)
consumer sales promotion method (380)
trade sales promotion method (380)
rebate (380)
coupon (380)
sample (381)
premium (381)
frequent-user incentive (381)
point-of-purchase display (381)
trade show (381)
buying allowance (382)
cooperative advertising (382)
publicity (382)
news release (382)
feature article (382)
captioned photograph (382)
press conference (382)

Discussion Questions

1. What are the most common marketing channels for consumer products? For industrial products?
2. What are the three levels of market coverage? What types of products is each used for?
3. List the services performed by wholesalers. For whom is each service performed?
4. Identify three kinds of full-service wholesalers. What factors are used to classify wholesalers into one of these categories?
5. What can nonstore retailers offer their customers that in-store retailers cannot?
6. What is physical distribution? Which major functions does it include?
7. Many producers sell to consumers both directly and through middlemen. How can such a producer justify competing with its own middlemen?
8. In what situations might a producer use agents or commission merchants rather than its own sales offices or branches?
9. If a middleman is eliminated from a marketing channel, under what conditions will costs decrease? Under what conditions will costs increase? Will the middleman's functions be eliminated? Explain.
10. What is integrated marketing communications, and why is it becoming increasingly accepted?
11. Identify and describe the major ingredients of a promotion mix.
12. Identify and give examples of the three major types of salespersons.
13. What are the major tasks involved in managing a sales force?
14. What are the major differences between consumer and trade sales promotion methods? Give examples of each.
15. What is the difference between publicity and public relations? What is the purpose of each?
16. Why do firms use event sponsorship?

Test Yourself

Matching Questions

1. _____ This type of market coverage provides the widest possible exposure in the marketplace.

2. _____ A middleman often hired on a commission basis.

3. _____ This middleman carries a few lines with many products within each line.

4. _____ The process involves receiving and filling customers' purchase orders.

5. _____ Manufacturers' seconds or off-season merchandise are examples of products sold.

6. _____ The process includes any nonpersonal, paid form of communication.

7. _____ The purpose is to increase demand for all brands of a product.

8. _____ A large specialty store that concentrates on a single product line and has low prices.

9. _____ A salesperson who handles repeat sales to maintain positive relationships with customers.

10. _____ News stories about products, employees, or a company that appear in the newspaper are examples.

   a. agent
   b. intensive distribution
   c. limited-line wholesaler
   d. category killer
   e. off-price retailer
   f. order processing
   g. advertising
   h. distribution channel
   i. catalog marketing
   j. primary-demand advertising
   k. publicity
   l. order taker

True False Questions

11. **T** **F** A direct channel of distribution includes both wholesalers and retailers.

12. **T** **F** A retailer buys and sells merchandise.

13. **T** **F** Exclusive distribution makes use of all available outlets for a product.

14. **T** **F** Inventory holding costs are the costs of storing products until they are purchased or shipped to customers.

15. **T** **F** Piggyback service is unique to air freight.

16. **T** **F** Institutional advertising promotes specific brands of products.

17. **T** **F** Advertising can be broadly classified into three groups: selective demand, institutional, and primary demand.

18. **T** **F** A major disadvantage of magazines is their lack of timeliness.

19. **T** **F** Radio advertising offers a high degree of selectivity.

20. **T** **F** News releases are the least used type of publicity.

Multiple-Choice Questions

21. _____ A women's apparel manufacturer most likely will use
   a. intensive distribution.
   b. selective distribution.
   c. exclusive distribution.
   d. high-style distribution.
   e. popular style distribution.

22. _____ Category management is
   a. a producer deciding which category to concentrate on for the next season.
   b. a retailer asking the supplier in a particular category how to stock the shelves.
   c. when suppliers tell the manufacturer which category to produce more of.
   d. when Home Depot decides which category sells the best and decides to concentrate on that category of goods.
   e. the combined efforts of producers and whole-salers to manage the wholesaler's inventory.

23. _____ Haley is shopping for a new outfit to wear to an awards banquet where she will be honored. She has found a beautiful outfit at Banana Republic and a new pair of shoes at Designer Shoe Warehouse. What type of stores are these?
   a. Warehouse club
   b. Convenience
   c. Specialty
   d. Department
   e. Off-price

24. _____ Which one of the following is an example of a category killer?
   a. Kmart
   b. 7-Eleven
   c. Home Depot
   d. Burlington Coat Factory
   e. Macy's

25. _____ Which activity combines inventory management, order processing, warehousing, material handling, and transportation?
   a. Marketing
   b. Merchandising
   c. Warehousing
   d. Physical distribution
   e. Transporting

26. _____ Choose the correct order of the following three of the eight steps in developing an advertising campaign.
   a. Create the advertising platform; identify and analyze the target audience; define the advertising objectives.
   b. Identify and analyze the target audience; create the advertising platform; define the advertising objectives.
   c. Identify and analyze the target audience; define the advertising objectives; create the advertising platform.
   d. Define the advertising objectives; identify and analyze the target audience; create the advertising platform.
   e. Define the advertising objectives; create the advertising platform; identify and analyze the target audience.

27. _____ Salespeople may be identified as
   a. experts, order makers, and support personnel.
   b. order preparers, order trackers, and order receivers.
   c. order getters, order takers, and support personnel.
   d. order getters, order makers, and order receivers.
   e. order getters, order dictators, and support personnel.

28. _____ The first step in the personal-selling process is
   a. product display.
   b. prospecting.
   c. approaching the prospect.
   d. organizing the sales pitch.
   e. making the presentation.

29. _____ Closing the sale is considered the critical point in the selling process. Many salespeople use a trial closing. Based on an assumption that the customer is going to buy, which of the following statements is an appropriate trial closing?
   a. "Will you be placing an order, Mrs. Johnston?"
   b. "Would you like the standard or the deluxe model?"
   c. "Here's my card. Give me a call if you would like to place an order."
   d. "Shall I give you a week to consider the offer?"
   e. "I'll put you down for the deluxe model. Is that your natural hair color?"

30. _____ Deloitte, a public accounting firm, helps to underwrite the musical production "Mama Mia" currently playing at the Theater Center. Why would the accounting firm do this? What is Deloitte creating?
   a. Point-of-purchase activity
   b. Sales promotion
   c. Public-relations activity
   d. Community-service activity
   e. Cooperative advertising

Answers to the Test Yourself questions appear at the end of the book on page TY-2.

Video Case

L.L.Bean Employs a Variety of Promotion Methods to Communicate with Customers

Perhaps best known for its beloved mail-order catalog, L.L.Bean was recently placed near the top of Photobrand's list of New England's most powerful brands, beating Ethan Allen and Yankee Candle. L.L.Bean has grown from its founding as a one-product firm in 1912 to a national brand with 14 stores in 10 different states and a thriving online store. Net sales are over $1.5 billion a year.

Marketing communications are more sophisticated now than they were when L.L.Bean created his first product, a waterproof boot, and publicized it with a homemade brochure. In its early days, the firm thrived on word-of-mouth communication about its reliability and the expert advice

of its founder, himself an avid outdoorsman. Determined to build his company and his mailing list, L.L.Bean poured all the company's profits into advertising and talked about the company with one and all. Said one neighbor at the time, "If you drop in just to shake his hand, you get home to find his catalog in your mailbox."

Now the company makes use of marketing database systems to manage and update its mailing lists. The L.L.Bean catalog swelled in size in the 1980s and 1990s, but it has slimmed down as the company's website has taken over some of the task of promoting the company's products. Still a major communication tool for the firm, the catalog is also a multiple-industry award-winner. The company uses computer-modeling tools to help it identify what customers want and sends them only the catalogs they desire. Still, says the vice president of stores, "What we find is most customers want some sort of touch point," and the catalog remains very popular.

Online orders recently surpassed mail and phone orders for the first time in the company's history. The relationship between the catalog and the website is complicated. As L.L.Bean's vice president for e-commerce explains, customers have begun to shift much of their buying to the Internet, but they still rely on the catalog to browse, plan, and get ideas. Customers take their L.L.Bean catalogs "to soccer games, they read them in the car," she says. "What's changed is what they do next"—often they go online to find more details about an item or to place an order.

L.L.Bean still places print advertising, sometimes small ads that simply offer a free catalog or remind customers that they already have the catalog at home. Since the catalog is expensive to produce, the company tries to support it with other marketing media so it doesn't get lost among all the other messages demanding customers' attention.

A big and growing area for the company's promotion efforts is the Internet, where it uses banner ads on popular sites like Hulu.com that let customers click through to the L.L.Bean online store. It also maintains a Facebook page, a Twitter account, and a YouTube channel. The company invests heavily in television advertising as well, particularly around the holidays. Local TV ads are concentrated in the areas around the company's retail stores.

L.L.Bean doesn't take the wide familiarity of its brand for granted. It also promotes its name through partnerships with environmentally conscious companies and organizations and through charitable giving, mainly to organizations committed to maintaining and protecting Earth's natural resources. The company recognizes, however, that a good product is at the heart of its success. "We really want to sell a good product, and we really guarantee that product," says the company's vice president of e-commerce. "We want to keep . . . the customer happy and keep that customer coming back to L.L.Bean over and over."[15]

Questions

1. What are the ingredients of L.L.Bean's promotion mix?
2. L.L.Bean is reaching into "alternative" promotions, including outfitting Weather Channel meteorologists around the United States and emblazoning its name on the tarp used by the Red Sox baseball team to protect the field during rain delays. What other kinds of promotional activities do you think would suit the company's outdoors image?
3. Do you think L.L.Bean's website will ever entirely take the place of its mail-order catalog? Why or why not?

Building Skills for Career Success

1. Social Media Exercise

Wholesaling, retailing, and physical distribution

Gamification is a new trend in social media that uses the ideas and theories behind gaming (rewards, competition, progressing through levels and so forth) to engage people online. Fantasy Shopper is a good example of combining the retail experience (in this case fashion retailing) with online games. For example, a luxury handbag by Stella McCartney is the prize in a online game to design the best virtual outfit using real items for sale in Matches, a real store. The players of the game choose the winner. Players visit a city and compete to find bargains and assemble the best outfits using virtual money to spend on goods actually sold in stores. The choices are published in Facebook newsfeeds and others vote on the looks. In addition to winning real prizes, players are rewarded virtually with badges and vouchers to use in real stores. This game is popular with women 20–25, and retailers have found that it helps them to promote their products while providing instant feedback about what is likely to sell. The real value to retailers is the amount of data generated and passed along by these "social shopping" firms based on the players' behavior. Visit Fantasy Shopper (www.fantasyshopper.com) and take a look about the games available.

1. For what types of retailers are these games most likely to be effective?
2. While Fantasy Shopper is marketed toward women 20–25, what other age and gender segments would be likely to participate in similar online games?

2. Building Team Skills

Surveys are a common tool in marketing research. The information they provide can reduce business risk and facilitate decision making. Retail outlets often survey their customers' wants and needs by distributing comment cards or questionnaires.

The following is an example of a customer survey that a local photography shop might distribute to its customers.

Assignment

1. Working in teams of three to five, choose a local retailer.
2. Classify the retailer according to the major types.
3. Design a survey to help the retailer to improve customer service. (You may find it beneficial to work with the retailer and actually administer the survey to customers. Prepare a report of the survey results.)
4. Present your findings to the class.

3. Researching Different Careers

When you are looking for a job, the people closest to you can be a great resource. Family members and friends may be able to answer your questions directly or put you in touch with someone else who can. This type of "networking" can lead to an "informational interview," in which you meet with someone who will answer your questions about a career or a company and who can provide inside information on related fields and other helpful hints.

Assignment

1. Choose a retailer or wholesaler and a position within the company that interests you.
2. Call the company and ask to speak to the person in that particular position. Explain that you are a college student interested in the position and ask to set up an informational interview.
3. Prepare a list of questions to ask in the interview. The questions should focus on:
   a. The training and experience recommended for the position
   b. How the person entered the position and advanced within the organization
   c. What he or she likes and dislikes about the work
   d. Present your findings to the class

Customer Survey

To help us to serve you better, please take a few minutes to answer the following questions. Your opinions are important to us.

1. Do you live/work in the area? (Circle one or both if they apply.)
2. Why did you choose us? (Circle all that apply.)

   Close to home   Quality

   Close to work   Full-service photography shop

   Convenience   Other

   Good service

3. How did you learn about us? (Circle one.)

   Newspaper

   Flyer/coupon

   Passing by

   Recommended by someone

   Other

4. How frequently do you have photos printed? (Please estimate.)

   ___ Times per month

   ___ Times per year

5. Which aspects of our photography shop do you think need improvement?
6. Our operating hours are from 8:00 a.m. to 7:00 p.m. weekdays and from 9:30 a.m. to 6:00 p.m. Saturdays. We are closed on Sundays and legal holidays. If changes in our operating hours would serve you better, please specify your preferences.
7. Age (Circle one.)

   Under 25

   26–39

   40–59

   Over 60

   Comments:

Running a Business
Part 5

Graeter's Is "Synonymous with Ice Cream"

When a 140-year-old company finally redesigns its logo, that's big news. Graeter's, the beloved Cincinnati-based maker of premium, hand-packed ice cream, is still managed by direct descendants of its founders. Its new logo is just one part of a major rebranding effort to support the company's first big planned expansion. "If we don't continue to improve and innovate, somebody will come and do it better than us," says Chip Graeter, the company's vice president of retail stores. "And we don't want that to happen."

Quality Builds the Brand

Graeter's considers as its competitors not only Häagen-Dazs and Ben & Jerry's, national premium ice-cream brands that have much bigger marketing budgets, but also all kinds of premium-quality desserts and edible treats. Taking that wide-angle view means its competition is both broad and fierce. One thing the company is firm about, however, is maintaining the quality of its dense, creamy product (it's so dense that one pint of Graeter's ice cream weighs about a pound). Graeter's quality standards call for adhering to its simple, original family recipe—which now includes more all-natural ingredients, like beet juice instead of food dye and dairy products from hormone-free cows—and an original, artisanal production process that yields only about two gallons per machine every 20 minutes. "We were always all-natural," says CEO Richard Graeter II, "but now we're being militant about it."

That hard-earned premium quality is what built the Graeter's brand from its earliest days when refrigeration was unknown and ice cream was a true novelty. Today, "Graeter's in Cincinnati is synonymous with ice cream," says a company executive. "People will say, 'Let's go get a Graeter's.' They don't say, 'Let's go get an ice cream.'" Quality is also what the current management team hopes will propel Graeter's beyond its current market, which consists of a few dozen company-owned retail stores in Ohio, Missouri, Kentucky, and nearby states, and the freezer cases of about 1,700 supermarkets and grocery stores, particularly the Kroger chain. Graeter's is also on the menu in some fine restaurants and country clubs. The company operates an online store and will ship ice cream overnight via UPS to any of the 48 continental states (California is its biggest shipping market).

Graeter's also sells a limited line of candies, cakes, and other bakery goods, and its ice-cream line includes smoothies and sorbets.

Expanding to New Markets

Graeter's ambitious expansion plans are backed by a recent increase in production capacity from one factory to three (one of the new factories was built, and the other purchased). The plans call for distributing Graeter's delectable, seasonal flavors to even more supermarkets and grocery stores, and for gradually opening new retail stores, perhaps as far away as Los Angeles and New York. The Kroger chain is Graeter's biggest distribution partner. Of the tens of thousands of brands Kroger carries, says the chain, pricey Graeter's commands the strongest brand loyalty. It was through Kroger, in fact, that Graeter's managers hit upon the idea of conducting a trial expansion to Denver, a new market for the brand.

Kroger owns the King Soopers chain of grocery stores in Denver, and research showed that more Denver ice-cream buyers choose premium brands than cheaper choices, suggesting that Graeter's might do well there. So Graeter's chose 12 flavors to send to 30 King Soopers stores in Denver as a test market, with the goal of selling two or three gallons a week. The test was an unqualified success. Within a few weeks, the company was selling an average of five gallons a week per store.

"I'd like to be coast to coast," admits Graeter's CEO. In fact, the management team would like to explore selling Graeter's in Canada, perhaps within the next five years. "The challenge, of course, is to preserve the integrity of the product as we grow. But we have done that for more than 100 years, and I'd argue that it's better now than ever."

Promoting the Brand

Graeter's had already gotten a big free boost from a positive mention on the *Oprah Winfrey Show* in 2002, when the influential talk-show host called it the best ice cream she had ever tasted. "We were shipping about 40 orders a day," says CEO Richard Graeter II. "After her show, the next day we probably shipped 400." National attention continues with occasional exposure on the Food Network, the Fine Living Channel, the Travel Channel, and even the History Channel.

"How does that happen?" asks one of the firm's executives. "It happens because we have a product and a process and a growth that is exciting."

Still, says George Denman, the company's vice president of sales and marketing, Graeter's faces the same challenge in new markets as any "small, regional niche player" and one with a limited marketing budget: "establishing a relationship with the consumer, building brand awareness [through] trial and repeat. . . . So obviously when we roll into a marketplace one of the first things we do is we demo the product. We get it out in front of the consumer and get them to taste it, because the product sells itself." The company has also been reducing its price to distributors, who pass the savings along to stores that can then advertise that Graeter's pints are on sale. "If a consumer has maybe been buying Ben & Jerry's and never considered ours, because maybe that dollar price point difference was too high, this gives her the opportunity to try us. And once she tries us, we know we've brand-switched that consumer right then," says Denman.

Marketing Communications

Through its Cincinnati-based ad agency, Graeter's does some local advertising, including attractive point-of-sale displays in supermarkets and grocery stores and some radio ads, occasional print ads, and billboards. The company launches small-scale promotions for the introduction of a new flavor or to celebrate National Ice Cream Month or other occasions. However, brand loyalty for this family business has grown mostly through word of mouth that endures across generations. "We are the beneficiary of that loyalty that our customers have built up over so many years, multiple generations," says one of the company's executives. "Our customers have told us they were introduced to the product through their grandmother, or a special time. . . . They don't come to our stores because they have to; they come because they want to."

"We use the traditional [marketing] methods," says Denman. "We are also doing nontraditional methods. We are looking at electronic couponing, where consumers will be able to go to our website as a new consumer . . . and secure a dollar-off coupon to try Graeter's, just for coming to our website or joining up on Facebook. We've done loyalty programs with Kroger where they have actually direct-mailed loyal consumers and offered . . . discounts as well. . . . So far it's worked well for us. We've had to go back and look at the return on investment on each of these programs and cut some things out and improve on some other things, but in the end we have been very pleased with the results."

"Quality . . . We Never Changed"

"We ship our product, and that was something that for the first hundred years you never thought about. I mean, who would think about shipping ice cream from Cincinnati to California? But it is our number-one market for shipping, so all those things you can change," says Richard Graeter, the CEO. "The most important thing, the quality of the product and how we make it, that we never changed."[16]

Questions

1. What are the elements of Graeter's marketing mix? Which are most likely to be affected by external forces in the marketing environment?

2. Graeter's ice-cream line includes smoothies and sorbets. Do you think it should consider other brand extensions such as yogurt, low-fat ice cream, coffee drinks, or other related products? Why or why not?

3. How might Graeter's capitalize on its valuable capacity for word-of-mouth promotion in expanding to new markets where, despite some national publicity like the *Oprah Winfrey Show*, its name is still not widely known?

Building a Business Plan: Part 5

This part is one of the most important components of your business plan. In this part, you will present the facts that you have gathered on the size and nature of your market(s). State market size in dollars and units. How many units and what is the dollar value of the products you expect to sell in a given time period? Indicate your primary and secondary sources of data and the methods you used to estimate total market size and your market share. Part 5 of your textbook covers all marketing-related topics. These chapters should help you to answer the questions in this part of the business plan.

The Marketing Plan Component

The marketing plan component is and should be unique to your business. Many assumptions or projections used in the analysis may turn out differently; therefore, this component should be flexible enough to be adjusted as needed. The marketing plan should include answers to at least the following questions:

5.1 What are your target markets, and what common identifiable need(s) can you satisfy?

5.2 What are the competitive, legal, political, economic, technological, and sociocultural factors affecting your marketing efforts?

5.3 What are the current needs of each target market? Describe the target market in terms of demographic, geographic, psychographic, and product-usage characteristics. What changes in the target market are anticipated?

5.4 What advantages and disadvantages do you have in meeting the target market's needs?

5.5 How will your product distribution, promotion, and price satisfy customer needs?

5.6 How effectively will your products meet these needs?

5.7 What are the relevant aspects of consumer behavior and product use?

5.8 What are your company's projected sales volume, market share, and profitability?

5.9 What are your marketing objectives? Include the following in your marketing objectives:

- Product introduction, improvement, or innovation
- Sales or market share
- Profitability
- Pricing
- Distribution
- Advertising (Prepare advertising samples for the appendix.)

Make sure that your marketing objectives are clearly written, measurable, and consistent with your overall marketing strategy.

5.10 How will the results of your marketing plan be measured and evaluated?

Review of Business Plan Activities

Remember that even though it will be time-consuming, developing a clear, well-written marketing plan is important. Therefore, make sure that you have checked the plan for any weaknesses or problems before proceeding to Part 6. Also, make certain that all your answers to the questions in this and other parts are consistent throughout the business plan. Finally, write a brief statement that summarizes all the information for this part of the business plan.

The information contained in this section will also assist you in completing the online *Interactive Business Plan*.

Endnotes

1. Based on information in Kim Leonard, "New Dick's Location Opens in Cranberry," *Pittsburgh Tribune-Review*, October 25, 2012, www.pittsburghlive.com; Teresa F. Lindeman, "Dick's Sporting Goods Tests Viability of Specialty Store in Shadyside," *Pittsburgh Post-Gazette*, August 21, 2012, www.post-gazette.com; Gary M. Stern, "Dick's Sporting Goods Knows about Location," *Investor's Business Daily*, August 20, 2012, p. A4 ; David Saito-Chung, "Dick's Is Still the Champ in Sports Retailing," *Investor's Business Daily*, August 20, 2012, p. B2; www.dickssportinggoods.com.

2. Suzy Hansen, "How Zara Grew into the World's Largest Fashion Retailer," *New York Times*, November 11, 2012, http://www.nytimes.com/2012/11/11/magazine/how-zara-grew-into-the-worlds-largest-fashion-retailer.html.

3. "Retail Trade, Geographic Area Series, Summary Statistics for the United States," U.S. Economic Census, 2007.

4. "U.S. Convenience Store Count," National Association of Convenience Stores, http://www.nacsonline.com/NACS/NEWS/FACTSHEETS/SCOPEOFINDUSTRY/Pages/IndustryStoreCount.aspx, accessed January 2, 2013.

5. Kathy Chu and Laurie Burkitt, "Retailers Adjust to New Pace in China," *Wall Street Journal*, November 6, 2012, http://online.wsj.com/article/SB10001424052970204755404578102301266588938.html.

6. "Fast Facts," Direct Selling 411, http://www.directselling411.com/about-direct-selling/, accessed January 2, 2013.

7. Do Not Call, "http://www.donotcall.gov," accessed January 2, 2013; Maya Jackson Randall, "FCC Cracks Down on Robocalls," *The Wall Street Journal*, February 15, 2012, http://online.wsj.com/article/SB10001424052970204792404577225922293962202.html, accessed January 2, 2013.

8. "Vending Machines of the Past and Present," *The Wall Street Journal*, March 22, 2012, http://online.wsj.com/article/SB10001424052702304724404577295671669812582.html#slide/1, accessed January 3, 2013; Zafar Aylin, "Prescription Pills, iPods, and Live Bait: There's a Vending Machine for That," *Time*, March 23, 2012, http://newsfeed.time.com/2012/03/23/prescription-pills-ipods-and-live-bait-theres-a-vending-machine-for-that/, accessed January 2, 2013.

9. Staff reporter, "Retail's New Motto is Experiences and Shopping," *SA Commercial Prop News*, March 19, 2012, www.sacommercialpropnews.co.za/commercial-property-research-report/4539-retail-s-new-motto-is-experiences-and-shopping.html, accessed January 2, 2013.

10. Susanne Vranica, "Ad-Spending Outlook Dims," *Wall Street Journal*, December 2, 2012, http://online.wsj.com/article/SB10001424127887324020804578151710820996072.html.

11. Corn Refiners Association, www.corn.org/, accessed January 3, 2013; Carey Gillam, "Sugar versus Corn Syrup: Sweeteners at center of bitter food fight," *Reuters*, September 5, 2012, http://www.reuters.com/article/2012/09/05/us-usa-sugar-lawsuit-idUSBRE8841IQ20120905, accessed January 4, 2013.

12. "Gulf of Mexico Restoration," *BP*, http://www.bp.com/sectionbodycopy.do?categoryId=41&contentId=7067505, accessed January 2, 2013.

13. Save Local, Constant Contact, http://search.constantcontact.com/savelocal/index.jsp, accessed January 3, 2013.

14. Red Bull Stratos, http://www.redbullstratos.com/, accessed January 3, 2013.

15. Based on company website http://www.llbean.com, accessed July 20, 2010; "Photobrand 25 Ranks ESPN, GE, and Dunkin' Donuts as New England's Most Powerful Brands for 2010," *PR Newswire*, June 1, 2010, http://www.prnewswire.com; Michael Arndt, "Customer Service Champs: L.L. Bean Follows Its Shoppers to the Web," *Bloomberg BusinessWeek*, February 18, 2010, http://www.businessweek.com; interviews with L.L. Bean employees and the video, "L.L. Bean Employs a Variety of Promotion Methods to Communicate with Customers".

16. Based on information from Kimberly L. Jackson, "Graeter's Premium Chocolate Chip Ice cream Lands at Stop & Shop," *Newark Star-Ledger (NJ)*, April 4, 2012, www.nj.com; "Graeter's Ice cream Debuts in Bay Area," *Tampa Bay Times (St. Petersburg, FL)*, January 10, 2012, p. 4B; Jim carper, "Graeter's Runs a Hands-on Ice cream Plant," *Dairy Foods*, August 2011, pp. 36+; Jim carper, "The Greater Good," *Dairy Foods*, August 2011, pp. 95+; "Graeter's Unveils New 'Mystery Flavor,'" *Dayton Daily News*, March 29, 2012, www.daytondailynews.com; Bob Driehaus, "A Cincinnati Ice Cream Maker Aims Big," *New York Times*, September 11, 2010, www.nytimes.com; Lucy May, "Graeter's Northern Kentucky Franchisee Puts Stores on the Block," *Business Courier*, August 6, 2010, http://cincinnati.bizjournals.com; www.graeters.com; interviews with company staff and Cengage videos about Graeter's.

Exploring Social Media and e-Business

Why Should You Care?

Question: How important is social media and e-business for a business today? Answer: Today, more and more businesses are using social media and e-business to reach new customers and increase sales and profits.

Learning Objectives

Once you complete this chapter, you will be able to:

1 Examine why it is important for a business to use social media.

2 Discuss how businesses use social media tools.

3 Explain the business objectives for using social media.

4 Describe how businesses develop a social media plan.

5 Explain the meaning of e-business.

6 Understand the fundamental models of e-business.

7 Identify the factors that will affect the future of the Internet, social media, and e-business.

Domino's Puts e-Business and Social Media on the Menu

More than half a century after Tom Monaghan bought a small pizza shop in Ypsilanti, Michigan, the business he renamed Domino's Pizza (www.dominos.com) delivers more than 400 million pizzas every year. The majority of the company's 10,000 stores in 70 countries are operated by franchisees, independent business owners who rely on Domino's brand image, operational processes, and cutting-edge technologies to build revenues and profits. In fact, technologies that hadn't been invented when the company was young now account for a lot of its success today.

For example, more than 30 percent of Domino's sales today start with an order placed online or via mobile app, in English or in Spanish. Customers have the option of using Domino's online tracking system to follow their orders minute by minute from kitchen to delivery, a feature the company is adding for in-store orders, as well. Customers can even see the name of the employee who makes their pizza. Supported by this sophisticated system, the number of digital transactions is growing year by year. Just as important, customers tend to spend a little more when they order with a click or a tap—and

they report higher satisfaction with the convenience and speed of digital ordering. No wonder Domino's rings up more than $1.6 billion in sales of pizzas, soft drinks, and side dishes.

Domino's makes good use of social media such as Facebook (where it has nearly 7.6 million "likes") and Twitter (more than 153,000 followers). Many of its advertising campaigns tie in with social media promotions such as discount codes mentioned in company tweets. To engage customers and reinforce its commitment to quality, Domino's invites customers to post photos on Facebook showing what their just-delivered pizzas look like. And the company makes a special effort to respond quickly to questions and complaints on Facebook and Twitter, knowing that its digital reputation is on the line.[1]

Did You Know?

Domino's rings up more than $1.6 billion in annual sales of pizzas, soft drinks, and side dishes.

For Domino's, the company profiled in the Inside Business feature for this chapter, pizza is big business. With 10,000 stores in 70 countries, this company sells a lot of pizza, soft drinks, and related food items. In order to generate more than $1.6 billion in sales, the company uses both social media and e-business to build revenues and profits. Today, Domino's is an excellent example of how social media and e-business are changing the way companies do business in today's competitive business environment.

Take a moment to think about how social media and e-business affect your own life. In just a few short years, it has changed the way we communicate with each other, it has changed the way we meet people, and it has changed the way we shop. In this chapter, we explore how these trends affect both individuals and businesses.

We begin this chapter by examining why social media is important for both individuals and business firms. Next, we discuss how companies can use social media to build relationships with customers, the goals for social media usage, and the steps required to build a social media plan and measure the effectiveness of a firm's social media activities. In the last part of this chapter, we take a close look at how firms use technology to conduct business on the Internet and what growth opportunities and challenges affect both social media and e-businesses.

WHY IS SOCIAL MEDIA IMPORTANT?

Learning Objective

1 Examine why it is important for a business to use social media.

If you are a "digital native" (anyone born after 1980), you know exactly what social media is because you have grown up with technology and are very comfortable sharing information about yourself. If you are anyone else, social media seems like a strange (but exciting) phenomenon where millions of people freely share, create, vote, and connect with other people effortlessly using Internet-based technologies.

What Is Social Media and How Popular Is It?

social media the online interactions that allow people and businesses to communicate and share ideas, personal information, and information about products and services

Today, there are many definitions of social media because it is still developing and continually changing. For our purposes, **social media** represents the online interactions that allow people and businesses to communicate and share ideas, personal information, and information about products and services. Simply put, social media is about people. It is about a culture of participation, meaning that people can now discuss, vote, create, connect, and advocate much easier than ever before. For example, you can post your plans for a weekend trip on Facebook. Then you can share a travel itinerary and chronicle your trip through videos, photos, and ratings on Facebook. People can also use Twitter to raise awareness about bone-marrow donations in order to help a friend find a match. While it's hard to imagine, many popular social media sites like Facebook and Twitter were just created in the past decade (see Figure 14-1).

So how popular is social media? A recent Pew Internet Research study showed that 69 percent of U.S. adults use social media sites such as Facebook, LinkedIn, Google+,

FIGURE 14-1 Timeline for the Development of Social Media

Like computer technology, developments in social media have been not only rapid, they have also changed the way people connect.

SOCIAL MEDIA BREAKTHROUGH	
1991	• AOL
1995	• Classmates.com; Yahoo
1996	• AOL instant messenger
1998	• MoveOn.org, Google
1999	• Napster, Blogger, Epinions, LiveJournal
2001	• Wikipedia, StumbleUpon
2002	• Friendster, Technorati
2003	• LinkedIn, Wordpress, MySpace, Hi5, Photobucket, Delicious
2004	• Gmail, Flickr, Facebook, Yelp, Digg
2005	• YouTube, Mashable, Reddit, Bebo
2006	• Twitter
2007	• Tumblr
2008	• Apple's App Store
2009	• Foursquare
2010	• Pinterest,
2011	• Google +
2012	• Facebook sells stock to the public
2013	• At the beginning of 2013, over two thirds of U.S. adults use social media
The Future	• Who knows what the next generation of social media will mean for both individuals and business?

© CENGAGE LEARNING 2015

Twitter, and Pinterest. By far the most popular of these sites is Facebook, which has more than 1 billion users worldwide. LinkedIn has 200 million users who use the site mainly for professional networking. Google+ has more than 135 million users, Twitter has 200 million users, and Pinterest has 40 million users. These numbers increase daily as consumers log onto social media from home, from work, and from mobile phones to stay in touch with family and friends, reconnect with old friends, share photos, and post messages about what's happening in their lives.[2]

Why Businesses Use Social Media

Social media has completely changed the business environment. Early on, companies saw potential in the sheer number of people using social media and that made using social media a top priority for many business firms. By using social media, companies could share information about their products and services and improve customer service. Now many companies, large and small, are using social media to learn about customers' likes and dislikes, seek public input about products and marketing, create a community feeling, polish brand image, and promote particular products. Macy's, for example, is active on Facebook, YouTube, Pinterest, Twitter, and a blog designed to be read on mobile screens. The company recently asked its 10 million-plus Facebook fans for advice about which colors to feature in jeans (the winners: bright blue, red, and orange) and which print dress to stock (the winner: a floral print).[3] Macy's maintains multiple Twitter accounts to highlight special in-store events, announce discounts and clearance sales, and recruit college students and graduates for internships and job opportunities. On Pinterest, Macy's various virtual bulletin boards hold thousands of "pinned" images representing the latest in beauty products, fashions, bridal registry items, and home décor. Its YouTube channel includes Macy's commercials, coverage of the annual Thanksgiving Day Parade, behind-the-scenes designer interviews, and videos about fashion trends. Many CEOs see social media as a way to increase transparency and empower employees, as well.[4] For more information about why businesses use social media (and the benefits for a business), see Figure 14-2.

A new kind of family time. Today, technology has changed the way people communicate and share ideas, personal information, and information about products and services. In this photo, mom, dad, and the kids could be looking at pictures of relatives or reading movie reviews or sending an e-mail to grandma—all social media activities.

© YURI ARCURS/SHUTTERSTOCK.COM

Concept Check

✓ According to material in this section, what are the reasons why people use social media?

✓ How has social media changed the environment for business firms?

FIGURE 14-2 The Five Most Important Benefits for a Business That Uses Social Media

While there are many reasons a business chooses to use social media, the number one reason is that social media generates exposure for a business.

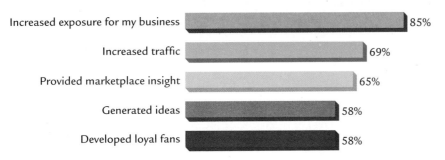

Increased exposure for my business	85%
Increased traffic	69%
Provided marketplace insight	65%
Generated ideas	58%
Developed loyal fans	58%

Source: Michael A. Stelzner, "2012 Social Media Marketing Industry Report," The SocialMediaExaminer.com website at www.socialmediaexaminer.com (accessed April 12, 2013).

The fact that so many people are actively sharing information about themselves and their likes and dislikes online for all to see was a driving force behind many companies' attempts to develop a social media presence. Unlike social media, traditional marketing messages were top down—meaning that companies used television and magazine ads to promote their product to a large audience without any opportunity for feedback. With social media, this is no longer the case. If people have bad experiences with a product or service, they tend to let the world know by writing about it on a blog, mentioning it on Facebook, or tweeting about it. Not long ago, one customer tweeted her annoyance after spending a frustrating 40 minutes on hold waiting to talk with a Citibank service representative. To her surprise, a Citibank representative quickly tweeted back to ask for the customer's phone number so the bank could solve the problem. The bank's @askCiti Twitter account now has as many as 17 representatives monitoring social media and tweeting to offer help, part of the bank's social media initiative to improve customer relations. As a result of Citibank's attention to social media, it receives tweeted compliments in addition to tweeted complaints. Other banks using social media to stay in touch with customers' concerns and comments include Bank of America, Capital One, JP Morgan Chase, TD Bank, and Wells Fargo. Speed is essential: In one study, 33 percent of the consumers surveyed said they'd recommend a firm that responded quickly to a social media complaint—even if the response didn't completely resolve the issue.[5] The bottom line: Because of social media, companies no longer have much control over what is said about their products or services, and many are not yet comfortable with the new roles set forth by a consumer-dominated culture.

Learning Objective

2 Discuss how businesses use social media tools.

SOCIAL MEDIA TOOLS FOR BUSINESS USE

For a business, part of what makes social media so challenging is the sheer number of ways to interact with other businesses and both existing and potential consumers. Companies are using social media because it allows the company to

- connect with customers;
- listen to its main stakeholders (including but not limited to customers);
- provide another means of customer service;
- develop content that is valuable to customers; and
- engage customers in product development and formulation.

social content sites allow companies to create and share information about their products and services

Social content sites allow companies to create and share information about their products and services via blogs, videos, photos, and podcasts. For businesses selling to other businesses, social content sites can also include webinars and online promotional materials. For an overview of how businesses can use social media tools, take another look at Figure 14-2.

Business Use of Blogs

blog a website that allows a company to share information in order to not only increase the customer's knowledge about its products and services, but also to build trust

For businesses, blogs have become one of the most widely used tools for the effective use of social media. A **blog** is a website that allows a company to share information in order to increase customers' knowledge about its products and services, as well as to build trust. Once a story or information is posted, customers can provide feedback through comments, which is one of the most important ways of creating a conversation between business firms and consumers. Some experts believe that every company should have a blog that speaks to current and potential customers, not as customers, but as people.[6]

Blogs are effective at developing better relationships with customers, attracting new customers, telling stories about the company's products or services, and providing an active forum for testing new ideas. For example, even after Bill Marriott stepped down as CEO of Marriott International, he continued to record his comments about interesting travel destinations, current events, hotel openings, company policies, and family stories for the company's "Marriott on the Move" blog. The blog includes photos of people and places, plus an occasional video, and it invites public comments. Thanks to its distinctive voice and diverse content, Marriott on the Move is a "must follow" blog for many travelers. By one estimate, this blog has brought in $5 million worth of business for Marriott over a five-year period. The company also maintains a blog with news and updates about corporate earnings, and a culinary blog highlighting its food specialties.[7] By including information about webinars and promotional materials, blogs are also effective for businesses that are selling to other businesses.

Podcasts can be not only informative, but also inspirational. As the wife of a retired army sergeant and an army veteran herself, Victoria Parham knows what it is like to experience long separations, job instability, and single parenthood that come with the military lifestyle. Today she shares her experiences and solutions to everyday problems in a free twice-monthly podcast created to inspire, educate, and entertain military spouses.

Photos, Videos, and Podcasts

In addition to blogs, another tool for social content is **media sharing sites,** which allow users to upload photos, videos, and podcasts. Before participating in media sharing, consider the following three factors:

media sharing sites allow users to upload photos, videos, and podcasts

- Who will create the photos, videos, and podcasts that will be used?
- How will the content be distributed to interested businesses and consumers?
- How much will it cost to create and distribute the material?

Today, photo sharing provides a method for companies to tell a compelling story about its products or services through postings on either the company's website or a social media site.

Videos have also gained popularity because of their inherent ability to tell stories. Entertainment companies, for example, now traditionally use YouTube as a way to showcase movie trailers. And Home Depot has also posted great do-it-yourself videos on its YouTube channel. Companies know that YouTube and others sites are useful because they are already recognized by other businesses and consumers as a source of both entertainment and information.

Podcasts are digital audio or video files that people listen to or watch online on tablets, computers, MP3 players, or smartphones. Think of podcasts as radio shows that are distributed through various means (like iTunes) and not linked to a scheduled time period. The great thing about podcasts is that they are available for download at any time. Bill Marriott, former CEO of Marriott Hotels, has always used an audio recorder to "write" his blog entries. The company posts those podcasts for download on the Marriott on the Move blog, alongside the transcribed version that's posted on the blog itself.

podcasts digital audio or video files that people listen to or watch online on tablets, computers, MP3 players, or smartphones

Social Media Ratings

Social media enables shoppers to access opinions, recommendations, and referrals from others who have bought a product or service. This type of information is available via a social media site and can include reviews and ratings, as well as information on sales promotions programs like Groupon and LivingSocial. Both of these sites provide information about companies that offer deep discounts to customers that redeem an offer.

Sites for ratings and reviews are based on the idea that consumers trust the opinions of others when it comes to purchasing products and services. According to Nielsen Media Research, more than 70 percent of consumers said that they trust online consumer opinions.[8] Based on the early work of Amazon and eBay, new sites have sprung up allowing consumers to rate local businesses or compare products and services. One of the most popular, Yelp, combines customer ratings with social networking and is now the largest local review directory on the Web. Consumer reviews are especially influential in certain purchase situations. Travel services, for example, are an area where ratings make a difference in buying decisions. Knowing this, Wyndham Hotel Group puts the ratings of consumers who use TripAdvisor directly on its websites so travelers can see what others say about the hotels. By examining the reviews on other sites, plus any social media comments posted elsewhere, Wyndham can get a good sense of its online reputation and identify specific areas for improvement.[9]

Social Games

social game a multiplayer, competitive, goal-oriented activity with defined rules of engagement and online connectivity among a community of players

Social games are another area of growth in social media. A **social game** is "a multiplayer, competitive, goal-oriented activity with defined rules of engagement and online connectivity among a community of players."[10] One of the most important aspects of social media is entertainment and games like Angry Birds and FarmVille serve that purpose. Indeed, research shows that the "gamification" of social media is a huge trend because people like the competition, social status, and rewards that they can earn through social gaming.[11] For businesses that create games, it can be very profitable. Rovio Entertainment's Angry Birds social games have been downloaded more than 1 billion times, creating huge demand for game-related goods and services. In all, Rovio has made hundreds of millions of dollars from the sale of branded toys, T-shirts, key chains, and other merchandise, as well as from licensing fees for Angry Birds play areas and other entertainment services. While some businesses elect to create their own games, others promote particular brands or products within another firm's game. For example, Honda sponsored a promotion in which players of the Zynga social game, Words with Friends, earned extra points and special tips when they played and uncovered words that describe the new Honda Accord, words such as "tech" and "luxury."[12]

Concept Check

✓ What is a blog? How can a business use blogs to develop relationships with customers?

✓ What types of content can be used on a media sharing site? What factors should be considered when developing content for a media sharing site?

✓ Describe two ways that businesses can use "gamification" to generate sales revenue.

Learning Objective

3 Explain the business objectives for using social media.

ACHIEVING BUSINESS OBJECTIVES THROUGH SOCIAL MEDIA

Although the popularity of social media is a recent phenomenon, many businesses are already using it to achieve important objectives. Some of these goals are long-term—such as building brand awareness and brand reputation—while others are more short-term—such as increasing website traffic or generating sales leads. Regardless of how social media is used, there are a lot of business opportunities. In this section, we explore a few ways that companies have used social media effectively to achieve business objectives.

Social Media Communities

social media communities social networks based on the relationships among people

For a business, social media can be used to build a community. **Social media communities** are social networks based on the relationships among people.[13] These electronic communities encourage two-way communication, allow for people to develop profiles, and identify other people to connect with by using technology and the Internet. People in each community can be called friends, fans, followers, or connections. Popular social networking sites include Facebook (the largest), LinkedIn (for professionals), Twitter, Google+, YouTube, Pinterest, and many others. To see how many businesses use the top four social media community sites, see Figure 14-3.

For businesses using social media, the most popular social networking sites are Facebook, Twitter, LinkedIn, and blogs.

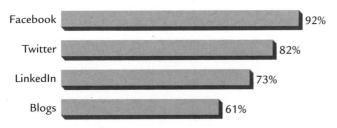

Facebook 92%
Twitter 82%
LinkedIn 73%
Blogs 61%

Source: Michael A. Stelzner, "2012 Social Media Marketing Industry Report," The SocialMediaExaminer.com website at www.socialmediaexaminer.com (accessed April 12, 2013).

There are social communities for every interest, ethnic group, and lifestyle. Different types of social communities include forums and wikis. A **forum** is an interactive version of a community bulletin board that focuses on threaded discussions. These are particularly popular with people who share a common interest such as video games. Another community based on social media is a wiki. A **wiki** is a collaborative online working space that enables members to contribute content that can be shared with other people. With wikis, members of the community are the editors and gatekeepers ensuring that the content is correct and updated. Wikipedia—the free online encyclopedia—is the best example of a wiki.

forum an interactive version of a community bulletin board that focuses on threaded discussions

wiki a collaborative online working space that enables members to contribute content that can be shared with other people

Today, many companies are using social media to build communities with other businesses and consumers in order to achieve business objectives. For the past few years, JP Morgan Chase has used a special Facebook page to involve the public in its Community Giving philanthropy program. The bank sets aside $5 million to give as grants to the nonprofit groups that receive the most votes on its Facebook page during each yearly two-week voting period. This community involvement program has so far provided grants to 500 charities in 41 states. It has also gained the Chase Community Giving page on Facebook nearly 4 million likes and attracted more than 340,000 yearly votes from the public.[14]

Crisis and Reputation Management

One of the most important reasons for listening to stakeholders is to determine whether there is a crisis brewing. A majority of companies believe that their company is less than a year away from some potential crisis moment and monitor social media for conversations that may predict a crisis.[15] Apple, one of the world's most admired and profitable technology companies, endured a reputation crisis not long ago when it decided to install the newly developed Apple Maps function instead of Google Maps when it upgraded its popular iPhone operating system. Google competes with Apple in several product categories, including mobile operating systems and Internet browsers, which may be why Apple decided to replace Google

AP IMAGES/EVAN VUCCI

Social media: A new way to handle a crisis. For years, Walmart—the world's largest retailer—has tried to repair a reputation that's been damaged by decades of criticism and legal problems. Now Walmart has a new public relations tool—social media—to not only monitor what people are saying about the company, but also to tell its side of the story when controversies develop.

Maps with its own mapping function. Unfortunately, the first version of Apple Maps lacked public transit information, misplaced or missed some major landmarks, and steered users off-course in some highly publicized situations. Within days of introducing Apple Maps, the company found itself criticized in the news media, bashed on Facebook and in the blogosphere, and satirized in tweets. Apple CEO Tim Cook quickly issued an apology, admitted the problems, and suggested that iPhone owners try other mapping programs while Apple Maps was being improved. Meanwhile, Google created a new mapping app for the iPhone that was downloaded 10 million times in the first two days of availability. Despite the Apple Maps controversy, new iPhone models have been big hits in the U.S. market, and the company's reputation has been improved because of the way it handled the Apple maps crisis.[16]

Listening to Stakeholders

Listening to people, whether they are customers or not, is always an important aspect of a company's social media plan. Indeed, listening is often the first step when developing a social media strategy. Listening to the conversations unfolding on Facebook or Twitter, for example, can be important to understanding just what people think about a company's products and services. By monitoring Facebook, Twitter, and other social media sites, Domino's Pizza found out that people were not very happy with its product quality. Customers described the sauce as "tasting like ketchup" and the crust as "tasting like cardboard." Unfortunately, there were enough comments of a similar nature for the company to use traditional marketing research to verify this information. They found the sentiment to be true and the company then developed a plan to reinvent every aspect of the company—and its pizza products. Did the plan work? Same store sales increased more than 14 percent.[17]

Targeting Customers

Millennials tech-savvy digital natives born after 1980

Many companies are using social media to increase awareness and build their brand among customers. It is especially valuable in targeting the Millennials. **Millennials** are tech-savvy digital natives born after 1980. When the U.K. fashion firm Burberry began researching the market for luxury apparel, it found that 60 percent of the world's population is under 30 years old. It also realized that this demographic group is increasingly affluent in developing nations. Therefore, the company decided to target Millennials worldwide as the key to revitalizing sales and building a loyal customer base for future success. Burberry's designers created new collections of styles that appeal to Millennials' fashion tastes while building on the company's 150-year heritage.

Despite high brand awareness, Burberry still faced a challenge in communicating its move toward hipper styles for today's Millennial lifestyle. To accomplish this, it engaged its tech-savvy target market through social media marketing. Burberry started live-streaming its fashion shows online and for viewing on mobile devices, allowing customers to place orders with a few clicks even before the end of a show. It tweeted a few photos of new styles in advance of new seasons to build anticipation; it posted YouTube videos to promote new looks and thank customers for their loyalty. With every new social site and new fashion season, Burberry has added to its digital marketing. One recent collection was introduced via Facebook, Twitter, YouTube, Instagram, Pinterest, and Google+, as well as several social media sites in China, where Burberry is recording double-digit sales increases. A special website, Burberry Bespoke, allows customers to design the details of their own trench coats for special order, and the company's Art of the Trench website and Tumblr mini-blogs feature photos of customers modeling their favorite Burberry trench. Thanks to its aggressive social media outreach, Burberry has attracted 15 million Facebook likes, 1.5 million Twitter followers, 21 million YouTube video views, and tens of thousands of followers on Instagram, Pinterest, and other networking sites.[18]

Social Media Marketing

According to a survey by eMarketer, 80 percent of U.S. companies with more than 100 employees are using social media tools for marketing products and services. Among small business, the rate of social media use for marketing is closer to 40 percent, and among businesses selling to other businesses, the rate is around 24 percent.[19] **Social media marketing** is the "utilization of social media technologies, channels, and software to create, communicate, deliver and exchange offerings that have value for an organization."[20] As companies become more comfortable with social media, we can expect even more companies to use social media to market products and services to their customers. Already, research indicates that companies are shifting their advertising money from traditional marketing (like television and magazines) to digital marketing (like Internet search engines and social media). Experts now predict that social media will account for 26 percent of all online spending by 2016.[21] The primary reason is simple. People are spending more time online.[22] Often the first step for a business that wants to use social media is to go to LinkedIn, Facebook, Twitter, or some other popular social media site. As you can tell from the information in Figure 14-4, companies like LinkedIn make using their technology as easy as possible to connect with potential or existing customers.

social media marketing the utilization of social media technologies, channels, and software to create, communicate, deliver, and exchange offerings that have value for an organization

FIGURE 14-4 LinkedIn's Marketing Solutions for Other Businesses

Like many popular social media communities, LinkedIn's marketing tools make it easy to connect with potential or existing customers.

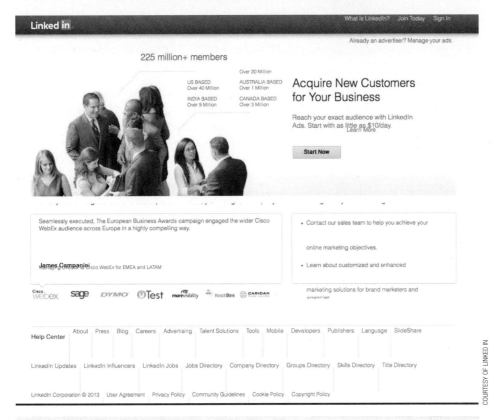

inbound marketing a marketing term that describes new ways of gaining attention and ultimately customers by creating content on a website that pulls customers in

crowdsourcing outsourcing tasks to a group of people in order to tap into the ideas of the crowd

Concept Check

✓ In your own words, describe how social media can help businesses to connect with other businesses and consumers.

✓ For a business, why are crisis and reputation management, listening to stakeholders, and targeting specific types of customers important activities?

✓ How can social media be used to market and advertise a firm's products or services?

✓ How can social media help a firm generate new product ideas and recruit employees?

Today, many companies have been quite successful using social media marketing not only to develop customer awareness, but also to obtain sales leads and increase actual sales. HubSpot, for example, is a software company that helps small and medium-sized companies develop inbound marketing programs. **Inbound marketing** is a marketing term that describes new ways of gaining attention, and ultimately, customers, by creating content on a website that pulls customers in. Tools used for inbound marketing programs include search engine optimization, blogging, videos, and social media. In order to market its software products, the software company HubSpot shunned traditional advertising and began to practice what it preached. First, the company developed its own inbound marketing program by creating valuable content and marketing information that was then distributed through social media and search engine websites. Companies interested in HubSpot's software were required to enter contact information (name, phone number, and e-mail address) in order to view the information. People provided contact information because they believed the company's software could help them improve their marketing activities. As a result of HubSpot's inbound marketing program, the cost of generating new sales leads was five to seven times less than leads generated by more traditional marketing activities and as a bonus they gained thousands of new customers.[23]

Companies like Dell also use social media to sell products and services. Unlike other companies experimenting with social media, Dell decided to be more visible and actively use social media to increase sales by using Twitter. The company has sold computers, monitors, printers, and other technology products by including links in its Twitter account to the DellOutlet website. While this represents a tiny percentage of Dell's total sales, it does show that products can be sold through social media.

As important as social media marketing is, it is only one aspect of digital marketing. Indeed, digital marketing or online marketing is comprised of several areas, including

- online public relations—developing social media press kits;
- search engine optimization—using keywords in the website in order to rank higher in search engine results;
- search engine marketing—buying ads like Google's AdWords to increase traffic to a company's website;
- display advertising—buying banner ads;
- e-mail marketing—targeting customers through opt-in e-mail campaigns; and
- content marketing—developing photos, videos, podcasts, blog posts, and other tools to increase the value to the customer.

Got an idea, then go to www.mystarbucksidea.com. For Starbucks, listening to customers is big business. Each year, Starbucks receives thousands of ideas and suggestions when customers post ideas and suggestions for new products, information about their in store experience, and how the company can become more involved in the community. For Starbucks, listening to customers and then implementing their ideas and suggestions is a great way to build loyalty.

AP IMAGES/TED S. WARREN

Generating New Product Ideas

Companies can use social media to conduct much of their consumer-based research. Using insight gained from Facebook or Twitter, for example, allows a company to modify existing products and services and develop new ones. **Crowdsourcing** involves outsourcing tasks to a group of people in order to tap into the ideas of the crowd. In some cases valuable information can be obtained by crowd voting. Frito Lay, for example, has used crowd voting for the last few years when they allowed people to create and then vote for their favorite television spots for its popular Doritos brand. The winners are then featured during the Super Bowl. Their effort "Crash the Super Bowl" has been wildly successful.[24]

Companies can even build communities for specific brands in order to obtain information and new ideas from consumers. A few years ago, Starbucks built a network called Mystarbucksidea .com that allowed customers to post ideas about how the company could improve. Since the creation of the website, thousands of ideas have been posted about Starbucks products, the customer's store experience, and the company's community involvement. The site also enables people to vote on the best ideas, many of which Starbucks has already implemented. For example, getting a free coffee on your birthday if you are a Gold Member or developing a VIP program were both originally customer ideas. Customers appreciate the ability to share their ideas when the company implements their ideas.[25]

Recruiting Employees

For years, companies have used current employees to recruit new employees based on the theory that "birds of a feather flock together." The concept is simple: Current employees' friends and family may prove to be good job candidates. Social media takes that concept to a whole new level. LinkedIn, the largest social network for professionals, has been used quite effectively by large corporations, small businesses, nonprofit organizations, and government agencies that want to recruit new employees. Because LinkedIn hosts more than 200 million professional profiles,

Career Success

Make a Good Impression Using Social Media

When you use social media to promote yourself to potential employers, what you post and how often you post can affect your ability to make a good impression.

- *Do: Show your professional side.* The first thing a visitor will notice is your photo—so be sure you look as professional as you would at an interview. Consider posting a brief "interview" video in which you answer a few questions that employers typically ask, such as what your career goals are or why you're interested in a particular industry. Include a contact link, with an e-mail address that matches the image you want to project.

- *Don't: Post inappropriate material.* One recruiter says he and his colleagues don't judge applicants based on their personal posts, but "we will judge their judgment for putting it on the Internet" if text or photos are offensive or racy. The head of a marketing research agency warns about using a lot of profanity online. An executive at the Hill Holliday ad agency doesn't like to "see a lot of posts about nothing or points of view that are judgmental or not open-minded. Inappropriate pictures can also [make] a bad impression."

- *Don't: Post too often.* Although many employers welcome active users of social media, they steer clear of applicants who post too often. "Too many Twitter posts from 9 to 5 might make us wonder how you find time for your real job," says the CEO of Zipcar.

Sources: Based on information in Rachel Barsky, "Career Tip Tuesday: How to Leverage Social Media in Your Job Search," *Fox News*, April 3, 2012, www.foxnews.com; Megan Marrs, "The First Step to Building Your Personal Brand," *Forbes*, February 14, 2012, www.forbes.com; Gerrit Hall, "4 Tips for Optimizing Your Resume with Social Media," *Mashable*, November 20, 2011, www.mashable.com; Scott Kirsner, "Social Media Advice for Job-Seekers," *Boston Globe*, September 9, 2011, www.boston.com.

© VICHIE81/SHUTTERSTOCK.COM

How do companies find the right employee? Answer: More and more companies are using social media sites to recruit employees. Sites like LinkedIn, the largest social network for professionals, are often used by both large and small companies to advertise current job openings and reach out to potential employees located not only in the United States, but also in other parts of the world.

employers using the site can save time, reduce their recruiting costs, and see more information about individual candidates. Companies like Accenture, Ford, General Electric, Home Depot, IBM, and Oracle have all had recruiting success with LinkedIn.[26]

DEVELOPING A SOCIAL MEDIA PLAN

Before developing a plan to use social media, it is important to determine how social media can improve the organization's overall performance and how it "fits" with a company's objectives and other promotional activities. For example, if a social media plan attempts to improve customer service, it needs to link to the company's other efforts to improve customer service.

Steps to Build a Social Media Plan

Once it is determined how social media links to the company's other activities, there are several steps that should be considered.

STEP 1: LISTEN TO DETERMINE OPPORTUNITIES Often social media is used to "listen" to what customers like and don't like about a company's products or services. For example, reading comments on social media sites can yield some insight into how consumers are reacting to a price increase for an existing product or service. Monitoring social media sites also allows managers and employees to enter the conversation and tell the company's side of the story. In addition, companies can monitor social media sites to gather information about competitors as well as what is being said about the industry.

After the listening phase, it is important to analyze the information to identify the company's strengths and weaknesses before taking the next step—setting objectives.

STEP 2: ESTABLISH SOCIAL MEDIA OBJECTIVES After listening to and analyzing the information obtained from social media sites, it is important to use that information to develop specific objectives. For social media, an objective is a statement about what a social media plan should accomplish. Each objective should be specific, measurable, achievable, realistic, and oriented toward the future.

For most companies, the most popular objectives are increasing brand awareness, acquiring new customers, introducing new products, retaining current customers, and gaining customer insight.[27] Other objectives that are often important include improving search engine ranking, showcasing public relations activities, increasing website traffic, and generating sales leads.[28] All objectives need to be linked to specific actions that can be used to accomplish each objective.

STEP 3: SEGMENT AND TARGET THE SOCIAL CUSTOMER Ideally, a company will have developed a customer profile that describes a typical customer in terms of age, income, gender, ethnicity, etc. When segmenting or targeting customers, it also helps to know how they think, how they spend their time, how much they buy, and how often they buy. More information about potential customers will help you develop a social media plan to achieve a company's objectives. Lack of information about customers can lead to wasted time and money and the inability to successfully achieve the firm's social media objectives. For example, most companies feel that they must use Facebook and Twitter. But if their core customer does not use these social media sites, then it does not make sense to use them. Additionally it is important to really understand how customers use social media.

- Do they create content like photos, videos, blog posts, etc?
- Do they use social media for ratings and reviews?

- Do they post product reviews and ratings on Facebook accounts?
- Do they spend a lot of time using social media?

In fact, a business should consider all available and relevant information about potential and existing customers when creating a social media plan. Some of the information that can help you target just the "right" social media customer is illustrated in Figure 14-5.

STEP 4: SELECT SOCIAL MEDIA TOOLS The search for the right social media tool(s) usually begins with the company's social media objectives, outlined in Step 2. It also helps to review the target customer or segment of the market the company is trying to reach (Step 3). With this information, the next step is to choose the right social media tools to reach the right customers. A company can use social communities, blogs, photos, videos, podcasts, or games to reach potential or existing customers. For example, if the goal is to recruit college students for college entry-level jobs, LinkedIn may be a good choice. Remember, it is not necessary (or even advisable) to use all of the above tools. It is also possible for a business to build a social media community—especially when the objective is to fund local community projects or charities.

STEP 5: IMPLEMENT AND INTEGRATE THE PLAN Once social media tools have been identified, a company can implement and integrate the social

FIGURE 14-5 Types of Information That Can Help Target Different Social Media Customers

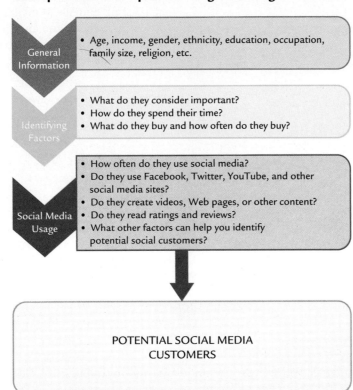

The more information you have about social media customers, the easier it is to develop a social media plan that targets the "right" customer.

General Information
- Age, income, gender, ethnicity, education, occupation, family size, religion, etc.

Identifying Factors
- What do they consider important?
- How do they spend their time?
- What do they buy and how often do they buy?

Social Media Usage
- How often do they use social media?
- Do they use Facebook, Twitter, YouTube, and other social media sites?
- Do they create videos, Web pages, or other content?
- Do they read ratings and reviews?
- What other factors can help you identify potential social customers?

POTENTIAL SOCIAL MEDIA CUSTOMERS

© CENGAGE LEARNING 2015

media plan. Because a social media plan doesn't necessarily have a start and stop date, it is different from traditional advertising campaigns. Some social media activities continue and have a life of their own. For example, Zappos, a very successful and well-respected online retailer, is a company who is always "on" in terms of its social media. Indeed, they do very little traditional advertising and instead rely on social media to promote products, monitor customer service, and enhance the company's reputation. Some companies, on the other hand, feel that it is important to have a mix of short- and long-term social media promotion. In this case, it's important to key the content and presentation to each social media site, and to coordinate the timing of promotions. For example, Coca-Cola is constantly adding new features to its Facebook page, which has more than 72 million likes. One day, the company might post its latest TV commercial. The next day, it might invite visitors to send branded greetings to friends from Coke's Facebook page. On Twitter, where Coca-Cola has over 1.8 million followers, it posts messages about new products and initiates discussions linked to its other promotional activities. Knowing that customers post 15,000 tweets about its brands every day, Coca-Cola monitors Twitter very carefully and responds quickly to questions and comments. Finally, like a growing number of companies, Coca-Cola integrates its social media and traditional marketing efforts for maximum impact. To illustrate, after the University of Alabama football team won its third Bowl Championship series title, Coca-Cola had a Coke Zero TV commercial ready for immediate release as a salute to the coach. The commercial was also posted on YouTube and other sites, with links to Coca-Cola's Facebook page and Twitter account, as well as to the University of Alabama's social media sites. To follow up on the Crimson Tide's win, Coca-Cola created commemorative packaging for Coke Zero beverages distributed in the Alabama area.[29]

To increase the effectiveness of social media, companies will often integrate online promotions with more traditional or offline promotions. For example, it is not unusual to see the Twitter icon at the end of a television commercial. This signals to consumers that more information about the product or service is provided on Twitter. Indeed, as companies increase the amount of money spent on digital marketing and social media, they will attempt to tie online and offline promotions together in order to get "more bang for the buck."

Measuring and Adapting a Social Media Plan

Because social media is a relatively new method of reaching customers, many companies struggle when attempting to measure social media. Often companies use the same measurements that have been used with long-established media channels like television and radio to determine the effect of social media on the customer's awareness of the company or a specific brand and if sales (and profits) are increasing. Generally, there are two types of social media measurement. While both quantitative and qualitative measurements can be used, most companies tend to use quantitative measurements.

Technology that satisfies needs online. Both large and small businesses are using social media to sell products and services to customers 24 hours a day and seven days a week. As an added bonus, today's technology can reach potential and existing customers any place in the world as long as customers have access to the Internet.

DAVID J. GREEN - LIFESTYLE 2 / ALAMY

QUANTITATIVE SOCIAL MEDIA MEASUREMENT **Quantitative social media measurement** consists of using numerical measurements, such as counting the number of website visitors, number of fans and followers, number of leads generated, and the number of new customers. As discussed previously, Coca-Cola counts not only the number of social media likes and followers but also the number of times its brands are mentioned each day. Business-to-business marketers frequently set additional goals to track how social media activities lead to sales contacts and then to purchases. For example, before Hitachi Data Systems launched the "Be a Star" campaign to promote its data storage products for corporations, it set objectives for the number of times its campaign website would be viewed, the number of contacts in social media, and the number of leads to be generated for the sales force. The six-month campaign combined a special website, a dedicated Facebook fan page, tweets identified with the campaign's hashtag, paid online advertising, and comments on the company's LinkedIn site. "Be a Star" campaign wound up exceeding all of Hitachi's objectives. It delivered 30,000 website views, sparked 9,000 social media dialogues with customers, and generated 359 sales leads.[30] Table 14-1 shows a few popular quantitative ways to measure social media.

A number of companies are using key performance indicators to measure their social media activities. **Key performance indicators (KPIs)** are measurements that define and measure the progress of an organization toward achieving its objectives. Generally, KPIs are *quantitative* (based on numbers like the number of Twitter followers).

If measuring the success or failure of social media activities with KPIs, the first step is to connect KPIs with objectives. The second step is to set a benchmark—a number that shows what success should look like. For example, Ford said that if 144,000 people visited the Ford Fiesta website within a specified time, it would indicate that the company's social media plan to introduce the new subcompact car to Millennials was successful. When measured, more than 300,000 people had visited the website.[31] Simply put: The company's social media plan was successful because it surpassed the original benchmark.

QUALITATIVE SOCIAL MEDIA MEASUREMENT **Qualitative social media measurement** is the process of accessing the opinions and beliefs about a brand. This process primarily uses sentiment analysis to categorize what is being said about a company. **Sentiment analysis** is a measurement that uses technology to detect

quantitative social media measurement using numerical measurements, such as counting the number of website visitors, number of fans and followers, number of leads generated, and the number of new customers

key performance indicators (KPIs) measurements that define and measure the progress of an organization toward achieving its objectives

qualitative social media measurement the process of accessing the opinions and beliefs about a brand and primarily uses sentiment analysis to categorize what is being said about a company

sentiment analysis a measurement that uses technology to detect the moods, attitudes, or emotions of people who experience a social media activity

TABLE 14-1 Quantitative Measurements for Selected Social Media Websites

Type of Social Media	Typical Measurements
Blogs	• Unique visitors • Number of views • Ratio of visitors to posted comments
Twitter	• Number of followers • Number of tweets and retweets • Click through rate (CTR) of tweeted links • Visits to website from tweeted links
Facebook	• Number of fans • Number of likes • Number of comments • Growth of wall response • Visits to websites from Facebook links
YouTube	• Number of videos • Number of visitors • Ratio of comments to the number of videos uploaded • Number of embedded links

© CENGAGE LEARNING 2015

the mood, attitudes, or emotions of people who experience a social media activity. Other measurements for determining customer sentiment include:

- *Customer satisfaction score*—defined as the relative satisfaction of customers.
- *Issue resolution rate*—the percentage of customer service inquiries resolved satisfactorily using social media.
- *Resolution time*—defined as the amount of time taken to resolve customer service issues.

When compared to quantitative measurement, it should be noted that many of these qualitative social media measurements are more subjective in nature.

The Cost of Maintaining a Social Media Plan

Basic Assumption: Social media is not free and can be quite expensive. Because social media costs both time and money, it is important to measure the success of a social media plan and make adjustments and changes if needed. Based on quantitative and qualitative measurements, the company may also try to determine if it is getting a positive return on its investment in social media.

After reviewing results for social media activities against pre-established benchmarks, it may be necessary to make changes and update the plan to increase the effectiveness of the social media plan. A social media plan, for example, must provide current and up-to-date information in order to keep customers coming back to see what's new. Without updates, customers lose interest and the amount of returning customers can drop dramatically. After all, one of the major objectives of social media activities is to provide customers and stakeholders with current and useful information about the company and its products or services. Once it is determined that updates and changes are needed, many of the same steps described in this section may be used to improve a firm's social media plan. It is also important to create future social media plans based on what worked and what didn't work in previous plans.

Social media is particularly important to businesses that use e-business to sell their products and services online. In the next section, we take a close look at how e-business firms are organized, satisfy needs online, and earn profits.

Concept Check

✓ What are the steps required to develop a social media plan?

✓ What is the difference between quantitative and qualitative measurements? Which type of measurement do you think is the most reliable when measuring the effectiveness of a company's social media plan?

Learning Objective

5 Explain the meaning of e-business.

e-business (electronic business) the organized effort of individuals to produce and sell, for a profit, the goods and services that satisfy society's needs *through the facilities available on the Internet*

DEFINING E-BUSINESS

In Chapter 1, we defined *business* as the organized effort of individuals to produce and sell, for a profit, the goods and services that satisfy society's needs. In a simple sense, then, **e-business** or **electronic business**, can be defined as the organized effort of individuals to produce and sell, for a profit, the goods and services that satisfy society's needs *through the facilities available on the Internet*. Sometimes people use the term *e-commerce* instead of *e-business*. In a strict sense, e-business is used when you're talking about all business activities and practices conducted on the Internet by an individual firm or industry. On the other hand, e-commerce is a part of e-business and usually refers only to buying and selling activities conducted online. In this chapter, we generally use the term *e-business* because of its broader definition and scope.

Organizing e-Business Resources

As noted in Chapter 1, to be organized, a business must combine *human, material, informational*, and *financial resources*. This is true of e-business, too (see Figure 14-6), but in this case, the resources may be more specialized than in a typical business. For example, people who can design, create, and maintain websites are only a fraction of the specialized human resources required by e-businesses. Material resources must include specialized computers, sophisticated equipment and software, and high-speed

FIGURE 14-6 Combining e-Business Resources

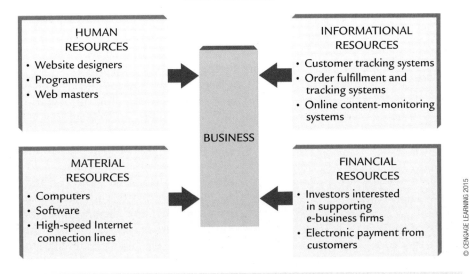

While all businesses use four resources (human, material, informational, and financial), these resources are typically more specialized when used in an e-business.

Internet connections. Computer programs that track the number of customers who view a firm's website are generally among the specialized informational resources required. Financial resources, the money required to start and maintain the firm and allow it to grow, usually reflect greater participation by individual entrepreneurs, venture capitalists, and investors willing to invest in a high-tech firm instead of conventional financial sources such as banks.

In an effort to reduce the cost of specialized resources that are used in e-business, many firms have turned to outsourcing. **Outsourcing** is the process of finding outside vendors and suppliers that provide professional help, parts, or materials at a lower cost. For example, a firm that needs specialized software to complete a project may turn to an outside firm located in another part of the United States, India, or an Eastern European country.

outsourcing the process of finding outside vendors and suppliers that provide professional help, parts, or materials at a lower cost

Satisfying Needs Online

Today more and more people are using computers, the Internet, and social media as a way to connect with people. The Internet can also be used to purchase products or services. Let's start with two basic assumptions.

- The Internet has created some new customer needs that did not exist before the creation of the Internet.
- e-Businesses can satisfy those needs, as well as more traditional ones.

Restoration Hardware (www.restorationhardware.com), for instance, gives customers anywhere in the world access to the same virtual store of hardware and decorative items. In

Want to shop 24 hours a day, seven days a week? Then go to Amazon's Website. Although Amazon originally was created to sell books online, today it's so much more. Amazon's product mix has expanded and now you can buy movies, products for the home, clothing, games, software, and even pet supplies. In fact, there's a good chance Amazon has the products you want. To take a look, go to www.amazon.com.

Entrepreneurial Success

Starting an Online Farmers' Market

How can grocery stores, restaurants, and consumers find out which local farmers have fresh foods for sale on any given day, get the price, and make a deal? This was a challenge that entrepreneur Heather Hilleren understood first-hand. During her years as a team leader for Whole Foods in Madison, Wisconsin, she saw how many steps were needed to identify local sources, confirm product availability, and check up-to-date prices before a purchase could be completed.

Hilleren realized that an online farmers' market could streamline the process for both buyers and sellers. In 2005, the year she completed her MBA at University of Wisconsin Business School, she launched Local Dirt (www.localdirt.com) as an online marketplace for restaurants, retailers, and consumers who want to buy fresh foods from local producers.

Today, more than 35,000 farms, farm cooperatives, and farmers' markets participate in Local Dirt, selling fruits, vegetables, poultry, and other locally produced foods to individuals, buying clubs, restaurants, wholesalers, and retailers. With a few clicks, farmers can list their seasonal items for sale—and, with a few clicks, buyers can place an order and arrange delivery.

Local Dirt has also teamed up with Locavore to offer a free app for locating local producers and determining which items are in season at any given time. Farmers can use the app to promote themselves and their local specialties. Day by day, more buyers and sellers are signing up with Local Dirt to save time, save money, and support local businesses.

Sources: Based on information in Roya Wolverson, "The Disrupters: Heather Hilleren, Local Dirt," *Time*, October 8, 2012, http://ideas.time.com; Danielle Gould, "Local Dirt Offers Up Local Farm Mapping and in Season Food Data," *Forbes*, March 28, 2012, www.forbes.com; Gwen Moran, "Online Network for Local Farmers Hits Pay Dirt," *Entrepreneur*, October 20, 2010, www.entrepreneur.com; http://localdirt.com.

addition to purchasing products, the Internet can be used by both individuals and business firms to obtain information. For example:

- Internet users can access newspapers, magazines, and radio and television programming at a time and place convenient to them.
- The Internet provides the opportunity for two-way interaction between an Internet firm and the viewer. For example, the CNN news site (www.cnn.com) and other news-content sites encourage dialogue among users.
- Customers can respond to information on the Internet by requesting more information or posing specific questions, which may lead to purchasing a product or service.
- Finally, the Internet allows customers to choose the content they are offered. Knowing the interests of a customer allows an Internet firm to direct appropriate, smart advertising to a specific customer. For the advertiser, knowing that its advertisements are being directed to the most likely customers represents a better way to spend advertising dollars.

Creating e-Business Profit

Business firms can increase profits either by increasing sales revenue or by reducing expenses through a variety of e-business activities.

INCREASING SALES REVENUE Each source of sales revenue flowing into a firm is referred to as a **revenue stream.** One way to increase revenues is to sell merchandise on the Internet. Because the opportunity to shop on the Internet is virtually unrestricted, traditional retailers like Macy's (www.macys.com) and Walmart (www.walmart.com) can obtain additional revenue by selling to a global customer base 24 hours a day, seven days a week. However, shifting revenues earned from customers inside a real store to revenues earned from these same customers online does not create any real new revenue for a firm. The goal is to find *new customers* and generate *new sales* so that *total revenues are increased.*

revenue stream a source of revenue flowing into a firm

Intelligent information systems also can help to generate sales revenue for Internet firms such as Amazon.com (www.amazon.com). Such systems store information about each customer's purchases, along with a variety of other information about the buyer's preferences. Using this information, the system can assist the customer the next time he or she visits the website. For example, if the customer has bought a Carrie Underwood CD in the past, the system might suggest CDs by similar artists who have either appeared on *American Idol* or won Country Music Awards.

Although some customers may not make a purchase online, the existence of the firm's website and the services and information it provides may lead to increased sales in the firm's physical stores. For example, Honda's website (www.honda.com) can provide basic comparative information for shoppers so that they are better prepared for their visit to an automobile showroom.

Concept Check

- ✓ What are the four major factors contained in the definition of e-business?
- ✓ How do e-businesses generate revenue streams, reduce expenses, and earn a profit?

In addition to selling products or services online, e-business revenue streams are created by advertising placed on Web pages and by subscription fees charged for access to online services and content. For example, Hoover's (www.hoovers.com), a comprehensive source for company and industry information, makes some of its online content free for anyone who visits the site, but more detailed information is available only by paid subscription. In addition, Hoover's receives revenue from companies acting as sponsors who advertise their products and services on the site.

Many Internet firms that distribute news, magazine and newspaper articles, and similar content generate revenue from commissions earned from sellers of products linked to the site. Online shopping malls, for example, now provide groups of related vendors of electronic equipment and computer hardware and software with a new method of selling their products and services. In many cases, the vendors share online sales revenues with the site owners.

REDUCING EXPENSES Reducing expenses is the second major way in which e-business can help to increase profitability. Providing online access to information that customers want can reduce the cost of dealing with customers. Sprint (www.sprint.com), for instance, is just one company that maintains an extensive website where potential customers can learn more about products and services, and where current customers can access personal account information, send questions to customer service, and purchase additional products or services. With such extensive online services, Sprint does not have to maintain as many physical store locations as it would without these online services. We examine more examples of how e-business contributes to profitability throughout this chapter, especially as we focus on some of the business models for activity on the Internet.

Personal Apps

What Do e-Businesses Sell?

These days, you can find e-businesses that sell almost anything. Many will help you recognize a new need by offering free trials of apps, games, or other digital products. This is a great way to find out whether the digital product is useful, convenient, and worth buying.

FUNDAMENTAL MODELS OF E-BUSINESS

Learning Objective
6 Understand the fundamental models of e-business.

One way to get a better sense of how businesses are adapting to the opportunities available on the Internet is to identify e-business models. A **business model** represents a group of common characteristics and methods of doing business to generate sales revenues and reduce expenses. Each of the models discussed in the following text represents a primary e-business model. Regardless of the type of business model, planning often depends on if the e-business is a new firm or an existing firm adding an online presence—see Figure 14-7. It also helps to keep in mind that in order to generate sales revenues and earn profits, a business—especially an e-business—must meet the needs of its customers.

business model represents a group of common characteristics and methods of doing business to generate sales revenues and reduce expenses

Business-to-Business (B2B) Model

Some firms use the Internet mainly to conduct business with other businesses. These firms are generally referred to as having a **business-to-business (or B2B) model**.

When examining B2B firms, two clear types emerge. In the first type, the focus is simply on facilitating sales transactions between businesses. For example, Dell

business-to-business (or B2B) model a model used by firms that conduct business with other businesses

The approach taken to creating an e-business plan will depend on whether you are establishing a new Internet business or adding an online component to an existing business.

SUCCESSFUL E-BUSINESS PLANNING

Starting a new Internet business	Building an online presence for an existing business

- Will the new e-business provide a product or service that meets customer needs?
- Who are the new firm's potential customers?
- How do promotion, pricing, and distribution affect the new e-business?
- Will the potential market generate enough sales and profits to justify the risk of starting an e-business?

- Is going online a logical way to increase sales and profits for the existing business?
- Are potential online customers different from the firm's traditional customers?
- Will the new e-business activities complement the firm's traditional activities?
- Does the firm have the time, talent, and financial resources to develop an online presence?

© CENGAGE LEARNING 2015

M40S PHOTOS / ALAMY

A new way to reach business customers around the globe. Alibaba.com is a business-to-business (B2B) global trade site that makes it easy for millions of importers and exporters to buy and sell products and services online. Because it meets the needs of its customers, Alibaba.com has become a successful company with offices in more than 70 cities around the globe.

manufactures computers to specifications that customers enter on the Dell website (www.dell.com). A large portion of Dell's online orders are from corporate clients who are well informed about the products they need and are looking for fairly priced, high-quality computer products that will be delivered quickly. By dealing directly with Dell, customers eliminate costs associated with wholesalers and retailers, thereby helping to reduce the price they pay for equipment.

A second, more complex type of B2B model involves a company and its suppliers. Today, suppliers use the Internet to bid on products and services they wish to sell to a customer and learn about the customer's rules and procedures that must be followed. For example, Ford has developed a B2B model to link thousands of suppliers that sell the automobile maker parts, supplies, and raw materials worth millions of dollars each year. Although the B2B site is expensive to start and maintain, there are significant savings for Ford. Given the potential savings, it is no wonder that many other manufacturers and their suppliers are beginning to use the same kind of B2B systems that are used by the automaker.

Business-to-Consumer (B2C) Model

In contrast with the B2B model, firms such as Barnes and Noble (www.barnesandnoble .com) and online retailer Lands' End (www.landsend.com) clearly are focused on individual consumers. These companies are referred to as having a **business-to-consumer (or B2C) model**. In a B2C situation, understanding how consumers behave online is critical to a firm's success. Typically, a business firm that uses a B2C model must answer the following questions:

business-to-consumer (or B2C) model a model used by firms that focus on conducting business with individual consumers

- Will consumers use websites merely to simplify and speed up comparison shopping?
- Will consumers purchase services and products online or end up buying at a traditional retail store?
- What sorts of products and services are best suited for online consumer shopping?

In addition to providing round-the-clock global access to all kinds of products and services, B2C firms often attempt to build long-term relationships with their customers. Often, firms will make a special effort to make sure that the customer is satisfied and that problems, if any, are solved quickly. Specialized software also can help build good customer relationships. Tracking the decisions and buying preferences as customers navigate a website, for instance, helps management to make well-informed decisions about how best to serve online customers. In essence, this is Orbitz's (www.orbitz.com) online selling approach. By tracking and analyzing customer data, the online travel company can provide individualized service to its customers. Although a "little special attention" may increase the cost of doing business for a B2C firm, the customer's repeated purchases will repay the investment many times over.

Today, B2B and B2C models are the most popular business models for e-business. And yet, there are other business models that perform specialized e-business activities to generate revenues. Most of the business models described in Table 14-2 are modified versions of the B2B and B2C models.

> ## Concept Check
>
> ✓ What are the two fundamental e-business models?
>
> ✓ Assume that you are the owner of a small company that produces outdoor living furniture. Describe how you could use the B2C business model to sell your products to consumers.

TABLE 14-2 Other Business Models That Perform Specialized e-Business Activities

Although modified versions of B2B or B2C, these business models perform specialized e-business activities to generate revenues.	
Advertising e-business model	Advertisements that are displayed on a firm's website in return for a fee. Examples include pop-up and banner advertisements on search engines and other popular Internet sites.
Brokerage e-business model	Online marketplaces where buyers and sellers are brought together to facilitate an exchange of goods and services. One example is eBay (www.ebay.com), which provides a site for buying and selling virtually anything.
Consumer-to-consumer model	Peer-to-peer software that allows individuals to share information over the Internet. Examples include Bit Torrent (www.bittorrent.com), which allows users to exchange digital media files.
Subscription and pay-per-view e-business models	Content that is available only to users who pay a fee to gain access to a website. Examples include investment information provided by Standard & Poor's (www.netadvantage.standardandpoors.com) and business research provided by Forrester Research, Inc. (www.forrester.com).

© CENGAGE LEARNING 2015

Learning Objective

7 Identify the factors that will affect the future of the Internet, social media, and e-business.

THE FUTURE OF THE INTERNET, SOCIAL MEDIA, AND E-BUSINESS

Since the beginning of commercial activity on the Internet, developments in computer technology, social media, and e-business have been rapid and formidable with spectacular successes such as Facebook, Amazon, Google, eBay, and Pinterest. However, a larger-than-usual number of technology companies struggled or even failed during the economic crisis. Today, most firms involved in the Internet, social media, and e-business use a more intelligent approach to development. The long-term view held by the vast majority of analysts is that the Internet, social media, and e-business will continue to expand to meet the needs of businesses and consumers.

Internet Growth Potential

To date, only a small percentage of the global population uses the Internet. In June 2012, estimates suggest that about 2.4 billion of the 7 billion people in the world use the Web.[32] Clearly, there is much more growth opportunity. Americans comprise just over 10 percent of all Internet users.[33] Of the almost 314 million people making up the American population, 245 million use the Internet. With approximately 78 percent of the American population already using the Internet, potential growth in the United States is limited.[34] On the other hand, the number of Internet users in the world's developing countries is expected to increase dramatically.

Although the number of global Internet users is expected to increase, that's only part of the story. Perhaps the more important question is why people are using the Internet. Primary reasons for using the Internet include the ability to connect with other people, to obtain information, or to purchase a firm's products or services. Of particular interest to business firms is the growth of social media. For example, Facebook now has more than 1 billion users worldwide. And because only 13 percent of the world population currently uses Facebook, the number of Facebook users is expected to continue to increase for years to come.[35] And the number of users for other social media sites like LinkedIn, Google+, Twitter, Pinterest, are also expected to increase.

Experts also predict that the number of companies using e-business to increase sales and reduce expenses will continue to increase. Firms that adapt existing business models to an online environment will continue to dominate development. For example, books, CDs, clothing, hotel accommodations, car rentals, and travel reservations are products and services well suited to online buying and selling. These products or services will continue to be sold in the traditional way, as well as in a more cost-effective and efficient fashion over the Internet.

Ethical and Legal Concerns

The social and legal concerns for the Internet, social media, and e-business extend beyond those shared by all businesses. Essentially, the Internet is a new "frontier" without borders and without much control by governments or other organizations.

ETHICS AND SOCIAL RESPONSIBILITY Socially responsible and ethical behavior by individuals and businesses on the Internet are major concerns. For example, an ethically questionable practice in cyberspace is the unauthorized access and use of information discovered through computerized tracking of users once they are connected to the Internet. Essentially, a user may visit a website and unknowingly receive a small piece of software code called a **cookie**. This cookie can track where the user goes on the Internet and measure how long the user stays at any particular website. Although this type of software may produce valuable customer information, it also can be viewed as an invasion of privacy, especially since users may not even be aware that their movements are being monitored.

cookie a small piece of software sent by a website that tracks an individual's Internet use

Besides the unauthorized use of cookies to track online behavior, there are several other threats to users' privacy and confidentiality. Monitoring an employee's computer usage may be intended to help employers police unauthorized Internet use on company time. However, the same records can also give a firm the opportunity to observe what otherwise might be considered private and confidential information. Today, legal experts suggest that, at the very least, employers need to disclose the level of surveillance to their employees and consider the corporate motivation for monitoring employees' behavior.

Some firms also practice data mining. **Data mining** refers to the practice of searching through data records looking for useful information. Customer registration forms typically require a variety of information before a user is given access to a site. Based on an individual's information, data mining analysis can then provide what might be considered private and confidential information about individuals. For instance, assume an individual frequents a website that provides information about a life-threatening disease. If this information is sent to an insurance company, the company might refuse to insure this individual, thinking that there is a higher risk associated with someone who wants more information about this disease.

data mining the practice of searching through data records looking for useful information

INTERNET CRIME Because the Internet is often regarded as an unregulated frontier, both individuals and business users must be particularly aware of online risks and dangers. For example, a general term that describes software designed to infiltrate a computer system without the user's consent is **malware**. Malware is often based on the creator's criminal or malicious intent and can include computer viruses, spyware, deceptive adware, and other software capable of criminal activities. A more specific term used to describe disruptive software is computer virus. The potentially devastating effects of both malware and computer viruses have given rise to a software security industry.

malware a general term that describes software designed to infiltrate a computer system without the user's consent

In addition to the risk of computer viruses, identity theft is one of the most common computer crimes that impacts both individuals and business users. A recent study conducted by Javelin Strategy and Research determined that over 5 percent of Americans were victims of identity theft in just one year.[36] Most consumers are also concerned about fraud. Because the Internet allows easy creation of websites, access from anywhere in the world, and anonymity for the creator, it is almost impossible to know with certainty that the website, organization, or individuals that you believe you are interacting with are what they seem. As always, caveat emptor ("let the buyer beware") is a good suggestion to follow whether on the Internet or not.

cloud computing a type of computer usage in which services stored on the Internet is provided to users on a temporary basis

Future Challenges for Computer Technology, Social Media, and e-Business

Today, more information is available than ever before. Although individuals and business users may think we are at the point of information overload, the amount of information will only increase in the future. In order to obtain more information in the future, both individuals and business users must consider the cost of obtaining information and computer technology. In an effort to reduce expenses and improve accessibility, some companies and individuals are now using cloud computing. **Cloud computing** is a type of computer usage in which services stored on the Internet is provided to users on a temporary basis. When cloud computing is used,

© DEVY/SHUTTERSTOCK.COM

With technology, the sky is the limit. Just when you think technology can't change, it takes another step higher, and this time it's in the clouds. Cloud computing—a type of technology in which services stored on the Internet are provided to users on a temporary basis—can reduce expenses and improve accessibility for both businesses and individuals.

Concept Check

✓ Experts predict that the Internet will continue to expand along with related technologies. What effect will this expansion have on businesses in the future?

✓ Give an example of an unethical use of computer technology by a business.

✓ What is the difference between internal and external forces that affect an e-business? How do they change the way an e-business operates?

a third party makes processing power, software applications, databases, and storage available for on-demand use from anywhere. Instead of running software and storing data on their employer's computer network or their individual computers, employees log onto the third party's system and use (and pay for) only the applications and data storage they actually need. In addition to just cost, there are a number of external and internal factors that a business must consider.

Although the environmental forces at work are complex, it is useful to think of them as either *internal* or *external* forces that affect how a business uses computer technology. Internal environmental forces are those that are closely associated with the actions and decisions taking place within a firm. As shown in Figure 14-8, typical internal forces include a firm's planning activities, organizational structure, human resources, management decisions, information database, and available financing. A shortage of skilled employees needed for a specialized project, for instance, can undermine a firm's ability to sell its services to clients. Unlike the external environmental forces affecting the firm, internal forces such as this one are more likely to be under the direct control of management. In this case, management can either hire the needed staff or choose to pass over a prospective project. In addition to the obvious internal factors that affect how a company operates, a growing number of firms are concerned about how their use of technology affects the environment. The term **green IT** is now used to describe all of a firm's activities to support a healthy environment and sustain the planet. Many offices, for example, are reducing the amount of paper they use by storing data and information on computers.

In contrast, external environmental forces affect a company's use of technology and originate outside the organization. These forces are unlikely to be controllable by a company. Instead, managers and employees of a company generally will react to

FIGURE 14-8 Internal and External Forces That Affect an e-Business

Today, managers and employees of an e-business must respond to internal forces within the organization and external forces outside the organization.

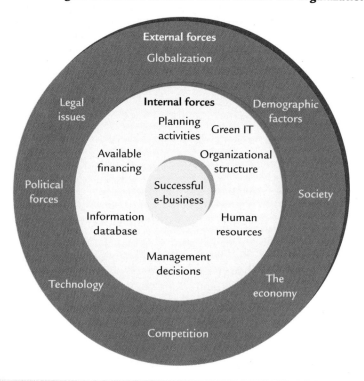

these forces, attempting to shield the organization from any undue negative effects and finding ways to take advantage of opportunities in an ever-changing technology environment. The primary external environmental forces affecting a company's use of technology include globalization, demographic, societal, economic, competitive, technological, and political and legal forces.

In this chapter, we have explored how both individuals and businesses use social media. We also examined how e-business is changing the way that firms do business. In Chapter 15, we examine a business firm's need for information and why accounting is a major source of information for business.

Summary

1 Examine why it is important for a business to use social media.

Millions of people of all ages use social media to interact with people and share ideas, personal information, and information about products and services. Today 69 percent of U.S. adults use some sort of social media platform like Facebook, LinkedIn, Google+, Twitter, or Pinterest according to a recent Pew Internet Research Study. The primary reason for using social media is to stay in touch with family and friends. Other reasons include reconnecting with friends and posting messages about what's in their lives. Early on, companies saw the potential in the sheer numbers of people using social media. Even though companies have used social media to share information about their products and services and improve customer service, many are still uncomfortable with this new method of communicating with customers because they do not have much control over what is said about their products or services.

2 Discuss how businesses use social media tools.

Companies use social media to connect with customers, listen to stakeholders, provide customer service, provide information to customers, and engage customers in product development. To share social content (information about products and services), companies can use blogs, photos, videos, and podcasts. In addition, social media also enables shoppers to access opinions, recommendations, and referrals from others within and outside their own social circle. Rating and review sites are based on the idea that people trust the opinions of others when it comes to purchasing products and services. Social games are another area of growth in social media. A social game (like Angry Birds or FarmVille)

is a multiplayer, competitive, goal-oriented activity with defined rules of engagement and online connectivity among a community of players. While some businesses elect to create their own game, others choose to place advertising into a game.

3 Explain the business objectives for using social media.

Although its popularity is a recent phenomenon, many businesses are already using social media to achieve important goals and objectives. In fact, there are many ways for businesses to use social media to take advantage of business opportunities to build connections with other businesses and consumers. For example, businesses can use social media to build a community. Social media communities are social networks based on the relationships among people. Today, there are social communities for every interest, ethnic group, and lifestyle. Different types of communities include both forums and wikis. Other reasons for using social media include crisis and reputation management, listening to stakeholders, targeting customers, social media marketing, generating new product ideas, and recruiting employees. For a business, social media marketing is especially important because it can not only develop customer awareness, but also obtain sales leads and increase actual sales.

4 Describe how businesses develop a social media plan.

Before developing a plan to use social media, it is important to determine how social media can improve the organization's overall performance and how it "fits" with a company's objectives and other promotional activities. Once it is determined how social media links to the company's other activities, the first step is to listen to what customers like and don't like about a company's products or services. Typically, the second step is to establish social media objectives that are specific, measurable, achievable, realistic, and time oriented. After listening and establishing objectives, the third step is to identify the customer or market segment a business is trying to reach with a social media promotion. The fourth step is to select the social media tool that will be used to reach customers. While it is not necessary (or even advisable) to use all of the available tools, a company can use social media communities, blogs, photos, videos, podcasts, or games to reach potential or existing customers. Once social media tools have been identified, a company can implement and integrate the social media plan.

Both quantitative and qualitative measurements can be used to determine the effectiveness of a social media plan. Quantitative social media measurement consists of using numerical measurements. Key performance indicators (KPIs), for example, are quantitative measurements. Qualitative measurement is the process of accessing the opinions and beliefs about a brand and primarily uses sentiment analysis to categorize what is being said about a company. Because social media costs both time and money, it is important to maintain, update, and measure the success of a social media plan and make adjustments and changes if needed.

5 Explain the meaning of e-business.

e-Business, or electronic business, can be defined as the organized effort of individuals to produce and sell, for a profit, the goods and services that satisfy society's needs *through the facilities available on the Internet.* The human, material, information, and financial resources that any business requires are highly specialized for e-business. In an effort to reduce the cost of e-business resources, many firms have turned to outsourcing.

Using e-business activities, it is possible to satisfy new customer needs created by the Internet as well as traditional ones in unique ways. Meeting customer needs is especially important when an e-business is trying to earn profits by increasing sales and reducing expenses. Each source of revenue flowing into the firm is referred to as a revenue stream.

6 Understand the fundamental models of e-business.

e-Business models focus attention on the identity of a firm's customers. Firms that use the Internet mainly to conduct business with other businesses generally are referred to as having a business-to-business, or B2B, model. When examining B2B firms, two clear types emerge. In the first type of B2B, the focus is simply on facilitating sales transactions between businesses. A second, more complex type of the B2B model involves a company and its suppliers. In contrast to the focus of the B2B model, firms such as Amazon or eBay clearly are focused on individual buyers and are thus referred to as having a business-to-consumer, or B2C, model. In a B2C situation, understanding how consumers behave online is critical to the firm's success. Successful B2C firms often make a special effort to build long-term relationships with their customers. While B2B and B2C models are the most popular e-business models, there are other models that perform specialized e-business activities to generate revenues (see Table 14-2).

7 Identify the factors that will affect the future of the Internet, social media, and e-business.

Since the beginning of commercial activity on the Internet, developments in computer technology, social media, and e-business have been rapid and formidable. Although a number of technology companies struggled or even failed during the economic crisis, most firms involved in computer technology, social media, and e-business today use a more intelligent approach to development. The long-term view held by the vast majority of analysts is that use of the Internet will continue to expand along with related technologies. Because approximately 78 percent of Americans now have access to the Internet, potential growth is limited in the United States. On the other hand, only 2.4 billion of the 7 billion people in the world use the Web. Clearly, the number of Internet users in the world's developing countries is expected to increase dramatically.

The future of computer technology and the Internet will be influenced by advances in technology, the increasing popularity of social media, and the increasing use of e-business. Other factors including ethics, social responsibility, and Internet crime will all impact the way that businesses and consumers use computer technology and the Internet. Although the environmental forces at work are complex, it is useful to think of them as either internal or external forces that affect how businesses use computer technology. Internal environmental forces are those that are closely associated with the actions and decisions taking place within a firm. In contrast, external environmental forces are those factors affecting an e-business originating outside an organization.

Key Terms

You should now be able to define and give an example relevant to each of the following terms:

social media (396)
social content sites (398)
blog (398)
media sharing sites (399)
podcasts (399)
social game (400)
social media
    communities (400)
forum (401)

wiki (401)
Millennials (402)
social media marketing (403)
inbound marketing (404)
crowdsourcing (404)
quantitative social media
    measurement (409)
key performance indicators
    (KPIs) (409)

qualitative social media
    measurement (409)
sentiment analysis
    (409)
e-business (electronic
    business) (410)
outsourcing (411)
revenue stream (412)
business model (413)

business-to-business (or
    B2B) model (413)
business-to-consumer (or
    B2C) model (415)
cookie (416)
data mining (417)
malware (417)
cloud computing (417)
green IT (418)

Discussion Questions

1. Given the fast pace of everyday life, most people often feel there is not enough time to do everything that needs to be done. Yet, people do find time to post personal information, photos, etc., on Facebook, Twitter, blogs, and other social media sites. Why do you think people are so fascinated with social media?

2. Assume you are the owner of a small company that produces a line of barbeque grills. Describe how you could use social media to connect with customers, improve customer service, increase sales, and reduce expenses.

3. How can a small cosmetics wholesaler located in Jacksonville, Florida use e-business and social media to increase its customer base, increase revenues, and reduce expenses?

4. Is outsourcing good for an e-business firm? The firm's employees? Explain your answer.

5. What distinguishes a B2B from a B2C e-business model?

6. Experts predict that the Internet, social media, and e-business will continue to expand along with related computer technologies. What effect will this expansion have on how businesses connect with customers in the future?

Test Yourself

Matching Questions

1. _____ Digital audio or video files that people listen to or watch online.

2. _____ People born after 1980 that are comfortable with technology, the Internet, and social media.

3. _____ The online interactions that allow people and businesses to share ideas, personal information, and information.

4. _____ A competitive activity with defined rules for a community of players.

5. _____ A website that pulls customers in to obtain more information.

6. _____ Allows users to upload multimedia content including photos, videos, and podcasts.

7. _____ Amazon.com makes a special effort to build long-term relationships with its customers.

8. _____ Software that tracks an individual's Internet use.

9. _____ All business activities that are conducted on the Internet.

10. _____ Its focus is to facilitate sales transactions between businesses.

    a. e-business
    b. media sharing sites
    c. podcasts
    d. inbound marketing
    e. social media
    f. Millennials
    g. social game
    h. business-to-business model
    i. business-to-consumer model
    j. revenue stream
    k. cookie
    l. malware

True False Questions

11. **T F** Just under 45 percent of U.S. adults use some sort of social media.

12. **T F** Engaging customers in generating new ideas for products or services is an unethical use of social media.

13. **T F** The cost to create and distribute photos, videos, and podcasts should be a consideration when a business is trying to decide if it should participate in media sharing.

14. **T F** Angry Birds is a popular blog.

15. **T F** A wiki is an online collaborative working space where people contribute content.

16. **T F** The two types of social media measurement are quantitative and qualitative.

17. **T F** Sources of revenue flowing into the firm are referred to as revenue channels.

18. **T F** Firms that tend to focus on conducting e-business with other businesses are referred to as having a B2B focus.

19. **T F** When General Electric uses the Internet to purchase materials from its suppliers, it is using a B2C business model.

20. **T F** Outsourcing is the process of finding outside vendors and suppliers that provide professional help, parts, or materials at a lower cost.

Multiple-Choice Questions

21. _____ Social media can most accurately be described as being about
   a. technology.
   b. people.
   c. the Web.
   d. new development.
   e. advertising.

22. _____ Which of the following describes an interactive community bulletin board?
   a. Blogs
   b. Podcasts
   c. Forums
   d. Social games
   e. Crowdsourcing

23. _____ What is a podcast?
   a. A multiplayer, competitive activity
   b. An interactive version of a community bulletin board
   c. A collaborative online working space
   d. A digital audio or video file
   e. A website to share information

24. _____ Which of the following companies was one of the early adopters of consumer ratings?
   a. Facebook
   b. Help.com
   c. MySpace
   d. Amazon
   e. SocialLiving

25. _____ Which of the following is the last step in building a social media plan?
   a. Establish social media objectives
   b. Listen to determine opportunities
   c. Segment and target the social media customer
   d. Select social media tools
   e. Implement and integrate the plan

26. _____ Each objective of a social media plan should be all of the following except
   a. measurable.
   b. specific.
   c. achievable.
   d. oriented toward the future.
   e. vague.

27. _____ Which of the following is *true* about social media measurement tools?
   a. Most companies use quantitative measurements.
   b. Companies should use the same measurements for online as for offline business activities.
   c. There are generally five types of social media measurement.
   d. Social media cannot be measured quantitatively.
   e. Most companies use qualitative measurements.

28. _____ A customer tracking system is an example of e-business _____ resources.
   a. human
   b. informational
   c. material
   d. financial
   e. supplemental

29. _____ What percentage of worldwide Internet users do Americans represent?
   a. 4
   b. 78
   c. 10
   d. 15
   e. 25

30. _____ Which of the types of resources needed for an e-business is Storybook.com most likely to receive from a venture capitalist?
   a. Software
   b. Human
   c. Financial
   d. Material
   e. Informational

Answers to the Test Yourself questions appear at the end of the book on page TY-2.

Video Case

Luke's Lobster: Entrepreneurs Use Social Networking to Claw Their Way Up the Food Chain

When Luke Holden decided to open up a restaurant in 2009, using social media to promote it seemed like a no-brainer. "Word-of-mouth from friends is stronger than any other form of advertising in my opinion," says the 27-year-old.

Holden didn't start out in the restaurant business, though. After graduating from Georgetown University, he went to work on Wall Street as a financial analyst. A couple of years later, the banking crisis hit. When many of his coworkers started getting laid off, he began thinking about a backup plan for himself.

One thing Holden had noticed about New York City was that there were no restaurants serving good lobster rolls for a decent price: "They were all selling for $24, but you got only a little lobster, a lot of mayo, and more filler," he says. The Maine native sensed an opportunity. Plus, he knew where to find a good lobster supplier: his dad, Jeff Holden, who owns a seafood processing company in Portland, Maine. Luke had worked for his father when he was younger. If he purchased seafood directly from his father, rather than through a wholesaler, he figured he could offer a big lobster roll for a small price.

Because the restaurant business in New York City is very competitive, Holden figured he better not quit his day job right away. Instead, he posted an ad on Craigslist to find a partner who could help him get the business up and running. That's how he came across Ben Conniff. Conniff was fresh out of Yale and looking to get into the restaurant business, too. After coming up with a business plan and raising some money, he and Holden hired some employees and opened Luke's Lobster, a tiny eatery in New York City's East Village. Conniff worked the day shift. Holden worked nights and weekends.

Fortunately, Luke's Lobster quickly found a following. Better yet, customers got online to rave about the restaurant's generously portioned rolls as well as their $15 price. Health- and environmentally conscious diners who want to know where their food is coming from were also attracted to the eatery. "We know the exact source of all our food," Holden says. "We can trace it from the bottom of the ocean to the East Village."

To further spread the word out about the restaurant, Holden and Conniff signed up with the social networking site Foursquare. Foursquare has a GPS-enabled, mobile-phone app that recommends businesses in the area where you're located based on what you and your friends in your network have said they like. People with the app can automatically "check in" with a business on Foursquare. They can let their friends know where they are and comment on their experience. When customers accumulate enough check-ins, they qualify for discounts and freebies. "Forget about loyalty cards and coupons. This makes it so it's more digital and virtual," Holden says about Foursquare. "It's a digital wallet that you can carry around, and it's constantly rewarding you."

In addition to using Foursquare to get customers in the door, Holden and Conniff use it to help manage Luke's. The data they get from Foursquare allows them to categorize their customers by gender, age, and arrival time. Analyzing the arrival times of customers helps the restaurant ramp up for busy periods and offer specials when business is slow.

The entrepreneurs didn't limit their social networking to Foursquare, however. They use a combination of Facebook, Twitter, Tumblr, Pinterest, and Vimeo to post photos and videos about Luke's, make announcements about specials and contests, and provide links to the restaurant's website and blog. The crew at Luke's also "listens" to what people on the Web are saying about the restaurant and replies to them. "Responding to folks who mention us is our way of bringing them into the family and incorporating their feedback into our business," Holden says.

Six months after setting up shop in the East Village, business was so good that Holden and Conniff were able to open up a second location. At that point, Holden felt comfortable enough to leave the banking business. Since then, the men have opened up more Luke's Lobster restaurants in New York City, and in Washington, D.C. In 2011, the Luke's chain rolled out a food truck in the New York area. The employees who work the truck use Twitter to update customers on its whereabouts.

Thanks to a good product and social networking strategy, New York City has been awash with information about Luke's Lobster. HauteLiving.com even named it the city's best lobster restaurant. What's interesting is that without doing any traditional advertising whatsoever, Holden and Conniff have achieved so much success—including landing a spot on the *Today Show* with Kathie Lee Gifford. With a little more angling, it's looking like they could net some cookbook or reality TV offers.[37]

Questions

1. What factors have contributed to the success of Luke's Lobster?
2. Why have Holden and Conniff shunned traditional advertising? Is that a good idea? Why or why not?
3. Pick another type of business and describe how it could use social media networking to promote its products or services?

Building Skills for Career Success

1. Social Media Exercise

The purpose of the first part of this chapter is to introduce you to social media and its importance to business. After reading the chapter, choose a business that you either know something about, want to start, or is the company you already work for.

Assignment

1. Develop a social media plan for that business using what you learned in this chapter.
2. What are the objectives of your social media plan?
3. What social media tools would you choose and why? How would you measure success?
4. Prepare a report that describes how this exercise has helped you understand the material in this chapter.

2. Building Team Skills

After graduating from college with a degree in marketing, your first job was working in the marketing department for a fast-food chain located in the southwestern part of the United States. After three years, you were promoted and became director of the chain's social media program. While monitoring posts about the company on Facebook and Twitter, you notice the following post from one of the firm's former employees.

> "Got fired today, but I was tired of serving low-quality food with expired expiration dates. Don't eat there or any of the chain's restaurants unless you want to get deathly ill."

To make matters worse, a couple of other employees who had recently been fired chimed in and made posts of a similar nature.

Assignment

1. Working in small teams, create a response that can be used to convince consumers that your company is committed to food freshness and quality and that these posts were made by employees who had been terminated.
2. Choose a spokesperson that will read your response to the rest of the class.
3. As a class, discuss the pros and cons of each response developed by each team.
4. Ask all members of the class to vote on the best response.
5. Finally, each team should prepare a report for the company's management that describes what happened and the response that was made to tell the company's side of this issue and restore consumer confidence in the firm's food products.

3. Researching Different Careers

Today, there are a wide assortment of career opportunities in companies that are involved in technology, social media, and e-business. In addition to existing businesses, there are new technology companies springing up every day. In many cases, these firms want people with a fresh outlook on how technology, social media, and e-business companies can differentiate their products or services from those of other companies in the same industry. They often prefer individuals without preconceived notions about how to proceed. Website managers, designers, creative artists, and content specialists are just a few of the positions available. Many large online job sites, such as Monster.com, can help you to find out about employment opportunities and the special skills required for various jobs.

Assignment

1. Identify a website that provides information about careers in technology, social media, or e-business.
2. Summarize the positions that appear to be in high demand.
3. What are some of the special skills required to fill these jobs?
4. What salaries and benefits typically are associated with these positions?
5. Which job seems most appealing to you personally? Why?

Endnotes

1. Based on information from The Domino's website at www.dominos.com accessed April 15, 2013; Brad Tuttle, "It's Official: We're Comfortable Ordering Pizza Online," *Time*, June 13, 2012, http://business.time.com; "Extra Large: CEO Has Global Vision for Media-Savvy Domino's," *Crain's Detroit Business*, November 7, 2011, p. 18; Lizzy Alfs, "$1B Milestone," *AnnArbor.com*, June 11, 2012, www.annarbor.com; Vanessa Van Landingham, "Domino's Unveils New Logo, New Unit Design," *Nation's Restaurant News*, September 3, 3012, p. 4.
2. Danny Goodwin, "LinkedIn Now Has More Than 200 Million Members," *ClickZ*, January 11, 2013, www.clickz.com; Joanna Brenner, "Pew Internet: Social Networking (Full Detail)," *Pew Internet and American Life Project*, November 13, 2012, www.pewinternet.org; Stephanie Mlot, "Infographic: 365 Days of Social Media," *PC Magazine*, January 3, 3013, www.pcmag.com.
3. Candice Choi and Christina Rexrode, "Facebook Users Hit 'Like,' Stores Jump into Action," *Associated Press*, December 18, 2012, www.google.com/hostednews.
4. Lauren Hockenson, "Making Fashion Personal: Macy's Smart Social Media Strategy," *Mashable*, March 14, 2012, http://mashable.com; Mark Fidelman, "IBM Study: If You Don't Have a Social CEO, You're Going to Be Less Competitive," *Forbes*, May 22, 2012, www.forbes.com.
5. Suzanne Kapner, "Citi Won't Sleep on Customer Tweets," *Wall Street Journal*, October 4, 2012, www.wsj.com; Gadi Benmark and Dan Singer, "Turn Customer Care into 'Social Care' to Break Away from the Competition," *Harvard Business Review*, December 19, 2012, http://blogs.hbr.org.
6. Michael Miller, *The Ultimate Web Marketing Guide* (Indianapolis: QUE, 2011), p. 315.

7. Shashi Bellamkonda, "D.C.-Area CEO Blogs to Follow," *Washington Business Journal*, December 24, 2012, www.bizjournals.com/washington; Michael S. Rosenwald, "Bill Marriott: Chairman of the Blog," *Washington Post*, June 18, 2012, www.washingtonpost.com.

8. Amy Dusto, "Consumers Increasingly Trust Online Reviews," *Internet Retailer*, April 17, 2012, www.internetretailer.com.

9. Jeff Higley, "Social Media Creates Revenue? Jury's Still Out," *Hotel News Now*, July 12, 2012, www.hotelnewnow.com; Adam Leposa, "Reputation Management: Metrics Matter in Online Reviews," *Hotel Management*, November 2012, p. 54.

10. Tracy L. Tuten and Michael R. Solomon, *Social Media Marketing* (Upper Saddle River, NJ: Pearson Publishing, 2013), p. 147.

11. Dave Chaffey, "2011 Marketing Trends," the Smart Insights website at www.smartinsights.com/digital-p.marketing-strategy/online-marketing-mix/2011-digital-marketing-trends/ accessed March 1, 2012.

12. Stephanie Mlot, "Angry Birds Lands 30 Million Christmas Week Downloads," *PC Magazine*, January 3, 2013, www.pcmag.com; Sven Grundberg, "Finland's Angry Birds Flock Takes Wing," *Wall Street Journal*, November 27, 2012, www.wsj.com; Shara Tibken, "Zynga Revs Up Mobile Ads with Honda Campaign," *CNet*, October 16, 2012, http://news.cnet.com.

13. Tracy L. Tuten and Michael R. Solomonm, *Social Media Marketing* (Upper Saddle River, NJ: Pearson Publishing, 2013), p. 5.

14. Brandon Gutman, "2012 Success Story: Chase Community Giving," *Forbes*, January 14, 2013, www.forbes.com; Cody Switzer, "Chase Online Contest Draws Ire for Technical Glitches," *Chronicle of Philanthropy*, September 10, 2012, http://philanthropy.com; www.facebook.com/ChaseCommunityGiving.

15. Stephanie Rosendahl, "Top 5 Tips for Reputation Management through Social Media," the Articlebase website at http://articlebase.com/internet-marketingarticles/top-5-tips-for-reputation-managmenet-through-social-media-4997832.html, accessed July 7, 2011.

16. Nick Wingfield and Claire Cain Miller, "Google Gains from Creating Apps for the Opposition," *New York Times*, January 13, 2013, www.nytimes.com; Bob Brown, "iOS 6 Maps Twitter Account Skewers Apple, Gets Suspended, Resurrects Itself," *Network World*, September 20, 2012, www.networkworld.com; Ian Sherr, "Apple Makes a Wrong Turn as Users Blast Map Switch," *Wall Street Journal*, September 28, 2012, www.wsj.com; "Apple's Maps Fiasco and the Mobile Arms Race," *Knowledge@Wharton*, October 10, 2012, http://knowledge.wharton.upenn.edu.

17. Emily Bryson York, "Domino's Reports 14 Percent Same-Store Sales Hike for First Quarter," the Advertising Age website at www.advertisingage.com, accessed April 1, 2012.

18. Gemma Taylor, "Burberry Total Sales Rise 9% in Q3," *Retail Gazette*, January 15, 2013, www.retailgazette.co.uk; Nina Easton, "Angela Ahrendts: The Secrets Behind Burberry's Growth," *Fortune*, June 19, 2012, http://management.fortune.cnn.com; Maureen Morrison, "A Focus on Digital Makes Burberry Relevant to a New Generation," *Advertising Age*, December 10, 2012, www.adage.com; Caryn Rousseau, "Classic Fashion Brand Burberry Goes Digital," *Bloomberg*, December 26, 2012, www.bloomberg.com; Di Gallo, "Luxury Brand Burberry Moves Beyond the Tartan," *Social Media Week*, August 14, 2012, http://socialmediaweek.org; Emily Cronin, "Burberry: Entrenched in the Digisphere," *Telegraph (London)*, November 24, 2012, http://fashion.telegraph.co.uk.

19. Vipin Mayar and Geoff Ramsey, *Digital Impact: The Two Secrets to Online Marketing Success* (Hoboken, NJ: John Wiley & Sons, 2011), pp. 141–43.

20. Tracy L. Tuten and Michael R. Solomon, *Social Media Marketing* (Upper Saddle River, NJ: Pearson Publishing, 2013), p. 5.

21. Shar VanBoskirk with Christine Spivey Overby, "US Interactive Marketing Forecast 2011 to 2016," the Forrester Research website at www.forrester.com accessed August 24, 2011.

22. "Consumers Spend Less Time with Traditional Media: US Interactive Marketing Forecast 2011 to 2016," the Forrester Research website at www.forrester.com accessed August 24, 2011.

23. Thomas Steenburgh, Jill Avery, and Naseem Dahoud, "Hubspot: Inbound Marketing and Web 2.0," *Harvard Business School*, January 24, 2011, 1–21.

24. The Dorito's Crash the Super Bowl website at www.crashthesuperbowl.com accessed May 2, 2012.

25. The Starbucks Idea website at www.mystarbucksidea.com accessed April 27, 2012.

26. Christopher Heine, "LinkedIn Hits Big Milestone; Brands Could Flock Next," *AdWeek*, January 9, 2013, www.adweek.com.

27. Melissa Barker, Donald Barker, Nicholas Bormann, and Krista E. Neher, *Social Media Marketing: A Strategic Approach* (Mason, OH: Cengage Publishing, 2013), p. 31.

28. Ibid.

29. Karlene Lukovitz, "Coke Zero Ad Salutes Crimson Tide Coach," *Media Post*, January 8, 2013, www.mediapost.com; Patricia Sellers, "Coke's Facebook Expert on How to Build a 'Social' Brand, *Fortune*, October 17, 2012, http://postcards.blogs.fortune.cnn.com; Jessi Hempel, "How Coke Got 52 Million Facebook Likes," *Fortune*, October 2, 2012, http://tech.fortune.cnn.com.

30. Kate Maddox, "Tob B2B Trends for 2013," *BtoB Online*, January 11, 2013, www.btobonline.com; Kate Maddox, "Hitachi Data Systems Extends Social Reach to Generate Leads," *BtoB Online*, May 14, 2012, www.btobonline.com.

31. John Deighton and Leora Kornfeld, "The Ford Fiesta," *Harvard Business School*, June 20, 2011, 1–24.

32. The Internet World Stats website at www.internetworldstats.com accessed April 29, 2012.

33. Ibid.

34. Ibid.

35. Ibid.

36. The Javelin Strategy and Research website at www.idsafety.net accessed April 29, 2012.

37. Based on information in the Luke's Lobster website at www.lukeslobster.com accessed April 15, 2013; "Foursquare: Social Media for Small Businesses," *CBSNews*, June 13, 2011, www.cbsnews.com; Katy Finneran, "Food Trucks' Tasty Tweets," *FOXBusiness*, May 13, 2011, http://foxbusiness.com; Dana Schuster, "On a Roll!" *New York Post*, May 11, 2011, www.nypost.com; Alexandra Wolfe, "Luke Holden's Luke's Lobster," *Businessweek*, October 14, 2010, www.businessweek.com; Benjamin Wallace, "On a Roll," *New York Magazine*, June 20, 2010, http://nymag.com.

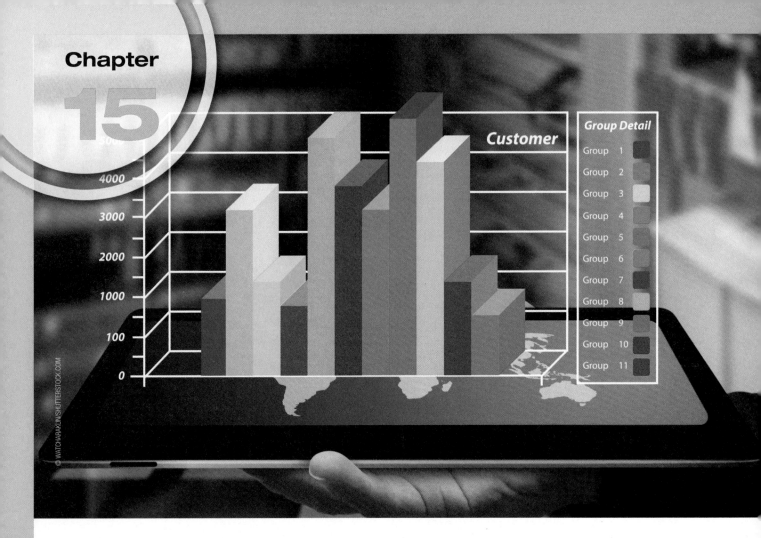

Using Management and Accounting Information

Why Should You Care?

Question: How important is management and accounting information for a successful business? Answer: It would be extremely difficult to manage even a small business without management and accounting information.

Learning Objectives

Once you complete this chapter, you will be able to:

1 Examine how information can reduce risk when making a decision.

2 Discuss management's information requirements.

3 Outline the five functions of an information system.

4 Explain why accurate accounting information and audited financial statements are important.

5 Read and interpret a balance sheet.

6 Read and interpret an income statement.

7 Describe business activities that affect a firm's cash flow.

8 Summarize how managers evaluate the financial health of a business.

Intuit Takes Technology into the Future

When Intuit (www.intuit.com) first introduced Quicken software in 1983 to help consumers and small businesses manage their money, the IBM PC was only two years old, software was sold on diskettes, and the World Wide Web hadn't even been invented. Now, three decades later, Intuit uses cloud computing, mobile apps, and other cutting-edge technologies to deliver specialized software and services that help small businesses handle accounting, finance, payroll, and other functions. It also offers a variety of products for consumers, including tax preparation software (TurboTax) and a free personal finance website (www.mint.com).

Worldwide, Intuit rings up over $4 billion in annual sales and invests hundreds of millions of dollars yearly to research and develop new software and new services. The company has also been acquiring other companies and products to expand the high-tech tools it offers for small businesses. For example, it recently purchased Demandforce, which provides systems for managing marketing and communications data and programs. By integrating Demandforce's marketing systems with its best-selling QuickBooks accounting system, Intuit enables small businesses to analyze historical transaction data and make more informed decisions about implementing customer-outreach programs.

Today, Intuit delivers most of its services on demand, via the Internet. As a result, small businesses have the option of using desktop computers, smart phones, or tablet computers to upload data, check trends, create reports, or schedule financial transactions in the office or on the go. In the coming years, Intuit plans to expand its in-the-cloud services through partnerships with other companies. Once these connections are in place, customers will be able to log in once for access to any of the partners' systems and services, and receive a single bill for all the services they utilize. This added efficiency will allow small businesses more time to focus on serving *their* customers, while helping Intuit increase profits and strengthen customer relationships for continued success.[1]

Did You Know?

Intuit rings up over $4 billion in annual sales worldwide and invests hundreds of millions of dollars each year to research and develop new products and technology.

Information—that's what this chapter is all about! We begin this chapter with information about Intuit—the company profiled in the Inside Business feature. For this financial software firm, one of its most important goals is to provide information that enables both business clients and consumers to manage their finances. Although Intuit was founded back in 1983, today the firm has evolved into a global leader in the financial software industry because of its investment in research to develop not only software but also the latest technology. With software for desktop computers and apps for both smart phones and tablet computers, Intuit makes it easy for its customers to obtain the information they need.

In this chapter, we begin by describing why employees need information. The first three major sections in this chapter answer the following questions:

- How can information reduce risk when making a decision?
- What is a management information system?
- How do employees use a management information system?

Next, we look at why accounting information is important, attempts to improve financial reporting, and careers in the accounting industry. Then we examine the basic accounting equation and the three most important financial statements: the balance sheet, the income statement, and the statement of cash flows. Finally, we take a look at how managers evaluate the firm's financial health.

Learning Objective

1 Examine how information can reduce risk when making a decision.

HOW CAN INFORMATION REDUCE RISK WHEN MAKING A DECISION?

As we noted in Chapter 1, information is one of the four major resources (along with material, human, and financial resources) managers must have to operate a business. Although a successful business uses all four resources efficiently, it is information that helps managers reduce risk when making a decision.

Information and Risk

To improve the decision-making process and reduce risk, the information used by individuals and business firms must be relevant or useful to meet a specific need. Using relevant information results in better decisions.

Relevant information → Better intelligence and knowledge → Better decisions

For businesses, better intelligence and knowledge that lead to better decisions are especially important because they can provide a *competitive edge* over competitors and improve a firm's *profits*.

Theoretically, with accurate and complete information, there is no risk whatsoever. On the other hand, a decision made without any information is a gamble. These two extreme situations are rare in business. For the most part, business decision makers see themselves located someplace between the extremes. As illustrated in Figure 15-1, when the amount of available information is high, there is less risk; when the amount of available information is low, there is more risk.

Suppose that a marketing manager for Procter & Gamble (P&G) responsible for the promotion of a well-known shampoo such as Pantene Pro-V has called a meeting of key people within her department to consider the selection of a new magazine advertisement. The company's advertising agency has submitted two new advertisements in sealed envelopes. Neither the manager nor any of her team has seen them before. Only one selection will be made for the new advertising campaign. Which advertisement should be chosen?

Without any further information, the team might as well make the decision by flipping a coin. If, however, team members were allowed to open the envelopes and examine the advertisements, they would have more information. If, in addition to allowing them to examine the advertisements, the marketing manager circulated a report containing the reactions of a group of target consumers to each of the two advertisements, the team would have even more information with which to work. Thus, information, when understood properly, produces knowledge and empowers managers and employees to make better decisions.

FIGURE 15-1 The Relationship Between Information and Risk

When the amount of available information is high, managers tend to make better decisions. On the other hand, when the amount of information is low, there is a high risk of making a poor decision.

Information Rules

Marketing research continues to show that discounts influence almost all car buyers. Simply put, if dealers lower their prices, they will sell more cars. This relationship between buyer behavior and price can be thought of as an information rule that usually will guide the marketing manager correctly. An information rule emerges when research confirms the same results each time that it studies the same or a similar set of circumstances.

Because of the volume of information they receive each day and their need to make decisions on a daily basis, businesspeople try to accumulate information rules to shorten the time they spend analyzing choices. Information rules are the "great simplifiers" for all decision makers. Business research is continuously looking for new rules that can be put to good use and looking to discredit old ones that are no longer valid. This ongoing process is necessary because business conditions rarely stay the same for very long.

The Difference Between Data and Information

Many people use the terms *data* and *information* interchangeably, but the two differ in important ways. **Data** are numerical or verbal descriptions that usually result from some sort of measurement. Your current wage level, the amount of last year's after-tax profit for ExxonMobil Corporation, and the current retail prices of Honda automobiles are all data. Most people think of data as being numerical only, but they can be nonnumerical as well. A description of an individual as a "tall, athletic person with short, dark hair" certainly would qualify as data.

Information is data presented in a form that is useful for a specific purpose. Suppose that a human resources manager wants to compare the wages paid to male and female employees over a period of five years. The manager might begin with a stack of computer printouts listing every person employed by the firm, along with

data numerical or verbal descriptions that usually result from some sort of measurement

information data presented in a form that is useful for a specific purpose

Technology giant! Cisco Systems is a company known for transforming how people connect, communicate, and collaborate. The technology giant is also a respected innovator that develops state-of-the-art equipment needed by employees, managers, and individuals to manage knowledge and information.

each employee's current and past wages. The manager would be hard pressed to make any sense of all the names and numbers. Such printouts consist of data rather than information.

Now suppose that the manager uses a computer to graph the average wages paid to men and to women in each of the five years. The result is information because the manager can use it to compare wages paid to men with those paid to women over the five-year period. For a manager, information presented in a practical, useful form, such as a graph, simplifies the decision-making process.

Knowledge Management

The average company maintains a great deal of data that can be transformed into information. Typical data include records pertaining to personnel, inventory, sales, and accounting. Often each type of data is stored in individual departments within an organization. However, the data can be used more effectively when they are organized into a database. A **database** is a single collection of data and information stored in one place that can be used by people throughout an organization to make decisions. Although databases are important, the way the data and information are used is even more important—and more valuable to the firm. As a result, management information experts now use the term **knowledge management (KM)** to describe a firm's procedures for generating, using, and sharing the data and information. Typically, data, information, databases, and KM all become important parts of a firm's management information system.

WHAT IS A MANAGEMENT INFORMATION SYSTEM?

A **management information system (MIS)** is a system that provides managers and employees with the information they need to perform their jobs as effectively as possible. The purpose of an MIS (sometimes referred to as an information technology system or simply IT system) is to distribute timely and useful information from both internal and external sources to the managers and employees who need it.

A Firm's Information Requirements

Employees and managers have to plan for the future, implement their plans in the present, and evaluate results against what has been accomplished in the past. Of course, the specific types of information they need depend on their work area and on their level within the firm.

Today, many firms are organized into five areas of management: *finance, operations, marketing, human resources,* and *administration.* Managers in each of these areas need specific information in order to make decisions (see Figure 15-2).

- *Financial managers* are obviously most concerned with a firm's finances. They must ensure that the firm's managers and employees, lenders and suppliers, stockholders and potential investors, and government agencies have the information they need to measure the financial health of the firm.
- *Operations managers* are concerned with present and future sales levels, current inventory levels of work in process and finished goods, and the availability and cost of the resources required to produce products and services.
- *Marketing managers* need to have detailed information about a firm's products and services and those offered by competitors. Such information includes pricing strategies, new promotional campaigns, and products that competitors are test marketing. Information concerning the firm's customers, current and projected market share, and new and pending product legislation is also important to marketing managers.
- *Human resources managers* must be aware of anything that pertains to a firm's employees. Key examples include current wage levels and benefits packages

FIGURE 15-2 Management Information System (MIS)

After an MIS is installed, employers and managers can get information directly from the MIS without having to go through other people in the organization.

MANAGEMENT INFORMATION SYSTEM

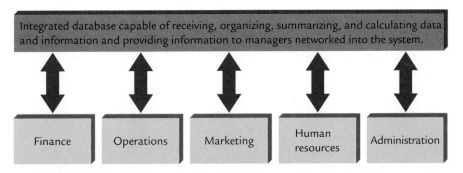

Integrated database capable of receiving, organizing, summarizing, and calculating data and information and providing information to managers networked into the system.

| Finance | Operations | Marketing | Human resources | Administration |

Source: Adapted from Ricky W. Griffin, *Management* (Mason, OH: Cengage Learning, 2013). Reprinted with permission.

both within the firm and in firms that compete for valuable employees, current legislation and court decisions that affect employment practices, and the firm's plans for growth, expansion, or mergers.

- *Administrative managers* are responsible for the overall management of the organization. Thus, they are concerned with the coordination of information—just as they are concerned with the coordination of material, human, and financial resources.

Administrative managers must ensure that the information is used in a consistent manner throughout the firm. Suppose, for example, that General Electric (GE) is designing a new plant in China to manufacture energy-efficient light bulbs that will open in five years. GE's management will want answers to many questions: Is the capacity of the plant consistent with marketing plans based on sales projections? Will human resources managers be able to recruit U.S. employees with the appropriate skills who are willing to relocate to a foreign country and hire and train Chinese workers to staff the plant? And do sales projections indicate enough income to cover the expected cost of the plant? Next, administrative managers must make sure that all managers and employees are able to use the information technology that is available. Certainly, this requires that all employees receive the skills training required to access the information. Finally, administrative managers must commit to the costs of updating the firm's MIS and providing additional training when necessary.

Costs and Limits of the System

Can employees, managers, and executives have too much information? The answer is yes. The truth is that each group needs relevant information that helps them make better decisions.

Is all this information really necessary? Today, we live in an information society—that is, a society in which large groups of individuals, employees, and managers generate or depend on information to perform everyday tasks. As a result, all three groups often complain that they have too much information. For many, the problem is not lack of information, but how to determine what information is really needed?

And yet, too much information that must be analyzed can lead to information overload. Another problem related to information overload is the amount of worthless information, junk e-mails, and advertising that contribute to information overload. Just for a moment, think about the time employees spend reading e-mails that have been sent to everyone in a firm instead of the one or two people who really need to receive the e-mail. Unfortunately, there are other misuses of information technology that do nothing but rob employees of time that could be devoted to more productive activities. In addition to lower employee productivity, the cost of computers, software, and related equipment can be staggering. Although it would be nice for all employees to have new computers and the latest software applications, in reality, even the largest and most profitable business firms cannot afford to waste money on unnecessary computer hardware and software. One of the main goals of a firm's information technology officer is to make sure that a firm has the equipment necessary to provide information the employees need to make effective decisions—*at a reasonable cost.*

In reality, an MIS must be tailored to the needs of the organization it serves. In some firms, a tendency to save on initial costs may result in a system that is too small or overly simple. Such a system generally ends up serving only one or two management levels or a single department. Managers in other departments "give up" on the system as soon as they find that it cannot process their data.

Almost as bad is an MIS that is too large or too complex for the organization. Unused capacity and complexity do nothing but increase the cost of owning and operating the system. In addition, a system that is difficult to use probably will not be used at all.

Concept Check

✓ How do the information requirements of managers differ by management area?

✓ What happens if a business has a management information system that is too large?

✓ What happens if a business has a management information system that is too small?

Learning Objective

3 Outline the five functions of an information system.

HOW DO EMPLOYEES USE A MANAGEMENT INFORMATION SYSTEM?

To provide information, an MIS must perform five specific functions. It must (1) collect data, (2) store the data, (3) update the data, (4) process the data into information, and (5) present the information to users (see Figure 15-3).

Step 1: Collecting Data

A firm's employees, with the help of an MIS system, must gather the data and information needed to establish the firm's *database.* The database should include all past and current data that may be useful in managing the firm. Clearly, the data entered into the system must be *relevant* to the needs of the firm's managers. And perhaps most important, the data must be *accurate.* Irrelevant data are simply useless; inaccurate data can be disastrous. There are two data sources: *internal* and *external.*

Typically, most of the data gathered for an MIS come from internal sources. The most common internal sources of information are managers and employees, company records and reports, accounting data, and minutes of meetings.

External sources of data include customers, suppliers, financial institutions and banks, trade and business publications, industry conferences, online computer services, lawyers, government sources, and firms that specialize in gathering marketing research for organizations.

Whether the source of the data is internal or external, always remember the following three cautions:

1. The cost of obtaining data from some external sources, such as marketing research firms, can be quite high.
2. Outdated or incomplete data usually yield inaccurate information.
3. Although computers generally do not make mistakes, the people who use them can make or cause errors. When data (or information) and your judgment disagree, always check the data.

FIGURE 15-3 Five Management Information System Functions

Every MIS must be tailored to the organization it serves and must perform five functions.

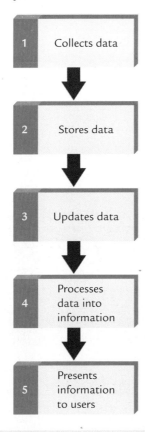

1 Collects data

2 Stores data

3 Updates data

4 Processes data into information

5 Presents information to users

© CENGAGE LEARNING 2015

Step 2: Storing Data

An MIS must be capable of storing data until they are needed. Typically, the method chosen to store data depends on the size and needs of the organization. Small businesses may enter data and then store them directly on an employee's computer. Generally, medium-sized to large businesses store data in a larger computer system and provide access to employees through a computer network.

Step 3: Updating Data

Today, an MIS must be able to update stored data regularly to ensure that the information presented to managers and employees is accurate, complete, and up-to-date. The frequency with which the data are updated depends on how fast they change and how often they are used. When it is vital to have current data, updating may occur as soon as the new data are available. For example, Macy's, a national retailer that sells a wide range of merchandise including apparel and accessories for men, women, and children, cosmetics, home furnishing, and other consumer goods, has cash registers that automatically transmit data on each item sold in each store to a central computer. The computer adjusts the store's inventory records accordingly. In addition to maintaining accurate inventory records, sales representatives can tell customers where they can obtain merchandise if the store where they are shopping is out of the merchandise they want. Data and information may also be entered into a firm's data bank at certain intervals—every 24 hours, weekly, or monthly.

How Much Should Businesses Know About Internet Users?

When you click to conduct an online search or to download a digital coupon, businesses can follow your electronic movements. Tracking online behavior helps businesses make better decisions about targeting communications and tailoring offers to an individual's needs and interests. Yet the public may not always understand what information is being gathered, how long it will be held, how it will be used, or who can see it. This raises questions about how much data should businesses be able to collect about Internet users—and whether consumers should be able to avoid or minimize tracking of their online movements.

Privacy advocates worry about the potential for identity theft and the possibility that data may be shared without consent. They also express concern that businesses might restrict access to some products based on what consumers do or say online. For example, would a bank consider a consumer's history of visiting Internet gambling sites when determining which financial services products to offer or approve? Businesses point out the benefits of collecting data to personalize website functionality

based on each user's preferences and previous visits. They also look at behavioral data when planning new products and services.

The controversy has become even more heated as people flock to social media. As experts debate the limits of online privacy, regulators are formulating new privacy protections, makers of Web browsers are adding anti-tracking features, and industry groups are discussing ways to allow consumers to opt out of tracking if they choose. So how much should businesses be able to find out about what consumers say or do online?

Sources: Based on information in Natasha Singer, "Mediator Joins Contentious Effort to Add a 'Do Not Track' Option to Web Browsing," *New York Times*, November 28, 2012, www.nytimes.com; Julia Angwin, "A Search for Privacy in a Nonprivate Age," *Wall Street Journal*, November 16, 2012, www.wsj.com; Julia Angwin, Scott Thurm, and Michael Hickins, "Lawmaker Introduces New Privacy Bill," *Wall Street Journal*, February 11, 2011, www.wsj.com; Wendy Davis, "Report: Marketers Limit Behavioral Targeting Due to Privacy Worries," *Media Post*, May 2, 2010, www.mediapost.com; Emily Steel and Julia Angwin, "The Web's Cutting Edge, Anonymity in Name Only," *Wall Street Journal*, August 3, 2010, www.wsj.com.

Step 4: Processing Data

data processing the transformation of data into a form that is useful for a specific purpose

Some data are used in the form in which they are stored, whereas other data require processing to extract, highlight, or summarize the information they contain. **Data processing** is the transformation of data into a form that is useful for a specific purpose.

For verbal data, this processing consists mainly of extracting the pertinent material from storage and combining it into a report. Most business data, however, are in the form of numbers—large groups of numbers, such as daily sales totals or production costs for a specific product. Fortunately, computers can be programmed to process such large volumes of numbers quickly. While such groups of numbers may be difficult to handle and to comprehend, their contents can be summarized through the use of statistics. A **statistic** is a measure that summarizes a particular characteristic of an entire group of numbers.

statistic a measure that summarizes a particular characteristic of an entire group of numbers

Step 5: Presenting Information

An MIS must be capable of presenting information in a usable form. That is, the method of presentation—reports, tables, graphs, or charts, for example—must be appropriate for the information itself and for the uses to which it will be put.

BUSINESS REPORTS Verbal information may be presented in list or paragraph form. Employees often are asked to prepare formal business reports. A typical business report includes

- An introduction
- The body of the report
- The conclusions
- The recommendations

The *introduction*, which sets the stage for the remainder of the report, describes the problem to be studied in the report, identifies the research techniques that were used, and previews the material that will be presented in the report. The *body* of the report should objectively describe the facts that were discovered in the process of completing the report. The body also should provide a foundation for the conclusions and the recommendations. The *conclusions* are statements of fact that describe the findings contained in the report. Conclusions should be specific, practical, and based on the evidence in the report. The *recommendations* section presents suggestions on how the problem might be solved. Like the conclusions, the recommendations should be specific, practical, and based on the evidence.

VISUAL DISPLAYS AND TABLES A visual display can also be used to present information and may be a diagram that represents several items of information in a manner that makes comparison easier. Figure 15-4 illustrates examples of visual displays including graphs, bar charts, and pie charts generated by a computer.

A tabular display is used to present verbal or numerical information in columns and rows. It is most useful in presenting information about two or more related variables. A table, for example, can be used to illustrate the number of salespeople in each region of the country, sales for different types of products, and total sales for all products (see Table 15-1). Information that is to be manipulated—for example, to calculate loan payments—is usually displayed in tabular form.

Tabular displays generally have less impact than visual displays. However, displaying the information that could be contained in a multicolumn table such as the one shown in Table 15-1 would require several bar or pie charts.

PATRICK LA ROQUE/ALAMY

Who are the people who use information? Although the primary users of information are a firm's managers and employees, parties outside the organization—lenders, suppliers, stockholders, and government agencies—are also interested in the firm's information. In fact, both managers and employees and outside groups often examine a firm's annual report to determine the financial health of a firm.

Making Smart Decisions

How do managers and employees sort out relevant and useful information from the spam, junk mail, and useless data? In addition to the steps described in the last section (collecting data, storing data, updating data, processing data, and presenting information) three different software applications can actually help to improve and speed the decision-making process for people at different levels within an organization. First, a **decision-support system (DSS)** is a type of software program that provides relevant data and information to help a firm's employees make decisions. It also can be used to determine the effect of changing different variables and answer "what if" type questions. For example, a manager at Michigan-based Pulte Homes may use a DSS to determine prices for new homes built in an upscale, luxury subdivision. By entering the number of homes that will be built along with different costs associated with land, labor, materials, building permits, promotional costs, and all other costs, a DSS can help to determine a base price for each new home. It is also possible to increase or decrease the building costs and determine new home prices for each set of assumptions with a DSS. Although similar to a DSS, an **executive information system (EIS)** is a computer-based system that facilitates and supports the decision-making needs of top managers and senior executives by providing easy access to both internal and external information.

decision-support system (DSS) a type of software program that provides relevant data and information to help a firm's employees make decisions

executive information system (EIS) a computer-based system that facilitates and supports the decision-making needs of top managers and senior executives by providing easy access to both internal and external information

FIGURE 15-4 Typical Visual Displays Used in Business Presentations

Visual displays help businesspeople present information in a form that can be understood easily.

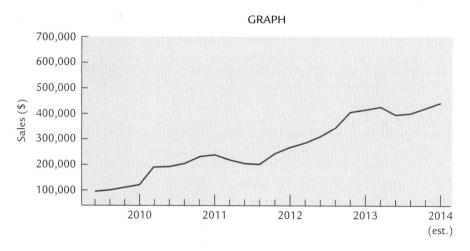

GRAPH

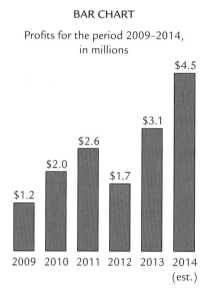

BAR CHART

Profits for the period 2009–2014, in millions

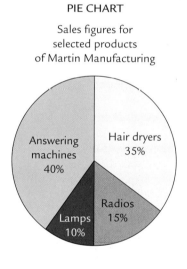

PIE CHART

Sales figures for selected products of Martin Manufacturing

TABLE 15-1 Typical Three-Column Table Used in Business Presentations

Tables are most useful for displaying information about two or more variables.

All-Star Technology Projected Sales

Section of the Country	Number of Salespeople	Consumer Products ($)	Industrial Products ($)
Eastern territory	15	1,500,000	3,500,000
Midwestern territory	20	2,000,000	5,000,000
Western territory	10	1,000,000	4,000,000
TOTAL	45	4,500,000	12,500,000

© CENGAGE LEARNING 2015

Word processing	Users can prepare and edit written documents and store them in the computer or on a memory device.
Desktop publishing	Users can combine text and graphics in professional reports, newsletters, and pamphlets.
Accounting	Users can record routine financial transactions and prepare financial reports at the end of the accounting period.
Database management	Users can electronically store large amounts of data and transform the data into information.
Graphics	Users can display and print pictures, drawings, charts, and diagrams.
Spreadsheets	Users can organize numerical data into a grid of rows and columns.

© CENGAGE LEARNING 2015

An **expert system** is a type of computer program that uses artificial intelligence to imitate a human's ability to think. An expert system uses a set of rules that analyze information supplied by the user about a particular activity or problem. Based on the information supplied, the expert system then provides recommendations or suggests specific actions in order to help make decisions. Expert systems, for example, have been used to schedule manufacturing tasks, diagnose illnesses, determine credit limits for credit card customers, evaluate loan applications, and develop electronic games.

expert system a type of computer program that uses artificial intelligence to imitate a human's ability to think

Business Application Software

Early software typically performed a single function. Today, however, *integrated* software combines many functions in a single package. Integrated packages allow for the easy linking of text, numerical data, graphs, photographs, and even audiovisual clips. A business report prepared using the Microsoft Office package, for instance, can include all these components.

Integration offers at least two other benefits. Once data have been entered into an application in an integrated package, the data can be used in another integrated package without having to reenter the data. In addition, once a user learns one application, it is much easier to learn another application in an integrated package. From a career standpoint, you should realize that employers will assume that you possess, or will possess after training, a high degree of working comfort with several of the software applications described in Table 15-2.

Concept Check

✓ List the five functions of an MIS.

✓ What are the components of a typical business report?

✓ What types of information could be illustrated in a visual display? In a tabular display?

✓ Describe the three types of computer applications that help employees, managers, and executives make smart decisions.

WHY ACCOUNTING INFORMATION IS IMPORTANT

In today's competitive business environment, all successful firms use information to make decisions. In order to obtain needed information, firms use an MIS like the one described in the first part of this chapter. Executives, managers, and employees also rely on the firm's accounting system to provide needed financial information. **Accounting** is the process of systematically collecting, analyzing, and reporting financial information. Just for a moment, think about the following three questions:

1. How much profit did a business earn last year?
2. How much tax does a business owe the Internal Revenue Service?
3. How much cash does a business have to pay lenders and suppliers?

Learning Objective

4 Explain why accurate accounting information and audited financial statements are important.

accounting the process of systematically collecting, analyzing, and reporting financial information

In each case, the firm's accountants and its accounting system provide the answers to these questions and many others. Although accounting information can be used to answer questions about what has happened in the past, it can also be used to help make decisions about the future.

Because the information provided by a firm's accountants and its accounting system is so important, managers and other groups interested in a business firm's financial records must be able to "trust the numbers." To improve the accuracy of a firm's accounting information and its financial statements, businesses rely on audits conducted by accountants employed by public accounting firms.

Why Audited Financial Statements Are Important?

audit an examination of a company's financial statements and the accounting practices that produced them

generally accepted accounting principles (GAAPs) an accepted set of guidelines and practices for U.S. companies reporting financial information and for the accounting profession

An **audit** is an examination of a company's financial statements and the accounting practices that produced them. The purpose of an audit is to make sure that a firm's financial statements have been prepared in accordance with **generally accepted accounting principles (GAAPs)**. GAAPs have been developed to provide an accepted set of guidelines and practices for U.S. companies reporting financial information and the accounting profession. At the time of publication, the Financial Accounting Standards Board (FASB), which establishes and improves accounting standards for U.S. companies, is working toward establishing a new set of standards that combines GAAPs with the International Financial Reporting Standards (IFRS) to create one set of accounting standards that can be used by both U.S. and multinational firms. Created by the International Accounting Standards Board, IFRS are now used in more than 100 different countries around the world. For multinational firms like Royal Dutch Shell, ExxonMobil, Walmart, and Toyota, the benefits of global accounting standards are huge because preparing financial statements and accounting records that meet global standards saves both time and money. According to many accounting experts, the United States is on a path toward the adoption of IFRS, the question is when.[2]

If an accountant determines that a firm's financial statements present financial information fairly and conform to GAAPs, then he or she will issue the following statement:

In our opinion, the financial statements . . . present fairly, in all material respects the financial position of the company . . . in conformity with generally accepted accounting principles.

Although an audit and the resulting report do not *guarantee* that a company has not "cooked" the books, it does imply that, on the whole, the company has followed GAAPs. Bankers, creditors, investors, and government agencies are willing to rely on an auditor's opinion because of the historically ethical reputation and independence of auditors and accounting firms. Finally, it should be noted that without the audit function and GAAPs, there would be very little oversight or supervision. The validity of a firm's financial statements and its accounting records would drop quickly, and firms would find it difficult to obtain debt financing, acquire goods and services from suppliers, find investor financing, or prepare documents requested by government agencies.

COMSTOCK IMAGES/GETTY IMAGES

Does this executive trust the numbers? Good question! A firm's managers and employees must have accurate accounting information to make decisions and plan for the future. Other groups including investors, lenders, and suppliers also must "trust" accounting information to determine the financial health of a company. In fact, without accurate accounting information, the numbers are just that numbers.

Accounting Fraud, Ethical Behavior, and Reform

Which of the following firms has been convicted or accused of accounting fraud?

   a. Lehman Brothers (Banking in the United States)

   b. Sino-Forest (Forestry Operations in China)

   c. Fannie Mae (Home Mortgages in United States)

   d. Autonomy Software (Software Development in Britain)

   e. All of the above

Unfortunately, the answer to the question is e—all of the above. Each company is a large business that has been plagued by accounting problems. In some cases, the accounting problems led to bankruptcy for Lehman Brothers and Sino-Forest Corporation. In other cases, the value of the corporation's stock plummeted because the firm had inflated sales or underreported expenses. And as you can tell from the options to the above question, the companies can operate in any industry and be located any place on the globe. The bottom line: The accounting problems at these companies—and similar problems at even more companies—have forced many investors, lenders and suppliers, and government regulators to question the motives behind fraudulent and unethical accounting practices.

Today, much of the pressure on corporate executives to "cook" the books is driven by the desire to look good to Wall Street analysts and investors. If a company reports sales and profit figures that are lower than expected, the company's stock value can drop dramatically. Greed—especially when executive salaries and bonuses are tied to a company's stock value—is another factor that can lead some corporate executives to use unethical accounting methods to inflate a firm's sales revenues and profit amount.

Unfortunately, the ones hurt when companies (and their accountants) report inaccurate or misleading accounting information often are not the high-paid corporate executives. In many cases, it's the employees who lose their jobs when the company files for bankruptcy, as well as the money they invested in the company's retirement program. In addition, investors, lenders, and suppliers who relied on fraudulent accounting information in order to make a decision to invest in or lend money to the company also usually experience a loss.

To help ensure that corporate financial information is accurate and to prevent the type of accounting scandals that have occurred in the past, Congress enacted the Sarbanes–Oxley Act in 2002. Key components include the following:[3]

- The Securities and Exchange Commission (SEC) is required to establish a full-time five-member federal oversight board that will police the accounting industry.
- Chief executive and financial officers are required to certify periodic financial reports and are liable for intentional violations of securities reporting requirements.
- Accounting firms are prohibited from providing many types of nonaudit and consulting services to the companies they audit.
- Auditors must maintain financial documents and audit work papers for five years.
- Auditors, accountants, and employees can be imprisoned for up to 20 years and subject to fines for destroying financial documents and willful violations of the securities laws.
- A public corporation must change its lead auditing firm every five years.
- There is added protection for whistle-blowers who report violations of the Sarbanes–Oxley Act.

Although most people welcome the Sarbanes–Oxley Act, complex rules make compliance more expensive and time-consuming for corporate management and more difficult for accounting firms. Yet, most people agree that the cost of compliance is justified.

Different Types of Accounting

Although many people think that all accountants do the same tasks, there are special areas of expertise within the accounting industry. In fact, accounting is usually broken down into two broad categories: managerial and financial.

Managerial accounting provides managers and employees within the organization with the information needed to make decisions about a firm's financing, investing, marketing, and operating activities. By using managerial accounting information, both managers and employees can evaluate how well they have done in the past and what they can expect in the future.

Financial accounting, on the other hand, generates financial statements and reports for interested people outside of an organization. Typically, stockholders, financial analysts, bankers, lenders, suppliers, government agencies, and other interested groups use the information provided by financial accounting to determine how well a business firm has achieved its goals. In addition to managerial and financial accounting, additional special areas of accounting include the following:

managerial accounting
provides managers and employees with the information needed to make decisions about a firm's financing, investing, marketing, and operating activities

financial accounting generates financial statements and reports for interested people outside an organization

- *Cost accounting*—determining the cost of producing specific products or services;
- *Tax accounting*—planning tax strategy and preparing tax returns for firms or individuals;
- *Government accounting*—providing basic accounting services to ensure that tax revenues are collected and used to meet the goals of state, local, and federal agencies; and
- *Not-for-profit accounting*—helping not-for-profit organizations to account for all donations and expenditures.

Careers in Accounting

What is the typical day like for accountants? While each day may be different than the next and depending on if they are self-employed, work for a business firm, or work for an accounting firm, accountants typically do the following:

- Inspect a firm's accounting systems to ensure the business is using generally accepted accounting procedures.
- Examine financial statements to be sure that they are accurate.
- Calculate the amount of taxes owed, prepare tax returns, and ensure that taxes are paid properly and on time.
- Organize and maintain financial records.
- Assist employees, managers, and owners to improve financial decisions.
- Suggest ways to reduce costs, enhance revenues, and improve profits.

According to the *Occupational Outlook Handbook*, published by the Department of Labor, job opportunities for accountants, as well as auditors in the accounting area, are expected to experience a 16 percent increase or about average employment growth between now and the year 2020.[4] And more good news: Starting salaries for employees in the accounting industry are often higher than the starting salaries for other entry-level positions.

Accounting can be an exciting and rewarding career. To be successful in the accounting industry, employees must

certified public accountant (CPA) an individual who has met state requirements for accounting education and experience and has passed a rigorous accounting examination

- be responsible, honest, and ethical;
- have a strong background in financial management;
- know how to use a computer and software to process data into accounting information; and
- be able to communicate with people who need accounting information.

Today, accountants generally are classified as either private accountants or public accountants. A *private accountant* is employed by a specific organization. On the other hand, a *public accountant* works on a fee basis for clients and may be self-employed or be the employee of an accounting firm. Accounting firms range in size from one-person operations to huge international firms with hundreds of accounting partners and thousands of employees. Today, the largest accounting firms, sometimes referred to as the "Big Four," are PricewaterhouseCoopers (PwC), Ernst & Young, KPMG, and Deloitte Touche Tohmatsu.

Typically, public accounting firms include on their staffs at least one **certified public accountant (CPA)**, an individual who has met state requirements for accounting education and experience and has passed a rigorous accounting examination. More information about general requirements and the CPA profession can be obtained by contacting the American Institute of CPAs (AICPA) at www.aicpa.org. State requirements usually include a college degree or a specified number of hours of college course work and generally from one to three years of on-the-job experience. Details regarding specific state requirements for practice as a CPA can be obtained by contacting the state's board of accountancy.

Certification as a CPA brings both status and responsibility. Publicly traded corporations, for example, must hire an independent CPA to audit their financial statements. Fees for the services provided by CPAs generally range from $50 to $300 an hour.

THE ACCOUNTING EQUATION AND THE BALANCE SHEET

At the beginning of this chapter, *information* was defined as data presented in a form that is useful for a specific purpose. Now, we examine how financial *data* is transformed into financial *information* and reported on three very important financial statements—the balance sheet, income statement, and statement of cash flows. We begin by describing why the fundamental accounting equation is the basis for a firm's balance sheet.

The Accounting Equation

The accounting equation is a simple statement that forms the basis for the accounting process. This equation shows the relationship between a firm's assets, liabilities, and owners' equity.

- **Assets** are the resources a business owns—cash, inventory, equipment, and real estate.
- **Liabilities** are the firm's debts—borrowed money it owes to others that must be repaid.
- **Owners' equity** is the difference between total assets and total liabilities—what would be left for the owners if the firm's assets were sold and the money used to pay off its liabilities.

The relationship between assets, liabilities, and owners' equity is shown by the following **accounting equation**:

$$\text{Assets} = \text{Liabilities} + \text{Owners' equity}$$

The dollar total of all of a firm's assets cannot equal more than the total funds obtained by borrowing money (liabilities) and the investment of the owner(s).

Concept Check

✓ What purpose do audits and GAAPs serve in today's business world?

✓ How do the major provisions of the Sarbanes–Oxley Act affect a public company's audit procedures?

✓ Based on the information in this section, would you choose accounting as a career?

Learning Objective

5 Read and interpret a balance sheet.

assets the resources that a business owns

liabilities a firm's debts and obligations

owners' equity the difference between a firm's assets and its liabilities

accounting equation the basis for the accounting process: *assets = liabilities + owners' equity*

double-entry bookkeeping
system a system in which each
financial transaction is recorded as
two separate accounting entries to
maintain the balance shown in the
accounting equation

Whether a business is a small corner grocery store or a global giant like Procter & Gamble, the total dollar amount for assets must equal the sum of its liabilities and owners' equity. To use this equation, a firm's accountants must record raw data—that is, the firm's day-to-day financial transactions—using the double-entry system of bookkeeping. The **double-entry bookkeeping system** is a system in which each financial transaction is recorded as two separate accounting entries to maintain the balance shown in the accounting equation. At the end of a specific accounting period, all of the financial transactions can now be summarized in the firm's financial statements. This information is presented in a standardized format to make the statements as accessible as possible to the various people who may be interested in the firm's financial affairs—managers, employees, lenders, suppliers, stockholders, potential investors, and government agencies. In fact, the form of the financial statements is pretty much the same for all businesses, from a neighborhood video store or small dry cleaner to giant conglomerates such as Home Depot, Boeing, and Bank of America. A firm's financial statements are prepared at least once a year and included in the firm's annual report. An **annual report** is a report distributed to stockholders and other interested parties that describes a firm's operating activities and its financial condition. Most firms also have financial statements prepared semiannually, quarterly, or monthly.

annual report a report distributed to stockholders and other
interested parties that describes
the firm's operating activities and
its financial condition

The Balance Sheet

Question: *Where could you find the total amount of assets, liabilities, and owners' equity for Hershey Foods Corporation?*

Answer: The firm's balance sheet.

balance sheet (or statement of
financial position) a summary
of the dollar amounts of a firm's
assets, liabilities, and owners'
equity accounts at the end of a
specific accounting period

A **balance sheet** (sometimes referred to as a **statement of financial position**) is a summary of the dollar amounts of a firm's assets, liabilities, and owners' equity accounts at the end of a specific accounting period. The balance sheet must demonstrate that assets are equal to liabilities plus owners' equity, and the accounting equation is still in balance. Most people think of a balance sheet as a statement that reports the financial condition of a business firm such as the Hershey Foods Corporation, but balance sheets apply to individuals, too. For example, Marty Campbell graduated from college three years ago and obtained a position as a sales representative for an office supply firm. After going to work, he established a checking and savings account and purchased an automobile, stereo, television, and furniture for his apartment. Marty paid cash for some purchases, but he had to borrow money to pay for the larger ones. Figure 15-5 shows Marty's current personal balance sheet.

Marty Campbell's assets total $26,500, and his liabilities amount to $10,000. Although the difference between total assets and total liabilities is referred to as *owners' equity* or *stockholders' equity* for a business, it is normally called *net worth* for an individual. As reported on Marty's personal balance sheet, net worth is $16,500. The total assets ($26,500) and the total liabilities *plus* net worth ($26,500) are equal. Thus, the accounting equation (Assets = Liabilities + Owners' equity) is still in balance.

Figure 15-6 shows the balance sheet for Northeast Art Supply, a small corporation that sells picture frames, paints, canvases, and other artists' supplies to retailers in New England. Note that assets are reported on the left side of the statement, and liabilities and stockholders' equity are reported on the right side. Let's work through the different accounts in Figure 15-6.

Assets

liquidity the ease with which an
asset can be converted into cash

On a balance sheet, assets are listed in order from the *most liquid* to the *least liquid*. The **liquidity** of an asset is the ease with which it can be converted into cash.

FIGURE 15-5 Personal Balance Sheet

Often, individuals determine their net worth, or owners' equity, by subtracting
the value of their liabilities from the value of their assets.

Marty Campbell
Personal Balance Sheet
December 31, 20XX

ASSETS		LIABILITIES	
Cash	$ 2,500	Automobile loan	$ 9,500
Savings account	5,000	Credit card balance	500
Automobile	15,000	TOTAL LIABILITIES	$10,000
Stereo	1,000		
Television	500		
Furniture	2,500	NET WORTH (Owners' Equity)	16,500
TOTAL ASSETS	$26,500	TOTAL LIABILITIES AND NET WORTH	$26,500

© CENGAGE LEARNING 2015

FIGURE 15-6 Business Balance Sheet

A balance sheet (sometimes referred to as a statement of financial position) summarizes a firm's assets,
liabilities, and owners' equity. Note that assets ($340,000) equal liabilities plus owners' equity ($340,000)
and the accounting equation is still in balance.

NORTHEAST ART SUPPLY, INC.

Balance Sheet
December 31, 20XX

ASSETS

				LIABILITIES AND STOCKHOLDERS' EQUITY		
Current assets				**Current liabilities**		
Cash		$ 59,000		Accounts payable	$ 35,000	
Marketable securities		10,000		Notes payable	25,675	
Accounts receivable	$ 40,000			Salaries payable	4,000	
Less allowance for doubtful accounts	2,000	38,000		Taxes payable	5,325	
Notes receivable		32,000		Total current liabilities		$ 70,000
Merchandise inventory		41,000				
Prepaid expenses		2,000				
Total current assets			$182,000	**Long-term liabilities**		
				Mortgage payable on store equipment	$ 40,000	
				Total long-term liabilities		$ 40,000
Fixed assets						
Delivery equipment	$110,000			TOTAL LIABILITIES		$110,000
Less accumulated depreciation	20,000	$ 90,000				
Furniture and store equipment	$62,000					
Less accumulated depreciation	15,000	47,000		**Stockholders' equity**		
Total fixed assets			137,000	Common stock (25,000×$6)	$ 150,000	
				Retained earnings	80,000	
Intangible assets						
Patents		$ 21,000				
Total intangible assets			21,000	TOTAL OWNERS' EQUITY		230,000
TOTAL ASSETS			$340,000	TOTAL LIABILITIES AND OWNERS' EQUITY		$340,000

© CENGAGE LEARNING 2015

Checking it once, checking it twice. . . . Before determining the total value of a firm's assets, accountants must determine the value of each type of inventory a firm has on hand to meet customer demand. Accurate accounting procedures for inventory can also determine when it is time to order more inventory.

current assets assets that can be converted quickly into cash or that will be used in one year or less

fixed assets assets that will be held or used for a period longer than one year

depreciation the process of apportioning the cost of a fixed asset over the period during which it will be used

Concept Check

✓ How are current assets distinguished from fixed assets?

✓ Why are fixed assets depreciated on a firm's balance sheet?

✓ How do you determine the dollar amount of owners' equity for a sole proprietorship, or a partnership, or a corporation?

✓ If a business firm has assets worth $170,000 and liabilities that total $40,000, what is the value of the owners' equity?

CURRENT ASSETS **Current assets** are assets that can be converted quickly into cash or that will be used in one year or less. Because cash is the most liquid asset, it is listed first. Next are *marketable securities*—stocks, bonds, and other investments—that can be converted into cash in a matter of days.

Next are the firm's receivables. Its *accounts receivable*, which result from allowing customers to make credit purchases, generally are paid within 30 to 60 days. However, the firm expects that some of these debts will not be collected. Thus, it has reduced its accounts receivables by a 5 percent *allowance for doubtful accounts*. The firm's *notes receivable* are receivables for which customers have signed promissory notes. They generally are repaid over a longer period of time than the firm's accounts receivable.

Northeast's *merchandise inventory* represents the value of goods on hand for sale to customers. Since Northeast Art Supply is a wholesale operation, the inventory listed in Figure 15-6 represents finished goods ready for sale to retailers. For a manufacturing firm, merchandise inventory also may represent raw materials that will become part of a finished product or work that has been partially completed but requires further processing.

Northeast Art's last current asset is *prepaid expenses*, which are assets that have been paid for in advance but have not yet been used. An example is insurance premiums. They are usually paid at the beginning of the policy year. The unused portion (say, for the last four months of the time period covered by the policy) is a prepaid expense. For Northeast Art, all current assets total $182,000.

FIXED ASSETS **Fixed assets** are assets that will be held or used for a period longer than one year. They generally include land, buildings, and equipment used in the continuing operation of the business. Although Northeast Art owns no land or buildings, it does own delivery equipment that originally cost $110,000. It also owns furniture and store equipment that originally cost $62,000.

Note that the values of both fixed assets are decreased by their *accumulated depreciation*. **Depreciation** is the process of apportioning the cost of a fixed asset over the period during which it will be used, that is, its useful life. The depreciation amount allotted to each year is an expense for that year, and the value of the asset must be reduced by the amount of depreciation expense. In the case of Northeast's delivery equipment, $20,000 of its value has been depreciated since it was purchased. Its value at this time is thus $110,000 less $20,000, or $90,000. In a similar fashion, the original value of furniture and store equipment ($62,000) has been reduced by depreciation totaling $15,000. Furniture and store equipment now has a reported value of $47,000. For Northeast Art, all fixed assets total $137,000.

INTANGIBLE ASSETS **Intangible assets** are assets that do not exist physically but that have a value based on the rights or privileges they confer on a firm. They include patents, copyrights, trademarks, and goodwill. By their nature, intangible assets are long-term assets—they are of value to the firm for a number of years.

Northeast Art Supply lists a *patent* for a special oil paint that the company purchased from the inventor. The firm's accountants estimate that the patent has a current market value of $21,000. The firm's intangible assets total $21,000. Now it is possible to total all three types of assets for Northeast Art. As calculated in Figure 15-6, total assets are $340,000.

Liabilities and Owners' Equity

The liabilities and the owners' equity accounts complete the balance sheet. The firm's liabilities are separated into two categories—current and long-term liabilities.

CURRENT LIABILITIES A firm's **current liabilities** are debts that will be repaid in one year or less. Northeast Art Supply purchased merchandise from its suppliers on credit. Thus, its balance sheet includes an entry for accounts payable. *Accounts payable* are short-term obligations that arise as a result of a firm making credit purchases.

Notes payable are obligations that have been secured with promissory notes. They are usually short-term obligations, but they may extend beyond one year. Only those that must be paid within the year are listed under current liabilities.

Northeast Art also lists *salaries payable* and *taxes payable* as current liabilities. These are both expenses that have been incurred during the current accounting period but will be paid in the next accounting period. For Northeast Art, current liabilities total $70,000.

LONG-TERM LIABILITIES **Long-term liabilities** are debts that need not be repaid for at least one year. Northeast Art lists only one long-term liability—a $40,000 *mortgage payable* for store equipment. As you can see in Figure 15-6, Northeast Art's current and long-term liabilities total $110,000.

OWNERS' OR STOCKHOLDERS' EQUITY For a sole proprietorship or partnership, the owners' equity is shown as the difference between assets and liabilities. In a partnership, each partner's share of the ownership is reported separately in each owner's name. For a corporation, the owners' equity usually is referred to as *stockholders' equity*. The dollar amount reported on the balance sheet is the total value of stock plus retained earnings that have accumulated to date. **Retained earnings** are the portion of a business's profits not distributed to stockholders.

The original investment by the owners of Northeast Art Supply was $150,000 and was obtained by selling 25,000 shares at $6 per share. In addition, $80,000 of Northeast Art's earnings have been reinvested in the business since it was founded. Thus, owners' equity totals $230,000.

As the two grand totals in Figure 15-6 show, Northeast Art's assets and the sum of its liabilities and owners' equity are equal—at $340,000. The accounting equation (Assets = Liabilities + Owners' equity) is still in balance.

Personal Apps

Smart Career Moves

Before you accept a company's job offer or buy its stock, check financials and its business situation. Are profits increasing or decreasing? How is it handling its debt? What are its plans for expansion?

© SAMUEL BORGES PHOTOGRAPHY/SHUTTERSTOCK.COM

intangible assets assets that do not exist physically but that have a value based on the rights or privileges they confer on a firm

current liabilities debts that will be repaid in one year or less

long-term liabilities debts that need not be repaid for at least one year

retained earnings the portion of a business's profits not distributed to stockholders

THE INCOME STATEMENT

Question: *Where can you find the profit or loss amount for Apple, Inc.?*

Answer: The firm's income statement.

income statement a summary of a firm's revenues and expenses during a specified accounting period

An **income statement** is a summary of a firm's revenues and expenses during a specified accounting period—one month, three months, six months, or a year. The income statement is sometimes called the *earnings statement* or *the statement of income and expenses*. Let's begin our discussion by constructing a personal income statement for Marty Campbell. Having worked as a sales representative for an office supply firm for the past three years, Marty now earns $33,600 a year, or $2,800 a month. After deductions, his take-home pay is $1,900 a month. As illustrated in Figure 15-7, Marty's typical monthly expenses include payments for an automobile loan, credit card purchases, apartment rent, utilities, food, clothing, and recreation and entertainment.

Although the difference between income and expenses is referred to as *profit* or *loss* for a business, it is normally referred to as a *cash surplus* or *cash deficit* for an individual. Fortunately for Marty, he has a surplus of $250 at the end of each month. He can use this surplus for savings, investing, or paying off debts. It is also possible to use the information from a personal income statement to construct a personal budget. A *personal budget* is a specific plan for spending your income—over the next month, for example.

Figure 15-8 shows the income statement for Northeast Art Supply. For a business,

Revenues *less* Cost of goods sold *less* Operating expenses equals Net income

FIGURE 15-7 Personal Income Statement

By subtracting expenses from income, anyone can construct a personal income statement and determine if he or she has a surplus or deficit at the end of each month.

Marty Campbell
Personal Income Statement
For the month ended December 31, 20XX

INCOME (Take-home pay)		$1,900
LESS MONTHLY EXPENSES		
Automobile loan	$ 250	
Credit card payment	100	
Apartment rent	500	
Utilities	200	
Food	250	
Clothing	100	
Recreation & entertainment	250	
TOTAL MONTHLY EXPENSES		1,650
CASH SURPLUS (or profit)		$ 250

FIGURE 15-8 Business Income Statement

An income statement summarizes a firm's revenues and expenses during a specified accounting period. For Northeast Art Supply, net income after taxes is $30,175.

NORTHEAST ART SUPPLY, INC.		Income Statement for the Year Ended December 31, 20XX
Revenues		
Gross sales		$465,000
Less sales returns and allowances	$ 9,500	
Less sales discounts	4,500	14,000
Net sales		$451,000
Cost of goods sold		
Beginning inventory, January 1, 20XX		$ 40,000
Purchases	$346,000	
Less purchase discounts	11,000	
Net purchases		335,000
Cost of goods available for sale		$375,000
Less ending inventory December 31, 20XX		41,000
Cost of goods sold		334,000
Gross profit		$117,000
Operating expenses		
Selling expenses		
Sales salaries	$ 22,000	
Advertising	4,000	
Sales promotion	2,500	
Depreciation—store equipment	3,000	
Depreciation—delivery equipment	4,000	
Miscellaneous selling expenses	1,500	
Total selling expenses		$ 37,000
General expenses		
Office salaries	$ 28,500	
Rent	8,500	
Depreciation—furniture	1,500	
Utilities expense	2,500	
Insurance expense	1,000	
Miscellaneous expense	500	
Total general expense		42,500
Total operating expenses		79,500
Net income from operations		$ 37,500
Less interest expense		2,000
NET INCOME BEFORE TAXES		$ 35,500
Less federal income taxes		5,325
NET INCOME AFTER TAXES		$ 30,175

© CENGAGE LEARNING 2015

Revenues

Revenues are the dollar amounts earned by a firm from selling goods, providing services, or performing business activities. Like most businesses, Northeast Art Supply obtains its revenues solely from the sale of its products or services. The revenues section of its income statement begins with gross sales. **Gross sales** are the total dollar amount of all goods and services sold during the accounting period. Deductions made from this amount are

- *sales returns*—merchandise returned to the firm by its customers;
- *sales allowances*—price reductions offered to customers who accept slightly damaged or soiled merchandise; and
- *sales discounts*—price reductions offered to customers who pay their bills promptly.

The remainder is the firm's net sales. **Net sales** are the actual dollar amounts received by the firm for the goods and services it has sold after adjustment for returns, allowances, and discounts. For Northeast Art, net sales are $451,000.

revenues the dollar amounts earned by a firm from selling goods, providing services, or performing business activities

gross sales the total dollar amount of all goods and services sold during the accounting period

net sales the actual dollar amounts received by a firm for the goods and services it has sold after adjustment for returns, allowances, and discounts

Entrepreneurial Success

Accounting for First-Time Entrepreneurs

How can a firm be profitable but have no cash? The founder of a small soap-making supply firm was spending money to develop profitable new products more quickly than she was generating cash from sales. She needed to focus on her *statement of cash flows* and on her *cost of goods sold*. She did, and within a few years, she had built the company into a million-dollar business. Entrepreneurs in her situation need to control expenses and have sufficient cash flow to get through occasional unprofitable periods. It also makes sense to have money in the bank to see you through the rough times that may come.

What about being so busy selling to new customers that the firm doesn't do much to collect on outstanding invoices? A partner in a commercial tile company was pleased that he had more than $100,000 in accounts receivable—until he learned that some unpaid bills were so old that those customers had gone out of business. Now he pays more attention to his *accounts receivables*, and he doesn't sell to customers until they settle their outstanding balances. Some experts advise entrepreneurs to collect receivables within 30 days of making the sale.

Finally, record *revenues* at the proper time. One entrepreneur booked revenues in December when customers left deposits for custom-made furniture. Because he didn't deliver the items until January, the full sales should have been recorded in that month. Correcting this changed his firm's revenues and profitability for both years.

Sources: Based on information in Jason Federer, "4 Ways Entrepreneurs Can Reduce Risk," *Go Articles.com*, January 18, 2013, www.goarticles.com; Deanna Pogorelc, "Accounting 101 for the First-Time Entrepreneur," *Entrepreneurship.org*, March 22, 2012, www.entrepreneurship.org; Darren Dahl, "Basics of Accounting for Entrepreneurs," *New York Times*, August 3, 2011, www.nytimes.com; Don Sadler, "It's All in the Numbers," *Costco Connection*, April 2012, p. 43; "Pay Yourself First," *SCORE*, July 28, 2011, www.score.org.

Cost of Goods Sold

The standard method of determining the **cost of goods sold** by a retailing or a wholesaling firm can be summarized as follows:

Cost of goods sold = Beginning inventory + Net purchases − Ending inventory

According to Figure 15-8, Northeast Art Supply began its accounting period on January 1 with a merchandise inventory that cost $40,000. During the next 12 months, the firm purchased merchandise valued at $346,000. After deducting *purchase discounts*, however, it paid only $335,000 for this merchandise. Thus, during the year, Northeast had total *goods available for sale* valued at $40,000 plus $335,000, for a total of $375,000.

Twelve months later, at the end of the accounting period on December 31, Northeast had sold all but $41,000 worth of the available goods. The cost of goods sold by Northeast was therefore $375,000 less ending inventory of $41,000, or $334,000. It is now possible to calculate gross profit. A firm's **gross profit** is its net sales *less* the cost of goods sold. For Northeast Art Supply, gross profit was $117,000.

Operating Expenses

A firm's **operating expenses** are all business costs other than the cost of goods sold. Total operating expenses generally are divided into two categories: selling expenses or general expenses.

Selling expenses are costs related to the firm's marketing activities. For Northeast Art Supply, selling expenses total $37,000. *General expenses* are costs incurred in managing a business, in this case, a total of $42,500. Now it is possible

Sometimes the inventory you sell is really pretty! For a product like spring flowers, the right amount of inventory is very important. The goal for plant retailers is to make sure that customers can purchase the flowers they want and that the flowers are available at the right time. On the other hand, without inventory, sales decrease and customers often go to another retailer that has the merchandise the customers want.

cost of goods sold the dollar amount equal to beginning inventory *plus* net purchases *less* ending inventory

to total both selling and general expenses. As Figure 15-8 shows, total operating expenses for the accounting period are $79,500.

Net Income

When revenues exceed expenses, the difference is called **net income**. When expenses exceed revenues, the difference is called **net loss**. As Figure 15-8 shows, Northeast Art's *net income from operations* is computed as gross profit ($117,000) less total operating expenses ($79,500). For Northeast Art, net income from operations is $37,500. From this amount, *interest expense* of $2,000 is deducted to obtain a *net income before taxes* of $35,500. The interest expense is deducted in this section of the income statement because it is not an operating expense. Rather, it is an expense that results from financing the business.

Northeast Art's *federal income taxes* are $5,325. Although these taxes may or may not be payable immediately, they are definitely an expense that must be deducted from income. This leaves Northeast Art with a *net income after taxes* of $30,175. This amount may be used to pay a dividend to stockholders, it may be retained or reinvested in the firm, it may be used to reduce the firm's debts, or all three.

THE STATEMENT OF CASH FLOWS

Cash is vital to any business. In 1987, the SEC and the FASB required all publicly traded companies to include a statement of cash flows, along with their balance sheet and income statement, in their annual report. The **statement of cash flows** illustrates how the company's operating, investing, and financing activities affect cash during an accounting period. Whereas a firm's balance sheet reports dollar values for assets, liabilities, and owners' equity and an income statement reports the firm's dollar amount of profit or loss, the statement of cash flows focuses on how much cash is on hand to pay the firm's bills. Executives and managers can also use the information on a firm's statement of cash flows to determine how much cash is available to pay dividends to stockholders. Finally, the information on the statement of cash flows can be used to evaluate decisions related to a firm's future investments and financing needs. Outside stakeholders including investors, lenders, and suppliers are also interested in a firm's statement of cash flows. Investors want to know if a firm can pay dividends. Before extending credit to a firm, lenders and suppliers often use the information on the statement of cash flows to evaluate the firm's ability to repay its debts.

A statement of cash flows for Northeast Art Supply is illustrated in Figure 15-9. It provides information concerning the company's cash receipts and cash payments and is organized around three different activities: operating, investing, and financing.

- *Cash flows from operating activities.* This is the first section of a statement of cash flows. It addresses the firm's primary revenue source—providing goods and services. Typical adjustments include adding the amount of depreciation to a firm's net income. Other adjustments for increase or decrease in amounts for accounts receivable, inventory, accounts payable, and income taxes payable are also required to reflect a true picture of cash flows from operating activities.
- *Cash flows from investing activities.* The second section of the statement is concerned with cash flow from investments. This includes the purchase and sale of land, equipment, and other assets and investments.
- *Cash flows from financing activities.* The third and final section deals with the cash flow from all financing activities. It reports changes in debt obligation and owners' equity accounts. This includes loans and repayments, the sale and repurchase of the company's own stock, and cash dividends.

gross profit a firm's net sales *less* the cost of goods sold

Concept Check

✓ What is the difference between a balance sheet and an income statement?

✓ Explain how a retailing firm would determine the cost of goods sold during an accounting period.

✓ If a retailer has revenues of $700,000, cost of goods sold that total $270,000, and operating expenses that total $200,000, what is its net income before taxes?

Learning Objective

7 Describe business activities that affect a firm's cash flow.

operating expenses all business costs other than the cost of goods sold

net income occurs when revenues exceed expenses

net loss occurs when expenses exceed revenues

statement of cash flows a statement that illustrates how the company's operating, investing, and financing activities affect cash during an accounting period

FIGURE 15-9 Statement of Cash Flows

A statement of cash flows summarizes how a firm's operating, investing, and financing activities affect its cash during a specified period—one month, three months, six months, or a year. For Northeast Art Supply, the amount of cash at the end of the year reported on the statement of cash flows is $59,000— the same amount reported for the cash account on the firm's balance sheet.

NORTHEAST ART SUPPLY, INC.

Statement of Cash Flows
for the Year Ended
December 31, 20XX

Cash flows from operating activities

Net Income		$30,175
Adjustments to reconcile net income to net cash flows		
Depreciation	$ 8,500	
Decrease in accounts receivable	1,000	
Increase in inventory	(5,000)	
Increase in accounts payable	6,000	
Increase in income taxes payable	3,000	13,500
Net cash provided by operating activities		$43,675
Cash flows from investing activities		
Purchase of equipment	$ (2,000)	
Purchase of investments	(10,000)	
Sale of investments	20,000	
Net cash provided by investing activities		8,000
Cash flows from financing activities		
Payments on debt	$(23,000)	
Payment of dividends	(5,000)	
Net cash provided by financing activities		(28,000)
NET INCREASE IN CASH		$23,675
Cash at beginning of year		35,325
CASH AT END OF YEAR		$59,000

© CENGAGE LEARNING 2015

Concept Check

✓ What is the purpose of the statement of cash flows?

✓ In a statement of cash flows, what is included in the operating activities section? In the investing activities section? In the financial activities section?

The totals of all three activities are added to the beginning cash balance to determine the ending cash balance. For Northeast Art Supply, the ending cash balance is $59,000. Note that this is the same amount reported for the cash account on the firm's balance sheet. Together, the statement of cash flows, balance sheet, and income statement illustrate the results of past business decisions and reflect the firm's ability to pay debts and dividends and to finance new growth.

Learning Objective

8 Summarize how managers evaluate the financial health of a business.

EVALUATING FINANCIAL STATEMENTS

All three financial statements—the balance sheet, the income statement, and the statement of cash flows—can provide answers to a variety of questions about a firm's ability to do business and stay in business, its profitability, and its value as an investment. To evaluate a firm's financial health, often the first step is to compare a firm's financial data with other firms in similar industries and with its own financial results over recent accounting periods.

Comparing Financial Data

Many firms compare their financial results with those of competing firms, with industry averages, and with their own financial results. Comparisons are possible as long as accountants follow GAAPs. Except for minor differences in format and terms, the balance sheet, income statement, and statement of cash flows of Procter & Gamble, for example, will be similar to those of other large corporations, such as Clorox, Colgate-Palmolive, and Unilever, in the consumer goods industry. Comparisons among firms give executives, managers, and employees a general idea of a firm's relative effectiveness and its standing within the industry. Competitors' financial statements can be obtained from their annual reports—if they are public corporations. Industry averages are published by reporting services such as D&B (formerly Dun & Bradstreet) and Hoover's, Inc., as well as by some industry trade associations.

Today, most corporations include in their annual reports comparisons of the important elements of their financial statements for recent years. For example, Figure 15-10 shows such comparisons—of revenue, research and development (R&D), operating income, and sales and marketing expenses—for Microsoft Corporation, a world leader in the computer software industry. By examining these data, an operating

FIGURE 15-10 Comparisons of Present and Past Financial Statements for Microsoft Corporation

Most corporations include in their annual reports comparisons of the important elements of their financial statements for recent years.

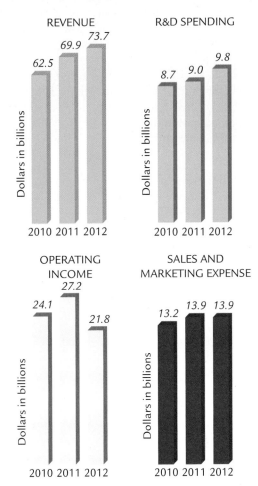

Source: Adapted from the Microsoft Corporation 2012 Annual Report, www.microsoft.com (accessed January 24, 2013).

manager can tell whether R&D expenditures have been increasing or decreasing over the past three years. The vice president of marketing can determine if the total amount of sales and marketing expenses is changing. Stockholders and potential investors, on the other hand, may be more concerned with increases or decreases in Microsoft's revenues and operating income over the same time period. Still another type of analysis of a firm's financial health involves computation of financial ratios.

Financial Ratios

A **financial ratio** is a number that shows the relationship between two elements of a firm's financial statements. While it is possible to calculate many different financial ratios, we'll only discuss three different ratios that are used to measure a firm's profitability, its ability to pay its debts, and how often it sells its inventory. Like the individual elements in financial statements, these ratios can be compared with those of competitors, with industry averages, and with the firm's past ratios from previous accounting periods. The information required to form these ratios is found in a firm's balance sheet, income statement, and statement of cash flows (in our examples for Northeast Art Supply, Figures 15-6, 15-8, and 15-9).

Evaluating financial statements is serious business. Even after a firm's financial statements are prepared, accountants often dig deeper and prepare audits to make sure that accounting information is accurate. They also calculate financial ratios to measure a firm's profitability, its ability to pay its debts, and how well it manages inventory.

financial ratio a number that shows the relationship between two elements of a firm's financial statements

return on sales (or profit margin) a financial ratio calculated by dividing net income after taxes by net sales

MEASURING A FIRM'S ABILITY TO EARN PROFITS A firm's net income after taxes indicates whether the firm is profitable. It does not, however, indicate how effectively the firm's resources are being used. For this latter purpose, a return on sales ratio can be computed. **Return on sales (or profit margin)** is a financial ratio calculated by dividing net income after taxes by net sales. For Northeast Art Supply,

$$\text{Return on sales} = \frac{\text{Net income after taxes}}{\text{Net sales}} = \frac{\$30,175}{\$451,000}$$

$$= 0.067, \text{ or } 6.7 \text{ percent}$$

The return on sales indicates how effectively the firm is transforming sales into profits. A higher return on sales is better than a low one. Today, the average return on sales for all business firms is between 4 and 5 percent. With a return on sales of 6.7 percent, Northeast Art Supply is above average. A low return on sales can be increased by reducing expenses, increasing sales, or both.

current ratio a financial ratio computed by dividing current assets by current liabilities

MEASURING A FIRM'S ABILITY TO PAY ITS DEBTS A current ratio can be used to evaluate a firm's ability to pay its current liabilities. A firm's **current ratio** is computed by dividing current assets by current liabilities. For Northeast Art Supply,

$$\text{Current ratio} = \frac{\text{Current assets}}{\text{Current liabilities}} = \frac{\$182,000}{\$70,000} = 2.6$$

This means that Northeast Art Supply has $2.60 of current assets for every $1 of current liabilities. The average current ratio for all industries is 2.0, but it varies greatly from industry to industry. A high current ratio indicates that a firm can pay its current liabilities. A low current ratio can be improved by repaying current liabilities, by reducing dividend payments to stockholders to increase the firm's cash balance, or by obtaining additional cash from investors.

MEASURING HOW WELL A FIRM MANAGES ITS INVENTORY A firm's **inventory turnover** is the number of times the firm sells its merchandise inventory in one year. It is approximated by dividing the cost of goods sold in one year by the average value of the inventory.

The average value of the inventory can be found by adding the beginning inventory value and the ending inventory value (given on the income statement) and dividing the sum by 2. For Northeast Art Supply, average inventory is $40,500. Thus

$$\text{Inventory turnover} = \frac{\text{cost of goods sold}}{\text{average inventory}} = \frac{\$334,000}{\$40,500}$$

$$= 8.2 \text{ times per year}$$

Northeast Art Supply sells its merchandise inventory 8.2 times each year, or about once every 45 days. The average inventory turnover for all firms is about 9 times per year, but turnover rates vary widely from industry to industry. For example, supermarkets may have inventory turnover rates of 20 or higher, whereas inventory turnover rates for furniture stores are generally well below the national average. The quickest way to improve inventory turnover is to order merchandise in smaller quantities at more frequent intervals.

Like the three ratios described in this section, the calculations for other financial ratios, including return on owners' equity, earnings per share, working capital, and debt-to-equity, are based on the information contained in a firm's balance sheet, income statement, and statement of cash flows. For more detailed information on ratio analysis, you may want to read more on the topic in an accounting or finance textbook or use an Internet search engine.

This chapter ends our discussion of management and accounting information. In Chapter 16, we see why firms need financing, how they obtain it, and how they ensure that funds are used effectively in keeping with the organization's goals.

inventory turnover a financial ratio calculated by dividing the cost of goods sold in one year by the average value of the inventory

Concept Check

✓ What are the benefits of comparing a firm's current financial information with information for previous accounting periods, with industry averages, and with financial information for competitors?

✓ Explain the calculation procedures for and significance of each of the following:

a. Return on sales.

b. The current ratio.

c. Inventory turnover.

Looking for Success? *Get Flashcards, Quizzes, Games, Crosswords, and more @ www.cengagebrain.com.*

Summary

1 Examine how information can reduce risk when making a decision.

The more information a manager has, the less risk there is that a decision will be incorrect. Information produces knowledge and empowers managers and employees to make better decisions. Because of the volume of information they receive each day and their need to make decisions on a daily basis, businesspeople use information rules to shorten the time spent analyzing choices. Information rules emerge when business research confirms the same results each time it studies the same or a similar set of circumstances. Although many people use the terms *data* and *information* interchangeably, there is a difference. Data are numerical or verbal descriptions that usually result from some sort of measurement. Information is data presented in a form that is useful for

a specific purpose. A database is a single collection of data and information stored in one place that can be used by people throughout an organization to make decisions. Although databases are important, the way the data and information are used is even more important. As a result, management information experts now use the term *knowledge management* (KM) to describe a firm's procedures for generating, using, and sharing the data and information.

2 Discuss management's information requirements.

A management information system (MIS) is a means of providing managers with the information they need to perform their jobs as effectively as possible. The purpose of an MIS (sometimes referred to as an information technology system or simply IT system) is to distribute timely and useful information from both internal and external sources to the decision makers who need it. The specific types of information managers need depend on their area of management and level within the firm. The size and complexity of an MIS must be tailored to the information needs of the organization it serves.

3 Outline the five functions of an information system.

The five functions performed by an MIS system are collecting data, storing data, updating data, processing data into information, and presenting information. Data may be collected from internal sources and external sources. An MIS must be able to store data until they are needed and to update them regularly to ensure that the information presented to managers and employees is accurate, complete, and timely. Data processing is the MIS function that transforms stored data into a form useful for a specific purpose. Finally, the processed data (which now can be called information) must be presented for use. Verbal information generally is presented in the form of a report. Numerical information most often is displayed in graphs, charts, or tables. In addition to the five basic functions performed by an MIS, managers and employees can use a decision-support system (DSS), an executive information system (EIS), expert system, and business application software to make decisions and to report data and information.

4 Explain why accurate accounting information and audited financial statements are important.

Accounting is the process of systematically collecting, analyzing, and reporting financial information. It can be used to answer questions about what has happened in the past; it also can be used to help make decisions about the future. The purpose of an audit is to make sure that a firm's financial statements have been prepared in accordance with generally accepted accounting principles. To help ensure that corporate financial information is accurate and in response to the accounting scandals that surfaced in the last few years, the Sarbanes–Oxley Act was signed into law. This law contains a number of provisions designed to restore public confidence in the accounting industry. Although many people think all accountants do the same thing, typical areas of expertise include managerial, financial, cost, tax, government, and not-for-profit. A private accountant is employed by a private firm. A public accountant performs accounting work for various individuals or firms on a fee basis. Most accounting firms include on their staffs at least one CPA.

5 Read and interpret a balance sheet.

A balance sheet (sometimes referred to as a statement of financial position) is a summary of a firm's

assets, liabilities, and owners' equity accounts at the end of an accounting period. This statement must demonstrate that the accounting equation is in balance. On the balance sheet, assets are categorized as current, fixed, or intangible. Similarly, liabilities can be divided into current liabilities and long-term liabilities. For a sole proprietorship or partnership, owners' equity is shown as the difference between assets and liabilities. For corporations, the owners' equity section reports the values of stock and retained earnings.

6 Read and interpret an income statement.

An income statement is a summary of a firm's financial operations during the specified accounting period. On the income statement, the company's gross profit is computed by subtracting the cost of goods sold from net sales. Operating expenses and interest expense then are deducted to compute net income before taxes. Finally, income taxes are deducted to obtain the firm's net income after taxes.

7 Describe business activities that affect a firm's cash flow.

Since 1987, the Securities and Exchange Commission (SEC) and the Financial Accounting Standards Board (FASB) have required all publicly traded companies to include a statement of cash flows in their annual reports. This statement illustrates how the company's operating, investing, and financing activities affect cash during an accounting period. Together, the cash flow statement, balance sheet, and income statement illustrate the results of past decisions and the business's ability to pay debts and dividends as well as to finance new growth.

8 Summarize how managers evaluate the financial health of a business.

The firm's financial statements and its accounting information become more meaningful when compared with information for competitors, for the industry in which the firm operates, and corresponding information for previous years. Such comparisons permit managers, employees, lenders, investors, and other interested people to pick out trends in growth, borrowing, income, and other business variables and to determine whether the firm is on the way to accomplishing its long-term goals. A number of financial ratios can be computed from the information in a firm's financial statements. These ratios provide a picture of a firm's profitability, its ability to pay its debts, and how often it sells its inventory. Like the information on the firm's financial statements, these ratios can and should be compared with information for competitors, for the industry in which the firm operates, and corresponding information for previous years.

Key Terms

You should now be able to define and give an example relevant to each of the following terms:

data (429)
information (429)
database (430)
knowledge management (KM) (430)
management information system (MIS) (430)
data processing (434)
statistic (434)
decision-support system (DSS) (435)
executive information system (EIS) (435)
expert system (437)

accounting (437)
audit (438)
generally accepted accounting principles (GAAPs) (438)
managerial accounting (440)
financial accounting (440)
certified public accountant (CPA) (441)
assets (441)
liabilities (441)
owners' equity (441)
accounting equation (441)

double-entry bookkeeping system (442)
annual report (442)
balance sheet (or statement of financial position) (442)
liquidity (442)
current assets (444)
fixed assets (444)
depreciation (444)
intangible assets (445)
current liabilities (445)
long-term liabilities (445)
retained earnings (445)
income statement (446)

revenues (447)
gross sales (447)
net sales (447)
cost of goods sold (448)
gross profit (449)
operating expenses (449)
net income (449)
net loss (449)
statement of cash flows (449)
financial ratio (452)
return on sales (or profit margin) (452)
current ratio (452)
inventory turnover (453)

Discussion Questions

1. Do managers really need all the kinds of information discussed in this chapter? If not, which kinds can they do without?
2. How can confidential data and information (such as the wages of individual employees) be kept confidential and yet still be available to managers who need them?
3. Bankers usually insist that prospective borrowers submit audited financial statements along with a loan application. Why should financial statements be audited by a CPA?
4. What can be said about a firm whose owners' equity is a negative amount? How could such a situation come about?
5. Do the balance sheet, income statement, and statement of cash flows contain all the information you might want as a potential lender or stockholder? What other information would you like to examine?
6. Of the three financial ratios discussed in this chapter, which do you think is the most important financial ratio? Why?

Test Yourself

Matching Questions

1. _____ Data that have been processed.
2. _____ A term for the debts of a firm.
3. _____ It is the difference between a firm's assets and its liabilities.
4. _____ It transforms data into useful information.
5. _____ Inventories are an example.
6. _____ The ease with which assets can be converted into cash.
7. _____ This statement reveals the financial position of the firm.
8. _____ It illustrates how operating, investing, and financing activities affect cash.
9. _____ It incorporates a firm's procedures for generating, using, and sharing the data and information contained in the firm's database.
10. _____ The result of dividing current assets by current liabilities.

a. assets
b. balance sheet
c. cost of goods sold
d. current ratio
e. data processing
f. information
g. liabilities
h. liquidity
i. knowledge management
j. owners' equity
k. public accountant
l. statement of cash flows

True False Questions

11. **T   F**   The more information a manager has, the less risk there is that a decision will be incorrect.

12. **T   F**   A single collection of data stored in one place is called a data center.

13. **T   F**   Information is defined as numerical or verbal descriptions that usually result from sort of measurement.

14. **T   F**   In a business report, the conclusions present suggestions on how the problem might be solved.

15. **T   F**   An expert system uses artificial intelligence to imitate a human's ability to think.

16. **T   F**   There is added protection for whistle-blowers who report violations of the Sarbanes–Oxley Act.

17. **T   F**   A private accountant is an accountant whose services may be hired on a fee basis by individuals or business firms.

18. **T   F**   The accounting equation is assets + liabilities = owners' equity.

19. **T   F**   Marketable securities can be converted into cash in a matter of days.

20. **T   F**   Stockholders' equity represents the total value of a corporation's stock plus retained earnings that have accumulated to date.

Multiple-Choice Questions

21. _____ Which statement is not true about a balance sheet?
   a. It provides proof that Assets = Liabilities + Owners' equity.
   b. It lists the current, fixed, and intangible assets.
   c. It summarizes the firm's revenues and expenses during one accounting period.
   d. It gives the liabilities of the firm.
   e. It shows the owners' equity in the business.

22. _____ The board of directors decided to pay 50 percent of the firm's $460,000 earnings in dividends to the stockholders. The firm has retained earnings of $680,000 on the books. After the dividends are paid, which of the following statements is true about the firm's retained earnings account?
   a. The new value of the firm's retained earnings is $910,000.
   b. The new value of the firm's retained earnings is $450,000.
   c. The firm failed to reach its profit goal.
   d. Each shareholder will receive more than he or she received last year.
   e. The firm's retained earnings are too high.

23. _____ A firm had gross profits from sales in the amount of $180,000, operating expenses of $90,000, and federal incomes taxes of $20,000. What was the firm's net income after taxes?
   a. $10,000
   b. $20,000
   c. $70,000
   d. $90,000
   e. $200,000

24. _____ The Sarbanes–Oxley Act
   a. requires the SEC to establish a federal oversight board for the accounting industry.
   b. requires CEOs to certify periodic financial statements.
   c. subjects auditors, accountants, and employees to imprisonment for destroying financial documents.
   d. prohibits many types of consulting services by accounting firms.
   e. All of the above are true.

25. _____ You are a purchasing manager in a large firm and are responsible for deciding on and ordering the appropriate software program that allows the user to prepare and edit letters and store them on a computer memory stick. Which type of program will you order?
   a. Spreadsheet
   b. Word processing
   c. Graphics
   d. Communications
   e. Database

26. _____ An income statement is sometimes called the
   a. statement of financial position.
   b. owners' equity statement.
   c. earnings statement.
   d. statement of cash inflow.
   e. statement of revenues.

27. _____ When a company reports financial numbers that are lower than expected, generally
   a. the company's stock value will increase.
   b. the company's stock value will decrease.
   c. the company will restate its earnings amount.
   d. the stockholders' will immediately ask for an audit.
   e. the corporate officers will resign and new officers will be appointed.

28. _____ An audit is
   a. performed by the firm's private bookkeepers.
   b. not necessary if the firm used accepted bookkeeping procedures.
   c. required by many lenders who are trying to validate a firm's accounting statements.
   d. a waste of the firm's resources.
   e. a guarantee that a firm hasn't "cooked" the books.

29. _____ Management information systems
     a. collect data, hire personnel, and evaluate workers.
     b. store data, present data to users, and make final decisions.
     c. collect, store, update, process, and present data.
     d. supervise personnel, reprimand workers, and conduct follow-up evaluations.
     e. collect relevant information.

30. _____ As an administrative manager, you must ensure that
     a. information is protected from employees.
     b. information is used in a consistent manner.
     c. the smart group receives the data first.
     d. the promotional campaigns are aired on time.
     e. new product planning is on schedule.

Answers to the Test Yourself questions appear at the end of the book on page TY-2.

Video Case
Making the Numbers or Faking the Numbers?

Will sales and profits meet the expectations of investors and Wall Street analysts? Managers at public corporations must answer this important question quarter after quarter, year after year. In an ideal world—one in which there is never an economic crisis, expenses never go up, and customers never buy competing products—the corporation's price for a share of its stock would soar, and investors would cheer as every financial report showed ever-higher sales revenues, profit margins, and earnings.

In the real world, however, many uncontrollable and unpredictable factors can affect a corporation's performance. Customers may buy fewer units or postpone purchases, competitors may introduce superior products, expenses may rise, interest rates may climb, and buying power may plummet. Faced with the prospect of releasing financial results that fall short of Wall Street's expectations, managers may feel intense pressure to "make the numbers" using a variety of accounting techniques.

For example, executives and board members at Groupon—the premier source for consumers who want to take advantage of daily deals—found itself having to answer difficult questions about how it reported revenues, expenses, and its internal accounting controls. What's worse, the questions came just a few months after it sold stock to the public. As a result of increased scrutiny by both regulators and investors, the company was forced to reexamine its accounting practices and tighten its audit procedures.

Under the Sarbanes–Oxley Act, the CEO and CFO now must certify the corporation's financial reports. (For more information about Sarbanes–Oxley, visit www.aicpa.org, the website of the American Institute of Certified Public Accountants.) Immediately after this legislation became effective, hundreds of companies restated their earnings, a sign that stricter accounting controls were having the intended effect. "I don't mean to sugarcoat the figure on restatements," says Steve Odland, the former CEO of Office Depot, "but I think it is positive—it shows a healthy system." Yet not all earnings restatements are due to accounting irregularities. "The general impression of the public is that accounting rules are black and white," he adds. "They are often anything but

that, and in many instances the changes in earnings came after new interpretations by the chief accountant of the SEC."

Now that stricter regulation has been in force for some time, fewer and fewer corporations are announcing restatements. In fact, the number of corporations restating earnings has declined since it peaked in 2006. The chief reason for the decline is that corporations and their accounting firms have learned to dig deeper and analyze the process used to produce the figures for financial statements, as well as checking the numbers themselves.

Because accounting rules are open to interpretation, managers sometimes find themselves facing ethical dilemmas when a corporation feels pressure to live up to Wall Street's expectations. Consider the hypothetical situation at Commodore Appliances, a fictional company that sells to Home Depot, Lowe's, and other major retail chains. Margaret, the vice president of sales, has told Rob, a district manager, that the company's sales are down 10 percent in the current quarter. She points out that sales in Rob's district are down 20 percent and states that higher-level managers want him to improve this month's figures using "book and hold," which means recording future sales transactions in the current period.

Rob hesitates, saying that the company is gaining market share and that he needs more time to get sales momentum going. He thinks "book and hold" is not a good business practice, even if it is legal. Margaret hints that Rob will lose his job if his sales figures don't look better and stresses that he will need the book-and-hold approach for one month only. Rob realizes that if he doesn't go along, he won't be working at Commodore for very much longer.

Meeting with Kevin, one of Commodore's auditors, Rob learns that book and hold meets GAAPs. Kevin emphasizes that customers must be willing to take title to the goods before they're delivered or billed. Any book-and-hold sales must be real, backed by documentation such as e-mails to and from buyers, and the transactions must be completed in the near future.

Rob is at a crossroads: His sales figures must be higher if Commodore is to achieve its performance targets, yet he doesn't know exactly when (or if) he actually would complete any book-and-hold sales he might report this month. He doesn't want to mislead anyone, but he also doesn't want to lose his job or put other people's jobs in jeopardy by refusing to do what he is being asked to do. Rob is confident that he can improve his district's sales over the long term. However, Commodore's executives are pressuring Rob to make the sales figures look better right now. What should he do?[5]

Questions

1. What are the ethical and legal implications of using accounting practices such as the book-and-hold technique to accelerate revenues and inflate corporate earnings?
2. Why would Commodore's auditor insist that Rob document any sales booked under the book-and-hold technique?
3. If you were in Rob's situation, would you agree to use the book-and-hold technique this month to accelerate revenues? Justify your decision.
4. Imagine that Commodore has taken out a multimillion-dollar loan that must be repaid next year. How might the lender react if it learned that Commodore was using the book-and-hold method to make revenues look higher than they really are?

Building Skills for Career Success

1. Using Social Media

All of the Big Four accounting firms are active on Twitter, as well as posting messages, content, and photos on Facebook, listing job openings on LinkedIn, and posting videos on YouTube. The idea is to connect with clients and potential job candidates, interact with clients and potential clients, engage employees, showcase the firm's expertise, and polish their reputations.

Assignment

1. Choose one of the Big Four accounting firms and take a look at its Twitter, Facebook, LinkedIn, or YouTube websites.
2. How does the accounting firm you chose use social media? Are they trying to reach potential job candidates, existing clients and potential clients, or employees?
3. Do you think that social media is an effective way for an accounting firm to reach the target audience?

2. Building Team Skills

This has been a bad year for Miami-based Park Avenue Furniture. The firm increased sales revenues to $1,400,000, but total expenses ballooned to $1,750,000. Although management realized that some of the firm's expenses were out of control, including cost of goods sold ($700,000), salaries ($450,000), and advertising costs ($140,000), it could not contain expenses. As a result, the furniture retailer lost $350,000. To make matters worse, the retailer applied for a $350,000 loan at Fidelity National Bank and was turned down. The bank officer, Mike Nettles, said that the firm already had too much debt. At that time, liabilities totaled $420,000; owners' equity was $600,000.

Assignment

1. In groups of three or four, analyze the financial condition of Park Avenue Furniture.

2. Discuss why you think the bank officer turned down Park Avenue's loan request.
3. Prepare a detailed plan of action to improve the financial health of Park Avenue Furniture over the next 12 months.

3. Researching Different Careers

To improve productivity, employers expect employees to use computers and computer software. Typical business applications include e-mail, word processing, spreadsheets, and graphics. By improving your skills in these areas, you can increase your chances not only of being employed but also of being promoted once you are employed.

Assignment

1. Assess your computer skills by placing a check in the appropriate column in the following table:

Software	Skill Level			
	None	Low	Average	High
e-Mail				
Word processing				
Desktop publishing				
Accounting				
Database management				
Graphics				
Spreadsheet				
Internet research				

2. Describe your self-assessment in a written report. Specify the skills in which you need to become more proficient, and outline a plan for doing this.

Endnotes

1. Based on information in Doug Tsuruoka, "Intuit on Track for Double-Digit FY '13 Growth: CFO," *Investor's Business Daily*, November 19, 2012, http://investors.com; R. Wang, "How Intuit Uses Cloud Computing," *Forbes*, February 9, 2012, www.forbes.com; Chris Kanaracus, "Intuit Ties QuickBooks to Demandforce marketing software," *PC World*, November 1, 2012, www.pcworld.com; www.intuit.com.

2. John Smith, EU's McCreevy, IASB's Smith on Financial Reporting in a Changing World FEI Financial Reporting Blog website at http://financailexecutives.blogspot.com, accessed May 8, 2009.

3. "Summary of the Provisions of the Sarbanes–Oxley Act of 2002," the AICPA website at www.aicpa.org, accessed January 23, 2013.

4. *Occupational Outlook Handbook*, The U.S. Bureau of Labor Statistics website at www.bls.gov/oco/ocos001.htm, accessed January 23, 2013.

5. Based on information from Jonathon Weil, "Groupon IPO Scandal Is the Sleaze that's Legal," the Bloomberg website at www.bloomberg.com, accessed April 4, 2012; Walter Pavlo, "Groupon Accounting Scandal, and We're Surprised," the Forbes website at www.forbes.com, accessed April 3, 2012; The Office Depot website at www.officedepot.com, accessed April 12, 2012; Matt Krantz, "Companies Are Making Fewer Accounting Mistakes," *USA Today*, March 1, 2010, www.usatoday.com; Jane Sasseen, "White-Collar Crime: Who Does Time?" *BusinessWeek*, February 6, 2006, www.businessweek.com; Stephen Labaton, "Four Years Later, Enron's Shadow Lingers as Change Comes Slowly," *New York Times*, January 5, 2006, C1; *Making the Numbers at Commodore Appliance* (Cengage video).

Chapter 16

Mastering Financial Management

Why Should You Care?

The old saying goes, "Money makes the world go around." For business firms, this is true. It's hard to operate a business without money. In this chapter, we discuss how financial management is used to obtain money and ensure that it is used effectively.

Learning Objectives

Once you complete this chapter, you will be able to:

1 Understand why financial management is important in today's uncertain economy.

2 Identify a firm's short- and long-term financial needs.

3 Summarize the process of planning for financial management.

4 Identify the services provided by banks and financial institutions for their business customers.

5 Describe the advantages and disadvantages of different methods of short-term debt financing.

6 Evaluate the advantages and disadvantages of equity financing.

7 Evaluate the advantages and disadvantages of long-term debt financing.

How Cisco Finances Future Growth

Founded in 1984 to make switches and routers for computer systems, Cisco Systems (www.cisco.com) approaches its fourth decade in business with billions of dollars on hand to fuel plans for future growth. The company sells networking gear, software, and services in over 160 countries, employing 67,000 people and ringing up $46 billion in annual revenue.

One way Cisco maintains its market leadership in the fast-paced technology industry is by investing more than $5 billion, year after year, to research and develop innovative products and processes for Internet-based communication and collaboration. As a result, Cisco files for hundreds of patents each year, a key element in its strategy for ongoing success. The company also buys companies to strengthen or complement its position in key areas. Not long ago, it acquired NDS Group, to profit from the boom in digital delivery of television programming across multiple devices. Earlier, it had acquired WebEx, which offers web-based conferencing services, to accelerate expansion in the fast-growing market for online collaboration.

How does Cisco find the billions it needs for R&D and acquisitions every year? First, it always keeps money in the bank, as well as marketable securities it can convert into cash on short notice as needed. Second, the company sometimes uses long-term debt financing to raise money. Since it became a publicly traded corporation in 1990, Cisco has issued corporate bonds only four times. Most recently, it sold $4 billion worth of unsecured bonds at historically low interest rates, knowing that the cost of borrowing was inexpensive enough to justify taking on repayments for up to six years. The company used some of that money to buy back shares of its common stock, which were trading at low prices during the recent period of economic turmoil. By taking good care of its financial situation today, Cisco will be ready for the challenges and opportunities of growth in the future.[1]

Did You Know?

Cisco is a global powerhouse in networking technology, with $46 billion in annual revenue and 67,000 employees in over 160 countries.

Question: How important is financial management for a business firm like Cisco Systems—the company profiled in the Inside Business feature for this chapter?

Answer: Very Important! Without financial management the company would not be able to pay its bills, fund the research needed to develop new products and services, and acquire other companies to maintain its market leadership. And without financial management, a business firm would not be able to borrow money (debt capital) or obtain money from stockholders (equity capital). The fact is that finances are necessary for the efficient operation of any business firm. Without money, creditors and lenders can't be paid, employees don't get paychecks, and the business may close its doors and cease to exist. On the other hand, when a company—like Cisco Systems—manages its finances it can not only pay its bills and employees, but can grow and expand in order to meet the needs of its customers and society.

In this chapter we examine why financial management is important. Then, we discuss how firms find the financing required to meet two needs of all business organizations: the need for money to start a business and keep it going, and the need to manage that money effectively. We also look at how firms develop financial plans and evaluate financial performance. Then we examine typical banking services and compare various methods of obtaining short-term and long-term financing.

WHY FINANCIAL MANAGEMENT?

Financial management can make the difference between success and failure for both large and small businesses. For example, executives at Ford used aggressive financial planning to anticipate the automaker's need for financing during the recent economic crisis. To avoid the same fate as General Motors and Chrysler—bankruptcy—Ford's financial managers borrowed money in anticipation

Learning Objective

1 Understand why financial management is important in today's uncertain economy.

CHRIS HOWES/WILD PLACES PHOTOGRAPHY/ALAMY

How do managers decide how much inventory is needed? One of the most perplexing problems financial managers must deal with is the amount of inventory a retail store needs. If a retailer has too much inventory, then too much money is tied up in merchandise that is not selling. If a retailer has too little inventory, it may not have enough merchandise to meet consumer demand.

of a downturn in the company's sales and profits. Ford also sold both stocks and bonds to raise the money it needed to keep the company operating during the crisis and even build for the future. Did that financial plan work? The answer: A definite yes! Today, Ford is selling more cars, developing environmentally friendly engines, creating concept cars for the future, and has returned to profitability.

Managers and employees must find the money needed to keep a business operating and pay lenders and suppliers, employees, and fund all the goals and objectives that a successful business wants to achieve. A business that cannot pay its bills may have to close its doors and even be forced to file for bankruptcy protection. Fortunately, the number of business firms filing for bankruptcy has decreased when compared to the large number of firms filing bankruptcy during the worst part of the recent economic crisis, as illustrated in Figure 16-1. And now that the nation's economy is improving, the number of bankruptcies should continue to decline.

The Need for Financial Management

financial management all the activities concerned with obtaining money and using it effectively

Financial management consists of all the activities concerned with obtaining money and using it effectively. To some extent, financial management can be viewed as a two-sided problem. On one side, the uses of funds often dictate the type or types of financing needed by a business. On the other side, the activities a business can undertake are determined by the types of financing available. Financial managers must ensure that funds are available when needed, that they are obtained at the lowest

FIGURE 16-1 Business Bankruptcies in the United States

The number of businesses that filed for bankruptcy increased during the economic crisis. (*Note*: At the time of publication, 2012 was the most recent year for which complete statistics were available.)

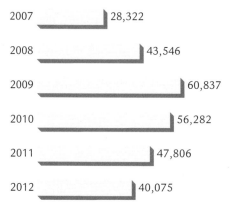

Year	Bankruptcies
2007	28,322
2008	43,546
2009	60,837
2010	56,282
2011	47,806
2012	40,075

Source: Based on The American Bankruptcy Institute website at www.abiworld.org (accessed June 11, 2013).

possible cost, and that they are used as efficiently as possible. In addition, proper financial management must also ensure that:

- Financing priorities are established in line with organizational goals and objectives.
- Spending is planned and controlled.
- Sufficient financing is available when it is needed, both now and in the future.
- A firm's credit customers pay their bills on time, and the number of past due accounts is reduced.
- Bills are paid promptly to protect the firm's credit rating and its ability to borrow money.
- The funds required for paying the firm's taxes are available when needed to meet tax deadlines.
- Excess cash is invested in certificates of deposit (CDs), government securities, or conservative, marketable securities.

Financial Reform After the Economic Crisis

The job of financial managers became a bit easier as the economy stabilized. Still, it became apparent that something needed to be done to stabilize the financial system and prevent future economic meltdowns. In the wake of the crisis that affected both business firms and individuals, a cry for more regulations and reforms became a high priority. To meet this need, President Obama signed the Dodd–Frank Wall Street Reform and Consumer Protection Act into law on July 21, 2010. Even with the new regulations, some experts say the law did not go far enough while others argue it went too far. Although the U.S. Senate and House of Representatives debate additional regulations, the goals are to hold Wall Street firms accountable for their actions, end taxpayer bailouts, tighten regulations for major financial firms, and increase government oversight. There has also been debate about limiting the amount of executive pay and bonuses, limiting the size of the largest financial firms, and curbing speculative investment techniques that were used by banks before the crisis.

New regulations will also protect American families from unfair, abusive financial and banking practices. For business firms, the impact of new regulations could increase the time and cost of obtaining both short- and long-term financing.

Careers in Finance

A career in finance can be rewarding. As an added bonus, the Bureau of Labor Statistics projects there will be about a 9 percent increase in the number of jobs in the financial sector of the economy between now and 2020.[2]

Today, there are many different types of positions in finance. At the executive level, most large business firms have a chief financial officer for financial management. A **chief financial officer (CFO)** is a high-level corporate executive who manages a firm's finances and reports directly to the company's chief executive officer or president. Some firms prefer to use the titles vice president of financial management, treasurer, or controller instead of the CFO title for executive-level positions in the finance area.

Although some executives in finance do make $300,000 a year or more, many entry-level and lower-level positions that pay quite a bit less are available. Banks, insurance companies, and investment firms obviously have a need for workers who can manage and analyze financial data. So do businesses involved in manufacturing, services, and marketing. Colleges and universities, not-for-profit organizations, and government entities at all levels also need finance workers.

People in finance must have certain traits and skills. One of the most important priorities for someone interested in a finance career is honesty. Be warned: Investors, lenders, and other corporate executives expect financial managers to be above

chief financial officer (CFO) a high-level corporate executive who manages a firm's finances and reports directly to the company's chief executive officer or president

reproach. Moreover, both federal and state government entities have enacted legislation to ensure that corporate financial statements reflect the "real" status of a firm's financial position. In addition to honesty, managers and employees in the finance area must:

1. Have a strong background in accounting or mathematics.
2. Know how to use a computer to analyze data.
3. Be an expert at both written and oral communication.

Typical job titles in finance include bank officer, consumer credit officer, financial analyst, financial planner, loan officer, insurance analyst, and investment account executive. Depending on qualifications, work experience, and education, starting salaries generally begin at $25,000 to $35,000 a year, but it is not uncommon for college graduates to earn higher salaries. In addition to salary, many employees have attractive benefits and other perks that make a career in financial management attractive.

Concept Check

✓ For a business firm, what type of activities does financial management involve?

✓ How has financial management changed after the recent economic crisis?

✓ To be successful, what traits and skills does an employee in the finance industry need?

Learning Objective

2 Identify a firm's short- and long-term financial needs.

short-term financing money that will be used for one year or less

cash flow the movement of money into and out of an organization

THE NEED FOR FINANCING

Money is needed both to start a business and to keep it going. The original investment of the owners, along with money they may have borrowed, should be enough to open the doors. After that, ideally sales revenues should be used to pay the firm's expenses and provide a profit as well.

This is exactly what happens in a successful firm—over the long run. However, income and expenses may vary from month to month or from year to year. Temporary financing may be needed when expenses are high or sales are low. Then, too, situations such as the opportunity to purchase a new facility or expand an existing plant may require more money than is currently available within a firm.

Short-Term Financing

Short-term financing is money that will be used for one year or less. As illustrated in Table 16-1, there are many short-term financing needs, but three deserve special attention. First, certain business practices may affect a firm's cash flow and create a need for short-term financing. **Cash flow** is the movement of money into and out of an organization. The goal is to have sufficient money coming into the firm in any period to cover the firm's expenses during that period. This goal, however, is not always achieved. For example, California-based Callaway Golf offers credit to retailers and wholesalers that carry the firm's golf clubs, balls, clothing, and golf accessories. Credit purchases made by Callaway's retailers generally are not paid until 30 to 60 days (or more) after the transaction. Callaway therefore may need short-term financing to pay its bills until its customers have paid theirs.

A second major need for short-term financing is speculative production. **Speculative production** refers to the time lag between the actual production of goods and when the goods are sold. Consider what happens when a firm such as Connecticut-based Stanley Black & Decker begins to manufacture power and small hand tools for sale during the Christmas season. Manufacturing begins in

© LENETSTAN/SHUTTERSTOCK.COM

A career in finance can mean more than money! While most people think a job in finance is all about "money," there are other attractive perks and benefits. According to the U.S. Bureau of Labor Statistics, jobs in finance are expected to increase about 9 percent between now and the year 2020. And there are finance jobs in all-types of companies, schools and universities, not-for-profit organizations, and government entities. You could even become a financial planner and help people manage their money.

TABLE 16-1 Comparison of Short- and Long-Term Financing

Whether a business seeks short- or long-term financing depends on what the money will be used for.	
Corporate Cash Needs	
Short-Term Financing Needs	**Long-Term Financing Needs**
Cash-flow problems	Business start-up costs
Speculative production	Mergers and acquisitions
Current inventory needs	New product development
Monthly expenses	Long-term marketing activities
Short-term promotional needs	Replacement of equipment
Unexpected emergencies	Expansion of facilities

© CENGAGE LEARNING 2015

March, April, and May, and the firm negotiates short-term financing to buy materials and supplies, to pay wages and rent, and to cover inventory costs until its products eventually are sold to wholesalers and retailers later in the year. Take a look at Figure 16-2. Although Stanley Black & Decker manufactures and sells finished products all during the year, expenses peak during the first part of the year. During this same period, sales revenues are low. Once the firm's finished products are shipped to retailers and wholesalers and payment is received (usually within 30 to 60 days), sales revenues are used to repay short-term financing.

A third need for short-term financing is to increase inventory. Retailers that range in size from Walmart to the neighborhood drugstore need short-term financing to build up their inventories before peak selling periods. For example, Dallas-based Bruce Miller Nurseries must increase the number of shrubs, trees, and flowering plants that it makes available for sale during the spring and

speculative production the time lag between the actual production of goods and when the goods are sold

FIGURE 16-2 Cash Flow for a Manufacturing Business

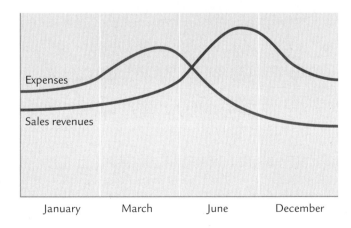

Manufacturers such as Stanley Black & Decker often use short-term financing to pay expenses during the production process. Once goods are shipped to retailers and wholesalers and payment is received, sales revenues are used to repay short-term financing.

Expenses

Sales revenues

January   March   June   December

© CENGAGE LEARNING 2015

long-term financing money that will be used for longer than one year

Business success often begins with a financial plan. Before the merchandise in this IKEA warehouse can be sold, it must be purchased from manufacturers or suppliers and then stored until it is needed in the retailer's stores. *Successful* businesses often use sound financial planning built on the firm's goals and objectives, different types of budgets, and available sources of funds to make sure financing is available to purchase inventory and other necessities needed to operate a business.

summer growing seasons. To obtain this merchandise inventory from growers or wholesalers, it uses short-term financing and repays the loans when the merchandise is sold.

Long-Term Financing

Long-term financing is money that will be used for longer than one year. Long-term financing obviously is needed to start a new business. As Table 16-1 shows, it is also needed for business mergers and acquisitions, new product development, long-term marketing activities, replacement of equipment that has become obsolete, and expansion of facilities.

The amounts of long-term financing needed by large firms can seem almost unreal. The 3M Company—a large multinational corporation known for research and development—spent $1.6 billion in 2012 and has invested more than $7 billion over the last five years to develop new products designed to make people's lives easier and safer.[3]

The Risk–Return Ratio

According to financial experts, business firms will find it more difficult to raise both short- and long-term financing in the future for two reasons. First, financial reform and increased regulations will lengthen the process required to obtain financing. Second, both lenders and investors are more cautious about who receives financing. As a result of these two factors, financial managers must develop a strong financial plan that describes how the money will be used and how it will be repaid.

When developing a financial plan for a business, a financial manager must also consider the risk–return ratio when making decisions that affect the firm's finances. The **risk–return ratio** is based on the principle that a high-risk decision should generate higher financial returns for a business. On the other hand, more conservative decisions (with less risk) often generate lesser returns. Although financial managers want higher returns, they often must strive for a balance between risk and return. For example, Ohio-based American Electric Power may consider investing millions of dollars to fund research into new solar technology that could enable the company to use the sun to generate electrical power. Yet, financial managers (along with other managers throughout the organization) must determine the potential return before committing to such a costly research project.

PLANNING—THE BASIS OF SOUND FINANCIAL MANAGEMENT

In Chapter 6, we defined a *plan* as an outline of the actions by which an organization intends to accomplish its goals and objectives. A **financial plan**, then, is a plan for obtaining and using the money needed to implement an organization's goals and objectives.

Developing the Financial Plan

Financial planning (like all planning) begins with establishing a set of valid goals and objectives. Financial managers must then determine how much money is needed to accomplish each goal and objective. Finally, financial managers must identify available sources of financing and decide which to use. The three steps involved in financial planning are illustrated in Figure 16-3.

Concept Check

✓ How does short-term financing differ from long-term financing? Give two business uses for each type of financing.

✓ What is speculative production? How is it related to a firm's cash-flow problems?

Learning Objective

3 Summarize the process of planning for financial management.

risk–return ratio a ratio based on the principle that a high-risk decision should generate higher financial returns for a business and more conservative decisions often generate lower returns

financial plan a plan for obtaining and using the money needed to implement an organization's goals and objectives

FIGURE 16-3 The Three Steps of Financial Planning

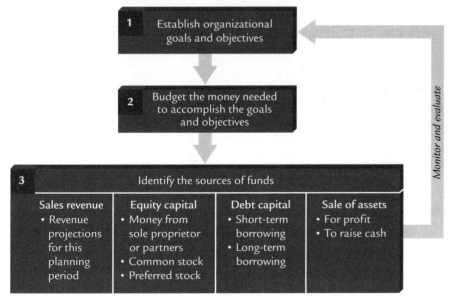

After a financial plan has been developed, it must be monitored continually to ensure that it actually fulfills the firm's goals.

1 Establish organizational goals and objectives

2 Budget the money needed to accomplish the goals and objectives

3 Identify the sources of funds

Sales revenue	Equity capital	Debt capital	Sale of assets
• Revenue projections for this planning period	• Money from sole proprietor or partners • Common stock • Preferred stock	• Short-term borrowing • Long-term borrowing	• For profit • To raise cash

Monitor and evaluate

© CENGAGE LEARNING 2015

ESTABLISHING ORGANIZATIONAL GOALS AND OBJECTIVES As pointed out in Chapter 6, a *goal* is an end result that an organization expects to achieve over a one- to ten-year period. An *objective* was defined in Chapter 6 as a specific statement detailing what an organization intends to accomplish over a shorter period of time. If goals and objectives are not specific and measurable, they cannot be translated into dollar costs, and financial planning cannot proceed. For large corporations, both goals and objectives can be expensive. For example, have you ever wondered how much McDonald's spends on advertising? Well, to reach the nearly 69 million customers it serves each day in 119 countries, the world's most famous fast-food restaurant chain spends over $768 million each year.[4]

BUDGETING FOR FINANCIAL NEEDS Once planners know what the firm's goals and objectives are for a specific period—say, the next calendar year—they can construct a budget that projects the costs the firm will incur and the sales revenues it will receive. Specifically, a **budget** is a financial statement that projects income, expenditures, or both over a specified future period.

Usually, the budgeting process begins with the construction of departmental budgets for sales and various types of expenses. Financial managers can easily combine each department's budget for sales and expenses into a company-wide cash budget. A **cash budget** estimates cash receipts and cash expenditures over a specified period. Notice in the cash budget for Stars and Stripes Clothing, shown in Figure 16-4, cash sales and collections are listed at the top for each calendar quarter. Payments for purchases and routine expenses are listed in the middle section. Using this information, it is possible to calculate the anticipated cash gain or loss at the end of each quarter for this retail clothing store.

Most firms today use one of two approaches to budgeting. In the *traditional* approach, each new budget is based on the dollar amounts contained in the budget for the preceding year. These amounts are modified to reflect any revised goals, and managers are required to justify only new expenditures. The problem with this approach is that it leaves room for padding budget items to protect the (sometimes selfish) interests of the manager or his or her department.

budget a financial statement that projects income, expenditures, or both over a specified future period

cash budget a financial statement that estimates cash receipts and cash expenditures over a specified period

FIGURE 16-4 Cash Budget for Stars and Stripes Clothing

A company-wide cash budget projects sales, collections, purchases, and expenses over a specified period to anticipate cash surpluses and deficits.

STARS AND STRIPES CLOTHING
Cash Budget   From January 1, 2013 to December 31, 2013

	First Quarter ($)	Second Quarter ($)	Third Quarter ($)	Fourth Quarter ($)	Total ($)
Cash sales and collections	150,000	160,000	150,000	185,000	645,000
Less payments					
Purchases	110,000	80,000	90,000	60,000	340,000
Wages/salaries	25,000	20,000	25,000	30,000	100,000
Rent	10,000	10,000	12,000	12,000	44,000
Other expenses	4,000	4,000	5,000	6,000	19,000
Taxes	8,000	8,000	10,000	10,000	36,000
Total payments	157,000	122,000	142,000	118,000	539,000
Cash gain or (loss)	(7,000)	38,000	8,000	67,000	106,000

This problem is essentially eliminated through zero-base budgeting. **Zero-base budgeting** is a budgeting approach in which every expense in every budget must be justified.

To develop a plan for long-term financing needs, managers often construct a capital budget. A **capital budget** estimates a firm's expenditures for major assets, including new product development, expansion of facilities, replacement of obsolete equipment, and mergers and acquisitions. For example, 3G Capital Management and Berkshire Hathaway purchased Heinz—a company known for manufacturing ketchup. Berkshire Hathaway, a company known for purchasing well-managed and innovative companies, constructed a capital budget to determine the best way to finance its part of the $28 billion 2013 acquisition.[5]

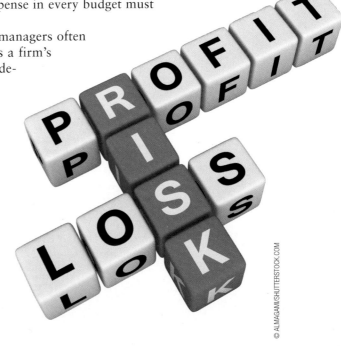

IDENTIFYING SOURCES OF FUNDS The four primary sources of funds, listed in Figure 16-3, are sales revenue, equity capital, debt capital, and proceeds from the sale of assets. Future sales revenue generally provides the greatest part of a firm's financing. Figure 16-4 shows that for Stars and Stripes Clothing, sales for the year are expected to cover all expenses and to provide a cash gain of $106,000. However, Stars and Stripes has a problem in the first quarter, when sales are expected to fall short of expenses by $7,000. In fact, one of the primary reasons for financial planning is to provide management with adequate lead time to solve this type of cash-flow problem.

A second type of funding is **equity capital**. For a sole proprietorship or partnership, equity capital is provided by the owner or owners of the business. For a corporation, equity capital is money obtained from the sale of shares of ownership in the business. Equity capital is used almost exclusively for long-term financing.

A third type of funding is **debt capital**, which is borrowed money. Debt capital may be borrowed for either short- or long-term use—and a short-term loan seems made to order for Stars and Stripes Clothing's shortfall problem. The firm probably would borrow the needed $7,000 (or perhaps a bit more) at some point during the first quarter and repay it from second-quarter sales revenue.

Proceeds from the sale of assets are the fourth type of funding. Selling assets is a drastic step. However, it may be a reasonable last resort when sales revenues are declining and equity capital or debt capital cannot be found. Assets also may be sold to increase a firm's cash balance or when they are no longer needed or do not "fit" with the company's core business. In 2012, Citigroup, one of the world's largest financial institutions, agreed to sell its part in India's Housing Development Finance Corporation for $2 billion. Citigroup will use the cash it receives from the sale to meet increased capital requirements required by government regulators.[6]

Monitoring and Evaluating Financial Performance

It is important to ensure that financial plans are implemented properly and to catch potential problems before they become major ones. Despite efforts to raise additional financing, reduce expenses, increase sales to become profitable, and negotiate a new labor agreement with the union representing employees, Hostess Brands—the maker of Twinkies and Wonder Bread—shut down all operations in late 2012. Eventually, the firm's assets were sold in order to pay creditors and lenders.[7]

zero-base budgeting a budgeting approach in which every expense in every budget must be justified

capital budget a financial statement that estimates a firm's expenditures for major assets and its long-term financing needs

equity capital money received from the owners or from the sale of shares of ownership in a business

debt capital borrowed money obtained through loans of various types

Concept Check

✓ What is the function of a cash budget? A capital budget?

✓ What is the difference between equity capital and debt capital?

✓ Describe the four sources of funds for a business.

✓ How does a financial manager monitor and evaluate a firm's financing?

© ALMAGAMI/SHUTTERSTOCK.COM

To prevent such problems, financial managers should establish a means of monitoring financial performance. Interim budgets (weekly, monthly, or quarterly) may be prepared for comparison purposes. These comparisons point up areas that require additional or revised planning—or at least areas calling for a more careful investigation. Budget comparisons can also be used to improve the firm's future budgets.

Learning Objective

4 Identify the services provided by banks and financial institutions for their business customers.

FINANCIAL SERVICES PROVIDED BY BANKS AND OTHER FINANCIAL INSTITUTIONS

For a business owner, it helps to know your banker. Banking services can be divided into three broad categories: traditional services, electronic banking services, and international services.

Traditional Banking Services for Business Clients

Traditional services provided by banks and other financial institutions include savings and checking accounts, loans, processing credit- and debit-card transactions, and providing professional advice.

SAVINGS AND CHECKING ACCOUNTS Savings accounts provide a safe place to store money and a very conservative means of investing. The usual *passbook savings account* earns between 0.10 and 0.50 percent in banks and savings and loan associations (S&Ls) and slightly more in credit unions. A business with excess cash it is willing to leave on deposit with a bank for a set period of time can earn a higher rate of interest. To do so, the business firm buys a certificate of deposit. A **certificate of deposit (CD)** is a document stating that the bank will pay the depositor a guaranteed interest rate on money left on deposit for a specified period of time. At the time of publication, CDs were paying between 0.30 and 1 percent. The rate can vary depending on the financial institution and the amount of time until maturity.

Business firms (and individuals) also deposit money in checking accounts so that they can write checks to pay for purchases. A **check** is a written order for a bank or other financial institution to pay a stated dollar amount to the business or person indicated on the face of the check. For businesses, monthly charges are based on the average daily balance in the checking account and/or the number of checks written.

BUSINESS LOANS Banks, savings and loan associations, credit unions, and other financial institutions provide short- and long-term loans to businesses. *Short-term business loans* must be repaid within one year or less. Typical uses for the money obtained through short-term loans include solving cash-flow problems, purchasing inventory, and meeting unexpected emergencies. To help ensure that short-term money will be available when needed, many firms establish a line of credit. A **line of credit** is a loan that is approved before the money is actually needed. Because all the necessary paperwork is already completed and the loan is preapproved, the business can obtain the money later without delay, as soon as it is required. Even with a line of credit, a firm may not be able to borrow money if the bank does not have sufficient funds available. For this reason, some firms prefer a **revolving credit agreement**, which is a guaranteed line of credit. Under this type of agreement, the bank guarantees that the money will be available when the borrower needs it. In return for the guarantee, the bank charges a commitment fee ranging from 0.25 to

certificate of deposit (CD) A document stating that the bank will pay the depositor a guaranteed interest rate on money left on deposit for a specified period of time

check a written order for a bank or other financial institution to pay a stated dollar amount to the business or person indicated on the face of the check

line of credit a loan that is approved before the money is actually needed

revolving credit agreement a guaranteed line of credit

1.0 percent of the *unused* portion of the revolving credit agreement. The usual interest is charged for the portion that *is* borrowed.

Long-term business loans are repaid over a period of years. The average length of a long-term business loan is generally 3 to 7 years but sometimes as long as 15 to 20 years. Long-term loans are used most often to finance the expansion of buildings and retail facilities, mergers and acquisitions, replacement of equipment, or product development. Most lenders require some type of collateral for long-term loans. **Collateral** is real estate or property (e.g., stocks, bonds, equipment, or any other asset of value) pledged as security for a loan.

Repayment terms and interest rates for both short- and long-term loans are arranged between the lender and the borrower. For businesses, repayment terms may include monthly, quarterly, semiannual, or annual payments.

THE BASICS OF GETTING A LOAN According to many financial experts, preparation is the key when applying for a business loan. In reality, preparation begins before you ever apply for the loan. To begin the process, you should get to know potential lenders before requesting debt financing. Although there may be many potential lenders that can provide the money you need, the logical place to borrow money is where your business does its banking. This fact underscores the importance of maintaining adequate balances in the firm's bank accounts. Before applying for a loan, you may also want to check your firm's credit rating with a national credit bureau such as D&B (formerly known as Dun & Bradstreet). Typically, business owners will be asked to fill out a loan application. In addition to the loan application, the lender will also want to see your current business plan. Be sure to explain what your business is, how much funding you require to accomplish your goals, and how the loan will be repaid. Most lenders insist that you submit current financial statements that have been prepared by an independent certified public accountant. Then compile a list of references that includes your suppliers, other lenders, or the professionals with whom you are associated. You may also be asked to discuss the loan request with a loan officer. Hopefully, your loan request will be approved. If not, try to determine why your loan request was rejected. Think back over the loan process and determine what you could do to improve your chances of getting a loan the next time you apply.

Even "big" banks want more customers. Bank of America, one of the largest bank in the United States, still wants your business. Like many competitors, the bank offers cash back, competitive rates for savings and loans, online banking, and many other services to attract new customers. Check out the latest promotions at www.bankofamerica.com.

collateral real estate or property pledged as security for a loan

Why Has the Use of Credit Transactions Increased?

At the beginning of 2013, it was estimated that 160 million Americans use their credit cards to pay for everything from tickets on American Airlines to Zebco fishing gear.[8] Why have credit cards become so popular? For a merchant, the answer is obvious. By depositing charge slips in a bank or other financial institution, the merchant can convert credit-card sales into cash. In return for processing the merchant's credit-card transactions, the financial institution charges a fee that generally ranges between 1.5 and 4 percent. Typically, small, independent businesses pay more than larger stores or chain stores. Let's assume that you use a Visa credit card to purchase a microwave oven for $300 from Gold Star Appliances, a small retailer in Richardson, Texas. At the end of the day, the retailer deposits your charge slip, along with other charge slips, checks, and currency collected during the day, at its bank. If the bank charges Gold Star Appliances 4 percent to process each credit-card transaction, the bank deducts a processing fee of $12 ($300 × 0.04 = $12) for the customer's credit-card transaction and immediately deposits the remainder ($288) in Gold Star Appliances' account. The number of credit-card transactions, the total dollar amount of credit sales, and how well the merchant can negotiate the fees the financial institution charges determine actual fees.

Do not confuse debit cards with credit cards. Although they may look alike, there are important differences. A **debit card** electronically subtracts the amount of a customer's purchase from her or his bank account at the moment the purchase is made. (By contrast, when you use your credit card, the credit-card company extends short-term financing, and you do not make payment until you receive your next statement.) At the beginning of 2013, approximately 190 million Americans had at least one debit card.[9] Debit cards are used most commonly to obtain cash at automatic teller machines (ATMs) and to purchase products and services from retailers.

debit card a card that electronically subtracts the amount of a customer's purchase from her or his bank account at the moment the purchase is made

Electronic Banking Services

An **electronic funds transfer (EFT) system** is a means of performing financial transactions through a computer terminal. The following four EFT applications are changing how banks help firms do business:

electronic funds transfer (EFT) system a means of performing financial transactions through a computer terminal

1. *Automatic teller machines (ATMs)*. An ATM is an electronic bank teller—a machine that provides almost any service a human teller can provide. Once the customer is properly identified, the machine dispenses cash from the customer's checking or savings account or makes a cash advance charged to a credit card. ATMs are located in bank parking lots, supermarkets, drugstores, and even gas stations. Customers have access to them at all times of the day or night. There may be a fee for each transaction.
2. *Automated clearinghouses (ACHs)*. Designed to reduce the number of paper checks, automated clearinghouses process checks, recurring bill payments, Social Security benefits, and employee salaries. For example, large companies use the ACH network to transfer wages and salaries directly into their employees' bank accounts, thus eliminating the need to make out individual paychecks.
3. *Point-of-sale (POS) terminals*. A POS terminal is a computerized cash register located in a retail store and connected to a bank's computer. Assume you want to pay for purchases at a Walmart Supercenter. You begin the process by pulling your bank credit or debit card through a magnetic card reader. A central processing center notifies a computer at your bank that you want to make a purchase. The bank's computer immediately adds the amount to your account for a credit-card transaction. In a similar process, the bank's computer deducts the amount of the purchase from your bank account if you use a debit card. Finally, the amount of your purchase is added to the store's account. The Walmart store then is notified that the transaction is complete, and the cash register prints out your receipt.
4. *Electronic check conversion (ECC)*. Electronic check conversion is a process used to convert information from a paper check into an electronic payment for merchandise, services, or bills. When you give your completed check to a store cashier at a Best Buy store, the check is processed through an electronic system that captures your banking information and the dollar amount of the check. Once the check is processed, you are asked to sign a receipt, and you get a voided (canceled) check back for your records. Finally, the funds to pay for your transaction are transferred into the business firm's account. ECC also can be used for checks you mail to pay for a purchase or to pay on an account.

Bankers and business owners generally are pleased with EFT systems. EFTs are fast, and they eliminate the costly processing of checks. However, some customers are reluctant to use online banking or EFT systems. Some simply do not like "the technology," whereas others fear that the computer will garble their accounts.

Early on, in 1978, Congress responded to such fears by passing the Electronic Funds Transfer Act, which protects the customer in case the bank makes an error or the customer's credit or debit card is stolen.

International Banking Services

For international businesses, banking services are extremely important. Depending on the needs of an international firm, a bank can help by providing a letter of credit or a banker's acceptance.

A **letter of credit** is a legal document issued by a bank or other financial institution guaranteeing to pay a seller a stated amount for a specified period of time—usually thirty to sixty days. (With a letter of credit, certain conditions, such as delivery of the merchandise, may be specified before payment is made.)

A **banker's acceptance** is a written order for a bank to pay a third party a stated amount of money on a specific date. (With a banker's acceptance, no conditions are specified. It is simply an order to pay without any strings attached.)

Both a letter of credit and a banker's acceptance are popular methods of paying for import and export transactions. Imagine that you are a business owner in the United States who wants to purchase some leather products from a small business in Florence, Italy. You offer to pay for the merchandise with your company's check drawn on an American bank, but the Italian business owner is worried about payment. To solve the problem, your bank can issue either a letter of credit or a banker's acceptance to guarantee that payment will be made. In addition to a letter of credit and a banker's acceptance, banks also can use EFT technology to speed international banking transactions.

One other international banking service should be noted. Banks and other financial institutions provide for currency exchange. If you place an order for Japanese merchandise valued at $50,000, how do you pay for the order? Do you use U.S. dollars or Japanese yen? To solve this problem, you can use the bank's currency-exchange service. To make payment, you can use either currency, and if necessary, the bank will exchange one currency for the other to complete your transaction.

letter of credit a legal document issued by a bank or other financial institution guaranteeing to pay a seller a stated amount for a specified period of time

banker's acceptance a written order for a bank to pay a third party a stated amount of money on a specific state

Concept Check

✓ Describe the traditional banking services provided by financial institutions.

✓ What are the major advantages of electronic banking services?

✓ How can a bank or other financial institution help American businesses to compete in the global marketplace?

SOURCES OF SHORT-TERM DEBT FINANCING

Learning Objective

5 Describe the advantages and disadvantages of different methods of short-term debt financing.

The decision to borrow money does not necessarily mean that a firm is in financial trouble. On the contrary, astute financial management often means regular, responsible borrowing of many different kinds to meet different needs. In this section, we examine the sources of *short-term debt financing* available to businesses. In the next two sections, we look at long-term financing options: equity capital and debt capital.

Sources of Unsecured Short-Term Financing

Short-term debt financing is usually easier to obtain than long-term debt financing for three reasons:

1. For the lender, the shorter repayment period means less risk of nonpayment.
2. The dollar amounts of short-term loans are usually smaller than those of long-term loans.
3. A close working relationship normally exists between the short-term borrower and the lender.

Most lenders do not require collateral for short-term financing. If they do, it is usually because they are concerned about the size of a particular loan, the borrowing firm's poor credit rating, or the general prospects of repayment. Remember in the last section that *collateral* was defined as real estate or property pledged as security for a loan.

Entrepreneurs can always use more capital. Even though Body Rest Mattress Company in St. Petersburg, Florida, was successful, Carl and Emma Calhoun found that obtaining short-term financing was difficult during the economic crisis. Traditional sources of financing—banks and other financial institutions—tightened the requirements for obtaining unsecured loans or in many cases rejected loan requests.

unsecured financing financing that is not backed by collateral

trade credit a type of short-term financing extended by a seller who does not require immediate payment after delivery of merchandise

promissory note a written pledge by a borrower to pay a certain sum of money to a creditor at a specified future date

Unsecured financing is financing that is not backed by collateral. A company seeking unsecured short-term financing has several options.

TRADE CREDIT Manufacturers and wholesalers often provide financial aid to retailers by allowing them 30 to 60 days (or more) in which to pay for merchandise. This delayed payment, known as **trade credit**, is a type of short-term financing extended by a seller who does not require immediate payment after delivery of merchandise. It is the most popular form of short-term financing, because most manufacturers and wholesalers do not charge interest for trade credit. In fact, from 70 to 90 percent of all transactions between businesses involve some trade credit.

Let us assume that Discount Tire Stores receives a shipment of tires from a manufacturer. Along with the merchandise, the manufacturer sends an invoice that states the terms of payment. Discount Tire now has two options for payment. First, the retailer may pay the invoice promptly and take advantage of any cash discount the manufacturer offers. Cash-discount terms are specified on the invoice. For instance, "2/10, net 30" means that the customer—Discount Tire—may take a "2" percent discount if it pays the invoice within ten days of the invoice date. Let us assume that the dollar amount of the invoice is $200,000. In this case, the cash discount is $4,000 ($200,000 × 0.02 = $4,000). If the cash discount is taken, Discount Tire only has to pay the manufacturer $196,000 ($200,000 − $4,000 = $196,000).

A second option is to wait until the end of the credit period before making payment. If payment is made between 11 and 30 days after the date of the invoice, Discount Tire must pay the entire amount. As long as payment is made before the end of the credit period, the retailer maintains the ability to purchase additional merchandise using the trade-credit arrangement.

PROMISSORY NOTES ISSUED TO SUPPLIERS A **promissory note** is a written pledge by a borrower to pay a certain sum of money to a creditor at a specified future date. Suppliers uneasy about extending trade credit may be less reluctant to offer credit to customers who sign promissory notes. Unlike trade credit, however, promissory notes usually require the borrower to pay interest. Although repayment periods may extend to one year, most short-term promissory notes are repaid in 60 to 180 days.

A promissory note offers two important advantages to the firm extending the credit.

1. A promissory note is legally binding and an enforceable contract.
2. A promissory note is a negotiable instrument.

Because a promissory note is negotiable, the manufacturer, wholesaler, or company extending credit may be able to discount, or sell, the note to its own bank. If the note is discounted, the dollar amount received by the company extending credit is slightly less than the maturity value because the bank charges a fee for the service. The supplier recoups most of its money immediately, and the bank collects the maturity value when the note matures.

MCT/MCCLATCHY-TRIBUNE/GETTY IMAGES

UNSECURED BANK LOANS Banks and other financial institutions offer unsecured short-term loans to businesses at interest rates that vary with each borrower's credit rating. The **prime interest rate** is the lowest rate charged by a bank for a short-term loan. Figure 16-5 traces the fluctuations in the average prime rate charged by U.S. banks from 1990 to February 2013. This lowest rate generally is reserved for large corporations with excellent credit ratings. Organizations with good to high credit ratings may pay the prime rate plus "2" percent. Firms with questionable credit ratings may have to pay the prime rate plus "4" percent. (The fact that a banker charges a higher interest rate for a higher-risk loan is a practical application of the risk–return ratio discussed earlier in this chapter.) Of course, if the banker believes that loan repayment may be a problem, the borrower's loan application may well be rejected.

When a business obtains a short-term bank loan, interest rates and repayment terms may be negotiated. As a condition of the loan, a bank may require that a *compensating balance* be kept on deposit at the bank. Compensating balances, if required, are typically 10 to 20 percent of the borrowed funds. The bank may also require that every commercial borrower *clean up* (pay off completely) its short-term loans at least once each year and not use it again for a period of 30 to 60 days.

prime interest rate the lowest rate charged by a bank for a short-term loan

COMMERCIAL PAPER Large firms with excellent credit reputations like Microsoft, Procter & Gamble, and Caterpillar can raise large sums of money quickly by issuing commercial paper. **Commercial paper** is a short-term promissory note issued by a large corporation. The maturity date for commercial paper is normally 270 days or less.

Commercial paper is secured only by the reputation of the issuing firm; no collateral is involved. The interest rate a corporation pays when it sells commercial paper is tied to its credit rating and its ability to repay the commercial paper. In most cases, corporations selling commercial paper pay interest rates slightly below the interest rates charged by banks for short-term loans. Thus, selling commercial paper is cheaper than getting short-term financing from a bank.

Although it is possible to purchase commercial paper in smaller denominations, larger amounts—$100,000 or more—are quite common. Money obtained by selling commercial paper is most often used to purchase inventory, finance a firm's accounts receivables, pay salaries and other necessary expenses, and solve cash-flow problems.

commercial paper a short-term promissory note issued by a large corporation.

FIGURE 16-5 Average Prime Interest Rate Paid by U.S. Businesses, 1990–February 2013

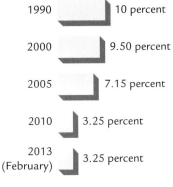

The prime rate is the interest rate charged by U.S. banks when businesses with the "best" credit ratings borrow money. All other businesses pay higher interest rates than the prime rate.

1990		10 percent
2000		9.50 percent
2005		7.15 percent
2010		3.25 percent
2013 (February)		3.25 percent

Source: Federal Reserve Bank website, www.federalreserve.gov (accessed March 7, 2013).

Sources of Secured Short-Term Financing

If a business cannot obtain enough money through unsecured financing, it must put up collateral to obtain additional short-term financing. Almost any asset can serve as collateral. However, *inventories* and *accounts receivable* are the assets most commonly pledged for short-term financing. Even when it is willing to pledge collateral to back up a loan, a firm that is financially weak may have difficulty obtaining short-term financing.

LOANS SECURED BY INVENTORY Normally, manufacturers, wholesalers, and retailers have large amounts of money invested in finished goods. In addition, manufacturers carry raw materials and work-in-process inventories. All three types of inventory may be pledged as collateral for short-term loans. However, lenders prefer the much more salable finished merchandise to raw materials or work-in-process inventories.

A lender may insist that inventory used as collateral be stored in a public warehouse. In such a case, the receipt issued by the warehouse is retained by the lender. Without this receipt, the public warehouse will not release the merchandise. The lender releases the warehouse receipt—and the merchandise—to the borrower when the borrowed money is repaid. In addition to paying the interest on the loan, the borrower must pay for storage in the public warehouse. As a result, this type of loan is more expensive than an unsecured short-term loan.

LOANS SECURED BY RECEIVABLES As defined in Chapter 15, *accounts receivable* are amounts owed to a firm by its customers. A firm can pledge its accounts receivable as collateral to obtain short-term financing. A lender may advance 70 to 80 percent of the dollar amount of the receivables. First, however, it conducts a thorough investigation to determine the *quality* of the receivables. (The quality of the receivables is the credit standing of the firm's customers, coupled with the customers' ability to repay their credit obligations when they are due.) If a favorable determination is made, the loan is approved. When the borrowing firm collects from a customer whose account has been pledged as collateral, generally it must turn the money over to the lender as partial repayment of the loan. An alternative approach is to notify the borrowing firm's credit customers to make their payments directly to the lender.

Factoring Accounts Receivable

factor a firm that specializes in buying other firms' accounts receivable

Accounts receivable may be used in one other way to help raise short-term financing: They can be sold to a factoring company (or factor). A **factor** is a firm that specializes in buying other firms' accounts receivable. The factor buys the accounts receivable for less than their face value; however, it collects the full dollar amount when each account is due. The factor's profit thus is the difference between the face value of the accounts receivable and the amount the factor has paid for them. Generally, the amount of profit the factor receives is based on the risk the factor assumes. Risk, in this case, is the probability that the accounts receivable will not be repaid when they mature.

Even though the firm selling its accounts receivable gets less than face value, it does receive needed cash immediately. Moreover, it has shifted both the task of collecting and the risk of nonpayment to the factor, which now owns the accounts receivable. Generally, customers whose accounts receivable have been factored are given instructions to make their payments directly to the factor.

Cost Comparisons

Table 16-2 compares the various types of short-term financing. As you can see, trade credit is the least expensive. Factoring of accounts receivable is typically the highest-cost method shown.

For many purposes, short-term financing suits a firm's needs perfectly. At other times, however, long-term financing may be more appropriate. In this case, a business may try to raise equity capital or long-term debt capital.

Concept Check

✓ How important is trade credit as a source of short-term financing?

✓ Why would a supplier require a customer to sign a promissory note?

✓ What is the prime rate? Who gets the prime rate?

✓ Explain how factoring works. Of what benefit is factoring to a firm that sells its receivables?

TABLE 16-2 Comparison of Short-Term Financing Methods

Type of Financing	Cost	Repayment Period	Businesses That May Use It	Comments
Trade credit	Low, if any	30–60 days	All businesses with good credit	Usually no finance charge
Promissory note issued to suppliers	Moderate	One year or less	All businesses	Usually unsecured but requires legal document
Unsecured bank loan	Moderate	One year or less	All businesses	Promissory note is required and compensating balance may be required
Commercial paper	Moderate	270 days or less	Large corporations with high credit ratings	Available only to large firms
Secured loan	High	One year or less	Firms with questionable credit ratings	Inventory or accounts receivable often used as collateral
Factoring	High	None	Firms that have large numbers of credit customers	Accounts receivable sold to a factor

© CENGAGE LEARNING 2015

SOURCES OF EQUITY FINANCING

Learning Objective

6 **Evaluate the advantages and disadvantages of equity financing.**

Sources of long-term financing vary with the size and type of business. As mentioned earlier, a sole proprietorship or partnership acquires equity capital (sometimes referred to as *owners' equity*) when the owner or partners invest money in the business. For corporations, equity-financing options include the sale of stock and the use of profits not distributed to owners. All three types of businesses can also obtain venture capital and use long-term debt capital (borrowed money) to meet their financial needs.

initial public offering (IPO) occurs when a corporation sells common stock to the general public for the first time

Selling Stock

Some equity capital is used to start every business—sole proprietorship, partnership, or corporation. In the case of corporations, stockholders who buy shares in the company provide equity capital.

INITIAL PUBLIC OFFERING AND THE PRIMARY MARKET An **initial public offering (IPO)** occurs when a corporation sells common stock to the general public for the first time. In mid-2012, Facebook used an IPO to raise capital, and it was one of the largest IPOs in recent history. And at the time of the publication of your text, there are more social media and technology companies using IPOs to raise capital. Corporations in other industries also use IPOs to raise money. In fact, as illustrated in Figure 16-6, the largest IPOs—Visa, Facebook, General Motors, AT&T Wireless, and Kraft Foods—for U.S. companies involve companies from a number of different industries.

© TUPUNGATO/SHUTTERSTOCK.COM

Just a piece of paper—or is it? In fact, a piece of paper can be worth a lot of money when it is a stock certificate. A corporation sells stock to raise needed financing for expansion and to pay for other long-term financial needs. On the other hand, investors purchase stock because they can profit from their investment if the price of the corporation's stock increases and a corporation pays dividends.

FIGURE 16-6 The All-Time Largest Initial Public Offerings for U.S. Companies

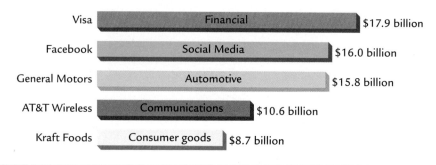

These five corporations raised billions of dollars by selling stock. Visa—the record holder for U.S. companies—raised almost $18 billion when it sold stock for the first time in 2008.

Visa	Financial	$17.9 billion
Facebook	Social Media	$16.0 billion
General Motors	Automotive	$15.8 billion
AT&T Wireless	Communications	$10.6 billion
Kraft Foods	Consumer goods	$8.7 billion

Source: Renaissance Capital, Greenwich, CT (www.renaissancecapital.com), (accessed March 7, 2013).

primary market a market in which an investor purchases financial securities (via an investment bank) directly from the issuer of those securities

investment banking firm an organization that assists corporations in raising funds, usually by helping to sell new issues of stocks, bonds, or other financial securities

secondary market a market for existing financial securities that are traded between investors

Established companies that plan to raise capital by selling subsidiaries to the public can also use IPOs. In 2013, Pfizer sold shares in its animal health division and raised over $2 billion. Monies from the IPO will be used to increase the parent company's cash balance, allow Pfizer to concentrate on its core business, and provide funding for growth opportunities and expansion.[10] In addition to using an IPO to increase the cash balance for the parent company, corporations often sell shares in a subsidiary when shares can be sold at a profit or when the subsidiary no longer fits with its current business plan. Finally, some corporations will sell a subsidiary that is growing more slowly than the rest of the company's operating divisions.

When a corporation uses an IPO to raise capital, the stock is sold in the primary market. The **primary market** is a market in which an investor purchases financial securities (via an investment bank) directly from the issuer of the securities. An **investment banking firm** is an organization that assists corporations in raising funds, usually by helping to sell new issues of stocks, bonds, or other financial securities.

Although a corporation can have only one IPO, it can sell additional stock after the IPO, assuming that there is a market for the company's stock. Even though the cost of selling stock (often referred to as *flotation costs*) is high, the *ongoing* costs associated with this type of equity financing are low for two reasons. First, the corporation does not have to repay money obtained from the sale of stock because the corporation is under no legal obligation to do so. If you purchase corporate stock and later decide to sell your stock, you may sell it to another investor—not the corporation.

A second advantage of selling stock is that a corporation is under no legal obligation to pay dividends to stockholders. As noted in Chapter 4, a *dividend* is a distribution of earnings to the stockholders of a corporation. For any reason (e.g., if a company has a bad year), the board of directors can vote to omit dividend payments. Earnings then are retained for use in funding business operations. Of course, corporate management may hear from unhappy stockholders if expected dividends are omitted too frequently.

THE SECONDARY MARKET Although a share of corporate stock is only sold one time in the primary market, the stock can be sold again and again in the secondary market. The **secondary market** is a market for existing financial securities that are traded between investors. Although a corporation does not receive money each time its stock is bought or sold in the secondary market, the ability to obtain cash

Investor Relations in the Social Media Era

Tweeting about earnings? Increasingly, public corporations are communicating with their investors via Twitter, Facebook, YouTube, LinkedIn, and other social media. Companies still publish annual reports (in print and online) and hold annual meetings (in person and via webcast). In addition, because stockholders and potential investors want easy access to the latest financial news, companies like Alcoa, Dell, and eBay now use social media to provide official updates. Although the timing and content of these messages must comply with regulatory requirements, the ability to connect quickly and directly with investors is vital at a time when rumors can fly around the world at the click of a mouse.

Alcoa, for example, uses its Facebook page to announce quarterly earnings figures and link to executive webcasts. It also uses its Twitter account to call attention to specific results and invite comments from its followers. For investors who want to dig deeper into quarterly or annual financial reports, the investor relations department shares its electronic presentations on SlideShare.

Thanks to Twitter, YouTube, a dedicated investor relations blog, and other social media, Dell reaches more than five million people when it presents its quarterly financial results. And the online auction site eBay live-tweets earnings results as the CEO announces them. Watch for corporate investor relations departments to become even more social in the years ahead.

Sources: Based on information in Rachel Koning Beals, "Investors Increasingly Tap Social Media for Stock Tips," *U.S. News & World Report*, January 31, 2012, http://money.usnews.com/money; Dominic Jones, "Social Media Investor Relations Reaches Tipping Point," *IR Web Report*, April 14, 2011, http://irwebreport.com; Dave Hogan, "Investor Relations and Social Media: Together at Last," *PR News Online*, May 9, 2011, www.prnewsonline.com; Jennifer Van Grove, "Investor Relations Tool Helps Fortune 500 Companies Get Social," *Mashable*, June 8, 2011, www.mashable.com.

---

by selling stock investments is one reason why investors purchase corporate stock. Without the secondary market, investors would not purchase stock in the primary market because there would be no way to sell shares to other investors. Usually, secondary-market transactions are completed through a securities exchange or the over-the-counter (OTC) market.

A **securities exchange** is a marketplace where member brokers meet to buy and sell securities. Generally, securities issued by larger corporations are traded at the New York Stock Exchange (NYSE) (now owned by the NYSE Euronext), or at regional exchanges located in different parts of the country. The securities of very large corporations may be traded at more than one of these exchanges. Securities of firms also may be listed on foreign securities exchanges—in Tokyo or London, for example.

securities exchange
a marketplace where member brokers meet to buy and sell securities

Stocks issued by several thousand companies are traded in the OTC market. The **over-the-counter (OTC) market** is a network of dealers who buy and sell the stocks of corporations that are not listed on a securities exchange. The term *over-the-counter* was coined more than 100 years ago when securities actually were sold "over the counter" in stores and banks. Many stocks are traded through an *electronic* exchange called the Nasdaq (pronounced "nazzdack"). The Nasdaq is now one of the largest securities markets in the world. Today, the Nasdaq is known for its forward-looking, innovative, growth companies, including Intel, Microsoft, Cisco Systems, and Dell Computer.

over-the-counter (OTC) market
a network of dealers who buy and sell the stocks of corporations that are not listed on a securities exchange

There are two types of stock: common and preferred. Each type has advantages and drawbacks as a means of long-term financing.

COMMON STOCK A share of **common stock** represents the most basic form of corporate ownership. In return for the financing provided by selling common stock, management must make certain concessions to stockholders that may restrict or change corporate policies. Every corporation must hold an annual meeting, at which the holders of common stock may vote for the board of directors. Often, stockholders are also asked to approve or disapprove of major corporate actions.

common stock stock whose owners may vote on corporate matters but whose claims on profits and assets are subordinate to the claims of others

Social Media

Talk to Chuck

Founded in 1971, the Charles Schwab Corporation is a brokerage firm and banking company with extensive product lines including checking accounts, mortgages, brokerage and retirement accounts, mutual funds, stocks and bonds, and more.

© CHARLES SCHWAB

While some financial service firms have been slow to adopt social media, due in part to the risk of violating the rules of the Financial Industry Regulatory Authority (FINRA), Schwab has long been viewed as a leader in the use of social media. The Schwab promotional campaign "Talk to Chuck" invited investors to check out the company as an option to more traditional investment companies. Take a look at www.charlesschwab.com. You can also find Schwab on Facebook, Twitter, and YouTube.

Few investors will buy common stock unless they believe that their investment will increase in value. As already mentioned, stockholders may receive dividends if the corporation's board of directors approves a dividend distribution. Additional information on the reasons why investors purchase stocks and how to evaluate stock investments is provided in Appendix A, "Understanding Personal Finances and Investments."

PREFERRED STOCK As noted in Chapter 4, the owners of **preferred stock** must receive their dividends before holders of common stock receive theirs. Also, preferred stockholders know the dollar amount of their dividend because it is stated on the stock certificate. When compared to common stockholders, preferred stockholders also have first claim (after creditors) on assets if the corporation is dissolved or declares bankruptcy. Even so, as with common stock, the board of directors must approve dividends on preferred stock, and this type of financing does not represent a debt that must be legally repaid. In return for preferential treatment, preferred stockholders generally give up the right to vote at a corporation's annual meeting.

Although a corporation usually issues only one type of common stock, it may issue many types of preferred stock with varying dividends or dividend rates. For example, New York–based Consolidated Edison has one common-stock issue but three preferred-stock issues.[11]

Retained Earnings

Most large corporations distribute only a portion of their after-tax earnings to stockholders. The portion of a corporation's profits *not* distributed to stockholders is called **retained earnings**. Because they are undistributed profits, retained earnings are considered a form of equity financing.

The amount of retained earnings in any year is determined by corporate management and approved by the board of directors. Most small and growing corporations pay no cash dividend—or a very small dividend—to their stockholders. All or most earnings are reinvested in the business for research and development, expansion, or the funding of major projects. Reinvestment tends to increase the value of the firm's stock while it provides essentially cost-free financing for the business. More mature corporations may distribute 40 to 60 percent of their after-tax profits as dividends. Utility companies and other corporations with very stable earnings often pay out as much as 80 to 90 percent of what they earn. For a large corporation, retained earnings can amount to a hefty bit of financing. For example, as reported in its last annual report, the total amount of retained earnings for General Electric was over $144 billion.[12]

Venture Capital and Private Placements

To establish a new business or expand an existing one, an entrepreneur may try to obtain venture capital. In Chapter 5, we defined *venture capital* as money invested in small (and sometimes struggling) firms that have the potential to become very successful. Most venture capital firms do not invest in the typical small business—a

preferred stock stock whose owners usually do not have voting rights but whose claims on dividends and assets are paid before those of common-stock owners

retained earnings the portion of a corporation's profits not distributed to stockholders

neighborhood convenience store or a local dry cleaner—but in firms that have the potential to become extremely profitable. Today, most venture capital firms are investing in companies that build the nation's infrastructure, develop computer software, or provide consumer information or social media services. For example, Zynga—the fast-growing company behind such popular games as FarmVille—received venture capital before selling stock to the public.[13]

Generally, a venture capital firm consists of a pool of investors, a partnership established by a wealthy family, or a joint venture formed by corporations with money to invest. In return for financing, these investors generally receive an equity or ownership position in the business and share in its profits. Although venture capital firms are willing to take chances, they have also been more selective about where they invest their money after the recent economic crisis.

Another method of raising capital is through a private placement. A **private placement** occurs when stock and other corporate securities are sold directly to insurance companies, pension funds, or large institutional investors. When compared with selling stocks and other corporate securities to the public, there are often fewer government regulations and the cost is generally less when the securities are sold through a private placement. Typically, terms between the buyer and seller are negotiated when a private placement is used to raise capital.

SOURCES OF LONG-TERM DEBT FINANCING

As pointed out earlier in this chapter, businesses borrow money on a short-term basis for many valid reasons other than desperation. There are equally valid reasons for long-term borrowing. In addition to using borrowed money to meet the long-term needs listed in Table 16-1, successful businesses often use the financial leverage it creates to improve their financial performance. **Financial leverage** is the use of borrowed funds to increase the return on owners' equity. The principle of financial leverage works as long as a firm's earnings are larger than the interest charged for the borrowed money.

To understand how financial leverage can increase a firm's return on owners' equity, study the information for Texas-based Cypress Springs Plastics presented in Table 16-3. Pete Johnston, the owner of the firm, is trying to decide how best to finance a $100,000 purchase of new high-tech manufacturing equipment.

- He could borrow the money and pay 7 percent annual interest.
- He could invest an additional $100,000 in the firm.

Assuming that the firm earns $95,000 a year and that annual interest for this loan totals $7,000 ($100,000 × 0.07 = $7,000), the return on owners' equity for Cypress Springs Plastics would be higher if the firm borrowed the additional financing. Return on owners' equity is determined by dividing a firm's profit by the dollar amount of owners' equity. Based on the calculations illustrated in Table 16-3, Cypress Springs Plastics' return on owners' equity equals 17.6 percent if Johnston borrows the additional $100,000. The firm's return on owners' equity would decrease to 15.8 percent if Johnston invests an additional $100,000 in the business.

The most obvious danger when using financial leverage is that the firm's earnings may be lower than expected. If this situation occurs, the fixed interest charge actually works to reduce or eliminate the return on owners' equity. Of course, borrowed money eventually must be repaid.

For a small business, long-term debt financing is generally limited to loans. Large corporations have the additional option of issuing corporate bonds.

Long-Term Loans

Many businesses satisfy their long-term financing needs, such as those listed in Table 16-1, with loans from commercial banks and other financial institutions. Manufacturers and suppliers of heavy machinery may also provide long-term debt financing by granting credit to their customers.

private placement occurs when stock and other corporate securities are sold directly to insurance companies, pension funds, or large institutional investors

Concept Check

✓ What are the advantages of financing through the sale of stock?

✓ From a corporation's point of view, how does preferred stock differ from common stock?

✓ What is venture capital?

Learning Objective

7 Evaluate the advantages and disadvantages of long-term debt financing.

financial leverage the use of borrowed funds to increase the return on owners' equity

TABLE 16-3 Analysis of the Effect of Additional Capital from Debt or Equity for Cypress Springs Plastics, Inc.

Additional Debt		Additional Equity	
Owners' equity	$500,000	Owners' equity	$500,000
Additional equity	+0	Additional equity	+100,000
Total owner's equity	$500,000	Total owner's equity	$600,000
Loan (@ 7%)	+100,000	No loan	+0
Total capital	$600,000	Total capital	$600,000
Year-End Earnings			
Gross profit	$95,000	Gross profit	$95,000
Less loan interest	−7,000	No interest	−0
Profit	$88,000	Profit	$95,000
Return on owners' equity	17.6%	Return on owners' equity	15.8%
($88,000 ÷ $500,000 = 17.6%)		($95,000 ÷ $600,000 = 15.8%)	

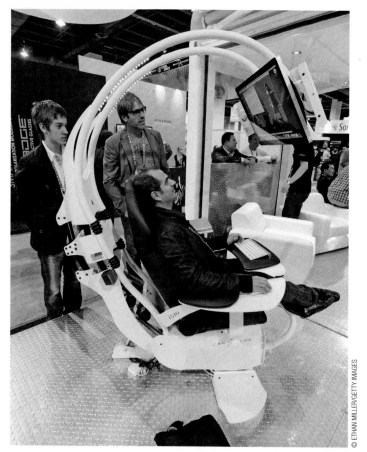

The office of the future. While this product may look like something that should be on the next spaceship to the moon, it is a state-of-the-art office chair designed for people who spend long hours in front of computer monitors. The chair was created by Modern Work Environment (MWE) Lab. Companies that develop innovative products like this one need financing, and they generally have two choices. They can obtain financing from owners and investors or they can borrow money.

TERM-LOAN AGREEMENTS A **term-loan agreement** is a promissory note that requires a borrower to repay a loan in monthly, quarterly, semiannual, or annual installments. As discussed earlier in this chapter, repayment may be as long as 15 to 20 years, but long-term business loans normally are repaid in 3 to 7 years.

Assume that Pete Johnston, the owner of Cypress Springs Plastics, decides to borrow $100,000 and take advantage of the principle of financial leverage illustrated in Table 16-3. Although the firm's return on owners' equity does increase, interest must be paid each year and, eventually, the loan must be repaid. To pay off a $100,000 loan over a three-year period with annual payments, Cypress Springs Plastics must pay $33,333 on the loan balance plus $7,000 annual interest, or a total of $40,333 the first year. Although the amount of interest decreases each year because of the previous year's payment on the loan balance, annual payments of this amount are still a large commitment for a small firm such as Cypress Springs Plastics.

The interest rate and repayment terms for term loans often are based on factors such as the reasons for borrowing, the borrowing firm's credit rating, and the value of collateral. Although long-term loans occasionally may be unsecured, the lender usually requires some type of collateral. Acceptable collateral includes real estate, stocks, bonds, equipment, or any asset with value. Lenders may also require that borrowers maintain a minimum amount of working capital.

Corporate Bonds

In addition to loans, large corporations may choose to issue bonds in denominations of $1,000 to $50,000. Although the usual face value for corporate bonds is

$1,000, the total face value of all the bonds in an issue usually amounts to millions of dollars. In fact, one of the reasons why corporations sell bonds is so that they can borrow a lot of money from a lot of different bondholders and raise larger amounts of money than could be borrowed from one lender. A **corporate bond** is a corporation's written pledge that it will repay a specified amount of money with interest. Interest rates for corporate bonds vary with the financial health of the company issuing the bond. Specific factors that increase or decrease the interest rate that a corporation must pay when it issues bonds include

- The corporation's ability to pay interest each year until maturity.
- The corporation's ability to repay the bond at maturity.

For bond investors, the interest rate on corporate bonds is an example of the risk–return ratio discussed earlier in this chapter. Simply put: Investors expect more interest if there is more risk with more speculative bond issues—see Figure 16-7. As a result, corporations must pay higher interest if investors are concerned about continued interest payments or eventual repayment of a corporate bond.

The **maturity date** is the date on which the corporation is to repay the borrowed money. Today, most corporate bonds are registered bonds. A **registered bond** is a bond registered in the owner's name by the issuing company. Many corporations do not issue actual bonds. Instead, the bonds are recorded electronically, and the specific details regarding the bond issue, along with the current owner's name and address, are maintained by computer. Computer entries are safer because they cannot be stolen, misplaced, or destroyed, and make it easier to transfer when a bond is sold.

Until a bond's maturity, a corporation pays interest to the bond owner at the stated rate. For example, owners of American & Foreign Power Company bonds that mature in 2030 receive 5 percent per year for each bond. For each $1,000 bond issued, the corporation must pay bondholders $50 ($1,000 × 0.05 = $50) each year. Because interest for corporate bonds is usually paid semiannually, the owner of an American & Foreign Power bond will receive a $25 payment every six months for each bond they own. On the maturity date, a registered owner will receive cash equaling the face value of the bond.

Personal Apps

You Are a CFO!

As CFO of your life, you should put your financial house in order before you apply for any loan. Be sure to check your credit report in advance to see how it looks, and think about how you'll repay the loan. Apply only when you know your finances are ready for the spotlight.

term-loan agreement a promissory note that requires a borrower to repay a loan in monthly, quarterly, semiannual, or annual installments

corporate bond a corporation's written pledge that it will repay a specified amount of money with interest

maturity date the date on which a corporation is to repay borrowed money

registered bond a bond registered in the owner's name by the issuing company

FIGURE 16-7 The Risk–Return Ratio for Corporate Bond Investors

High-quality corporate bonds pay less interest when compared to bonds that are more speculative.

LESS RISK Bonds with less risk have lower interest rates

lower Interest rates higher

MORE RISK Bonds with more risk have higher interest rates

© CENGAGE LEARNING 2015

TYPES OF BONDS Corporate bonds are generally classified as debentures, mortgage bonds, or convertible bonds. Most corporate bonds are debenture bonds. A **debenture bond** is a bond backed only by the reputation of the issuing corporation. To make its bonds more appealing to investors, a corporation may issue mortgage bonds. A **mortgage bond** is a corporate bond secured by various assets of the issuing firm. Typical corporate assets that are used as collateral for a mortgage bond include real estate, machinery, and equipment that is not pledged as collateral for other debt obligations. The corporation can also issue convertible bonds. A **convertible bond** can be exchanged, at the owner's option, for a specified number of shares of the corporation's common stock. An Advanced Micro Devices (AMD) bond that matures in 2015 is convertible: Each bond can be converted to 35.6125 shares of AMD common stock.[14] A corporation can gain in three ways by issuing convertible bonds. First, convertibles usually carry a lower interest rate than nonconvertible bonds. Second, the conversion feature attracts investors who are interested in the speculative gain that conversion to common stock may provide. Third, if the bondholder converts to common stock, the corporation no longer has to redeem the bond at maturity.

REPAYMENT PROVISIONS FOR CORPORATE BONDS Maturity dates for bonds generally range from 10 to 30 years after the date of issue. Some bonds are callable before the maturity date; that is, a corporation can buy back, or redeem, them. For these bonds, the corporation may pay the bond owner a call premium. The amount of the call premium, if any, is specified, along with other provisions, in the bond indenture. The **bond indenture** is a legal document that details all the conditions relating to a bond issue.

A corporation may use one of three methods to ensure that it has sufficient funds available to redeem a bond issue. First, it can issue the bonds as **serial bonds**, which are bonds of a single issue that mature on different dates. For example, a company may use a 25-year $50 million bond issue to finance its expansion. None of the bonds mature during the first 15 years. Thereafter, 10 percent of the bonds mature each year until all the bonds are retired at the end of the 25th year. Second, the corporation can establish a sinking fund. A **sinking fund** is a sum of money to which deposits are made each year for the purpose of redeeming a bond issue. When Union Pacific Corporation sold a $275 million bond issue, the company agreed to contribute to a sinking fund until the bond's maturity in the year 2025.[15] Third, a corporation can pay off an old bond issue by selling new bonds. Although this may appear to perpetuate the corporation's long-term debt, a number of utility companies and railroads use this repayment method.

A corporation that issues bonds must also appoint a **trustee**, an individual or an independent firm that acts as the bond owner's representative. A trustee's duties are handled most often by a commercial bank or other large financial institution. The corporation must report to the trustee periodically regarding its ability to make interest payments and eventually redeem the bonds. In turn, the trustee transmits this information to the bond owners, along with its own evaluation of the corporation's ability to pay.

Cost Comparisons

Table 16-4 compares some of the methods that can be used to obtain long-term equity *and* debt financing. Although the initial flotation cost of issuing stock is high, selling common stock is generally a popular option for most financial managers. Once the stock is sold and upfront costs are paid, the *ongoing* costs of using stock to finance a business are low. The type of long-term financing that generally has the highest *ongoing* costs is a long-term loan (debt).

To a great extent, firms are financed through the investments of individuals—money that people have deposited in banks or have used to purchase stocks, mutual funds, and bonds. In Appendix A, we look at how you can invest your money in business.

---

debenture bond a bond backed only by the reputation of the issuing corporation

mortgage bond a corporate bond secured by various assets of the issuing firm

convertible bond a bond that can be exchanged, at the owner's option, for a specified number of shares of the corporation's common stock

bond indenture a legal document that details all the conditions relating to a bond issue

serial bonds bonds of a single issue that mature on different dates

sinking fund a sum of money to which deposits are made each year for the purpose of redeeming a bond issue

trustee an individual or an independent firm that acts as a bond owner's representative

---

Concept Check

✓ Describe how financial leverage can increase return on owners' equity.

✓ For a corporation, what are the advantages of corporate bonds over long-term loans?

✓ Describe the three methods used to ensure that funds are available to redeem corporate bonds at maturity.

TABLE 16-4 Comparison of Long-Term Financing Methods

Type of Financing	Repayment	Repayment Period	Cost/Dividends Interest	Businesses That May Use It
Equity				
Common stock	No	None	High initial cost; low ongoing costs because dividends not required	All corporations that sell stock to investors
Preferred stock	No	None	Dividends not required but must be paid before common stockholders receive any dividends	Large corporations that have an established investor base of common stockholders
Debt				
Long-term loan	Yes	Usually 3–7 years	Interest rates between 3.50 and 12 percent depending on economic conditions, the financial stability of the company requesting the loan, and the amount of the loan	All firms that can meet the lender's repayment and collateral requirements
Corporate bond	Yes	Usually 10–30 years	Interest rates between 3 and 9 percent depending on the financial stability of the company issuing the bonds and economic conditions	Large corporations that are financially healthy

Looking for Success? *Get Flashcards, Quizzes, Games, Crosswords, and more @ www.cengagebrain.com.*

Summary

1 Understand why financial management is important in today's uncertain economy.

Financial management consists of all activities concerned with obtaining money and using it effectively. Financial management can be viewed as a two-sided problem. On one side, the uses of funds often dictate the type or types of financing needed by a business. On the other side, the activities a business can undertake are determined by the types of financing available. Financial managers must ensure that funds are available when needed, that they are obtained at the lowest possible cost, and that they are used as efficiently as possible. In the wake of the economic crisis, the Dodd–Frank Wall Street Reform and Consumer Protection Act was signed into law. And today, there is an ongoing debate if more regulations are needed. Still, there are a number of rewarding jobs in finance for qualified job applicants.

2 Identify a firm's short- and long-term financial needs.

Short-term financing is money that will be used for one year or less. There are many short-term needs, but cash flow, speculative production, and inventory are three for which financing is often required. Long-term financing is money that will be used for more than one year. Such financing may be required for a business start-up, for a merger or an acquisition, for new product development, for long-term marketing activities, for replacement of equipment, or for expansion of facilities. According to financial experts, business firms will find it more difficult to raise both short- and long-term financing in the future because of increased regulations and more cautious lenders. Financial managers must also consider the risk–return ratio when making financial decisions. The risk–return ratio is based on the principle that a high-risk decision should generate higher financial returns for a business. On the other hand, more conservative decisions generate lesser returns.

3 Summarize the process of planning for financial management.

A financial plan begins with an organization's goals and objectives. Next, a firm's goals and objectives are "translated" into departmental budgets that detail expected income and expenses. From these budgets, which may be combined into an overall cash budget, the financial manager determines what funding will be needed and where it may be obtained. Whereas departmental and cash budgets emphasize short-term financing needs, a capital budget can be used to estimate a firm's expenditures for major assets and its long-term financing needs. The four principal sources of financing are sales revenues, equity capital, debt capital, and proceeds from the sale of assets. Once the needed funds have been obtained, the financial manager is responsible for monitoring and evaluating the firm's financial activities.

4 Identify the services provided by banks and financial institutions for their business customers.

Banks and other financial institutions offer today's business customers a tempting array of services. Among the most important and attractive banking services are savings accounts and certificates of deposit, checking accounts, short- and long-term loans, and credit-card and debit-card processing. Increased use of electronic funds transfer systems (automated teller machines, automated clearinghouse systems, point-of-sale terminals, and electronic check conversion) also will change the way that business firms bank and conduct typical business transactions. For firms in the global marketplace, a bank can provide letters of credit and banker's acceptances that will reduce the risk of nonpayment for sellers. Banks and financial institutions also can provide currency exchange to reduce payment problems for import or export transactions.

5 Describe the advantages and disadvantages of different methods of short-term debt financing.

Most short-term financing is unsecured; that is, no collateral is required. Sources of unsecured short-term financing include trade credit, promissory notes issued to suppliers, unsecured bank loans, and commercial paper. Sources of secured short-term financing include loans secured by inventory and accounts receivable. A firm may also sell its receivables to factors. Trade credit is the least-expensive source of short-term

financing. The cost of financing through other sources generally depends on the source and on the credit rating of the firm that requires the financing. Factoring is generally the most expensive approach.

6 Evaluate the advantages and disadvantages of equity financing.

The first time a corporation sells stock to the general public is referred to as an initial public offering (IPO). With an IPO, the stock is sold in the primary market. Once sold in the primary market, investors buy and sell stock in the secondary market. Usually, secondary market transactions are completed through a securities exchange or the over-the-counter market. Common stock is voting stock; holders of common stock elect the corporation's directors and often must approve changes to the corporate charter. Holders of preferred stock must be paid dividends before holders of common stock are paid any dividends. Another source of equity funding is retained earnings, which is the portion of a business's profits *not* distributed to stockholders. Venture capital—money invested in small (and sometimes struggling) firms that have the potential to become very successful—is yet another source of equity funding. Finally, a private placement can be used to sell stocks and other corporate securities.

7 Evaluate the advantages and disadvantages of long-term debt financing.

For a small business, debt financing is generally limited to loans. Large corporations have the additional option of issuing corporate bonds. Regardless of whether the business is small or large, it can take advantage of financial leverage. Financial leverage is the use of borrowed funds to increase the return on owners' equity. The rate of interest for long-term loans usually depends on the financial status of the borrower, the reason for borrowing, and the kind of collateral pledged to back up the loan. Long-term business loans are normally repaid in 3 to 7 years but can be as long as 15 to 20 years. Money realized from the sale of corporate bonds must be repaid when the bonds mature. In addition, the corporation must pay interest on that money from the time the bonds are sold until maturity. The interest rate the corporation must pay often depends on the financial health of the firm issuing bonds. Maturity dates for bonds generally range from 10 to 30 years after the date of issue. Three types of bonds—debentures, mortgage bonds, and convertible bonds—are sold to raise debt capital. When comparing the cost of long-term financing, the ongoing costs of using stock (equity) to finance a business are low. The most expensive is a long-term loan (debt).

Key Terms

You should now be able to define and give an example relevant to each of the following terms:

financial management (462)
chief financial officer
  (CFO) (463)
short-term financing (464)
cash flow (464)
speculative production
  (465)
long-term financing (466)
risk–return ratio (467)
financial plan (467)
budget (468)
cash budget (468)
zero-base budgeting (469)
capital budget (469)
equity capital (469)

debt capital (469)
certificate of deposit
  (470)
check (470)
line of credit (470)
revolving credit agreement
  (470)
collateral (471)
debit card (472)
electronic funds transfer
  system (EFT) (472)
letter of credit (473)
banker's acceptance (473)
unsecured financing (474)
trade credit (474)

promissory note (474)
prime interest rate (475)
commercial paper (475)
factor (476)
initial public offering
  (IPO) (477)
primary market (478)
investment banking
  firm (478)
secondary market (478)
securities exchange (479)
over-the-counter (OTC)
  market (479)
common stock (479)
preferred stock (480)

retained earnings (480)
private placement (481)
financial leverage (481)
term-loan agreement
  (483)
corporate bond (483)
maturity date (483)
registered bond (483)
debenture bond (484)
mortgage bond (484)
convertible bond (484)
bond indenture (484)
serial bonds (484)
sinking fund (484)
trustee (484)

Discussion Questions

1. During the recent economic crisis, many financial managers and corporate officers have been criticized for (a) poor decisions, (b) lack of ethical behavior, (c) large salaries, (d) lucrative severance packages worth millions of dollars, and (e) extravagant lifestyles. Is this criticism justified? Justify your opinion.

2. If you were the financial manager of Stars and Stripes Clothing, what would you do with the excess cash that the firm expects in the second and fourth quarters? (See Figure 16-4.)

3. Develop a *personal* cash budget for the next six months. Explain what you would do if there are budget shortfalls or excess cash amounts at the end of any month during the six-month period.

4. Why would a lender offer unsecured short-term loans when it could demand collateral?

5. How can a small-business owner or corporate manager use financial leverage to improve the firm's profits and return on owners' equity?

6. In what circumstances might a large corporation sell stock rather than bonds to obtain long-term financing? In what circumstances would it sell bonds rather than stock?

Test Yourself

Matching Questions

1. _____ It is the movement of money into and out of a business organization.

2. _____ Determining a firm's financial needs is one of its important functions.

3. _____ A loan that is approved before the money is actually needed.

4. _____ Funding that comes from the sale of stock.

5. _____ Payments are usually made in 30 to 60 days from the invoice date.

6. _____ Must receive dividends before common stockholders.

7. _____ It is pledged as security for a loan.

8. _____ A method of financing that is a legally binding and enforceable and often issued to suppliers.

9. _____ The deposits are used for redeeming a bond issue.

10. _____ This investment is backed by the reputation of the issuing corporation.

a. cash flow
b. collateral
c. debenture bond
d. equity capital

e. financial management
f. letter of credit
g. line of credit
h. preferred stock
i. private placement
j. promissory note
k. sinking fund
l. trade credit

True False Questions

11. **T F** Long-term financing is generally used to open new businesses.

12. **T F** A budget is a historical record of the previous year's financial activities.

13. **T F** When you use a debit card to make a purchase, a financial institution is extending credit to you and expects to be paid in the future.

14. **T F** With a banker's acceptance, certain conditions, such as delivery of the merchandise, may be specified before payment is made.

15. **T F** Most lenders do not require collateral for short-term financing.

16. **T F** A revolving credit agreement is a guaranteed line of credit.

17. **T F** Factoring of accounts receivable typically is the highest cost method of short-term financing.

18. **T F** Normally, the usual repayment period for a long-term loan is three to seven years.

19. **T F** The usual face value for most corporate bonds is $5,000.

20. **T F** A capital budget estimates a firm's expenditures for labor costs and other monthly expenses.

Multiple Choice Questions

21. _____ A written order for a bank or other financial institution to pay a stated dollar amount to a specified business or person is called a
a. check.
b. deposit slip.
c. notes receivable.
d. receipt.
e. debit memorandum.

22. _____ Judy Martinez, owner of Judy's Fashions, received a $12,000 tax refund. She deposited the money in Chase Bank. The terms of the agreement are that she must leave the money on deposit for three years and the bank will pay her 1 percent interest. Her account is a
a. line of credit.
b. certificate of deposit.
c. checking account.
d. commercial paper agreement.
e. savings account.

23. _____ An invoice in the amount of $200 carries cash terms of "2/10, net 30." If the buyer takes advantage of the discount terms, how much will the buyer pay?
a. $100
b. $120
c. $140
d. $160
e. $196

24. _____ When a firm sells its accounts receivable to raise short-term cash, it is engaging in a strategy called

a. factoring.
b. financial planning.
c. equity financing.
d. debt financing.
e. drafting.

25. _____ Retained earnings, as a form of equity financing, are
a. gross earnings.
b. profits before taxes.
c. profits after taxes.
d. undistributed profits.
e. total owners' equity.

26. _____ Since prices are extremely low, the Pipeline Supply Company wants to purchase a special line of pipes from a company going out of business. Pipeline, however, will need to borrow money to make this deal. Which assets will Pipeline most commonly pledge as collateral for this short-term loan?
a. delivery equipment
b. notes payable
c. manufacturing equipment
d. owners' equity
e. inventory

27. _____ The most basic form of corporate ownership that has voting rights is
a. preferred stock.
b. common stock.
c. retained stock.
d. deferred value stock.
e. treasury stock.

28. _____ A short-term promissory note issued by large corporations is known as
   a. debenture agreement.
   b. equity agreement.
   c. commercial paper.
   d. draft agreement.
   e. loan commitment.

29. _____ Each of the following causes a cash flow problem except
   a. embezzlement of company funds.
   b. an unexpected slow selling season.
   c. a large number of credit sales.
   d. slow-paying customers.
   e. customers who pay on time.

30. _____ The primary sources of funds available to a business include all of the following *except*
   a. debt capital.
   b. equity capital.
   c. sales revenue.
   d. government grants.
   e. sale of assets.

Answers to the Test Yourself questions appear at the end of the book on page TY-2.

Video Case
Financial Planning Equals Profits for Nederlander Concerts

Nederlander Concerts is in the business of booking, promoting, and producing live music shows in the western United States. The company presents artists ranging from James Taylor to Flogging Molly, Bruce Springsteen, Bonnie Raitt, and the Allman Brothers Band. But, according to Adam Friedman, Nederlander's former CEO, "We're not trying to be necessarily a national player or an international player. We seek out opportunities that fit within and leverage our existing portfolio of small- to mid-size venues. . . . It's one of the few remaining family-run entertainment enterprises worldwide. . . . What this means for us on a day-to-day basis is that we can focus on running the business. We're not as guided by Wall Street, we don't have the same constraints, we don't have the same reporting responsibilities, and it allows us to focus on . . . our business strategy for development."

Of course, being a privately owned company and not needing to respond to shareholders (Wall Street) doesn't mean that Nederlander has *no* reporting responsibilities. As Friedman explains, "We assess at the beginning of the year not only concert revenue and expenses but also special event revenue." Nederlander owns some theaters, amphitheaters, and arenas, and it sometimes rents space for concerts and events along the West Coast. "When we rent the facilities to, for example, movie premieres here in Los Angeles, what kind of revenue are we going to see? What kind of expenses are attended to generating that revenue? What's our fixed overhead for the year? Who's on the payroll, whether full-time, or part-time, or seasonal, and how much does it cost us to run the business on a day-to-day basis in order to secure those revenues and pay those expenses? That's wrapped up into an annual budget at the beginning of every year, which is kind of a guideline for me to know how we achieve growth. It also allows me to communicate to our owners what our growth orientation is for that given year. . . . Every event has its own profit and loss statement . . . which is a mini version of that annual plan," says Friedman.

In addition to daily, weekly, and quarterly event reports, Nederlander's financial team generates daily and weekly reports of ticket sales. Monthly reports on company-wide performance feed into quarterly and annual reports. Each annual report is compared to that year's budget. The finance department tallies hundreds of transactions in order to arrive at some of these annual numbers, which are reported to the company's owners to ensure that the company is running as profitably as it can be.

Nederlander's managers say growth in the concert industry must be measured in the long term because the business is cyclical and the cost of real estate is so high that short-term profit is hard to generate. Still, the company is in a strong financial position (it is part of a profitable global theater-ownership company called the Nederlander Organization), so it can afford to fund its own growth and expansion, or it can borrow on favorable terms. "We're very fortunate to have an ownership that is very well capitalized with over 80 years in the business," says Friedman. "Our balance sheet is so strong that we have the ability to tap into debt financing if it makes the most sense. . . . or [use] the corporate treasury. . . . If it makes more sense to borrow the money, we will, and we're typically able to do that on very favorable rates because of very long-term banking relationships."

It can be thrilling to meet some of the artists the company books. "But at the end of the day, it's a business," Friedman points out. "If we're not successful in growing our revenue and managing our expense, ultimately we won't be profitable, and our ownership will not be happy with those results."[16]

1. Here's what Nederlander's chief operating officer has to say about its business model: "A show has a short lifetime. You go and sell two months out, and the tickets have no value on any day but the day of the show. So it's a very interesting model in that sense." How do you think the short life of the company's products affects its financial planning?

2. The company uses its own arenas and theaters about 90 percent of the time. What are some of the possible advantages and disadvantages of owning its own venues?

3. Why would Nederlander choose to sometimes borrow funds for expansion if it has capital of its own?

Building Skills for Career Success

1. Social Media Exercise

Turbo Tax is probably one of the best-known tax preparation services in the world. One of the reasons for its popularity is that it provides software that small business firms and individuals really need to make financial decisions and prepare tax returns. Another reason for its popularity is the company's use of social media through various platforms that include building an online community of users, using Twitter, and developing a YouTube channel. Each video on the TurboTax channel illustrates how a company can use social media to provide valuable information to customers. You can check out Turbo Tax videos at www.youtube.com/user/TurboTax.

1. Visit the YouTube channel for Turbo Tax (www.youtube.com/user/TurboTax). Do you think social media is an effective method of obtaining the tax information you might need to prepare your taxes?
2. Can you think of other companies that could use videos on a YouTube channel to share information that their customers could use?

2. Building Team Skills

Suppose that for the past three years you have been repairing lawn mowers in your garage. Your business has grown steadily, and you recently hired two part-time workers. Your garage is no longer adequate for your business; it is also in violation of the city code, and you have already been fined for noncompliance. You have decided that it is time to find another location for your shop and that it also would be a good time to expand your business. If the business continues to grow in the new location, you plan to hire a full-time employee to repair small appliances. You are concerned, however, about how you will get the money to move your shop and get it established in a new location.

Assignment

1. With all class members participating, use brainstorming to identify the following:
   a. The funds you will need to accomplish your business goals

   b. The sources of short-term financing available to you
   c. Problems that might prevent you from getting a short-term loan
   d. How you will repay the money if you get a loan
2. Have a classmate write the ideas on the board.
3. Discuss how you can overcome any problems that might hamper your current chances of getting a loan and how your business can improve its chances of securing short-term loans in the future.
4. Summarize what you learned from participating in this exercise.

3. Researching Different Careers

Financial managers are responsible for determining the best way to raise funds, for ensuring that the funds are used to accomplish their firm's goals and objectives, and for developing and implementing their firm's financial plan. Their decisions have a direct impact on the firm's level of success.

Assignment

1. Investigate the job of financial manager by searching the library or Internet, by interviewing a financial manager, or both.
2. Find answers to the following questions:
   a. What skills do financial managers need?
   b. How much education is required?
   c. What is the starting salary? Top salary?
   d. What will the job of financial manager be like in the future?
   e. What opportunities are available?
   f. What types of firms are most likely to hire financial managers? What is the employment potential?
3. Prepare a report on your findings.

Running a Business
Part 6

Graeter's Recipe for Growth: New Systems, Social Media, and Financing

Graeter's still makes ice cream by hand, just like the founders did in 1870. But in every other respect, it's a very different business from the mom-and-pop firm founded by the great-grandparents of Richard, Robert, and Chip Graeter. With the rise of communication technologies such as social media, Graeter's can stay in touch with customers and see what people say about its brand. Technology is also a factor in the new systems Graeter's recently installed to keep the business running smoothly as it pursues fast-paced growth. Just as important, the company has arranged financing to support its long-term plans for national expansion.

Graeter's Social Side

Even a small business can have a big presence in social media. Graeter's has designated an employee to manage all of the company's activities on Facebook, Twitter, and YouTube. With 155,000 Facebook "likes," Graeter's engages its brand fans in conversations about new or favorite flavors, the size of its chocolate chunks, and more. It posts a new message or photo every few days, and reveals the names of mystery flavors on Facebook in advance of other publicity. As a result, fans return to its Facebook page often. In addition, Graeter's tweets frequently and periodically posts videos on its YouTube channel. Graeter's also monitors "mentions" of its brand on other social-media sites. For example, hundreds of consumers have shared images of Graeter's ice cream on the Pinterest site. As other people add their comments and click to "like," the conversation continues and the word of mouth builds buzz for Graeter's.

New Growth, New Systems

Paul Porcino, a consultant working with the Graeter family, observes that small, entrepreneurial firms often have only "a very small amount of information, and . . . it hasn't been pulled together in any meaningful way." The first step was to define what Graeter's executives needed to know to run the business. For example, they needed to be able to track unit sales online, in each store, and to each wholesale customer, and to measure both costs and profitability by product and distribution channel.

Despite some technical challenges during implementation, Graeter's has already experienced some of the benefits of collecting better information. When management noticed that overall bakery sales weren't up to par, "we had to adjust," comments Porcino. The remedy was surprising: "We actually reduced the number of products we were selling in the store. . . . It wasn't very clear exactly how much we were selling, but at least [we had] the good-enough gut sense in terms of the ones that were not selling, and we . . . adjusted the total inventory line."

Counting on Accounting

Graeter's controller, David Blink, is responsible for preparing "all financial statements, all reports, payroll, [and] any ad hoc reports that any of the managers would need. I handle a lot of the reporting for the retail side as well as the manufacturing side," he says. With these reports in hand, the Graeter's team can make informed decisions about how many seasonal employees to hire, which products to keep, how much to invest in new equipment, and other issues that arise day by day. Although an outside payroll company actually prints the employees' checks, Blink's department collects and analyzes payroll data as input for management decisions.

Money Matters

With expansion on the menu, the Graeter's recognized they needed a new production facility. After scouting possible locations, Graeter's signed a 20-year deal with Cincinnati, paying a token amount for land and borrowing $10 million from the city to pay for construction of a new 28,000-square-foot factory. The loan carried low interest rates and would be repaid over 20 years. In turn, Cincinnati issued $10 million in bonds to provide Graeter's with this funding. The package of financial incentives that Graeter's received toward its new Bond Hill factory was worth $3.3 million. In exchange, Graeter's committed to "stay and grow" in Cincinnati for at least 20 years, creating dozens of new jobs when the facility opened in 2010 and additional jobs as Graeter's growth continued.

© iSTOCKPHOTO.COM/LUNVO

As opening day for the Bond Hill facility approached, Graeter's was presented with an unexpected opportunity. Its largest franchisee wanted to sell the franchise operation, complete with stores and an ice-cream factory, and Graeter's had the right to buy the franchise back. "That was not planned, not part of our strategic vision," explains Richard Graeter, "but the opportunity came up, and we had to look at it." After examining what the business had done in the past and where it was going in the future, the three great-grandsons of Graeter's founders put together the financing to buy the stores and factory from the franchisee. Now Graeter's has the right combination of ingredients for expanding from coast to coast and beyond.[17]

Questions

1. Suppose you were writing a social media plan for Graeter's, with two objectives: to improve brand awareness in new markets and to build online orders during holiday periods. What quantitative and qualitative measurements would you use to evaluate the results of your plan?

2. Graeter's uses information to track cash, sales revenue, and expenses on a daily basis. How does this type of accounting system facilitate effective decision making?

3. What kinds of questions do you think Cincinnati officials asked Graeter's owners before agreeing to loan the company $10 million? Why would Graeter's go with this financing arrangement rather than borrowing from a bank to pay for the Bond Hill factory?

Building a Business Plan: Part 6

Now that you have a marketing plan, the next big and important step is to prepare an information and financial plan. One of the biggest mistakes an entrepreneur makes when faced with a need for financing is not being prepared. The information contained in Chapter 14 (Exploring Social Media and e-Business), Chapter 15 (Using Management and Accounting Information), and Chapter 16 (Mastering Financial Management) will help you prepare this section of the business plan and determine the amount of financing you need to start your business. With the help of information in the last three chapters of the text, the task may be easier than you think.

In this last section, you should also provide some information about your exit strategy, and discuss any potential trends, problems, or risks that you may encounter. Now is also the time to go back and prepare the executive summary, which should be placed at the beginning of the business plan.

The Information and Accounting Plan Component

Information and accounting systems are important if your business is to succeed. Your information plan should answer at least the following questions:

6.1. How will you gather information about competitors, their products, and the prices that they charge for their products and services?
6.2. Explain how you will develop a management information system to collect, store, update, process data, and present information.
6.3. Will your business have an e-business component? If so, explain how you sell your products or services online.
6.4. Are there ways that you can use social media to promote products and services and reach out to your customers?
6.5. Who will create and maintain the accounting system that you use to record routine business transactions for your business?
6.6. Will you hire an accountant to prepare financial statements for your firm?

The Financial Plan Component

Your financial plan should answer at least the following questions about the investment needed, sales and cash-flow forecasts, breakeven analysis, and sources of funding:

6.7. What is the actual amount of money you need to open your business (start-up budget) and the amount needed to keep it open (operating budget)? Prepare a realistic budget.
6.8. How much money do you have, and how much money will you need to start your business and stay in business?
6.9. Prepare a projected income statement by month for the first year of operation and by quarter for the second and third years.
6.10. Prepare projected balance sheets for each of the first three years of operation.
6.11. Prepare a breakeven analysis. How many units of your products or service will have to be sold to cover your costs?
6.12. Reinforce your final projections by comparing them with industry averages for your chosen industry.

The Exit Strategy Component

Your exit strategy component should at least include answers to the following questions:

6.13. How do you intend to get yourself (and your money) out of the business?
6.14. Will your children take over the business, or do you intend to sell it later?
6.15. Do you intend to grow the business to the point of an IPO?
6.16. How will investors get their money back?

The Critical Risks and Assumptions Component

Your critical risks and assumptions component should answer at least the following questions:

6.17. What will you do if your market does not develop as quickly as you predicted? What if your market develops too quickly?
6.18. What will you do if your competitors underprice or make your product obsolete?
6.19. What will you do if there is an unfavorable industry-wide trend?
6.20. What will happen if trained workers are not available as predicted?
6.21. What will you do if there is an erratic supply of products or raw materials?

The Appendix Component

Supplemental information and documents often are included in an appendix. Here are a few examples of some documents that can be included:

- Résumés of owners and principal managers
- Advertising samples and brochures
- An organization chart
- Floor plans

Review of Business Plan Activities

As you have discovered, writing a business plan involves a long series of interrelated steps. As with any project involving a number of complex steps and calculations, your business plan should be reviewed carefully and revised before you present it to potential investors.

Remember, there is one more component you need to prepare after your business plan is completed: The executive summary should be written last, but because of its importance, it appears after the introduction.

The Executive Summary Component

In the executive summary, give a one- to two-page overview of your entire business plan. This is the most important part of the business plan and is of special interest to busy bankers, investors, and other interested parties. Remember, this section is a summary; more detailed information is provided in the remainder of your business plan.

Make sure that the executive summary captures the reader's attention instantly in the first sentence by using a key selling point or benefit of the business.

Your executive summary should include answers to at least the following:

6.22. *Company information*. What product or service do you provide? What is your competitive advantage? When will the company be formed? What are your company objectives? What is the background of you and your management team?

6.23. *Market opportunity*. What is the expected size and growth rate of your market, your expected market share, and any relevant market trends?

Once again, review your answers to all the questions in the preceding parts to make sure that they are all consistent throughout the entire business plan.

Although many would-be entrepreneurs are excited about the prospects of opening their own business, remember that it takes a lot of hard work, time, and in most cases a substantial amount of money. While the business plan provides an enormous amount of information about your business, it is only the first step. Once it is completed, it is now your responsibility to implement the plan. Good luck in your business venture.

The information contained in "Building a Business Plan" will also assist you in completing the online *Interactive Business Plan*.

Endnotes

1. Based on information in Jeffrey Burt, "Cisco Sees Revenue Jump 6 percent as It Expands Business Reach," *eWeek*, November 13, 2012, www.eweek.com; Quentin Hardy, "Cisco's Net Income Climbs, Beating Wall St. Forecasts," *New York Times*, November 13, 2012, www.nytimes.com; Noah Buhayar, "Cisco Adds to Technology Issuance with $4 Billion Debt Sale," *Bloomberg*, March 9, 2011, www.bloomberg.com; www.cisco.com.
2. The U.S. Bureau of Labor Statistics at http://bls.gov (accessed March 5, 2013).
3. The 3M Corporation website at www.3m.com (accessed March 5, 2013).
4. The McDonald's Corporate website at www.aboutmcdonalds.com (accessed March 4, 2013).
5. Dan Primack, "Buffettt: Heinz Is Not a 'Private Equity' Deal," The CNNMoney website at http://finance.fortune.cnn.com (accessed March 5, 2013).
6. Kenneth Rapozza, "Looking for Cash, Citigroup Selling India Bank Position," the Forbes website at www.forbes.com (accessed February 23, 2012).
7. "Hostess Brands Is Closed," The Hostess Brands website at www.hostessbrands.com (accessed November 21, 2012).
8. U.S. Census Bureau, Statistical Abstract of the United States, 2012 (Washington, D.C.: U.S. Government Printing Office, p. 740).
9. Ibid.
10. Steve Schaefer, "Puppies Over Pills: Pfizer Spinout Zoetisshines in Biggest IPO Since Facebook," the Forbes website at www.forbes.com (accessed February 1, 2013).
11. The Consolidated Edison Company of New York website at www.conedison.com (accessed March 8, 2013).
12. The General Electric website at www.ge.com (accessed September 7, 2013).
13. Russ Garland, "Zynga Inc: Venture Capital Investment Up Despite Fund-Raising Constraints," the 4-Traders.com website at www.4-traders.com (accessed January 20, 2012).
14. The Advanced Micro Devices corporate website at www.amd.com (accessed March 8, 2013).
15. *Mergent Transportation Manual* (New York: Mergent, Inc., 2009), 64.
16. Based on information from the company website www.nederlanderconcerts.com (accessed March 9, 2013); Nederlander Organization company overview, *BusinessWeek*, www.businessweek.com (accessed August 20, 2010); Hannah Heineman, "Moving Forward on Capital Improvement Projects," *Santa Monica Mirror*, July 28, 2010, www.smmirror.com; Steve Knopper, "Tour Biz Strong in Weak Economy," *Rolling Stone*, October 2, 2008, 11–12; Ray Waddell, "Nederlander/Viejas Deal Offers Touring Opportunities," *Billboard*, January 10, 2008, www.billboard.com; interviews with Nederlander employees and the video "Financial Planning and Budgets Equal Profits for Nederlander Concerts."
17. Sources: Based on information from the Graeter's company website at www.graeter.com (accessed March 10, 2013); Kimberly L. Jackson, "Graeter's Premium Chocolate Chip Ice Cream Lands at Stop & Shop," *Newark Star-Ledger (NJ)*, April 4, 2012, www.nj.com; "Graeter's Ice Cream Debuts in Bay Area," *Tampa Bay Times (St. Petersburg, FL)*, January 10, 2012, p. 4B; Jim Carper, "Graeter's Runs a Hands-on Ice Cream Plant," *Dairy Foods*, August 2011, pp. 36+; Jim Carper, "The Greater Good," *Dairy Foods*, August 2011, pp. 95+; "Graeter's Unveils New 'Mystery Flavor,'" *Dayton Daily News*, March 29, 2012, www.daytondailynews.com; Bob Driehaus, "A Cincinnati Ice Cream Maker Aims Big," *New York Times*, September 11, 2010, www.nytimes.com; Lucy May, "Graeter's Northern Kentucky Franchisee Puts Stores on the Block," *Business Courier*, August 6, 2010, http://cincinnati.bizjournals.com; www.graeters.com; interviews with company staff and Cengage videos about Graeter's.

Answer Key

CHAPTER 1

1. g   2. c   3. j   4. e   5. d   6. b
7. f   8. a   9. h   10. i   11. F   12. F
13. T   14. F   15. T   16. T   17. F   18. T
19. F   20. T   21. a   22. c   23. d   24. e
25. d   26. b   27. d   28. c   29. d   30. e

CHAPTER 2

1. j   2. g   3. e   4. k   5. a   6. l
7. d   8. i   9. f   10. b   11. T   12. F
13. F   14. T   15. F   16. T   17. T   18. F
19. T   20. F   21. b   22. e   23. d   24. a
25. d   26. c   27. e   28. c   29. b   30. d

CHAPTER 3

1. i   2. d   3. g   4. j   5. h   6. l
7. e   8. f   9. a   10. c   11. F   12. T
13. T   14. F   15. T   16. F   17. F   18. T
19. F   20. T   21. c   22. d   23. c   24. c
25. a   26. c   27. e   28. c   29. b   30. c

CHAPTER 4

1. j   2. i   3. k   4, f   5. l   6. h
7. b   8. d   9. c   10. a   11. F   12. F
13. T   14. F   15. T   16. F   17. T   18. F
19. T   20. T   21. d   22. d   23. c   24. e
25. e   26. c   27. b   28. a   29. d   30. d

CHAPTER 5

1. i   2. e   3. k   4. a   5. d   6. f
7. b   8. g   9. j   10. l   11. T   12. F
13. F   14. T   15. F   16. F   17. F   18. F
19. F   20. T   21. b   22. e   23. a   24. d
25. c   26. d   27. e   28. e   29. b   30. c

CHAPTER 6

1. g   2. i   3. j   4. b   5. f   6. c
7. d   8. k   9. e   10. l   11. F   12. F
13. T   14. F   15. T   16. F   17. F   18. F
19. T   20. T   21. b   22. e   23. b   24. a
25. d   26. b   27. b   28. d   29. c   30. a

CHAPTER 7

1. c   2. j   3. f   4. e   5. b   6. k
7. h   8. d   9. g   10. l   11. T   12. F
13. T   14. T   15. F   16. T   17. F   18. F
19. F   20. T   21. d   22. d   23. e   24. b
25. a   26. c   27. d   28. b   29. a   30. d

CHAPTER 8

1. e   2. a   3. g   4. f   5. l   6. b
7. k   8. j   9. d   10. i   11. f   12. t
13. f   14. f   15. t   16. f   17. f   18. t
19. f   20. t   21. b   22. b   23. a   24. d
25. e   26. d   27. c   28. d   29. e   30. c

CHAPTER 9

1. h   2. e   3. i   4. k   5. b   6. c
7. j   8. f   9. a   10. d   11. T   12. F
13. T   14. T   15. F   16. T   17. F   18. F
19. T   20. F   21. d   22. a   23. a   24. a
25. d   26. d   27. b   28. a   29. a   30. a

CHAPTER 10

1. g   2. k   3. d   4. e   5. j   6. c
7. h   8. b   9. f   10. i   11. T   12. F
13. T   14. F   15. F   16. F   17. T   18. T
19. F   20. T   21. b   22. c   23. a   24. a
25. e   26. a   27. c   28. b   29. c   30. a

CHAPTER 11

1. f   2. g   3. c   4. e   5. b   6. i
7. k   8. a   9. l   10. j   11. T   12. F
13. F   14. T   15. T   16. T   17. F   18. F
19. T   20. T   21. a   22. b   23. b   24. a
25. c   26. c   27. c   28. e   29. e   30. b

CHAPTER 12

1. b   2. c   3. a   4. e   5. g   6. f
7. j   8. i   9. h   10. l   11. F   12. F
13. F   14. T   15. T   16. F   17. T   18. T
19. T   20. F   21. d   22. b   23. c   24. b
25. c   26. d   27. a   28. c   29. d   30. c

CHAPTER 13

1. b   2. a   3. c   4. f   5. e   6. g
7. j   8. d   9. l   10. k   11. F   12. T
13. F   14. T   15. F   16. F   17. T   18. T
19. T   20. F   21. b   22. b   23. c   24. c
25. d   26. c   27. c   28. b   29. b   30. c

CHAPTER 14

1. c   2. f   3. e   4. g   5. d   6. b
7. i   8. k   9. a   10. h   11. F   12. F
13. T   14. F   15. T   16. T   17. F   18. T
19. F   20. T   21. b   22. c   23. d   24. d
25. e   26. e   27. a   28. b   29. c   30. c

CHAPTER 15

1. f   2. g   3. j   4. e   5. a   6. h
7. b   8. l   9. i   10. d   11. T   12. F
13. F   14. F   15. T   16. T   17. F   18. F
19. T   20. T   21. c   22. a   23. c   24. e
25. b   26. c   27. b   28. c   29. c   30. b

CHAPTER 16

1. a   2. e   3. g   4. d   5. l   6. h
7. b   8. j   9. k   10. c   11. T   12. F
13. F   14. F   15. T   16. T   17. T   18. T
19. F   20. F   21. a   22. b   23. e   24. a
25. d   26. e   27. b   28. c   29. e   30. d

Glossary

A

absolute advantage the ability to produce a specific product more efficiently than any other nation.

accessory equipment standardized equipment used in a firm's production or office activities.

accountability the obligation of a worker to accomplish an assigned job or task.

accounting the process of systematically collecting, analyzing, and reporting financial information.

accounting equation the basis for the accounting process: assets = liabilities + owners' equity.

ad hoc committee a committee created for a specific short-term purpose.

administrative manager a manager who is not associated with any specific functional area but who provides overall administrative guidance and leadership.

advertising a paid nonpersonal message communicated to a select audience through a mass medium.

advertising agency an independent firm that plans, produces, and places advertising for its clients.

affirmative action program a plan designed to increase the number of minority employees at all levels within an organization.

agent a middleman that expedites exchanges, represents a buyer or a seller, and often is hired permanently on a commission basis.

alien corporation a corporation chartered by a foreign government and conducting business in the United States.

analytic skills the ability to identify problems correctly, generate reasonable alternatives, and select the "best" alternatives to solve problems.

analytical process a process in operations management in which raw materials are broken into different component parts.

annual report a report distributed to stockholders and other interested parties that describes the firm's operating activities and its financial condition.

assets the resources that a business owns.

audit an examination of a company's financial statements and the accounting practices that produced them.

authority the power, within an organization, to accomplish an assigned job or task.

autocratic leadership task-oriented leadership style in which workers are told what to do and how to accomplish it without having a say in the decision-making process.

automatic vending the use of machines to dispense products.

automation the total or near-total use of machines to do work.

B

balance of payments the total flow of money into a country minus the total flow of money out of that country over some period of time.

balance of trade the total value of a nation's exports minus the total value of its imports over some period of time.

balance sheet (or statement of financial position) a summary of the dollar amounts of a firm's assets, liabilities, and owners' equity accounts at the end of a specific accounting period.

banker's acceptance a written order for a bank to pay a third party a stated amount of money on a specific state.

barter a system of exchange in which goods or services are traded directly for other goods or services without using money.

behavior modification a systematic program of reinforcement to encourage desirable behavior.

benchmarking a process used to evaluate the products, processes, or management practices of another organization that is superior in some way in order to improve quality.

bill of lading document issued by a transport carrier to an exporter to prove that merchandise has been shipped.

blog a website that allows a company to share information in order to not only increase the customer's knowledge about its products and services but also to build trust.

board of directors the top governing body of a corporation, the members of which are elected by the stockholders.

bond indenture a legal document that details all the conditions relating to a bond issue.

brand a name, term, symbol, design, or any combination of these that identifies a seller's products as distinct from those of other sellers.

brand equity marketing and financial value associated with a brand's strength in a market.

brand extension using an existing brand to brand a new product in a different product category.

brand loyalty extent to which a customer is favorable toward buying a specific brand.

brand mark the part of a brand that is a symbol or distinctive design.

brand name the part of a brand that can be spoken.

breakeven quantity the number of units that must be sold for the total revenue (from all units sold) to equal the total cost (of all units sold).

broker a middleman that specializes in a particular commodity, represents either a buyer or a seller, and is likely to be hired on a temporary basis.

budget a financial statement that projects income, expenditures, or both over a specified future period.

bundle pricing packaging together two or more complementary products and selling them for a single price.

business the organized effort of individuals to produce and sell, for a profit, the goods and services that satisfy society's needs.

business buying behavior the purchasing of products by producers, resellers, governmental units, and institutions.

business cycle the recurrence of periods of growth and recession in a nation's economic activity.

business ethics the application of moral standards to business situations.

business model represents a group of common characteristics and methods of doing business to generate sales revenues and reduce expenses.

business plan a carefully constructed guide for the person starting a business.

business product a product bought for resale, for making other products, or for use in a firm's operations.

business service an intangible product that an organization uses in its operations.

business-to-business (or B2B) model a model used by firms that conduct business with other businesses.

business-to-consumer (or B2C) model a model used by firms that focus on conducting business with individual consumers.

buying allowance a temporary price reduction to resellers for purchasing specified quantities of a product.

buying behavior the decisions and actions of people involved in buying and using products.

C

capacity the amount of products or services that an organization can produce in a given time.

capital budget a financial statement that estimates a firm's expenditures for major assets and its long-term financing needs.

capital-intensive technology a process in which machines and equipment do most of the work.

capitalism an economic system in which individuals own and operate the majority of businesses that provide goods and services.

captioned photograph a picture accompanied by a brief explanation.

captive pricing pricing the basic product in a product line low, but pricing related items at a higher level.

carrier a firm that offers transportation services.

cash budget a financial statement that estimates cash receipts and cash expenditures over a specified period.

cash flow the movement of money into and out of an organization.

catalog marketing a type of marketing in which an organization provides a catalog from which customers make selections and place orders by mail, telephone, or the Internet.

category killer a very large specialty store that concentrates on a single product line and competes on the basis of low prices and product availability.

caveat emptor a Latin phrase meaning "let the buyer beware."

centralized organization an organization that systematically works to concentrate authority at the upper levels of the organization.

certificate of deposit (CD) a document stating that the bank will pay the depositor a guaranteed interest rate on money left on deposit for a specified period of time.

certified public accountant (CPA) an individual who has met state requirements for accounting education and experience and has passed a rigorous accounting examination.

chain of command the line of authority that extends from the highest to the lowest levels of an organization.

chain retailer a company that operates more than one retail outlet.

check a written order for a bank or other financial institution to pay a stated dollar amount to the business or person indicated on the face of the check.

chief financial officer (CFO) a high-level corporate executive who manages a firm's finances and reports directly to the company's chief executive officer or president.

closed corporation a corporation whose stock is owned by relatively few people and is not sold to the general public.

cloud computing a type of computer usage in which services stored on the Internet is provided to users on a temporary basis.

code of ethics a guide to acceptable and ethical behavior as defined by the organization.

collateral real estate or property pledged as security for a loan.

command economy an economic system in which the government decides what goods and services will be produced, how they will be produced, for whom available goods and services will be produced, and who owns and controls the major factors of production.

commercial paper a short-term promissory note issued by a large corporation..

commission a payment that is a percentage of sales revenue.

common stock stock owned by individuals or firms who may vote on corporate matters but whose claims on profits and assets are subordinate to the claims of others.

communication skills the ability to speak, listen, and write effectively.

community shopping center a planned shopping center that includes one or two department stores and some specialty stores, along with convenience stores.

comparable worth a concept that seeks equal compensation for jobs requiring about the same level of education, training, and skills.

comparative advantage the ability to produce a specific product more efficiently than any other product.

comparison discounting setting a price at a specific level and comparing it with a higher price.

compensation the payment employees receive in return for their labor.

competition rivalry among businesses for sales to potential customers.

compensation system the policies and strategies that determine employee compensation.

component part an item that becomes part of a physical product and is either a finished item ready for assembly or a product that needs little processing before assembly.

computer-aided design (CAD) the use of computers to aid in the development of products.

computer-aided manufacturing (CAM) the use of computers to plan and control manufacturing processes.

computer-integrated manufacturing (CIM) a computer system that not only helps to design products but also controls the machinery needed to produce the finished product.

conceptual skills the ability to think in abstract terms.

consumer buying behavior the purchasing of products for personal or household use, not for business purposes.

consumerism all activities undertaken to protect the rights of consumers.

consumer price index (CPI) a monthly index that measures the changes in prices of a fixed basket of goods purchased by a typical consumer in an urban area.

consumer product a product purchased to satisfy personal and family needs.

consumer sales promotion method a sales promotion method designed to attract consumers to particular retail stores and to motivate them to purchase certain new or established products.

contingency plan a plan that outlines alternative courses of action that may be taken if an organization's other plans are disrupted or become ineffective.

continuous process a manufacturing process in which a firm produces the same product(s) over a long period of time.

controlling the process of evaluating and regulating ongoing activities to ensure that goals are achieved.

convenience product a relatively inexpensive, frequently purchased item for which buyers want to exert only minimal effort.

convenience store a small food store that sells a limited variety of products but remains open well beyond normal business hours.

convertible bond a bond that can be exchanged, at the owner's option, for a specified number of shares of the corporation's common stock.

cookie a small piece of software sent by a website that tracks an individual's Internet use.

cooperative advertising an arrangement whereby a manufacturer agrees to pay a certain amount of a retailer's media cost for advertising the manufacturer's products.

core competencies approaches and processes that a company performs well that may give it an advantage over its competitors.

corporate bond a corporation's written pledge that it will repay a specified amount of money with interest.

corporate culture the inner rites, rituals, heroes, and values of a firm.

corporate officers the chairman of the board, president, executive vice presidents, corporate secretary, treasurer, and any other top executive appointed by the board of directors.

corporation an artificial person created by law with most of the legal rights of a real person, including the rights to start and operate a business, to buy or sell property, to borrow money, to sue or be sued, and to enter into binding contracts.

cost of goods sold the dollar amount equal to beginning inventory plus net purchases less ending inventory.

countertrade an international barter transaction.

coupon reduces the retail price of a particular item by a stated amount at the time of purchase.

creative selling selling products to new customers and increasing sales to present customers.

cross-functional team a team of individuals with varying specialties, expertise, and skills that are brought together to achieve a common task.

crowdsourcing outsourcing tasks to a group of people in order to tap into the ideas of the crowd.

cultural (workplace) diversity differences among people in a workforce owing to race, ethnicity, and gender.

currency devaluation the reduction of the value of a nation's currency relative to the currencies of other countries.

current assets assets that can be converted quickly into cash or that will be used in one year or less.

current liabilities debts that will be repaid in one year or less.

current ratio a financial ratio computed by dividing current assets by current liabilities.

customary pricing pricing on the basis of tradition.

customer lifetime value a measure of a customer's worth (sales minus costs) to a business over one's lifetime.

customer relationship management (CRM) using information about customers to create marketing strategies that develop and sustain desirable customer relationships.

D

data numerical or verbal descriptions that usually result from some sort of measurement.

database a single collection of data and information stored in one place that can be used by people throughout an organization to make decisions.

data mining the practice of searching through data records looking for useful information.

data processing the transformation of data into a form that is useful for a specific purpose.

debenture bond a bond backed only by the reputation of the issuing corporation.

debit card a card that electronically subtracts the amount of a customer's purchase from her or his bank account at the moment the purchase is made.

debt capital borrowed money obtained through loans of various types.

decentralized organization an organization in which management consciously attempts to spread authority widely in the lower levels of the organization.

decision making the act of choosing one alternative from a set of alternatives.

decision-support system (DSS) a type of software program that provides relevant data and information to help a firm's employees make decisions.

deflation a general decrease in the level of prices.

delegation assigning part of a manager's work and power to other workers.

demand the quantity of a product that buyers are willing to purchase at each of various prices.

departmentalization the process of grouping jobs into manageable units.

departmentalization by customer grouping activities according to the needs of various customer populations.

departmentalization by function grouping jobs that relate to the same organizational activity.

departmentalization by location grouping activities according to the defined geographic area in which they are performed.

departmentalization by product grouping activities related to a particular product or service.

department store a retail store that (1) employs 25 or more persons and (2) sells at least home furnishings, appliances, family apparel, and household linens and dry goods, each in a different part of the store.

depreciation the process of apportioning the cost of a fixed asset over the period during which it will be used.

depression a severe recession that lasts longer than a typical recession and has a larger decline in business activity when compared to a recession.

design planning the development of a plan for converting an idea into an actual product or service.

directing the combined processes of leading and motivating.

direct marketing the use of the telephone, Internet, and nonpersonal media to introduce products to customers, who then can purchase them via mail, telephone, or the Internet.

direct-response marketing a type of marketing in which a retailer advertises a product and makes it available through mail, telephone, or online orders.

direct selling the marketing of products to customers through face-to-face sales presentations at home or in the workplace.

discount a deduction from the price of an item.

discount store a self-service general-merchandise outlet that sells products at lower-than-usual prices.

discretionary income disposable income less savings and expenditures on food, clothing, and housing.

disposable income personal income less all additional personal taxes.

distribution channel (or marketing channel) a sequence of marketing organizations that directs a product from the producer to the ultimate user.

dividend a distribution of earnings to the stockholders of a corporation.

domestic corporation a corporation in the state in which it is incorporated.

domestic system a method of manufacturing in which an entrepreneur distributes raw materials to various homes, where families process them into finished goods to be offered for sale by the merchant entrepreneur.

double-entry bookkeeping system a system in which each financial transaction is recorded as two separate accounting entries to maintain the balance shown in the accounting equation.

draft issued by the exporter's bank, ordering the importer's bank to pay for the merchandise, thus guaranteeing payment once accepted by the importer's bank.

dumping exportation of large quantities of a product at a price lower than that of the same product in the home market.

E

e-business (electronic business) the organized effort of individuals to produce and sell, for a profit, the products and services that satisfy society's needs through the facilities available on the Internet.

economic community an organization of nations formed to promote the free movement of resources and products among its members and to create common economic policies.

economic model of social responsibility the view that society will benefit most when business is left alone to produce and market profitable products that society needs.

economy the way in which people deal with the creation and distribution of wealth.

electronic funds transfer (EFT) system a means of performing financial transactions through a computer terminal.

embargo a complete halt to trading with a particular nation or in a particular product.

employee benefit a reward in addition to regular compensation that is provided indirectly to employees.

employee ownership a situation in which employees own the company they work for by virtue of being stockholders.

employee training the process of teaching operations and training employees how to do their present jobs more effectively and efficiently.

empowerment making employees more involved in their jobs by increasing their participation in decision making.

entrepreneur a person who risks time, effort, and money to start and operate a business.

entrepreneurial leadership personality-based leadership style in which the manager seeks to inspire workers with a vision of what can be accomplished to benefit all stakeholders.

Equal Employment Opportunity Commission (EEOC) a government agency with the power to investigate complaints of employment discrimination and the power to sue firms that practice it.

equity capital money received from the owners or from the sale of shares of ownership in a business.

equity theory a theory of motivation based on the premise that people are motivated to obtain and preserve equitable treatment for themselves.

esteem needs our need for respect, recognition, and a sense of our own accomplishment and worth.

ethics the study of right and wrong and of the morality of the choices individuals make.

everyday low prices (EDLPs) setting a low price for products on a consistent basis.

exclusive distribution the use of only a single retail outlet for a product in a large geographic area.

executive information system (EIS) a computer-based system that facilitates and supports the decision-making needs of top managers and senior executives by providing easy access to both internal and external information.

expectancy theory a model of motivation based on the assumption that motivation depends on how much we want something and on how likely we think we are to get it.

expert system a type of computer program that uses artificial intelligence to imitate a human's ability to think.

Export-Import Bank of the United States an independent agency of the U.S. government whose function is to assist in financing the exports of American firms.

exporting selling and shipping raw materials or products to other nations.

express warranty a written explanation of the producer's responsibilities in the event that a product is found to be defective or otherwise unsatisfactory.

external recruiting the attempt to attract job applicants from outside an organization.

F

factor a firm that specializes in buying other firms' accounts receivable.

factors of production resources used to produce goods and services.

factory system a system of manufacturing in which all the materials, machinery, and workers required to manufacture a product are assembled in one place.

family branding the strategy in which a firm uses the same brand for all or most of its products.

feature article a piece (of up to 3,000 words) prepared by an organization for inclusion in a particular publication.

federal deficit a shortfall created when the federal government spends more in a fiscal year than it receives.

financial accounting generates financial statements and reports for interested people outside an organization.

financial leverage the use of borrowed funds to increase the return on owners' equity.

financial management all the activities concerned with obtaining money and using it effectively.

financial manager a manager who is primarily responsible for an organization's financial resources.

financial plan a plan for obtaining and using the money needed to implement an organization's goals and objectives.

financial ratio a number that shows the relationship between two elements of a firm's financial statements.

first-line manager a manager who coordinates and supervises the activities of operating employees.

fiscal policy government influence on the amount of savings and expenditures; accomplished by altering the tax structure and by changing the levels of government spending.

fixed assets assets that will be held or used for a period longer than one year.

fixed cost a cost incurred no matter how many units of a product are produced or sold.

flexible benefit plan compensation plan whereby an employee receives a predetermined amount of benefit dollars to spend on a package of benefits he or she has selected to meet individual needs.

flexible manufacturing system (FMS) a single production system that combines electronic machines and CIM.

flextime a system in which employees set their own work hours within employer-determined limits.

foreign corporation a corporation in any state in which it does business except the one in which it is incorporated.

foreign-exchange control a restriction on the amount of a particular foreign currency that can be purchased or sold.

form utility utility created by people converting raw materials, finances, and information into finished products.

forum an interactive version of a community bulletin board that focuses on threaded discussions.

franchise a license to operate an individually owned business as though it were part of a chain of outlets or stores.

franchisee a person or organization purchasing a franchise.

franchising the actual granting of a franchise.

franchisor an individual or organization granting a franchise.

free enterprise the system of business in which individuals are free to decide what to produce, how to produce it, and at what price to sell it.

frequent-user incentive a program developed to reward customers who engage in repeat (frequent) purchases.

full-service wholesaler a middleman that performs the entire range of wholesaler functions.

functional middleman a middleman that helps in the transfer of ownership of products but does not take title to the products.

G

General Agreement on Tariffs and Trade (GATT) an international organization of 158 nations dedicated to reducing or eliminating tariffs and other barriers to world trade.

generally accepted accounting principles (GAAPs) an accepted set of guidelines and practices for companies reporting financial information and for the accounting profession.

general-merchandise wholesaler a middleman that deals in a wide variety of products.

general partner a person who assumes full or shared responsibility for operating a business.

generic product (or brand) a product with no brand at all.

goal an end result that an organization is expected to achieve over a one- to ten-year period.

goal-setting theory a theory of motivation suggesting that employees are motivated to achieve goals that they and their managers establish together.

grapevine the informal communications network within an organization.

green IT a term used to describe all of a firm's activities to support a healthy environment and sustain the planet.

gross domestic product (GDP) the total dollar value of all goods and services produced by all people within the boundaries of a country during a one-year period.

gross profit a firm's net sales less the cost of goods sold.

gross sales the total dollar amount of all goods and services sold during the accounting period.

H

hard-core unemployed workers with little education or vocational training and a long history of unemployment.

hostile takeover a situation in which the management and board of directors of a firm targeted for acquisition disapprove of the merger.

hourly wage a specific amount of money paid for each hour of work.

human resources management (HRM) all the activities involved in acquiring, maintaining, and developing an organization's human resources.

human resources manager a person charged with managing an organization's human resources programs.

human resources planning the development of strategies to meet a firm's future human resources needs.

hygiene factors job factors that reduce dissatisfaction when present to an acceptable degree but that do not necessarily result in high levels of motivation.

I

import duty (tariff) a tax levied on a particular foreign product entering a country.

importing purchasing raw materials or products in other nations and bringing them into one's own country.

import quota a limit on the amount of a particular good that may be imported into a country during a given period of time.

inbound marketing a marketing term that describes new ways of gaining attention and ultimately customers by creating content on a website that pulls customers in.

incentive payment a payment in addition to wages, salary, or commissions.

income statement a summary of a firm's revenues and expenses during a specified accounting period.

independent retailer a firm that operates only one retail outlet.

individual branding the strategy in which a firm uses a different brand for each of its products.

inflation a general rise in the level of prices.

informal group a group created by the members themselves to accomplish goals that may or may not be relevant to an organization.

informal organization the pattern of behavior and interaction that stems from personal rather than official relationships.

information data presented in a form that is useful for a specific purpose.

initial public offering (IPO) occurs when a corporation sells common stock to the general public for the first time.

inspection the examination of the quality of work-in-process.

institutional advertising advertising designed to enhance a firm's image or reputation.

intangible assets assets that do not exist physically but that have a value based on the rights or privileges they confer on a firm.

integrated marketing communications coordination of promotion efforts to ensure maximal informational and persuasive impact on customers.

intensive distribution the use of all available outlets for a product.

intermittent process a manufacturing process in which a firm's manufacturing machines and equipment are changed to produce different products.

internal recruiting considering present employees as applicants for available positions.

International business all business activities that involve exchanges across national boundaries.

International Monetary Fund (IMF) an international bank with 188 member nations that makes short-term loans to developing countries experiencing balance-of-payment deficits.

International Organization for Standardization (ISO) a network of national standards institutes and similar organizations from over 160 different countries that is charged with developing standards for quality products and services that are traded throughout the globe.

interpersonal skills the ability to deal effectively with other people.

inventory control the process of managing inventories in such a way as to minimize inventory costs, including both holding costs and potential stock-out costs.

inventory turnover a financial ratio calculated by dividing the cost of goods sold in one year by the average value of the inventory.

investment banking firm an organization that assists corporations in raising funds, usually by helping to sell new issues of stocks, bonds, or other financial securities.

invisible hand a term created by Adam Smith to describe how an individual's personal gain benefits others and a nation's economy.

J

job analysis a systematic procedure for studying jobs to determine their various elements and requirements.

job description a list of the elements that make up a particular job.

job enlargement expanding a worker's assignments to include additional but similar tasks.

job enrichment a motivation technique that provides employees with more variety and responsibility in their jobs.

job evaluation the process of determining the relative worth of the various jobs within a firm.

job redesign a type of job enrichment in which work is restructured to cultivate the worker-job match.

job rotation the systematic shifting of employees from one job to another.

job sharing an arrangement whereby two people share one full-time position.

job specialization the separation of all organizational activities into distinct tasks and the assignment of different tasks to different people.

job specification a list of the qualifications required to perform a particular job.

joint venture an agreement between two or more groups to form a business entity in order to achieve a specific goal or to operate for a specific period of time.

just-in-time inventory system a system designed to ensure that materials or supplies arrive at a facility just when they are needed so that storage and holding costs are minimized.

K

key performance indicators (KPIs) measurements that define and measure the progress of an organization toward achieving its objectives.

knowledge management (KM) a firm's procedures for generating, using, and sharing the data and information.

L

labeling the presentation of information on a product or its package.

labor-intensive technology a process in which people must do most of the work.

leadership the ability to influence others.

leading the process of influencing people to work toward a common goal.

lean manufacturing a concept built on the idea of eliminating waste from all of the activities required to produce a product or service.

letter of credit issued by a bank on request of an importer stating that the bank will pay an amount of money to a stated beneficiary.

liabilities a firm's debts and obligations.

licensing a contractual agreement in which one firm permits another to produce and market its product and use its brand name in return for a royalty or other compensation.

lifestyle shopping center an open-air-environment shopping center with upscale chain specialty stores.

limited liability a feature of corporate ownership that limits each owner's financial liability to the amount of money that he or she has paid for the corporation's stock.

limited-liability company (LLC) a form of business ownership that combines the benefits of a corporation and a partnership while avoiding some of the restrictions and disadvantages of those forms of ownership.

limited-line wholesaler a middleman that stocks only a few product lines but carries numerous product items within each line.

limited partner a person who invests money in a business but has no management responsibility or liability for losses beyond the amount he or she invested in the partnership.

line-and-staff structure an organizational structure that utilizes the chain of command from a line structure in combination with the assistance of staff managers.

line extension development of a new product that is closely related to one or more products in the existing product line but designed specifically to meet somewhat different customer needs.

line managers a position in which a person makes decisions and gives orders to subordinates to achieve the organization's goals.

line of credit a loan that is approved before the money is actually needed.

line structure an organizational structure in which the chain of command goes directly from person to person throughout the organization.

liquidity the ease with which an asset can be converted into cash.

long-term financing money that will be used for longer than one year.

long-term liabilities debts that need not be repaid for at least one year.

lump-sum salary increase an entire pay raise taken in one lump sum.

M

macroeconomics the study of the national economy and the global economy.

major equipment large tools and machines used for production purposes.

Malcolm Baldrige National Quality Award an award given by the President of the United States to organizations judged to be outstanding in specific managerial tasks that lead to improved quality for both products and services.

malware a general term that describes software designed to infiltrate a computer system without the user's consent.

management the process of coordinating people and other resources to achieve the goals of an organization.

management by objectives (MBO) a motivation technique in which managers and employees collaborate in setting goals.

management development the process of preparing managers and other professionals to assume increased responsibility in both present and future positions.

management information system (MIS) a system that provides managers and employees with the information they need to perform their jobs as effectively as possible.

managerial accounting provides managers and employees with the information needed to make decisions about a firm's financing, investing, marketing, and operating activities.

manufacturer (or producer) brand a brand that is owned by a manufacturer.

market a group of individuals or organizations, or both, that need products in a given category and that have the ability, willingness, and authority to purchase them.

market economy an economic system in which businesses and individuals decide what to produce and buy, and the market determines quantities sold and prices.

marketing the activity, set of institutions, and processes for creating, communicating, delivering, and exchanging offerings that have value for customers, clients, partners, and society at large.

marketing concept a business philosophy that a firm should provide goods and services that satisfy customers' needs through a coordinated set of activities that allow the firm to achieve its objectives.

marketing information system a system for managing marketing information that is gathered continually from internal and external sources.

marketing manager a manager who is responsible for facilitating the exchange of products between an organization and its customers or clients.

marketing mix a combination of product, price, distribution, and promotion developed to satisfy a particular target market.

marketing plan a written document that specifies an organization's resources, objectives, strategy, and implementation and control efforts to be used in marketing a specific product or product group.

market price the price at which the quantity demanded is exactly equal to the quantity supplied.

market segment a group of individuals or organizations within a market that share one or more common characteristics.

market segmentation the process of dividing a market into segments and directing a marketing mix at a particular segment or segments rather than at the total market.

marketing research the process of systematically gathering, recording, and analyzing data concerning a particular marketing problem.

marketing strategy a plan that will enable an organization to make the best use of its resources and advantages to meet its objectives.

markup the amount a seller adds to the cost of a product to determine its basic selling price.

Maslow's hierarchy of needs a sequence of human needs in the order of their importance.

mass production a manufacturing process that lowers the cost required to produce a large number of identical or similar products over a long period of time.

materials handling the actual physical handling of goods, in warehouses as well as during transportation.

materials requirements planning (MRP) a computerized system that integrates production planning and inventory control.

matrix structure an organizational structure that combines vertical and horizontal lines of authority, usually by superimposing product departmentalization on a functionally departmentalized organization.

maturity date the date on which a corporation is to repay borrowed money.

media sharing sites allow users to upload photos, videos, and podcasts.

merchant middleman a middleman that actually takes title to products by buying them.

merchant wholesaler a middleman that purchases goods in large quantities and sells them to other wholesalers or retailers and to institutional, farm, government, professional, or industrial users.

merger the purchase of one corporation by another.

microeconomics the study of the decisions made by individuals and businesses.

middleman (or marketing intermediary) a marketing organization that links a producer and user within a marketing channel.

middle manager a manager who implements the strategy and major policies developed by top management.

Millennials tech-savvy digital natives born after 1980.

minority a racial, religious, political, national, or other group regarded as different from the larger group of which it is a part and that is often singled out for unfavorable treatment.

mission a statement of the basic purpose that makes an organization different from others.

missionary salesperson a salesperson—generally employed by a manufacturer—who visits retailers to persuade them to buy the manufacturer's products.

mixed economy an economy that exhibits elements of both capitalism and socialism.

monetary policies Federal Reserve's decisions that determine the size of the supply of money in the nation and the level of interest rates.

monopolistic competition a market situation in which there are many buyers along with a relatively large number of sellers who differentiate their products from the products of competitors.

monopoly a market (or industry) with only one seller, and there are barriers to keep other firms from entering the industry.

morale an employee's feelings about the job, about superiors, and about the firm itself.

mortgage bond a corporate bond secured by various assets of the issuing firm.

motivating the process of providing reasons for people to work in the best interests of an organization.

motivation the individual internal process that energizes, directs, and sustains behavior; the personal "force" that causes you or me to behave in a particular way.

motivation factors job factors that increase motivation, although their absence does not necessarily result in dissatisfaction.

motivation-hygiene theory the idea that satisfaction and dissatisfaction are separate and distinct dimensions.

multilateral development bank (MDB) an internationally supported bank that provides loans to developing countries to help them grow.

multinational enterprise a firm that operates on a worldwide scale without ties to any specific nation or region.

multiple-unit pricing the strategy of setting a single price for two or more units.

N

national debt the total of all federal deficits.

need a personal requirement.

negotiated pricing establishing a final price through bargaining.

neighborhood shopping center a planned shopping center consisting of several small convenience and specialty stores.

net income occurs when revenues exceed expenses.

net loss occurs when expenses exceed revenues.

net sales the actual dollar amounts received by a firm for the goods and services it has sold after adjustment for returns, allowances, and discounts.

network structure an organizational structure in which administration is the primary function, and most other functions are contracted out to other firms.

news release a typed page of about 300 words provided by an organization to the media as a form of publicity.

non-price competition competition based on factors other than price.

nonstore retailing a type of retailing whereby consumers purchase products without visiting a store.

nontariff barrier a nontax measure imposed by a government to favor domestic over foreign suppliers.

not-for-profit corporation a corporation organized to provide a social, educational, religious, or other service rather than to earn a profit.

O

objective a specific statement detailing what an organization intends to accomplish over a shorter period of time.

odd-number pricing the strategy of setting prices using odd numbers that are slightly below whole-dollar amounts.

off-price retailer a store that buys manufacturers' seconds, overruns, returns, and off-season merchandise for resale to consumers at deep discounts.

oligopoly a market (or industry) in which there are few sellers.

online retailing retailing that makes products available to buyers through computer connections.

open corporation a corporation whose stock can be bought and sold by any individual.

operating expenses all business costs other than the cost of goods sold.

operational plan a type of plan designed to implement tactical plans.

operations management all the activities required to produce goods and services.

operations manager a manager who manages the systems that convert resources into goods and services.

order getter a salesperson who is responsible for selling a firm's products to new customers and increasing sales to present customers.

order processing activities involved in receiving and filling customers' purchase orders.

order taker a salesperson who handles repeat sales in ways that maintain positive relationships with customers.

organization a group of two or more people working together to achieve a common set of goals.

organizational height the number of layers, or levels, of management in a firm.

organization chart a diagram that represents the positions and relationships within an organization.

organizing the grouping of resources and activities to accomplish some end result in an efficient and effective manner.

orientation the process of acquainting new employees with an organization.

outsourcing the process of finding outside vendors and suppliers that provide professional help, parts, or materials at a lower cost.

over-the-counter (OTC) market a network of dealers who buy and sell the stocks of corporations that are not listed on a securities exchange.

owners' equity the difference between a firm's assets and its liabilities.

P

packaging all the activities involved in developing and providing a container with graphics for a product.

participative leadership leadership style in which all members of a team are involved in identifying essential goals and developing strategies to reach those goals.

partnership a voluntary association of two or more persons to act as co-owners of a business for profit.

part-time work permanent employment in which individuals work less than a standard work week.

penetration pricing the strategy of setting a low price for a new product.

perfect (or pure) competition the market situation in which there are many buyers and sellers of a product, and no single buyer or seller is powerful enough to affect the price of that product.

performance appraisal the evaluation of employees' current and potential levels of performance to allow managers to make objective human resources decisions.

periodic discounting temporary reduction of prices on a patterned or systematic basis.

personal income the income an individual receives from all sources less the Social Security taxes the individual must pay.

personal selling personal communication aimed at informing customers and persuading them to buy a firm's products.

physical distribution all those activities concerned with the efficient movement of products from the producer to the ultimate user.

physiological needs the things we require for survival.

piece-rate system a compensation system under which employees are paid a certain amount for each unit of output they produce.

place utility utility created by making a product available at a location where customers wish to purchase it.

plan an outline of the actions by which an organization intends to accomplish its goals and objectives.

planning establishing organizational goals and deciding how to accomplish them.

planning horizon the period during which an operational plan will be in effect.

plant layout the arrangement of machinery, equipment, and personnel within a production facility.

podcasts digital audio or video files that people listen to or watch online on tablets, computers, MP3 players, or smartphones.

point-of-purchase display promotional material placed within a retail store.

pollution the contamination of water, air, or land through the actions of people in an industrialized society.

possession utility utility created by transferring title (or ownership) of a product to a buyer.

preferred stock stock owned by individuals or firms who usually do not have voting rights but whose claims on dividends are paid before those of common-stock owners.

premium a gift that a producer offers a customer in return for buying its product.

premium pricing pricing the highest-quality or most-versatile products higher than other models in the product line.

press conference a meeting at which invited media personnel hear important news announcements and receive supplementary textual materials and photographs.

price the amount of money a seller is willing to accept in exchange for a product at a given time and under given circumstances.

price competition an emphasis on setting a price equal to or lower than competitors' prices to gain sales or market share.

price leaders products priced below the usual markup, near cost, or below cost.

price lining the strategy of selling goods only at certain predetermined prices that reflect definite price breaks.

price skimming the strategy of charging the highest possible price for a product during the introduction stage of its life-cycle.

primary-demand advertising advertising whose purpose is to increase the demand for all brands of a product within a specific industry.

primary market a market in which an investor purchases financial securities (via an investment bank) directly from the issuer of those securities.

prime interest rate the lowest rate charged by a bank for a short-term loan.

private placement occurs when stock and other corporate securities are sold directly to insurance companies, pension funds, or large institutional investors.

problem the discrepancy between an actual condition and a desired condition.

problem-solving team a team of knowledgeable employees brought together to tackle a specific problem.

process material a material that is used directly in the production of another product but is not readily identifiable in the finished product.

producer price index (PPI) an index that measures prices that producers receive for their finished goods.

product everything one receives in an exchange, including all tangible and intangible attributes and expected benefits; it may be a good, a service, or an idea.

product deletion the elimination of one or more products from a product line.

product design the process of creating a set of specifications from which a product can be produced.

product differentiation the process of developing and promoting differences between one's product and all similar products.

productivity the average level of output per worker per hour.

product life-cycle a series of stages in which a product's sales revenue and profit increase, reach a peak, and then decline.

product line a group of similar products that differ only in relatively minor characteristics.

product mix all the products a firm offers for sale.

product modification the process of changing one or more of a product's characteristics.

profit what remains after all business expenses have been deducted from sales revenue.

profit-sharing the distribution of a percentage of a firm's profit among its employees.

promissory note a written pledge by a borrower to pay a certain sum of money to a creditor at a specified future date.

promotion communication about an organization and its products that is intended to inform, persuade, or remind target-market members.

promotion mix the particular combination of promotion methods a firm uses to reach a target market.

proxy a legal form listing issues to be decided at a stockholders' meeting and enabling stockholders to transfer their voting rights to some other individual or individuals.

proxy fight a technique used to gather enough stockholder votes to control a targeted company.

publicity communication in news-story form about an organization, its products, or both.

public relations communication activities used to create and maintain favorable relationships between an organization and various public groups, both internal and external.

purchasing all the activities involved in obtaining required materials, supplies, components, and parts from other firms.

Q

qualitative social media measurement the process of accessing the opinions and beliefs about a brand and primarily uses sentiment analysis to categorize what is being said about a company.

quality circle a team of employees who meet on company time to solve problems of product quality.

quality control the process of ensuring that goods and services are produced in accordance with design specifications.

quantitative social media measurement using numerical measurements, such as counting the number of website visitors, number of fans and followers, number of leads generated, and the number of new customers.

R

random discounting temporary reduction of prices on an unsystematic basis.

raw material a basic material that actually becomes part of a physical product; usually comes from mines, forests, oceans, or recycled solid wastes.

rebate a return of part of the purchase price of a product.

recession two or more consecutive three-month periods of decline in a country's GDP.

recruiting the process of attracting qualified job applicants.

reference pricing pricing a product at a moderate level and positioning it next to a more expensive model or brand.

regional shopping center a planned shopping center containing large department stores, numerous specialty stores, restaurants, movie theaters, and sometimes even hotels.

registered bond a bond registered in the owner's name by the issuing company.

reinforcement theory a theory of motivation based on the premise that rewarded behavior is likely to be repeated, whereas punished behavior is less likely to recur.

relationship marketing establishing long-term, mutually satisfying buyer–seller relationships.

replacement chart a list of key personnel and their possible replacements within a firm.

research and development (R&D) a set of activities intended to identify new ideas that have the potential to result in new goods and services.

reshoring a situation in which U.S. manufacturers bring manufacturing jobs back to the United States.

responsibility the duty to do a job or perform a task.

retailer a middleman that buys from producers or other middlemen and sells to consumers.

retained earnings the portion of a corporation's profits not distributed to stockholders.

return on sales (or profit margin) a financial ratio calculated by dividing net income after taxes by net sales.

revenues the dollar amounts earned by a firm from selling goods, providing services, or performing business activities.

revenue stream a source of revenue flowing into a firm.

revolving credit agreement a guaranteed line of credit.

risk-return ratio a ratio based on the principle that a high-risk decision should generate higher financial returns for a business and more conservative decisions often generate lower returns.

Robotics the use of programmable machines to perform a variety of tasks by manipulating materials and tools.

S

safety needs the things we require for physical and emotional security.

salary a specific amount of money paid for an employee's work during a set calendar period, regardless of the actual number of hours worked.

sales forecast an estimate of the amount of a product that an organization expects to sell during a certain period of time based on a specified level of marketing effort.

sales promotion the use of activities or materials as direct inducements to customers or salespersons.

sales support personnel employees who aid in selling but are more involved in locating prospects, educating customers, building goodwill for the firm, and providing follow-up service.

sample a free product given to customers to encourage trial and purchase.

Sarbanes-Oxley Act of 2002 provides sweeping new legal protection for employees who report corporate misconduct.

scheduling the process of ensuring that materials and other resources are at the right place at the right time.

scientific management the application of scientific principles to management of work and workers.

S-corporation a corporation that is taxed as though it were a partnership.

secondary market a market for existing financial securities that are traded between investors.

secondary-market pricing setting one price for the primary target market and a different price for another market.

securities exchange a marketplace where member brokers meet to buy and sell securities.

selection the process of gathering information about applicants for a position and then using that information to choose the most appropriate applicant.

selective-demand (or brand) advertising advertising that is used to sell a particular brand of product.

selective distribution the use of only a portion of the available outlets for a product in each geographic area.

self-actualization needs the need to grow and develop and to become all that we are capable of being.

self-managed teams groups of employees with the authority and skills to manage themselves.

sentiment analysis a measurement that uses technology to detect the moods, attitudes, or emotions of people who experience a social media activity.

serial bonds bonds of a single issue that mature on different dates.

Service Corps of Retired Executives (SCORE) a group of businesspeople who volunteer their services to small businesses through the SBA.

service economy an economy in which more effort is devoted to the production of services than to the production of goods.

shopping product an item for which buyers are willing to expend considerable effort on planning and making the purchase.

short-term financing money that will be used for one year or less.

sinking fund a sum of money to which deposits are made each year for the purpose of redeeming a bond issue.

Six Sigma a disciplined approach that relies on statistical data and improved methods to eliminate defects for a firm's products and services.

skills inventory a computerized data bank containing information on the skills and experience of all present employees.

small business one that is independently owned and operated for profit and is not dominant in its field.

Small Business Administration (SBA) a governmental agency that assists, counsels, and protects the interests of small businesses in the United States.

small-business development centers (SBDCs) university-based groups that provide individual counseling and practical training to owners of small businesses.

small-business institutes (SBIs) groups of senior and graduate students in business administration who provide management counseling to small businesses.

small-business investment companies (SBICs) privately owned firms that provide venture capital to small enterprises that meet their investment standards.

social audit a comprehensive report of what an organization has done and is doing with regard to social issues that affect it.

social content sites allow companies to create and share information about their products and services.

social game a multiplayer, competitive, goal-oriented activity with defined rules of engagement and online connectivity among a community of players.

social media the online interaction that allows people and businesses to communicate and share ideas, personal information, and information about products or services.

social media communities social networks based on the relationships among people.

social media marketing the utilization of social media technologies, channels, and software to create, communicate, deliver, and exchange offerings that have value for an organization.

social needs the human requirements for love and affection and a sense of belonging.

social responsibility the recognition that business activities have an impact on society and the consideration of that impact in business decision making.

socioeconomic model of social responsibility the concept that business should emphasize not only profits but also the impact of its decisions on society.

sole proprietorship a business that is owned (and usually operated) by one person.

span of management (or span of control) the number of workers who report directly to one manager.

special-event pricing advertised sales or price cutting linked to a holiday, season, or event.

specialization the separation of a manufacturing process into distinct tasks and the assignment of the different tasks to different individuals.

specialty-line wholesaler a middleman that carries a select group of products within a single line.

specialty product an item that possesses one or more unique characteristics for which a significant group of buyers is willing to expend considerable purchasing effort.

speculative production the time lag between the actual production of goods and when the goods are sold.

staff managers a position created to provide support, advice, and expertise within an organization.

stakeholders all the different people or groups of people who are affected by an organization's policies, decisions, and activities.

standard of living a loose, subjective measure of how well off an individual or a society is, mainly in terms of want satisfaction through goods and services.

standing committee a relatively permanent committee charged with performing some recurring task.

statement of cash flows a statement that illustrates how the company's operating, investing, and financing activities affect cash during an accounting period.

statistic a measure that summarizes a particular characteristic of an entire group of numbers.

stock the shares of ownership of a corporation.

stockholder a person who owns a corporation's stock.

store (or private brand) a brand that is owned by an individual wholesaler or retailer.

strategic alliance a partnership formed to create competitive advantage on a worldwide basis.

strategic plan an organization's broadest plan, developed as a guide for major policy setting and decision making.

strategic planning process the establishment of an organization's major goals and objectives and the allocation of resources to achieve them.

supermarket a large self-service store that sells primarily food and household products.

superstore a large retail store that carries not only food and nonfood products ordinarily found in supermarkets but also additional product lines.

supply an item that facilitates production and operations but does not become part of a finished product.

supply the quantity of a product that producers are willing to sell at each of various prices.

supply-chain management long-term partnership among channel members working together to create a distribution system that reduces inefficiencies, costs, and redundancies while creating a competitive advantage and satisfying customers.

sustainability creating and maintaining the conditions under which humans and nature can exist in productive harmony while fulfilling the social, economic, and other requirements of present and future generations.

SWOT analysis the identification and evaluation of a firm's strengths, weaknesses, opportunities, and threats.

syndicate a temporary association of individuals or firms organized to perform a specific task that requires a large amount of capital.

synthetic process a process in operations management in which raw materials or components are combined to create a finished product.

T

tactical plan a smaller scale plan developed to implement a strategy.

target market a group of individuals or organizations, or both, for which a firm develops and maintains a marketing mix suitable for the specific needs and preferences of that group.

task force a committee established to investigate a major problem or pending decision.

team two or more workers operating as a coordinated unit to accomplish a specific task or goal.

technical salesperson a salesperson who assists a company's current customers in technical matters.

technical skills specific skills needed to accomplish a specialized activity.

telecommuting working at home all the time or for a portion of the work week.

telemarketing the performance of marketing-related activities by telephone.

television home shopping a form of selling in which products are presented to television viewers, who can buy them by calling a toll-free number and paying with a credit card.

tender offer an offer to purchase the stock of a firm targeted for acquisition at a price just high enough to tempt stockholders to sell their shares.

term-loan agreement a promissory note that requires a borrower to repay a loan in monthly, quarterly, semiannual, or annual installments.

Theory X a concept of employee motivation generally consistent with Taylor's scientific management; assumes that employees dislike work and will function only in a highly controlled work environment.

Theory Y a concept of employee motivation generally consistent with the ideas of the human relations movement; assumes responsibility and work toward organizational goals, and by doing so they also achieve personal rewards.

Theory Z the belief that some middle ground between type A and type J practices is best for American business.

time utility utility created by making a product available when customers wish to purchase it.

top manager an upper-level executive who guides and controls the overall fortunes of an organization.

total cost the sum of the fixed costs and the variable costs attributed to a product.

total quality management (TQM) the coordination of efforts directed at improving customer satisfaction, increasing employee participation, strengthening supplier partnerships, and facilitating an organizational atmosphere of continuous quality improvement.

total revenue the total amount received from the sales of a product.

trade credit a type of short-term financing extended by a seller who does not require immediate payment after delivery of merchandise.

trade deficit a negative balance of trade.

trade name the complete and legal name of an organization.

trade salesperson a salesperson—generally employed by a food producer or processor—who assists customers in promoting products, especially in retail stores.

trade sales promotion method a sales promotion method designed to encourage wholesalers and retailers to stock and actively promote a manufacturer's product.

trademark a brand name or brand mark that is registered with the U.S. Patent and Trademark Office and thus is legally protected from use by anyone except its owner.

trade show an industry-wide exhibit at which many sellers display their products.

trading company provides a link between buyers and sellers in different countries.

traditional specialty store a store that carries a narrow product mix with deep product lines.

transfer pricing prices charged in sales between an organization's units.

transportation the shipment of products to customers.

trustee an individual or an independent firm that acts as a bond owner's representative.

U

undifferentiated approach directing a single marketing mix at the entire market for a particular product.

unemployment rate the percentage of a nation's labor force unemployed at any time.

unlimited liability a legal concept that holds a business owner personally responsible for all the debts of the business.

unsecured financing financing that is not backed by collateral.

utility the ability of a good or service to satisfy a human need.

V

variable cost a cost that depends on the number of units produced.

venture capital money that is invested in small (and sometimes struggling) firms that have the potential to become very successful.

virtual team a team consisting of members who are geographically dispersed but communicate electronically.

W

wage survey a collection of data on prevailing wage rates within an industry or a geographic area.

warehouse club a large-scale members-only establishment that combines features of cash-and-carry wholesaling with discount retailing.

warehouse showroom a retail facility in a large, low-cost building with a large on-premises inventory and minimal service.

warehousing the set of activities involved in receiving and storing goods and preparing them for reshipment.

whistle-blowing informing the press or government officials about unethical practices within one's organization.

wholesaler a middleman that sells products to other firms.

wiki a collaborative online working space that enables members to contribute content that can be shared with other people.

World Trade Organization (WTO) powerful successor to GATT that incorporates trade in goods, services, and ideas.

Z

zero-base budgeting a budgeting approach in which every expense in every budget must be justified.

Name Index

Google, 239, 252, 267, 268, 330, 335, 401, 404, 416
Google+, 396, 400, 402, 416
Gorman, Leon, 180
Goscha, John, 332
gotomeeting.com, 248
Government Accountability Office (GAO), 72
Graeter, Chip, 95, 155, 234, 390, 491
Graeter, Louis Charles, 95, 155
Graeter, Regina, 95, 155
Graeter, Richard II, 95, 155, 234, 390, 491, 492
Graeter, Robert (Bob), 95, 155, 234, 491
Graeter's Ice Cream, 7, 95–96, 155–156, 234–235, 293–294, 390–391, 491–492
Great Clips hair salons, 148
Green Dot Corp, 131
Griswold, Daniel T., 69
Grosnickle, Karolyn, 35
Groupon, 399, 457
Gruma SA, 83
Gurung, Prabal, 304

H

Häagen-Dazs, 96, 390
Habitat for Humanity, 117
Halliburton, 37
Halogen Software, 242
Halvorsen, Elizabeth, 142
Hard Rock Cafe, 216
Harkness, John, 57
Harrington, Emily, 142
Harvard Business School, 300
Hasbro, 227
Heinz, 338
Heinz Ketchup, 328
Hendricks, Brian, 133
Hershey Foods Corporation, 442
Herzberg, Frederick, 271
Hewlett-Packard (HP), 34, 37, 223
Hewson, Marillyn, 171
Hilleren, Heather, 412
Hispanic PR Wire, 113
Hitachi Data Systems, 409
H.J. Heinz, 334
Hochberg, Fred P., 87
Holden, Luke, 423
Home Depot, 185, 363, 399, 406, 442, 457
Honda, 21, 22, 209, 333, 412
Honeywell, 223
Hoover's Inc., 413, 451
Horatio Alger Award, 3
Horizon Ventures, 12
Housing Development Finance Corporation, 469
H&R Block, 8, 144, 210, 211
HubSpot, 404
Hufbauer, Gary, 72
Hulu.com, 388

Human Proteome Folding Project, 42
The Human Side of Enterprise (McGregor), 273
Hurt, Alan, 57

I

IBM, 42, 141, 185, 223, 276, 335, 336, 406, 427
Illumina, Inc., 227
Ingersoll Rand, 243
Innovision Technologies, 131
Instagram, 310, 402
Intel Corporation, 9, 144, 207, 209, 479
Inter-American Development Bank (IDB), 87, 88
Intergovernmental Panel on Climate Change, 56
International Accounting Standards Board, 438
International Financial Reporting Standards (IFRS), 438
International Franchise Association, 148
International Monetary Fund (IMF), 74, 88
International Organization for Standardization (ISO), 224
International Trade Administration, 86, 87, 90
Intuit, 427
Isenberg, Daniel, 133
IVY Planning Group, 105

J

Jaguar, 42
Javelin Strategy and Research, 417
JCPenney, 102, 363
Jell-O, 336
Johns Manville building products, 101
Johnson & Johnson, 25
Johnston, Pete, 481, 482
Jones, Gareth, 197
Jordan, Kim, 172
JPMorgan Chase & Co., 118, 398, 401
Jubilant Foodworks, 84
Junior's Restaurant, 103

K

Kaminesky, Ken, 310
Karl, 15
Kelley, Harry, 138
Kellogg's, 185, 210, 328, 333
Kelly, Terri, 184
Kenmore, 334
Kennedy, John F., 58, 60, 77
Klein, Marvin, 62
Klippert, Joel, 30
Klippert, LeeAnn, 30
KlipTech, 30

Kmart, 111, 364
Koch, Jim, 331
Koehn, Nancy F., 133
Kohler, 300
Kozlowski, Leo Dennis, 35
KPMG, 441
Kraft Foods, Inc., 8, 477, 478
Kroger, 7, 363, 390
Kroopf, Jackson, 138
Krummer, Robert, Jr., 138

L

La Boulange bakery, 163
LAB Series, 304
Lamy, Pascal, 78, 89
Lands' End, 357, 415
Lavrov, Sergey, 71
Le Cirque, 342
Lehman Brothers, 439
Lenor, 328
Lenovo, 73
Levi Strauss, 220, 333
LEXIS-NEXIS, 312
Lincoln Electric, 227
LinkedIn, 5, 246, 247, 249, 253, 396, 400, 403, 405, 406, 416, 479
LiveOps, 276
LivingSocial, 399
Liz Claiborne, 227
L.L.Bean, Inc., 134, 180, 357, 387–388
Local Dirt, 412
Lockheed Martin, 42, 223
Loopt, 131
Lowe's, 363, 457
Luke's Lobster, 423
Lupron cancer drug, 34

M

Macaroni Grill restaurants, 376
Macy's, 68, 412
Madoff, Bernard "Bernie,", 34, 35
Maggiano's Little Italy Restaurant, 213
Magic Bullet, 366
Malcolm Baldrige National Quality Award, 222
ManPower Group, 245
Mantega, Guido, 93
Marathon Oil Corporation, 210
Marks, Richard, 35
Marriott, 143, 309
Marriott, Bill, 399
Marriott International, 4, 399
Mars, 110
Marshall, John, 109
Martin, Lockheed, 171
Mary Kay, 358, 365
Maslow, Abraham, 270
Massachusetts Export Center, 149
Master Lock, 209
Mattel, Inc., 19
Maxim Integrated Products, Inc., 219

SCORE (Service Corps of Retired Executives), 115, 141–142
Sears Holdings Corporation, 111
Sears, Richard, 111
Sears, Roebuck & Co., 114, 136, 357, 362, 363
See's Candies, 101
Service Corps of Retired Executives (SCORE), 115, 141–142
ServiceMaster, 136
Seton Hall University, 35
7-Eleven, 161, 364
Seven-Up, 145
Shake Weight, 366
Shaw Industries, 101
Shell, Richard, 143
Signs By Tomorrow, 146
Sino-Forest, 439
Sinopec Group, 85
Six Sigma, 223, 230
Skida, 138
Skoda, 298
Skype, 248, 284, 287
Slater, Samuel, 23
Small Business Training Network (SBTN), 141
Smartfood, 102
"Smart Fridge,", 215, 216
Smith, Adam, 12, 13, 15, 27, 186, 187
Smith, Gary, 105
Smith, Janet, 105
Snuggie, 366
Society for Human Resource Management, 188
Sodexho, 243
Sony Corporation, 3, 9, 84, 111, 336
Sorber, Brig, 153
Sorber, Jon, 153
Southwest Airlines, 167, 211, 253
Springhill, 310
Springsteen, Bruce, 489
Sprint Nextel, 413
Stanley Black & Decker, Inc., 464, 465
Stanley Home Products, 365
Staples, Inc., 144, 331
Starbucks, 2, 47, 163, 170, 281, 357, 404, 405
StartUpPc, 133
State Grid, 85
Stav, Julie, 6
Stephenson, Randall, 44
Strand, Cheryl, 132
SUBWAY, 145, 147, 148
Summify, 120
Summly, 12
Sutarik, Mike, 57

T

TAP Pharmaceutical Products, Inc., 34
Target, 363
Taylor, Frederick W., 268

Taylor, James, 489
TCBY Enterprises, Inc., 147
TD Bank, 398
Teavana tea chain, 163
Telephone Pioneers of America, 44
Texas Instruments (TI), 40
Thomasville, 21
Thornton, Beth, 143
Thorp, Lauren, 300
3M Company, 56, 214
Tindell, Kip, 263
T.J. Maxx, 365
T-Mobile, 120, 125
Toluna, 312
Toyota Motor Corp., 16, 22, 85, 175, 218, 221, 223, 298
Toyota Way, 223
Trammel, Angela, 146
Trammel, Ernest, 146
Trans-Pacific Partnership (TPP), 80
Tree City, 138
Trimit (application), 12
Trism (application), 6
TTK Group, 84
Tumblr, 423
Tupperware, 365
Twitter, 5, 9, 25, 86, 115, 120, 162, 170, 246, 253, 310, 320, 336, 388, 395, 397, 400, 402, 403, 404, 405, 409, 423, 479, 480, 491
Two Men and a Truck, 153
Tyco International, Ltd, 35

U

Ulukaya, Hamdi, 173
Umba Box, 300
Under Armour, 357
Underwood, Carrie, 412
Unilever, 25, 96, 376, 451
Union Carbide, 83
Union Pacific Corporation, 484
United Parcel Service (UPS), 96, 396
U.S. Commercial Service, 149
U.S. Department of Commerce, 71
U.S. Environmental Protection Agency (EPA), 25, 54
U.S. Government Printing Office, 143
U.S. Navy, 174
U.S. Patent and Trademark Office, 333, 336
U.S. Postal Service, 242
U.S. Small Business Administration (SBA), 128, 135, 141–144
U.S. West, 313

V

VB Solutions, Inc., 133
Verizon Communications, 125, 252, 346, 374
Vimeo, 423
Virgin Group, 168, 191

Visa, 471, 477, 478
Volkswagen, 72, 93, 111, 298
VPI Pet Insurance, 337
Vroom, Victor, 276

W

Wall Street Journal, 457–458, 463, 489
Walmart, 9, 42, 43, 85, 102, 118, 119, 331, 357, 363, 364, 365, 369, 370, 412
Walton, Sam, 9, 119
Watermark Designs, 209
The Wealth of Nations (Smith), 12, 186
Wegmans Food Markets, 268
Weisberg, Syd, 62
Wells Fargo, 398
Wendy's International, 148
Whataburger, 219
Whirlpool Corporation, 93, 195, 333
White Hen Pantry, 364
Winfrey, Oprah, 96
Withey, Annie, 102
W.L. Gore & Associates, 184
Workday, Inc., 169
World Bank, 88
WorldCom, 36, 37
World Community Grid, 42
The World Is Flat (Friedman), 66
World Trade Organization, 71, 78, 89
Wrike, 282
Wu, Jason, 304
Wyndham Hotel Group, 400

X

Xerox, 55, 134, 336

Y

Yankee Candle, 387
Yelp, 400
Yoplait yogurt, 81
Young Eagles, 42
YouTube, 115, 239, 253, 292, 336, 388, 397, 399, 400, 402, 409, 479, 480, 491

Z

Zappos, 171, 203–204, 408
Zara, 307, 361
Zebco, 471
Zipcar, 304, 405
Zoom Box, 57
Zurita, Ivan, 93
Zynga, 400, 481

Subject Index

A

absolute advantage, 67–68
accessibility, transportation mode, 370, 371
accessory equipment, 325
accountability, creating, 190
accounting
  careers in, 440–441
  defined, 437
  equation, 441–442
  fraud, 439
  types of, 440
accounts payable, 445
accounts receivable, 444
  factoring, 476
  of a firm, 444
  pledged for short-term financing, 476
accumulated depreciation, 444
acid rain, 55
acquisition, 119–120
  of people, 239–240
  trends for the future, 121
adaptations, 331
ad hoc committee, 199
adjourning stage, of team development, 286
administrative managers, 169, 431
advertising, 372
  campaign, execution of, 376
  campaign, major steps in developing, 374–376
  defined, 372
  false and misleading, 37
  social and legal considerations, 377
  types of, 373–374
advertising agency, 376
advertising appropriation, 374
advertising e-business model, 415
advertising message, 375
advertising money, shifting to digital marketing, 403
advertising objectives, 374
advertising platform, 374
advisory authority, 194
advisory positions, 185
aesthetic modifications, of existing products, 329
affirmative action, 52–53, 259

Affordable Care Act (2010), 258
Age Discrimination in Employment Act (1967-1986), 258
agent, 362
aircraft emissions, 55, 56
air pollution, 56, 57
air transport, 370–371
alien corporation, 111
allocator, price serving function of, 339
allowance, 348
  for doubtful accounts, 444
alternatives, 174
American Recovery and Reinvestment Act (2009), 54
Americans with Disabilities Act (ADA) (1990), 258, 259–260
analytical process, in operations management, 210
analytic skills, of managers, 6, 170
anational company, 85
annual meetings, 479, 480
annual reports, 442, 479, 489
app business, building a million-dollar, 12
applied research, 213
appraisal errors, avoiding, 256
Armenia, economic growth, 75
articles of incorporation, 111
articles of partnership, 106, 107
ASEAN-5 countries, 74
Asian countries, economic growth, 89
assembly line, 217, 218
assessment centers, 249
assets, 441, 442–445
  proceeds from the sale of, 469
Association of Southeast Asian Nations, 80
associations, of brand, 335
attrition, cutbacks through, 242
audit, 438
authority
  within an organization, 172
  decentralization of, 191–192
  delegation of, 190–191
  granting, 190
authors, e-mail addresses of, 8
autocratic leadership, 172
automatic vending, 366
automation, 216, 226–228
Azerbaijan, economic growth, 75

B

balance of payments, 70
balance of trade, 18, 68, 69
balance sheet, 442, 443
bar chart, example, 436
barter, 22
basic research, 213
basis, for segmentation, 306
B2B firms, types of, 413–414
"Be a Star" campaign, 409
behavior modification, 280
benchmarking, 175, 223
benchmarks, setting, 409
benefits, 240
benefits-to-the-community component, of a business plan, 99
bilingual skills, from cultural diversity, 244
bill of lading, 82
"Blast! Then Refine,", 174
blogs, 398–399, 409
board of directors, 112–113
Boeing Ethics Line, 58
bond indenture, 484
bonds
  types of, 484
"book and hold," 457–458
brainstorming, 174
branches, of an exporting firm, 82–83
brand awareness, 335
brand equity, 335
brand extensions, 337
branding, 333–337
  benefits of, 334–335
  strategies, 336
brand insistence, 335
brand loyalty, 334
brand mark, 333
brand names, 333, 336
brand preference, 334–335
brand recognition, 334
brands, 333
  choosing and protecting, 335–336
  top ten most valuable, 335
  types of, 333–334
Brazil, 93
breakeven quantity, 342, 343
bribes, as unethical, 36
broker, 362

inventory turnover, 453
investing activities, cash flows from, 449
investment banking firms, 478
investments
   frozen in a partnership, 109
   return on, 341
investor relations, in social media era, 479
investors, 34
invisible hand, 12
Iran, embargoes against, 71
Isenberg Entrepreneur Test, 133
ISO 9000, 223–224
ISO 14000, 223–224
issue resolution rate, 410

J

Japan, projected growth, 74
jet aircraft, carbon monoxide and
   hydrocarbon emitted by, 56
job analysis, 240, 245
job applicants, attracting qualified, 246
jobbers, 362
job description, 245
job design, 186–188
job enlargement, 279
job enrichment, 279–280
job evaluation, 250
job posting, 247
job redesign, 279–280
job rotation, 188
job sharing, 281–282
jobs, loss of from trade restrictions, 73
job specialization, 186–187
job specification, 245
joint ventures, 83, 118
judgmental appraisal methods, 255–256
just-in-time (JIT) inventory system, 221

K

Kefauver-Harris Drug Amendments
   (1962), 51
Kennedy Round (1964-1967), 77–78
key performance indicators (KPIs), 409
Kindle, inventing, 160
knowledge management (KM), 430

L

label, 338
labeling, 338–339
labor, 11
labor-intensive technology, 216
Labor-Management Relations Act
   (1947), 257, 258
labor unions, 45
laid off, employees, 242
laissez faire capitalism, 12, 13
land and natural resources, 11
land pollution, 56–57
Latin America, projected growth
   rates, 74

"lattice" structure, 184
lawsuits, product liability, 49
leadership, 172–173
leading, 165
lean manufacturing, 225
legal and regulatory forces, in the
   marketing environment, 309
legal monopoly, 22
letter of credit, 82
liabilities, 441, 445
licensing, 81
lifestyle shopping center, 367
limited liability
   of corporations, 114
   for malpractice of other partners, 108
limited-liability company (LLC)
   advantages and disadvantages of,
     108
   taxed like a partnership, 116
limited-liability partnership (LLP), 108
limited-line retailers, 364
limited-line wholesaler, 362
limited monopoly, 22
limited partners, 106
limited partnerships, 106
limited potential, of small
   businesses, 138
line-and-staff structure, 194–195
line authority, 194
line extensions, 330, 337
line managers, 193
line of credit, 470
line structure, 193–194
liquidity
   of an asset, 442
LLC. See limited-liability
   company (LLC)
LLP. See limited-liability partnership
   (LLP)
load flexibility, transportation mode,
   370, 371
loans
   basics of getting, 471
   by inventory, 476
   receivables, 476
location, departmentalization by, 189
"long" product line, 216
long-term debt financing, sources of,
   481–485
long-term financing, 465, 466
long-term liabilities, 445
long-term loans, 481–482, 485
loss, 9, 446
lower-level managers, abilities of, 191
lump-sum salary increases, 251
Lupron cancer drug, 34

M

macroeconomics, 11
"Made in America,", 72, 73, 209
"Made in the United States" label, 25

magnitude
   of a conversion process, 211
Magnuson-Moss Warranty-Federal
   Trade Commission Act (1975), 51
major equipment, 325
major events, shaping nation's economy
   from 1940 to 2000, 23
Malcolm Baldrige National Quality
   Award, 222
male and female workers, relative
   earnings of, 53
malware, 417
management, 160
   areas of, 430–431
   defined, 160–161
   functions, 162–167
   levels of, 167–168
   resources of, 161
   span of, 192–193
Management Assistance Program,
   SBA's, 141
management by objectives (MBO),
   278–279
management courses, offered by
   SBA, 141
management development, 253
management disagreement, in
   partnerships, 122
management functions, 6
management information system
   (MIS), 430–432
   costs and limits of, 431–432
   employees using, 432–437
management process, functions of,
   162–167
management skills
   improving, 6
   limited for sole proprietors, 104
management specialization, areas of,
   168–169
managerial accounting, 440
managerial decision making, 173–175
managers
   coordinated effort of all three levels
     of, 168
   kinds of, 167–169
   skills of, 7
   skills of successful, 170–171
managing, total quality, 175–176
manufacturers, 333
   U.S., 208–210
manufacturer's agents, 362
manufacturing businesses, 9
marketable securities, 444
market coverage, level of, 360
market demand
   comparing with capacity, 219
   estimating, 219
   exceeding capacity, 219
market economy, 13
marketing channel, 357
marketing-communications mix, 372

sales offices, of an exporting firm, 83
sales orientation, of business, 302
salespersons, kinds of, 377–378
sales promotion, 373, 379
　methods, 380
　objectives, 379–380
　selection of methods, 380–382
sales revenue
　exchanged for additional resources, 14
　increasing, 412–413
　relationship with profit, 10
sales support personnel, 377–378
sample, 381
Sarbanes-Oxley Act (2002), 38, 41,
　439, 457
satisfaction, of employees, 271–272
"satisfice," making decisions that, 174
satisfiers, 272
Saudi Arabia, 67, 74
savings accounts, 470
SBA. See Small Business
　Administration (SBA)
SBDCs. See small-business
　development centers (SBDCs)
SBICs. See small-business investment
　companies (SBICs)
SBIs. See Small-business institutes
　(SBIs)
SBTN. See Small Business Training
　Network (SBTN)
scarcity, dealing with, 11
scheduling, materials and resources,
　221–222
scientific management, 268–269
SCORE. See Service Corps of Retired
　Executives (SCORE)
S-corporations
　advantages and disadvantages
　　of, 117
　Graeter's as, 155
　taxed like a partnership, 122
screening, of new products, 331
search engines
　optimization, 404
seasonal discounts, 348
secondary information, sources of,
　313, 314
secondary market, 478–480
secondary-market pricing, 345
secrecy, lack of for open
　corporations, 116
secured loan, 477
securities exchange, 479
segmentation bases, variety of, 307
selection, 240, 247–249
selective-demand (or brand) advertising,
　373, 374
selective distribution, 360
self-actualization needs, 271
self-managed teams, 284
selling expenses, 448
sense of involvement, of workers, 270

sentiment analysis, 409–410
serial bonds, 484
service businesses, 8
Service Corps of Retired Executives
　(SCORE), 141–142
service economy, 24, 212
service industries, 130
service, right to, 50
services, 323
　adjusting to meet demand, 219–220
　consumed immediately, 213
　evaluating the quality of a firm's, 213
　increasing importance of, 212–213
　labor-intensive, 216
setting standards, 167
shares of ownership, of a
　corporation, 110
shark repellents, 119
Sherman Antitrust Act (1890), 46
shopping product, 324
"short" product line, 216
short-term financing, 464–466, 473–477
　comparison of methods, 477
　sources of secured, 476
　sources of unsecured, 473–475
significant others, affecting ethics, 37
simulations, 254
single line retailers, 364–365
sinking fund, 484
site selection, 216–219
situational factors, buying process
　influenced by, 315
Six Sigma, 223
skills inventory, 242
Skype/gotomeeting.com, for
　interviewing, 248
Small Business Administration (SBA),
　128, 141–144
small-business development centers
　(SBDCs), 143
small businesses
　advantages of remaining small, 136–137
　defined, 131
　disadvantages of, 137–138
　failure of, 6
　global perspectives, 149
　importance in U.S. economy, 129
　industries attracting, 130–131
　minority-owned, 142–143
　prone to failure, 133
　during the recession, 129
　size standards, 129
　solving unemployment problems, 136
Small-business institutes (SBIs), 142
small-business investment companies
　(SBICs), 144
small-business owners, teenagers
　as, 133
small-business sector, 129–130
Small Business Training Network
　(SBTN), 141
smart decisions, making, 435–437

social acceptance, of a group, 270
social audit, 58
social content sites, 398
social customer, segmenting and
　targeting, 406–407
social entrepreneurs, 57
social factors, 37–38, 315
social games, 400
socialism, 14–15
socialist nations, transitioning to a free-
　market economy, 15
social media
　achieving business objectives
　　through, 400–406
　advancing your career, 5
　building relationships with
　　customers, 213
　businesses using, 397–398
　challenges for, 417–419
　communities, 400–401
　defined, 25
　described, 396–397
　employee use of, 171
　importance of, 395–398
　making a good impression, 405
　policy, 253
　Raleigh active in, 320
　reasons for using, 397–398
　reviews and ratings on, 399–400
　small businesses marketing on, 336
　timeline of, 396
　tools for business use, 398–400
social media marketing, 403–404
social media measurement, types of,
　408–410
social media objectives, establishing, 406
social media plan
　cost of maintaining, 410
　developing, 406–408
　implementing and integrating,
　　407–408
　measuring and adapting, 408–410
　steps to building, 406–408
social media sites
　for professionals, 253
social media tools, selecting, 407
social needs, 271
social responsibility, 42–48
　arguments for/against increased, 47
　developing a program of, 58
　evolution of in business, 45–46
　funding the program, 59
　historical evolution of business,
　　45–46
　implementing a program of, 58–59
　on the Internet, 416–417
　pros and cons of, 47–48
　views of, 46–48
social responsibility record, of a firm, 10
Social Security account, 252
society, impact of business decisions
　on, 47